D0815093

The Booker T. Washington Reader

Up From Slavery: An Autobiography
My Larger Education
Character Building
The Negro Problem

Wilder Publications, LLC.
PO Box 3005
Radford VA 24143-3005

ISBN 10: 1-60459-200-1
ISBN 13: 978-1-60459-200-9

Up From Slavery: An Autobiography

Table of Contents

Preface

This volume is the outgrowth of a series of articles, dealing with incidents in my life, which were published consecutively in the Outlook. While they were appearing in that magazine I was constantly surprised at the number of requests which came to me from all parts of the country, asking that the articles be permanently preserved in book form. I am most grateful to the Outlook for permission to gratify these requests.

I have tried to tell a simple, straightforward story, with no attempt at embellishment. My regret is that what I have attempted to do has been done so imperfectly. The greater part of my time and strength is required for the executive work connected with the Tuskegee Normal and Industrial Institute, and in securing the money necessary for the support of the institution. Much of what I have said has been written on board trains, or at hotels or railroad stations while I have been waiting for trains, or during the moments that I could spare from my work while at Tuskegee. Without the painstaking and generous assistance of Mr. Max Bennett Thrasher I could not have succeeded in any satisfactory degree.

Introduction

The details of Mr. Washington's early life, as frankly set down in "Up from Slavery," do not give quite a whole view of his education. He had the training that a colored youth receives at Hampton, which, indeed, the autobiography does explain. But the reader does not get his intellectual pedigree, for Mr. Washington himself, perhaps, does not as clearly understand it as another man might. The truth is he had a training during the most impressionable period of his life that was very extraordinary, such a training as few men of his generation have had. To see its full meaning one must start in the Hawaiian Islands half a century or more ago. There Samuel Armstrong, a youth of missionary parents, earned enough money to pay his expenses at an American college. Equipped with this small sum and the earnestness that the undertaking implied, he came to Williams College when Dr. Mark Hopkins was president. Williams College had many good things for youth in that day, as it has in this, but the greatest was the strong personality of its famous president. Every student does not profit by a great teacher; but perhaps no young man ever came under the influence of Dr. Hopkins, whose whole nature was so ripe for profit by such an experience as young Armstrong. He lived in the family of President Hopkins, and thus had a training that was wholly out of the common; and this training had much to do with the development of his own strong character, whose originality and force we are only beginning to appreciate.

In turn, Samuel Armstrong, the founder of Hampton Institute, took up his work as a trainer of youth. He had very raw material, and doubtless most of his pupils failed to get the greatest lessons from him; but, as he had been a peculiarly receptive pupil of Dr. Hopkins, so Booker Washington became a peculiarly receptive pupil of his. To the formation of Mr. Washington's character, then, went the missionary zeal of New England, influenced by one of the strongest personalities in modern education, and the wide-reaching moral earnestness of General Armstrong himself These influences are easily recognizable in Mr. Washington to-day by men who knew Dr. Hopkins and General Armstrong.

I got the cue to Mr. Washington's character from a very simple incident many years ago. I had never seen him, and I knew little about him, except that he was the head of a school at Tuskegee, Alabama. I had occasion to write to him, and I addressed him as "The Rev. Booker T. Washington." In his reply there was no mention of my addressing him as a clergyman. But when I had occasion to write to him again, and persisted in making him a preacher, his second letter brought a postscript: "I have no claim to 'Rev.'" I knew most of the colored men who at that time had become prominent as leaders of their race, but I had not then known one who was neither a politician nor a preacher; and I had not heard of the head of an important colored school who was not a preacher. "A new kind of man in the colored world," I said to myself—"a new kind of man surely if he looks upon his task as an economic one instead of a theological one." I wrote him an apology for mistaking him for a preacher.

The first time that I went to Tuskegee I was asked to make an address to the school on Sunday evening. I sat upon the platform of the large chapel and looked forth on a thousand colored faces, and the choir of a hundred or more behind me sang a familiar religious melody, and the whole company joined in the chorus with unction. I was the only white man under the roof, and the scene and the songs made an impression on me that I shall never forget. Mr. Washington arose and asked them to sing one after another of the old melodies that I had heard all my life; but I had never before heard them sung by a thousand voices nor by the voices of educated Negroes. I had associated them with the Negro of the past, not with the Negro who was struggling upward. They brought to my mind the plantation, the cabin, the slave, not the freedman in quest of education. But on the plantation and in the cabin they had never been sung as these thousand students sang them. I saw again all the old plantations that I had ever seen; the whole history of the Negro ran through my mind; and the inexpressible pathos of his life found expression in these songs as I had never before felt it.

And the future? These were the ambitious youths of the race, at work with an earnestness that put to shame the conventional student life of most educational institutions. Another song rolled up along the rafters. And as soon as silence came, I found myself in front of this extraordinary mass of faces, thinking not of them, but of that long and unhappy chapter in our country's history which followed the one great structural mistake of the Fathers of the Republic; thinking of the one continuous great problem that generations of statesmen had wrangled over, and a million men fought about, and that had so dwarfed the mass of English men in the Southern States as to hold them back a hundred years behind their fellows in every other part of the world—in England, in Australia, and in the Northern and Western States; I was thinking of this dark shadow that had oppressed every large-minded statesman from Jefferson to Lincoln. These thousand young men and women about me were victims of it. I, too, was an innocent victim of it. The whole Republic was a victim of that fundamental error of importing Africa into America. I held firmly to the first article of my faith that the Republic must stand fast by the principle of a fair ballot; but I recalled the wretched mess that Reconstruction had made of it; I recalled the low level of public life in all the "black" States. Every effort of philanthropy seemed to have miscarried, every effort at correcting abuses seemed of doubtful value, and the race friction seemed to become severer. Here was the century-old problem in all its pathos seated singing before me. Who were the more to be pitied—these innocent victims of an ancient wrong, or I and men like me, who had inherited the problem? I had long ago thrown aside illusions and theories, and was willing to meet the facts face to face, and to do whatever in God's name a man might do towards saving the next generation from such a burden. But I felt the weight of twenty well-nigh hopeless years of thought and reading and observation; for the old difficulties remained and new ones had sprung up. Then I saw clearly that the way out of a century of blunders had been made by this man who stood beside me and was introducing me to this audience. Before me was the material he had used. All about me was the indisputable evidence that he had found the natural line of development. He had shown the way. Time and patience and encouragement and work would do the rest.

It was then more clearly than ever before that I understood the patriotic significance of Mr. Washington's work. It is this conception of it and of him that I have ever since carried with me. It is on this that his claim to our gratitude rests.

To teach the Negro to read, whether English, or Greek, or Hebrew, butters no parsnips. To make the Negro work, that is what his master did in one way and hunger has done in another; yet both these left Southern life where they found it. But to teach the Negro to do skillful work, as men of all the races that have risen have worked,—responsible work, which *is* education and character; and most of all when Negroes so teach Negroes to do this that they will teach others with a missionary zeal that puts all ordinary philanthropic efforts to shame,—this is to change the whole economic basis of life and the whole character of a people.

The plan itself is not a new one. It was worked out at Hampton Institute, but it was done at Hampton by white men. The plan had, in fact, been many times theoretically laid down by thoughtful students of Southern life. Handicrafts were taught in the days of slavery on most well-managed plantations. But Tuskegee is, nevertheless, a brand-new chapter in the history of the Negro, and in the history of the knottiest problem we have ever faced. It not only makes "a carpenter of a man; it makes a man of a carpenter." In one sense, therefore, it is of greater value than any other institution for the training of men and women that we have, from Cambridge to Palo Alto. It is almost the only one of which it may be said that it points the way to a new epoch in a large area of our national life.

To work out the plan on paper, or at a distance—that is one thing. For a white man to work it out—that too, is an easy thing. For a colored man to work it out in the South, where, in its constructive period, he was necessarily misunderstood by his own people as well as by the whites, and where he had to adjust it at every step to the strained race relations—that is so very different and more difficult a thing that the man who did it put the country under lasting obligations to him.

It was not and is not a mere educational task. Anybody could teach boys trades and give them an elementary education. Such tasks have been done since the beginning of civilization. But this task had to be done with the rawest of raw material, done within the civilization of the dominant race, and so done as not to run across race lines and social lines that are the strongest forces in the community. It had to be done for the benefit of the whole community. It had to be done, moreover, without local help, in the face of the direst poverty, done by begging, and done in spite of the ignorance of one race and the prejudice of the other.

No man living had a harder task, and a task that called for more wisdom to do it right. The true measure of Mr. Washington's success is, then, not his teaching the pupils of Tuskegee, nor even gaining the support of philanthropic persons at a distance, but this—that every Southern white man of character and of wisdom has been won to a cordial recognition of the value of the work, even men who held and still hold to the conviction that a mere book education for the Southern blacks under present conditions is a positive evil. This is a demonstration of the efficiency of the Hampton-Tuskegee idea that stands like the demonstration of the value of democratic institutions themselves—a demonstration made so clear in spite of the greatest odds that it is no longer open to argument.

Consider the change that has come in twenty years in the discussion of the Negro problem. Two or three decades ago social philosophers and statisticians and well-meaning philanthropists were still talking and writing about the deportation of the Negroes, or about their settlement within some restricted area, or about their settling in all parts of the Union, or about their decline through their neglect of their children, or about their rapid multiplication till they should expel the whites from the South—of every sort of nonsense under heaven. All this has given place to the simple plan of an indefinite extension among the neglected classes of both races of the Hampton-Tuskegee system of training. The "problem" in one sense has disappeared. The future will have for the South swift or slow development of its masses and of its soil in proportion to the swift or slow development of this kind of training. This change of view is a true measure of Mr. Washington's work.

The literature of the Negro in America is colossal, from political oratory through abolitionism to "Uncle Tom's Cabin" and "Cotton is King"—a vast mass of books which many men have read to the waste of good years (and I among them); but the only books that I have read a second time or ever care again to read in the whole list (most of them by tiresome and unbalanced "reformers") are "Uncle Remus" and "Up from Slavery"; for these are the great literature of the subject. One has all the best of the past, the other foreshadows a better future; and the men who wrote them are the only men who have written of the subject with that perfect frankness and perfect knowledge and perfect poise whose other name is genius.

Mr. Washington has won a world-wide fame at an early age. His story of his own life already has the distinction of translation into more languages, I think, than any other American book; and I suppose that he has as large a personal acquaintance among men of influence as any private citizen now living.

His own teaching at Tuskegee is unique. He lectures to his advanced students on the art of right living, not out of text-books, but straight out of life. Then he sends them into the country to visit Negro families. Such a student will come back with a minute report of the way in which the family that he has seen lives, what their earnings are, what they do well and what they do ill; and he will explain how they might live better. He constructs a definite plan for the betterment of that particular family out of the resources that they have. Such a student, if he be bright, will profit more by an experience like this than he could profit by all the books on sociology and economics that ever were written. I talked with a boy at Tuskegee who had made such a study as this, and I could not keep from contrasting his knowledge and enthusiasm with what I heard in a class room at a Negro university in one of the Southern cities, which is conducted on the idea that a college course will save the soul. Here the class was reciting a lesson from an abstruse text-book on economics, reciting it by rote, with so obvious a failure to assimilate it that the waste of labor was pitiful.

I asked Mr. Washington years ago what he regarded as the most important result of his work, and he replied:

"I do not know which to put first, the effect of Tuskegee's work on the Negro, or the effect on the attitude of the white man to the Negro."

The race divergence under the system of miseducation was fast getting wider. Under the influence of the Hampton-Tuskegee idea the races are coming into a closer sympathy and into an honorable and helpful relation. As the Negro becomes economically independent, he becomes a responsible part of the Southern life; and the whites so recognize him. And this must be so from the nature of things. There is nothing artificial about it. It is development in a perfectly natural way. And the Southern whites not only so recognize it, but they are imitating it in the teaching of the neglected masses of their own race. It has thus come about that the school is taking a more direct and helpful hold on life in the South than anywhere else in the country. Education is not a thing apart from life—not a "system," nor a philosophy; it is direct teaching how to live and how to work.

To say that Mr. Washington has won the gratitude of all thoughtful Southern white men, is to say that he has worked with the highest practical wisdom at a large constructive task; for no plan for the up-building of the freedman could succeed that ran counter to Southern opinion. To win the support of Southern opinion and to shape it was a necessary part of the task; and in this he has so well succeeded that the South has a sincere and high regard for him. He once said to me that he recalled the day, and remembered it thankfully, when he grew large enough to regard a Southern white man as he regarded a Northern one. It is well for our common country that the day is come when he and his work are regarded as highly in the South as in any other part of the Union. I think that no man of our generation has a more noteworthy achievement to his credit than this; and it is an achievement of moral earnestness of the strong character of a man who has done a great national service.

Walter H. Page.

A Slave Among Slaves

I was born a slave on a plantation in Franklin County, Virginia. I am not quite sure of the exact place or exact date of my birth, but at any rate I suspect I must have been born somewhere and at some time. As nearly as I have been able to learn, I was born near a cross-roads post-office called Hale's Ford, and the year was 1858 or 1859. I do not know the month or the day. The earliest impressions I can now recall are of the plantation and the slave quarters—the latter being the part of the plantation where the slaves had their cabins.

My life had its beginning in the midst of the most miserable, desolate, and discouraging surroundings. This was so, however, not because my owners were especially cruel, for they were not, as compared with many others. I was born in a typical log cabin, about fourteen by sixteen feet square. In this cabin I lived with my mother and a brother and sister till after the Civil War, when we were all declared free.

Of my ancestry I know almost nothing. In the slave quarters, and even later, I heard whispered conversations among the colored people of the tortures which the slaves, including, no doubt, my ancestors on my mother's side, suffered in the middle passage of the slave ship while being conveyed from Africa to America. I have been unsuccessful in securing any information that would throw any accurate light upon the history of my family beyond my mother. She, I remember, had a half-brother and a half-sister. In the days of slavery not very much attention was given to family history and family records—that is, black family records. My mother, I suppose, attracted the attention of a purchaser who was afterward my owner and hers. Her addition to the slave family attracted about as much attention as the purchase of a new horse or cow. Of my father I know even less than of my mother. I do not even know his name. I have heard reports to the effect that he was a white man who lived on one of the near-by plantations. Whoever he was, I never heard of his taking the least interest in me or providing in any way for my rearing. But I do not find especial fault with him. He was simply another unfortunate victim of the institution which the Nation unhappily had engrafted upon it at that time.

The cabin was not only our living-place, but was also used as the kitchen for the plantation. My mother was the plantation cook. The cabin was without glass windows; it had only openings in the side which let in the light, and also the cold, chilly air of winter. There was a door to the cabin—that is, something that was called a door—but the uncertain hinges by which it was hung, and the large cracks in it, to say nothing of the fact that it was too small, made the room a very uncomfortable one. In addition to these openings there was, in the lower right-hand corner of the room, the "cat-hole,"—a contrivance which almost every mansion or cabin in Virginia possessed during the ante-bellum period. The "cat-hole" was a square opening, about seven by eight inches, provided for the purpose of letting the cat pass in and out of the house at will during the night. In the case of our particular cabin I could never understand the necessity for this convenience, since there were at least a half-dozen other places in the cabin that would have accommodated the cats. There was no wooden floor in our cabin, the naked earth being used as a floor. In the center of the earthen floor there was a large, deep opening covered with boards, which was used as a place in which to store sweet potatoes during the winter. An impression of this potato-hole is very distinctly engraved upon my memory, because I recall that during the process of putting the potatoes in or taking them out I would often come into possession of one or two, which I roasted and thoroughly enjoyed. There was no cooking-stove on our plantation, and all the cooking for the whites and slaves my mother had to do over an open fireplace, mostly in pots and "skillets." While the poorly built cabin caused us to suffer with cold in the winter, the heat from the open fireplace in summer was equally trying.

The early years of my life, which were spent in the little cabin, were not very different from those of thousands of other slaves. My mother, of course, had little time in which to give attention to the training of her children during the day. She snatched a few moments for our care in the early morning before her work began, and at night after the day's work was done. One of my earliest recollections is that of my mother cooking a chicken late at night, and awakening her children for the purpose of feeding them. How or where she got it I do not know. I presume, however, it was procured from our owner's farm. Some people may call this theft. If such a thing were to happen now, I should condemn it as theft myself. But taking place at the time it did, and for the reason that it did, no one could ever make me believe that my mother was guilty of thieving. She was simply a victim of the system of slavery. I cannot remember having slept in a bed until after our family was declared free by the Emancipation Proclamation. Three children—John, my older brother, Amanda, my sister, and myself—had a pallet on the dirt floor, or, to be more correct, we slept in and on a bundle of filthy rags laid upon the dirt floor.

I was asked not long ago to tell something about the sports and pastimes that I engaged in during my youth. Until that question was asked it had never occurred to me that there was no period of my life that was devoted to play. From the time that I can remember anything, almost every day of my life had been occupied in some kind of labor; though I think I would now be a more useful man if I had had time for sports. During the period that I spent in slavery I was not large enough to be of much service, still I was occupied most of the time in cleaning the yards, carrying water to the men in the fields, or going to the mill to which I used to take the corn, once a week, to be ground. The mill was about three miles from the plantation. This work I always dreaded. The heavy bag of corn would be thrown across the back of the horse, and the corn divided about evenly on each side; but in some way, almost without exception, on these trips, the corn would so shift as to become unbalanced and would fall off the horse, and often I would fall with it. As I was not strong enough to reload the corn upon the horse, I would have to wait, sometimes for many hours, till a chance passer-by came along who would help me out of my trouble. The hours while waiting for some one were usually spent in crying. The time consumed in this way made me late in reaching the mill, and by the time I got my corn ground and reached home it would be far into the night. The road was a lonely one, and often led through dense forests. I was always frightened. The woods were said to be full of soldiers who had deserted from the army, and I had been told that the first thing a deserter did to a Negro boy when he found him alone was to cut off his ears. Besides, when I was late in getting home I knew I would always get a severe scolding or a flogging.

I had no schooling whatever while I was a slave, though I remember on several occasions I went as far as the schoolhouse door with one of my young mistresses to carry her books. The picture of several dozen boys and girls in a schoolroom engaged in study made a deep impression upon me, and I had the feeling that to get into a schoolhouse and study in this way would be about the same as getting into paradise.

So far as I can now recall, the first knowledge that I got of the fact that we were slaves, and that freedom of the slaves was being discussed, was early one morning before day, when I was awakened by my mother kneeling over her children and fervently praying that Lincoln and his armies might be successful, and that one day she and her children might be free. In this connection I have never been able to understand how the slaves throughout the South, completely ignorant as were the masses so far as books or newspapers were concerned, were able to keep themselves so accurately and completely informed about the great National questions that were agitating the country. From the time that Garrison, Lovejoy, and others began to agitate for freedom, the slaves throughout the South kept in close touch with the progress of the movement. Though I was a mere child during the preparation for the Civil War and during the war itself, I now recall the many late-at-night whispered discussions that I heard my mother and the other slaves on the plantation indulge in. These discussions showed that they understood the situation, and that they kept themselves informed of events by what was termed the "grape-vine" telegraph.

During the campaign when Lincoln was first a candidate for the Presidency, the slaves on our far-off plantation, miles from any railroad or large city or daily newspaper, knew what the issues involved were. When war was begun between the North and the South, every slave on our plantation felt and knew that, though other issues were discussed, the primal one was that of slavery. Even the most ignorant members of my race on the remote plantations felt in their hearts, with a certainty that admitted of no doubt, that the freedom of the slaves would be the one great result of the war, if the northern armies conquered. Every success of the Federal armies and every defeat of the Confederate forces was watched with the keenest and most intense interest. Often the slaves got knowledge of the results of great battles before the white people received it. This news was usually gotten from the colored man who was sent to the post-office for the mail. In our case the post-office was about three miles from the plantation, and the mail came once or twice a week. The man who was sent to the office would linger about the place long enough to get the drift of the conversation from the group of white people who naturally congregated there, after receiving their mail, to discuss the latest news. The mail-carrier on his way back to our master's house would as naturally retail the news that he had secured among the slaves, and in this way they often heard of important events before the white people at the "big house," as the master's house was called.

I cannot remember a single instance during my childhood or early boyhood when our entire family sat down to the table together, and God's blessing was asked, and the family ate a meal in a civilized manner. On the plantation in Virginia, and even later, meals were gotten by the children very much as dumb animals get theirs. It was a piece of bread here and a scrap of meat there. It was a cup of milk at one time and some potatoes at another. Sometimes a portion of our family would eat out of the skillet or pot, while some one else would eat from a tin plate held on the knees, and often using nothing but the hands with which to hold the food. When I had grown to sufficient size, I was required to go to the "big house" at meal-times to fan the flies from the table by means of a large set of paper fans operated by a pulley. Naturally much of the conversation of the white people turned upon the subject of freedom and the war, and I absorbed a good deal of it. I remember that at one time I saw two of my young mistresses and some lady visitors eating ginger-cakes, in the yard. At that time those cakes seemed to me to be absolutely the most tempting and desirable things that I had ever seen; and I then and there resolved that, if I ever got free, the height of my ambition would be reached if I could get to the point where I could secure and eat ginger-cakes in the way that I saw those ladies doing.

Of course as the war was prolonged the white people, in many cases, often found it difficult to secure food for themselves. I think the slaves felt the deprivation less than the whites, because the usual diet for slaves was corn bread and pork, and these could be raised on the plantation; but coffee, tea, sugar, and other articles which the whites had been accustomed to use could not be raised on the plantation, and the conditions brought about by the war frequently made it impossible to secure these things. The whites were often in great straits. Parched corn was used for coffee, and a kind of black molasses was used instead of sugar. Many times nothing was used to sweeten the so-called tea and coffee.

The first pair of shoes that I recall wearing were wooden ones. They had rough leather on the top, but the bottoms, which were about an inch thick, were of wood. When I walked they made a fearful noise, and besides this they were very inconvenient, since there was no yielding to the natural pressure of the foot. In wearing them one presented and exceedingly awkward appearance. The most trying ordeal that I was forced to endure as a slave boy, however, was the wearing of a flax shirt. In the portion of Virginia where I lived it was common to use flax as part of the clothing for the slaves. That part of the flax from which our clothing was made was largely the refuse, which of course was the cheapest and roughest part. I can scarcely imagine any torture, except, perhaps, the pulling of a tooth, that is equal to that caused by putting on a new flax shirt for the first time. It is almost equal to the feeling that one would experience if he had a dozen or more chestnut burrs, or a hundred small pin-points, in contact with his flesh. Even to this day I can recall accurately the tortures that I underwent when putting on one of these garments. The fact that my flesh was soft and tender added to the pain. But I had no choice. I had to wear the flax shirt or none; and had it been left to me to choose, I should have chosen to wear no covering. In connection with the flax shirt, my brother John, who is several years older than I am, performed one of the most generous acts that I ever heard of one slave relative doing for another. On several occasions when I was being forced to wear a new flax shirt, he generously agreed to put it on in my stead and wear it for several days, till it was "broken in." Until I had grown to be quite a youth this single garment was all that I wore.

One may get the idea, from what I have said, that there was bitter feeling toward the white people on the part of my race, because of the fact that most of the white population was away fighting in a war which would result in keeping the Negro in slavery if the South was successful. In the case of the slaves on our place this was not true, and it was not true of any large portion of the slave population in the South where the Negro was treated with anything like decency. During the Civil War one of my young masters was killed, and two were severely wounded. I recall the feeling of sorrow which existed among the slaves when they heard of the death of "Mars' Billy." It was no sham sorrow, but real. Some of the slaves had nursed "Mars' Billy"; others had played with him when he was a child. "Mars' Billy" had begged for mercy in the case of others when the overseer or master was thrashing them. The sorrow in the slave quarter was only second to that in the "big house." When the two young masters were brought home wounded, the sympathy of the slaves was shown in many ways. They were just as anxious to assist in the nursing as the family relatives of the wounded. Some of the slaves would even beg for the privilege of sitting up at night to nurse their wounded masters. This tenderness and sympathy on the part of those held in bondage was a result of their kindly and generous nature. In order to defend and protect the women and children who were left on the plantations when the white males went to war, the slaves would have laid down their lives. The slave who was selected to sleep in the "big house" during the absence of the males was considered to have the place of honor. Any one attempting to harm "young Mistress" or "old Mistress" during the night would have had to cross the dead body of the slave to do so. I do not know how many have noticed it, but I think that it will be found to be true that there are few instances, either in slavery or freedom, in which a member of my race has been known to betray a specific trust.

As a rule, not only did the members of my race entertain no feelings of bitterness against the whites before and during the war, but there are many instances of Negroes tenderly carrying for their former masters and mistresses who for some reason have become poor and dependent since the war. I know of instances where the former masters of slaves have for years been supplied with money by their former slaves to keep them from suffering. I have known of still other cases in which the former slaves have assisted in the education of the descendants of their former owners. I know of a case on a large plantation in the South in which a young white man, the son of the former owner of the estate, has become so reduced in purse and self-control by reason of drink that he is a pitiable creature; and yet, notwithstanding the poverty of the colored people themselves on this plantation, they have for years supplied this young white man with the necessities of life. One sends him a little coffee or sugar, another a little meat, and so on. Nothing that the colored people possess is too good for the son of "old Mars' Tom," who will perhaps never be permitted to suffer while any remain on the place who knew directly or indirectly of "old Mars' Tom."

I have said that there are few instances of a member of my race betraying a specific trust. One of the best illustrations of this which I know of is in the case of an ex-slave from Virginia whom I met not long ago in a little town in the state of Ohio. I found that this man had made a contract with his master, two or three years previous to the Emancipation Proclamation, to the effect that the slave was to be permitted to buy himself, by paying so much per year for his body; and while he was paying for himself, he was to be permitted to labor where and for whom he pleased. Finding that he could secure better wages in Ohio, he went there. When freedom came, he was still in debt to his master some three hundred dollars. Notwithstanding that the Emancipation Proclamation freed him from any obligation to his master, this black man walked the greater portion of the distance back to where his old master lived in Virginia, and placed the last dollar, with interest, in his hands. In talking to me about this, the man told me that he knew that he did not have to pay the debt, but that he had given his word to the master, and his word he had never broken. He felt that he could not enjoy his freedom till he had fulfilled his promise.

From some things that I have said one may get the idea that some of the slaves did not want freedom. This is not true. I have never seen one who did not want to be free, or one who would return to slavery.

I pity from the bottom of my heart any nation or body of people that is so unfortunate as to get entangled in the net of slavery. I have long since ceased to cherish any spirit of bitterness against the Southern white people on account of the enslavement of my race. No one section of our country was wholly responsible for its introduction, and, besides, it was recognized and protected for years by the General Government. Having once got its tentacles fastened on to the economic and social life of the Republic, it was no easy matter for the country to relieve itself of the institution. Then, when we rid ourselves of prejudice, or racial feeling, and look facts in the face, we must acknowledge that, notwithstanding the cruelty and moral wrong of slavery, the ten million Negroes inhabiting this country, who themselves or whose ancestors went through the school of American slavery, are in a stronger and more hopeful condition, materially, intellectually, morally, and religiously, than is true of an equal number of black people in any other portion of the globe. This is so to such an extend that Negroes in this country, who themselves or whose forefathers went through the school of slavery, are constantly returning to Africa as missionaries to enlighten those who remained in the fatherland. This I say, not to justify slavery—on the other hand, I condemn it as an institution, as we all know that in America it was established for selfish and financial reasons, and not from a missionary motive—but to call attention to a fact, and to show how Providence so often uses men and institutions to accomplish a purpose. When persons ask me in these days how, in the midst of what sometimes seem hopelessly discouraging conditions, I can have such faith in the future of my race in this country, I remind them of the wilderness through which and out of which, a good Providence has already led us.

Ever since I have been old enough to think for myself, I have entertained the idea that, notwithstanding the cruel wrongs inflicted upon us, the black man got nearly as much out of slavery as the white man did. The hurtful influences of the institution were not by any means confined to the Negro. This was fully illustrated by the life upon our own plantation. The whole machinery of slavery was so constructed as to cause labor, as a rule, to be looked upon as a badge of degradation, of inferiority. Hence labor was something that both races on the slave plantation sought to escape. The slave system on our place, in a large measure, took the spirit of self-reliance and self-help out of the white people. My old master had many boys and girls, but not one, so far as I know, ever mastered a single trade or special line of productive industry. The girls were not taught to cook, sew, or to take care of the house. All of this was left to the slaves. The slaves, of course, had little personal interest in the life of the plantation, and their ignorance prevented them from learning how to do things in the most improved and thorough manner. As a result of the system, fences were out of repair, gates were hanging half off the hinges, doors creaked, window-panes were out, plastering had fallen but was not replaced, weeds grew in the yard. As a rule, there was food for whites and blacks, but inside the house, and on the dining-room table, there was wanting that delicacy and refinement of touch and finish which can make a home the most convenient, comfortable, and attractive place in the world. Withal there was a waste of food and other materials which was sad. When freedom came, the slaves were almost as well fitted to begin life anew as the master, except in the matter of book-learning and ownership of property. The slave owner and his sons had mastered no special industry. They unconsciously had imbibed the feeling that manual labor was not the proper thing for them. On the other hand, the slaves, in many cases, had mastered some handicraft, and none were ashamed, and few unwilling, to labor.

Finally the war closed, and the day of freedom came. It was a momentous and eventful day to all upon our plantation. We had been expecting it. Freedom was in the air, and had been for months. Deserting soldiers returning to their homes were to be seen every day. Others who had been discharged, or whose regiments had been paroled, were constantly passing near our place. The "grape-vine telegraph" was kept busy night and day. The news and mutterings of great events were swiftly carried from one plantation to another. In the fear of "Yankee" invasions, the silverware and other valuables were taken from the "big house," buried in the woods, and guarded by trusted slaves. Woe be to any one who would have attempted to disturb the buried treasure. The slaves would give the Yankee soldiers food, drink, clothing—anything but that which had been specifically intrusted to their care and honor. As the great day drew nearer, there was more singing in the slave quarters than usual. It was bolder, had more ring, and lasted later into the night. Most of the verses of the plantation songs had some reference to freedom. True, they had sung those same verses before, but they had been careful to explain that the "freedom" in these songs referred to the next world, and had no connection with life in this world. Now they gradually threw off the mask, and were not afraid to let it be known that the "freedom" in their songs meant freedom of the body in this world. The night before the eventful day, word was sent to the slave quarters to the effect that something unusual was going to take place at the "big house" the next morning. There was little, if any, sleep that night. All as excitement and expectancy. Early the next morning word was sent to all the slaves, old and young, to gather at the house. In company with my mother, brother, and sister, and a large number of other slaves, I went to the master's house. All of our master's family were either standing or seated on the veranda of the house, where they could see what was to take place and hear what was said. There was a feeling of deep interest, or perhaps sadness, on their faces, but not bitterness. As I now recall the impression they made upon me, they did not at the moment seem to be sad because of the loss of property, but rather because of parting with those whom they had reared and who were in many ways very close to them. The most distinct thing that I now recall in connection with the scene was that some man who seemed to be a stranger (a United States officer, I presume) made a little speech and then read a rather long paper—the Emancipation Proclamation, I think. After the reading we were told that we were all free, and could go when and where we pleased. My mother, who was standing by my side, leaned over and kissed her children, while tears of joy ran down her cheeks. She explained to us what it all meant, that this was the day for which she had been so long praying, but fearing that she would never live to see.

For some minutes there was great rejoicing, and thanksgiving, and wild scenes of ecstasy. But there was no feeling of bitterness. In fact, there was pity among the slaves for our former owners. The wild rejoicing on the part of the emancipated colored people lasted but for a brief period, for I noticed that by the time they returned to their cabins there was a change in their feelings. The great responsibility of being free, of having charge of themselves, of having to think and plan for themselves and their children, seemed to take possession of them. It was very much like suddenly turning a youth of ten or twelve years out into the world to provide for himself. In a few hours the great questions with which the An-glo-Saxon race had been grappling for centuries had been thrown upon these people to be solved. These were the questions of a home, a living, the rearing of children, education, citizenship, and the establishment and support of churches. Was it any wonder that within a few hours the wild rejoicing ceased and a feeling of deep gloom seemed to pervade the slave quarters? To some it seemed that, now that they were in actual possession of it, freedom was a more serious thing than they had expected to find it. Some of the slaves were seventy or eighty years old; their best days were gone. They had no strength with which to earn a living in a strange place and among strange people, even if they had been sure where to find a new place of abode. To this class the problem seemed especially hard. Besides, deep down in their hearts there was a strange and peculiar attachment to "old Master" and "old Missus," and to their children, which they found it hard to think of breaking off. With these they had spent in some cases nearly a half-century, and it was no light thing to think of parting. Gradually, one by one, stealthily at first, the older slaves began to wander from the slave quarters back to the "big house" to have a whispered conversation with their former owners as to the future.

Boyhood Days

After the coming of freedom there were two points upon which practically all the people on our place were agreed, and I found that this was generally true throughout the South: that they must change their names, and that they must leave the old plantation for at least a few days or weeks in order that they might really feel sure that they were free.

In some way a feeling got among the colored people that it was far from proper for them to bear the surname of their former owners, and a great many of them took other surnames. This was one of the first signs of freedom. When they were slaves, a colored person was simply called "John" or "Susan." There was seldom occasion for more than the use of the one name. If "John" or "Susan" belonged to a white man by the name of "Hatcher," sometimes he was called "John Hatcher," or as often "Hatcher's John." But there was a feeling that "John Hatcher" or "Hatcher's John" was not the proper title by which to denote a freeman; and so in many cases "John Hatcher" was changed to "John S. Lincoln" or "John S. Sherman," the initial "S" standing for no name, it being simply a part of what the colored man proudly called his "entitles."

As I have stated, most of the colored people left the old plantation for a short while at least, so as to be sure, it seemed, that they could leave and try their freedom on to see how it felt. After they had remained away for a while, many of the older slaves, especially, returned to their old homes and made some kind of contract with their former owners by which they remained on the estate.

My mother's husband, who was the stepfather of my brother John and myself, did not belong to the same owners as did my mother. In fact, he seldom came to our plantation. I remember seeing his there perhaps once a year, that being about Christmas time. In some way, during the war, by running away and following the Federal soldiers, it seems, he found his way into the new state of West Virginia. As soon as freedom was declared, he sent for my mother to come to the Kanawha Valley, in West Virginia. At that time a journey from Virginia over the mountains to West Virginia was rather a tedious and in some cases a painful undertaking. What little clothing and few household goods we had were placed in a cart, but the children walked the greater portion of the distance, which was several hundred miles.

I do not think any of us ever had been very far from the plantation, and the taking of a long journey into another state was quite an event. The parting from our former owners and the members of our own race on the plantation was a serious occasion. From the time of our parting till their death we kept up a correspondence with the older members of the family, and in later years we have kept in touch with those who were the younger members. We were several weeks making the trip, and most of the time we slept in the open air and did our cooking over a log fire out-of-doors. One night I recall that we camped near an abandoned log cabin, and my mother decided to build a fire in that for cooking, and afterward to make a "pallet" on the floor for our sleeping. Just as the fire had gotten well started a large black snake fully a yard and a half long dropped down the chimney and ran out on the floor. Of course we at once abandoned that cabin. Finally we reached our destination—a little town called Malden, which is about five miles from Charleston, the present capital of the state.

At that time salt-mining was the great industry in that part of West Virginia, and the little town of Malden was right in the midst of the salt-furnaces. My stepfather had already secured a job at a salt-furnace, and he had also secured a little cabin for us to live in. Our new house was no better than the one we had left on the old plantation in Virginia. In fact, in one respect it was worse. Notwithstanding the poor condition of our plantation cabin, we were at all times sure of pure air. Our new home was in the midst of a cluster of cabins crowded closely together, and as there were no sanitary regulations, the filth about the cabins was often intolerable. Some of our neighbors were colored people, and some were the poorest and most ignorant and degraded white people. It was a motley mixture. Drinking, gambling, quarrels, fights, and shockingly immoral practices were frequent. All who lived in the little town were in one way or another connected with the salt business. Though I was a mere child, my stepfather put me and my brother at work in one of the furnaces. Often I began work as early as four o'clock in the morning.

The first thing I ever learned in the way of book knowledge was while working in this salt-furnace. Each salt-packer had his barrels marked with a certain number. The number allotted to my stepfather was "18." At the close of the day's work the boss of the packers would come around and put "18" on each of our barrels, and I soon learned to recognize that figure wherever I saw it, and after a while got to the point where I could make that figure, though I knew nothing about any other figures or letters.

From the time that I can remember having any thoughts about anything, I recall that I had an intense longing to learn to read. I determined, when quite a small child, that, if I accomplished nothing else in life, I would in some way get enough education to enable me to read common books and newspapers. Soon after we got settled in some manner in our new cabin in West Virginia, I induced my mother to get hold of a book for me. How or where she got it I do not know, but in some way she procured an old copy of Webster's "blue-back" spelling-book, which contained the alphabet, followed by such meaningless words as "ab," "ba," "ca," "da." I began at once to devour this book, and I think that it was the first one I ever had in my hands. I had learned from somebody that the way to begin to read was to learn the alphabet, so I tried in all the ways I could think of to learn it,—all of course without a teacher, for I could find no one to teach me. At that time there was not a single member of my race anywhere near us who could read, and I was too timid to approach any of the white people. In some way, within a few weeks, I mastered the greater portion of the alphabet. In all my efforts to learn to read my mother shared fully my ambition, and sympathized with me and aided me in every way that she could. Though she was totally ignorant, she had high ambitions for her children, and a large fund of good, hard, common sense, which seemed to enable her to meet and master every situation. If I have done anything in life worth attention, I feel sure that I inherited the disposition from my mother.

In the midst of my struggles and longing for an education, a young colored boy who had learned to read in the state of Ohio came to Malden. As soon as the colored people found out that he could read, a newspaper was secured, and at the close of nearly every day's work this young man would be surrounded by a group of men and women who were anxious to hear him read the news contained in the papers. How I used to envy this man! He seemed to me to be the one young man in all the world who ought to be satisfied with his attainments.

About this time the question of having some kind of a school opened for the colored children in the village began to be discussed by members of the race. As it would be the first school for Negro children that had ever been opened in that part of Virginia, it was, of course, to be a great event, and the discussion excited the wildest interest. The most perplexing question was where to find a teacher. The young man from Ohio who had learned to read the papers was considered, but his age was against him. In the midst of the discussion about a teacher, another young colored man from Ohio, who had been a soldier, in some way found his way into town. It was soon learned that he possessed considerable education, and he was engaged by the colored people to teach their first school. As yet no free schools had been started for colored people in that section, hence each family agreed to pay a certain amount per month, with the understanding that the teacher was to "board 'round"—that is, spend a day with each family. This was not bad for the teacher, for each family tried to provide the very best on the day the teacher was to be its guest. I recall that I looked forward with an anxious appetite to the "teacher's day" at our little cabin.

This experience of a whole race beginning to go to school for the first time, presents one of the most interesting studies that has ever occurred in connection with the development of any race. Few people who were not right in the midst of the scenes can form any exact idea of the intense desire which the people of my race showed for an education. As I have stated, it was a whole race trying to go to school. Few were too young, and none too old, to make the attempt to learn. As fast as any kind of teachers could be secured, not only were day-schools filled, but night-schools as well. The great ambition of the older people was to try to learn to read the Bible before they died. With this end in view men and women who were fifty or seventy-five years old would often be found in the night-school. Some day-schools were formed soon after freedom, but the principal book studied in the Sunday-school was the spelling-book. Day-school, night-school, Sunday-school, were always crowded, and often many had to be turned away for want of room.

The opening of the school in the Kanawha Valley, however, brought to me one of the keenest disappointments that I ever experienced. I had been working in a salt-furnace for several months, and my stepfather had discovered that I had a financial value, and so, when the school opened, he decided that he could not spare me from my work. This decision seemed to cloud my every ambition. The disappointment was made all the more severe by reason of the fact that my place of work was where I could see the happy children passing to and from school mornings and afternoons. Despite this disappointment, however, I determined that I would learn something, anyway. I applied myself with greater earnestness than ever to the mastering of what was in the "blue-back" speller.

My mother sympathized with me in my disappointment, and sought to comfort me in all the ways she could, and to help me find a way to learn. After a while I succeeded in making arrangements with the teacher to give me some lessons at night, after the day's work was done. These night lessons were so welcome that I think I learned more at night than the other children did during the day. My own experiences in the night-school gave me faith in the night-school idea, with which, in after years, I had to do both at Hampton and Tuskegee. But my boyish heart was still set upon going to the day-school, and I let no opportunity slip to push my case. Finally I won, and was permitted to go to the school in the day for a few months, with the understanding that I was to rise early in the morning and work in the furnace till nine o'clock, and return immediately after school closed in the afternoon for at least two more hours of work.

The schoolhouse was some distance from the furnace, and as I had to work till nine o'clock, and the school opened at nine, I found myself in a difficulty. School would always be begun before I reached it, and sometimes my class had recited. To get around this difficulty I yielded to a temptation for which most people, I suppose, will condemn me; but since it is a fact, I might as well state it. I have great faith in the power and influence of facts. It is seldom that anything is permanently gained by holding back a fact. There was a large clock in a little office in the furnace. This clock, of course, all the hundred or more workmen depended upon to regulate their hours of beginning and ending the day's work. I got the idea that the way for me to reach school on time was to move the clock hands from half-past eight up to the nine o'clock mark. This I found myself doing morning after morning, till the furnace "boss" discovered that something was wrong, and locked the clock in a case. I did not mean to inconvenience anybody. I simply meant to reach that schoolhouse in time.

When, however, I found myself at the school for the first time, I also found myself confronted with two other difficulties. In the first place, I found that all the other children wore hats or caps on their heads, and I had neither hat nor cap. In fact, I do not remember that up to the time of going to school I had ever worn any kind of covering upon my head, nor do I recall that either I or anybody else had even thought anything about the need of covering for my head. But, of course, when I saw how all the other boys were dressed, I began to feel quite uncomfortable. As usual, I put the case before my mother, and she explained to me that she had no money with which to buy a "store hat," which was a rather new institution at that time among the members of my race and was considered quite the thing for young and old to own, but that she would find a way to help me out of the difficulty. She accordingly got two pieces of "homespun" (jeans) and sewed them together, and I was soon the proud possessor of my first cap.

The lesson that my mother taught me in this has always remained with me, and I have tried as best as I could to teach it to others. I have always felt proud, whenever I think of the incident, that my mother had strength of character enough not to be led into the temptation of seeming to be that which she was not—of trying to impress my schoolmates and others with the fact that she was able to buy me a "store hat" when she was not. I have always felt proud that she refused to go into debt for that which she did not have the money to pay for. Since that time I have owned many kinds of caps and hats, but never one of which I have felt so proud as of the cap made of the two pieces of cloth sewed together by my mother. I have noted the fact, but without satisfaction, I need not add, that several of the boys who began their careers with "store hats" and who were my schoolmates and used to join in the sport that was made of me because I had only a "homespun" cap, have ended their careers in the penitentiary, while others are not able now to buy any kind of hat.

My second difficulty was with regard to my name, or rather A name. From the time when I could remember anything, I had been called simply "Booker." Before going to school it had never occurred to me that it was needful or appropriate to have an additional name. When I heard the schoolroll called, I noticed that all of the children had at least two names, and some of them indulged in what seemed to me the extravagance of having three. I was in deep perplexity, because I knew that the teacher would demand of me at least two names, and I had only one. By the time the occasion came for the enrolling of my name, an idea occurred to me which I thought would make me equal to the situation; and so, when the teacher asked me what my full name was, I calmly told him "Booker Washington," as if I had been called by that name all my life; and by that name I have since been known. Later in my life I found that my mother had given me the name of "Booker Taliaferro" soon after I was born, but in some way that part of my name seemed to disappear and for a long while was forgotten, but as soon as I found out about it I revived it, and made my full name "Booker Taliaferro Washington." I think there are not many men in our country who have had the privilege of naming themselves in the way that I have.

More than once I have tried to picture myself in the position of a boy or man with an honored and distinguished ancestry which I could trace back through a period of hundreds of years, and who had not only inherited a name, but fortune and a proud family homestead; and yet I have sometimes had the feeling that if I had inherited these, and had been a member of a more popular race, I should have been inclined to yield to the temptation of depending upon my ancestry and my color to do that for me which I should do for myself. Years ago I resolved that because I had no ancestry myself I would leave a record of which my children would be proud, and which might encourage them to still higher effort.

The world should not pass judgment upon the Negro, and especially the Negro youth, too quickly or too harshly. The Negro boy has obstacles, discouragements, and temptations to battle with that are little know to those not situated as he is. When a white boy undertakes a task, it is taken for granted that he will succeed. On the other hand, people are usually surprised if the Negro boy does not fail. In a word, the Negro youth starts out with the presumption against him.

The influence of ancestry, however, is important in helping forward any individual or race, if too much reliance is not placed upon it. Those who constantly direct attention to the Negro youth's moral weaknesses, and compare his advancement with that of white youths, do not consider the influence of the memories which cling about the old family homesteads. I have no idea, as I have stated elsewhere, who my grandmother was. I have, or have had, uncles and aunts and cousins, but I have no knowledge as to where most of them are. My case will illustrate that of hundreds of thousands of black people in every part of our country. The very fact that the white boy is conscious that, if he fails in life, he will disgrace the whole family record, extending back through many generations, is of tremendous value in helping him to resist temptations. The fact that the individual has behind and surrounding him proud family history and connection serves as a stimulus to help him to overcome obstacles when striving for success.

The time that I was permitted to attend school during the day was short, and my attendance was irregular. It was not long before I had to stop attending day-school altogether, and devote all of my time again to work. I resorted to the night-school again. In fact, the greater part of the education I secured in my boyhood was gathered through the night-school after my day's work was done. I had difficulty often in securing a satisfactory teacher. Sometimes, after I had secured some one to teach me at night, I would find, much to my disappointment, that the teacher knew but little more than I did. Often I would have to walk several miles at night in order to recite my night-school lessons. There was never a time in my youth, no matter how dark and discouraging the days might be, when one resolve did not continually remain with me, and that was a determination to secure an education at any cost.

Soon after we moved to West Virginia, my mother adopted into our family, notwithstanding our poverty, an orphan boy, to whom afterward we gave the name of James B. Washington. He has ever since remained a member of the family.

After I had worked in the salt-furnace for some time, work was secured for me in a coal-mine which was operated mainly for the purpose of securing fuel for the salt-furnace. Work in the coal-mine I always dreaded. One reason for this was that any one who worked in a coal-mine was always unclean, at least while at work, and it was a very hard job to get one's skin clean after the day's work was over. Then it was fully a mile from the opening of the coal-mine to the face of the coal, and all, of course, was in the blackest darkness. I do not believe that one ever experiences anywhere else such darkness as he does in a coal-mine. The mine was divided into a large number of different "rooms" or departments, and, as I never was able to learn the location of all these "rooms," I many times found myself lost in the mine. To add to the horror of being lost, sometimes my light would go out, and then, if I did not happen to have a match, I would wander about in the darkness until by chance I found some one to give me a light. The work was not only hard, but it was dangerous. There was always the danger of being blown to pieces by a premature explosion of powder, or of being crushed by falling slate. Accidents from one or the other of these causes were frequently occurring, and this kept me in constant fear. Many children of the tenderest years were compelled then, as is now true I fear, in most coal-mining districts, to spend a large part of their lives in these coal-mines, with little opportunity to get an education; and, what is worse, I have often noted that, as a rule, young boys who begin life in a coal-mine are often physically and mentally dwarfed. They soon lose ambition to do anything else than to continue as a coal-miner.

In those days, and later as a young man, I used to try to picture in my imagination the feelings and ambitions of a white boy with absolutely no limit placed upon his aspirations and activities. I used to envy the white boy who had no obstacles placed in the way of his becoming a Congressman, Governor, Bishop, or President by reason of the accident of his birth or race. I used to picture the way that I would act under such circumstances; how I would begin at the bottom and keep rising until I reached the highest round of success.

In later years, I confess that I do not envy the white boy as I once did. I have learned that success is to be measured not so much by the position that one has reached in life as by the obstacles which he has overcome while trying to succeed. Looked at from this standpoint, I almost reached the conclusion that often the Negro boy's birth and connection with an unpopular race is an advantage, so far as real life is concerned. With few exceptions, the Negro youth must work harder and must perform his tasks even better than a white youth in order to secure recognition. But out of the hard and unusual struggle through which he is compelled to pass, he gets a strength, a confidence, that one misses whose pathway is comparatively smooth by reason of birth and race.

From any point of view, I had rather be what I am, a member of the Negro race, than be able to claim membership with the most favored of any other race. I have always been made sad when I have heard members of any race claiming rights or privileges, or certain badges of distinction, on the ground simply that they were members of this or that race, regardless of their own individual worth or attainments. I have been made to feel sad for such persons because I am conscious of the fact that mere connection with what is known as a superior race will not permanently carry an individual forward unless he has individual worth, and mere connection with what is regarded as an inferior race will not finally hold an individual back if he possesses intrinsic, individual merit. Every persecuted individual and race should get much consolation out of the great human law, which is universal and eternal, that merit, no matter under what skin found, is, in the long run, recognized and rewarded. This I have said here, not to call attention to myself as an individual, but to the race to which I am proud to belong.

The Struggle For An Education

One day, while at work in the coal-mine, I happened to overhear two miners talking about a great school for colored people somewhere in Virginia. This was the first time that I had ever heard anything about any kind of school or college that was more pretentious than the little colored school in our town.

In the darkness of the mine I noiselessly crept as close as I could to the two men who were talking. I heard one tell the other that not only was the school established for the members of any race, but the opportunities that it provided by which poor but worthy students could work out all or a part of the cost of a board, and at the same time be taught some trade or industry.

As they went on describing the school, it seemed to me that it must be the greatest place on earth, and not even Heaven presented more attractions for me at that time than did the Hampton Normal and Agricultural Institute in Virginia, about which these men were talking. I resolved at once to go to that school, although I had no idea where it was, or how many miles away, or how I was going to reach it; I remembered only that I was on fire constantly with one ambition, and that was to go to Hampton. This thought was with me day and night.

After hearing of the Hampton Institute, I continued to work for a few months longer in the coal-mine. While at work there, I heard of a vacant position in the household of General Lewis Ruffner, the owner of the salt-furnace and coal-mine. Mrs. Viola Ruffner, the wife of General Ruffner, was a "Yankee" woman from Vermont. Mrs. Ruffner had a reputation all through the vicinity for being very strict with her servants, and especially with the boys who tried to serve her. Few of them remained with her more than two or three weeks. They all left with the same excuse: she was too strict. I decided, however, that I would rather try Mrs. Ruffner's house than remain in the coal-mine, and so my mother applied to her for the vacant position. I was hired at a salary of $5 per month.

I had heard so much about Mrs. Ruffner's severity that I was almost afraid to see her, and trembled when I went into her presence. I had not lived with her many weeks, however, before I began to understand her. I soon began to learn that, first of all, she wanted everything kept clean about her, that she wanted things done promptly and systematically, and that at the bottom of everything she wanted absolute honesty and frankness. Nothing must be sloven or slipshod; every door, every fence, must be kept in repair.

I cannot now recall how long I lived with Mrs. Ruffner before going to Hampton, but I think it must have been a year and a half. At any rate, I here repeat what I have said more than once before, that the lessons that I learned in the home of Mrs. Ruffner were as valuable to me as any education I have ever gotten anywhere else. Even to this day I never see bits of paper scattered around a house or in the street that I do not want to pick them up at once. I never see a filthy yard that I do not want to clean it, a paling off of a fence that I do not want to put it on, an unpainted or unwhitewashed house that I do not want to pain or whitewash it, or a button off one's clothes, or a grease-spot on them or on a floor, that I do not want to call attention to it.

From fearing Mrs. Ruffner I soon learned to look upon her as one of my best friends. When she found that she could trust me she did so implicitly. During the one or two winters that I was with her she gave me an opportunity to go to school for an hour in the day during a portion of the winter months, but most of my studying was done at night, sometimes alone, sometimes under some one whom I could hire to teach me. Mrs. Ruffner always encouraged and sympathized with me in all my efforts to get an education. It was while living with her that I began to get together my first library. I secured a dry-goods box, knocked out one side of it, put some shelves in it, and began putting into it every kind of book that I could get my hands upon, and called it my "library."

Notwithstanding my success at Mrs. Ruffner's I did not give up the idea of going to the Hampton Institute. In the fall of 1872 I determined to make an effort to get there, although, as I have stated, I had no definite idea of the direction in which Hampton was, or of what it would cost to go there. I do not think that any one thoroughly sympathized with me in my ambition to go to Hampton unless it was my mother, and she was troubled with a grave fear that I was starting out on a "wild-goose chase." At any rate, I got only a half-hearted consent from her that I might start. The small amount of money that I had earned had been consumed by my stepfather and the remainder of the family, with the exception of a very few dollars, and so I had very little with which to buy clothes and pay my traveling expenses. My brother John helped me all that he could, but of course that was not a great deal, for his work was in the coal-mine, where he did not earn much, and most of what he did earn went in the direction of paying the household expenses.

Perhaps the thing that touched and pleased me most in connection with my starting for Hampton was the interest that many of the older colored people took in the matter. They had spent the best days of their lives in slavery, and hardly expected to live to see the time when they would see a member of their race leave home to attend a boarding-school. Some of these older people would give me a nickel, others a quarter, or a handkerchief.

Finally the great day came, and I started for Hampton. I had only a small, cheap satchel that contained a few articles of clothing I could get. My mother at the time was rather weak and broken in health. I hardly expected to see her again, and thus our parting was all the more sad. She, however, was very brave through it all. At that time there were no through trains connecting that part of West Virginia with eastern Virginia. Trains ran only a portion of the way, and the remainder of the distance was traveled by stage-coaches.

The distance from Malden to Hampton is about five hundred miles. I had not been away from home many hours before it began to grow painfully evident that I did not have enough money to pay my fair to Hampton. One experience I shall long remember. I had been traveling over the mountains most of the afternoon in an old-fashion stage-coach, when, late in the evening, the coach stopped for the night at a common, unpainted house called a hotel. All the other passengers except myself were whites. In my ignorance I supposed that the little hotel existed for the purpose of accommodating the passengers who traveled on the stage-coach. The difference that the color of one's skin would make I had not thought anything about. After all the other passengers had been shown rooms and were getting ready for supper, I shyly presented myself before the man at the desk. It is true

I had practically no money in my pocket with which to pay for bed or food, but I had hoped in some way to beg my way into the good graces of the landlord, for at that season in the mountains of Virginia the weather was cold, and I wanted to get indoors for the night. Without asking as to whether I had any money, the man at the desk firmly refused to even consider the matter of providing me with food or lodging. This was my first experience in finding out what the color of my skin meant. In some way I managed to keep warm by walking about, and so got through the night. My whole soul was so bent upon reaching Hampton that I did not have time to cherish any bitterness toward the hotel-keeper.

By walking, begging rides both in wagons and in the cars, in some way, after a number of days, I reached the city of Richmond, Virginia, about eighty-two miles from Hampton. When I reached there, tired, hungry, and dirty, it was late in the night. I had never been in a large city, and this rather added to my misery. When I reached Richmond, I was completely out of money. I had not a single acquaintance in the place, and, being unused to city ways, I did not know where to go. I applied at several places for lodging, but they all wanted money, and that was what I did not have. Knowing nothing else better to do, I walked the streets. In doing this I passed by many a food-stands where fried chicken and half-moon apple pies were piled high and made to present a most tempting appearance. At that time it seemed to me that I would have promised all that I expected to possess in the future to have gotten hold of one of those chicken legs or one of those pies. But I could not get either of these, nor anything else to eat.

I must have walked the streets till after midnight. At last I became so exhausted that I could walk no longer. I was tired, I was hungry, I was everything but discouraged. Just about the time when I reached extreme physical exhaustion, I came upon a portion of a street where the board sidewalk was considerably elevated. I waited for a few minutes, till I was sure that no passers-by could see me, and then crept under the sidewalk and lay for the night upon the ground, with my satchel of clothing for a pillow. Nearly all night I could hear the tramp of feet over my head. The next morning I found myself somewhat refreshed, but I was extremely hungry, because it had been a long time since I had had sufficient food. As soon as it became light enough for me to see my surroundings I noticed that I was near a large ship, and that this ship seemed to be unloading a cargo of pig iron. I went at once to the vessel and asked the captain to permit me to help unload the vessel in order to get money for food. The captain, a white man, who seemed to be kind-hearted, consented. I worked long enough to earn money for my breakfast, and it seems to me, as I remember it now, to have been about the best breakfast that I have ever eaten.

My work pleased the captain so well that he told me if I desired I could continue working for a small amount per day. This I was very glad to do. I continued working on this vessel for a number of days. After buying food with the small wages I received there was not much left to add on the amount I must get to pay my way to Hampton. In order to economize in every way possible, so as to be sure to reach Hampton in a reasonable time, I continued to sleep under the same sidewalk that gave me shelter the first night I was in Richmond. Many years after that the colored citizens of Richmond very kindly tendered me a reception at which there must have been two thousand people present. This reception was held not far from the spot where I slept the first night I spent in the city, and I must confess that my mind was more upon the sidewalk that first gave me shelter than upon the recognition, agreeable and cordial as it was.

When I had saved what I considered enough money with which to reach Hampton, I thanked the captain of the vessel for his kindness, and started again. Without any unusual occurrence I reached Hampton, with a surplus of exactly fifty cents with which to begin my education. To me it had been a long, eventful journey; but the first sight of the large, three-story, brick school building seemed to have rewarded me for all that I had undergone in order to reach the place. If the people who gave the money to provide that building could appreciate the influence the sight of it had upon me, as well as upon thousands of other youths, they would feel all the more encouraged to make such gifts. It seemed to me to be the largest and most beautiful building I had ever seen. The sight of it seemed to give me new life. I felt that a new kind of existence had now begun—that life would now have a new meaning. I felt that I had reached the promised land, and I resolved to let no obstacle prevent me from putting forth the highest effort to fit myself to accomplish the most good in the world.

As soon as possible after reaching the grounds of the Hampton Institute, I presented myself before the head teacher for an assignment to a class. Having been so long without proper food, a bath, and a change of clothing, I did not, of course, make a very favorable impression upon her, and I could see at once that there were doubts in her mind about the wisdom of admitting me as a student. I felt that I could hardly blame her if she got the idea that I was a worthless loafer or tramp. For some time she did not refuse to admit me, neither did she decide in my favor, and I continued to linger about her, and to impress her in all the ways I could with my worthiness. In the meantime I saw her admitting other students, and that added greatly to my discomfort, for I felt, deep down in my heart, that I could do as well as they, if I could only get a chance to show what was in me.

After some hours had passed, the head teacher said to me: "The adjoining recitation-room needs sweeping. Take the broom and sweep it."

It occurred to me at once that here was my chance. Never did I receive an order with more delight. I knew that I could sweep, for Mrs. Ruffner had thoroughly taught me how to do that when I lived with her.

I swept the recitation-room three times. Then I got a dusting-cloth and dusted it four times. All the woodwork around the walls, every bench, table, and desk, I went over four times with my dusting-cloth. Besides, every piece of furniture had been moved and every closet and corner in the room had been thoroughly cleaned. I had the feeling that in a large measure my future dependent upon the impression I made upon the teacher in the cleaning of that room. When I was through, I reported to the head teacher. She was a "Yankee" woman who knew just where to look for dirt. She went into the room and inspected the floor and closets; then she took her handkerchief and rubbed it on the woodwork about the walls, and over the table and benches. When she was unable to find one bit of dirt on the floor, or a particle of dust on any of the furniture, she quietly remarked, "I guess you will do to enter this institution."

I was one of the happiest souls on Earth. The sweeping of that room was my college examination, and never did any youth pass an examination for entrance into Harvard or Yale that gave him more genuine satisfaction. I have passed several examinations since then, but I have always felt that this was the best one I ever passed.

I have spoken of my own experience in entering the Hampton Institute. Perhaps few, if any, had anything like the same experience that I had, but about the same period there were hundreds who found their way to Hampton and other institutions after experiencing something of the same difficulties that I went through. The young men and women were determined to secure an education at any cost.

The sweeping of the recitation-room in the manner that I did it seems to have paved the way for me to get through Hampton. Miss Mary F. Mackie, the head teacher, offered me a position as janitor. This, of course, I gladly accepted, because it was a place where I could work out nearly all the cost of my board. The work was hard and taxing but I stuck to it. I had a large number of rooms to care for, and had to work late into the night, while at the same time I had to rise by four o'clock in the morning, in order to build the fires and have a little time in which to prepare my lessons. In all my career at Hampton, and ever since I have been out in the world, Miss Mary F. Mackie, the head teacher to whom I have referred, proved one of my strongest and most helpful friends. Her advice and encouragement were always helpful in strengthening to me in the darkest hour.

I have spoken of the impression that was made upon me by the buildings and general appearance of the Hampton Institute, but I have not spoken of that which made the greatest and most lasting impression on me, and that was a great man—the noblest, rarest human being that it has ever been my privilege to meet. I refer to the late General Samuel C. Armstrong.

It has been my fortune to meet personally many of what are called great characters, both in Europe and America, but I do not hesitate to say that I never met any man who, in my estimation, was the equal of General Armstrong. Fresh from the degrading influences of the slave plantation and the coal-mines, it was a rare privilege for me to be permitted to come into direct contact with such a character as General Armstrong. I shall always remember that the first time I went into his presence he made the impression upon me of being a perfect man: I was made to feel that there was something about him that was superhuman. It was my privilege to know the General personally from the time I entered Hampton till he died, and the more I saw of him the greater he grew in my estimation. One might have removed from Hampton all the buildings, class-rooms, teachers, and industries, and given the men and women there the opportunity of coming into daily contact with General Armstrong, and that alone would have been a liberal education. The older I grow, the more I am convinced that there is no education which one can get from books and costly apparatus that is equal to that which can be gotten from contact with great men and women. Instead of studying books so constantly, how I wish that our schools and colleges might learn to study men and things!

General Armstrong spent two of the last six months of his life in my home at Tuskegee. At that time he was paralyzed to the extent that he had lost control of his body and voice in a very large degree. Notwithstanding his affliction, he worked almost constantly night and day for the cause to which he had given his life. I never saw a man who so completely lost sight of himself. I do not believe he ever had a selfish thought. He was just as happy in trying to assist some other institution in the South as he was when working for Hampton. Although he fought the Southern white man in the Civil War, I never heard him utter a bitter word against him afterward. On the other hand, he was constantly seeking to find ways by which he could be of service to the Southern whites.

It would be difficult to describe the hold that he had upon the students at Hampton, or the faith they had in him. In fact, he was worshiped by his students. It never occurred to me that General Armstrong could fail in anything that he undertook. There is almost no request that he could have made that would not have been complied with. When he was a guest at my home in Alabama, and was so badly paralyzed that he had to be wheeled about in an invalid's chair, I recall that one of the General's former students had occasion to push his chair up a long, steep hill that taxed his strength to the utmost. When the top of the hill was reached, the former pupil, with a glow of happiness on his face, exclaimed, "I am so glad that I have been permitted to do something that was real hard for the General before he dies!" While I was a student at Hampton, the dormitories became so crowded that it was impossible to find room for all who wanted to be admitted. In order to help remedy the difficulty, the General conceived the plan of putting up tents to be used as rooms. As soon as it became known that General Armstrong would be pleased if some of the older students would live in the tents during the winter, nearly every student in school volunteered to go.

I was one of the volunteers. The winter that we spent in those tents was an intensely cold one, and we suffered severely—how much I am sure General Armstrong never knew, because we made no complaints. It was enough for us to know that we were pleasing General Armstrong, and that we were making it possible for an additional number of students to secure an education. More than once, during a cold night, when a stiff gale would be blowing, our tend was lifted bodily, and we would find ourselves in the open air. The General would usually pay a visit to the tents early in the morning, and his earnest, cheerful, encouraging voice would dispel any feeling of despondency.

I have spoken of my admiration for General Armstrong, and yet he was but a type of that Christlike body of men and women who went into the Negro schools at the close of the war by the hundreds to assist in lifting up my race. The history of the world fails to show a higher, purer, and more unselfish class of men and women than those who found their way into those Negro schools.

Life at Hampton was a constant revelation to me; was constantly taking me into a new world. The matter of having meals at regular hours, of eating on a tablecloth, using a napkin, the use of the bath-tub and of the tooth-brush, as well as the use of sheets upon the bed, were all new to me.

I sometimes feel that almost the most valuable lesson I got at the Hampton Institute was in the use and value of the bath. I learned there for the first time some of its value, not only in keeping the body healthy, but in inspiring self-respect and promoting virtue. In all my travels in the South and elsewhere since leaving Hampton I have always in some way sought my daily bath. To get it sometimes when I have been the guest of my own people in a single-roomed cabin has not always been easy to do, except by slipping away to some stream in the woods. I have always tried to teach my people that some provision for bathing should be a part of every house.

For some time, while a student at Hampton, I possessed but a single pair of socks, but when I had worn these till they became soiled, I would wash them at night and hang them by the fire to dry, so that I might wear them again the next morning.

The charge for my board at Hampton was ten dollars per month. I was expected to pay a part of this in cash and to work out the remainder. To meet this cash payment, as I have stated, I had just fifty cents when I reached the institution. Aside from a very few dollars that my brother John was able to send me once in a while, I had no money with which to pay my board. I was determined from the first to make my work as janitor so valuable that my services would be indispensable. This I succeeded in doing to such an extent that I was soon informed that I would be allowed the full cost of my board in return for my work. The cost of tuition was seventy dollars a year. This, of course, was wholly beyond my ability to provide. If I had been compelled to pay the seventy dollars for tuition, in addition to providing for my board, I would have been compelled to leave the Hampton school. General Armstrong, however, very kindly got Mr. S. Griffitts Morgan, of New Bedford, Mass., to defray the cost of my tuition during the whole time that I was at Hampton. After I finished the course at Hampton and had entered upon my lifework at Tuskegee, I had the pleasure of visiting Mr. Morgan several times.

After having been for a while at Hampton, I found myself in difficulty because I did not have books and clothing. Usually, however, I got around the trouble about books by borrowing from those who were more fortunate than myself. As to clothes, when I reached Hampton I had practically nothing. Everything that I possessed was in a small hand satchel. My anxiety about clothing was increased because of the fact that General Armstrong made a personal inspection of the young men in ranks, to see that their clothes were clean. Shoes had to be polished, there must be no buttons off the clothing, and no grease-spots. To wear one suit of clothes continually, while at work and in the schoolroom, and at the same time keep it clean, was rather a hard problem for me to solve. In some way I managed to get on till the teachers learned that I was in earnest and meant to succeed, and then some of them were kind enough to see that I was partly supplied with second-hand clothing that had been sent in barrels from the North. These barrels proved a blessing to hundreds of poor but deserving students. Without them I question whether I should ever have gotten through Hampton.

When I first went to Hampton I do not recall that I had ever slept in a bed that had two sheets on it. In those days there were not many buildings there, and room was very precious. There were seven other boys in the same room with me; most of them, however, students who had been there for some time. The sheets were quite a puzzle to me. The first night I slept under both of them, and the second night I slept on top of them; but by watching the other boys I learned my lesson in this, and have been trying to follow it ever since and to teach it to others.

I was among the youngest of the students who were in Hampton at the time. Most of the students were men and women—some as old as forty years of ago. As I now recall the scene of my first year, I do not believe that one often has the opportunity of coming into contact with three or four hundred men and women who were so tremendously in earnest as these men and women were. Every hour was occupied in study or work. Nearly all had had enough actual contact with the world to teach them the need of education. Many of the older ones were, of course, too old to master the text-books very thoroughly, and it was often sad to watch their struggles; but they made up in earnest much of what they lacked in books. Many of them were as poor as I was, and, besides having to wrestle with their books, they had to struggle with a poverty which prevented their having the necessities of life. Many of them had aged parents who were dependent upon them, and some of them were men who had wives whose support in some way they had to provide for.

The great and prevailing idea that seemed to take possession of every one was to prepare himself to lift up the people at his home. No one seemed to think of himself. And the officers and teachers, what a rare set of human beings they were! They worked for the students night and day, in seasons and out of season. They seemed happy only when they were helping the students in some manner. Whenever it is written—and I hope it will be—the part that the Yankee teachers played in the education of the Negroes immediately after the war will make one of the most thrilling parts of the history off this country. The time is not far distant when the whole South will appreciate this service in a way that it has not yet been able to do.

Helping Others

At the end of my first year at Hampton I was confronted with another difficulty. Most of the students went home to spend their vacation. I had no money with which to go home, but I had to go somewhere. In those days very few students were permitted to remain at the school during vacation. It made me feel very sad and homesick to see the other students preparing to leave and starting for home. I not only had no money with which to go home, but I had none with which to go anywhere.

In some way, however, I had gotten hold of an extra, second-hand coat which I thought was a pretty valuable coat. This I decided to sell, in order to get a little money for traveling expenses. I had a good deal of boyish pride, and I tried to hide, as far as I could, from the other students the fact that I had no money and nowhere to go. I made it known to a few people in the town of Hampton that I had this coat to sell, and, after a good deal of persuading, one colored man promised to come to my room to look the coat over and consider the matter of buying it. This cheered my drooping spirits considerably. Early the next morning my prospective customer appeared. After looking the garment over carefully, he asked me how much I wanted for it. I told him I thought it was worth three dollars. He seemed to agree with me as to price, but remarked in the most matter-of-fact way: "I tell you what I will do; I will take the coat, and will pay you five cents, cash down, and pay you the rest of the money just as soon as I can get it." It is not hard to imagine what my feelings were at the time.

With this disappointment I gave up all hope of getting out of the town of Hampton for my vacation work. I wanted very much to go where I might secure work that would at least pay me enough to purchase some much-needed clothing and other necessities. In a few days practically all the students and teachers had left for their homes, and this served to depress my spirits even more.

After trying for several days in and near the town of Hampton, I finally secured work in a restaurant at Fortress Monroe. The wages, however, were very little more than my board. At night, and between meals, I found considerable time for study and reading; and in this direction I improved myself very much during the summer.

When I left school at the end of my first year, I owed the institution sixteen dollars that I had not been able to work out. It was my greatest ambition during the summer to save money enough with which to pay this debt. I felt that this was a debt of honor, and that I could hardly bring myself to the point of even trying to enter school again till it was paid. I economized in every way that I could think of—did my own washing, and went without necessary garments—but still I found my summer vacation ending and I did not have the sixteen dollars.

One day, during the last week of my stay in the restaurant, I found under one of the tables a crisp, new ten-dollar bill. I could hardly contain myself, I was so happy. As it was not my place of business I felt it to be the proper thing to show the money to the proprietor. This I did. He seemed as glad as I was, but he coolly explained to me that, as it was his place of business, he had a right to keep the money, and he proceeded to do so. This, I confess, was another pretty hard blow to me. I will not say that I became discouraged, for as I now look back over my life I do not recall that I ever became discouraged over anything that I set out to accomplish. I have begun everything with the idea that I could succeed, and I never had much patience with the multitudes of people who are always ready to explain why one cannot succeed. I determined to face the situation just as it was. At the end of the week I went to the treasurer of the Hampton Institute, General J.F.B. Marshall, and told him frankly my condition. To my gratification he told me that I could reenter the institution, and that he would trust me to pay the debt when I could. During the second year I continued to work as a janitor.

The education that I received at Hampton out of the text-books was but a small part of what I learned there. One of the things that impressed itself upon me deeply, the second year, was the unselfishness of the teachers. It was hard for me to understand how any individuals could bring themselves to the point where they could be so happy in working for others. Before the end of the year, I think I began learning that those who are happiest are those who do the most for others. This lesson I have tried to carry with me ever since.

I also learned a valuable lesson at Hampton by coming into contact with the best breeds of live stock and fowls. No student, I think, who has had the opportunity of doing this could go out into the world and content himself with the poorest grades.

Perhaps the most valuable thing that I got out of my second year was an understanding of the use and value of the Bible. Miss Nathalie Lord, one of the teachers, from Portland, Me., taught me how to use and love the Bible. Before this I had never cared a great deal about it, but now I learned to love to read the Bible, not only for the spiritual help which it gives, but on account of it as literature. The lessons taught me in this respect took such a hold upon me that at the present time, when I am at home, no matter how busy I am, I always make it a rule to read a chapter or a portion of a chapter in the morning, before beginning the work of the day.

Whatever ability I may have as a public speaker I owe in a measure to Miss Lord. When she found out that I had some inclination in this direction, she gave me private lessons in the matter of breathing, emphasis, and articulation. Simply to be able to talk in public for the sake of talking has never had the least attraction to me. In fact, I consider that there is nothing so empty and unsatisfactory as mere abstract public speaking; but from my early childhood I have had a desire to do something to make the world better, and then to be able to speak to the world about that thing.

The debating societies at Hampton were a constant source of delight to me. These were held on Saturday evening; and during my whole life at Hampton I do not recall that I missed a single meeting. I not only attended the weekly debating society, but was instrumental in organizing an additional society. I noticed that between the time when supper was over and the time to begin evening study there were about twenty minutes which the young men usually spent in idle gossip. About twenty of us formed a society for the purpose of utilizing this time in debate or in practice in public speaking. Few persons ever derived more happiness or benefit from the use of twenty minutes of time than we did in this way.

At the end of my second year at Hampton, by the help of some money sent me by my mother and brother John, supplemented by a small gift from one of the teachers at Hampton, I was enabled to return to my home in Malden, West Virginia, to spend my vacation. When I reached home I found that the salt-furnaces were not running, and that the coal-mine was not being operated on account of the miners being out on "strike." This was something which, it seemed, usually occurred whenever the men got two or three months ahead in their savings. During the strike, of course, they spent all that they had saved, and would often return to work in debt at the same wages, or would move to another mine at considerable expense. In either case, my observations convinced me that the miners were worse off at the end of the strike. Before the days of strikes in that section of the country, I knew miners who had considerable money in the bank, but as soon as the professional labor agitators got control, the savings of even the more thrifty ones began disappearing.

My mother and the other members of my family were, of course, much rejoiced to see me and to note the improvement that I had made during my two years' absence. The rejoicing on the part of all classes of the colored people, and especially the older ones, over my return, was almost pathetic. I had to pay a visit to each family and take a meal with each, and at each place tell the story of my experiences at Hampton. In addition to this I had to speak before the church and Sunday-school, and at various other places. The thing that I was most in search of, though, work, I could not find. There was no work on account of the strike. I spent nearly the whole of the first month of my vacation in an effort to find something to do by which I could earn money to pay my way back to Hampton and save a little money to use after reaching there.

Toward the end of the first month, I went to place a considerable distance from my home, to try to find employment. I did not succeed, and it was night before I got started on my return. When I had gotten within a mile or so of my home I was so completely tired out that I could not walk any farther, and I went into an old, abandoned house to spend the remainder of the night. About three o'clock in the morning my brother John found me asleep in this house, and broke to me, as gently as he could, the sad news that our dear mother had died during the night.

This seemed to me the saddest and blankest moment in my life. For several years my mother had not been in good health, but I had no idea, when I parted from her the previous day, that I should never see her alive again. Besides that, I had always had an intense desire to be with her when she did pass away. One of the chief ambitions which spurred me on at Hampton was that I might be able to get to be in a position in which I could better make my mother comfortable and happy. She had so often expressed the wish that she might be permitted to live to see her children educated and started out in the world.

In a very short time after the death of my mother our little home was in confusion. My sister Amanda, although she tried to do the best she could, was too young to know anything about keeping house, and my stepfather was not able to hire a housekeeper. Sometimes we had food cooked for us, and sometimes we did not. I remember that more than once a can of tomatoes and some crackers constituted a meal. Our clothing went uncared for, and everything about our home was soon in a tumble-down condition. It seems to me that this was the most dismal period of my life.

My good friend, Mrs. Ruffner, to whom I have already referred, always made me welcome at her home, and assisted me in many ways during this trying period. Before the end of the vacation she gave me some work, and this, together with work in a coal-mine at some distance from my home, enabled me to earn a little money.

At one time it looked as if I would have to give up the idea of returning to Hampton, but my heart was so set on returning that I determined not to give up going back without a struggle. I was very anxious to secure some clothes for the winter, but in this I was disappointed, except for a few garments which my brother John secured for me. Notwithstanding my need of money and clothing, I was very happy in the fact that I had secured enough money to pay my traveling expenses back to Hampton. Once there, I knew that I could make myself so useful as a janitor that I could in some way get through the school year.

Three weeks before the time for the opening of the term at Hampton, I was pleasantly surprised to receive a letter from my good friend Miss Mary F. Mackie, the lady principal, asking me to return to Hampton two weeks before the opening of the school, in order that I might assist her in cleaning the buildings and getting things in order for the new school year. This was just the opportunity I wanted. It gave me a chance to secure a credit in the treasurer's office. I started for Hampton at once.

During these two weeks I was taught a lesson which I shall never forget. Miss Mackie was a member of one of the oldest and most cultured families of the North, and yet for two weeks she worked by my side cleaning windows, dusting rooms, putting beds in order, and what not. She felt that things would not be in condition for the opening of school unless every window-pane was perfectly clean, and she took the greatest satisfaction in helping to clean them herself. The work which I have described she did every year that I was at Hampton.

It was hard for me at this time to understand how a woman of her education and social standing could take such delight in performing such service, in order to assist in the elevation of an unfortunate race. Ever since then I have had no patience with any school for my race in the South which did not teach its students the dignity of labor.

During my last year at Hampton every minute of my time that was not occupied with my duties as janitor was devoted to hard study. I was determined, if possible, to make such a record in my class as would cause me to be placed on the "honor roll" of Commencement speakers. This I was successful in doing. It was June of 1875 when I finished the regular course of study at Hampton. The greatest benefits that I got out of my at the Hampton Institute, perhaps, may be classified under two heads:—

First was contact with a great man, General S.C. Armstrong, who, I repeat, was, in my opinion, the rarest, strongest, and most beautiful character that it has ever been my privilege to meet.

Second, at Hampton, for the first time, I learned what education was expected to do for an individual. Before going there I had a good deal of the then rather prevalent idea among our people that to secure an education meant to have a good, easy time, free from all necessity for manual labor. At Hampton I not only learned that it was not a disgrace to labor, but learned to love labor, not alone for its financial value, but for labor's own sake and for the independence and self-reliance which the ability to do something which the world wants done brings. At that institution I got my first taste of what it meant to live a life of unselfishness, my first knowledge of the fact that the happiest individuals are those who do the most to make others useful and happy.

I was completely out of money when I graduated. In company with our other Hampton students, I secured a place as a table waiter in a summer hotel in Connecticut, and managed to borrow enough money with which to get there. I had not been in this hotel long before I found out that I knew practically nothing about waiting on a hotel table. The head waiter, however, supposed that I was an accomplished waiter. He soon gave me charge of the table at which their sat four or five wealthy and rather aristocratic people. My ignorance of how to wait upon them was so apparent that they scolded me in such a severe manner that I became frightened and left their table, leaving them sitting there without food. As a result of this I was reduced from the position of waiter to that of a dish-carrier.

But I determined to learn the business of waiting, and did so within a few weeks and was restored to my former position. I have had the satisfaction of being a guest in this hotel several times since I was a waiter there.

At the close of the hotel season I returned to my former home in Malden, and was elected to teach the colored school at that place. This was the beginning of one of the happiest periods of my life. I now felt that I had the opportunity to help the people of my home town to a higher life. I felt from the first that mere book education was not all that the young people of that town needed. I began my work at eight o'clock in the morning, and, as a rule, it did not end until ten o'clock at night. In addition to the usual routine of teaching, I taught the pupils to comb their hair, and to keep their hands and faces clean, as well as their clothing. I gave special attention to teaching them the proper use of the tooth-brush and the bath. In all my teaching I have watched carefully the influence of the tooth-brush, and I am convinced that there are few single agencies of civilization that are more far-reaching.

There were so many of the older boys and girls in the town, as well as men and women, who had to work in the daytime and still were craving an opportunity for an education, that I soon opened a night-school. From the first, this was crowded every night, being about as large as the school that I taught in the day. The efforts of some of the men and women, who in many cases were over fifty years of age, to learn, were in some cases very pathetic.

My day and night school work was not all that I undertook. I established a small reading-room and a debating society. On Sundays I taught two Sunday-schools, one in the town of Malden in the afternoon, and the other in the morning at a place three miles distant from Malden. In addition to this, I gave private lessons to several young men whom I was fitting to send to the Hampton Institute. Without regard to pay and with little thought of it, I taught any one who wanted to learn anything that I could teach him. I was supremely happy in the opportunity of being able to assist somebody else. I did receive, however, a small salary from the public fund, for my work as a public-school teacher.

During the time that I was a student at Hampton my older brother, John, not only assisted me all that he could, but worked all of the time in the coal-mines in order to support the family. He willingly neglected his own education that he might help me. It was my earnest wish to help him to prepare to enter Hampton, and to save money to assist him in his expenses there. Both of these objects I was successful in accomplishing. In three years my brother finished the course at Hampton, and he is now holding the important position of Superintendent of Industries at Tuskegee. When he returned from Hampton, we both combined our efforts and savings to send our adopted brother, James, through the Hampton Institute. This we succeeded in doing, and he is now the postmaster at the Tuskegee Institute. The year 1877, which was my second year of teaching in Malden, I spent very much as I did the first.

It was while my home was at Malden that what was known as the "Ku Klux Klan" was in the height of its activity. The "Ku Klux" were bands of men who had joined themselves together for the purpose of regulating the conduct of the colored people, especially with the object of preventing the members of the race from exercising any influence in politics. They corresponded somewhat to the "patrollers" of whom I used to hear a great deal during the days of slavery, when I was a small boy. The "patrollers" were bands of white men—usually young men—who were organized largely for the purpose of regulating the conduct of the slaves at night in such matters as preventing the slaves from going from one plantation to another without passes, and for preventing them from holding any kind of meetings without permission and without the presence at these meetings of at least one white man.

Like the "patrollers" the "Ku Klux" operated almost wholly at night. They were, however, more cruel than the "patrollers." Their objects, in the main, were to crush out the political aspirations of the Negroes, but they did not confine themselves to this, because schoolhouses as well as churches were burned by them, and many innocent persons were made to suffer. During this period not a few colored people lost their lives.

As a young man, the acts of these lawless bands made a great impression upon me. I saw one open battle take place at Malden between some of the colored and white people. There must have been not far from a hundred persons engaged on each side; many on both sides were seriously injured, among them General Lewis Ruffner, the husband of my friend Mrs. Viola Ruffner. General Ruffner tried to defend the colored people, and for this he was knocked down and so seriously wounded that he never completely recovered. It seemed to me as I watched this struggle between members of the two races, that there was no hope for our people in this country. The "Ku Klux" period was, I think, the darkest part of the Reconstruction days.

I have referred to this unpleasant part of the history of the South simply for the purpose of calling attention to the great change that has taken place since the days of the "Ku Klux." To-day there are no such organizations in the South, and the fact that such ever existed is almost forgotten by both races. There are few places in the South now where public sentiment would permit such organizations to exist.

The Reconstruction Period

The years from 1867 to 1878 I think may be called the period of Reconstruction. This included the time that I spent as a student at Hampton and as a teacher in West Virginia. During the whole of the Reconstruction period two ideas were constantly agitating in the minds of the colored people, or, at least, in the minds of a large part of the race. One of these was the craze for Greek and Latin learning, and the other was a desire to hold office.

It could not have been expected that a people who had spent generations in slavery, and before that generations in the darkest heathenism, could at first form any proper conception of what an education meant. In every part of the South, during the Reconstruction period, schools, both day and night, were filled to overflowing with people of all ages and conditions, some being as far along in age as sixty and seventy years. The ambition to secure an education was most praiseworthy and encouraging. The idea, however, was too prevalent that, as soon as one secured a little education, in some unexplainable way he would be free from most of the hardships of the world, and, at any rate, could live without manual labor. There was a further feeling that a knowledge, however little, of the Greek and Latin languages would make one a very superior human being, something bordering almost on the supernatural. I remember that the first colored man whom I saw who knew something about foreign languages impressed me at the time as being a man of all others to be envied.

Naturally, most of our people who received some little education became teachers or preachers. While among those two classes there were many capable, earnest, godly men and women, still a large proportion took up teaching or preaching as an easy way to make a living. Many became teachers who could do little more than write their names. I remember there came into our neighborhood one of this class, who was in search of a school to teach, and the question arose while he was there as to the shape of the earth and how he could teach the children concerning the subject. He explained his position in the matter by saying that he was prepared to teach that the earth was either flat or round, according to the preference of a majority of his patrons.

The ministry was the profession that suffered most—and still suffers, though there has been great improvement—on account of not only ignorant but in many cases immoral men who claimed that they were "called to preach." In the earlier days of freedom almost every colored man who learned to read would receive "a call to preach" within a few days after he began reading. At my home in West Virginia the process of being called to the ministry was a very interesting one. Usually the "call" came when the individual was sitting in church. Without warning the one called would fall upon the floor as if struck by a bullet, and would lie there for hours, speechless and motionless. Then the news would spread all through the neighborhood that this individual had received a "call." If he were inclined to resist the summons, he would fall or be made to fall a second or third time. In the end he always yielded to the call. While I wanted an education badly, I confess that in my youth I had a fear that when I had learned to read and write very well I would receive one of these "calls"; but, for some reason, my call never came.

When we add the number of wholly ignorant men who preached or "exhorted" to that of those who possessed something of an education, it can be seen at a glance that the supply of ministers was large. In fact, some time ago I knew a certain church that had a total membership of about two hundred, and eighteen of that number were ministers. But, I repeat, in many communities in the South the character of the ministry is being improved, and I believe that within the next two or three decades a very large proportion of the unworthy ones will have disappeared. The "calls" to preach, I am glad to say, are not nearly so numerous now as they were formerly, and the calls to some industrial occupation are growing more numerous. The improvement that has taken place in the character of the teachers is even more marked than in the case of the ministers.

During the whole of the Reconstruction period our people throughout the South looked to the Federal Government for everything, very much as a child looks to its mother. This was not unnatural. The central government gave them freedom, and the whole Nation had been enriched for more than two centuries by the labor of the Negro. Even as a youth, and later in manhood, I had the feeling that it was cruelly wrong in the central government, at the beginning of our freedom, to fail to make some provision for the general education of our people in addition to what the states might do, so that the people would be the better prepared for the duties of citizenship.

It is easy to find fault, to remark what might have been done, and perhaps, after all, and under all the circumstances, those in charge of the conduct of affairs did the only thing that could be done at the time. Still, as I look back now over the entire period of our freedom, I cannot help feeling that it would have been wiser if some plan could have been put in operation which would have made the possession of a certain amount of education or property, or both, a test for the exercise of the franchise, and a way provided by which this test should be made to apply honestly and squarely to both the white and black races.

Though I was but little more than a youth during the period of Reconstruction, I had the feeling that mistakes were being made, and that things could not remain in the condition that they were in then very long. I felt that the Reconstruction policy, so far as it related to my race, was in a large measure on a false foundation, was artificial and forced. In many cases it seemed to me that the ignorance of my race was being used as a tool with which to help white men into office, and that there was an element in the North which wanted to punish the Southern white men by forcing the Negro into positions over the heads of the Southern whites. I felt that the Negro would be the one to suffer for this in the end. Besides, the general political agitation drew the attention of our people away from the more fundamental matters of perfecting themselves in the industries at their doors and in securing property.

The temptations to enter political life were so alluring that I came very near yielding to them at one time, but I was kept from doing so by the feeling that I would be helping in a more substantial way by assisting in the laying of the foundation of the race through a generous education of the hand, head, and heart. I saw colored men who were members of the state legislatures, and county officers, who, in some cases, could not read or write, and whose morals were as weak as their education. Not long ago, when passing through the streets of a certain city in the South, I heard some brick-masons calling out, from the top of a two-story brick building on which they were working, for the "Governor" to "hurry up and bring up some more bricks." Several times I heard the command, "Hurry up, Governor!" "Hurry up, Governor!" My curiosity was aroused to such an extent that I made inquiry as to who the "Governor" was, and soon found that he was a colored man who at one time had held the position of Lieutenant-Governor of his state.

But not all the colored people who were in office during Reconstruction were unworthy of their positions, by any means. Some of them, like the late Senator B.K. Bruce, Governor Pinchback, and many others, were strong, upright, useful men. Neither were all the class designated as carpetbaggers dishonorable men. Some of them, like ex-Governor Bullock, of Georgia, were men of high character and usefulness.

Of course the colored people, so largely without education, and wholly without experience in government, made tremendous mistakes, just as many people similarly situated would have done. Many of the Southern whites have a feeling that, if the Negro is permitted to exercise his political rights now to any degree, the mistakes of the Reconstruction period will repeat themselves. I do not think this would be true, because the Negro is a much stronger and wiser man than he was thirty-five years ago, and he is fast learning the lesson that he cannot afford to act in a manner that will alienate his Southern white neighbors from him. More and more I am convinced that the final solution of the political end of our race problem will be for each state that finds it necessary to change the law bearing upon the franchise to make the law apply with absolute honesty, and without opportunity for double dealing or evasion, to both races alike. Any other course my daily observation in the South convinces me, will be unjust to the Negro, unjust to the white man, and unfair to the rest of the state in the Union, and will be, like slavery, a sin that at some time we shall have to pay for.

In the fall of 1878, after having taught school in Malden for two years, and after I had succeeded in preparing several of the young men and women, besides my two brothers, to enter the Hampton Institute, I decided to spend some months in study at Washington, D.C. I remained there for eight months. I derived a great deal of benefit from the studies which I pursued, and I came into contact with some strong men and women. At the institution I attended there was no industrial training given to the students, and I had an opportunity of comparing the influence of an institution with no industrial training with that of one like the Hampton Institute, that emphasizes the industries. At this school I found the students, in most cases, had more money, were better dressed, wore the latest style of all manner of clothing, and in some cases were more brilliant mentally. At Hampton it was a standing rule that, while the institution would be responsible for securing some one to pay the tuition for the students, the men and women themselves must provide for their own board, books, clothing, and room wholly by work, or partly by work and partly in cash. At the institution at which I now was, I found that a large portion of the students by some means had their personal expenses paid for them. At Hampton the student was constantly making the effort through the industries to help himself, and that very effort was of immense value in character-building. The students at the other school seemed to be less self-dependent. They seemed to give more attention to mere outward appearances.

In a word, they did not appear to me to be beginning at the bottom, on a real, solid foundation, to the extent that they were at Hampton. They knew more about Latin and Greek when they left school, but they seemed to know less about life and its conditions as they would meet it at their homes. Having lived for a number of years in the midst of comfortable surroundings, they were not as much inclined as the Hampton students to go into the country districts of the South, where there was little of comfort, to take up work for our people, and they were more inclined to yield to the temptation to become hotel waiters and Pullman-car porters as their life-work.

During the time I was a student at Washington the city was crowded with colored people, many of whom had recently come from the South. A large proportion of these people had been drawn to Washington because they felt that they could lead a life of ease there. Others had secured minor government positions, and still another large class was there in the hope of securing Federal positions. A number of colored men—some of them very strong and brilliant—were in the House of Representatives at that time, and one, the Hon. B.K. Bruce, was in the Senate. All this tended to make Washington an attractive place for members of the colored race. Then, too, they knew that at all times they could have the protection of the law in the District of Columbia. The public schools in Washington for colored people were better then than they were elsewhere. I took great interest in studying the life of our people there closely at that time. I found that while among them there was a large element of substantial, worthy citizens, there was also a superficiality about the life of a large class that greatly alarmed me. I saw young colored men who were not earning more than four dollars a week spend two dollars or more for a buggy on Sunday to ride up and down Pennsylvania Avenue in, in order that they might try to convince the world that they were worth thousands. I saw other young men who received seventy-five or one hundred dollars per month from the Government, who were in debt at the end of every month. I saw men who but a few months previous were members of Congress, then without employment and in poverty. Among a large class there seemed to be a dependence upon the Government for every conceivable thing. The members of this class had little ambition to create a position for themselves, but wanted the Federal officials to create one for them. How many times I wished them, and have often wished since, that by some power of magic I might remove the great bulk of these people into the county districts and plant them upon the soil, upon the solid and never deceptive foundation of Mother Nature, where all nations and races that have ever succeeded have gotten their start,—a start that at first may be slow and toilsome, but one that nevertheless is real.

In Washington I saw girls whose mothers were earning their living by laundering. These girls were taught by their mothers, in rather a crude way it is true, the industry of laundering. Later, these girls entered the public schools and remained there perhaps six or eight years. When the public school course was finally finished, they wanted more costly dresses, more costly hats and shoes. In a word, while their wants have been increased, their ability to supply their wants had not been increased in the same degree. On the other hand, their six or eight years of book education had weaned them away from the occupation of their mothers. The result of this was in too many cases that the girls went to the bad. I often thought how much wiser it would have been to give these girls the same amount of maternal training—and I favor any kind of training, whether in the languages or mathematics, that gives strength and culture to the mind —but at the same time to give them the most thorough training in the latest and best methods of laundering and other kindred occupations.

Black Race And Red Race

During the year that I spent in Washington, and for some little time before this, there had been considerable agitation in the state of West Virginia over the question of moving the capital of the state from Wheeling to some other central point. As a result of this, the Legislature designated three cities to be voted upon by the citizens of the state as the permanent seat of government. Among these cities was Charleston, only five miles from Malden, my home. At the close of my school year in Washington I was very pleasantly surprised to receive, from a committee of three white people in Charleston, an invitation to canvass the state in the interests of that city. This invitation I accepted, and spent nearly three months in speaking in various parts of the state. Charleston was successful in winning the prize, and is now the permanent seat of government.

The reputation that I made as a speaker during this campaign induced a number of persons to make an earnest effort to get me to enter political life, but I refused, still believing that I could find other service which would prove of more permanent value to my race. Even then I had a strong feeling that what our people most needed was to get a foundation in education, industry, and property, and for this I felt that they could better afford to strive than for political preferment. As for my individual self, it appeared to me to be reasonably certain that I could succeed in political life, but I had a feeling that it would be a rather selfish kind of success—individual success at the cost of failing to do my duty in assisting in laying a foundation for the masses.

At this period in the progress of our race a very large proportion of the young men who went to school or to college did so with the expressed determination to prepare themselves to be great lawyers, or Congressmen, and many of the women planned to become music teachers; but I had a reasonably fixed idea, even at that early period in my life, that there was a need for something to be done to prepare the way for successful lawyers, Congressmen, and music teachers.

I felt that the conditions were a good deal like those of an old colored man, during the days of slavery, who wanted to learn how to play on the guitar. In his desire to take guitar lessons he applied to one of his young masters to teach him, but the young man, not having much faith in the ability of the slave to master the guitar at his age, sought to discourage him by telling him: "Uncle Jake, I will give you guitar lessons; but, Jake, I will have to charge you three dollars for the first lesson, two dollars for the second lesson, and one dollar for the third lesson. But I will charge you only twenty-five cents for the last lesson."

Uncle Jake answered: "All right, boss, I hires you on dem terms. But, boss! I wants yer to be sure an' give me dat las' lesson first."

Soon after my work in connection with the removal of the capital was finished, I received an invitation which gave me great joy and which at the same time was a very pleasant surprise. This was a letter from General Armstrong, inviting me to return to Hampton at the next Commencement to deliver what was called the "post-graduate address." This was an honor which I had not dreamed of receiving. With much care I prepared the best address that I was capable of. I chose for my subject "The Force That Wins."

As I returned to Hampton for the purpose of delivering this address, I went over much of the same ground—now, however, covered entirely by railroad—that I had traversed nearly six years before, when I first sought entrance into Hampton Institute as a student. Now I was able to ride the whole distance in the train. I was constantly contrasting this with my first journey to Hampton. I think I may say, without seeming egotism, that it is seldom that five years have wrought such a change in the life and aspirations of an individual.

At Hampton I received a warm welcome from teachers and students. I found that during my absence from Hampton the institute each year had been getting closer to the real needs and conditions of our people; that the industrial reaching, as well as that of the academic department, had greatly improved. The plan of the school was not modeled after that of any other institution then in existence, but every improvement was made under the magnificent leadership of General Armstrong solely with the view of meeting and helping the needs of our people as they presented themselves at the time. Too often, it seems to me, in missionary and educational work among underdeveloped races, people yield to the temptation of doing that which was done a hundred years before, or is being done in other communities a thousand miles away. The temptation often is to run each individual through a certain educational mold, regardless of the condition of the subject or the end to be accomplished. This was not so at Hampton Institute.

The address which I delivered on Commencement Day seems to have pleased every one, and many kind and encouraging words were spoken to me regarding it. Soon after my return to my home in West Virginia, where I had planned to continue teaching, I was again surprised to receive a letter from General Armstrong, asking me to return to Hampton partly as a teacher and partly to pursue some supplementary studies. This was in the summer of 1879. Soon after I began my first teaching in West Virginia I had picked out four of the brightest and most promising of my pupils, in addition to my two brothers, to whom I have already referred, and had given them special attention, with the view of having them go to Hampton. They had gone there, and in each case the teachers had found them so well prepared that they entered advanced classes. This fact, it seems, led to my being called back to Hampton as a teacher. One of the young men that I sent to Hampton in this way is now Dr. Samuel E. Courtney, a successful physician in Boston, and a member of the School Board of that city.

About this time the experiment was being tried for the first time, by General Armstrong, of education Indians at Hampton. Few people then had any confidence in the ability of the Indians to receive education and to profit by it. General Armstrong was anxious to try the experiment systematically on a large scale. He secured from the reservations in the Western states over one hundred wild and for the most part perfectly ignorant Indians, the greater proportion of whom were young men. The special work which the General desired me to do was be a sort of "house father" to the Indian young men—that is, I was to live in the building with them and have the charge of their discipline, clothing, rooms, and so on. This was a very tempting offer, but I had become so much absorbed in my work in West Virginia that I dreaded to give it up. However, I tore myself away from it. I did not know how to refuse to perform any service that General Armstrong desired of me.

On going to Hampton, I took up my residence in a building with about seventy-five Indian youths. I was the only person in the building who was not a member of their race. At first I had a good deal of doubt about my ability to succeed. I knew that the average Indian felt himself above the white man, and, of course, he felt himself far above the Negro, largely on account of the fact of the Negro having submitted to slavery—a thing which the Indian would never do. The Indians, in the Indian Territory, owned a large number of slaves during the days of slavery. Aside from this, there was a general feeling that the attempt to education and civilize the red men at Hampton would be a failure. All this made me proceed very cautiously, for I felt keenly the great responsibility. But I was determined to succeed. It was not long before I had the complete confidence of the Indians, and not only this, but I think I am safe in saying that I had their love and respect. I found that they were about like any other human beings; that they responded to kind treatment and resented ill-treatment. They were continually planning to do something that would add to my happiness and comfort. The things that they disliked most, I think, were to have their long hair cut, to give up wearing their blankets, and to cease smoking; but no white American ever thinks that any other race is wholly civilized until he wears the white man's clothes, eats the white man's food, speaks the white man's language, and professes the white man's religion.

When the difficulty of learning the English language was subtracted, I found that in the matter of learning trades and in mastering academic studies there was little difference between the colored and Indian students. It was a constant delight to me to note the interest which the colored students took in trying to help the Indians in every way possible. There were a few of the colored students who felt that the Indians ought not to be admitted to Hampton, but these were in the minority. Whenever they were asked to do so, the Negro students gladly took the Indians as room-mates, in order that they might teach them to speak English and to acquire civilized habits.

I have often wondered if there was a white institution in this country whose students would have welcomed the incoming of more than a hundred companions of another race in the cordial way that these black students at Hampton welcomed the red ones. How often I have wanted to say to white students that they lift themselves up in proportion as they help to lift others, and the more unfortunate the race, and the lower in the scale of civilization, the more does one raise one's self by giving the assistance.

This reminds me of a conversation which I once had with the Hon. Frederick Douglass. At one time Mr. Douglass was traveling in the state of Pennsylvania, and was forced, on account of his color, to ride in the baggage-car, in spite of the fact that he had paid the same price for his passage that the other passengers had paid. When some of the white passengers went into the baggage-car to console Mr. Douglass, and one of them said to him: "I am sorry, Mr. Douglass, that you have been degraded in this manner," Mr. Douglass straightened himself up on the box upon which he was sitting, and replied: "They cannot degrade Frederick Douglass. The soul that is within me no man can degrade. I am not the one that is being degraded on account of this treatment, but those who are inflicting it upon me."

In one part of the country, where the law demands the separation of the races on the railroad trains, I saw at one time a rather amusing instance which showed how difficult it sometimes is to know where the black begins and the white ends.

There was a man who was well known in his community as a Negro, but who was so white that even an expert would have hard work to classify him as a black man. This man was riding in the part of the train set aside for the colored passengers. When the train conductor reached him, he showed at once that he was perplexed. If the man was a Negro, the conductor did not want to send him to the white people's coach; at the same time, if he was a white man, the conductor did not want to insult him by asking him if he was a Negro. The official looked him over carefully, examining his hair, eyes, nose, and hands, but still seemed puzzled. Finally, to solve the difficulty, he stooped over and peeped at the man's feet. When I saw the conductor examining the feet of the man in question, I said to myself, "That will settle it;" and so it did, for the trainman promptly decided that the passenger was a Negro, and let him remain where he was. I congratulated myself that my race was fortunate in not losing one of its members.

My experience has been that the time to test a true gentleman is to observe him when he is in contact with individuals of a race that is less fortunate than his own. This is illustrated in no better way than by observing the conduct of the old-school type of Southern gentleman when he is in contact with his former slaves or their descendants.

An example of what I mean is shown in a story told of George Washington, who, meeting a colored man in the road once, who politely lifted his hat, lifted his own in return. Some of his white friends who saw the incident criticized Washington for his action. In reply to their criticism George Washington said: "Do you suppose that I am going to permit a poor, ignorant, colored man to be more polite than I am?"

While I was in charge of the Indian boys at Hampton, I had one or two experiences which illustrate the curious workings of caste in America. One of the Indian boys was taken ill, and it became my duty to take him to Washington, deliver him over to the Secretary of the Interior, and get a receipt for him, in order that he might be returned to his Western reservation. At that time I was rather ignorant of the ways of the world. During my journey to Washington, on a steamboat, when the bell rang for dinner, I was careful to wait and not enter the dining room until after the greater part of the passengers had finished their meal. Then, with my charge, I went to the dining saloon. The man in charge politely informed me that the Indian could be served, but that I could not. I never could understand how he knew just where to draw the color line, since the Indian and I were of about the same complexion. The steward, however, seemed to be an expert in this manner. I had been directed by the authorities at Hampton to stop at a certain hotel in Washington with my charge, but when I went to this hotel the clerk stated that he would be glad to receive the Indian into the house, but said that he could not accommodate me.

An illustration of something of this same feeling came under my observation afterward. I happened to find myself in a town in which so much excitement and indignation were being expressed that it seemed likely for a time that there would be a lynching. The occasion of the trouble was that a dark-skinned man had stopped at the local hotel. Investigation, however, developed the fact that this individual was a citizen of Morocco, and that while traveling in this country he spoke the English language. As soon as it was learned that he was not an

American Negro, all the signs of indignation disappeared. The man who was the innocent cause of the excitement, though, found it prudent after that not to speak English.

At the end of my first year with the Indians there came another opening for me at Hampton, which, as I look back over my life now, seems to have come providentially, to help to prepare me for my work at Tuskegee later. General Armstrong had found out that there was quite a number of young colored men and women who were intensely in earnest in wishing to get an education, but who were prevented from entering Hampton Institute because they were too poor to be able to pay any portion of the cost of their board, or even to supply themselves with books. He conceived the idea of starting a night-school in connection with the Institute, into which a limited number of the most promising of these young men and women would be received, on condition that they were to work for ten hours during the day, and attend school for two hours at night. They were to be paid something above the cost of their board for their work. The greater part of their earnings was to be reserved in the school's treasury as a fund to be drawn on to pay their board when they had become students in the day-school, after they had spent one or two years in the night-school. In this way they would obtain a start in their books and a knowledge of some trade or industry, in addition to the other far-reaching benefits of the institution.

General Armstrong asked me to take charge of the night-school, and I did so. At the beginning of this school there were about twelve strong, earnest men and women who entered the class. During the day the greater part of the young men worked in the school's sawmill, and the young men worked in the laundry. The work was not easy in either place, but in all my teaching I never taught pupils who gave me much genuine satisfaction as these did. They were good students, and mastered their work thoroughly. They were so much in earnest that only the ringing of the retiring-bell would make them stop studying, and often they would urge me to continue the lessons after the usual hour for going to bed had come.

These students showed so much earnestness, both in their hard work during the day, as well as in their application to their studies at night, that I gave them the name of "The Plucky Class"—a name which soon grew popular and spread throughout the institution. After a student had been in the night-school long enough to prove what was in him, I gave him a printed certificate which read something like this:—

"This is to certify that James Smith is a member of The Plucky Class of the Hampton Institute, and is in good and regular standing."

The students prized these certificates highly, and they added greatly to the popularity of the night-school. Within a few weeks this department had grown to such an extent that there were about twenty-five students in attendance. I have followed the course of many of these twenty-five men and women ever since then, and they are now holding important and useful positions in nearly every part of the South. The night-school at Hampton, which started with only twelve students, now numbers between three and four hundred, and is one of the permanent and most important features of the institution.

Early Days At Tuskegee

During the time that I had charge of the Indians and the night-school at Hampton, I pursued some studies myself, under the direction of the instructors there. One of these instructors was the Rev. Dr. H.B. Frissell, the present Principal of the Hampton Institute, General Armstrong's successor.

In May, 1881, near the close of my first year in teaching the night-school, in a way that I had not dared expect, the opportunity opened for me to begin my life-work. One night in the chapel, after the usual chapel exercises were over, General Armstrong referred to the fact that he had received a letter from some gentlemen in Alabama asking him to recommend some one to take charge of what was to be a normal school for the colored people in the little town of Tuskegee in that state. These gentlemen seemed to take it for granted that no colored man suitable for the position could be secured, and they were expecting the General to recommend a white man for the place. The next day General Armstrong sent for me to come to his office, and, much to my surprise, asked me if I thought I could fill the position in Alabama. I told him that I would be willing to try. Accordingly, he wrote to the people who had applied to him for the information, that he did not know of any white man to suggest, but if they would be willing to take a colored man, he had one whom he could recommend. In this letter he gave them my name.

Several days passed before anything more was heard about the matter. Some time afterward, one Sunday evening during the chapel exercises, a messenger came in and handed the general a telegram. At the end of the exercises he read the telegram to the school. In substance, these were its words: "Booker T. Washington will suit us. Send him at once."

There was a great deal of joy expressed among the students and teachers, and I received very hearty congratulations. I began to get ready at once to go to Tuskegee. I went by way of my old home in West Virginia, where I remained for several days, after which I proceeded to Tuskegee. I found Tuskegee to be a town of about two thousand inhabitants, nearly one-half of whom were colored. It was in what was known as the Black Belt of the South. In the county in which Tuskegee is situated the colored people outnumbered the whites by about three to one. In some of the adjoining and near-by counties the proportion was not far from six colored persons to one white.

I have often been asked to define the term "Black Belt." So far as I can learn, the term was first used to designated a part of the country which was distinguished by the color of the soil. The part of the country possessing this thick, dark, and naturally rich soil was, of course, the part of the South where the slaves were most profitable, and consequently they were taken there in the largest numbers. Later, and especially since the war, the term seems to be used wholly in a political sense—that is, to designate the counties where the black people outnumber the white.

Before going to Tuskegee I had expected to find there a building and all the necessary apparatus ready for me to begin teaching. To my disappointment, I found nothing of the kind. I did find, though, that which no costly building and apparatus can supply,—hundreds of hungry, earnest souls who wanted to secure knowledge.

Tuskegee seemed an ideal place for the school. It was in the midst of the great bulk of the Negro population, and was rather secluded, being five miles from the main line of railroad, with which it was connected by a short line. During the days of slavery, and since, the town had been a center for the education of the white people. This was an added advantage, for the reason that I found the white people possessing a degree of culture and education that is not surpassed by many localities. While the colored people were ignorant, they had not, as a rule, degraded and weakened their bodies by vices such as are common to the lower class of people in the large cities. In general, I found the relations between the two races pleasant. For example, the largest, and I think at that time the only hardware store in the town was owned and operated jointly by a colored man and a white man. This copartnership continued until the death of the white partner.

I found that about a year previous to my going to Tuskegee some of the colored people who had heard something of the work of education being done at Hampton had applied to the state Legislature, through their representatives, for a small appropriation to be used in starting a normal school in Tuskegee. This request the Legislature had complied with to the extent of granting an annual appropriation of two thousand dollars. I soon learned, however, that this money could be used only for the payment of the salaries of the instructors, and that there was no provision for securing land, buildings, or apparatus. The task before me did not seem a very encouraging one. It seemed much like making bricks without straw. The colored people were overjoyed, and were constantly offering their services in any way in which they could be of assistance in getting the school started.

My first task was to find a place in which to open the school. After looking the town over with some care, the most suitable place that could be secured seemed to be a rather dilapidated shanty near the colored Methodist church, together with the church itself as a sort of assembly-room. Both the church and the shanty were in about as bad condition as was possible. I recall that during the first months of school that I taught in this building it was in such poor repair that, whenever it rained, one of the older students would very kindly leave his lessons and hold an umbrella over me while I heard the recitations of the others. I remember, also, that on more than one occasion my landlady held an umbrella over me while I ate breakfast.

At the time I went to Alabama the colored people were taking considerable interest in politics, and they were very anxious that I should become one of them politically, in every respect. They seemed to have a little distrust of strangers in this regard. I recall that one man, who seemed to have been designated by the others to look after my political destiny, came to me on several occasions and said, with a good deal of earnestness: "We wants you to be sure to vote jes' like we votes. We can't read de newspapers very much, but we knows how to vote, an' we wants you to vote jes' like we votes." He added: "We watches de white man, and we keeps watching de white man till we finds out which way de white man's gwine to vote;

an' when we finds out which way de white man's gwine to vote, den we votes 'xactly de other way. Den we knows we's right."

I am glad to add, however, that at the present time the disposition to vote against the white man merely because he is white is largely disappearing, and the race is learning to vote from principle, for what the voter considers to be for the best interests of both races.

I reached Tuskegee, as I have said, early in June, 1881. The first month I spent in finding accommodations for the school, and in traveling through Alabama, examining into the actual life of the people, especially in the court districts, and in getting the school advertised among the glass of people that I wanted to have attend it. The most of my traveling was done over the country roads, with a mule and a cart or a mule and a buggy wagon for conveyance. I ate and slept with the people, in their little cabins. I saw their farms, their schools, their churches. Since, in the case of the most of these visits, there had been no notice given in advance that a stranger was expected, I had the advantage of seeing the real, everyday life of the people.

In the plantation districts I found that, as a rule, the whole family slept in one room, and that in addition to the immediate family there sometimes were relatives, or others not related to the family, who slept in the same room. On more than one occasion I went outside the house to get ready for bed, or to wait until the family had gone to bed. They usually contrived some kind of a place for me to sleep, either on the floor or in a special part of another's bed. Rarely was there any place provided in the cabin where one could bathe even the face and hands, but usually some provision was made for this outside the house, in the yard.

The common diet of the people was fat pork and corn bread. At times I have eaten in cabins where they had only corn bread and "black-eye peas" cooked in plain water. The people seemed to have no other idea than to live on this fat meat and corn bread,—the meat, and the meal of which the bread was made, having been bought at a high price at a store in town, notwithstanding the face that the land all about the cabin homes could easily have been made to produce nearly every kind of garden vegetable that is raised anywhere in the country. Their one object seemed to be to plant nothing but cotton; and in many cases cotton was planted up to the very door of the cabin.

In these cabin homes I often found sewing-machines which had been bought, or were being bought, on instalments, frequently at a cost of as much as sixty dollars, or showy clocks for which the occupants of the cabins had paid twelve or fourteen dollars. I remember that on one occasion when I went into one of these cabins for dinner, when I sat down to the table for a meal with the four members of the family, I noticed that, while there were five of us at the table, there was but one fork for the five of us to use. Naturally there was an awkward pause on my part. In the opposite corner of that same cabin was an organ for which the people told me they were paying sixty dollars in monthly instalments. One fork, and a sixty-dollar organ!

In most cases the sewing-machine was not used, the clocks were so worthless that they did not keep correct time—and if they had, in nine cases out of ten there would have been no one in the family who could have told the time of day—while the organ, of course, was rarely used for want of a person who could play upon it.

In the case to which I have referred, where the family sat down to the table for the meal at which I was their guest, I could see plainly that this was an awkward and unusual proceeding, and was done in my honor. In most cases, when the family got up in the morning, for example, the wife would put a piece of meat in a frying-pan and put a lump of dough in a "skillet," as they called it. These utensils would be placed on the fire, and in ten or fifteen minutes breakfast would be ready. Frequently the husband would take his bread and meat in his hand and start for the field, eating as he walked. The mother would sit down in a corner and eat her breakfast, perhaps from a plate and perhaps directly from the "skillet" or frying-pan, while the children would eat their portion of the bread and meat while running about the yard. At certain seasons of the year, when meat was scarce, it was rarely that the children who were not old enough or strong enough to work in the fields would have the luxury of meat.

The breakfast over, and with practically no attention given to the house, the whole family would, as a general thing, proceed to the cotton-field. Every child that was large enough to carry a hoe was put to work, and the baby—for usually there was at least one baby—would be laid down at the end of the cotton row, so that its mother could give it a certain amount of attention when she had finished chopping her row. The noon meal and the supper were taken in much the same way as the breakfast.

All the days of the family would be spent after much this same routine, except Saturday and Sunday. On Saturday the whole family would spent at least half a day, and often a whole day, in town. The idea in going to town was, I suppose, to do shopping, but all the shopping that the whole family had money for could have been attended to in ten minutes by one person. Still, the whole family remained in town for most of the day, spending the greater part of the time in standing on the streets, the women, too often, sitting about somewhere smoking or dipping snuff. Sunday was usually spent in going to some big meeting. With few exceptions, I found that the crops were mortgaged in the counties where I went, and that the most of the colored farmers were in debt. The state had not been able to build schoolhouses in the country districts, and, as a rule, the schools were taught in churches or in log cabins. More than once, while on my journeys, I found that there was no provision made in the house used for school purposes for heating the building during the winter, and consequently a fire had to be built in the yard, and teacher and pupils passed in and out of the house as they got cold or warm. With few exceptions, I found the teachers in these country schools to be miserably poor in preparation for their work, and poor in moral character. The schools were in session from three to five months. There was practically no apparatus in the schoolhouses, except that occasionally there was a rough blackboard. I recall that one day I went into a schoolhouse—or rather into an abandoned log cabin that was being used as a schoolhouse—and found five pupils who were studying a lesson from one book. Two of these, on the front seat, were using the book between them; behind these were two others peeping over the shoulders of the first two, and behind the four was a fifth little fellow who was peeping over the shoulders of all four.

What I have said concerning the character of the schoolhouses and teachers will also apply quite accurately as a description of the church buildings and the ministers.

I met some very interesting characters during my travels. As illustrating the peculiar mental processes of the country people, I remember that I asked one colored man, who was about sixty years old, to tell me something of his history. He said that he had been born in Virginia, and sold into Alabama in 1845. I asked him how many were sold at the same time. He said, "There were five of us; myself and brother and three mules."

In giving all these descriptions of what I saw during my mouth of travel in the country around Tuskegee, I wish my readers to keep in mind the fact that there were many encouraging exceptions to the conditions which I have described. I have stated in such plain words what I saw, mainly for the reason that later I want to emphasize the encouraging changes that have taken place in the community, not wholly by the work of the Tuskegee school, but by that of other institutions as well.

Teaching School In A Stable and a Hen-House

I confess that what I saw during my month of travel and investigation left me with a very heavy heart. The work to be done in order to lift these people up seemed almost beyond accomplishing. I was only one person, and it seemed to me that the little effort which I could put forth could go such a short distance toward bringing about results. I wondered if I could accomplish anything, and if it were worth while for me to try.

Of one thing I felt more strongly convinced than ever, after spending this month in seeing the actual life of the colored people, and that was that, in order to lift them up, something must be done more than merely to imitate New England education as it then existed. I saw more clearly than ever the wisdom of the system which General Armstrong had inaugurated at Hampton. To take the children of such people as I had been among for a month, and each day give them a few hours of mere book education, I felt would be almost a waste of time.

After consultation with the citizens of Tuskegee, I set July 4, 1881, as the day for the opening of the school in the little shanty and church which had been secured for its accommodation. The white people, as well as the colored, were greatly interested in the starting of the new school, and the opening day was looked forward to with much earnest discussion. There were not a few white people in the vicinity of Tuskegee who looked with some disfavor upon the project. They questioned its value to the colored people, and had a fear that it might result in bringing about trouble between the races. Some had the feeling that in proportion as the Negro received education, in the same proportion would his value decrease as an economic factor in the state. These people feared the result of education would be that the Negroes would leave the farms, and that it would be difficult to secure them for domestic service.

The white people who questioned the wisdom of starting this new school had in their minds pictures of what was called an educated Negro, with a high hat, imitation gold eye-glasses, a showy walking-stick, kid gloves, fancy boots, and what not—in a word, a man who was determined to live by his wits. It was difficult for these people to see how education would produce any other kind of a colored man.

In the midst of all the difficulties which I encountered in getting the little school started, and since then through a period of nineteen years, there are two men among all the many friends of the school in Tuskegee upon whom I have depended constantly for advice and guidance; and the success of the undertaking is largely due to these men, from whom I have never sought anything in vain. I mention them simply as types. One is a white man and an ex-slaveholder, Mr.

George W. Campbell; the other is a black man and an ex-slave, Mr. Lewis Adams. These were the men who wrote to General Armstrong for a teacher.

Mr. Campbell is a merchant and banker, and had had little experience in dealing with matters pertaining to education. Mr. Adams was a mechanic, and had learned the trades of shoemaking, harness-making, and tinsmithing during the days of slavery. He had never been to school a day in his life, but in some way he had learned to read and write while a slave. From the first, these two men saw clearly what my plan of education was, sympathized with me, and supported me in every effort. In the days which were darkest financially for the school, Mr. Campbell was never appealed to when he was not willing to extend all the aid in his power. I do not know two men, one an ex-slaveholder, one an ex-slave, whose advice and judgment I would feel more like following in everything which concerns the life and development of the school at Tuskegee than those of these two men.

I have always felt that Mr. Adams, in a large degree, derived his unusual power of mind from the training given his hands in the process of mastering well three trades during the days of slavery. If one goes to-day into any Southern town, and asks for the leading and most reliable colored man in the community, I believe that in five cases out of ten he will be directed to a Negro who learned a trade during the days of slavery.

On the morning that the school opened, thirty students reported for admission. I was the only teacher. The students were about equally divided between the sexes. Most of them lived in Macon County, the county in which Tuskegee is situated, and of which it is the county-seat. A great many more students wanted to enter the school, but it had been decided to receive only those who were above fifteen years of age, and who had previously received some education. The greater part of the thirty were public-school teachers, and some of them were nearly forty years of age. With the teachers came some of their former pupils, and when they were examined it was amusing to note that in several cases the pupil entered a higher class than did his former teacher. It was also interesting to note how many big books some of them had studied, and how many high-sounding subjects some of them claimed to have mastered. The bigger the book and the longer the name of the subject, the prouder they felt of their accomplishment. Some had studied Latin, and one or two Greek. This they thought entitled them to special distinction.

In fact, one of the saddest things I saw during the month of travel which I have described was a young man, who had attended some high school, sitting down in a one-room cabin, with grease on his clothing, filth all around him, and weeds in the yard and garden, engaged in studying a French grammar.

The students who came first seemed to be fond of memorizing long and complicated "rules" in grammar and mathematics, but had little thought or knowledge of applying these rules to their everyday affairs of their life. One subject which they liked to talk about, and tell me that they had mastered, in arithmetic, was "banking and discount," but I soon found out that neither they nor almost any one in the neighborhood in which they had lived had ever had a bank account. In registering the names of the students, I found that almost every one of them had one or more middle initials. When I asked what the "J" stood for, in the name of John J. Jones, it was explained to me that this was a part of his "entitles." Most of the students wanted to get an education because they thought it would enable them to earn more money as school-teachers.

Notwithstanding what I have said about them in these respects, I have never seen a more earnest and willing company of young men and women than these students were. They were all willing to learn the right thing as soon as it was shown them what was right. I was determined to start them off on a solid and thorough foundation, so far as their books were concerned. I soon learned that most of them had the merest smattering of the high-sounding things that they had studied. While they could locate the Desert of Sahara or the capital of China on an artificial globe, I found out that the girls could not locate the proper places for the knives and forks on an actual dinner-table, or the places on which the bread and meat should be set.

I had to summon a good deal of courage to take a student who had been studying cube root and "banking and discount," and explain to him that the wisest thing for him to do first was thoroughly master the multiplication table.

The number of pupils increased each week, until by the end of the first month there were nearly fifty. Many of them, however, said that, as they could remain only for two or three months, they wanted to enter a high class and get a diploma the first year if possible.

At the end of the first six weeks a new and rare face entered the school as a co-teacher. This was Miss Olivia A. Davidson, who later became my wife. Miss Davidson was born in Ohio, and received her preparatory education in the public schools of that state. When little more than a girl, she heard of the need of teachers in the South. She went to the state of Mississippi and began teaching there. Later she taught in the city of Memphis. While teaching in Mississippi, one of her pupils became ill with smallpox. Every one in the community was so frightened that no one would nurse the boy. Miss Davidson closed her school and remained by the bedside of the boy night and day until he recovered. While she was at her Ohio home on her vacation, the worst epidemic of yellow fever broke out in Memphis, Tenn., that perhaps has ever occurred in the South. When she heard of this, she at once telegraphed the Mayor of Memphis, offering her services as a yellow-fever nurse, although she had never had the disease.

Miss Davidon's experience in the South showed her that the people needed something more than mere book-learning. She heard of the Hampton system of education, and decided that this was what she wanted in order to prepare herself for better work in the South. The attention of Mrs. Mary Hemenway, of Boston, was attracted to her rare ability. Through Mrs. Hemenway's kindness and generosity, Miss Davidson, after graduating at Hampton, received an opportunity to complete a two years' course of training at the Massachusetts State Normal School at Framingham.

Before she went to Framingham, some one suggested to Miss Davidson that, since she was so very light in color, she might find it more comfortable not to be known as a colored women in this school in Massachusetts. She at once replied that under no circumstances and for no considerations would she consent to deceive any one in regard to her racial identity.

Soon after her graduation from the Framingham institution, Miss Davidson came to Tuskegee, bringing into the school many valuable and fresh ideas as to the best methods of teaching, as well as a rare moral character and a life of unselfishness that I think has seldom been equaled. No single individual did more toward laying the foundations of the Tuskegee Institute so as to insure the successful work that has been done there than Olivia A. Davidson.

Miss Davidson and I began consulting as to the future of the school from the first. The students were making progress in learning books and in development their minds; but it became apparent at once that, if we were to make any permanent impression upon those who had come to us for training we must do something besides teach them mere books. The students had come from homes where they had had no opportunities for lessons which would teach them how to care for their bodies. With few exceptions, the homes in Tuskegee in which the students boarded were but little improvement upon those from which they had come. We wanted to teach the students how to bathe; how to care for their teeth and clothing. We wanted to teach them what to eat, and how to eat it properly, and how to care for their rooms. Aside from this, we wanted to give them such a practical knowledge of some one industry, together with the spirit of industry, thrift, and economy, that they would be sure of knowing how to make a living after they had left us. We wanted to teach them to study actual things instead of mere books alone.

We found that the most of our students came from the country districts, where agriculture in some form or other was the main dependence of the people. We learned that about eighty-five per cent of the colored people in the Gulf states depended upon agriculture for their living. Since this was true, we wanted to be careful not to education our students out of sympathy with agricultural life, so that they would be attracted from the country to the cities, and yield to the temptation of trying to live by their wits. We wanted to give them such an education as would fit a large proportion of them to be teachers, and at the same time cause them to return to the plantation districts and show the people there how to put new energy and new ideas into farming, as well as into the intellectual and moral and religious life of the people.

All these ideas and needs crowded themselves upon us with a seriousness that seemed well-night overwhelming. What were we to do? We had only the little old shanty and the abandoned church which the good colored people of the town of Tuskegee had kindly loaned us for the accommodation of the classes. The number of students was increasing daily. The more we saw of them, and the more we traveled through the country districts, the more we saw that our efforts were reaching, to only a partial degree, the actual needs of the people whom we wanted to lift up through the medium of the students whom we should education and send out as leaders.

The more we talked with the students, who were then coming to us from several parts of the state, the more we found that the chief ambition among a large proportion of them was to get an education so that they would not have to work any longer with their hands.

This is illustrated by a story told of a colored man in Alabama, who, one hot day in July, while he was at work in a cotton-field, suddenly stopped, and, looking toward the skies, said: "O Lawd, de cottom am so grassy, de work am so hard, and the sun am so hot dat I b'lieve dis darky am called to preach!"

About three months after the opening of the school, and at the time when we were in the greatest anxiety about our work, there came into market for sale an old and abandoned plantation which was situated about a mile from the town of Tuskegee. The mansion house—or "big house," as it would have been called—which had been occupied by the owners during slavery, had been burned. After making a careful examination of the place, it seemed to be just the location that we wanted in order to make our work effective and permanent.

But how were we to get it? The price asked for it was very little —only five hundred dollars—but we had no money, and we were strangers in the town and had no credit. The owner of the land agreed to let us occupy the place if we could make a payment of two hundred and fifty dollars down, with the understanding that the remaining two hundred and fifty dollars must be paid within a year. Although five hundred dollars was cheap for the land, it was a large sum when one did not have any part of it.

In the midst of the difficulty I summoned a great deal of courage and wrote to my friend General J.F.B. Marshall, the Treasurer of the Hampton Institute, putting the situation before him and beseeching him to lend me the two hundred and fifty dollars on my own personal responsibility. Within a few days a reply came to the effect that he had no authority to lend me the money belonging to the Hampton Institute, but that he would gladly lend me the amount needed from his own personal funds.

I confess that the securing of this money in this way was a great surprise to me, as well as a source of gratification. Up to that time I never had had in my possession so much money as one hundred dollars at a time, and the loan which I had asked General Marshall for seemed a tremendously large sum to me. The fact of my being responsible for the repaying of such a large amount of money weighed very heavily upon me.

I lost no time in getting ready to move the school on to the new farm. At the time we occupied the place there were standing upon it a cabin, formerly used as a dining room, an old kitchen, a stable, and an old hen-house. Within a few weeks we had all of these structures in use. The stable was repaired and used as a recitation-room, and very presently the hen-house was utilized for the same purpose.

I recall that one morning, when I told an old colored man who lived near, and who sometimes helped me, that our school had grown so large that it would be necessary for us to use the hen-house for school purposes, and that I wanted him to help me give it a thorough cleaning out the next day, he replied, in the most earnest manner: "What you mean, boss? You sholy ain't gwine clean out de hen-house in de day-time?"

Nearly all the work of getting the new location ready for school purposes was done by the students after school was over in the afternoon. As soon as we got the cabins in condition to be used, I determined to clear up some land so that we could plant a crop. When I explained my plan to the young men, I noticed that they did not seem to take to it very kindly. It was hard for them to see the connection between clearing land and an education. Besides, many of them had been school-teachers, and they questioned whether or not clearing land would be in keeping with their dignity. In order to relieve them from any embarrassment, each afternoon after school I took my axe and led the way to the woods. When they saw that I was not afraid or ashamed to work, they began to assist with more enthusiasm. We kept at the work each afternoon, until we had cleared about twenty acres and had planted a crop.

In the meantime Miss Davidson was devising plans to repay the loan. Her first effort was made by holding festivals, or "suppers." She made a personal canvass among the white and colored families in the town of Tuskegee, and got them to agree to give something, like a cake, a chicken, bread, or pies, that could be sold at the festival. Of course the colored people were glad to give anything that they could spare, but I want to add that Miss Davidson did not apply to a single white family, so far as I now remember, that failed to donate something; and in many ways the white families showed their interested in the school.

Several of these festivals were held, and quite a little sum of money was raised. A canvass was also made among the people of both races for direct gifts of money, and most of those applied to gave small sums. It was often pathetic to note the gifts of the older colored people, most of whom had spent their best days in slavery. Sometimes they would give five cents, sometimes twenty-five cents. Sometimes the contribution was a quilt, or a quantity of sugarcane. I recall one old colored women who was about seventy years of age, who came to see me when we were raising money to pay for the farm. She hobbled into the room where I was, leaning on a cane. She was clad in rags; but they were clean. She said: "Mr. Washin'ton, God knows I spent de bes' days of my life in slavery. God knows I's ignorant an' poor; but," she added, "I knows what you an' Miss Davidson is tryin' to do. I knows you is tryin' to make better men an' better women for de colored race. I ain't got no money, but I wants you to take dese six eggs, what I's been savin' up, an' I wants you to put dese six eggs into the eddication of dese boys an' gals."

Since the work at Tuskegee started, it has been my privilege to receive many gifts for the benefit of the institution, but never any, I think, that touched me so deeply as this one.

Anxious Days and Sleepless Nights

The coming of Christmas, that first year of our residence in Alabama, gave us an opportunity to get a farther insight into the real life of the people. The first thing that reminded us that Christmas had arrived was the "foreday" visits of scores of children rapping at our doors, asking for "Chris'mus gifts! Chris'mus gifts!" Between the hours of two o'clock and five o'clock in the morning I presume that we must have had a half-hundred such calls. This custom prevails throughout this portion of the South to-day.

During the days of slavery it was a custom quite generally observed throughout all the Southern states to give the colored people a week of holiday at Christmas, or to allow the holiday to continue as long as the "yule log" lasted. The male members of the race, and often the female members, were expected to get drunk. We found that for a whole week the colored people in and around Tuskegee dropped work the day before Christmas, and that it was difficult for any one to perform any service from the time they stopped work until after the New Year. Persons who at other times did not use strong drink thought it quite the proper thing to indulge in it rather freely during the Christmas week. There was a widespread hilarity, and a free use of guns, pistols, and gunpowder generally. The sacredness of the season seemed to have been almost wholly lost sight of.

During this first Christmas vacation I went some distance from the town to visit the people on one of the large plantations. In their poverty and ignorance it was pathetic to see their attempts to get joy out of the season that in most parts of the country is so sacred and so dear to the heart. In one cabin I notice that all that the five children had to remind them of the coming of Christ was a single bunch of firecrackers, which they had divided among them. In another cabin, where there were at least a half-dozen persons, they had only ten cents' worth of ginger-cakes, which had been bought in the store the day before. In another family they had only a few pieces of sugarcane. In still another cabin I found nothing but a new jug of cheap, mean whiskey, which the husband and wife were making free use of, notwithstanding the fact that the husband was one of the local ministers. In a few instances I found that the people had gotten hold of some bright-colored cards that had been designed for advertising purposes, and were making the most of these. In other homes some member of the family had bought a new pistol. In the majority of cases there was nothing to be seen in the cabin to remind one of the coming of the Savior, except that the people had ceased work in the fields and were lounging about their homes. At night, during Christmas week, they usually had what they called a "frolic," in some cabin on the plantation. That meant a kind of rough dance, where there was likely to be a good deal of whiskey used, and where there might be some shooting or cutting with razors.

While I was making this Christmas visit I met an old colored man who was one of the numerous local preachers, who tried to convince me, from the experience Adam had in the Garden of Eden, that God had cursed all labor, and that, therefore, it was a sin for any man to work. For that reason this man sought to do as little work as possible. He seemed at that time to be supremely happy, because he was living, as he expressed it, through one week that was free from sin.

In the school we made a special effort to teach our students the meaning of Christmas, and to give them lessons in its proper observance. In this we have been successful to a degree that makes me feel safe in saying that the season now has a new meaning, not only through all that immediate region, but, in a measure, wherever our graduates have gone.

At the present time one of the most satisfactory features of the Christmas and Thanksgiving season at Tuskegee is the unselfish and beautiful way in which our graduates and students spend their time in administering to the comfort and happiness of others, especially the unfortunate. Not long ago some of our young men spent a holiday in rebuilding a cabin for a helpless colored women who was about seventy-five years old. At another time I remember that I made it known in chapel, one night, that a very poor student was suffering from cold, because he needed a coat. The next morning two coats were sent to my office for him.

I have referred to the disposition on the part of the white people in the town of Tuskegee and vicinity to help the school. From the first, I resolved to make the school a real part of the community in which it was located. I was determined that no one should have the feeling that it was a foreign institution, dropped down in the midst of the people, for which they had no responsibility and in which they had no interest. I noticed that the very fact that they had been asking to contribute toward the purchase of the land made them begin to feel as if it was going to be their school, to a large degree. I noted that just in proportion as we made the white people feel that the institution was a part of the life of the community, and that, while we wanted to make friends in Boston, for example, we also wanted to make white friends in Tuskegee, and that we wanted to make the school of real service to all the people, their attitude toward the school became favorable.

Perhaps I might add right here, what I hope to demonstrate later, that, so far as I know, the Tuskegee school at the present time has no warmer and more enthusiastic friends anywhere than it has among the white citizens of Tuskegee and throughout the state of Alabama and the entire South. From the first, I have advised our people in the South to make friends in every straightforward, manly way with their next-door neighbor, whether he be a black man or a white man. I have also advised them, where no principle is at stake, to consult the interests of their local communities, and to advise with their friends in regard to their voting.

For several months the work of securing the money with which to pay for the farm went on without ceasing. At the end of three months enough was secured to repay the loan of two hundred and fifty dollars to General Marshall, and within two months more we had secured the entire five hundred dollars and had received a deed of the one hundred acres of land. This gave us a great deal of satisfaction. It was not only a source of satisfaction to secure a permanent location for the school, but it was equally satisfactory to know that the greater part of the money with which it was paid for had been gotten from the white and colored people in the town of Tuskegee. The most of this money was obtained by holding festivals and concerts, and from small individual donations.

Our next effort was in the direction of increasing the cultivation of the land, so as to secure some return from it, and at the same time give the students training in agriculture. All the industries at Tuskegee have been started in natural and logical order, growing out of the needs of a community settlement. We began with farming, because we wanted something to eat.

Many of the students, also, were able to remain in school but a few weeks at a time, because they had so little money with which to pay their board. Thus another object which made it desirable to get an industrial system started was in order to make in available as a means of helping the students to earn money enough so that they might be able to remain in school during the nine months' session of the school year.

The first animal that the school came into possession of was an old blind horse given us by one of the white citizens of Tuskegee. Perhaps I may add here that at the present time the school owns over two hundred horses, colts, mules, cows, calves, and oxen, and about seven hundred hogs and pigs, as well as a large number of sheep and goats.

The school was constantly growing in numbers, so much so that, after we had got the farm paid for, the cultivation of the land begun, and the old cabins which we had found on the place somewhat repaired, we turned our attention toward providing a large, substantial building. After having given a good deal of thought to the subject, we finally had the plans drawn for a building that was estimated to cost about six thousand dollars. This seemed to us a tremendous sum, but we knew that the school must go backward or forward, and that our work would mean little unless we could get hold of the students in their home life.

One incident which occurred about this time gave me a great deal of satisfaction as well as surprise. When it became known in the town that we were discussing the plans for a new, large building, a Southern white man who was operating a sawmill not far from Tuskegee came to me and said that he would gladly put all the lumber necessary to erect the building on the grounds, with no other guarantee for payment than my word that it would be paid for when we secured some money. I told the man frankly that at the time we did not have in our hands one dollar of the money needed. Notwithstanding this, he insisted on being allowed to put the lumber on the grounds. After we had secured some portion of the money we permitted him to do this.

Miss Davidson again began the work of securing in various ways small contributions for the new building from the white and colored people in and near Tuskegee. I think I never saw a community of people so happy over anything as were the colored people over the prospect of this new building. One day, when we were holding a meeting to secure funds for its erection, an old, ante-bellum colored man came a distance of twelve miles and brought in his ox-cart a large hog. When the meeting was in progress, he rose in the midst of the company and said that he had no money which he could give, but he had raised two fine hogs, and that he had brought one of them as a contribution toward the expenses of the building. He closed his announcement by saying: "Any nigger that's got any love for his race, or any respect for himself, will bring a hog to the next meeting." Quite a number of men in the community also volunteered to give several days' work, each, toward the erection of the building.

After we had secured all the help that we could in Tuskegee, Miss Davidson decided to go North for the purpose of securing additional funds. For weeks she visited individuals and spoke in churches and before Sunday schools and other organizations. She found this work quite trying, and often embarrassing. The school was not known, but she was not long in winning her way into the confidence of the best people in the North.

The first gift from any Northern person was received from a New York lady whom Miss Davidson met on the boat that was bringing her North. They fell into a conversation, and the Northern lady became so much interested in the effort being made at Tuskegee that before they parted Miss Davidson was handed a check for fifty dollars. For some time before our marriage, and also after it, Miss Davidson kept up the work of securing money in the North and in the South by interesting people by personal visits and through correspondence. At the same time she kept in close touch with the work at Tuskegee, as lady principal and classroom teacher. In addition to this, she worked among the older people in and near Tuskegee, and taught a Sunday school class in the town. She was never very strong, but never seemed happy unless she was giving all of her strength to the cause which she loved. Often, at night, after spending the day in going from door to door trying to interest persons in the work at Tuskegee, she would be so exhausted that she could not undress herself. A lady upon whom she called, in Boston, afterward told me that at one time when Miss Davidson called her to see and send up her card the lady was detained a little before she could see Miss Davidson, and when she entered the parlor she found Miss Davidson so exhausted that she had fallen asleep.

While putting up our first building, which was named Porter Hall, after Mr. A.H. Porter, of Brooklyn, N.Y., who gave a generous sum toward its erection, the need for money became acute. I had given one of our creditors a promise that upon a certain day he should be paid four hundred dollars. On the morning of that day we did not have a dollar. The mail arrived at the school at ten o'clock, and in this mail there was a check sent by Miss Davidson for exactly four hundred dollars. I could relate many instances of almost the same character. This four hundred dollars was given by two ladies in Boston. Two years later, when the work at Tuskegee had grown considerably, and when we were in the midst of a season when we were so much in need of money that the future looked doubtful and gloomy, the same two Boston ladies sent us six thousand dollars. Words cannot describe our surprise, or the encouragement that the gift brought to us. Perhaps I might add here that for fourteen years these same friends have sent us six thousand dollars a year.

As soon as the plans were drawn for the new building, the students began digging out the earth where the foundations were to be laid, working after the regular classes were over. They had not fully outgrown the idea that it was hardly the proper thing for them to use their hands, since they had come there, as one of them expressed it, "to be educated, and not to work." Gradually, though, I noted with satisfaction that a sentiment in favor of work was gaining ground. After a few weeks of hard work the foundations were ready, and a day was appointed for the laying of the corner-stone.

When it is considered that the laying of this corner-stone took place in the heart of the South, in the "Black Belt," in the center of that part of our country that was most devoted to slavery; that at that time slavery had been abolished only about sixteen years; that only sixteen years before no Negro could be taught from books without the teacher receiving the condemnation of the law or of public sentiment—when all this is considered, the scene that was witnessed on that spring day at Tuskegee was a remarkable one. I believe there are few places in the world where it could have taken place.

The principal address was delivered by the Hon. Waddy Thompson, the Superintendent of Education for the county. About the corner-stone were gathered the teachers, the students, their parents and friends, the county officials—who were white—and all the leading white men in that vicinity, together with many of the black men and women whom the same white people but a few years before had held a title to as property. The members of both races were anxious to exercise the privilege of placing under the corner-stone some memento.

Before the building was completed we passed through some very trying seasons. More than once our hearts were made to bleed, as it were, because bills were falling due that we did not have the money to meet. Perhaps no one who has not gone through the experience, month after month, of trying to erect buildings and provide equipment for a school when no one knew where the money was to come from, can properly appreciate the difficulties under which we labored. During the first years at Tuskegee I recall that night after night I would roll and toss on my bed, without sleep, because of the anxiety and uncertainty which we were in regarding money. I knew that, in a large degree, we were trying an experiment—that of testing whether or not it was possible for Negroes to build up and control the affairs of a large education institution. I knew that if we failed it would injure the whole race. I knew that the presumption was against us. I knew that in the case of white people beginning such an enterprise it would be taken for granted that they were going to succeed, but in our case I felt that people would be surprised if we succeeded. All this made a burden which pressed down on us, sometimes, it seemed, at the rate of a thousand pounds to the square inch.

In all our difficulties and anxieties, however, I never went to a white or a black person in the town of Tuskegee for any assistance that was in their power to render, without being helped according to their means. More than a dozen times, when bills figuring up into the hundreds of dollars were falling due, I applied to the white men of Tuskegee for small loans, often borrowing small amounts from as many as a half-dozen persons, to meet our obligations. One thing I was determined to do from the first, and that was to keep the credit of the school high; and this, I think I can say without boasting, we have done all through these years.

I shall always remember a bit of advice given me by Mr. George W. Campbell, the white man to whom I have referred to as the one who induced General Armstrong to send me to Tuskegee. Soon after I entered upon the work Mr. Campbell said to me, in his fatherly way: "Washington, always remember that credit is capital."

At one time when we were in the greatest distress for money that we ever experienced, I placed the situation frankly before General Armstrong. Without hesitation he gave me his personal check for all the money which he had saved for his own use. This was not the only time that General Armstrong helped Tuskegee in this way. I do not think I have ever made this fact public before.

During the summer of 1882, at the end of the first year's work of the school, I was married to Miss Fannie N. Smith, of Malden, W. Va. We began keeping house in Tuskegee early in the fall. This made a home for our teachers, who now had been increase to four in number. My wife was also a graduate of the Hampton Institute. After earnest and constant work in the interests of the school, together with her housekeeping duties, my wife passed away in May, 1884. One child, Portia M. Washington, was born during our marriage.

From the first, my wife most earnestly devoted her thoughts and time to the work of the school, and was completely one with me in every interest and ambition. She passed away, however, before she had an opportunity of seeing what the school was designed to be.

A Harder Task Than Making Bricks Without Straw

From the very beginning, at Tuskegee, I was determined to have the students do not only the agricultural and domestic work, but to have them erect their own buildings. My plan was to have them, while performing this service, taught the latest and best methods of labor, so that the school would not only get the benefit of their efforts, but the students themselves would be taught to see not only utility in labor, but beauty and dignity; would be taught, in fact, how to lift labor up from mere drudgery and toil, and would learn to love work for its own sake. My plan was not to teach them to work in the old way, but to show them how to make the forces of nature—air, water, steam, electricity, horse-power—assist them in their labor.

At first many advised against the experiment of having the buildings erected by the labor of the students, but I was determined to stick to it. I told those who doubted the wisdom of the plan that I knew that our first buildings would not be so comfortable or so complete in their finish as buildings erected by the experienced hands of outside workmen, but that in the teaching of civilization, self-help, and self-reliance, the erection of buildings by the students themselves would more than compensate for any lack of comfort or fine finish.

I further told those who doubted the wisdom of this plan, that the majority of our students came to us in poverty, from the cabins of the cotton, sugar, and rice plantations of the South, and that while I knew it would please the students very much to place them at once in finely constructed buildings, I felt that it would be following out a more natural process of development to teach them how to construct their own buildings. Mistakes I knew would be made, but these mistakes would teach us valuable lessons for the future.

During the now nineteen years' existence of the Tuskegee school, the plan of having the buildings erected by student labor has been adhered to. In this time forty buildings, counting small and large, have been built, and all except four are almost wholly the product of student labor. As an additional result, hundreds of men are now scattered throughout the South who received their knowledge of mechanics while being taught how to erect these buildings. Skill and knowledge are now handed down from one set of students to another in this way, until at the present time a building of any description or size can be constructed wholly by our instructors and students, from the drawing of the plans to the putting in of the electric fixtures, without going off the grounds for a single workman.

Not a few times, when a new student has been led into the temptation of marring the looks of some building by lead pencil marks or by the cuts of a jack-knife, I have heard an old student remind him: "Don't do that. That is our building. I helped put it up."

In the early days of the school I think my most trying experience was in the matter of brick making. As soon as we got the farm work reasonably well started, we directed our next efforts toward the industry of making bricks. We needed these for use in connection with the erection of our own buildings; but there was also another reason for establishing this industry. There was no brickyard in the town, and in addition to our own needs there was a demand for bricks in the general market.

I had always sympathized with the "Children of Israel," in their task of "making bricks without straw," but ours was the task of making bricks with no money and no experience.

In the first place, the work was hard and dirty, and it was difficult to get the students to help. When it came to brick making, their distaste for manual labor in connection with book education became especially manifest. It was not a pleasant task for one to stand in the mud-pit for hours, with the mud up to his knees. More than one man became disgusted and left the school.

We tried several locations before we opened up a pit that furnished brick clay. I had always supposed that brick making was very simple, but I soon found out by bitter experience that it required special skill and knowledge, particularly in the burning of the bricks. After a good deal of effort we molded about twenty-five thousand bricks, and put them into a kiln to be burned. This kiln turned out to be a failure, because it was not properly constructed or properly burned. We began at once, however, on a second kiln. This, for some reason, also proved a failure. The failure of this kiln made it still more difficult to get the students to take part in the work. Several of the teachers, however, who had been trained in the industries at Hampton, volunteered their services, and in some way we succeeded in getting a third kiln ready for burning. The burning of a kiln required about a week. Toward the latter part of the week, when it seemed as if we were going to have a good many thousand bricks in a few hours, in the middle of the night the kiln fell. For the third time we had failed.

The failure of this last kiln left me without a single dollar with which to make another experiment. Most of the teachers advised the abandoning of the effort to make bricks. In the midst of my troubles I thought of a watch which had come into my possession years before. I took the watch to the city of Montgomery, which was not far distant, and placed it in a pawn-shop. I secured cash upon it to the amount of fifteen dollars, with which to renew the brick making experiment. I returned to Tuskegee, and, with the help of the fifteen dollars, rallied our rather demoralized and discouraged forces and began a fourth attempt to make bricks. This time, I am glad to say, we were successful. Before I got hold of any money, the time-limit on my watch had expired, and I have never seen it since; but I have never regretted the loss of it.

Brick making has now become such an important industry at the school that last season our students manufactured twelve hundred thousand of first-class bricks, of a quality stable to be sold in any market. Aside from this, scores of young men have mastered the brick making trade—both the making of bricks by hand and by machinery—and are now engaged in this industry in many parts of the South.

The making of these bricks taught me an important lesson in regard to the relations of the two races in the South. Many white people who had had no contact with the school, and perhaps no sympathy with it, came to us to buy bricks because they found out that ours were good bricks. They discovered that we were supplying a real want in the community. The making of these bricks caused many of the white residents of the neighborhood to begin to feel that the education of the Negro was not making him worthless, but that in educating our students we were adding something to the wealth and comfort of the community. As the people of the neighborhood came to us to buy bricks, we got acquainted with them; they traded with us and we with them. Our business interests became intermingled. We had something which they wanted; they had something which we wanted. This, in a large measure, helped to lay the foundation for the pleasant relations that have continued to exist between us and the white people in that section, and which now extend throughout the South.

Wherever one of our brick makers has gone in the South, we find that he has something to contribute to the well-being of the community into which he has gone; something that has made the community feel that, in a degree, it is indebted to him, and perhaps, to a certain extent, dependent upon him. In this way pleasant relations between the races have been simulated.

My experience is that there is something in human nature which always makes an individual recognize and reward merit, no matter under what color of skin merit is found. I have found, too, that it is the visible, the tangible, that goes a long ways in softening prejudices. The actual sight of a first-class house that a Negro has built is ten times more potent than pages of discussion about a house that he ought to build, or perhaps could build.

The same principle of industrial education has been carried out in the building of our own wagons, carts, and buggies, from the first. We now own and use on our farm and about the school dozens of these vehicles, and every one of them has been built by the hands of the students. Aside from this, we help supply the local market with these vehicles. The supplying of them to the people in the community has had the same effect as the supplying of bricks, and the man who learns at Tuskegee to build and repair wagons and carts is regarded as a benefactor by both races in the community where he goes. The people with whom he lives and works are going to think twice before they part with such a man.

The individual who can do something that the world wants done will, in the end, make his way regardless of race. One man may go into a community prepared to supply the people there with an analysis of Greek sentences. The community may not at the time be prepared for, or feel the need of, Greek analysis, but it may feel its need of bricks and houses and wagons. If the man can supply the need for those, then, it will lead eventually to a demand for the first product, and with the demand will come the ability to appreciate it and to profit by it.

About the time that we succeeded in burning our first kiln of bricks we began facing in an emphasized form the objection of the students to being taught to work. By this time it had gotten to be pretty well advertised throughout the state that every student who came to Tuskegee, no matter what his financial ability might be, must learn some industry. Quite a number of letters came from parents protesting against their children engaging in labor while they were in the school. Other parents came to the school to protest in person. Most of the new students brought a written or a verbal request from their parents to the effect that they wanted their children taught nothing but books. The more books, the larger they were, and the longer the titles printed upon them, the better pleased the students and their parents seemed to be.

I gave little heed to these protests, except that I lost no opportunity to go into as many parts of the state as I could, for the purpose of speaking to the parents, and showing them the value of industrial education. Besides, I talked to the students constantly on the subject. Notwithstanding the unpopularity of industrial work, the school continued to increase in numbers to such an extent that by the middle of the second year there was an attendance of about one hundred and fifty, representing almost all parts of the state of Alabama, and including a few from other states.

In the summer of 1882 Miss Davidson and I both went North and engaged in the work of raising funds for the completion of our new building. On my way North I stopped in New York to try to get a letter of recommendation from an officer of a missionary organization who had become somewhat acquainted with me a few years previous. This man not only refused to give me the letter, but advised me most earnestly to go back home at once, and not make any attempt to get money, for he was quite sure that I would never get more than enough to pay my traveling expenses. I thanked him for his advice, and proceeded on my journey.

The first place I went to in the North, was Northampton, Mass., where I spent nearly a half-day in looking for a colored family with whom I could board, never dreaming that any hotel would admit me. I was greatly surprised when I found that I would have no trouble in being accommodated at a hotel.

We were successful in getting money enough so that on Thanksgiving Day of that year we held our first service in the chapel of Porter Hall, although the building was not completed.

In looking about for some one to preach the Thanksgiving sermon, I found one of the rarest men that it has ever been my privilege to know. This was the Rev. Robert C. Bedford, a white man from Wisconsin, who was then pastor of a little colored Congregational church in Montgomery, Ala. Before going to Montgomery to look for some one to preach this sermon I had never heard of Mr. Bedford. He had never heard of me. He gladly consented to come to Tuskegee and hold the Thanksgiving service. It was the first service of the kind that the colored people there had ever observed, and what a deep interest they manifested in it! The sight of the new building made it a day of Thanksgiving for them never to be forgotten.

Mr. Bedford consented to become one of the trustees of the school, and in that capacity, and as a worker for it, he has been connected with it for eighteen years. During this time he has borne the school upon his heart night and day, and is never so happy as when he is performing some service, no matter how humble, for it. He completely obliterates himself in everything, and looks only for permission to serve where service is most disagreeable, and where others would not be attracted. In all my relations with him he has seemed to me to approach as nearly to the spirit of the Master as almost any man I ever met.

A little later there came into the service of the school another man, quite young at the time, and fresh from Hampton, without whose service the school never could have become what it is. This was Mr. Warren Logan, who now for seventeen years has been the treasurer of the Institute, and the acting principal during my absence. He has always shown a degree of unselfishness and an amount of business tact, coupled with a clear judgment, that has kept the school in good condition no matter how long I have been absent from it. During all the financial stress through which the school has passed, his patience and faith in our ultimate success have not left him.

As soon as our first building was near enough to completion so that we could occupy a portion of it—which was near the middle of the second year of the school—we opened a boarding department. Students had begun coming from quite a distance, and in such increasing numbers that we felt more and more that we were merely skimming over the surface, in that we were not getting hold of the students in their home life.

We had nothing but the students and their appetites with which to begin a boarding department. No provision had been made in the new building for a kitchen and dining room; but we discovered that by digging out a large amount of earth from under the building we could make a partially lighted basement room that could be used for a kitchen and dining room. Again I called on the students to volunteer for work, this time to assist in digging out the basement. This they did, and in a few weeks we had a place to cook and eat in, although it was very rough and uncomfortable. Any one seeing the place now would never believe that it was once used for a dining room.

The most serious problem, though, was to get the boarding department started off in running order, with nothing to do with in the way of furniture, and with no money with which to buy anything. The merchants in the town would let us have what food we wanted on credit. In fact, in those earlier years I was constantly embarrassed because people seemed to have more faith in me than I had in myself. It was pretty hard to cook, however, with stoves, and awkward to eat without dishes. At first the cooking was done out-of-doors, in the old-fashioned, primitive style, in pots and skillets placed over a fire. Some of the carpenters' benches that had been used in the construction of the building were utilized for tables. As for dishes, there were too few to make it worth while to spend time in describing them.

No one connected with the boarding department seemed to have any idea that meals must be served at certain fixed and regular hours, and this was a source of great worry. Everything was so out of joint and so inconvenient that I feel safe in saying that for the first two weeks something was wrong at every meal. Either the meat was not done or had been burnt, or the salt had been left out of the bread, or the tea had been forgotten.

Early one morning I was standing near the dining-room door listening to the complaints of the students. The complaints that morning were especially emphatic and numerous, because the whole breakfast had been a failure. One of the girls who had failed to get any breakfast came out and went to the well to draw some water to drink and take the place of the breakfast which she had not been able to get. When she reached the well, she found that the rope was broken and that she could get no water. She turned from the well and said, in the most discouraged tone, not knowing that I was where I could hear her, "We can't even get water to drink at this school." I think no one remark ever came so near discouraging me as that one.

At another time, when Mr. Bedford—whom I have already spoken of as one of our trustees, and a devoted friend of the institution—was visiting the school, he was given a bedroom immediately over the dining room. Early in the morning he was awakened by a rather animated discussion between two boys in the dining room below. The discussion was over the question as to whose turn it was to use the coffee-cup that morning. One boy won the case by proving that for three mornings he had not had an opportunity to use the cup at all.

But gradually, with patience and hard work, we brought order out of chaos, just as will be true of any problem if we stick to it with patience and wisdom and earnest effort.

As I look back now over that part of our struggle, I am glad to see that we had it. I am glad that we endured all those discomforts and inconveniences. I am glad that our students had to dig out the place for their kitchen and dining room. I am glad that our first boarding-place was in the dismal, ill-lighted, and damp basement. Had we started in a fine, attractive, convenient room, I fear we would have "lost our heads" and become "stuck up." It means a great deal, I think, to start off on a foundation which one has made for one's self.

When our old students return to Tuskegee now, as they often do, and go into our large, beautiful, well-ventilated, and well-lighted dining room, and see tempting, well-cooked food—largely grown by the students themselves—and see tables, neat tablecloths and napkins, and vases of flowers upon the tables, and hear singing birds, and note that each meal is served exactly upon the minute, with no disorder, and with almost no complaint coming from the hundreds that now fill our dining room, they, too, often say to me that they are glad that we started as we did, and built ourselves up year by year, by a slow and natural process of growth.

Making Their Beds Before They Could Lie On Them

A little later in the history of the school we had a visit from General J.F.B. Marshall, the Treasurer of the Hampton Institute, who had had faith enough to lend us the first two hundred and fifty dollars with which to make a payment down on the farm. He remained with us a week, and made a careful inspection of everything. He seemed well pleased with our progress, and wrote back interesting and encouraging reports to Hampton. A little later Miss Mary F. Mackie, the teacher who had given me the "sweeping" examination when I entered Hampton, came to see us, and still later General Armstrong himself came.

At the time of the visits of these Hampton friends the number of teachers at Tuskegee had increase considerably, and the most of the new teachers were graduates of the Hampton Institute. We gave our Hampton friends, especially General Armstrong, a cordial welcome. They were all surprised and pleased at the rapid progress that the school had made within so short a time. The colored people from miles around came to the school to get a look at General Armstrong, about whom they had heard so much. The General was not only welcomed by the members of my own race, but by the Southern white people as well.

This first visit which General Armstrong made to Tuskegee gave me an opportunity to get an insight into his character such as I had not before had. I refer to his interest in the Southern white people. Before this I had had the thought that General Armstrong, having fought the Southern white man, rather cherished a feeling of bitterness toward the white South, and was interested in helping only the colored man there. But this visit convinced me that I did not know the greatness and the generosity of the man. I soon learned, by his visits to the Southern white people, and from his conversations with them, that he was as anxious about the prosperity and the happiness of the white race as the black. He cherished no bitterness against the South, and was happy when an opportunity offered for manifesting his sympathy. In all my acquaintance with General Armstrong I never heard him speak, in public or in private, a single bitter word against the white man in the South. From his example in this respect I learned the lesson that great men cultivate love, and that only little men cherish a spirit of hatred. I learned that assistance given to the weak makes the one who gives it strong; and that oppression of the unfortunate makes one weak.

It is now long ago that I learned this lesson from General Armstrong, and resolved that I would permit no man, no matter what his color might be, to narrow and degrade my soul by making me hate him. With God's help, I believe that I have completely rid myself of any ill feeling toward the Southern white man for any wrong that he may have inflicted upon my race. I am made to feel just as happy now when I am rendering service to Southern white men as when the service is rendered to a member of my own race. I pity from the bottom of my heart any individual who is so unfortunate as to get into the habit of holding race prejudice.

The more I consider the subject, the more strongly I am convinced that the most harmful effect of the practice to which the people in certain sections of the South have felt themselves compelled to resort, in order to get rid of the force of the Negroes' ballot, is not wholly in the wrong done to the Negro, but in the permanent injury to the morals of the white man. The wrong to the Negro is temporary, but to the morals of the white man the injury is permanent. I have noted time and time again that when an individual perjures himself in order to break the force of the black man's ballot, he soon learns to practice dishonesty in other relations of life, not only where the Negro is concerned, but equally so where a white man is concerned. The white man who begins by cheating a Negro usually ends by cheating a white man. The white man who begins to break the law by lynching a Negro soon yields to the temptation to lynch a white man. All this, it seems to me, makes it important that the whole Nation lend a hand in trying to lift the burden of ignorance from the South.

Another thing that is becoming more apparent each year in the development of education in the South is the influence of General Armstrong's idea of education; and this not upon the blacks alone, but upon the whites also. At the present time there is almost no Southern state that is not putting forth efforts in the direction of securing industrial education for its white boys and girls, and in most cases it is easy to trace the history of these efforts back to General Armstrong.

Soon after the opening of our humble boarding department students began coming to us in still larger numbers. For weeks we not only had to contend with the difficulty of providing board, with no money, but also with that of providing sleeping accommodations. For this purpose we rented a number of cabins near the school. These cabins were in a dilapidated condition, and during the winter months the students who occupied them necessarily suffered from the cold. We charge the students eight dollars a month—all they were able to pay—for their board. This included, besides board, room, fuel, and washing. We also gave the students credit on their board bills for all the work which they did for the school which was of any value to the institution. The cost of tuition, which was fifty dollars a year for each student, we had to secure then, as now, wherever we could.

This small charge in cash gave us no capital with which to start a boarding department. The weather during the second winter of our work was very cold. We were not able to provide enough bed-clothes to keep the students warm. In fact, for some time we were not able to provide, except in a few cases, bedsteads and mattresses of any kind. During the coldest nights I was so troubled about the discomfort of the students that I could not sleep myself. I recall that on several occasions I went in the middle of the night to the shanties occupied by the young men, for the purpose of confronting them. Often I found some of them sitting huddled around a fire, with the one blanket which we had been able to provide wrapped around them, trying in this way to keep warm. During the whole night some of them did not attempt to lie down. One morning, when the night previous had been unusually cold, I asked those of the students in the chapel who thought that they had been frostbitten during the night to raise their hands. Three hands went up. Notwithstanding these experiences, there was almost no complaining on the part of the students. They knew that we were doing the best that we could for them. They were happy in the privilege of being permitted to enjoy any kind of opportunity that would enable them to improve their condition. They were constantly asking what they might do to lighten the burdens of the teachers.

I have heard it stated more than once, both in the North and in the South, that colored people would not obey and respect each other when one member of the race is placed in a position of authority over others. In regard to this general belief and these statements, I can say that during the nineteen years of my experience at Tuskegee I never, either by word or act, have been treated with disrespect by any student or officer connected with the institution. On the other hand, I am constantly embarrassed by the many acts of thoughtful kindness. The students do not seem to want to see me carry a large book or a satchel or any kind of a burden through the grounds. In such cases more than one always offers to relieve me. I almost never go out of my office when the rain is falling that some student does not come to my side with an umbrella and ask to be allowed to hold it over me.

While writing upon this subject, it is a pleasure for me to add that in all my contact with the white people of the South I have never received a single personal insult. The white people in and near Tuskegee, to an especial degree, seem to count it as a privilege to show me all the respect within their power, and often go out of their way to do this.

Not very long ago I was making a journey between Dallas (Texas) and Houston. In some way it became known in advance that I was on the train. At nearly every station at which the train stopped, numbers of white people, including in most cases of the officials of the town, came aboard and introduced themselves and thanked me heartily for the work that I was trying to do for the South.

On another occasion, when I was making a trip from Augusta, Georgia, to Atlanta, being rather tired from much travel, I road in a Pullman sleeper. When I went into the car, I found there two ladies from Boston whom I knew well. These good ladies were perfectly ignorant, it seems, of the customs of the South, and in the goodness of their hearts insisted that I take a seat with them in their section. After some hesitation I consented. I had been there but a few minutes when one of them, without my knowledge, ordered supper to be served for the three of us. This embarrassed me still further. The car was full of Southern white men, most of whom had their eyes on our party. When I found that supper had been ordered, I tried to contrive some excuse that would permit me to leave the section, but the ladies insisted that I must eat with them. I finally settled back in my seat with a sigh, and said to myself, "I am in for it now, sure."

To add further to the embarrassment of the situation, soon after the supper was placed on the table one of the ladies remembered that she had in her satchel a special kind of tea which she wished served, and as she said she felt quite sure the porter did not know how to brew it properly, she insisted upon getting up and preparing and serving it herself. At last the meal was over; and it seemed the longest one that I had ever eaten. When we were through, I decided to get myself out of the embarrassing situation and go to the smoking-room, where most of the men were by that time, to see how the land lay. In the meantime, however, it had become known in some way throughout the car who I was. When I went into the smoking-room I was never more surprised in my life than when each man, nearly every one of them a citizen of Georgia, came up and introduced himself to me and thanked me earnestly for the work that I was trying to do for the whole South.

This was not flattery, because each one of these individuals knew that he had nothing to gain by trying to flatter me.

From the first I have sought to impress the students with the idea that Tuskegee is not my institution, or that of the officers, but that it is their institution, and that they have as much interest in it as any of the trustees or instructors. I have further sought to have them feel that I am at the institution as their friend and adviser, and not as their overseer. It has been my aim to have them speak with directness and frankness about anything that concerns the life of the school. Two or three times a year I ask the students to write me a letter criticizing or making complaints or suggestions about anything connected with the institution. When this is not done, I have them meet me in the chapel for a heart-to-heart talk about the conduct of the school. There are no meetings with our students that I enjoy more than these, and none are more helpful to me in planning for the future. These meetings, it seems to me, enable me to get at the very heart of all that concerns the school. Few things help an individual more than to place responsibility upon him, and to let him know that you trust him. When I have read of labor troubles between employers and employees, I have often thought that many strikes and similar disturbances might be avoided if the employers would cultivate the habit of getting nearer to their employees, of consulting and advising with them, and letting them feel that the interests of the two are the same. Every individual responds to confidence, and this is not more true of any race than of the Negroes. Let them once understand that you are unselfishly interested in them, and you can lead them to any extent.

It was my aim from the first at Tuskegee to not only have the buildings erected by the students themselves, but to have them make their own furniture as far as was possible. I now marvel at the patience of the students while sleeping upon the floor while waiting for some kind of a bedstead to be constructed, or at their sleeping without any kind of a mattress while waiting for something that looked like a mattress to be made.

In the early days we had very few students who had been used to handling carpenters' tools, and the bedsteads made by the students then were very rough and very weak. Not unfrequently when I went into the students' rooms in the morning I would find at least two bedsteads lying about on the floor. The problem of providing mattresses was a difficult one to solve. We finally mastered this, however, by getting some cheap cloth and sewing pieces of this together as to make large bags. These bags we filled with the pine straw—or, as it is sometimes called, pine needles—which we secured from the forests near by. I am glad to say that the industry of mattress-making has grown steadily since then, and has been improved to such an extent that at the present time it is an important branch of the work which is taught systematically to a number of our girls, and that the mattresses that now come out of the mattress-shop at Tuskegee are about as good as those bought in the average store. For some time after the opening of the boarding department we had no chairs in the students' bedrooms or in the dining rooms. Instead of chairs we used stools which the students constructed by nailing together three pieces of rough board. As a rule, the furniture in the students' rooms during the early days of the school consisted of a bed, some stools, and sometimes a rough table made by the students. The plan of having the students make the furniture is still followed, but the number of pieces in a room has been increased, and the workmanship has so improved that little fault can be found with the articles now. One thing that I have always insisted upon at Tuskegee is that everywhere there should be absolute cleanliness. Over and over again the students were reminded in those first years—and are reminded now—that people would excuse us for our poverty, for our lack of comforts and conveniences, but that they would not excuse us for dirt.

Another thing that has been insisted upon at the school is the use of the tooth-brush. "The gospel of the tooth-brush," as General Armstrong used to call it, is part of our creed at Tuskegee. No student is permitted to retain who does not keep and use a tooth-brush. Several times, in recent years, students have come to us who brought with them almost no other article except a tooth-brush. They had heard from the lips of other students about our insisting upon the use of this, and so, to make a good impression, they brought at least a tooth-brush with them. I remember that one morning, not long ago, I went with the lady principal on her usual morning tour of inspection of the girls' rooms. We found one room that contained three girls who had recently arrived at the school. When I asked them if they had tooth-brushes, one of the girls replied, pointing to a brush: "Yes, sir. That is our brush. We bought it together, yesterday." It did not take them long to learn a different lesson.

It has been interesting to note the effect that the use of the tooth-brush has had in bringing about a higher degree of civilization among the students. With few exceptions, I have noticed that, if we can get a student to the point where, when the first or second tooth-brush disappears, he of his own motion buys another, I have not been disappointed in the future of that individual. Absolute cleanliness of the body has been insisted upon from the first. The students have been taught to bathe as regularly as to take their meals. This lesson we began teaching before we had anything in the shape of a bath-house. Most of the students came from plantation districts, and often we had to teach them how to sleep at night; that is, whether between the two sheets—after we got to the point where we could provide them two sheets—or under both of them. Naturally I found it difficult to teach them to sleep between two sheets when we were able to supply but one. The importance of the use of the night-gown received the same attention.

For a long time one of the most difficult tasks was to teach the students that all the buttons were to be kept on their clothes, and that there must be no torn places or grease-spots. This lesson, I am pleased to be able to say, has been so thoroughly learned and so faithfully handed down from year to year by one set of students to another that often at the present time, when the students march out of the chapel in the evening and their dress is inspected, as it is every night, not one button is found to be missing.

Raising Money

When we opened our boarding department, we provided rooms in the attic of Porter Hall, our first building, for a number of girls. But the number of students, of both sexes, continued to increase. We could find rooms outside the school grounds for many of the young men, but the girls we did not care to expose in this way. Very soon the problem of providing more rooms for the girls, as well as a larger boarding department for all the students, grew serious. As a result, we finally decided to undertake the construction of a still larger building—a building that would contain rooms for the girls and boarding accommodations for all.

After having had a preliminary sketch of the needed building made, we found that it would cost about ten thousand dollars. We had no money whatever with which to begin; still we decided to give the needed building a name. We knew we could name it, even though we were in doubt about our ability to secure the means for its construction. We decided to call the proposed building Alabama Hall, in honor of the state in which we were laboring. Again Miss Davidson began making efforts to enlist the interest and help of the colored and white people in and near Tuskegee. They responded willingly, in proportion to their means. The students, as in the case of our first building, Porter Hall, began digging out the dirt in order to allow the laying of the foundations.

When we seemed at the end of our resources, so far as securing money was concerned, something occurred which showed the greatness of General Armstrong—something which proved how far he was above the ordinary individual. When we were in the midst of great anxiety as to where and how we were to get funds for the new building, I received a telegram from General Armstrong asking me if I could spend a month traveling with him through the North, and asking me, if I could do so, to come to Hampton at once. Of course I accepted General Armstrong's invitation, and went to Hampton immediately. On arriving there I found that the General had decided to take a quartet of singers through the North, and hold meetings for a month in important cities, at which meetings he and I were to speak. Imagine my surprise when the General told me, further, that these meetings were to be held, not in the interests of Hampton, but in the interests of Tuskegee, and that the Hampton Institute was to be responsible for all the expenses.

Although he never told me so in so many words, I found that General Armstrong took this method of introducing me to the people of the North, as well as for the sake of securing some immediate funds to be used in the erection of Alabama Hall. A weak and narrow man would have reasoned that all the money which came to Tuskegee in this way would be just so much taken from the Hampton Institute; but none of these selfish or short-sighted feelings ever entered the breast of General Armstrong. He was too big to be little, too good to be mean. He knew that the people in the North who gave money gave it for the purpose of helping the whole cause of Negro civilization, and not merely for the advancement of any one school. The General knew, too, that the way to strengthen Hampton was to make it a center of unselfish power in the working out of the whole Southern problem.

In regard to the addresses which I was to make in the North, I recall just one piece of advice which the General gave me. He said: "Give them an idea for every word." I think it would be hard to improve upon this advice; and it might be made to apply to all public speaking. From that time to the present I have always tried to keep his advice in mind.

Meetings were held in New York, Brooklyn, Boston, Philadelphia, and other large cities, and at all of these meetings General Armstrong pleased, together with myself, for help, not for Hampton, but for Tuskegee. At these meetings an especial effort was made to secure help for the building of Alabama Hall, as well as to introduce the school to the attention of the general public. In both these respects the meetings proved successful.

After that kindly introduction I began going North alone to secure funds. During the last fifteen years I have been compelled to spend a large proportion of my time away from the school, in an effort to secure money to provide for the growing needs of the institution. In my efforts to get funds I have had some experiences that may be of interest to my readers. Time and time again I have been asked, by people who are trying to secure money for philanthropic purposes, what rule or rules I followed to secure the interest and help of people who were able to contribute money to worthy objects. As far as the science of what is called begging can be reduced to rules, I would say that I have had but two rules. First, always to do my whole duty regarding making our work known to individuals and organizations; and, second, not to worry about the results. This second rule has been the hardest for me to live up to. When bills are on the eve of falling due, with not a dollar in hand with which to meet them, it is pretty difficult to learn not to worry, although I think I am learning more and more each year that all worry simply consumes, and to no purpose, just so much physical and mental strength that might otherwise be given to effective work. After considerable experience in coming into contact with wealthy and noted men, I have observed that those who have accomplished the greatest results are those who "keep under the body"; are those who never grow excited or lose self-control, but are always calm, self-possessed, patient, and polite. I think that President William McKinley is the best example of a man of this class that I have ever seen.

In order to be successful in any kind of undertaking, I think the main thing is for one to grow to the point where he completely forgets himself; that is, to lose himself in a great cause. In proportion as one loses himself in the way, in the same degree does he get the highest happiness out of his work.

My experience in getting money for Tuskegee has taught me to have no patience with those people who are always condemning the rich because they are rich, and because they do not give more to objects of charity. In the first place, those who are guilty of such sweeping criticisms do not know how many people would be made poor, and how much suffering would result, if wealthy people were to part all at once with any large proportion of their wealth in a way to disorganize and cripple great business enterprises. Then very few persons have any idea of the large number of applications for help that rich people are constantly being flooded with. I know wealthy people who receive as much as twenty calls a day for help. More than once when I have gone into the offices of rich men, I have found half a dozen persons waiting to see them, and all come for the same purpose, that of securing money. And all these calls in person, to say nothing of the applications received through the mails. Very few people have any idea of the amount of money given away by persons who never permit their names to be known. I have often heard persons condemned for not giving away money, who, to my own knowledge, were giving away thousands of dollars every year so quietly that the world knew nothing about it.

As an example of this, there are two ladies in New York, whose names rarely appear in print, but who, in a quiet way, have given us the means with which to erect three large and important buildings during the last eight years. Besides the gift of these buildings, they have made other generous donations to the school. And they not only help Tuskegee, but they are constantly seeking opportunities to help other worthy causes.

Although it has been my privilege to be the medium through which a good many hundred thousand dollars have been received for the work at Tuskegee, I have always avoided what the world calls "begging." I often tell people that I have never "begged" any money, and that I am not a "beggar." My experience and observation have convinced me that persistent asking outright for money from the rich does not, as a rule, secure help. I have usually proceeded on the principle that persons who possess sense enough to earn money have sense enough to know how to give it away, and that the mere making known of the facts regarding Tuskegee, and especially the facts regarding the work of the graduates, has been more effective than outright begging. I think that the presentation of facts, on a high, dignified plane, is all the begging that most rich people care for.

While the work of going from door to door and from office to office is hard, disagreeable, and costly in bodily strength, yet it has some compensations. Such work gives one a rare opportunity to study human nature. It also has its compensations in giving one an opportunity to meet some of the best people in the world—to be more correct, I think I should say the best people in the world. When one takes a broad survey of the country, he will find that the most useful and influential people in it are those who take the deepest interest in institutions that exist for the purpose of making the world better.

At one time, when I was in Boston, I called at the door of a rather wealthy lady, and was admitted to the vestibule and sent up my card. While I was waiting for an answer, her husband came in, and asked me in the most abrupt manner what I wanted. When I tried to explain the object of my call, he became still more ungentlemanly in his words and manner, and finally grew so excited that I left the house without waiting for a reply from the lady. A few blocks from that house I called to see a gentleman who received me in the most cordial manner. He wrote me his check for a generous sum, and then, before I had had an opportunity to thank him, said: "I am so grateful to you, Mr. Washington, for giving me the opportunity to help a good cause. It is a privilege to have a share in it. We in Boston are constantly indebted to you for doing our work." My experience in securing money convinces me that the first type of man is growing more rare all the time, and that the latter type is increasing; that is, that, more and more, rich people are coming to regard men and women who apply to them for help for worthy objects, not as beggars, but as agents for doing their work.

In the city of Boston I have rarely called upon an individual for funds that I have not been thanked for calling, usually before I could get an opportunity to thank the donor for the money. In that city the donors seem to feel, in a large degree, that an honor is being conferred upon them in their being permitted to give. Nowhere else have I met with, in so large a measure, this fine and Christlike spirit as in the city of Boston, although there are many notable instances of it outside that city. I repeat my belief that the world is growing in the direction of giving. I repeat that the main rule by which I have been guided in collecting money is to do my full duty in regard to giving people who have money an opportunity for help.

In the early years of the Tuskegee school I walked the streets or traveled country roads in the North for days and days without receiving a dollar. Often as it happened, when during the week I had been disappointed in not getting a cent from the very individuals from whom I most expected help, and when I was almost broken down and discouraged, that generous help has come from some one who I had had little idea would give at all.

I recall that on one occasion I obtained information that led me to believe that a gentleman who lived about two miles out in the country from Stamford, Conn., might become interest in our efforts at Tuskegee if our conditions and needs were presented to him. On an unusually cold and stormy day I walked the two miles to see him. After some difficulty I succeeded in securing an interview with him. He listened with some degree of interest to what I had to say, but did not give me anything. I could not help having the feeling that, in a measure, the three hours that I had spent in seeing him had been thrown away. Still, I had followed my usual rule of doing my duty. If I had not seen him, I should have felt unhappy over neglect of duty.

Two years after this visit a letter came to Tuskegee from this man, which read like this: "Enclosed I send you a New York draft for ten thousand dollars, to be used in furtherance of your work. I had placed this sum in my will for your school, but deem it wiser to give it to you while I live. I recall with pleasure your visit to me two years ago."

I can hardly imagine any occurrence which could have given me more genuine satisfaction than the receipt of this draft. It was by far the largest single donation which up to that time the school had ever received. It came at a time when an unusually long period had passed since we had received any money. We were in great distress because of lack of funds, and the nervous strain was tremendous. It is difficult for me to think of any situation that is more trying on the nerves than that of conducting a large institution, with heavy obligations to meet, without knowing where the money is to come from to meet these obligations from month to month.

In our case I felt a double responsibility, and this made the anxiety all the more intense. If the institution had been officered by white persons, and had failed, it would have injured the cause of Negro education; but I knew that the failure of our institution, officered by Negroes, would not only mean the loss of a school, but would cause people, in a large degree, to lose faith in the ability of the entire race. The receipt of this draft for ten thousand dollars, under all these circumstances, partially lifted a burden that had been pressing down upon me for days.

From the beginning of our work to the present I have always had the feeling, and lose no opportunity to impress our teachers with the same idea, that the school will always be supported in proportion as the inside of the institution is kept clean and pure and wholesome.

The first time I ever saw the late Collis P. Huntington, the great railroad man, he gave me two dollars for our school. The last time I saw him, which was a few months before he died, he gave me fifty thousand dollars toward our endowment fund. Between these two gifts there were others of generous proportions which came every year from both Mr. and Mrs. Huntington.

Some people may say that it was Tuskegee's good luck that brought to us this gift of fifty thousand dollars. No, it was not luck. It was hard work. Nothing ever comes to me, that is worth having, except as the result of hard work. When Mr. Huntington gave me the first two dollars, I did not blame him for not giving me more, but made up my mind that I was going to convince him by tangible results that we were worthy of larger gifts. For a dozen years I made a strong effort to convince Mr. Huntington of the value of our work. I noted that just in proportion as the usefulness of the school grew, his donations increased. Never did I meet an individual who took a more kindly and sympathetic interest in our school than did Mr. Huntington. He not only gave money to us, but took time in which to advise me, as a father would a son, about the general conduct of the school.

More than once I have found myself in some pretty tight places while collecting money in the North. The following incident I have never related but once before, for the reason that I feared that people would not believe it. One morning I found myself in Providence, Rhode Island, without a cent of money with which to buy breakfast. In crossing the street to see a lady from whom I hoped to get some money, I found a bright new twenty-five-cent piece in the middle of the street track. I not only had this twenty-five cents for my breakfast, but within a few minutes I had a donation from the lady on whom I had started to call.

At one of our Commencements I was bold enough to invite the Rev. E. Winchester Donald, D.D., rector of Trinity Church, Boston, to preach the Commencement sermon. As we then had no room large enough to accommodate all who would be present, the place of meeting was under a large improvised arbor, built partly of brush and partly of rough boards. Soon after Dr. Donald had begun speaking, the rain came down in torrents, and he had to stop, while someone held an umbrella over him.

The boldness of what I had done never dawned upon me until I saw the picture made by the rector of Trinity Church standing before that large audience under an old umbrella, waiting for the rain to cease so that he could go on with his address.

It was not very long before the rain ceased and Dr. Donald finished his sermon; and an excellent sermon it was, too, in spite of the weather. After he had gone to his room, and had gotten the wet threads of his clothes dry, Dr. Donald ventured the remark that a large chapel at Tuskegee would not be out of place. The next day a letter came from two ladies who were then traveling in Italy, saying that they had decided to give us the money for such a chapel as we needed.

A short time ago we received twenty thousand dollars from Mr. Andrew Carnegie, to be used for the purpose of erecting a new library building. Our first library and reading-room were in a corner of a shanty, and the whole thing occupied a space about five by twelve feet. It required ten years of work before I was able to secure Mr. Carnegie's interest and help. The first time I saw him, ten years ago, he seemed to take but little interest in our school, but I was determined to show him that we were worthy of his help. After ten years of hard work I wrote him a letter reading as follows:

December 15, 1900.
Mr. Andrew Carnegie, 5 W. Fifty-first St., New York.

Dear Sir: Complying with the request which you made of me when I saw you at your residence a few days ago, I now submit in writing an appeal for a library building for our institution.

We have 1100 students, 86 officers and instructors, together with their families, and about 200 colored people living near the school, all of whom would make use of the library building.

We have over 12,000 books, periodicals, etc., gifts from our friends, but we have no suitable place for them, and we have no suitable reading-room.

Our graduates go to work in every section of the South, and whatever knowledge might be obtained in the library would serve to assist in the elevation of the whole Negro race.

Such a building as we need could be erected for about $20,000. All of the work for the building, such as brick making, brick-masonry, carpentry, blacksmithing, etc., would be done by the students. The money which you would give would not only supply the building, but the erection of the building would give a large number of students an opportunity to learn the building trades, and the students would use the money paid to them to keep themselves in school. I do not believe that a similar amount of money often could be made go so far in uplifting a whole race.

If you wish further information, I shall be glad to furnish it.

Yours truly,

Booker T. Washington, Principal.

The next mail brought back the following reply: "I will be very glad to pay the bills for the library building as they are incurred, to the extent of twenty thousand dollars, and I am glad of this opportunity to show the interest I have in your noble work."

I have found that strict business methods go a long way in securing the interest of rich people. It has been my constant aim at Tuskegee to carry out, in our financial and other operations, such business methods as would be approved of by any New York banking house.

I have spoken of several large gifts to the school; but by far the greater proportion of the money that has built up the institution has come in the form of small donations from persons of moderate means. It is upon these small gifts, which carry with them the interest of hundreds of donors, that any philanthropic work must depend largely for its support. In my efforts to get money I have often been surprised at the patience and deep interest of the ministers, who are besieged on every hand and at all hours of the day for help. If no other consideration had convinced me of the value of the Christian life, the Christlike work which the Church of all denominations in America has done during the last thirty-five years for the elevation of the black man would have made me a Christian. In a large degree it has been the pennies, the nickels, and the dimes which have come from the Sunday-schools, the Christian Endeavor societies, and the missionary societies, as well as from the church proper, that have helped to elevate the Negro at so rapid a rate.

This speaking of small gifts reminds me to say that very few Tuskegee graduates fail to send us an annual contribution. These contributions range from twenty-five cents up to ten dollars.

Soon after beginning our third year's work we were surprised to receive money from three special sources, and up to the present time we have continued to receive help from them. First, the State Legislature of Alabama increased its annual appropriation from two thousand dollars to three thousand dollars; I might add that still later it increased this sum to four thousand five hundred dollars a year. The effort to secure this increase was led by the Hon. M.F. Foster, the member of the Legislature from Tuskegee. Second, we received one thousand dollars from the John F. Slater Fund. Our work seemed to please the trustees of this fund, as they soon began increasing their annual grant. This has been added to from time to time until at present we receive eleven thousand dollars annually from the Fund. The other help to which I have referred came in the shape of an allowance from the Peabody Fund. This was at first five hundred dollars, but it has since been increased to fifteen hundred dollars.

The effort to secure help from the Slater and Peabody Funds brought me into contact with two rare men—men who have had much to do in shaping the policy for the education of the Negro. I refer to the Hon. J.L.M. Curry, of Washington, who is the general agent for these two funds, and Mr. Morris K. Jessup, of New York. Dr. Curry is a native of the South, an ex-Confederate soldier, yet I do not believe there is any man in the country who is more deeply interest in the highest welfare of the Negro than Dr. Curry, or one who is more free from race prejudice. He enjoys the unique distinction of possessing to an equal degree of confidence of the black man and the Southern white man. I shall never forget the first time I met him. It was in Richmond, Va., where he was then living. I had heard much about him. When I first went into his presence, trembling because of my youth and inexperience, he took me by the hand so cordially, and spoke such encouraging words, and gave me such helpful advice regarding the proper course to pursue, that I came to know him then, as I have known him ever since, as a high example of one who is constantly and unselfishly at work for the betterment of humanity.

Mr. Morris K. Jessup, the treasurer of the Slater Fund, I refer to because I know of no man of wealth and large and complication business responsibilities who gives not only money but his time and thought to the subject of the proper method of elevating the Negro to the extent that is true of Mr. Jessup. It is very largely through this effort and influence that during the last few years the subject of industrial education has assumed the importance that it has, and been placed on its present footing.

Two Thousand Miles For A Five-Minute Speech

Soon after the opening of our boarding department, quite a number of students who evidently were worthy, but who were so poor that they did not have any money to pay even the small charges at the school, began applying for admission. This class was composed of both men and women. It was a great trial to refuse admission to these applicants, and in 1884 we established a night-school to accommodate a few of them.

The night-school was organized on a plan similar to the one which I had helped to establish at Hampton. At first it was composed of about a dozen students. They were admitted to the night-school only when they had no money with which to pay any part of their board in the regular day-school. It was further required that they must work for ten hours during the day at some trade or industry, and study academic branches for two hours during the evening. This was the requirement for the first one or two years of their stay. They were to be paid something above the cost of their board, with the understanding that all of their earnings, except a very small part, were to be reserved in the school's treasury, to be used for paying their board in the regular day-school after they had entered that department. The night-school, started in this manner, has grown until there are at present four hundred and fifty-seven students enrolled in it alone.

There could hardly be a more severe test of a student's worth than this branch of the Institute's worth. It is largely because it furnishes such a good opportunity to test the backbone of a student that I place such high value upon our night-school. Any one who is willing to work ten hours a day at the brick-yard, or in the laundry, through one or two years, in order that he or she may have the privilege of studying academic branches for two hours in the evening, has enough bottom to warrant being further educated.

After the student has left the night-school he enters the day-school, where he takes academic branches four days in a week, and works at his trade two days. Besides this he usually works at his trade during the three summer months. As a rule, after a student has succeeded in going through the night-school test, he finds a way to finish the regular course in industrial and academic training. No student, no matter how much money he may be able to command, is permitted to go through school without doing manual labor. In fact, the industrial work is now as popular as the academic branches. Some of the most successful men and women who have graduated from the institution obtained their start in the night-school.

While a great deal of stress is laid upon the industrial side of the work at Tuskegee, we do not neglect or overlook in any degree the religious and spiritual side. The school is strictly undenominational, but it is thoroughly Christian, and the spiritual training or the students is not neglected. Our preaching service, prayer-meetings, Sunday-school, Christian Endeavor Society, Young Men's Christian Association, and various missionary organizations, testify to this.

In 1885, Miss Olivia Davidson, to whom I have already referred as being largely responsible for the success of the school during its early history, and I were married. During our married life she continued to divide her time and strength between our home and the work for the school. She not only continued to work in the school at Tuskegee, but also kept up her habit of going North to secure funds. In 1889 she died, after four years of happy married life and eight years of hard and happy work for the school. She literally wore herself out in her never ceasing efforts in behalf of the work that she so dearly loved. During our married life there were born to us two bright, beautiful boys, Booker Taliaferro and Ernest Davidson. The older of these, Booker, has already mastered the brick-maker's trade at Tuskegee.

I have often been asked how I began the practice of public speaking. In answer I would say that I never planned to give any large part of my life to speaking in public. I have always had more of an ambition to DO things than merely to talk *about* doing them. It seems that when I went North with General Armstrong to speak at the series of public meetings to which I have referred, the President of the National Educational Association, the Hon. Thomas W. Bicknell, was present at one of those meetings and heard me speak. A few days afterward he sent me an invitation to deliver an address at the next meeting of the Educational Association. This meeting was to be held in Madison, Wis. I accepted the invitation. This was, in a sense, the beginning of my public-speaking career.

On the evening that I spoke before the Association there must have been not far from four thousand persons present. Without my knowing it, there were a large number of people present from Alabama, and some from the town of Tuskegee. These white people afterward frankly told me that they went to this meeting expecting to hear the South roundly abused, but were pleasantly surprised to find that there was no word of abuse in my address. On the contrary, the South was given credit for all the praiseworthy things that it had done. A white lady who was teacher in a college in Tuskegee wrote back to the local paper that she was gratified, as well as surprised, to note the credit which I gave the white people of Tuskegee for their help in getting the school started. This address at Madison was the first that I had delivered that in any large measure dealt with the general problem of the races. Those who heard it seemed to be pleased with what I said and with the general position that I took.

When I first came to Tuskegee, I determined that I would make it my home, that I would take as much pride in the right actions of the people of the town as any white man could do, and that I would, at the same time, deplore the wrong-doing of the people as much as any white man. I determined never to say anything in a public address in the North that I would not be willing to say in the South. I early learned that it is a hard matter to convert an individual by abusing him, and that this is more often accomplished by giving credit for all the praiseworthy actions performed than by calling attention alone to all the evil done.

While pursuing this policy I have not failed, at the proper time and in the proper manner, to call attention, in no uncertain terms, to the wrongs which any part of the South has been guilty of. I have found that there is a large element in the South that is quick to respond to straightforward, honest criticism of any wrong policy. As a rule, the place to criticize the South, when criticism is necessary, is in the South—not in Boston. A Boston man who came to Alabama to criticize Boston would not effect so much good, I think, as one who had his word of criticism to say in Boston.

In this address at Madison I took the ground that the policy to be pursued with references to the races was, by every honorable means, to bring them together and to encourage the cultivation of friendly relations, instead of doing that which would embitter. I further contended that, in relation to his vote, the Negro should more and more consider the interests of the community in which he lived, rather than seek alone to please some one who lived a thousand miles away from him and from his interests.

In this address I said that the whole future of the Negro rested largely upon the question as to whether or not he should make himself, through his skill, intelligence, and character, of such undeniable value to the community in which he lived that the community could not dispense with his presence. I said that any individual who learned to do something better than anybody else—learned to do a common thing in an uncommon manner—had solved his problem, regardless of the color of his skin, and that in proportion as the Negro learned to produce what other people wanted and must have, in the same proportion would he be respected.

I spoke of an instance where one of our graduates had produced two hundred and sixty-six bushels of sweet potatoes from an acre of ground, in a community where the average production had been only forty-nine bushels to the acre. He had been able to do this by reason of his knowledge of the chemistry of the soil and by his knowledge of improved methods of agriculture. The white farmers in the neighborhood respected him, and came to him for ideas regarding the raising of sweet potatoes. These white farmers honored and respected him because he, by his skill and knowledge, had added something to the wealth and the comfort of the community in which he lived. I explained that my theory of education for the Negro would not, for example, confine him for all time to farm life—to the production of the best and the most sweet potatoes—but that, if he succeeded in this line of industry, he could lay the foundations upon which his children and grand-children could grow to higher and more important things in life.

Such, in brief, were some of the views I advocated in this first address dealing with the broad question of the relations of the two races, and since that time I have not found any reason for changing my views on any important point.

In my early life I used to cherish a feeling of ill will toward any one who spoke in bitter terms against the Negro, or who advocated measures that tended to oppress the black man or take from him opportunities for growth in the most complete manner. Now, whenever I hear any one advocating measures that are meant to curtail the development of another, I pity the individual who would do this. I know that the one who makes this mistake does so because of his own lack of opportunity for the highest kind of growth. I pity him because I know that he is trying to stop the progress of the world, and because I know that in time the development and the ceaseless advance of humanity will make him ashamed of his weak and narrow position. One might as well try to stop the progress of a mighty railroad train by throwing his body across the track, as to try to stop the growth of the world in the direction of giving mankind more intelligence, more culture, more skill, more liberty, and in the direction of extending more sympathy and more brotherly kindness.

The address which I delivered at Madison, before the National Educational Association, gave me a rather wide introduction in the North, and soon after that opportunities began offering themselves for me to address audiences there.

I was anxious, however, that the way might also be opened for me to speak directly to a representative Southern white audience. A partial opportunity of this kind, one that seemed to me might serve as an entering wedge, presented itself in 1893, when the international meeting of Christian Workers was held at Atlanta, Ga. When this invitation came to me, I had engagements in Boston that seemed to make it impossible for me to speak in Atlanta. Still, after looking over my list of dates and places carefully, I found that I could take a train from Boston that would get me into Atlanta about thirty minutes before my address was to be delivered, and that I could remain in that city before taking another train for Boston. My invitation to speak in Atlanta stipulated that I was to confine my address to five minutes. The question, then, was whether or not I could put enough into a five-minute address to make it worth while for me to make such a trip.

I knew that the audience would be largely composed of the most influential class of white men and women, and that it would be a rare opportunity for me to let them know what we were trying to do at Tuskegee, as well as to speak to them about the relations of the races. So I decided to make the trip. I spoke for five minutes to an audience of two thousand people, composed mostly of Southern and Northern whites. What I said seemed to be received with favor and enthusiasm. The Atlanta papers of the next day commented in friendly terms on my address, and a good deal was said about it in different parts of the country. I felt that I had in some degree accomplished my object—that of getting a hearing from the dominant class of the South.

The demands made upon me for public addresses continued to increase, coming in about equal numbers from my own people and from Northern whites. I gave as much time to these addresses as I could spare from the immediate work at Tuskegee. Most of the addresses in the North were made for the direct purpose of getting funds with which to support the school. Those delivered before the colored people had for their main object the impressing upon them the importance of industrial and technical education in addition to academic and religious training.

I now come to that one of the incidents in my life which seems to have excited the greatest amount of interest, and which perhaps went further than anything else in giving me a reputation that in a sense might be called National. I refer to the address which I delivered at the opening of the Atlanta Cotton states and International Exposition, at Atlanta, Ga., September 18, 1895.

So much has been said and written about this incident, and so many questions have been asked me concerning the address, that perhaps I may be excused for taking up the matter with some detail. The five-minute address in Atlanta, which I came from Boston to deliver, was possibly the prime cause for an opportunity being given me to make the second address there. In the spring of 1895 I received a telegram from prominent citizens in Atlanta asking me to accompany a committee from that city to Washington for the purpose of appearing before a committee of Congress in the interest of securing Government help for the Exposition. The committee was composed of about twenty-five of the most prominent and most influential white men of Georgia. All the members of this committee were white men except Bishop Grant, Bishop Gaines, and myself. The

Mayor and several other city and state officials spoke before the committee. They were followed by the two colored bishops. My name was the last on the list of speakers. I had never before appeared before such a committee, nor had I ever delivered any address in the capital of the Nation. I had many misgivings as to what I ought to say, and as to the impression that my address would make. While I cannot recall in detail what I said, I remember that I tried to impress upon the committee, with all the earnestness and plainness of any language that I could command, that if Congress wanted to do something which would assist in ridding the South of the race question and making friends between the two races, it should, in every proper way, encourage the material and intellectual growth of both races. I said that the Atlanta Exposition would present an opportunity for both races to show what advance they had made since freedom, and would at the same time afford encouragement to them to make still greater progress.

I tried to emphasize the fact that while the Negro should not be deprived by unfair means of the franchise, political agitation alone would not save him, and that back of the ballot he must have property, industry, skill, economy, intelligence, and character, and that no race without these elements could permanently succeed. I said that in granting the appropriation Congress could do something that would prove to be of real and lasting value to both races, and that it was the first great opportunity of the kind that had been presented since the close of the Civil War.

I spoke for fifteen or twenty minutes, and was surprised at the close of my address to receive the hearty congratulations of the Georgia committee and of the members of Congress who were present. The Committee was unanimous in making a favorable report, and in a few days the bill passed Congress. With the passing of this bill the success of the Atlanta Exposition was assured.

Soon after this trip to Washington the directors of the Exposition decided that it would be a fitting recognition of the colored race to erect a large and attractive building which should be devoted wholly to showing the progress of the Negro since freedom. It was further decided to have the building designed and erected wholly by Negro mechanics. This plan was carried out. In design, beauty, and general finish the Negro Building was equal to the others on the grounds.

After it was decided to have a separate Negro exhibit, the question arose as to who should take care of it. The officials of the Exposition were anxious that I should assume this responsibility, but I declined to do so, on the plea that the work at Tuskegee at that time demanded my time and strength. Largely at my suggestion, Mr. I. Garland Penn, of Lynchburg, Va., was selected to be at the head of the Negro department. I gave him all the aid that I could. The Negro exhibit, as a whole, was large and creditable. The two exhibits in this department which attracted the greatest amount of attention were those from the Hampton Institute and the Tuskegee Institute. The people who seemed to be the most surprised, as well as pleased, at what they saw in the Negro Building were the Southern white people.

As the day for the opening of the Exposition drew near, the Board of Directors began preparing the program for the opening exercises. In the discussion from day to day of the various features of this program, the question came up as to the advisability of putting a member of the Negro race on for one of the opening addresses, since the Negroes had been asked to take such a prominent part in the Exposition. It was argued, further, that such recognition would mark the good feeling prevailing between the two races. Of course there were those who were opposed to any such recognition of the rights of the Negro, but the Board of Directors, composed of men who represented the best and most progressive element in the South, had their way, and voted to invite a black man to speak on the opening day. The next thing was to decide upon the person who was thus to represent the Negro race. After the question had been canvassed for several days, the directors voted unanimously to ask me to deliver one of the opening-day addresses, and in a few days after that I received the official invitation.

The receiving of this invitation brought to me a sense of responsibility that it would be hard for any one not placed in my position to appreciate. What were my feelings when this invitation came to me? I remembered that I had been a slave; that my early years had been spent in the lowest depths of poverty and ignorance, and that I had had little opportunity to prepare me for such a responsibility as this. It was only a few years before that time that any white man in the audience might have claimed me as his slave; and it was easily possible that some of my former owners might be present to hear me speak.

I knew, too, that this was the first time in the entire history of the Negro that a member of my race had been asked to speak from the same platform with white Southern men and women on any important National occasion. I was asked now to speak to an audience composed of the wealth and culture of the white South, the representatives of my former masters. I knew, too, that while the greater part of my audience would be composed of Southern people, yet there would be present a large number of Northern whites, as well as a great many men and women of my own race.

I was determined to say nothing that I did not feel from the bottom of my heart to be true and right. When the invitation came to me, there was not one word of intimation as to what I should say or as to what I should omit. In this I felt that the Board of Directors had paid a tribute to me. They knew that by one sentence I could have blasted, in a large degree, the success of the Exposition. I was also painfully conscious of the fact that, while I must be true to my own race in my utterances, I had it in my power to make such an ill-timed address as would result in preventing any similar invitation being extended to a black man again for years to come. I was equally determined to be true to the North, as well as to the best element of the white South, in what I had to say.

The papers, North and South, had taken up the discussion of my coming speech, and as the time for it drew near this discussion became more and more widespread. Not a few of the Southern white papers were unfriendly to the idea of my speaking. From my own race I received many suggestions as to what I ought to say. I prepared myself as best I could for the address, but as the eighteenth of September drew nearer, the heavier my heart became, and the more I feared that my effort would prove a failure and a disappointment.

The invitation had come at a time when I was very busy with my school work, as it was the beginning of our school year. After preparing my address, I went through it, as I usually do with those utterances which I consider particularly important, with Mrs. Washington, and she approved of what I intended to say. On the sixteenth of September, the day before I was to start for Atlanta, so many of the Tuskegee teachers expressed a desire to hear my address that I consented to read it to them in a body. When I had done so, and had heard their criticisms and comments, I felt somewhat relieved, since they seemed to think well of what I had to say.

On the morning of September 17, together with Mrs. Washington and my three children, I started for Atlanta. I felt a good deal as I suppose a man feels when he is on his way to the gallows. In passing through the town of Tuskegee I met a white farmer who lived some distance out in the country. In a jesting manner this man said: "Washington, you have spoken before the Northern white people, the Negroes in the South, and to us country white people in the South; but Atlanta, to-morrow, you will have before you the Northern whites, the Southern whites, and the Negroes all together. I am afraid that you have got yourself in a tight place." This farmer diagnosed the situation correctly, but his frank words did not add anything to my comfort.

In the course of the journey from Tuskegee to Atlanta both colored and white people came to the train to point me out, and discussed with perfect freedom, in my hearings, what was going to take place the next day. We were met by a committee in Atlanta. Almost the first thing that I heard when I got off the train in that city was an expression something like this, from an old colored man near by: "Dat's de man of my race what's gwine to make a speech at de Exposition to-morrow. I'se sho' gwine to hear him."

Atlanta was literally packed, at the time, with people from all parts of the country, and with representatives of foreign governments, as well as with military and civic organizations. The afternoon papers had forecasts of the next day's proceedings in flaring headlines. All this tended to add to my burden. I did not sleep much that night. The next morning, before day, I went carefully over what I planned to say. I also kneeled down and asked God's blessing upon my effort. Right here, perhaps, I ought to add that I make it a rule never to go before an audience, on any occasion, without asking the blessing of God upon what I want to say.

I always make it a rule to make especial preparation for each separate address. No two audiences are exactly alike. It is my aim to reach and talk to the heart of each individual audience, taking it into my confidence very much as I would a person. When I am speaking to an audience, I care little for how what I am saying is going to sound in the newspapers, or to another audience, or to an individual. At the time, the audience before me absorbs all my sympathy, thought, and energy.

Early in the morning a committee called to escort me to my place in the procession which was to march to the Exposition grounds. In this procession were prominent colored citizens in carriages, as well as several Negro military organizations. I noted that the Exposition officials seemed to go out of their way to see that all of the colored people in the procession were properly placed and properly treated. The procession was about three hours in reaching the Exposition grounds, and during all of this time the sun was shining down upon us disagreeably hot. When we reached the grounds, the heat, together with my nervous anxiety, made me feel as if I were about ready to collapse, and to feel that my address was not going to be a success. When I entered the audience-room, I found it packed with humanity from bottom to top, and there were thousands outside who could not get in.

The room was very large, and well suited to public speaking. When I entered the room, there were vigorous cheers from the colored portion of the audience, and faint cheers from some of the white people. I had been told, while I had been in Atlanta, that while many white people were going to be present to hear me speak, simply out of curiosity, and that others who would be present would be in full sympathy with me, there was a still larger element of the audience which would consist of those who were going to be present for the purpose of hearing me make a fool of myself, or, at least, of hearing me say some foolish thing so that they could say to the officials who had invited me to speak, "I told you so!"

One of the trustees of the Tuskegee Institute, as well as my personal friend, Mr. William H. Baldwin, Jr. was at the time General Manager of the Southern Railroad, and happened to be in Atlanta on that day. He was so nervous about the kind of reception that I would have, and the effect that my speech would produce, that he could not persuade himself to go into the building, but walked back and forth in the grounds outside until the opening exercises were over.

The Atlanta Exposition Address

The Atlanta Exposition, at which I had been asked to make an address as a representative of the Negro race, as stated in the last chapter, was opened with a short address from Governor Bullock. After other interesting exercises, including an invocation from Bishop Nelson, of Georgia, a dedicatory ode by Albert Howell, Jr., and addresses by the President of the Exposition and Mrs. Joseph Thompson, the President of the Woman's Board, Governor Bullock introduce me with the words, "We have with us to-day a representative of Negro enterprise and Negro civilization."

When I arose to speak, there was considerable cheering, especially from the colored people. As I remember it now, the thing that was uppermost in my mind was the desire to say something that would cement the friendship of the races and bring about hearty cooperation between them. So far as my outward surroundings were concerned, the only thing that I recall distinctly now is that when I got up, I saw thousands of eyes looking intently into my face. The following is the address which I delivered:—

Mr. President and Gentlemen of the Board of Directors and Citizens.

One-third of the population of the South is of the Negro race. No enterprise seeking the material, civil, or moral welfare of this section can disregard this element of our population and reach the highest success. I but convey to you, Mr. President and Directors, the sentiment of the masses of my race when I say that in no way have the value and manhood of the American Negro been more fittingly and generously recognized than by the managers of this magnificent Exposition at every stage of its progress. It is a recognition that will do more to cement the friendship of the two races than any occurrence since the dawn of our freedom.

Not only this, but the opportunity here afforded will awaken among us a new era of industrial progress. Ignorant and inexperienced, it is not strange that in the first years of our new life we began at the top instead of at the bottom; that a seat in Congress or the state legislature was more sought than real estate or industrial skill; that the political convention or stump speaking had more attractions than starting a dairy farm or truck garden.

A ship lost at sea for many days suddenly sighted a friendly vessel. From the mast of the unfortunate vessel was seen a signal, "Water, water; we die of thirst!" The answer from the friendly vessel at once came back, "Cast down your bucket where you are." A second time the signal, "Water, water; send us water!" ran up from the distressed vessel, and was answered, "Cast down your bucket where you are." And a third and fourth signal for water was answered, "Cast down your bucket where you are." The captain of the distressed vessel, at last heading the injunction, cast down his bucket, and it came up full of fresh, sparkling water from the mouth of the Amazon River. To those of my race who depend on bettering their condition in a foreign land or who underestimate the importance of cultivating friendly relations with the Southern white man, who is their next-door neighbor, I would say: "Cast down your bucket where you are"—cast it down in making friends in every manly way of the people of all races by whom we are surrounded.

Cast it down in agriculture, mechanics, in commerce, in domestic service, and in the professions. And in this connection it is well to bear in mind that whatever other sins the South may be called to bear, when it comes to business, pure and simple, it is in the South that the Negro is given a man's chance in the commercial world, and in nothing is this Exposition more eloquent than in emphasizing this chance. Our greatest danger is that in the great leap from slavery to freedom we may overlook the fact that the masses of us are to live by the productions of our hands, and fail to keep in mind that we shall prosper in proportion as we learn to dignify and glorify common labor and put brains and skill into the common occupations of life; shall prosper in proportion as we learn to draw the line between the superficial and the substantial, the ornamental gewgaws of life and the useful. No race can prosper till it learns that there is as much dignity in tilling a field as in writing a poem. It is at the bottom of life we must begin, and not at the top. Nor should we permit our grievances to overshadow our opportunities.

To those of the white race who look to the incoming of those of foreign birth and strange tongue and habits of the prosperity of the South, were I permitted I would repeat what I say to my own race: "Cast down your bucket where you are." Cast it down among the eight millions of Negroes whose habits you know, whose fidelity and love you have tested in days when to have proved treacherous meant the ruin of your firesides. Cast down your bucket among these people who have, without strikes and labor wars, tilled your fields, cleared your forests, built your railroads and cities, and brought forth treasures from the bowels of the earth, and helped make possible this magnificent representation of the progress of the South. Casting down your bucket among my people, helping and encouraging them as you are doing on these grounds, and to education of head, hand, and heart, you will find that they will buy your surplus land, make blossom the waste places in your fields, and run your factories. While doing this, you can be sure in the future, as in the past, that you and your families will be surrounded by the most patient, faithful, law-abiding, and unresentful people that the world has seen. As we have proved our loyalty to you in the past, nursing your children, watching by the sick-bed of your mothers and fathers, and often following them with tear-dimmed eyes to their graves, so in the future, in our humble way, we shall stand by you with a devotion that no foreigner can approach, ready to lay down our lives, if need be, in defense of yours, interlacing our industrial, commercial, civil, and religious life with yours in a way that shall make the interests of both races one. In all things that are purely social we can be as separate as the fingers, yet one as the hand in all things essential to mutual progress.

There is no defense or security for any of us except in the highest intelligence and development of all. If anywhere there are efforts tending to curtail the fullest growth of the Negro, let these efforts be turned into stimulating, encouraging, and making him the most useful and intelligent citizen. Effort or means so invested will pay a thousand per cent interest. These efforts will be twice blessed—"blessing him that gives and him that takes."

There is no escape through law of man or God from the inevitable:—

The laws of changeless justice bind
Oppressor with oppressed;
And close as sin and suffering joined
We march to fate abreast.

Nearly sixteen millions of hands will aid you in pulling the load upward, or they will pull against you the load downward. We shall constitute one-third and more of the ignorance and crime of the South, or one-third its intelligence and progress; we shall contribute one-third to the business and industrial prosperity of the South, or we shall prove a veritable body of death, stagnating, depressing, retarding every effort to advance the body politic.

Gentlemen of the Exposition, as we present to you our humble effort at an exhibition of our progress, you must not expect overmuch. Starting thirty years ago with ownership here and there in a few quilts and pumpkins and chickens (gathered from miscellaneous sources), remember the path that has led from these to the inventions and production of agricultural implements, buggies, steam-engines, newspapers, books, statuary, carving, paintings, the management of drug-stores and banks, has not been trodden without contact with thorns and thistles. While we take pride in what we exhibit as a result of our independent efforts, we do not for a moment forget that our part in this exhibition would fall far short of your expectations but for the constant help that has come to our education life, not only from the Southern states, but especially from Northern philanthropists, who have made their gifts a constant stream of blessing and encouragement.

The wisest among my race understand that the agitation of questions of social equality is the extremest folly, and that progress in the enjoyment of all the privileges that will come to us must be the result of severe and constant struggle rather than of artificial forcing. No race that has anything to contribute to the markets of the world is long in any degree ostracized. It is important and right that all privileges of the law be ours, but it is vastly more important that we be prepared for the exercises of these privileges. The opportunity to earn a dollar in a factory just now is worth infinitely more than the opportunity to spend a dollar in an opera-house.

In conclusion, may I repeat that nothing in thirty years has given us more hope and encouragement, and drawn us so near to you of the white race, as this opportunity offered by the Exposition; and here bending, as it were, over the altar that represents the results of the struggles of your race and mine, both starting practically empty-handed three decades ago, I pledge that in your effort to work out the great and intricate problem which God has laid at the doors of the South, you shall have at all times the patient, sympathetic help of my race; only let this be constantly in mind, that, while from representations in these buildings of the product of field, of forest, of mine, of factory, letters, and art, much good will come, yet far above and beyond material benefits will be that higher good, that, let us pray God, will come, in a blotting out of sectional differences and racial animosities and suspicions, in a determination to administer absolute justice, in a willing obedience among all classes to the mandates of law. This, this, coupled with our material prosperity, will bring into our beloved South a new heaven and a new earth.

The first thing that I remember, after I had finished speaking, was that Governor Bullock rushed across the platform and took me by the hand, and that others did the same. I received so many and such hearty congratulations that I found it difficult to get out of the building. I did not appreciate to any degree, however, the impression which my address seemed to have made, until the next morning, when I went into the business part of the city. As soon as I was recognized, I was surprised to find myself pointed out and surrounded by a crowd of men who wished to shake hands with me. This was kept up on every street on to which I went, to an extent which embarrassed me so much that I went back to my boarding-place. The next morning I returned to Tuskegee. At the station in Atlanta, and at almost all of the stations at which the train stopped between that city and Tuskegee, I found a crowd of people anxious to shake hands with me.

The papers in all parts of the United States published the address in full, and for months afterward there were complimentary editorial references to it. Mr. Clark Howell, the editor of the Atlanta Constitution, telegraphed to a New York paper, among other words, the following, "I do not exaggerate when I say that Professor Booker T. Washington's address yesterday was one of the most notable speeches, both as to character and as to the warmth of its reception, ever delivered to a Southern audience. The address was a revelation. The whole speech is a platform upon which blacks and whites can stand with full justice to each other."

The Boston Transcript said editorially: "The speech of Booker T. Washington at the Atlanta Exposition, this week, seems to have dwarfed all the other proceedings and the Exposition itself. The sensation that it has caused in the press has never been equaled."

I very soon began receiving all kinds of propositions from lecture bureaus, and editors of magazines and papers, to take the lecture platform, and to write articles. One lecture bureau offered me fifty thousand dollars, or two hundred dollars a night and expenses, if I would place my services at its disposal for a given period. To all these communications I replied that my life-work was at Tuskegee; and that whenever I spoke it must be in the interests of Tuskegee school and my race, and that I would enter into no arrangements that seemed to place a mere commercial value upon my services.

Some days after its delivery I sent a copy of my address to the President of the United States, the Hon. Grover Cleveland. I received from him the following autograph reply:—

Gray Gables, Buzzard's Bay, Mass.,
October 6, 1895.
Booker T. Washington, Esq.:
My Dear Sir: I thank you for sending me a copy of your address delivered at the Atlanta Exposition.

I thank you with much enthusiasm for making the address. I have read it with intense interest, and I think the Exposition would be fully justified if it did not do more than furnish the opportunity for its delivery. Your words cannot fail to delight and encourage all who wish well for your race; and if our colored fellow-citizens do not from your utterances gather new hope and form new determinations to gain every valuable advantage offered them by their citizenship, it will be strange indeed.

Yours very truly,
Grover Cleveland.

Later I met Mr. Cleveland, for the first time, when, as President, he visited the Atlanta Exposition. At the request of myself and others he consented to spend an hour in the Negro Building, for the purpose of inspecting the Negro exhibit and of giving the colored people in attendance an opportunity to shake hands with him. As soon as I met Mr. Cleveland I became impressed with his simplicity, greatness, and rugged honesty. I have met him many times since then, both at public functions and at his private residence in Princeton, and the more I see of him the more I admire him. When he visited the Negro Building in Atlanta he seemed to give himself up wholly, for that hour, to the colored people. He seemed to be as careful to shake hands with some old colored "auntie" clad partially in rags, and to take as much pleasure in doing so, as if he were greeting some millionaire. Many of the colored people took advantage of the occasion to get him to write his name in a book or on a slip of paper. He was as careful and patient in doing this as if he were putting his signature to some great state document.

Mr. Cleveland has not only shown his friendship for me in many personal ways, but has always consented to do anything I have asked of him for our school. This he has done, whether it was to make a personal donation or to use his influence in securing the donations of others. Judging from my personal acquaintance with Mr. Cleveland, I do not believe that he is conscious of possessing any color prejudice. He is too great for that. In my contact with people I find that, as a rule, it is only the little, narrow people who live for themselves, who never read good books, who do not travel, who never open up their souls in a way to permit them to come into contact with other souls—with the great outside world. No man whose vision is bounded by color can come into contact with what is highest and best in the world. In meeting men, in many places, I have found that the happiest people are those who do the most for others; the most miserable are those who do the least. I have also found that few things, if any, are capable of making one so blind and narrow as race prejudice. I often say to our students, in the course of my talks to them on Sunday evenings in the chapel, that the longer I live and the more experience I have of the world, the more I am convinced that, after all, the one thing that is most worth living for—and dying for, if need be—is the opportunity of making some one else more happy and more useful.

The colored people and the colored newspapers at first seemed to be greatly pleased with the character of my Atlanta address, as well as with its reception. But after the first burst of enthusiasm began to die away, and the colored people began reading the speech in cold type, some of them seemed to feel that they had been hypnotized. They seemed to feel that I had been too liberal in my remarks toward the Southern whites, and that I had not spoken out strongly enough for what they termed the "rights" of my race. For a while there was a reaction, so far as a certain element of my own race was concerned, but later these reactionary ones seemed to have been won over to my way of believing and acting.

While speaking of changes in public sentiment, I recall that about ten years after the school at Tuskegee was established, I had an experience that I shall never forget. Dr. Lyman Abbott, then the pastor of Plymouth Church, and also editor of the Outlook (then the Christian Union), asked me to write a letter for his paper giving my opinion of the exact condition, mental and moral, of the colored ministers in the South, as based upon my observations. I wrote the letter, giving the exact facts as I conceived them to be. The picture painted was a rather black one—or, since I am black, shall I say "white"? It could not be otherwise with a race but a few years out of slavery, a race which had not had time or opportunity to produce a competent ministry.

What I said soon reached every Negro minister in the country, I think, and the letters of condemnation which I received from them were not few. I think that for a year after the publication of this article every association and every conference or religious body of any kind, of my race, that met, did not fail before adjourning to pass a resolution condemning me, or calling upon me to retract or modify what I had said. Many of these organizations went so far in their resolutions as to advise parents to cease sending their children to Tuskegee. One association even appointed a "missionary" whose duty it was to warn the people against sending their children to Tuskegee. This missionary had a son in the school, and I noticed that, whatever the "missionary" might have said or done with regard to others, he was careful not to take his son away from the institution. Many of the colored papers, especially those that were the organs of religious bodies, joined in the general chorus of condemnation or demands for retraction.

During the whole time of the excitement, and through all the criticism, I did not utter a word of explanation of retraction. I knew that I was right, and that time and the sober second thought of the people would vindicate me. It was not long before the bishops and other church leaders began to make careful investigation of the conditions of the ministry, and they found out that I was right. In fact, the oldest and most influential bishop in one branch of the Methodist Church said that my words were far too mild. Very soon public sentiment began making itself felt, in demanding a purifying of the ministry. While this is not yet complete by any means, I think I may say, without egotism, and I have been told by many of our most influential ministers, that my words had much to do with starting a demand for the placing of a higher type of men in the pulpit. I have had the satisfaction of having many who once condemned me thank me heartily for my frank words.

The change of the attitude of the Negro ministry, so far as regards myself, is so complete that at the present time I have no warmer friends among any class than I have among the clergymen. The improvement in the character and life of the Negro ministers is one of the most gratifying evidences of the progress of the race. My experience with them, as well as other events in my life, convince me that the thing to do, when one feels sure that he has said or done the right thing, and is condemned, is to stand still and keep quiet. If he is right, time will show it.

In the midst of the discussion which was going on concerning my Atlanta speech, I received the letter which I give below, from Dr. Gilman, the President of Johns Hopkins University, who had been made chairman of the judges of award in connection with the Atlanta Exposition:—

Johns Hopkins University, Baltimore,
President's Office, September 30, 1895.
Dear Mr. Washington: Would it be agreeable to you to be one of the Judges of Award in the Department of Education at Atlanta? If so, I shall be glad to place your name upon the list. A line by telegraph will be welcomed.
Yours very truly,
D.C. Gilman

I think I was even more surprised to receive this invitation than I had been to receive the invitation to speak at the opening of the Exposition. It was to be a part of my duty, as one of the jurors, to pass not only upon the exhibits of the colored schools, but also upon those of the white schools. I accepted the position, and spent a month in Atlanta in performance of the duties which it entailed. The board of jurors was a large one, containing in all of sixty members. It was about equally divided between Southern white people and Northern white people. Among them were college presidents, leading scientists and men of letters, and specialists in many subjects. When the group of jurors to which I was assigned met for organization, Mr. Thomas Nelson Page, who was one of the number, moved that I be made secretary of that division, and the motion was unanimously adopted. Nearly half of our division were Southern people. In performing my duties in the inspection of the exhibits of white schools I was in every case treated with respect, and at the close of our labors I parted from my associates with regret.

I am often asked to express myself more freely than I do upon the political condition and the political future of my race. These recollections of my experience in Atlanta give me the opportunity to do so briefly. My own belief is, although I have never before said so in so many words, that the time will come when the Negro in the South will be accorded all the political rights which his ability, character, and material possessions entitle him to. I think, though, that the opportunity to freely exercise such political rights will not come in any large degree through outside or artificial forcing, but will be accorded to the Negro by the Southern white people themselves, and that they will protect him in the exercise of those rights. Just as soon as the South gets over the old feeling that it is being forced by "foreigners," or "aliens," to do something which it does not want to do, I believe that the change in the direction that I have indicated is going to begin. In fact, there are indications that it is already beginning in a slight degree.

Let me illustrate my meaning. Suppose that some months before the opening of the Atlanta Exposition there had been a general demand from the press and public platform outside the South that a Negro be given a place on the opening program, and that a Negro be placed upon the board of jurors of award. Would any such recognition of the race have taken place? I do not think so. The Atlanta officials went as far as they did because they felt it to be a pleasure, as well as a duty, to reward what they considered merit in the Negro race. Say what we will, there is something in human nature which we cannot blot out, which makes one man, in the end, recognize and reward merit in another, regardless of color or race.

I believe it is the duty of the Negro—as the greater part of the race is already doing—to deport himself modestly in regard to political claims, depending upon the slow but sure influences that proceed from the possession of property, intelligence, and high character for the full recognition of his political rights. I think that the according of the full exercise of political rights is going to be a matter of natural, slow growth, not an over-night, gourd-vine affair. I do not believe that the Negro should cease voting, for a man cannot learn the exercise of self-government by ceasing to vote, any more than a boy can learn to swim by keeping out of the water, but I do believe that in his voting he should more and more be influenced by those of intelligence and character who are his next-door neighbors.

I know colored men who, through the encouragement, help, and advice of Southern white people, have accumulated thousands of dollars' worth of property, but who, at the same time, would never think of going to those same persons for advice concerning the casting of their ballots. This, it seems to me, is unwise and unreasonable, and should cease. In saying this I do not mean that the Negro should truckle, or not vote from principle, for the instant he ceases to vote from principle he loses the confidence and respect of the Southern white man even.

I do not believe that any state should make a law that permits an ignorant and poverty-stricken white man to vote, and prevents a black man in the same condition from voting. Such a law is not only unjust, but it will react, as all unjust laws do, in time; for the effect of such a law is to encourage the Negro to secure education and property, and at the same time it encourages the white man to remain in ignorance and poverty. I believe that in time, through the operation of intelligence and friendly race relations, all cheating at the ballot-box in the South will cease. It will become apparent that the white man who begins by cheating a Negro out of his ballot soon learns to cheat a white man out of his, and that the man who does this ends his career of dishonesty by the theft of property or by some equally serious crime. In my opinion, the time will come when the South will encourage all of its citizens to vote. It will see that it pays better, from every standpoint, to have healthy, vigorous life than to have that political stagnation which always results when one-half of the population has no share and no interest in the Government.

As a rule, I believe in universal, free suffrage, but I believe that in the South we are confronted with peculiar conditions that justify the protection of the ballot in many of the states, for a while at least, either by an education test, a property test, or by both combined; but whatever tests are required, they should be made to apply with equal and exact justice to both races.

The Secret Of Success In Public Speaking

As to how my address at Atlanta was received by the audience in the Exposition building, I think I prefer to let Mr. James Creelman, the noted war correspondent, tell. Mr. Creelman was present, and telegraphed the following account to the New York World:—

Atlanta, September 18.
While President Cleveland was waiting at Gray Gables to-day, to send the electric spark that started the machinery of the Atlanta Exposition, a Negro Moses stood before a great audience of white people and delivered an oration that marks a new epoch in the history of the South; and a body of Negro troops marched in a procession with the citizen soldiery of Georgia and Louisiana. The whole city is thrilling to-night with a realization of the extraordinary significance of these two unprecedented events. Nothing has happened since Henry Grady's immortal speech before the New England society in New York that indicates so profoundly the spirit of the New South, except, perhaps, the opening of the Exposition itself.

When Professor Booker T. Washington, Principal of an industrial school for colored people in Tuskegee, Ala. stood on the platform of the Auditorium, with the sun shining over the heads of his auditors into his eyes, and with his whole face lit up with the fire of prophecy, Clark Howell, the successor of Henry Grady, said to me, "That man's speech is the beginning of a moral revolution in America."

It is the first time that a Negro has made a speech in the South on any important occasion before an audience composed of white men and women. It electrified the audience, and the response was as if it had come from the throat of a whirlwind.

Mrs. Thompson had hardly taken her seat when all eyes were turned on a tall tawny Negro sitting in the front row of the platform. It was Professor Booker T. Washington, President of the Tuskegee (Alabama) Normal and Industrial Institute, who must rank from this time forth as the foremost man of his race in America. Gilmore's Band played the "Star-Spangled Banner," and the audience cheered. The tune changed to "Dixie" and the audience roared with shrill "hi-yis." Again the music changed, this time to "Yankee Doodle," and the clamor lessened.

All this time the eyes of the thousands present looked straight at the Negro orator. A strange thing was to happen. A black man was to speak for his people, with none to interrupt him. As Professor Washington strode to the edge of the stage, the low, descending sun shot fiery rays through the windows into his face. A great shout greeted him. He turned his head to avoid the blinding light, and moved about the platform for relief. Then he turned his wonderful countenance to the sun without a blink of the eyelids, and began to talk.

There was a remarkable figure; tall, bony, straight as a Sioux chief, high forehead, straight nose, heavy jaws, and strong, determined mouth, with big white teeth, piercing eyes, and a commanding manner. The sinews stood out on his bronzed neck, and his muscular right arm swung high in the air, with a lead-pencil grasped in the clinched brown fist. His big feet were planted squarely, with the heels together and the toes turned out. His voice range out clear and true, and he paused impressively as he made each point. Within ten minutes the multitude was in an uproar of enthusiasm—handkerchiefs were waved, canes were flourished, hats were tossed in the air. The fairest women of Georgia stood up and cheered. It was as if the orator had bewitched them.

And when he held his dusky hand high above his head, with the fingers stretched wide apart, and said to the white people of the South on behalf of his race, "In all things that are purely social we can be as separate as the fingers, yet one as the hand in all things essential to mutual progress," the great wave of sound dashed itself against the walls, and the whole audience was on its feet in a delirium of applause, and I thought at that moment of the night when Henry Grady stood among the curling wreaths of tobacco-smoke in Delmonico's banquet-hall and said, "I am a Cavalier among Roundheads."

I have heard the great orators of many countries, but not even Gladstone himself could have pleased a cause with most consummate power than did this angular Negro, standing in a nimbus of sunshine, surrounded by the men who once fought to keep his race in bondage. The roar might swell ever so high, but the expression of his earnest face never changed.

A ragged, ebony giant, squatted on the floor in one of the aisles, watched the orator with burning eyes and tremulous face until the supreme burst of applause came, and then the tears ran down his face. Most of the Negroes in the audience were crying, perhaps without knowing just why.

At the close of the speech Governor Bullock rushed across the stage and seized the orator's hand. Another shout greeted this demonstration, and for a few minutes the two men stood facing each other, hand in hand.

So far as I could spare the time from the immediate work at Tuskegee, after my Atlanta address, I accepted some of the invitations to speak in public which came to me, especially those that would take me into territory where I thought it would pay to plead the cause of my race, but I always did this with the understanding that I was to be free to talk about my life-work and the needs of my people. I also had it understood that I was not to speak in the capacity of a professional lecturer, or for mere commercial gain.

In my efforts on the public platform I never have been able to understand why people come to hear me speak. This question I never can rid myself of. Time and time again, as I have stood in the street in front of a building and have seen men and women passing in large numbers into the audience room where I was to speak, I have felt ashamed that I should be the cause of people—as it seemed to me—wasting a valuable hour of their time. Some years ago I was to deliver an address before a literary society in Madison, Wis. An hour before the time set for me to speak, a fierce snow-storm began, and continued for several hours. I made up my mind that there would be no audience, and that I should not have to speak, but, as a matter of duty, I went to the church, and found it packed with people. The surprise gave me a shock that I did not recover from during the whole evening.

People often ask me if I feel nervous before speaking, or else they suggest that, since I speak often, they suppose that I get used to it. In answer to this question I have to say that I always suffer intensely from nervousness before speaking. More than once, just before I was to make an important address, this nervous strain has been so great that I have resolved never again to speak in public. I not only feel nervous before speaking, but after I have finished I usually feel a sense of regret, because it seems to me as if I had left out of my address the main thing and the best thing that I had meant to say.

There is a great compensation, though, for this preliminary nervous suffering, that comes to me after I have been speaking for about ten minutes, and have come to feel that I have really mastered my audience, and that we have gotten into full and complete sympathy with each other. It seems to me that there is rarely such a combination of mental and physical delight in any effort as that which comes to a public speaker when he feels that he has a great audience completely within his control. There is a thread of sympathy and oneness that connects a public speaker with his audience, that is just as strong as though it was something tangible and visible. If in an audience of a thousand people there is one person who is not in sympathy with my views, or is inclined to be doubtful, cold, or critical, I can pick him out. When I have found him I usually go straight at him, and it is a great satisfaction to watch the process of his thawing out. I find that the most effective medicine for such individuals is administered at first in the form of a story, although I never tell an anecdote simply for the sake of telling one. That kind of thing, I think, is empty and hollow, and an audience soon finds it out.

I believe that one always does himself and his audience an injustice when he speaks merely for the sake of speaking. I do not believe that one should speak unless, deep down in his heart, he feels convinced that he has a message to deliver. When one feels, from the bottom of his feet to the top of his head, that he has something to say that is going to help some individual or some cause, then let him say it; and in delivering his message I do not believe that many of the artificial rules of elocution can, under such circumstances, help him very much. Although there are certain things, such as pauses, breathing, and pitch of voice, that are very important, none of these can take the place of soul in an address. When I have an address to deliver, I like to forget all about the rules for the proper use of the English language, and all about rhetoric and that sort of thing, and I like to make the audience forget all about these things, too.

Nothing tends to throw me off my balance so quickly, when I am speaking, as to have some one leave the room. To prevent this, I make up my mind, as a rule, that I will try to make my address so interesting, will try to state so many interesting facts one after another, that no one can leave. The average audience, I have come to believe, wants facts rather than generalities or sermonizing. Most people, I think, are able to draw proper conclusions if they are given the facts in an interesting form on which to base them.

As to the kind of audience that I like best to talk to, I would put at the top of the list an organization of strong, wide-awake, business men, such, for example, as is found in Boston, New York, Chicago, and Buffalo. I have found no other audience so quick to see a point, and so responsive. Within the last few years I have had the privilege of speaking before most of the leading organizations of this kind in the large cities of the United States. The best time to get hold of an organization of business men is after a good dinner, although I think that one of the worst instruments of torture that was ever invented is the custom which makes it necessary for a speaker to sit through a fourteen-course dinner, every minute of the time feeling sure that his speech is going to prove a dismal failure and disappointment.

I rarely take part in one of these long dinners that I do not wish that I could put myself back in the little cabin where I was a slave boy, and again go through the experience there—one that I shall never forget—of getting molasses to eat once a week from the "big house." Our usual diet on the plantation was corn bread and pork, but on Sunday morning my mother was permitted to bring down a little molasses from the "big house" for her three children, and when it was received how I did wish that every day was Sunday! I would get my tin plate and hold it up for the sweet morsel, but I would always shut my eyes while the molasses was being poured out into the plate, with the hope that when I opened them I would be surprised to see how much I had got. When I opened my eyes I would tip the plate in one direction and another, so as to make the molasses spread all over it, in the full belief that there would be more of it and that it would last longer if spread out in this way. So strong are my childish impressions of those Sunday morning feasts that it would be pretty hard for any one to convince me that there is not more molasses on a plate when it is spread all over the plate than when it occupies a little corner—if there is a corner in a plate. At any rate, I have never believed in "cornering" syrup. My share of the syrup was usually about two tablespoonfuls, and those two spoonfuls of molasses were much more enjoyable to me than is a fourteen-course dinner after which I am to speak.

Next to a company of business men, I prefer to speak to an audience of Southern people, of either race, together or taken separately. Their enthusiasm and responsiveness are a constant delight. The "amens" and "dat's de truf" that come spontaneously from the colored individuals are calculated to spur any speaker on to his best efforts. I think that next in order of preference I would place a college audience. It has been my privilege to deliver addresses at many of our leading colleges including Harvard, Yale, Williams, Amherst, Fisk University, the University of Pennsylvania, Wellesley, the University of Michigan, Trinity College in North Carolina, and many others.

It has been a matter of deep interest to me to note the number of people who have come to shake hands with me after an address, who say that this is the first time they have ever called a Negro "Mister."

When speaking directly in the interests of the Tuskegee Institute, I usually arrange, some time in advance, a series of meetings in important centers. This takes me before churches, Sunday-schools, Christian Endeavor Societies, and men's and women's clubs. When doing this I sometimes speak before as many as four organizations in a single day.

Three years ago, at the suggestion of Mr. Morris K. Jessup, of New York, and Dr. J.L.M. Curry, the general agent of the fund, the trustees of the John F. Slater Fund voted a sum of money to be used in paying the expenses of Mrs. Washington and myself while holding a series of meetings among the colored people in the large centers of Negro population, especially in the large cities of the ex-slaveholding states. Each year during the last three years we have devoted some weeks to this work. The plan that we have followed has been for me to speak in the morning to the ministers, teachers, and professional men. In the afternoon Mrs. Washington would speak to the women alone, and in the evening I spoke to a large mass-meeting. In almost every case the meetings have been attended not only by the colored people in large numbers, but by the white people. In

Chattanooga, Tenn., for example, there was present at the mass-meeting an audience of not less than three thousand persons, and I was informed that eight hundred of these were white. I have done no work that I really enjoyed more than this, or that I think has accomplished more good.

These meetings have given Mrs. Washington and myself an opportunity to get first-hand, accurate information as to the real condition of the race, by seeing the people in their homes, their churches, their Sunday-schools, and their places of work, as well as in the prisons and dens of crime. These meetings also gave us an opportunity to see the relations that exist between the races. I never feel so hopeful about the race as I do after being engaged in a series of these meetings. I know that on such occasions there is much that comes to the surface that is superficial and deceptive, but I have had experience enough not to be deceived by mere signs and fleeting enthusiasms. I have taken pains to go to the bottom of things and get facts, in a cold, business-like manner.

I have seen the statement made lately, by one who claims to know what he is talking about, that, taking the whole Negro race into account, ninety per cent of the Negro women are not virtuous. There never was a baser falsehood uttered concerning a race, or a statement made that was less capable of being proved by actual facts.

No one can come into contact with the race for twenty years, as I have done in the heart of the South, without being convinced that the race is constantly making slow but sure progress materially, educationally, and morally. One might take up the life of the worst element in New York City, for example, and prove almost anything he wanted to prove concerning the white man, but all will agree that this is not a fair test.

Early in the year 1897 I received a letter inviting me to deliver an address at the dedication of the Robert Gould Shaw monument in Boston. I accepted the invitation. It is not necessary for me, I am sure, to explain who Robert Gould Shaw was, and what he did. The monument to his memory stands near the head of the Boston Common, facing the State House. It is counted to be the most perfect piece of art of the kind to be found in the country.

The exercises connected with the dedication were held in Music Hall, in Boston, and the great hall was packed from top to bottom with one of the most distinguished audiences that ever assembled in the city. Among those present were more persons representing the famous old anti-slavery element that it is likely will ever be brought together in the country again. The late Hon. Roger Wolcott, then Governor of Massachusetts, was the presiding officer, and on the platform with him were many other officials and hundreds of distinguished men. A report of the meeting which appeared in the Boston Transcript will describe it better than any words of mine could do:—

The core and kernel of yesterday's great noon meeting, in honor of the Brotherhood of Man, in Music Hall, was the superb address of the Negro President of Tuskegee. "Booker T. Washington received his Harvard A.M. last June, the first of his race," said Governor Wolcott, "to receive an honorary degree from the oldest university in the land, and this for the wise leadership of his people." When Mr. Washington rose in the flag-filled, enthusiasm-warmed, patriotic, and glowing atmosphere of Music Hall, people felt keenly that here was the civic justification of the old abolition spirit of Massachusetts; in his person the proof of her ancient and indomitable faith; in his strong through and rich oratory, the crown and glory of the old war days of suffering and strife. The scene was full of historic beauty and deep significance. "Cold" Boston was alive with the fire that is always hot in her heart for righteousness and truth. Rows and rows of people who are seldom seen at any public function, whole families of those who are certain to be out of town on a holiday, crowded the place to overflowing. The city was at her birthright fete in the persons of hundreds of her best citizens, men and women whose names and lives stand for the virtues that make for honorable civic pride.

Battle-music had filled the air. Ovation after ovation, applause warm and prolonged, had greeted the officers and friends of Colonel Shaw, the sculptor, St. Gaudens, the memorial Committee, the Governor and his staff, and the Negro soldiers of the Fifty-fourth Massachusetts as they came upon the platform or entered the hall. Colonel Henry Lee, of Governor Andrew's old staff, had made a noble, simple presentation speech for the committee, paying tribute to Mr. John M. Forbes, in whose stead he served. Governor Wolcott had made his short, memorable speech, saying, "Fort Wagner marked an epoch in the history of a race, and called it into manhood." Mayor Quincy had received the monument for the city of Boston. The story of Colonel Shaw and his black regiment had been told in gallant words, and then, after the singing of

Mine eyes have seen the glory
Of the coming of the Lord,

Booker Washington arose. It was, of course, just the moment for him. The multitude, shaken out of its usual symphony-concert calm, quivered with an excitement that was not suppressed. A dozen times it had sprung to its feet to cheer and wave and hurrah, as one person. When this man of culture and voice and power, as well as a dark skin, began, and uttered the names of Stearns and of Andrew, feeling began to mount. You could see tears glisten in the eyes of soldiers and civilians. When the orator turned to the colored soldiers on the platform, to the color-bearer of Fort Wagner, who smilingly bore still the flag he had never lowered even when wounded, and said, "To you, to the scarred and scattered remnants of the Fifty-fourth, who, with empty sleeve and wanting leg, have honored this occasion with your presence, to you, your commander is not dead. Though Boston erected no monument and history recorded no story, in you and in the loyal race which you represent, Robert Gould Shaw would have a monument which time could not wear away," then came the climax of the emotion of the day and the hour. It was Roger Wolcott, as well as the Governor of Massachusetts, the individual representative of the people's sympathy as well as the chief magistrate, who had sprung first to his feet and cried, "Three cheers to Booker T. Washington!"

Among those on the platform was Sergeant William H. Carney, of New Bedford, Mass., the brave colored officer who was the color-bearer at Fort Wagner and held the American flag. In spite of the fact that a large part of his regiment was killed, he escape, and exclaimed, after the battle was over, "The old flag never touched the ground."

This flag Sergeant Carney held in his hands as he sat on the platform, and when I turned to address the survivors of the colored regiment who were present, and referred to Sergeant Carney, he rose, as if by instinct, and raised the flag. It has been my privilege to witness a good many satisfactory and rather sensational demonstrations in connection with some of my public addresses, but in dramatic effect I have never seen or experienced anything which equaled this. For a number of minutes the audience seemed to entirely lose control of itself.

In the general rejoicing throughout the country which followed the close of the Spanish-American war, peace celebrations were arranged in several of the large cities. I was asked by President William R. Harper, of the University of Chicago, who was chairman of the committee of invitations for the celebration to be held in the city of Chicago, to deliver one of the addresses at the celebration there. I accepted the invitation, and delivered two addresses there during the Jubilee week. The first of these, and the principal one, was given in the Auditorium, on the evening of Sunday, October 16. This was the largest audience that I have ever addressed, in any part of the country; and besides speaking in the main Auditorium, I also addressed, that same evening, two overflow audiences in other parts of the city.

It was said that there were sixteen thousand persons in the Auditorium, and it seemed to me as if there were as many more on the outside trying to get in. It was impossible for any one to get near the entrance without the aid of a policeman. President William McKinley attended this meeting, as did also the members of his Cabinet, many foreign ministers, and a large number of army and navy officers, many of whom had distinguished themselves in the war which had just closed. The speakers, besides myself, on Sunday evening, were Rabbi Emil G. Hirsch, Father Thomas P. Hodnett, and Dr. John H. Barrows.

The Chicago Times-Herald, in describing the meeting, said of my address:—

He pictured the Negro choosing slavery rather than extinction; recalled Crispus Attucks shedding his blood at the beginning of the American Revolution, that white Americans might be free, while black Americans remained in slavery; rehearsed the conduct of the Negroes with Jackson at New Orleans; drew a vivid and pathetic picture of the Southern slaves protecting and supporting the families of their masters while the latter were fighting to perpetuate black slavery; recounted the bravery of colored troops at Port Hudson and Forts Wagner and Pillow, and praised the heroism of the black regiments that stormed El Caney and Santiago to give freedom to the enslaved people of Cuba, forgetting, for the time being, the unjust discrimination that law and custom make against them in their own country.

In all of these things, the speaker declared, his race had chosen the better part. And then he made his eloquent appeal to the consciences of the white Americans: "When you have gotten the full story or the heroic conduct of the Negro in the Spanish-American war, have heard it from the lips of Northern soldier and Southern soldier, from ex-abolitionist and ex-masters, then decide within yourselves whether a race that is thus willing to die for its country should not be given the highest opportunity to live for its country."

The part of the speech which seems to arouse the wildest and most sensational enthusiasm was that in which I thanked the President for his recognition of the Negro in his appointments during the Spanish-American war. The President was sitting in a box at the right of the stage. When I addressed him I turned toward the box, and as I finished the sentence thanking him for his generosity, the whole audience rose and cheered again and again, waving handkerchiefs and hats and canes, until the President arose in the box and bowed his acknowledgments. At that the enthusiasm broke out again, and the demonstration was almost indescribable.

One portion of my address at Chicago seemed to have been misunderstood by the Southern press, and some of the Southern papers took occasion to criticize me rather strongly. These criticisms continued for several weeks, until I finally received a letter from the editor of the Age-Herald, published in Birmingham, Ala., asking me if I would say just what I meant by this part of the address. I replied to him in a letter which seemed to satisfy my critics. In this letter I said that I had made it a rule never to say before a Northern audience anything that I would not say before an audience in the South. I said that I did not think it was necessary for me to go into extended explanations; if my seventeen years of work in the heart of the South had not been explanation enough, I did not see how words could explain. I said that I made the same plea that I had made in my address at Atlanta, for the blotting out of race prejudice in "commercial and civil relations." I said that what is termed social recognition was a question which I never discussed, and then I quoted from my Atlanta address what I had said there in regard to that subject.

In meeting crowds of people at public gatherings, there is one type of individual that I dread. I mean the crank. I have become so accustomed to these people now that I can pick them out at a distance when I see them elbowing their way up to me. The average crank has a long beard, poorly cared for, a lean, narrow face, and wears a black coat. The front of his vest and coat are slick with grease, and his trousers bag at the knees.

In Chicago, after I had spoken at a meeting, I met one of these fellows. They usually have some process for curing all of the ills of the world at once. This Chicago specimen had a patent process by which he said Indian corn could be kept through a period of three or four years, and he felt sure that if the Negro race in the South would, as a whole, adopt his process, it would settle the whole race question. It mattered nothing that I tried to convince him that our present problem was to teach the Negroes how to produce enough corn to last them through one year. Another Chicago crank had a scheme by which he wanted me to join him in an effort to close up all the National banks in the country. If that was done, he felt sure it would put the Negro on his feet.

The number of people who stand ready to consume one's time, to no purpose, is almost countless. At one time I spoke before a large audience in Boston in the evening. The next morning I was awakened by having a card brought to my room, and with it a message that some one was anxious to see me. Thinking that it must be something very important, I dressed hastily and went down. When I reached the hotel office I found a blank and innocent-looking individual waiting for me, who coolly remarked: "I heard you talk at a meeting last night. I rather liked your talk, and so I came in this morning to hear you talk some more."

I am often asked how it is possible for me to superintend the work at Tuskegee and at the same time be so much away from the school. In partial answer to this I would say that I think I have learned, in some degree at least, to disregard the old maxim which says, "Do not get others to do that which you can do yourself." My motto, on the other hand, is, "Do not do that which others can do as well."

One of the most encouraging signs in connection with the Tuskegee school is found in the fact that the organization is so thorough that the daily work of the school is not dependent upon the presence of any one individual. The whole executive force, including instructors and clerks, now numbers eighty-six. This force is so organized and subdivided that the machinery of the school goes on day by day like clockwork. Most of our teachers have been connected with the institutions for a number of years, and are as much interested in it as I am. In my absence, Mr. Warren Logan, the treasurer, who has been at the school seventeen years, is the executive. He is efficiently supported by Mrs. Washington, and by my faithful secretary, Mr. Emmett J. Scott, who handles the bulk of my correspondence and keeps me in daily touch with the life of the school, and who also keeps me informed of whatever takes place in the South that concerns the race. I owe more to his tact, wisdom, and hard work than I can describe.

The main executive work of the school, whether I am at Tuskegee or not, centers in what we call the executive council. This council meets twice a week, and is composed of the nine persons who are at the head of the nine departments of the school. For example: Mrs. B.K. Bruce, the Lady Principal, the widow of the late ex-senator Bruce, is a member of the council, and represents in it all that pertains to the life of the girls at the school. In addition to the executive council there is a financial committee of six, that meets every week and decides upon the expenditures for the week. Once a month, and sometimes oftener, there is a general meeting of all the instructors. Aside from these there are innumerable smaller meetings, such as that of the instructors in the Phelps Hall Bible Training School, or of the instructors in the agricultural department.

In order that I may keep in constant touch with the life of the institution, I have a system of reports so arranged that a record of the school's work reaches me every day of the year, no matter in what part of the country I am. I know by these reports even what students are excused from school, and why they are excused—whether for reasons of ill health or otherwise. Through the medium of these reports I know each day what the income of the school in money is; I know how many gallons of milk and how many pounds of butter come from the dairy; what the bill of fare for the teachers and students is; whether a certain kind of meat was boiled or baked, and whether certain vegetables served in the dining room were bought from a store or procured from our own farm. Human nature I find to be very much the same the world over, and it is sometimes not hard to yield to the temptation to go to a barrel of rice that has come from the store—with the grain all prepared to go in the pot—rather than to take the time and trouble to go to the field and dig and wash one's own sweet potatoes, which might be prepared in a manner to take the place of the rice.

I am often asked how, in the midst of so much work, a large part of which is for the public, I can find time for any rest or recreation, and what kind of recreation or sports I am fond of. This is rather a difficult question to answer. I have a strong feeling that every individual owes it to himself, and to the cause which he is serving, to keep a vigorous, healthy body, with the nerves steady and strong, prepared for great efforts and prepared for disappointments and trying positions. As far as I can, I make it a rule to plan for each day's work—not merely to go through with the same routine of daily duties, but to get rid of the routine work as early in the day as possible, and then to enter upon some new or advance work. I make it a rule to clear my desk every day, before leaving my office, of all correspondence and memoranda, so that on the morrow I can begin a NEW day of work. I make it a rule never to let my work drive me, but to so master it, and keep it in such complete control, and to keep so far ahead of it, that I will be the master instead of the servant. There is a physical and mental and spiritual enjoyment that comes from a consciousness of being the absolute master of one's work, in all its details, that is very satisfactory and inspiring. My experience teachers me that, if one learns to follow this plan, he gets a freshness of body and vigor of mind out of work that goes a long way toward keeping him strong and healthy. I believe that when one can grow to the point where he loves his work, this gives him a kind of strength that is most valuable.

When I begin my work in the morning, I expect to have a successful and pleasant day of it, but at the same time I prepare myself for unpleasant and unexpected hard places. I prepared myself to hear that one of our school buildings is on fire, or has burned, or that some disagreeable accident has occurred, or that some one has abused me in a public address or printed article, for something that I have done or omitted to do, or for something that he had heard that I had said—probably something that I had never thought of saying.

In nineteen years of continuous work I have taken but one vacation. That was two years ago, when some of my friends put the money into my hands and forced Mrs. Washington and myself to spend three months in Europe. I have said that I believe it is the duty of every one to keep his body in good condition. I try to look after the little ills, with the idea that if I take care of the little ills the big ones will not come. When I find myself unable to sleep well, I know that something is wrong. If I find any part of my system the least weak, and not performing its duty, I consult a good physician. The ability to sleep well, at any time and in any place, I find of great advantage. I have so trained myself that I can lie down for a nap of fifteen or twenty minutes, and get up refreshed in body and mind.

I have said that I make it a rule to finish up each day's work before leaving it. There is, perhaps, one exception to this. When I have an unusually difficult question to decide—one that appeals strongly to the emotions—I find it a safe rule to sleep over it for a night, or to wait until I have had an opportunity to talk it over with my wife and friends.

As to my reading; the most time I get for solid reading is when I am on the cars. Newspapers are to me a constant source of delight and recreation. The only trouble is that I read too many of them. Fiction I care little for. Frequently I have to almost force myself to read a novel that is on every one's lips. The kind of reading that I have the greatest fondness for is biography. I like to be sure that I am reading about a real man or a real thing. I think I do not go too far when I say that I have read nearly every book and magazine article that has been written about Abraham Lincoln. In literature he is my patron saint.

Out of the twelve months in a year I suppose that, on an average, I spend six months away from Tuskegee. While my being absent from the school so much unquestionably has its disadvantages, yet there are at the same time some compensations. The change of work brings a certain kind of rest. I enjoy a ride of a long distance on the cars, when I am permitted to ride where I can be comfortable. I get rest on the cars, except when the inevitable individual who seems to be on every train approaches me with the now familiar phrase: "Isn't this Booker Washington? I want to introduce myself to you." Absence from the school enables me to lose sight of the unimportant details of the work, and study it in a broader and more comprehensive manner than I could do on the grounds. This absence also brings me into contact with the best work being done in educational lines, and into contact with the best educators in the land.

But, after all this is said, the time when I get the most solid rest and recreation is when I can be at Tuskegee, and, after our evening meal is over, can sit down, as is our custom, with my wife and Portia and Baker and Davidson, my three children, and read a story, or each take turns in telling a story. To me there is nothing on earth equal to that, although what is nearly equal to it is to go with them for an hour or more, as we like to do on Sunday afternoons, into the woods, where we can live for a while near the heart of nature, where no one can disturb or vex us, surrounded by pure air, the trees, the shrubbery, the flowers, and the sweet fragrance that springs from a hundred plants, enjoying the chirp of the crickets and the songs of the birds. This is solid rest.

My garden, also, what little time I can be at Tuskegee, is another source of rest and enjoyment. Somehow I like, as often as possible, to touch nature, not something that is artificial or an imitation, but the real thing. When I can leave my office in time so that I can spend thirty or forty minutes in spading the ground, in planting seeds, in digging about the plants, I feel that I am coming into contact with something that is giving me strength for the many duties and hard places that await me out in the big world. I pity the man or woman who has never learned to enjoy nature and to get strength and inspiration out of it.

Aside from the large number of fowls and animals kept by the school, I keep individually a number of pigs and fowls of the best grades, and in raising these I take a great deal of pleasure. I think the pig is my favorite animal. Few things are more satisfactory to me than a high-grade Berkshire or Poland China pig.

Games I care little for. I have never seen a game of football. In cards I do not know one card from another. A game of old-fashioned marbles with my two boys, once in a while, is all I care for in this direction. I suppose I would care for games now if I had had any time in my youth to give to them, but that was not possible.

Europe

In 1893 I was married to Miss Margaret James Murray, a native of Mississippi, and a graduate of Fisk University, in Nashville, Tenn., who had come to Tuskegee as a teacher several years before, and at the time we were married was filling the position of Lady Principal. Not only is Mrs. Washington completely one with me in the work directly connected with the school, relieving me of many burdens and perplexities, but aside from her work on the school grounds, she carries on a mothers' meeting in the town of Tuskegee, and a plantation work among the women, children, and men who live in a settlement connected with a large plantation about eight miles from Tuskegee. Both the mothers' meeting and the plantation work are carried on, not only with a view to helping those who are directly reached, but also for the purpose of furnishing object-lessons in these two kinds of work that may be followed by our students when they go out into the world for their own life-work.

Aside from these two enterprises, Mrs. Washington is also largely responsible for a woman's club at the school which brings together, twice a month, the women who live on the school grounds and those who live near, for the discussion of some important topic. She is also the President of what is known as the Federation of Southern Colored Women's Clubs, and is Chairman of the Executive Committee of the National Federation of Colored Women's Clubs.

Portia, the oldest of my three children, has learned dressmaking. She has unusual ability in instrumental music. Aside from her studies at Tuskegee, she has already begun to teach there.

Booker Taliaferro is my next oldest child. Young as he is, he has already nearly mastered the brickmason's trade. He began working at this trade when he was quite small, dividing his time between this and class work; and he has developed great skill in the trade and a fondness for it. He says that he is going to be an architect and brickmason. One of the most satisfactory letters that I have ever received from any one came to me from Booker last summer. When I left home for the summer, I told him that he must work at his trade half of each day, and that the other half of the day he could spend as he pleased. When I had been away from home two weeks, I received the following letter from him:

Tuskegee, Alabama.
My dear Papa: Before you left home you told me to work at my trade half of each day. I like my work so much that I want to work at my trade all day. Besides, I want to earn all the money I can, so that when I go to another school I shall have money to pay my expenses.
Your son,
Booker.

My youngest child, Earnest Davidson Washington, says that he is going to be a physician. In addition to going to school, where he studies books and has manual training, he regularly spends a portion of his time in the office of our resident physician, and has already learned to do many of the studies which pertain to a doctor's office.

The thing in my life which brings me the keenest regret is that my work in connection with public affairs keeps me for so much of the time away from my family, where, of all places in the world, I delight to be. I always envy the individual whose life-work is so laid that he can spend his evenings at home. I have sometimes thought that people who have this rare privilege do not appreciate it as they should. It is such a rest and relief to get away from crowds of people, and handshaking, and traveling, to get home, even if it be for but a very brief while.

Another thing at Tuskegee out of which I get a great deal of pleasure and satisfaction is in the meeting with our students, and teachers, and their families, in the chapel for devotional exercises every evening at half-past eight, the last thing before retiring for the night. It is an inspiring sight when one stands on the platform there and sees before him eleven or twelve hundred earnest young men and women; and one cannot but feel that it is a privilege to help to guide them to a higher and more useful life.

In the spring of 1899 there came to me what I might describe as almost the greatest surprise of my life. Some good ladies in Boston arranged a public meeting in the interests of Tuskegee, to be held in the Hollis Street Theater. This meeting was attended by large numbers of the best people of Boston, of both races. Bishop Lawrence presided. In addition to an address made by myself, Mr. Paul Lawrence Dunbar read from his poems, and Dr. W.E.B. Du Bois read an original sketch.

Some of those who attended this meeting noticed that I seemed unusually tired, and some little time after the close of the meeting, one of the ladies who had been interested in it asked me in a casual way if I had ever been to Europe. I replied that I never had. She asked me if I had ever thought of going, and I told her no; that it was something entirely beyond me. This conversation soon passed out of my mind, but a few days afterward I was informed that some friends in Boston, including Mr. Francis J. Garrison, had raised a sum of money sufficient to pay all the expenses of Mrs. Washington and myself during a three or four months' trip to Europe. It was added with emphasis that we MUST go. A year previous to this Mr. Garrison had attempted to get me to promise to go to Europe for a summer's rest, with the understanding that he would be responsible for raising the money among his friends for the expenses of the trip. At that time such a journey seemed so entirely foreign to anything that I should ever be able to undertake that I did confess I did not give the matter very serious attention; but later Mr. Garrison joined his efforts to those of the ladies whom I have mentioned, and when their plans were made known to me Mr. Garrison not only had the route mapped out, but had, I believe, selected the steamer upon which we were to sail.

The whole thing was so sudden and so unexpected that I was completely taken off my feet. I had been at work steadily for eighteen years in connection with Tuskegee, and I had never thought of anything else but ending my life in that way. Each day the school seemed to depend upon me more largely for its daily expenses, and I told these Boston friends that, while I thanked them sincerely for their thoughtfulness and generosity, I could not go to Europe, for the reason that the school could not live financially while I was absent. They then informed me that Mr. Henry L. Higginson, and some other good friends who I know do not want their names made public, were then raising a sum of money which would be sufficient to keep the school in operation while I was away. At this point I was compelled to surrender. Every avenue of escape had been closed.

Deep down in my heart the whole thing seemed more like a dream than like reality, and for a long time it was difficult for me to make myself believe that I was actually going to Europe. I had been born and largely reared in the lowest depths of slavery, ignorance, and poverty. In my childhood I had suffered for want of a place to sleep, for lack of food, clothing, and shelter. I had not had the privilege of sitting down to a dining-table until I was quite well grown. Luxuries had always seemed to me to be something meant for white people, not for my race. I had always regarded Europe, and London, and Paris, much as I regarded heaven. And now could it be that I was actually going to Europe? Such thoughts as these were constantly with me.

Two other thoughts troubled me a good deal. I feared that people who heard that Mrs. Washington and I were going to Europe might not know all the circumstances, and might get the idea that we had become, as some might say, "stuck up," and were trying to "show off." I recalled that from my youth I had heard it said that too often, when people of my race reached any degree of success, they were inclined to unduly exalt themselves; to try and ape the wealthy, and in so doing to lose their heads. The fear that people might think this of us haunted me a good deal. Then, too, I could not see how my conscience would permit me to spare the time from my work and be happy. It seemed mean and selfish in me to be taking a vacation while others were at work, and while there was so much that needed to be done. From the time I could remember, I had always been at work, and I did not see how I could spend three or four months in doing nothing. The fact was that I did not know how to take a vacation.

Mrs. Washington had much the same difficulty in getting away, but she was anxious to go because she thought that I needed the rest. There were many important National questions bearing upon the life of the race which were being agitated at that time, and this made it all the harder for us to decide to go. We finally gave our Boston friends our promise that we would go, and then they insisted that the date of our departure be set as soon as possible. So we decided upon May 10. My good friend Mr. Garrison kindly took charge of all the details necessary for the success of the trip, and he, as well as other friends, gave us a great number of letters of introduction to people in France and England, and made other arrangements for our comfort and convenience abroad. Good-bys were said at Tuskegee, and we were in New York May 9, ready to sail the next day. Our daughter Portia, who was then studying in South Framingham, Mass., came to New York to see us off. Mr. Scott, my secretary, came with me to New York, in order that I might clear up the last bit of business before I left. Other friends also came to New York to see us off. Just before we went on board the steamer another pleasant surprise came to us in the form of a letter from two generous ladies, stating that they had decided to give us the money with which to erect a new building to be used in properly housing all our industries for girls at Tuskegee.

We were to sail on the Friesland, of the Red Star Line, and a beautiful vessel she was. We went on board just before noon, the hour of sailing. I had never before been on board a large ocean steamer, and the feeling which took possession of me when I found myself there is rather hard to describe. It was a feeling, I think, of awe mingled with delight. We were agreeably surprised to find that the captain, as well as several of the other officers, not only knew who we were, but was expecting us and gave us a pleasant greeting. There were several passengers whom we knew, including Senator Sewell, of New Jersey, and Edward Marshall, the newspaper correspondent. I had just a little fear that we would not be treated civilly by some of the passengers. This fear was based upon what I had heard other people of my race, who had crossed the ocean, say about unpleasant experiences in crossing the ocean in American vessels. But in our case, from the captain down to the most humble servant, we were treated with the greatest kindness. Nor was this kindness confined to those who were connected with the steamer; it was shown by all the passengers also. There were not a few Southern men and women on board, and they were as cordial as those from other parts of the country.

As soon as the last good-bys were said, and the steamer had cut loose from the wharf, the load of care, anxiety, and responsibility which I had carried for eighteen years began to lift itself from my shoulders at the rate, it seemed to me, of a pound a minute. It was the first time in all those years that I had felt, even in a measure, free from care; and my feeling of relief it is hard to describe on paper. Added to this was the delightful anticipation of being in Europe soon. It all seemed more like a dream than like a reality.

Mr. Garrison had thoughtfully arranged to have us have one of the most comfortable rooms on the ship. The second or third day out I began to sleep, and I think that I slept at the rate of fifteen hours a day during the remainder of the ten days' passage. Then it was that I began to understand how tired I really was. These long sleeps I kept up for a month after we landed on the other side. It was such an unusual feeling to wake up in the morning and realize that I had no engagements; did not have to take a train at a certain hour; did not have an appointment to meet some one, or to make an address, at a certain hour. How different all this was from the experiences that I have been through when traveling, when I have sometimes slept in three different beds in a single night!

When Sunday came, the captain invited me to conduct the religious services, but, not being a minister, I declined. The passengers, however, began making requests that I deliver an address to them in the dining-saloon some time during the voyage, and this I consented to do. Senator Sewell presided at this meeting. After ten days of delightful weather, during which I was not seasick for a day, we landed at the interesting old city of Antwerp, in Belgium.

The next day after we landed happened to be one of those numberless holidays which the people of those countries are in the habit of observing. It was a bright, beautiful day. Our room in the hotel faced the main public square, and the sights there—the people coming in from the country with all kinds of beautiful flowers to sell, the women coming in with their dogs drawing large, brightly polished cans filled with milk, the people streaming into the cathedral—filled me with a sense of newness that I had never before experienced.

After spending some time in Antwerp, we were invited to go with a part of a half-dozen persons on a trip through Holland. This party included Edward Marshall and some American artists who had come over on the same steamer with us. We accepted the invitation, and enjoyed the trip greatly. I think it was all the more interesting and instructive because we went for most of the way on one of the slow, old-fashioned canal-boats. This gave us an opportunity of seeing and studying the real life of the people in the country districts. We went in this way as far as Rotterdam, and later went to The Hague, where the Peace Conference was then in session, and where we were kindly received by the American representatives.

The thing that impressed itself most on me in Holland was the thoroughness of the agriculture and the excellence of the Holstein cattle. I never knew, before visiting Holland, how much it was possible for people to get out of a small plot of ground. It seemed to me that absolutely no land was wasted. It was worth a trip to Holland, too, just to get a sight of three or four hundred fine Holstein cows grazing in one of those intensely green fields.

From Holland we went to Belgium, and made a hasty trip through that country, stopping at Brussels, where we visited the battlefield of Waterloo. From Belgium we went direct to Paris, where we found that Mr. Theodore Stanton, the son of Mrs. Elizabeth Cady Stanton, had kindly provided accommodations for us. We had barely got settled in Paris before an invitation came to me from the University Club of Paris to be its guest at a banquet which was soon to be given. The other guests were ex-President Benjamin Harrison and Archbishop Ireland, who were in Paris at the time. The American Ambassador, General Horace Porter, presided at the banquet. My address on this occasion seemed to give satisfaction to those who heard it. General Harrison kindly devoted a large portion of his remarks at dinner to myself and to the influence of the work at Tuskegee on the American race question. After my address at this banquet other invitations came to me, but I declined the most of them, knowing that if I accepted them all, the object of my visit would be defeated. I did, however, consent to deliver an address in the American chapel the following Sunday morning, and at this meeting General Harrison, General Porter, and other distinguished Americans were present.

Later we received a formal call from the American Ambassador, and were invited to attend a reception at his residence. At this reception we met many Americans, among them Justices Fuller and Harlan, of the United States Supreme Court. During our entire stay of a month in Paris, both the American Ambassador and his wife, as well as several other Americans, were very kind to us.

While in Paris we saw a good deal of the now famous American Negro painter, Mr. Henry O. Tanner, whom we had formerly known in America. It was very satisfactory to find how well known Mr. Tanner was in the field of art, and to note the high standing which all classes accorded to him. When we told some Americans that we were going to the Luxembourg Palace to see a painting by an American Negro, it was hard to convince them that a Negro had been thus honored. I do not believe that they were really convinced of the fact until they saw the picture for themselves. My acquaintance with Mr. Tanner reenforced in my mind the truth which I am constantly trying to impress upon our students at Tuskegee—and on our people throughout the country, as far as I can reach them with my voice—that any man, regardless of color, will be recognized and rewarded just in proportion as he learns to do something well—learns to do it better than some one else—however humble the thing may be. As I have said, I believe that my race will succeed in proportion as it learns to do a common thing in an uncommon manner; learns to do a thing so thoroughly that no one can improve upon what it has done; learns to make its services of indispensable value. This was the spirit that inspired me in my first effort at Hampton, when I was given the opportunity to sweep and dust that schoolroom. In a degree I felt that my whole future life depended upon the thoroughness with which I cleaned that room, and I was determined to do it so well that no one could find any fault with the job. Few people ever stopped, I found, when looking at his pictures, to inquire whether Mr. Tanner was a Negro painter, a French painter, or a German painter. They simply knew that he was able to produce something which the world wanted—a great painting—and the matter of his color did not enter into their minds. When a Negro girl learns to cook, to wash dishes, to sew, or write a book, or a Negro boy learns to groom horses, or to grow sweet potatoes, or to produce butter, or to build a house, or to be able to practice medicine, as well or better than some one else, they will be rewarded regardless of race or color. In the long run, the world is going to have the best, and any difference in race, religion, or previous history will not long keep the world from what it wants.

I think that the whole future of my race hinges on the question as to whether or not it can make itself of such indispensable value that the people in the town and the state where we reside will feel that our presence is necessary to the happiness and well-being of the community. No man who continues to add something to the material, intellectual, and moral well-being of the place in which he lives is long left without proper reward. This is a great human law which cannot be permanently nullified.

The love of pleasure and excitement which seems in a large measure to possess the French people impressed itself upon me. I think they are more noted in this respect than is true of the people of my own race. In point of morality and moral earnestness I do not believe that the French are ahead of my own race in America. Severe competition and the great stress of life have led them to learn to do things more thoroughly and to exercise greater economy; but time, I think, will bring my race to the same point. In the matter of truth and high honor I do not believe that the average Frenchman is ahead of the American Negro; while so far as mercy and kindness to dumb animals go, I believe that my race is far ahead. In fact, when I left France, I had more faith in the future of the black man in America than I had ever possessed.

From Paris we went to London, and reached there early in July, just about the height of the London social season. Parliament was in session, and there was a great deal of gaiety. Mr. Garrison and other friends had provided us with a large number of letters of introduction, and they had also sent letters to other persons in different parts of the United Kingdom, apprising these people of our coming. Very soon after reaching London we were flooded with invitations to attend all manner of social functions, and a great many invitations came to me asking that I deliver public addresses. The most of these invitations I declined, for the reason that I wanted to rest. Neither were we able to accept more than a small proportion of the other invitations. The Rev. Dr. Brooke Herford and Mrs. Herford, whom I had known in Boston, consulted with the American Ambassador, the Hon. Joseph Choate, and arranged for me to speak at a public meeting to be held in Essex Hall. Mr. Choate kindly consented to preside. The meeting was largely attended. There were many distinguished persons present, among them several members of Parliament, including Mr. James Bryce, who spoke at the meeting. What the American Ambassador said in introducing me, as well as a synopsis of what I said, was widely published in England and in the American papers at the time. Dr. and Mrs. Herford gave Mrs. Washington and myself a reception, at which we had the privilege of meeting some of the best people in England. Throughout our stay in London Ambassador Choate was most kind and attentive to us. At the Ambassador's reception I met, for the first time, Mark Twain.

We were the guests several times of Mrs. T. Fisher Unwin, the daughter of the English statesman, Richard Cobden. It seemed as if both Mr. and Mrs. Unwin could not do enough for our comfort and happiness. Later, for nearly a week, we were the guests of the daughter of John Bright, now Mrs. Clark, of Street, England. Both Mr. and Mrs. Clark, with their daughter, visited us at Tuskegee the next year. In Birmingham, England, we were the guests for several days of Mr. Joseph Sturge, whose father was a great abolitionist and friend of Whittier and Garrison. It was a great privilege to meet throughout England those who had known and honored the late William Lloyd Garrison, the Hon. Frederick Douglass, and other abolitionists. The English abolitionists with whom we came in contact never seemed to tire of talking about these two Americans. Before going to England I had had no proper conception of the deep interest displayed by the abolitionists of England in the cause of freedom, nor did I realize the amount of substantial help given by them.

In Bristol, England, both Mrs. Washington and I spoke at the Women's Liberal Club. I was also the principal speaker at the Commencement exercises of the Royal College for the Blind. These exercises were held in the Crystal Palace, and the presiding officer was the late Duke of Westminster, who was said to be, I believe, the richest man in England, if not in the world. The Duke, as well as his wife and their daughter, seemed to be pleased with what I said, and thanked me heartily. Through the kindness of Lady Aberdeen, my wife and I were enabled to go with a party of those who were attending the International Congress of Women, then in session in London, to see Queen Victoria, at Windsor Castle, where, afterward, we were all the guests of her Majesty at tea. In our party was Miss Susan B. Anthony, and I was deeply impressed with the fact that one did not often get an opportunity to see, during the same hour, two women so remarkable in different ways as Susan B. Anthony and Queen Victoria.

In the House of Commons, which we visited several times, we met Sir Henry M. Stanley. I talked with him about Africa and its relation to the American Negro, and after my interview with him I became more convinced than ever that there was no hope of the American Negro's improving his condition by emigrating to Africa.

On various occasions Mrs. Washington and I were the guests of Englishmen in their country homes, where, I think, one sees the Englishman at his best. In one thing, at least, I feel sure that the English are ahead of Americans, and that is, that they have learned how to get more out of life. The home life of the English seems to me to be about as perfect as anything can be. Everything moves like clockwork. I was impressed, too, with the deference that the servants show to their "masters" and "mistresses,"—terms which I suppose would not be tolerated in America. The English servant expects, as a rule, to be nothing but a servant, and so he perfects himself in the art to a degree that no class of servants in America has yet reached. In our country the servant expects to become, in a few years, a "master" himself. Which system is preferable? I will not venture an answer.

Another thing that impressed itself upon me throughout England was the high regard that all classes have for law and order, and the ease and thoroughness with which everything is done. The Englishmen, I found, took plenty of time for eating, as for everything else. I am not sure if, in the long run, they do not accomplish as much or more than rushing, nervous Americans do.

My visit to England gave me a higher regard for the nobility than I had had. I had no idea that they were so generally loved and respected by the classes, nor that I any correct conception of how much time and money they spent in works of philanthropy, and how much real heart they put into this work. My impression had been that they merely spent money freely and had a "good time."

It was hard for me to get accustomed to speaking to English audiences. The average Englishman is so serious, and is so tremendously in earnest about everything, that when I told a story that would have made an American audience roar with laughter, the Englishmen simply looked me straight in the face without even cracking a smile.

When the Englishman takes you into his heart and friendship, he binds you there as with cords of steel, and I do not believe that there are many other friendships that are so lasting or so satisfactory. Perhaps I can illustrate this point in no better way than by relating the following incident. Mrs. Washington and I were invited to attend a reception given by the Duke and Duchess of Sutherland, at Stafford House—said to be the finest house in London; I may add that I believe the Duchess of Sutherland is said to be the most beautiful woman in England. There must have been at least three hundred persons at this reception. Twice during the evening the Duchess sought us out for a conversation, and she asked me to write her when we got home, and tell her more about the work at Tuskegee. This I did. When Christmas came we were surprised and delighted to receive her photograph with her autograph on it. The correspondence has continued, and we now feel that in the Duchess of Sutherland we have one of our warmest friends.

After three months in Europe we sailed from Southampton in the steamship St. Louis. On this steamer there was a fine library that had been presented to the ship by the citizens of St. Louis, Mo. In this library I found a life of Frederick Douglass, which I began reading. I became especially interested in Mr. Douglass's description of the way he was treated on shipboard during his first or second visit to England. In this description he told how he was not permitted to enter the cabin, but had to confine himself to the deck of the ship. A few minutes after I had finished reading this description I was waited on by a committee of ladies and gentlemen with the request that I deliver an address at a concert which was to begin the following evening. And yet there are people who are bold enough to say that race feeling in America is not growing less intense! At this concert the Hon. Benjamin B. Odell, Jr., the present governor of New York, presided. I was never given a more cordial hearing anywhere. A large proportion of the passengers with Southern people. After the concert some of the passengers proposed that a subscription be raised to help the work at Tuskegee, and the money to support several scholarships was the result.

While we were in Paris I was very pleasantly surprised to receive the following invitation from the citizens of West Virginia and of the city near which I had spent my boyhood days:—

Charleston, W. Va., May 16, 1899.
Professor Booker T. Washington, Paris, France:
Dear Sir: Many of the best citizens of West Virginia have united in liberal expressions of admiration and praise of your worth and work, and desire that on your return from Europe you should favor them with your presence and with the inspiration of your words. We must sincerely indorse this move, and on behalf of the citizens of Charleston extend to your our most cordial invitation to have you come to us, that we may honor you who have done so much by your life and work to honor us.

We are,
Very truly yours,
The Common Council of the City of Charleston,
By W. Herman Smith, Mayor.

This invitation from the City Council of Charleston was accompanied by the following:—

Professor Booker T. Washington, Paris, France:

Dear Sir: We, the citizens of Charleston and West Virginia, desire to express our pride in you and the splendid career that you have thus far accomplished, and ask that we be permitted to show our pride and interest in a substantial way.

Your recent visit to your old home in our midst awoke within us the keenest regret that we were not permitted to hear you and render some substantial aid to your work, before you left for Europe.

In view of the foregoing, we earnestly invite you to share the hospitality of our city upon your return from Europe, and give us the opportunity to hear you and put ourselves in touch with your work in a way that will be most gratifying to yourself, and that we may receive the inspiration of your words and presence.

An early reply to this invitation, with an indication of the time you may reach our city, will greatly oblige,

Yours very respectfully,

The Charleston Daily Gazette, The Daily Mail-Tribune; G.W. Atkinson, Governor; E.L. Boggs, Secretary to Governor; Wm. M.O. Dawson, Secretary of State; L.M. La Follette, Auditor; J.R. Trotter, Superintendent of Schools; E.W. Wilson, ex-Governor; W.A. MacCorkle, ex-Governor; John Q. Dickinson, President Kanawha Valley Bank; L. Prichard, President Charleston National Bank; Geo. S. Couch, President Kanawha National Bank; Ed. Reid, Cashier Kanawha National Bank; Geo. S. Laidley, Superintended City Schools; L.E. McWhorter, President Board of Education; Chas. K. Payne, wholesale merchant; and many others.

This invitation, coming as it did from the City Council, the state officers, and all the substantial citizens of both races of the community where I had spent my boyhood, and from which I had gone a few years before, unknown, in poverty and ignorance, in quest of an education, not only surprised me, but almost unmanned me. I could not understand what I had done to deserve it all.

I accepted the invitation, and at the appointed day was met at the railway station at Charleston by a committee headed by ex-Governor W.A. MacCorkle, and composed of men of both races. The public reception was held in the Opera-House at Charleston. The Governor of the state, the Hon. George W. Atkinson, presided, and an address of welcome was made by ex-Governor MacCorkle. A prominent part in the reception was taken by the colored citizens. The Opera-House was filled with citizens of both races, and among the white people were many for whom I had worked when I was a boy. The next day Governor and Mrs. Atkinson gave me a public reception at the State House, which was attended by all classes.

Not long after this the colored people in Atlanta, Georgia, gave me a reception at which the Governor of the state presided, and a similar reception was given me in New Orleans, which was presided over by the Mayor of the city. Invitations came from many other places which I was not able to accept.

Last Words

Before going to Europe some events came into my life which were great surprises to me. In fact, my whole life has largely been one of surprises. I believe that any man's life will be filled with constant, unexpected encouragements of this kind if he makes up his mind to do his level best each day of his life—that is, tries to make each day reach as nearly as possible the high-water mark of pure, unselfish, useful living. I pity the man, black or white, who has never experienced the joy and satisfaction that come to one by reason of an effort to assist in making some one else more useful and more happy.

Six months before he died, and nearly a year after he had been stricken with paralysis, General Armstrong expressed a wish to visit Tuskegee again before he passed away. Notwithstanding the fact that he had lost the use of his limbs to such an extent that he was practically helpless, his wish was gratified, and he was brought to Tuskegee. The owners of the Tuskegee Railroad, white men living in the town, offered to run a special train, without cost, out of the main station—Chehaw, five miles away—to meet him. He arrived on the school grounds about nine o'clock in the evening. Some one had suggested that we give the General a "pine-knot torchlight reception." This plan was carried out, and the moment that his carriage entered the school grounds he began passing between two lines of lighted and waving "fat pine" wood knots held by over a thousand students and teachers. The whole thing was so novel and surprising that the General was completely overcome with happiness. He remained a guest in my home for nearly two months, and, although almost wholly without the use of voice or limb, he spent nearly every hour in devising ways and means to help the South. Time and time again he said to me, during this visit, that it was not only the duty of the country to assist in elevating the Negro of the South, but the poor white man as well. At the end of his visit I resolved anew to devote myself more earnestly than ever to the cause which was so near his heart. I said that if a man in his condition was willing to think, work, and act, I should not be wanting in furthering in every possible way the wish of his heart.

The death of General Armstrong, a few weeks later, gave me the privilege of getting acquainted with one of the finest, most unselfish, and most attractive men that I have ever come in contact with. I refer to the Rev. Dr. Hollis B. Frissell, now the Principal of the Hampton Institute, and General Armstrong's successor. Under the clear, strong, and almost perfect leadership of Dr. Frissell, Hampton has had a career of prosperity and usefulness that is all that the General could have wished for. It seems to be the constant effort of Dr. Frissell to hide his own great personality behind that of General Armstrong—to make himself of "no reputation" for the sake of the cause.

More than once I have been asked what was the greatest surprise that ever came to me. I have little hesitation in answering that question. It was the following letter, which came to me one Sunday morning when I was sitting on the veranda of my home at Tuskegee, surrounded by my wife and three children:—

Harvard University, Cambridge, May 28, 1896.
President Booker T. Washington,
My Dear Sir: Harvard University desired to confer on you at the approaching Commencement an honorary degree; but it is our custom to confer degrees only on gentlemen who are present. Our Commencement occurs this year on June 24, and your presence would be desirable from about noon till about five o'clock in the afternoon. Would it be possible for you to be in Cambridge on that day?
    Believe me, with great regard,
    Very truly yours,
    Charles W. Eliot.

This was a recognition that had never in the slightest manner entered into my mind, and it was hard for me to realize that I was to be honored by a degree from the oldest and most renowned university in America. As I sat upon my veranda, with this letter in my hand, tears came into my eyes. My whole former life—my life as a slave on the plantation, my work in the coal-mine, the times when I was without food and clothing, when I made my bed under a sidewalk, my struggles for an education, the trying days I had had at Tuskegee, days when I did not know where to turn for a dollar to continue the work there, the ostracism and sometimes oppression of my race,—all this passed before me and nearly overcame me.

I had never sought or cared for what the world calls fame. I have always looked upon fame as something to be used in accomplishing good. I have often said to my friends that if I can use whatever prominence may have come to me as an instrument with which to do good, I am content to have it. I care for it only as a means to be used for doing good, just as wealth may be used. The more I come into contact with wealthy people, the more I believe that they are growing in the direction of looking upon their money simply as an instrument which God has placed in their hand for doing good with. I never go to the office of Mr. John D. Rockefeller, who more than once has been generous to Tuskegee, without being reminded of this. The close, careful, and minute investigation that he always makes in order to be sure that every dollar that he gives will do the most good—an investigation that is just as searching as if he were investing money in a business enterprise—convinces me that the growth in this direction is most encouraging.

At nine o'clock, on the morning of June 24, I met President Eliot, the Board of Overseers of Harvard University, and the other guests, at the designated place on the university grounds, for the purpose of being escorted to Sanders Theater, where the Commencement exercises were to be held and degrees conferred. Among others invited to be present for the purpose of receiving a degree at this time were General Nelson A. Miles, Dr. Bell, the inventor of the Bell telephone, Bishop Vincent, and the Rev. Minot J. Savage. We were placed in line immediately behind the President and the Board of Overseers, and directly afterward the Governor of Massachusetts, escorted by the Lancers, arrived and took his place in the line of march by the side of President Eliot. In the line there were also various other officers and professors, clad in cap and gown. In this order we marched to Sanders Theater, where, after the usual Commencement exercises, came the conferring of the honorary degrees. This, it seems, is always considered the most interesting feature at Harvard. It is not known, until the individuals appear, upon whom the honorary degrees are to be conferred, and those receiving these honors are cheered by the students and others in proportion to their popularity. During the conferring of the degrees excitement and enthusiasm are at the highest pitch.

When my name was called, I rose, and President Eliot, in beautiful and strong English, conferred upon me the degree of Master of Arts. After these exercises were over, those who had received honorary degrees were invited to lunch with the President. After the lunch we were formed in line again, and were escorted by the Marshal of the day, who that year happened to be Bishop William Lawrence, through the grounds, where, at different points, those who had been honored were called by name and received the Harvard yell. This march ended at Memorial Hall, where the alumni dinner was served. To see over a thousand strong men, representing all that is best in State, Church, business, and education, with the glow and enthusiasm of college loyalty and college pride,—which has, I think, a peculiar Harvard flavor,—is a sight that does not easily fade from memory.

Among the speakers after dinner were President Eliot, Governor Roger Wolcott, General Miles, Dr. Minot J. Savage, the Hon. Henry Cabot Lodge, and myself. When I was called upon, I said, among other things:—

It would in some measure relieve my embarrassment if I could, even in a slight degree, feel myself worthy of the great honor which you do me to-day. Why you have called me from the Black Belt of the South, from among my humble people, to share in the honors of this occasion, is not for me to explain; and yet it may not be inappropriate for me to suggest that it seems to me that one of the most vital questions that touch our American life is how to bring the strong, wealthy, and learned into helpful touch with the poorest, most ignorant, and humblest, and at the same time make one appreciate the vitalizing, strengthening influence of the other. How shall we make the mansion on yon Beacon Street feel and see the need of the spirits in the lowliest cabin in Alabama cotton-fields or Louisiana sugar-bottoms? This problem Harvard University is solving, not by bringing itself down, but by bringing the masses up.

If my life in the past has meant anything in the lifting up of my people and the bringing about of better relations between your race and mine, I assure you from this day it will mean doubly more. In the economy of God there is but one standard by which an individual can succeed—there is but one for a race. This country demands that every race shall measure itself by the American standard. By it a race must rise or fall, succeed or fail, and in the last analysis mere sentiment counts for little.

During the next half-century and more, my race must continue passing through the severe American crucible. We are to be tested in our patience, our forbearance, our perseverance, our power to endure wrong, to withstand temptations, to economize, to acquire and use skill; in our ability to compete, to succeed in commerce, to disregard the superficial for the real, the appearance for the substance, to be great and yet small, learned and yet simple, high and yet the servant of all.

As this was the first time that a New England university had conferred an honorary degree upon a Negro, it was the occasion of much newspaper comment throughout the country. A correspondent of a New York Paper said:—

When the name of Booker T. Washington was called, and he arose to acknowledge and accept, there was such an outburst of applause as greeted no other name except that of the popular soldier patriot, General Miles. The applause was not studied and stiff, sympathetic and condoling; it was enthusiasm and admiration. Every part of the audience from pit to gallery joined in, and a glow covered the cheeks of those around me, proving sincere appreciation of the rising struggle of an ex-slave and the work he has accomplished for his race.

A Boston paper said, editorially:—

In conferring the honorary degree of Master of Arts upon the Principal of Tuskegee Institute, Harvard University has honored itself as well as the object of this distinction. The work which Professor Booker T. Washington has accomplished for the education, good citizenship, and popular enlightenment in his chosen field of labor in the South entitles him to rank with our national benefactors. The university which can claim him on its list of sons, whether in regular course or *honoris causa*, may be proud.

It has been mentioned that Mr. Washington is the first of his race to receive an honorary degree from a New England university. This, in itself, is a distinction. But the degree was not conferred because Mr. Washington is a colored man, or because he was born in slavery, but because he has shown, by his work for the elevation of the people of the Black Belt of the South, a genius and a broad humanity which count for greatness in any man, whether his skin be white or black.

Another Boston paper said:—

It is Harvard which, first among New England colleges, confers an honorary degree upon a black man. No one who has followed the history of Tuskegee and its work can fail to admire the courage, persistence, and splendid common sense of Booker T. Washington.

Well may Harvard honor the ex-slave, the value of whose services, alike to his race and country, only the future can estimate.

The correspondent of the New York Times wrote:—

All the speeches were enthusiastically received, but the colored man carried off the oratorical honors, and the applause which broke out when he had finished was vociferous and long-continued.

Soon after I began work at Tuskegee I formed a resolution, in the secret of my heart, that I would try to build up a school that would be of so much service to the country that the President of the United States would one day come to see it. This was, I confess, rather a bold resolution, and for a number of years I kept it hidden in my own thoughts, not daring to share it with any one.

In November, 1897, I made the first move in this direction, and that was in securing a visit from a member of President McKinley's Cabinet, the Hon. James Wilson, Secretary of Agriculture. He came to deliver an address at the formal opening of the Slater-Armstrong Agricultural Building, our first large building to be used for the purpose of giving training to our students in agriculture and kindred branches.

In the fall of 1898 I heard that President McKinley was likely to visit Atlanta, Georgia, for the purpose of taking part in the Peace Jubilee exercises to be held there to commemorate the successful close of the Spanish-American war. At this time I had been hard at work, together with our teachers, for eighteen years, trying to build up a school that we thought would be of service to the Nation, and I determined to make a direct effort to secure a visit from the President and his Cabinet. I went to Washington, and I was not long in the city before I found my way to the White House. When I got there I found the waiting rooms full of people, and my heart began to sink, for I feared there would not be much chance of my seeing the President that day, if at all. But, at any rate, I got an opportunity to see Mr. J. Addison Porter, the secretary to the President, and explained to him my mission. Mr. Porter kindly sent my card directly to the President, and in a few minutes word came from Mr. McKinley that he would see me.

How any man can see so many people of all kinds, with all kinds of errands, and do so much hard work, and still keep himself calm, patient, and fresh for each visitor in the way that President McKinley does, I cannot understand. When I saw the President he kindly thanked me for the work which we were doing at Tuskegee for the interests of the country. I then told him, briefly, the object of my visit. I impressed upon him the fact that a visit from the Chief Executive of the Nation would not only encourage our students and teachers, but would help the entire race. He seemed interested, but did not make a promise to go to Tuskegee, for the reason that his plans about going to Atlanta were not then fully made; but he asked me to call the matter to his attention a few weeks later.

By the middle of the following month the President had definitely decided to attend the Peace Jubilee at Atlanta. I went to Washington again and saw him, with a view of getting him to extend his trip to Tuskegee. On this second visit Mr. Charles W. Hare, a prominent white citizen of Tuskegee, kindly volunteered to accompany me, to reenforce my invitation with one from the white people of Tuskegee and the vicinity.

Just previous to my going to Washington the second time, the country had been excited, and the colored people greatly depressed, because of several severe race riots which had occurred at different points in the South. As soon as I saw the President, I perceived that his heart was greatly burdened by reason of these race disturbances. Although there were many people waiting to see him, he detained me for some time, discussing the condition and prospects of the race. He remarked several times that he was determined to show his interest and faith in the race, not merely in words, but by acts. When I told him that I thought that at that time scarcely anything would go father in giving hope and encouragement to the race than the fact that the President of the Nation would be willing to travel one hundred and forty miles out of his way to spend a day at a Negro institution, he seemed deeply impressed.

While I was with the President, a white citizen of Atlanta, a Democrat and an ex-slaveholder, came into the room, and the President asked his opinion as to the wisdom of his going to Tuskegee. Without hesitation the Atlanta man replied that it was the proper thing for him to do. This opinion was reenforced by that friend of the race, Dr. J.L.M. Curry. The President promised that he would visit our school on the 16th of December.

When it became known that the President was going to visit our school, the white citizens of the town of Tuskegee—a mile distant from the school—were as much pleased as were our students and teachers. The white people of this town, including both men and women, began arranging to decorate the town, and to form themselves into committees for the purpose of cooperating with the officers of our school in order that the distinguished visitor might have a fitting reception. I think I never realized before this how much the white people of Tuskegee and vicinity thought of our institution. During the days when we were preparing for the President's reception, dozens of these people came to me and said that, while they did not want to push themselves into prominence, if there was anything they could do to help, or to relieve me personally, I had but to intimate it and they would be only too glad to assist. In fact, the thing that touched me almost as deeply as the visit of the President itself was the deep pride which all classes of citizens in Alabama seemed to take in our work.

The morning of December 16th brought to the little city of Tuskegee such a crowd as it had never seen before. With the President came Mrs. McKinley and all of the Cabinet officers but one; and most of them brought their wives or some members of their families. Several prominent generals came, including General Shafter and General Joseph Wheeler, who were recently returned from the Spanish-American war. There was also a host of newspaper correspondents. The Alabama Legislature was in session in Montgomery at this time. This body passed a resolution to adjourn for the purpose of visited Tuskegee. Just before the arrival of the President's party the Legislature arrived, headed by the governor and other state officials.

The citizens of Tuskegee had decorated the town from the station to the school in a generous manner. In order to economize in the matter of time, we arranged to have the whole school pass in review before the President. Each student carried a stalk of sugar-cane with some open bolls of cotton fastened to the end of it. Following the students the work of all departments of the school passed in review, displayed on "floats" drawn by horses, mules, and oxen. On these floats we tried to exhibit not only the present work of the school, but to show the contrasts between the old methods of doing things and the new. As an example, we showed the old method of dairying in contrast with the improved methods, the old methods of tilling the soil in contrast with the new, the old methods of cooking and housekeeping in contrast with the new. These floats consumed an hour and a half of time in passing.

In his address in our large, new chapel, which the students had recently completed, the President said, among other things:—

To meet you under such pleasant auspices and to have the opportunity of a personal observation of your work is indeed most gratifying. The Tuskegee Normal and Industrial Institute is ideal in its conception, and has already a large and growing reputation in the country, and is not unknown abroad. I congratulate all who are associated in this undertaking for the good work which it is doing in the education of its students to lead lives of honor and usefulness, thus exalting the race for which it was established.

Nowhere, I think, could a more delightful location have been chosen for this unique educational experiment, which has attracted the attention and won the support even of conservative philanthropists in all sections of the country.

To speak of Tuskegee without paying special tribute to Booker T. Washington's genius and perseverance would be impossible. The inception of this noble enterprise was his, and he deserves high credit for it. His was the enthusiasm and enterprise which made its steady progress possible and established in the institution its present high standard of accomplishment. He has won a worthy reputation as one of the great leaders of his race, widely known and much respected at home and abroad as an accomplished educator, a great orator, and a true philanthropist.

The Hon. John D. Long, the Secretary of the Navy, said in part:—

I cannot make a speech to-day. My heart is too full—full of hope, admiration, and pride for my countrymen of both sections and both colors. I am filled with gratitude and admiration for your work, and from this time forward I shall have absolute confidence in your progress and in the solution of the problem in which you are engaged.

The problem, I say, has been solved. A picture has been presented to-day which should be put upon canvas with the pictures of Washington and Lincoln, and transmitted to future time and generations—a picture which the press of the country should spread broadcast over the land, a most dramatic picture, and that picture is this: The President of the United States standing on this platform; on one side the Governor of Alabama, on the other, completing the trinity, a representative of a race only a few years ago in bondage, the colored President of the Tuskegee Normal and Industrial Institute.

God bless the President under whose majesty such a scene as that is presented to the American people. God bless the state of Alabama, which is showing that it can deal with this problem for itself. God bless the orator, philanthropist, and disciple of the Great Master—who, if he were on earth, would be doing the same work—Booker T. Washington.

Postmaster General Smith closed the address which he made with these words:—

We have witnessed many spectacles within the last few days. We have seen the magnificent grandeur and the magnificent achievements of one of the great metropolitan cities of the South. We have seen heroes of the war pass by in procession. We have seen floral parades. But I am sure my colleagues will agree with me in saying that we have witnessed no spectacle more impressive and more encouraging, more inspiring for our future, than that which we have witnessed here this morning.

Some days after the President returned to Washington I received the letter which follows:—

Executive Mansion, Washington, Dec. 23, 1899.

Dear Sir: By this mail I take pleasure in sending you engrossed copies of the souvenir of the visit of the President to your institution. These sheets bear the autographs of the President and the members of the Cabinet who accompanied him on the trip. Let me take this opportunity of congratulating you most heartily and sincerely upon the great success of the exercises provided for and entertainment furnished us under your auspices during our visit to Tuskegee. Every feature of the program was perfectly executed and was viewed or participated in with the heartiest satisfaction by every visitor present. The unique exhibition which you gave of your pupils engaged in their industrial vocations was not only artistic but thoroughly impressive. The tribute paid by the President and his Cabinet to your work was none too high, and forms a most encouraging augury, I think, for the future prosperity of your institution. I cannot close without assuring you that the modesty shown by yourself in the exercises was most favorably commented upon by all the members of our party.

With best wishes for the continued advance of your most useful and patriotic undertaking, kind personal regards, and the compliments of the season, believe me, always,

Very sincerely yours,

John Addison Porter,

Secretary to the President.

To President Booker T. Washington, Tuskegee Normal and Industrial Institute, Tuskegee, Ala.

Twenty years have now passed since I made the first humble effort at Tuskegee, in a broken-down shanty and an old hen-house, without owning a dollar's worth of property, and with but one teacher and thirty students. At the present time the institution owns twenty-three hundred acres of land, one thousand of which are under cultivation each year, entirely by student labor. There are now upon the grounds, counting large and small, sixty-six buildings; and all except four of these have been almost wholly erected by the labor of our students. While the students are at work upon the land and in erecting buildings, they are taught, by competent instructors, the latest methods of agriculture and the trades connected with building.

There are in constant operation at the school, in connection with thorough academic and religious training, thirty industrial departments. All of these teach industries at which our men and women can find immediate employment as soon as they leave the institution. The only difficulty now is that the demand for our graduates from both white and black people in the South is so great that we cannot supply more than one-half the persons for whom applications come to us. Neither have we the buildings nor the money for current expenses to enable us to admit to the school more than one-half the young men and women who apply to us for admission.

In our industrial teaching we keep three things in mind: first, that the student shall be so educated that he shall be enabled to meet conditions as they exist now, in the part of the South where he lives—in a word, to be able to do the thing which the world wants done; second, that every student who graduates from the school shall have enough skill, coupled with intelligence and moral character, to enable him to make a living for himself and others; third, to send every graduate out feeling and knowing that labor is dignified and beautiful—to make each one love labor instead of trying to escape it. In addition to the agricultural training which we give to young men, and the training given to our girls in all the usual domestic employments, we now train a number of girls in agriculture each year. These girls are taught gardening, fruit-growing, dairying, bee-culture, and poultry-raising.

While the institution is in no sense denominational, we have a department known as the Phelps Hall Bible Training School, in which a number of students are prepared for the ministry and other forms of Christian work, especially work in the country districts. What is equally important, each one of the students works . . . each day at some industry, in order to get skill and the love of work, so that when he goes out from the institution he is prepared to set the people with whom he goes to labor a proper example in the matter of industry.

The value of our property is now over $700,000. If we add to this our endowment fund, which at present is $1,000,000, the value of the total property is now $1,700,000. Aside from the need for more buildings and for money for current expenses, the endowment fund should be increased to at least $3,000,000. The annual current expenses are now about $150,000. The greater part of this I collect each year by going from door to door and from house to house. All of our property is free from mortgage, and is deeded to an undenominational board of trustees who have the control of the institution.

From thirty students the number has grown to fourteen hundred, coming from twenty-seven states and territories, from Africa, Cuba, Porto Rico, Jamaica, and other foreign countries. In our departments there are one hundred and ten officers and instructors; and if we add the families of our instructors, we have a constant population upon our grounds of not far from seventeen hundred people.

I have often been asked how we keep so large a body of people together, and at the same time keep them out of mischief. There are two answers: that the men and women who come to us for an education are in earnest; and that everybody is kept busy. The following outline of our daily work will testify to this:—

5 a.m., rising bell; 5.50 a.m., warning breakfast bell; 6 a.m., breakfast bell; 6.20 a.m., breakfast over; 6.20 to 6.50 a.m., rooms are cleaned; 6.50, work bell; 7.30, morning study hours; 8.20, morning school bell; 8.25, inspection of young men's toilet in ranks; 8.40, devotional exercises in chapel; 8.55, "five minutes with the daily news;" 9 a.m., class work begins; 12, class work closes; 12.15 p.m., dinner; 1 p.m., work bell; 1.30 p.m., class work begins; 3.30 p.m., class work ends; 5.30 p.m., bell to "knock off" work; 6 p.m., supper; 7.10 p.m., evening prayers; 7.30 p.m., evening study hours; 8.45 p.m., evening study hour closes; 9.20 p.m., warning retiring bell; 9.30 p.m., retiring bell.

We try to keep constantly in mind the fact that the worth of the school is to be judged by its graduates. Counting those who have finished the full course, together with those who have taken enough training to enable them to do reasonably good work, we can safely say that at least six thousand men and women from Tuskegee are now at work in different parts of the South; men and women who, by their own example or by direct efforts, are showing the masses of our race now to improve their material, educational, and moral and religious life. What is equally important, they are exhibiting a degree of common sense and self-control which is causing better relations to exist between the races, and is causing the Southern white man to learn to believe in the value of educating the men and women of my race. Aside from this, there is the influence that is constantly being exerted through the mothers' meeting and the plantation work conducted by Mrs. Washington.

Wherever our graduates go, the changes which soon begin to appear in the buying of land, improving homes, saving money, in education, and in high moral characters are remarkable. Whole communities are fast being revolutionized through the instrumentality of these men and women.

Ten years ago I organized at Tuskegee the first Negro Conference. This is an annual gathering which now brings to the school eight or nine hundred representative men and women of the race, who come to spend a day in finding out what the actual industrial, mental, and moral conditions of the people are, and in forming plans for improvement. Out from this central Negro Conference at Tuskegee have grown numerous state an local conferences which are doing the same kind of work. As a result of the influence of these gatherings, one delegate reported at the last annual meeting that ten families in his community had bought and paid for homes. On the day following the annual Negro Conference, there is the "Workers' Conference." This is composed of officers and teachers who are engaged in educational work in the larger institutions in the South. The Negro Conference furnishes a rare opportunity for these workers to study the real condition of the rank and file of the people.

In the summer of 1900, with the assistance of such prominent colored men as Mr. T. Thomas Fortune, who has always upheld my hands in every effort, I organized the National Negro Business League, which held its first meeting in Boston, and brought together for the first time a large number of the colored men who are engaged in various lines of trade or business in different parts of the United States. Thirty states were represented at our first meeting. Out of this national meeting grew state and local business leagues.

In addition to looking after the executive side of the work at Tuskegee, and raising the greater part of the money for the support of the school, I cannot seem to escape the duty of answering at least a part of the calls which come to me unsought to address Southern white audiences and audiences of my own race, as well as frequent gatherings in the North. As to how much of my time is spent in this way, the following clipping from a Buffalo (N.Y.) paper will tell. This has reference to an occasion when I spoke before the National Educational Association in that city.

Booker T. Washington, the foremost educator among the colored people of the world, was a very busy man from the time he arrived in the city the other night from the West and registered at the Iroquois. He had hardly removed the stains of travel when it was time to partake of supper. Then he held a public levee in the parlors of the Iroquois until eight o'clock. During that time he was greeted by over two hundred eminent teachers and educators from all parts of the United States. Shortly after eight o'clock he was driven in a carriage to Music Hall, and in one hour and a half he made two ringing addresses, to as many as five thousand people, on Negro education. Then Mr. Washington was taken in charge by a delegation of colored citizens, headed by the Rev. Mr. Watkins, and hustled off to a small informal reception, arranged in honor of the visitor by the people of his race.

Nor can I, in addition to making these addresses, escape the duty of calling the attention of the South and of the country in general, through the medium of the press, to matters that pertain to the interests of both races. This, for example, I have done in regard to the evil habit of lynching. When the Louisiana State Constitutional Convention was in session, I wrote an open letter to that body pleading for justice for the race. In all such efforts I have received warm and hearty support from the Southern newspapers, as well as from those in all other parts of the country.

Despite superficial and temporary signs which might lead one to entertain a contrary opinion, there was never a time when I felt more hopeful for the race than I do at the present. The great human law that in the end recognizes and rewards merit is everlasting and universal. The outside world does not know, neither can it appreciate, the struggle that is constantly going on in the hearts of both the Southern white people and their former slaves to free themselves from racial prejudice; and while both races are thus struggling they should have the sympathy, the support, and the forbearance of the rest of the world.

As I write the closing words of this autobiography I find myself—not by design—in the city of Richmond, Virginia: the city which only a few decades ago was the capital of the Southern Confederacy, and where, about twenty-five years ago, because of my poverty I slept night after night under a sidewalk.

This time I am in Richmond as the guest of the colored people of the city; and came at their request to deliver an address last night to both races in the Academy of Music, the largest and finest audience room in the city. This was the first time that the colored people had ever been permitted to use this hall. The day before I came, the City Council passed a vote to attend the meeting in a body to hear me speak. The state Legislature, including the House of Delegates and the Senate, also passed a unanimous vote to attend in a body. In the presence of hundreds of colored people, many distinguished white citizens, the City Council, the state Legislature, and state officials, I delivered my message, which was one of hope and cheer; and from the bottom of my heart I thanked both races for this welcome back to the state that gave me birth.

My Larger Education

Table of Contents

Learning From Men and Things

It has been my fortune to be associated all my life with a problem-a hard, perplexing, but important problem. There was a time when I looked upon this fact as a great misfortune. It seemed to me a great hardship that I was born poor, and it seemed an even greater hardship that I should have been born a Negro. I did not like to admit, even to myself, that I felt this way about the matter, because it seemed to me an indication of weakness and cowardice for any man to complain about the condition he was born to. Later I came to the conclusion that it was not only weak and cowardly, but that it was a mistake to think of the matter in the way in which I had done. I came to see that, along with his disadvantages, the Negro in America had some advantages, and I made up my mind that opportunities that had been denied him from without could be more than made up by greater concentration and power within.

Perhaps I can illustrate what I mean by a fact I learned while I was in school. I recall my teacher's explaining to the class one day how it was that steam or any other form of energy, if allowed to escape and dissipate itself, loses its value as a motive power. Energy must be confined; steam must be locked in a boiler in order to generate power. The same thing seems to have been true in the case of the Negro. Where the Negro has met with discriminations and with difficulties because of his race, he has invariably tended to get up more steam. When this steam has been rightly directed and controlled, it has become a great force in the upbuilding of the race. If, on the contrary, it merely spent itself in fruitless agitation and hot air, no good has come of it.

Paradoxical as it may seem, the difficulties that the Negro has met since emancipation have, in my opinion, not always, but on the whole, helped him more than they have hindered him. For example, I think the progress which the Negro has made within less than half a century in the matter of learning to read and write the English language has been due in large part to the fact that, in slavery, this knowledge was forbidden him. My experience and observation have taught me that people, who try to withhold the best things in civilization from any group of people, or race of people, not infrequently aid that people to the very things that they are trying to withhold from them. I am sure that, in my own case, I should never have made the efforts that I did make in my early boyhood to get an education and still later to develop the Tuskegee Institute in Alabama if I had not been conscious of the fact that there were a large number of people in the world who did not believe that the Negro boy could learn or that members of the Negro race could build up and conduct a large institution of learning.

A wider acquaintance with men in all the different grades of life taught me that the Negro's case is not peculiar. The majority of successful men are persons who have had difficulties to overcome, problems to master; and, in overcoming those difficulties and mastering those problems, they have gained strength of mind and a clearness of vision that few persons who have lived a life of ease have been able to attain. Experience has taught me, in fact, that no man should be pitied because, every day in his life, he faces a hard, stubborn problem, but rather that it is the man who has no problem to solve, no hardships to face, who is to be pitied.

His misfortune consists in the fact that he has nothing in his life which will strengthen and form his character; nothing to call out his latent powers, and deepen and widen his hold on life. It has come home to me more in recent years that I have had, just because my life has been connected with a problem, some unusual opportunities. I have had unusual opportunities for example in getting an education in the broader sense of the word.

If I had not been born a slave, for example, I never could have had the opportunity, perhaps, of associating day by day with the most ignorant people, so far as books are concerned, and thus coming in contact with people of this class at first hand. The most fortunate part of my early experience was that which gave me the opportunity of getting into direct contact and of communing with and taking lessons from the old class of colored people who have been slaves. At the present time few experiences afford me more genuine pleasure than to get a day or a half a day off and go out into the country, miles from town and railroad, and spend the time in close contact with a colored farmer and his family.

And then I have felt for a long while that, if I had not been a slave and lived on a slave plantation, I never would have had the opportunity to learn nature, to love the soil, to love cows and pigs and trees and flowers and birds and worms and creeping things. I have always been intensely fond of outdoor life. Perhaps the explanation for this lies partly in the fact that I was born nearly out of doors. I have also, from my earliest childhood, been very fond of animals and fowls. When I was but a child, and a slave, I had close and interesting acquaintances with animals.

During my childhood days, as a slave, I did not see very much of my mother, since she was obliged to leave her children very early in the morning to begin her day's work. The early departure of my mother often made the matter of my securing breakfast uncertain. This led to my first intimate acquaintance with animals.

In those days it was the custom upon the plantation to boil the Indian corn that was fed to the cows and pigs. At times, when I had failed to get any other breakfast, I used to go to the places where the cows and pigs were fed and make my breakfast off this boiled corn, or else go to the place where it was the custom to boil the corn, and get my share there before it was taken to the animals.

If I was not there at the exact moment of feeding, I could still find enough corn scattered around the fence or the trough to satisfy me. Some people may think that this was a pretty bad way in which to get one's food, but, leaving out the name and the associations, there was nothing very bad about it. Anyone who has eaten hard-boiled corn knows it has a delicious taste. I never pass a pot of boiled corn now without yielding to the temptation to eat a few grams.

I think that I owe a great deal of my present strength and ability to work to my love of out-door life. It is true that the amount of time that I can spend in the open air is now very limited. Taken on an average, it is perhaps not more than an hour a day, but I make the most of that hour. In addition to this I get much pleasure out of the anticipation and the planning for that hour. When I am at my home at Tuskegee, I usually find a way, by rising early in the morning, to spend at least half an hour in my garden, or with my fowls, pigs, or cows. As far as I can get the time, I like to find the new eggs each morning myself, and when at home am selfish enough to permit no one else to do this in my place. As with the growing plants, there is a sense of freshness and newness and of restfulness in connection with the finding and handling of newly laid eggs that is delightful to me. Both the anticipation and the realization are most pleasing. I begin the day by seeing how many eggs I can find, or how many little chickens there are, that are just beginning to peep through the shells.

I am deeply interested in the different kinds of fowls, and, aside from the large number grown by the school in its poultry house and yards, I grow at my own home common chickens, Plymouth Rocks, Buff Cochins and Brahmas, Peking ducks, and fan-tailed pigeons.

The pig, I think, is my favorite animal. I do not know how this will strike the taste of my readers, but it is true. In addition to some common bred pigs, I keep a few Berkshires and some Poland Chinas; and it is a real pleasure to me to watch their development and increase from month to month. Practically all the pork used in my family is of my own raising.

This will, perhaps, illustrate what I mean when I say that I have gotten a large part of my education from actual contact with things, rather than through the medium of books. I like to touch things and handle them; I like to watch plants grow and observe the behavior of animals. For the same reason, I like to deal with things, as far as possible, at first hand, in the way that the carpenter deals with wood, the blacksmith with iron, and the farmer with the earth. I believe that there is something gained by getting acquainted, in the way which I have described, with the physical world about you that is almost indispensable.

A number of years ago, in a book called, "Up From Slavery," I told a story of my early life, describing the manner in which I got my early schooling and the circumstances under which I came to start the Tuskegee Normal and Industrial Institute. At the time that school was organized I had read very little, and, in fact, few books on the subject of teaching, and knew very little about the science of education and pedagogy. I had had the advantage of going through an exceptional school at Hampton and of coming in contact with an inspired teacher in General Armstrong; but I had never attempted to formulate the methods of teaching I used in that school, and I had very little experience in applying them to the new and difficult problems I met as soon as I attempted to conduct a school of my own. What I learned about the science of education I learned in my efforts in working out the plans for, and organizing and perfecting the educational methods at, Tuskegee.

The necessity of collecting large sums of money every year to carry on the work at Tuskegee compelled me to travel much and brought me in contact with all kinds of people. As soon as I began to meet educated and cultivated people, people who had had the advantage of study in higher institutions of learning, as well as the advantages of much reading and travel, I soon became conscious of my own disadvantages. I found that the people I met were able to speak fluently and with perfect familiarity about a great many things with which I was acquainted in only the vaguest sort of way. In speaking they used words and phrases from authors whom I had never read and often never heard of. All this made me feel more keenly my deficiencies, and the more I thought about it the more it troubled and worried me. It made me feel all the more badly because I discovered that, if I were to carry on the work I had undertaken to do, if I was ever going to accomplish any of the things that it seemed to me important to do, I should never find time, no matter how diligent and studious I might be, to overtake them and possess myself of the knowledge and familiarity with books for which I envied those persons who had been more highly educated than myself.

After a time, however, I found that while I was at a certain disadvantage among highly educated and cultivated people in certain directions, I had certain advantages over them in others. I found that the man who has an intimate acquaintance with some department of life through personal experience has a great advantage over persons who have gained their knowledge of life almost entirely through books. I found also that, by using my personal experience and observation; by making use of the stories that I had heard, as illustrations; by relating some incident that happened in my own case or some incident that I had heard from some one else, I could frequently express what I had to say in a much clearer and more impressive way than if I made use of the language of books or the statements and quotations from the authors of books. More than that, as I reflected upon the matter, I discovered that these authors, in their books, were after all merely making use of their own experiences or expressing ideas which they had worked out in actual life, and that to make use of their language and ideas was merely to get life second hand.

The result was that I made up my mind that I would try to make up for my defects in my knowledge of books by my knowledge of men and things. I said I would take living men and women for my study, and I would give the closest attention possible to everything that was going on in the world about me. I determined that I would get my education out of my work; I would learn about education in solving the problems of the school as they arose from day to day, and learn about life by learning to deal with men. I said to myself that I would try to learn something from every man I met; make him my text-book, read him, study him, and learn something from him. So I began deliberately to try to learn from men. I learned something from big men and something from little men, from the man with prejudice and the man without prejudice. As I studied and understood them, I found that I began to like men better; even those who treated me badly did not cause me to lose my temper or patience, as soon as I found that I could learn something from them.

For example, some years ago, I had an experience which taught me a lesson in politeness and liberality which I shall long remember. I was in a large city making calls on wealthy people in order to interest them in our work at Tuskegee Institute. I called at the office of a man, and he spoke to me in the most abrupt and insulting manner. He not only refused to give any money but spoke of my race in a manner that no gentleman of culture ought ever to permit himself to speak of another race. A few minutes later I called on another gentleman in the same city, who received me politely, thanked me for calling upon him, but explained that he was so situated that he could not help me. My interview with the first man occupied about twice as much of his time and my time as was true of the second gentleman. I learned from this experience that it takes no more time to be polite to every one than it does to be rude.

During the later years of my experience I have had the good fortune to study not only white men and learn from them, but colored men as well. In my earlier experiences I used to have sympathy with the colored people who were narrow and bitter toward white people. As I grew older I began to study that class of colored people, and I found that they did not get anywhere, that their bitterness and narrowness toward the white man did not hurt the white man or change his feeling toward the colored race, but that, in almost every case, the cherishing of such feeling toward the white man reacted upon the colored man and made him narrow and bitter.

In the chapters which follow, I have given some account of the way in which my work has brought me in contact, not so much with plants and animals and with physical objects, but rather with human institutions, with politics, with newspapers, with educational and social problems of various kinds and descriptions, and I have tried to indicate in every case the way in which I have been educated through them. One of the purposes in writing these later chapters from my experience is to complete the story of my education which I began in the book, "Up From Slavery"; to answer the questions I have frequently been asked as to how I have worked out for myself the educational methods which we are now using at Tuskegee; and, finally, to illustrate, for the benefit of the members of my own race, some of the ways in which a people who are struggling upward may turn disadvantages into opportunities; how they may gain within themselves something that will compensate them for what they have been deprived of from without.

If I have learned much from things, I have learned more from men. The work that I started to do brought me early in contact with some of the most generous, high-minded and public-spirited persons in the country. In the chapters that follow I have tried to indicate what I have learned from contact with those men. Perhaps I can best indicate the way in which I have been educated by my contact with these men if I tell something of my relations with one man from whom, after General Armstrong, my first teacher, I learned, perhaps, more than from any other. I refer to the late William H. Baldwin, Jr.

I well remember my first meeting with Mr. Baldwin, although the exact date has now slipped from my memory. He was at that time manager and vice-president of the Southern Railway, with headquarters in Washington, D. C. I had been given a letter to him by his father, in Boston. I found him one morning in his office and presented this letter, which he read over carefully, as was his custom in such matters. Then we began talking about the school at Tuskegee and its work. I had been in the room but a few minutes when the conviction forced itself upon me that I had met a man who could thoroughly understand me and whom I understood. Indeed, I had the feeling that I was in the presence of one in whose mind there was neither faltering nor concealment, and one from whom it would be impossible to hide a single thought or purpose. I never had occasion, during all the years that I knew Mr. Baldwin, to change the opinion formed of him at my first visit, or to feel that the understanding established between us then was ever clouded or diminished.

Mr. Baldwin did not at first manifest any definite interest in the work at Tuskegee. He said he would come down and "look us over" and if he found we were doing "the real thing," as he expressed it, he would do anything he could to help us.

Within a few weeks after this first meeting, Mr. Baldwin fulfilled his promise to "look us over" and see if we were doing "the real thing." He spent a busy day on the grounds of the institution, going through every department with the thoroughness of an experienced executive. He found, as a matter of course, a great many deficiencies in the details of the management and organization of the school, but he saw what the institution was striving to do and at once determined to help. In fact, from that time he never lost an opportunity to serve the institution in every possible way. He was just as deeply and as practically interested in everything that concerned the progress and reputation of the school and its work as anyone connected with it. I think I never met anyone who was more genuinely interested than Mr. Baldwin in the success of the Negro people. During his last visit to Tuskegee I remember that Mrs. Washington said to me one day that she would be glad when he went away. She meant that he sympathized too deeply, felt too profoundly the bigness of the task and the limitations under which the school was laboring. He was touched by everything he saw. The struggles of individual students and teachers whom he came to know weighed heavily on him and he needed to get out of the atmosphere of the school and its work, and rest. None of us realized at that time that the disease that finally took him away was already doing its fatal work.

William H. Baldwin, Jr., understood, as few men have, the Negro people, and, understanding them as he did, he was in full sympathy with their ambition to rise to a position of usefulness as large and as honorable as that of any other race. Persons who knew him only slightly, after hearing him express him on the race question, gained the impression that he was not in full sympathy with the deepest aspirations of the Negro people. But this impression was mistaken. He was, before all, anxious that the Negro people, in their struggle to go forward and succeed, should not mistake the appearance for the real thing. In his effort to have them avoid this danger he sometimes seemed to go too far.

But I would do injustice to the memory of Mr. Baldwin if, by anything I have written or said, I should leave the impression that, because he was interested in the welfare of the Negro, he was any the less interested in the progress of the white race in the South. He saw with perfect clearness that both races were, to a certain extent, hampered in their struggles upward by conditions which they had inherited and for which neither was wholly responsible. He saw, also, that in the long run the welfare of each was bound up with that of the other. Much as he did for Negro education, he never overlooked an opportunity to get money and secure support for the education of the unfortunate white people of the South.

Mr. Baldwin's greatest service to Tuskegee Institute was in the reorganization of the finances of the institution. When he first became one of the trustees, the business organization of the school, its finances, and the system of keeping the accounts were in a very uncertain and unsatisfactory condition. He began at once to look into our investments and to study the items of our annual budget. The school was growing rapidly. The number of productive industries carried on by the school, the large amount of building we were engaged in, and the large amount of business carried on between the different departments made the accounts of the school particularly complicated and the problem of a proper business organization a most important one.

As I look back over the years in which he and I worked together, it seems to me that the most pleasant and profitable hours I have ever known were spent with Mr. Baldwin in his library in Brooklyn, while we studied out together the problems and discussed the questions which this work involved. When I came to New York he would often invite me to his home and, as soon as dinner was over, we would spend three or four hours in his library, sometimes not breaking up our conference until after midnight.

Among other things I learned from Mr. Baldwin was that it is the smaller, the petty, things in life that divide people. It is the great tasks that bring men together. Any man who will take up his life in a broad spirit, not of class nor sect nor locality, but in the freer spirit which seeks to perform a work simply because it is good, that man can have the support and the friendship of the best and highest people in the world.

As I have said before, I do not regret that I was born a slave. I am not sorry that I found myself part of a problem; on the contrary, that problem has given direction and meaning to my life and has brought me friendships and comforts that I could have gotten in no other way.

Building A School Around A Problem

One of the first questions that I had to answer for myself after beginning my work at Tuskegee was how I was to deal with public opinion on the race question.

It may seem strange that a man who had started out with the humble purpose of establishing a little Negro industrial school in a small Southern country town should find himself, to any great extent, either helped or hindered in his work by what the general public was thinking and saying about any of the large social or educational problems of the day. But such was the case at that time in Alabama; and so it was that I had not gone very far in my work before I found myself trying to formulate clear and definite answers to some very fundamental questions.

The questions came to me in this way: Colored people wanted to know why I proposed to teach their children to work. They said that they and their parents had been compelled to work for two hundred and fifty years, and now they wanted their children to go to school so that they might be free and live like the white folks-without working. That was the way in which the average colored man looked at the matter. Some of the Southern white people, on the contrary, were opposed to any kind of education of the Negro. Others inquired whether I was merely going to train preachers and teachers, or whether I proposed to furnish them with trained servants.

Some of the people in the North understood that I proposed to train the Negro to be a mere "hewer of wood and drawer of water," and feared that my school would make no effort to prepare him to take his place in the community as a man and a citizen.

Of course all these different views about the kind of education that the Negro ought or ought not to have were deeply tinged with racial and sectional feelings. The rule of the "carpet-bag" government had just come to an end in Alabama. The masses of the white people were very bitter against the Negroes as a result of the excitement and agitation of the reconstruction period. On the other hand, the colored people-who had recently lost, to a very large extent, their place in the politics of the state-were greatly discouraged and disheartened. Many of them feared that they were going to be drawn back into slavery. At this time also there was still a great deal of bitterness between the North and the South in regard to anything that concerned political matters.

I found myself, as it were, at the angle where these opposing forces met. I saw that, in carrying out the work I had planned, I was likely to be opposed or criticized at some point by each of these parties. On the other hand, I saw just as clearly that in order to succeed I must in some way secure the support and sympathy of each of them. I knew, for example, that the South was poor and the North was rich. I knew that Northern people believed, as the South at that time did not believe, in the power of education to inspire, to uplift, and to regenerate the masses of the people. I knew that the North was eager to go forward and complete, with the aid of education, the work of liberation which had been begun with the sword, and that Northern people would be willing and glad to give their support to any school or other agency that proposed to do this work in a really fundamental way.

It was, at the same time, plain to me that no effort put forth in behalf of the members of my own race who were in the South was going to succeed unless it finally won the sympathy and support of the best white people in the South. I knew also-what many Northern people did not know or understand-that however much they might doubt the wisdom of educating the Negro, deep down in their hearts the Southern white people had a feeling of gratitude toward the Negro race; and I was convinced that in the long run any sound and sincere effort that was made to help the Negro was going to have the Southern white man's support. Finally, I had faith in the good common-sense of the masses of my own race. I felt confident that, if I were actually on the right track in the kind of education that I proposed to give them and at the same time remained honest and sincere in all my dealings with them, I was bound to win their support, not only for the school that I had started, but for all that I had in my mind to do for them.

Still it was often a puzzling and a trying problem to determine how best to win and hold the respect of all three of these classes of people, each of which looked with such different eyes and from such widely different points of view at what I was attempting to do. The temptation which presented itself to me in my dealings with these three classes of people was to show each group the side of the subject that it would be most willing to look at, and, at the same time, to keep silent about those matters in regard to which they were likely to differ with me. There was the temptation to say to the white man the thing that the white man wanted to hear; to say to the colored man the thing that he wanted to hear; to say one thing in the North and another in the South.

Perhaps I should have yielded to this temptation if I had not perceived that in the long run I should be found out, and that if I hoped to do anything of lasting value for my own people or for the South I must first get down to bedrock.

There is a story of an old colored minister, which I am fond of telling, that illustrates what I mean. The old fellow was trying to explain to a Sunday-school class how it was and why it was that Pharaoh and his party were drowned when they were trying to cross the Red Sea, and how it was and why it was that the Children of Israel crossed over dry-shod. He explained it in this wise:

"When the first party came along it was early in the morning and the ice was hard and thick, and the first party had no trouble in crossing over on the ice; but when Pharaoh and his party came along the sun was shining on the ice, and when they got on the ice it broke, and they went in and got drowned."

Now there happened to be in this class a young colored man who had had considerable schooling, and this young fellow turned to the old minister and said:

"Now, Mr. Minister, I do not understand that kind of explanation. I have been going to school and have been studying all these conditions, and my geography teaches me that ice does not freeze within a certain distance of the equator."

The old minister replied: "Now, I'se been expecting something just like this. There's always some fellow ready to spile all the theology. The time I'se talkin' about was before they had any jogerphies or ' quaters either."

Now this old man, in his plain and simple way, was trying to brush aside all artificiality and to get down to bedrock. So it was with me. There have always been a number of educated and clever persons among my race who are able to make plausible and fine-sounding statements about all the different phases of the Negro problem, but I saw clearly that I should have to follow the example of the old preacher and start on a solid basis in order to succeed in the work that I had undertaken. So, after thinking the matter all out as I have described, I made up my mind definitely on one or two fundamental points. I determined:

First, that I should at all times be perfectly frank and honest in dealing with each of the three classes of people that I have mentioned;

Second, that I should not depend upon any "short-cuts" or expedients merely for the sake of gaining temporary popularity or advantage, whether for the time being such action brought me popularity or the reverse. With these two points clear before me as my creed, I began going forward.

One thing which gave me faith at the outset, and increased my confidence as I went on, was the insight which I early gained into the actual relations of the races in the South. I observed, in the first place, that as a result of two hundred and fifty years of slavery the two races had become bound together in intimate ways that people outside of the South could not understand, and of which the white people and colored people themselves were perhaps not fully conscious. More than that, I perceived that the two races needed each other and that for many years to come no other laboring class of people would be able to fill the place occupied by the Negro in the life of the Southern white man.

I saw also one change that had been brought about as a result of freedom, a change which many Southern white men had, it seemed to me, failed to see. As long as slavery existed, the white man, for his own protection and in order to keep the Negro contented with his condition of servitude, was compelled to keep him in ignorance. In freedom, however, just the reverse condition exists. Now the white man is not only free to assist the Negro in his effort to rise, but he has every motive of self-interest to do so, since to uplift and educate the Negro would reduce the number of paupers and criminals of the race and increase the number and efficiency of its skilled laborers.

Clear ideas did not come into my mind on this subject at once. It was only gradually that I gained the notion that there had been two races in slavery; that both were now engaged in a struggle to adjust themselves to the new conditions; that the progress of each meant the advancement of the other; and that anything that I attempted to do for the members of my own race would be of no real value to them unless it was of equal value to the members of the white race by whom they were surrounded.

As this thought got hold in my mind and I began to see further into the nature of the task that I had undertaken to perform, much of the political agitation and controversy that divided the North from the South, the black man from the white, began to look unreal and artificial to me. It seemed as if the people who carried on political campaigns were engaged to a very large extent in a battle with shadows, and that these shadows represented the prejudices and animosities of a period that was now past.

On the contrary, the more I thought about it, the more it seemed to me that the kind of work that I had undertaken to do was a very real sort of thing. Moreover, it was a kind of work which tended not to divide, but to unite, all the opposing elements and forces, because it was a work of construction.

Having gone thus far, I began to consider seriously how I should proceed to gain the sympathy of each of the three groups that I have mentioned for the work that I had in hand.

I determined, first of all, that as far as possible I would try to gain the active support and cooperation in all that I undertook, of the masses of my own race. With this in view, before I began my work at Tuskegee, I spent several weeks traveling about among the rural communities of Macon County, of which Tuskegee is the county seat. During all this time I had an opportunity to meet and talk individually with a large number of people representing the rural classes, which constitute 80 per cent of the Negro population in the South. I slept in their cabins, ate their food, talked to them in their churches, and discussed with them in their own homes their difficulties and their needs. In this way I gained a kind of knowledge which has been of great value to me in all my work since.

As years went on, I extended these visits to the adjoining counties and adjoining states. Then, as the school at Tuskegee became better known, I took advantage of the invitations that came to me to visit more distant parts of the country, where I had an opportunity to learn still more about the actual life of the people and the nature of the difficulties with which they were struggling.

In all this, my purpose was to get acquainted with the masses of the people-to gain their confidence so that I might work with them and for them.

In the course of travel and observation I became more and more impressed with the influence that the organizations which colored people have formed among themselves exert upon the masses of the people.

The average man outside of the Negro race is likely to assume that the ten millions of colored people in this country are a mere disorganized and heterogeneous collection of individuals, herded together under one statistical label, without head or tail, and with no conscious common purpose. This is far from true. There are certain common interests that are peculiar to all Negroes, certain channels through which it is possible to touch and influence the whole people.

In my study of the race in what I may call its organized capacity, I soon learned that the most influential organization among Negroes is the Negro church. I question whether or not there is a group of ten millions of people anywhere, not excepting the Catholics that can be so readily reached and influenced through their church organizations as the ten millions of Negroes in the United States. Of these millions of black people there is only a very small percentage that does not have formal or informal connection with some church. The principal church groups are:

Baptists, African Methodists, African Methodist Episcopal Zionists, and Colored Methodists, to which I might add about a dozen smaller denominations.

I began my work of getting the support of these organizations by speaking (or lecturing, as they are accustomed to describe it) to the colored people in the little churches in the country surrounding the school at Tuskegee. When later I extended my journeys into other and more distant parts of the country, I began to get into touch with the leaders in the church and to learn something about the kind and extent of influence which these men exercise through the churches over the masses of the Negro people.

It has always been a great pleasure to me to meet and to talk in a plain, straightforward way with the common people of my own race wherever I have been able to meet them. But it is in the Negro churches that I have had my best opportunities for meeting and getting acquainted with them.

It has been my privilege to attend service in Trinity Church, Boston, where I heard Phillips Brooks. I have attended service in the Fifth Avenue Presbyterian Church in New York, where I heard the late Dr. John Hall. I have attended service in Westminster Abbey, in London. I have visited some of the great cathedrals in Europe when service was being held. But not any of these services have had for me the real interest that certain services among my own people have had. Let me describe the type of the service that I have enjoyed more than any other in all my experience in attending church, whether in America or Europe.

In Macon County, Ala., where I live, the colored people have a kind of church-service that is called an "all-day meeting." The ideal season for such meetings is about the middle of May. The church-house that I have in mind is located about ten miles from town. To get the most out of the "all-day meeting" one should make an early start, say eight o'clock. During the drive one drinks in the fresh fragrance of forests and wild flowers. The church building is located near a stream of water, not far from a large, cool spring, and in the midst of a grove or primitive forest. Here the colored people begin to come together by nine or ten o'clock in the morning. Some of them walk; most of them drive. A large number come in buggies, but many use the more primitive wagons or carts, drawn by mules, horses, or oxen. In these conveyances a whole family, from the youngest to the eldest, makes the journey together. All bring baskets of food, for the "all-day meeting" is a kind of Sunday picnic or festival. Preaching, preceded by much singing, begins at about eleven 0' clock. If the building is not large enough, the services are held out under the trees. Sometimes there is but one sermon; sometimes there are two or three sermons, if visiting ministers are present. The sermon over, there is more plantation singing. A collection is taken--sometimes two collections-then comes recess for dinner and recreation.

Sometimes I have seen at these "all-day meetings" as many as three thousand people present. No one goes away hungry. Large baskets, filled with the most tempting spring chicken or fresh pork, fresh vegetables, and all kinds of pies and cakes, are then opened. The people scatter in groups. Sheets or table-cloths are spread on the grass under a tree near the stream. Here old acquaintances are renewed; relatives meet members of the family whom they have not seen for months. Strangers, visitors, every one must be invited by some one else to dinner. Kneeling on the fresh grass or on broken branches of trees surrounding the food, dinner is eaten. The animals are fed and watered, and then at about three o'clock there is another sermon or two, with plenty of singing thrown in; then another collection, or perhaps two. In between these sermons I am invited to speak, and am very glad to accept the invitation. At about five o'clock the benediction is pronounced and the thousands quietly scatter to their homes with many good-bys and well-wishes. This, as I have said, is the kind of church-service that I like best. In the opportunities which I have to speak to such gatherings I feel that I have done some of my best work.

In carrying out the policy which I formed early, of making use of every opportunity to speak to the masses of the people, I have not only visited country churches and spoken at such "all-day meetings" as I have just described, but for years I have made it a practice to attend, whenever it has been possible for me to do so, every important ministers' meeting. I have also made it a practice to visit town and city churches and in this way to get acquainted with the ministers and meet the people.

During my many and long campaigns in the North, for the purpose of getting money to carry on Tuskegee Institute, it has been a great pleasure and satisfaction to me, after I have spoken in some white church or hall or at some banquet, to go directly to some colored church for a heart-to heart talk with my own people. The deep interest that they have shown in my work and the warmth and enthusiasm with which colored people invariably respond to anyone who talks to them frankly and sincerely in regard to matters that concern the welfare of the race, make it a pleasure to speak to them.

Many times on these trips to the North it has happened that colored audiences have waited until ten or eleven o'clock at night for my coming. This does not mean that colored people may not attend the other meetings which I address, but means simply that they prefer in most cases to have me to speak to them alone. When at last I have been able to reach the church or the hall where the audience was gathered, it has been such a pleasure to meet them that I have often found myself standing on my feet until after twelve o'clock. No one thing has given me more faith in the future of the race than the fact that Negro audiences will sit for two hours or more and listen with the utmost attention to a serious discussion of any subject that has to do with their interest as a people. This is just as true of the unlettered masses as it is of the more highly educated few.

Not long ago, for example, I spoke to a large audience in the Chamber of Commerce in Cleveland, Ohio. This audience was composed for the most part of white people, and the meeting continued rather late into the night. Immediately after this meeting I was driven to the largest colored church in Cleveland, where I found an audience of something like twenty-five hundred colored people waiting patiently for my appearance. The church building was crowded, and many of those present, I was told, had been waiting for two or three hours.

As I entered the building an unusual scene presented itself. Each member of the audience had been provided with a little American flag, and as I appeared upon the platform, the whole audience rose to its feet and began waving these flags. The reader can, perhaps, imagine the picture of twenty-five hundred enthusiastic people each of whom is wildly waving a flag. The scene was so animated and so unexpected that it made an impression on me that I shall never forget. For an hour and a half I spoke to this audience, and, although the building was crowded until there was apparently not an inch of standing room in it, scarcely a single person left the church during this time.

Another way in which I have gained the confidence and support of the millions of my race has been in meeting the religious leaders in their various state and national gatherings. For example, every year, for a number of years past, I have been invited to deliver an address before the National Colored Baptist Convention, which brings together four or five thousand religious leaders from all parts of the United States. In a similar way I meet, once in four years, the leaders in the various branches of the Methodist Church during their general conferences.

Invitations to address the different secret societies in their national gatherings frequently come to me also. Next to the church, I think it is safe to say that the secret societies or beneficial orders bring together greater numbers of colored people and exercise a larger influence upon the race than any other kind of organization. One can scarcely shake hands with a colored man without receiving some kind of grip which identifies him as a member of one or another of these many organizations.

I am reminded, in speaking of these secret societies, of an occasion at Little Rock, Ark., when, without meaning to do so, I placed my friends there in a very awkward position. It had been pretty widely advertised for some weeks before that I was to visit the city. Among the plans decided upon for my reception was a parade, in which all the secret and beneficial societies in Little Rock were to take part. Much was expected of this parade, because secret societies are numerous in Little Rock, and the occasions when they can all turn out together are rare.

A few days before I reached that city some one began to make inquiry as to which one of these orders I belonged to. When it finally became known among the rank and file that I was not a member of any of them, the committee which was preparing for the parade lost a great deal of its enthusiasm, and a sort of gloom settled down over the whole proceeding. The leading men told me that they found it quite a difficult task after that to make the people understand why they were asked to turn out to honor a person who was not a member of any of their organizations. Besides, it seemed unnatural that a Negro should not belong to some kind of order. Somehow or other, however, matters were finally straightened out; all the organizations turned out, and a most successful reception was the result.

Another agency which exercises tremendous power among Negroes is the Negro press. Few if any persons outside of the Negro race understand the power and influence of the Negro newspaper. In all, there are about two hundred newspapers published by colored men at different points in the United States. Many of them have only a small circulation and are, therefore, having a hard struggle for existence; but they are read in their local communities. Others have built up a national circulation and are conducted with energy and intelligence. With the exception of about three, these two hundred papers have stood loyally by me in all my plans and policies to uplift the race. I have called upon them freely to aid me in making known my plans and ideas, and they have always responded in a most generous fashion to all the demands that I have made upon them.

It has been suggested to me at different times that I should purchase a Negro newspaper in order that I might have an "organ" to make known my views on matters concerning the policies and interests of the race. Certain persons have suggested also that I pay money to certain of these papers in order to make sure that they support my views.

I confess that there have frequently been times when it seemed that the easiest way to combat some statement that I knew to be false, or to correct some impression which seemed to me peculiarly injurious, would be to have a paper of my own or to pay for the privilege of setting forth my own views in the editorial columns of some paper which I did not own.

I am convinced, however, that either of these two courses would have proved fatal. The minute it should become known-and it would be known-that I owned an "organ," the other papers would cease to support me as they now do. If I should attempt to use money with some papers, I should soon have to use it with all. If I should pay for the support of newspapers once, I should have to keep on paying all the time. Very soon I should have around me, if I should succeed in bribing them, merely a lot of hired men and no sincere and earnest supporters. Although I might gain for myself some apparent and temporary advantage in this way, I should destroy the value and influence of the very papers that support me. I say this because if I should attempt to hire men to write what they do not themselves believe, or only half believe, the articles or editorials they write would cease to have the true ring; and when they cease to have the true ring, they will exert little or no influence.

So, when I have encountered opposition or criticism in the press, I have preferred to meet it squarely. Frequently I have been able to profit by these criticisms of the newspapers. At other times, when I have felt that I was right and that those who criticized me were wrong, I have preferred to wait and let the results show. Thus, even when we differed with one another on minor points, I have usually succeeded in gaining the confidence and support of the editors of the different papers in regard to those matters and policies which seemed to me really important.

In traveling throughout the United States I have met the Negro editors. Many of them have been to Tuskegee. It has taken me twenty years to get acquainted with them and to know them intimately. In dealing with these men I have not found it necessary to hold them at arm's-length. On the contrary, I am in the habit of speaking with them frankly and openly in regard to my plans. A number of the men who own and edit Negro newspapers are graduates or former students of the Tuskegee Institute. I go into their offices and I go to their homes. We know one another; they are my friends, and I am their friend.

In dealing with newspaper people, whether they are white or black, there is no way of getting their sympathy and support like that of actually knowing the individual men, of meeting and talking with them frequently and frankly, and of keeping them in touch with everything you do or intend to do. Money cannot purchase or control this kind of friendship.

Whenever I am in a town or city where Negro newspapers are published, I make it a point to see the editors, to go to their offices, or to invite them to visit Tuskegee. Thus we keep in close, constant, and sympathetic touch with one another. When these papers write editorials endorsing any project that I am interested in, the editors speak with authority and with intelligence because of our close personal relations. There is no more generous and helpful class of men among the Negro race in America to-day than the owners and editors of Negro newspapers.

Many times I have been asked how it is that I have secured the confidence and good wishes of so large a number of the white people of the South.

My answer in brief is that I have tried to be perfectly frank and straightforward at all times in my relations with them. Sometimes they have opposed my actions, sometimes they have not, but I have never tried to deceive them. There are no people in the world which more quickly recognizes and appreciates the qualities of frankness and sincerity, whether they are exhibited in a friend or in an opponent, in a white man or in a black man, than the white people of the South.

In my experience in dealing with men of my race I have found that there is a class that has gained a good deal of fleeting popularity for possessing what was supposed to be courage in cursing and abusing all classes of Southern white people on all possible occasions. But, as I have watched the careers of this class of Negroes, in practically every case their popularity and influence with the masses of colored people have not been lasting. There are few races of people the masses of whom are endowed with more common-sense than the Negro, and in the long run these common people see things and men pretty much as they are.

On the other hand, there have always been in every Southern community a certain number of colored men who have sought to gain the friendship of the white people around them in ways that were more or less dishonest. For a number of years after the close of the Civil War, for example, it was natural that practically all the Negroes should be Republicans in politics. There were, however, in nearly every community in the South, one or two colored men who posed as Democrats. They thought that by pretending to favor the Democratic Party they might make themselves popular with their white neighbors and thus gain some temporary advantage. In the majority of cases the white people saw through their pretenses and did not have the respect for them that they had for the Negro who honestly voted with the party to which he felt that he belonged.

I remember hearing a prominent white Democrat remark not long ago that in the old days whenever a Negro Democrat entered his office he always took a tight grasp upon his pocket-book. I mention these facts because I am certain that wherever I have gained the confidence of the Southern people I have done so, not by opposing them and not by truckling to them, but by acting in a straightforward manner, always seeking their good-will, but never seeking it upon false pretenses.

I have made it a rule to talk to the Southern white people concerning what I might call their shortcomings toward the Negro rather than talk about them. In the last analysis, however, I have succeeded in getting the sympathy and support of so large a number of Southern white people because I have tried to recognize and to face conditions as they actually are, and have honestly tried to work with the best white people in the South to bring about a better condition.

From the first I have tried to secure the confidence and good-will of every white citizen in my own county. My experience teaches me that if a man has little or no influence with those by whose side he lives, as a rule there is something wrong with him. The best way to influence the Southern white man in your community, I have found, is to convince him that you are of value to that community. For example, if you are a teacher, the best way to get the influence of your white neighbors is to convince them that you are teaching something that will make the pupils that you educate able to do something better and more useful than they would otherwise be able to do; to show, in other words, that the education which they get adds something of value to the community.

In my own case, I have attempted from the beginning to let every white citizen in my own town see that I am as much interested in the common, every-day affairs of life as himself. I tried to let them see that the presence of Tuskegee Institute in the community means better farms and gardens, good housekeeping, good schools, law and order. As soon as the average white man is convinced that the education of the Negro makes of him a citizen who is not always "up in the air," but one who can apply his education to the things in which every citizen is interested, much of opposition, doubt, or indifference to Negro education will disappear.

During all the years that I have lived in Macon County, Ala., I have never had the slightest trouble in either registering or casting my vote at any election. Every white person in the county knows that I am going to vote in a way that will help the county in which I live.

Many nights I have been up with the sheriff of my county, in consultation concerning law and order, seeking to assist him in getting hold of and freeing the community of criminals. More than that, Tuskegee Institute has constantly sought, directly and indirectly, to impress upon the twenty-five or thirty thousand colored people in the surrounding county the importance of cooperating with the officers of the law in the detection and apprehension of criminals. The result is that we have one of the most orderly communities in the state. I do not believe that there is any county in the state, for example, where the prohibition laws are so strictly enforced as in Macon County, in spite of the fact that the Negroes in this county so largely outnumber the whites.

Whatever influence I have gained with the Northern white people has come about from the fact, I think, that they feel that I have tried to use their gifts honestly and in a manner to bring about real and lasting results. I learned long ago that in education as in other things nothing but honest work lasts; fraud and sham are bound to be detected in the end. I have learned, on the other hand, that if one does a good, honest job, even though it may be done in the middle of the night when no eyes see but one's own, the results will just as surely come to light.

My experience has taught me, for example, that if there is a filthy basement or a dirty closet anywhere in the remotest part of the school grounds it will be discovered. On the other hand, if every basement or every closet-no matter how remote from the center of the school activities-is kept clean, some one will find it and commend the care and the thoughtfulness that kept it clean.

It has always been my policy to make visitors to Tuskegee, feel that they are seeing more than they expected to see. When a person has contributed, say, $20,000 for the erection of a building, I have tried to provide a larger building, a better building, than the donor expected to see. This I have found can be brought about only by keeping one's eyes constantly on all the small details. I shall never forget a remark made to me by Mr. John D. Rockefeller when I was spending an evening at his house. It was to this effect: "Always be master of the details of your work; never have too many loose outer edges or fringes."

Then, in dealing with Northern people, I have always let them know that I did not want to get away from my own race; that I was just as proud of being a Negro as they were of being white people. No one can see through a sham more quickly, whether it be in speech or in dress, than the hardheaded Northern business man.

I once knew a fine young colored man who nearly ruined himself by pretending to be something that he was not. This young man was sent to England for several months of study. When he returned he seemed to have forgotten how to talk. He tried to ape the English accent, the English dress, the English walk. I was amused to notice sometimes, when he was off his guard, how he got his English pronunciation mixed with the ordinary American accent which he had used all of his life. So one day I quietly called him aside and said to him: "My friend, you are ruining yourself. Just drop all those frills and be yourself." I am glad to say that he had sense enough to take the advice in the right spirit, and from that time on he was a different man.

The most difficult and trying of the classes of persons with which I am brought in contact is the colored man or woman who is ashamed of his or her color, ashamed of his or her race and, because of this fact, is always in a bad temper. I have had opportunities, such as few colored men have had, of meeting and getting acquainted with many of the best white people, North and South. This has never led me to desire to get away from my own people. On the contrary, I have always returned to my own people and my own work with renewed interest.

I have never at any time asked or expected that anyone, in dealing with me, should overlook or forget that I am a Negro. On the contrary, I have always recognized that, when any special honor was conferred upon me, it was conferred not in spite of my being a Negro, but because I am a Negro, and because I have persistently identified myself with every interest and with every phase of the life of my own people.

Looking back over the twenty-five and more years that have passed since that time, I realize, as I did not at that time, how the better part of my education-the education that I got after leaving school-has been in the effort to work out those problems in a way that would gain the interest and the sympathy of all three of the classes directly concerned-the Southern white man, the Northern white man, and the Negro.

In order to gain consideration from these three classes for what I was trying to do I have had to enter sympathetically into the three different points of view entertained by those three classes; I have had to consider in detail how the work that I was trying to do was going to affect the interests of all three. To do this, and at the same time continue to deal frankly and honestly with each class, has been indeed a difficult and at times a puzzling task. It has not always been easy to stick to my work and keep myself free from the distracting influences of narrow and factional points of view; but, looking back on it all after a quarter of a century, I can see that it has been worth what it cost.

Some Exceptional Men And What I Have Learned From Them

There are some opportunities that come to the boy or girl who is born poor that the boy or girl who is born rich does not have. In the same way there are some advantages in belonging to a disadvantaged race. The individual or the race which has to face peculiar hardships and to overcome unusual difficulties gains an experience of men and things and gets into close and intimate touch with life in a way that is not possible to the man or woman in ordinary circumstances.

In the old slavery days, when any of the white folks were a little uncertain about the quality of a new family that had moved into the neighborhood, they always had one last resource for determining the character and the status of the new family. When in doubt, they could always rely on old "Aunt Jenny." After "Aunt Jenny" had visited the new family and returned with her report, the question was settled. Her decision was final, because "Aunt Jenny" knew. The old-fashioned house servants gained, through their peculiar experiences, a keen sense for what was called the "quality."

In freedom also the Negro has had special opportunities for finding out the character and the quality of the white people among whom he lives. If there is a man in the community who is habitually kind and considerate to the humblest people about him, the colored people know about that man. On the contrary, if there is a man in that community who is unfair and unjust in his dealings with them, the colored people know that man also.

In their own way and among themselves, the colored people in the South still have the habit of weighing and passing judgment on the white people in their community; and, nine times out of ten, their opinion of a man is pretty accurate. A man who can always be counted on to go out of his way to assist and protect the members of an unpopular race, and who is not afraid or ashamed to show that he is interested in the efforts of the colored people about him to improve their condition, is pretty likely to be a good citizen in other respects.

In the average Southern community, also, it is almost always the best people, those who are most highly cultured and religious, who know the colored people best. It is the best white people who go oftenest into the Negro churches or teach in the Negro Sunday-schools. It is to individual white men of this better class that the average colored people go most frequently for counsel and advice when they are in trouble.

The fact that I was born a Negro, and the further fact that I have all my life been engaged in a kind of work that was intended to uplift the masses of my people, has brought me in contact with many exceptional persons, both North and South. For example, it was because I was a poor boy and a Negro that I found my way to Hampton Institute, where I came under the influence of General

Armstrong, who, as teacher and friend, has had a larger influence upon my life than any other person I have ever known, except my mother. As it was in my boyhood, it has been in a greater degree in my later life; because of the work I was trying to do for the Negro race I have constantly been brought into contact with men of the very highest type, generous, high-minded, enlightened, and free. As I have already suggested, a large part of my education has been gained by my personal contact with these exceptional men.

There have been times in my life when I fear that I should have lost courage to go forward if I had not had constantly before me the example of other men, some of them obscure and almost unknown outside of the communities in which they lived, whose patient, unwavering cheerfulness and good-will, in spite of difficulties, have been a continued inspiration to me.

On my way to Tuskegee for the first time I met one of the finest examples of the type of man I have tried to describe. He was a railroad conductor and his name was Capt. Isaiah C. Howard. For many years he had charge of a train on the Western Railroad of Alabama, between Montgomery and Atlanta. I do not know where Captain Howard got his education, or how much he had studied books. I do know that he was born in the South and had spent all his life there. During a period of twenty years I rarely, if ever, met a higher type of the true gentleman, North or South.

I recall one occasion in particular when I was on his train between Atlanta and Montgomery during the Christmas holiday season, when the rougher and more ignorant of my race usually travel in large numbers, and when owing to the general license that has always prevailed during the holiday season, a certain class of colored people are likely to be more or less under the influence of whiskey.

After a time a disturbance arose in the crowd at the lower end of the car. When Captain Howard appeared, some of the men who had been drinking spoke to him in a way that most men, white or black, would have resented. In the case of some men, the language these Negroes used might easily have furnished an occasion for a shooting, the consequences of which it was not difficult for me to picture to myself. I was deeply touched to see how, like a wise and patient father, Captain Howard handled these rough fellows. He spoke to them calmly, without the least excitement in his voice or manner, and in a few moments he had obtained almost complete order in the car. After that he gave them a few words of very sensible advice which at once won their respect and gratitude, because they understood the spirit that prompted it.

During all the time that I traveled with him I never saw Captain Howard, even under the most trying circumstances, lose his temper or grow impatient with any class of colored people that he had to deal with. During the long trips that I used to make with him, whenever he had a little leisure time, he would drop down into the seat by my side and we would talk together, sometimes for an hour at a time, on the condition and prospects of the Negro in the South. I remember that he had very definite ideas in regard to the white man's duty and responsibility, and more than once he expressed to me his own reasons for believing that the Negro should be treated with patience and with justice. He used frequently to express the fear that, by allowing himself to get into the habit of treating Negroes with harshness, the white man in the South would be injured more than the Negro.

I have spoken of Captain Howard at some length because he represents a distinct class of white people in the South, of whom an increasing number may be found in nearly every Southern community. He possessed in a very high degree those qualities of kindness, self-control, and general good breeding which belong to the real aristocracy of the South. In his talks with me he frequently explained that he was no "professional" lover of the Negro; that, in fact, he had no special feeling for the Negro or against him, but was interested in seeing fair play for every race and every individual. He said that his real reason for wanting to give the Negro the same chance that other races have was that he loved the South, and he knew that there could be no permanent prosperity unless the lowest and poorest portion of the community was treated with the same justice as the highest and most powerful. I count it a part of my good fortune to have been thrown, early in my life in Alabama, in contact with such a man as Captain Howard. After knowing him I said to myself: "If, under the circumstances, a white man can learn to be fair to my race instead of hating it, a black man ought to be able to return the compliment."

In connection with my work in Alabama, I early made the acquaintance of another Southern white man, also an Alabamian by birth but of a different type, a man of education and high social and official standing-the late J. L. M. Curry.

It was my privilege to know Doctor Curry well during the last twenty years of his life. He had fought on the side of the Confederacy during the Civil War, he had served as a college professor and as United States Minister to Spain, and had held other high public positions. More than that, he represented, in his personal feelings and ways of thinking, all that was best in the life of the Southern white people.

Notwithstanding the high positions he had held in social and official life, Doctor Curry gave his latter years to the cause of education among the masses of white and colored people in the South, and was never happier than when engaged in this work.

I met Doctor Curry for the first time, in a business way, at Montgomery, Ala. While I was in the Capitol building I happened to be, for a few moments, in a room adjoining that in which Doctor Curry and some other gentlemen were talking, and could not avoid overhearing their conversation. They were speaking about Negro education. One of the state officials expressed some doubt about the propriety of a Southern gentleman taking an active part in the education of the Negro. While I am not able to give his exact words, Doctor Curry replied in substance that he did not believe that he or anyone else had ever lost anything, socially or in any other way, on account of his connection with Negro education.

"On the other hand," Doctor Curry continued, "I believe that Negro education has done a great deal more for me than I have ever been able to do for Negro education."

Then he went on to say that he had never visited a Negro school or performed a kindly act for a Negro man, woman, or child, that he himself was not made stronger and better for it.

Immediately after the Civil War, he said, he had been bitterly opposed to every movement that had been proposed to educate the Negro. After he came to visit some of the colored schools, however, and saw for himself the struggles that the colored people were making to get an education, his prejudice had changed into sympathy and admiration.

As far as my own experience goes-and I have heard the same thing said by others-there is no gentler, kindlier, or more generous type of man anywhere than those Southern white men who, born and bred to those racial and sectional differences which, after the Civil War, were mingled with and intensified by the bitterness of poverty and defeat, have struggled up to the point where they feel nothing but kind-ness to the people of all races and both sections. It is much easier for those who shared in the victory of the Civil War-I mean the Northern white man and the Negro-to emancipate themselves from racial and sectional narrowness.

There is another type of white man in the South who has aided me in getting a broader and more practical conception of my work. I refer to the man who has no special sentiment for or against the Negro, but appreciates the importance of the Negro race as a commercial asset-a man like Mr. John M. Parker, of New Orleans. Mr. Parker is the president of the Southern Industrial Congress, and is one of the largest planters in the Gulf States. His firm in New Orleans, I understand, buys and sells more cotton than any other firm in the world. Mr. Parker sees more clearly than any white man in the South with whom I have talked, the fact that it is important to the commercial progress of the country that the Negro should be treated with justice in the courts, in business, and in all the affairs of life. He realizes also that, in order that the Negro may have an incentive to work regularly, he must have his wants increased; and this can be brought about only through education.

I have heard many addresses to colored people in all parts of the country, but I have never heard words more sensible, practical, and to the point from the lips of any man than those of an address which Mr. Parker delivered before nearly a thousand Negro farmers at one of the annual Negro Conferences at the Tuskegee Institute. Mr. Parker has for years been a large employer of Negro labor on his plantation. He was thus able to speak to the farmers simply and frankly, and, even though he told them some rather unpleasant truths, the audience understood and appreciated not only what was said, but the spirit in which it was uttered.

The hope of the South, so far as the interests of the Negro are concerned, rests very largely upon men like Mr. Parker, who see the close connection between labor, industry, education, and political institutions, and have learned to face the race problem in a large and tolerant spirit, and are seeking to solve it in a practical way.

A quite different type of man with whom I have been thrown in frequent contact is Col. Henry Watterson, of the Louisville Courier-journal. Colonel Watterson seems to me to represent the Southern gentleman of the old school, a man of generous impulses, high ideals, and gracious manner. I have had frequent and long conversations with him about the Negro and about conditions in the South. If there is anywhere a man who has broader or more liberal ideas concerning the Negro, or any undeveloped race, I have not met him.

A few years ago, when a meeting had been arranged at Carnegie Hall, New York, in order to interest the public in the work of our school at Tuskegee, we were disappointed in securing a distinguished speaker from the South who had promised to be present. At the last moment the committee in charge telegraphed to Colonel Watterson. Although (because of the death of one of his children) he had made up his mind not to speak again in public for some time, Colonel Watterson went to New York from Louisville and made one of the most eloquent speeches in behalf of the Negro that I have ever heard. He told me at the time that nothing but his interest in the work that we were trying to do at Tuskegee would have induced him to leave home at that time.

Whenever I have been tempted to grow embittered or discouraged about conditions in the South, my acquaintance with such men as Mr. Parker and Colonel Watterson has given me new strength and increased my faith.

I have been fortunate also in the colored men with whom I have been associated. There is a class of Negroes in the South who are just as much interested as the best white people in the welfare of the communities in which they live. They are just as much· opposed as the best white people to anything that tends to stir up strife between the races. But there are two kinds of colored people, just as there are two kinds of white people.

There is a class of colored people who are narrow in their sympathies, short-sighted in their views, and bitter in their prejudices against the white people. When I first came to Alabama I had to decide whether I could unite with this class in a general crusade of denunciation against the white people of the South, in order to create sympathy in the North for the work that I was seeking to carry on, or whether I would consider the real interests of the masses of my race, and seek to preserve and promote the good relations that already existed between the races.

I do not deny that I was frequently tempted, during the early years of my work, to join in the general denunciation of the evils and injustice that I saw about me. But when I thought the matter over, I saw that such a course would accomplish no good and that it would do a great deal of harm. For one thing, it would serve only to mislead the masses of my own race in regard to the opportunities that existed right about them. Besides that, I saw that the masses of the Negro people had no disposition to carry on any general war against the white people. What they wanted was the help and encouragement of their white neighbors in their efforts to get an education and to improve themselves.

Among the colored men who saw all this quite as clearly as myself was Rufus Herron, of Camp Hill, Ala. He was born in slavery and had had almost no school advantages, but he was not lacking in practical wisdom and he was a leader in the community in which he lived. Some years ago, after he had harvested his cotton crop he called to see me at the Tuskegee Institute. He said that he had sold all of his cotton, had got a good price for it, had paid all his debts for the year, and had twenty dollars remaining. He handed me ten dollars and asked me to use it in the education of a student at Tuskegee. He returned to his home and gave the other ten to the teacher of the white school in his vicinity, and asked him to use it in the education of a white student.

Since that day I have come to know Rufus Herron well.

He never misses a session of the annual Tuskegee Negro conference. He is the kind of man that one likes to listen to because he always says something that goes straight to the point, and after he has covered the subject he stops. I do not think that I have ever talked with him that he did not have something to suggest in regard to the material, educational, and moral improvement of the people, or something that might promote better relations between white people and black people. If there is a white man, North or South, that has more love for his community or his country than Rufus Herron, it has not been my good fortune to meet him. In his feelings and ambitions he also is what I have called an aristocrat.

I have no disposition to deny to anyone, black or white, the privilege of speaking out and protesting against wrong and injustice, whenever and wherever they choose to do so. I would do injustice to the facts and to the masses of my people in the South, however, if I did not point out how much more useful a man like Rufus Herron has made his life than the man who spends his time and makes a profession of going about talking about his "rights" and stirring up bitterness between the white people and colored people. The salvation of the Negro race in America is to be worked out, for the most part, not by abstract argument and not by mere denunciation of wrong, but by actual achievement in constructive work.

In Nashville there is another colored man-a banker, a man of education, wealth, and culture. James c. Napier is about the same age as Rufus Herron. I have been closely associated with him for twenty years. I have been with him in the North and in the South; I have worked with him in conventions, and I have talked with him in private in my home and in his home. During all the years that I have known him I have never heard Mr. Napier express a narrow or bitter thought toward the white race. On the contrary, he has shown himself anxious to give publicity to the best deeds of the white people rather than the worst. During the greater part of my life I have done my work in association with such men as he. There is no part of the United States in which I have not met some of this type of colored men. I honor such men all the more because, had they chosen to do so, they could easily have made themselves and those about them continually miserable by dwelling upon the mean things which people say about the race or the injustices which are so often a part of the life of the Negro.

Let me add that, so far as I have been able to see, there is no real reason why a Negro in this country should make himself miserable or unhappy. The average white man in the United States has the idea that the average Negro spends most of his time in bemoaning the fact that he is not a white man, or in trying to devise some way by which he will be permitted to mingle, in a purely social way, with white people. This is far from the truth. In my intercourse with all classes of the Negro, North and South, it is a rare occurrence when the matter of getting away from the race, or of social intermingling with the white people, is so much as mentioned. It is especially true that intelligent Negroes find a satisfaction in social intercourse among themselves that is rarely known or understood by anyone outside of the Negro race. In their family life, in the secret societies and churches, as well as other organizations where colored people come together, the most absorbing topic of conversation invariably relates to some enterprise for the betterment of the race.

Among colored farmers, as among white farmers, the main topic of discussion is naturally the farm. The Negro is, in my opinion, naturally a farmer, and he is at his very best when he is in close contact with the soil. There is something in the atmosphere of the farm that develops and strengthens the Negro's natural common-sense. As a rule the Negro farmer has a rare gift of getting at the sense of things and of stating in picturesque language what he has learned. The explanation of it is, it seems to me, that the Negro farmer studies nature. In his own way he studies the soil, the development of plants and animals, the streams, the birds, and the changes of the seasons. He has a chance of getting the kind of knowledge that is valuable to him at firsthand.

In a visit some years ago to a Negro farmers' institute in the country, I got a lesson from an unlettered colored farmer which I have never forgotten. I had been invited by one of the Tuskegee graduates to go into the country some miles from Tuskegee to be present at this institute. When I entered the room the members of the institute were holding what they called their farmers' experience meeting. One colored farmer was asked to come up to the platform and give his experience. He was an old man, about sixty-five years of age. He had had no education in the book, but the teacher had reached him, as he had others in the community, and showed him how to improve his methods of farming. When this old man came up to the front of the room to tell his experience, he said: "I'se never had no chance to study no science, but since dis teacher has been here I'se been trying to make some science for myself."

Thereupon he laid upon the table by his side six stalks of cotton and began to describe in detail how, during the last ten years, he had gradually enriched his land so as to increase the number of bolls of cotton grown upon each individual stalk. He picked up one stalk and showed it to the audience; before the teacher came to the community, he said, and before he began to improve his land, his cotton produced only two bolls to the stalk. The second year he reached the point where, on the same land, he succeeded in producing four bolls on a stalk. Then he showed the second stalk to the audience. After that he picked up the third and fourth stalks, saying that during the last few years he had reached a point where a stalk produced eight bolls.

Finally he picked up the last stalk and said:

"This year I made cotton like dis"-and he showed a stalk containing fourteen bolls. Then the old fellow took his seat.

Some one in the audience from a distance arose and said: "Uncle, will you tell us your name?"

The old fellow arose and said: "Now, as you ask me for my name, I'll tell you. In de old days, before dis teacher come here, I lived in a little log-cabin on rented land, and had to mortgage my crop every year for food. When I didn't have nothin', in dem days, in my community dey used to call me 'Old Jim Hill.' But now I'se out 0' debt; I'se de deeds for fifty acres of land; and I lives in a nice house wid four rooms that's painted inside and outside; I'se got some money in de bank; I'se a taxpayer in my community; I'se edicated my children. And now, in my community, dey calls me 'Mr. James Hill. '"

The old fellow had not only learned to raise cotton during these ten years, but, so far as he was concerned, he had solved the race problem.

As one travels through the Southland, he is continually meeting old Negro farmers like the one that I have described. It has been one of the great satisfactions of my life to be able from time to time to go out into the heart of the country, on the plantations and on the farms where the masses of the colored people live. I like to get into the fields and into the woods where they are at work and talk with them. I like to attend their churches and Sunday-schools and camp-meetings and revival meetings. In this way I have gotten more material which has been of service to me in writing and speaking than I have ever gotten by reading books. There are no frills about the ordinary Negro farmer, no pretense. He, at least, is himself and no one else. There is no type of man that I more enjoy meeting and knowing.

A disadvantaged race has, too, the advantage of coming in contact with the best in the North, and this again has been my good fortune. There are two classes of people in the North-one that is just as narrow and unreasonable toward the white man at the South as any Southern white man can be toward the Negro or a Northern white man. I have always chosen to deal with the other white man at the North-the man with large and liberal views.

In saying this I make an exception of the "professional" friend of the Negro. I have little patience with the man who parades himself as the "professional" friend of any race. The "professional" friend of the Chinese or Japanese or Filipino is frequently a well-meaning person, but he is always tiresome. I like to meet the man who is interested in the Negro because he is a human being. I like to talk with the man who wants to help the Negro because he is a member of the human family, and because he believes that, in helping the Negro, he is helping to make this a better world to live in.

During the twenty-five years and more that I have been accustomed to go North every year to obtain funds with which to build up and support the Tuskegee Institute, I have made the acquaintance of a large number of exceptional people in that part of the country. Because I was seeking aid for Negro education, seeking assistance in giving opportunities to a neglected portion of our population, I had an opportunity to meet these people in a different and, perhaps, more intimate way than the average man. I had an opportunity to see a side of their lives of which many of their business acquaintances, perhaps, did not know the existence.

Few people, I dare say, who were acquainted with the late Mr. H. H. Rogers, former head of the Standard Oil Company, knew that he had any special interest or sympathy for the Negro. I remember well, however, an occasion when he showed this interest and sympathy. I was showing him one day the copy of a little Negro farmers' newspaper, published at Tuskegee, containing an account of the efforts the people in one of our country communities were making to raise a sum of money among themselves in order that they might receive the aid he had promised them in building a school house. As Mr. Rogers read the account of this school "rally," as it was called, and looked down the long list of names of the individuals who in order to make up the required sum, had contributed out of their poverty, some a penny, some five cents, some twenty-five, some a dollar and a few as much as five dollars, his eyes filled with tears. I do not think he ever before realized, as he did at that moment, the great power-and the great power for good-which his money gave them.

During the last years of his life, Mr. Rogers was greatly interested in the building of the Virginian Railway, which was constructed upon his own plans and almost wholly with his own capital, from Norfolk, Va., to Deep Water, W Va. One of the first things he did, after this new railway was completed, was to make arrangements for a special train in order that I might travel over and speak at the different towns to the colored people along the line and, at the same time, study their situation in order that something might be done to improve their condition. From his point of view, these people were part of the resources of the country which he wanted to develop. He desired to see the whole country, through which this railway passed, which, up to that time, had remained in a somewhat backward condition, made prosperous and flourishing and filled with thriving towns and with an industrious and happy people. He died, however, just as he seemed on the eve of realizing this dream.

For a number of years before his death, I knew Mr. H. H. Rogers intimately. I used to see him frequently in his office in New York; sometimes I made trips with him on his yacht. At such times I had opportunity to talk over in detail the work that I was trying to do. Mr. Rogers had one of the most powerful and resourceful minds of any man I ever met. His connection with large business affairs had given him a broad vision and practical grasp of public and social questions, and I learned much from my contact with him.

In this connection I might name another individual who represents another and entirely different type of man, with whom I have frequently come in contact during my travels through the Northern states. I refer to Mr. Oswald Garrison

Villard, editor of the New York Evening Post. Mr. Villard is not primarily a business man in the sense that Mr. Rogers was, and his interest in the education and progress of the Negro is of a very different kind from that of Mr. Rogers; at least he approaches the matter from a very different point of view.

Mr. Villard is the grandson of William Lloyd Garrison, the abolitionist. He is a literary man and idealist, and he cherishes all the intense zeal for the rights of the Negro which his grandfather before him displayed. He is anxious and determined that the Negro shall have every right and every opportunity that any other race of people has in this country. He is the outspoken opponent of every institution and every individual who seeks to limit in any way the freedom of any man or class of men anywhere. He has not only continued in the same way and by much the same methods that his grandfather used, to fight the battles for human liberty, but he has interested himself in the education of the Negro. It is due to the suggestion and largely to the work of Mr. Villard that Tuskegee, at the celebration of its twenty-fifth anniversary received the $150,000 memorial fund to commemorate the name and service of Mr. William H. Baldwin to Tuskegee and Negro education in the South. Mr. Villard has given much of his time and personal service to the work of helping and building up some of the smaller and struggling Negro schools in the South. He is a trustee of at least two of such institutions, being president of the board of trustees in one case, and takes an active part in the direction and control of their work. He has recently been active and, in fact, is largely responsible for the organization of the National Association for the Advancement of the Colored People, a sort of national vigilance committee, which will watch over and guard the rights and interests of the race, and seek through the courts, through legislation, and through other public and private means, to redress the wrongs from which the race now suffers in different parts of the country.

Perhaps I ought to add in fairness that, while I sympathize fully with Mr. Villard's purposes, I have frequently differed with him as to the methods he has used to accomplish them. Sometimes he has criticized me publicly in his newspaper and privately in conversation. Nevertheless, during all this time, I have always felt that I retained his friendship and good-will. I do not think there has ever been a time when I went to him with a request of any kind either for myself personally or to obtain his help in any way in the work in which I was engaged that he has not shown himself willing and anxious to do everything in his power to assist me. While I have not always been able to follow his suggestions, or agree with him as to the methods I should pursue, I have, nevertheless, I think, profited by his criticism and have always felt and appreciated the bracing effect upon public sentiment of his vigorous and uncompromising spirit.

I have learned also from Mr. Villard the lesson that persons who have a common purpose may still maintain helpful, friendly relations, even if they do differ as to details and choose to travel to the common goal by different roads.

Another man who has exercised a deep influence upon me is Robert C. Ogden. Some months after I became a student at Hampton Institute, Mr. Robert C. Ogden, in company with a number of other gentlemen from New York, came to Hampton on a visit. It was the first time I ever saw him and the first sight of a man of the physical, mental, and moral build of Mr. Ogden----strong, fresh, clean, vigorous-made an impression upon me that it is hard for anyone not in my situation to appreciate. The thing that impressed me most was this: Here was a man, intensely earnest and practical, a man who was deeply engrossed in business affairs, who still found time to turn aside from his business and give a portion of his time and thought to the elevation of an unfortunate race.

Mr. Ogden is a man of a very different type from either Mr. Rogers or Mr. Villard. He does not look at the question of uplifting the Negro as a question of rights and liberty exclusively: he does not think of it merely as a means of developing one of the neglected resources of the South. He looks upon it, if I may venture to say so, as a question of humanity. Mr. Ogden is intensely interested in human beings; he cannot think of an unfortunate individual or class of individuals without feeling a strong impulse to help them. He has spent a large portion of his time, energy, and fortune in inspiring a large number of other people with that same sentiment. I do not believe any man has done more than Mr. Ogden to spread, among the masses of the people, a spirit of unselfish service to the interests of humanity, irrespective of geographical, sectarian or racial distinction.

Perhaps I can in no better way give an idea of what Mr.

Ogden has accomplished in this direction than by giving a list of some of the activities in which he has been engaged. Mr. Ogden is: President and only Northern member of the Conference for Southern Education, President of the Southern Education Board, President of the Board of Trustees of Hampton Institute, Trustee of Tuskegee Institute, Trustee of the Anna T. Jeans Fund for Improvement of the Negro Common School, Member of the General Education Board.

From this it will be seen that Mr. Ogden is directly connected with almost every important movement for education in the South, whether for white people or for black

people. In addition to that he is president of the Board of Directors of the Union Theological Seminary of New York, member of the Sage Foundation Board, and of the Presbyterian Board of Home Missions. In all these different directions he has worked quietly, steadily, without stinting himself, for the good of the whole country. Many of the sentiments which he has expressed in his annual addresses at the meetings of these different organizations have in them the breadth of view of a real statesman. His idea was that in giving an equal opportunity for education to every class in the community he was laying the foundation for a real democracy. He spoke of the educational conference, for instance, as "a congress called by the voice of democracy"; and again he said of this same institution, "Its foundation is the proposition that every American child is entitled to an education."

In spite of what he has done in a multitude of ways to advance education, I have heard Mr. Ogden say, both in public and in private, that he was not an educated man. Perhaps he has not gotten so much education in the usual, formal, technical matter out of books as some other people. But through the study of books, or men, or things, Mr. Ogden has secured the finest kind of education, and deserves to be classed with the scholars of the world. So far as I have studied Mr. Ogden's career, it is of interest and value to the public in three directions:

First: He has been a successful business man.

Second: More than any other one individual except Gen. S. C. Armstrong, he has been the leader in a movement to educate the whole South, regardless of race or color.

Third: In many important matters relating to moral and religious education in the North, Mr. Ogden is an important leader. I know of few men in America whose life can be held up before young people as a model as can Mr. Ogden's life.

It would be difficult for me to describe or define the manner and extent to which I have been influenced and educated by my contact with Mr. Ogden. It was characteristic of him, that the only reason I came to know him is because I needed him, needed him in the work which I was trying to do. Had I not been a Negro I would probably never have had the rare experience of meeting and knowing intimately a man who stands so high in every walk of life as Mr. Robert C. Ogden. Had Mr. Ogden been a weak man, seeking his own peace of mind and social position, he would not have been brave enough and strong enough to ignore adverse criticism in his efforts to serve the unfortunate of both races in the South, and in that case I should probably not have made his acquaintance.

The men that I have mentioned are but types of many others, men intellectually and spiritually great, who, directly and indirectly, have given comfort, help, and counsel to the ten millions of my race in America.

My Experience With Reporters And Newspapers

I have learned much from reporters and newspapers. Seldom do I go into any city, or even step out on the platform between trains, but that it seems to me some newspaper reporter finds me. I used to be surprised at the unexpected places in which these representatives of the press would turn up, and still more surprised and sometimes embarrassed by the questions they would ask me. It seemed to me that, if there was any particular thing that I happened to know and did not feel at liberty to talk about, that would be the precise thing that the reporter who met me wanted to question me about. In such cases, too, the reporter usually got the information he wanted, or, if he didn't, I was sorry afterward, because if the actual facts had been published they would have done less damage than the half truths which he did get hold of.

I confess that when I was less experienced I used to dread reporters. For a long time I used to look upon a reporter as a kind of professional pry, a sort of social mischief-maker, who was constantly trying to find out something that would make trouble. The consequence was that when I met reporters I was likely to find myself laying plans to circumvent them and keep them in the dark in regard to my purposes and business.

A wide acquaintance with newspapers and newspaper men has completely changed my attitude toward them. In the first place I have discovered that reporters usually ask just the questions that the average man in the community in which the newspapers are located would ask if he had the courage to do so. The only difference is that the reporter comes out squarely and plumply and asks you the question that another person would ask indirectly of some one else.

For my part, I have found it both interesting and important to know what sort of questions the average man in the community was asking, for example about the progress of the Negro, or about my work. The sort of questions the reporters in the different parts of the country ask indicate pretty clearly, not only what the people in the community know about my work, but they tell me a great deal, also, about the feeling of the average man toward the members of my race in that community and toward the Negro generally. Not only do the newspaper reporters keep me informed, in the way I have described, in regard to a great many things I want to know, but frequently, by the questions that they ask, they enable me to correct false impressions and to give information which it seems important the public should have, in regard to the condition and progress of the Negro.

One other consideration has changed my attitude toward the reporters. As I have become better acquainted with newspapers I have come to understand the manner and extent to which they represent the interests and habits of thought of the people who read and support them. Any man who is engaged in any sort of work that makes constant demands upon the good-will and confidence of the public knows that it is important that he should have an opportunity to reach this public directly and to answer just the sort of questions the newspapers ask of him. As I have said, these inquiries represent the natural inquiries of the average man. If the newspaper did not ask and answer these questions, they would remain unanswered, or the public would get the information it wanted from some more indirect and less reliable source.

Several times, during the years that I have been at Tuskegee, a representative from some Southern paper or magazine has come to me to inquire in regard to some rumor or report that has got abroad in regard to conditions inside our school. In such cases I have simply told the reporter to take as much time as he chose and make as thorough an examination of the school and everything about it as he cared to. At the same time, I have assured him that he was perfectly free to ask any questions on any subject, of any person that he met on the grounds. In other words, I have given him every opportunity to go as far as he wanted, and to make his investigation as thorough as he desired.

Of course, in every institution as large as ours, there is abundant opportunity for a malicious or ill-disposed person to make injurious criticism, or to interpret what he learns in a way that would injure the institution. But in every such case, instead of printing anything derogatory to the school, the newspaper investigation has proved the most valuable sort of advertisement, and the rumors that had been floating about have been silenced. There is no means so effectual in putting an end to gossip as a newspaper investigation and report. On the other hand, I have found that there is no way of so quickly securing the good-will of a newspaper reporter as by showing him that you have if nothing to conceal.

Frequently I have heard people criticize the newspapers because they print and give currency to so much that is merely trivial; in other words, what we commonly speak of as gossip. What I know of the newspapers convinces me that they do not print one tenth of the reports that are sent in to them, and that a large part of the time of every newspaper man is spent in running down and proving the falsity of stories and rumors that have gained currency in the community as a result of the natural disposition of mankind to accept and believe any kind of statement that is sufficiently circumstantial and interesting. My own experience leads me to believe that if the newspaper performed no other service for the community but that of rooting out of the public mind the malice and prejudice that rest upon misinformation and gossip, it would justify its existence in this way alone.

In saying this, I do not overlook the fact that daily papers are responsible for giving currency to many statements that are false and misleading: that too frequently the emphasis is placed upon the things that are merely exciting, while important matters-or, at least, matters that seem important to some of us who are on the outside-are passed over in silence. To a very large extent the daily newspapers have merely taken up the work that was formerly performed by the village gossip, or by the men who sat around in the village store, talked politics, and made public opinion. The newspaper, however, does that work on a higher plane. It gives us a world-wide outlook, and it makes a commendable effort to get the truth. Even if, like the village gossip, it puts the emphasis sometimes on the wrong things and spends a lot of time over personal and unimportant matters, it at least brings all classes of people together in doing so. People who read the same newspaper are bound to feel neighborly, even though they may never meet one another, even though they live thousands of miles apart.

I have learned much from newspapers and from newspaper men. I think I have met all kinds of newspaper reporters, not only those who work on the conservative, but also those on the so-called "yellow" journals, and what I have seen of them convinces me that no class of men in the community work harder or more faithfully to perform the difficult tasks to which they are assigned or, considering all the circumstances, perform their work better. I confess that I have grown to the point where I always like to meet and talk with newspaper men, because they know the world, they know what is going on, and they know men. I have frequently been amazed, in talking with newspaper men, to learn the amount of accurate, intimate, and inside information that they had about public and even private matters, and at the insight they showed in weighing and judging public men and their actions.

One thing that has interested me in this connection has been the discovery that practically every large newspaper in the country has in its office a vast array of facts which, out of charity for the individuals concerned or because some public interest would be injured by their publication, never get into print. I am convinced that much more frequently than is supposed newspaper men show their interest in individuals and in the public welfare by what they withhold from publication rather than by what they actually do print. Considering that, under the conditions in which modern newspapers are conducted, any fact which would interest and excite the community has become a kind of commodity which it is the business of the newspaper to gather up and sell, it is surprising that these publications are as discriminating and as considerate as they are.

It seems to me, also, that there has been a noticeable improvement, in recent years, in the method of getting and preparing newspaper reports. I am not sure whether this is due more to the improvement in the class of men who represent the papers or whether it is due to a better understanding on the part of the public as to the methods of dealing with reporters; to a more definite recognition on the part of both the public and the newspapers of the responsible position which the modern newspaper occupies in the complex organization of modern social life. Both private individuals and public men seem to have recognized the fact that, in a country where the life of every individual touches so closely the life of every other, it is in the interest of all that each should work, as it were, in the open, where all the world may know and understand what he is doing.

On the other hand, newspapers have discovered that the only justification for putting any fact in a newspaper is that publication will serve some sort of public interest, and that, in the long run, the value of a piece of news and the reputation of a newspaper that prints it depend upon the absolute accuracy and trustworthiness of its reports.

I have learned something about newspapers and newspaper men from my own experience with them, but I have learned much, also, from the manner in which some of the best known men in this country have been accustomed to deal with them.

On several occasions when I was at the White House, during the time that Colonel Roosevelt was President, I saw him surrounded by half a dozen reporters representing great daily papers. I was greatly surprised on those occasions to observe that the President would talk to these reporters just as frankly and freely about matters pertaining to the government, and his plans and policies, as one partner in business would talk to another partner. While these men, as a result of the interview, would telegraph long dispatches to their papers, I am sure I am safe in saying that the President's confidence was rarely, if ever, betrayed.

It was largely through such frank interviews, taking the whole country into his confidence, as it were, that President Roosevelt was able, in so large a degree, to carry the whole country along with him. Ever since I have known Colonel Roosevelt, one of the things that I have observed in his career has been his ability and disposition to keep in close personal touch with the brightest newspaper men and magazine writers of the country. The newspaper men like him because he understands the conditions under which they work and at the same time recognizes the important part that they and their reports play in the actual, if not in the official, government in a democratic country like ours.

Another noted man whom it has been my privilege to see a good deal of, in connection with newspapers, is Mr. Andrew Carnegie. Not long ago I heard the question asked why it was that, while so many rich men were unpopular, Andrew Carnegie held the love and respect of the common people. From what I have seen of Mr. Carnegie I ascribe a good deal of his popularity to the can dour and good sense with which he deals with reporters and newspapers. Mr. Carnegie has something of Mr. Roosevelt's disposition to take reporters into his confidence. Both Colonel Roosevelt and Mr. Carnegie have known how to use newspapers as a means of letting the world know what they are doing and, in both cases, I believe that the popularity of these men is due, in very large part, to their ability to get into a sort of personal touch with the masses of the people through the newspapers.

In saying this I do not mean that either Colonel Roosevelt or Mr. Carnegie has made use of the newspapers merely for the sake of increasing their personal popularity. The man who is known, and has the confidence of the public, can, if he does not allow himself to be fooled by his own popularity, accomplish a great deal more, perform a much greater public service, than the man whose name is unknown.

In the case of both Colonel Roosevelt and Mr. Carnegie, the names of private individuals have, in each case, become associated in the public mind with certain large public interests. They have come to be, in a very real sense, public men because they have embodied in their persons and their lives certain important public interests. Although, so far as I know, he has never held public office of any kind, Mr. Carnegie is nevertheless a public man. Mr. Roosevelt has not ceased to be identified with certain important public interests; nor has he lost, to any great extent, political power because he is no longer President of the United States. The power which these men exercise upon the minds and hearts of the masses of their fellow countrymen is largely due to the fact that they were able to make the acquaintance of the public through the newspapers.

I have always counted it a great privilege that my name became associated, comparatively early in my life, with what has always seemed to me a great and important public interest, namely, a form of education which seems to me best suited to fit a recently enfranchised race for the duties and responsibilities of citizenship in a republic. The fact that I have been compelled to raise the larger part of the money for establishing this kind of education by direct appeals to the public has made my name pretty generally known. I am glad that this is true, for through the medium of the newspapers I have been able to get in touch with many hundreds and thousands of persons that I would never have been able to reach with my voice. All this has multiplied my powers for service a hundredfold.

Of course it is just as true that a man who has become well known and gained the confidence of the public through the medium of the press can use that power for purely selfish purposes, if he chooses, as that he can use it for the public welfare. I have no doubt that nearly every man who has in any way gained the confidence of the public has every year many opportunities for turning his popularity to private account. Several times in the course of a year, for example, someone makes me a present of shares of stock in some new concern, and, on several occasions, I have had deeds of lots in some land scheme or new town presented to me. I have made it a rule to promptly return every gift of that kind, first of all for the good business reason that it would not pay me to have my name connected with any enterprise, no matter how legitimate it might be, for which I could be personally responsible, and the use of my name, under such circumstances, so far as it influenced anyone to invest in the scheme, would be a fraud.

A second reason is my desire to keep faith with the public, if I may so express it. In order to do that, I have never been able to see how I could afford to give any of my time or attention to any enterprise or any kind of work that did not have to do specifically and directly with the work of Negro education, in the broad spirit in which I have interpreted it. I have already said that, in my early experience with newspaper reporters, I used to think it was necessary to be very careful in letting them know what my ambitions and aims in regard to my work were. But I have learned that it is pretty hard to keep anything from the newspapers that the newspapers think the public wants to know. As a result of what I have learned I try to be perfectly frank with newspaper men. For some years I have made it my custom to talk with them concerning all my plans and everything of a public nature in which I am interested. I talk with them just the same as I would with one of my friends or business acquaintances. When a reporter comes to interview me I tell him what I wish he might publish, and what I wish he would not publish. Frequently I have discovered that the newspaper man understood better than I how to state things in a way that should give the right impression to the public. This seems to be especially true of the Washington correspondents of the great dailies, who, considering the many important matters which they have to handle, exercise, it seems to me, a remarkable discretion as to what should, and should not, be printed.

Let me give an illustration: When Colonel Roosevelt was President, he invited me to come to the White House to read over an important part of one of his annual messages to Congress. The passage of his message in regard to which he consulted me referred to a subject upon which there was great interest at that time, and the newspaper reporters in Washington, and especially those on duty at the White House, had some inkling as to the subject that the President wished to discuss with me. I was with the President for a considerable time. When I came out of the President's office I was at once surrounded by half a dozen newspaper men who wished me to tell them, in detail, just what I had discussed with the President. After some hesitation I made up my mind to try the experiment of being perfectly frank with them. I gave them an outline of what was in the message and went into some detail in regard to our discussion of it. After I had given them the facts, I said to them: "Now, gentlemen, do you think that this is a subject that I ought to give out to the public at this time through the newspapers?"

Each one of them promptly replied that he did not think it was a matter that I ought to give out to the public. The result was that the next day not a single newspaper represented in this conversation had a line concerning the matter which had called me to the White House. This is an example of an experience which I have frequently had in dealing with reporters. If I had tried to hide something from them, or to deceive them, I suspect that some garbled report or misstatement of the facts would have been given to the public in regard to the matter.

There is always a question with me, and I presume there is with most public speakers, as to what is the best form of preparing and delivering a public address, and of getting the gist of it correctly and properly reported through the newspapers. When I first began speaking in public I used to follow the plan to a great extent of committing speeches to memory. This plan, however, I soon gave up. At present I do not commit speeches to memory, except on very important occasions, or when I am to speak on an entirely new subject.

The plan of writing out one's speech and reading it has its advantages, but it also has its disadvantages. A written speech is apt to sound stiff and formal; besides, if one depends upon a manuscript, he will not be able to adapt himself to the occasion. Writing out a speech, however, has the advantage of enabling one to give out something to the newspapers that will be absolutely accurate.

After trying both the plan of committing to memory and of writing out my addresses, I have struck upon a compromise which I find, in my case, answers the purpose pretty well. The plan which I now follow is this: I think out what I want to say pretty carefully. After having done that, I write head lines, or little suggestions that will call my attention to the points that I wish to make in covering my speech. After having thought out the general line of my speech, and then having prepared my head lines, I have for a number of years been accustomed to dictate my speech to a stenographer. By long practice, I have found that, after dictating my speech, I can take my head lines or memorandum sheet and follow the dictation almost exactly when I deliver my address. I give out all or a portion of the dictated address to the newspapers in advance. This the reporters consider an accommodation to them. It insures accuracy and at the same time leaves me free while speaking to throw aside the stiffness and formality that would naturally be necessary in reading an address or in delivering an address that had been committed to memory, and to take advantage of any local interests that would give a more lively color to what I have to say.

Another disadvantage of a written address, or of one committed to memory, is that it is difficult to adapt it to the interests of the immediate audience. To me, talking to an audience is like talking to an individual. Each audience has a personality of its own, and one can no more find two audiences that are exactly alike than he can find two individuals that are exactly alike. The speaker who fails to adapt himself to the conditions, surroundings, and general atmosphere of his audience in a large degree fails, I think, as a speaker. I have found that the best plan is, as I have stated, to study one's subject through and through, to saturate himself with it so that he is master of every detail, and then use head lines as a memorandum.

One of the questions which I suppose, every man who deals with the public has to meet sooner or later is how to deal with a false newspaper report. I have made it a rule never to deny a false report, except under very exceptional circumstances. In nine cases out of ten the denying of the report simply calls attention to the original statement in a way to magnify it. Many people who did not see the original false report will see the denial and will then begin to search for the original report to find out what it was. And then, unfortunately, there are always some newspapers that will spread a report that is not justified by facts, for the purpose of securing a denial or of exciting a discussion. My experience is that it always gives a certain dignity and standing to a slander or a falsehood to deny it. Every one likes a fight, and a controversy will frequently lend a fictitious interest and importance to comparatively trivial circumstances.

During a long period of years in dealing with the public I have been deceived only once in recent years by a newspaper reporter. This was the case of a man on a New York paper who got aboard a train with me, took a seat by my side, and began the discussion of a question which was much before the public at that time. He gave me the impression that he was a man engaged in business and was only incidentally interested in the subject under discussion. I talked with him pretty freely and frankly, as I would with any gentleman. My suspicions were not aroused until I noticed that suddenly and unceremoniously he left the train at a way station. I at once made up my mind that I had been talking, not to an individual but to the public. The next morning a long report of this interview appeared in his paper. I at once informed the managing editor of what had occurred.

I am not sure that anything definite came of my letter, but I believe that one way to improve the methods of the newspapers in dealing with individuals is to protest when you think you have been badly treated.

The important thing, it seems to me, about the newspaper is that it represents the interest and reflects the opinions and intelligence of the average man in the community where the paper is published. The local press reflects the local prejudice. Its failings are the common human failings. Its faults are the faults of the average man in the community, and on the whole it seems to me best that it should be so. If the newspapers were not a reflex of the minds of their readers, they would not be as interesting or as valuable as they are. We should not know the people about us as well as we do. As long as the newspaper exists we not only have a means of understanding how the average man thinks and feels, but we have a medium for reaching and influencing him. People who profess to have no respect for the newspapers as a rule, I fear, have very little understanding or respect for the average man.

The real trouble with the newspapers is that while they frequently exhibit the average man at his worst, they rarely show him at his best. In order to read the best about the average man we must still go to books or to magazines. The newspaper has the advantage that it touches real things and real persons, but it touches them only on the surface. For that reason I have found it safe never to give too much weight to what a newspaper says about a man either good or bad.

Nevertheless I have learned more from newspapers than I have from books. In fact, aside from what I have learned from actual contact with men and with things, I believe I have gained the greatest part of my education from newspapers. I am sure this is so if I include among the newspapers those magazines which deal with current topics. Certainly I have been stimulated in all my thinking more by news than I have by the general statements I have met in books. In this, as in other matters, I like to deal at first-hand with the raw material and this I find in the newspapers more than in books.

Frequently I have heard persons speak of the newspaper as if it's only purpose in making its reports was to tear down rather than build up. It is certainly true that newspapers are rather ruthless in the way in which they seem to bring every man, particularly every public man, to the bar of public opinion and make him explain and justify his work.

Nevertheless it is important that every man who is in any way engaged, directly or indirectly, in performing any kind of public service should never be permitted to forget that the only title to place or privilege that any man enjoys in the community is ultimately based on the service that he performs. I believe that any man, public or private, who meets newspaper men and deals with the newspaper in that spirit, will find himself helped immensely in his work by the press rather than injured.

For my own part I feel sure that I owe much of such success as I have been able to achieve to the sympathy and interest which the newspaper press, North and South, has shown in the work that I have been trying to do. Largely through the medium of the newspapers I have been able to come into contact with the larger public outside of my community and the circle of my immediate friends and, by this means, to make the school at Tuskegee, not merely a private philanthropy, but in the truest sense of that word a public institution, supported by the public and conducted not in the interest of anyone race or section, merely, but in the interest of the whole country.

The Intellectuals and the Boston Mob

It makes a great deal of difference in the life of a race, as it does in the life of an individual, whether the world expects much or little of that individual or of that race. I suppose that every boy and every girl born in poverty have felt at some time in their lives the weight of the world against them. What the people in the communities did not expect them to do it was hard for them to convince themselves that they could do.

After I got so that I could read a little, I used to take a great deal of satisfaction in the lives of men who had risen by their own efforts from poverty to success. It is a great thing for a boy to be able to read books of that kind. It not only inspires him with the desire to do something and make something of his life, but it teaches him that success depends upon his ability to do something useful, to perform some kind of service that the world wants.

The trouble in my case, as in that of other colored boys of any age, was that the stories we read in school were all concerned with the success and achievements of white boys and men. Occasionally I spoke to some of my schoolmates in regard to the characters of whom I had read, but they invariably reminded me that the stories I had been reading had to do with the members of another race. Sometimes I tried to argue the matter with them, saying that what others had done some of us might also be able to do, and that the lack of a past in our race was no reason why it should not have a future.

They replied that our case was entirely different. They said, in effect, that because of our color and because we carried in our faces the brand of a race that had been in slavery, white people did not want us to succeed.

In the end I usually wound up the discussion by recalling the life of Frederick Douglass, reminding them of the high position which he had reached and of the great service which he had performed for his own race and for the cause of human freedom in the long anti-slavery struggle.

Even before I had learned to read books or newspapers, I remember hearing my mother and other colored people in our part of the country speak about Frederick Douglass's wonderful life and achievements. I heard so much about Douglass when I was a boy that one of the reasons why I wanted to go to school and learn to read was that I might read for myself what he had written and said. In fact, one of the first books that I remember reading was his own story of his life, which Mr. Douglass published under the title of "My Life and Times." This book made a deep impression upon me, and I read it many times.

After I became a student at Hampton, under Gen. Samuel C. Armstrong, I heard a great deal more about Frederick Douglass, and I followed all his movements with intense interest. At the same time I began to learn something about other prominent and successful colored men who were at that time the leaders of my race in the United States. These were such men as Congressmen John M. Langston, of Virginia; United States Senator Blanche K. Bruce, of Mississippi; Lieut. Gov. P.B.S. Pinchback, of Louisiana; Congressman John R. Lynch of Mississippi; and others whose names were household words among the masses of colored people at that time. I read with the greatest eagerness everything I could get hold of regarding the prominent Negro characters of that period, and was a faithful student of their lives and deeds. Later on I had the privilege of meeting and knowing all of these men, but at that time I little thought that it would ever be my fortune to meet and know any of them.

On one occasion, when I happened to be in Washington, I heard that Frederick Douglass was going to make a speech in a near-by town. I had never seen him nor heard him speak, so I took advantage of the opportunity. I was profoundly impressed both by the man and by the address, but I did not dare approach even to shake hands with him. Some three or four years after I had organized the Tuskegee Institute I invited Mr. Douglass to make a visit to the school and to speak at the commencement exercises of the school He came and spoke to a great audience, many of whom had driven thirty or forty miles to hear the great orator and leader of the race. In the course of time I invited all of the prominent colored men whose names I have mentioned, as well as others, to come to Tuskegee and speak to our students and to the colored people in our community.

As a matter of course, the speeches (as well as the writings) of most of these men were concerned for the most part with the past history, or with the present and future political problems, of the Negro race. Mr. Douglass's great life-work had been in the political agitation that led to the destruction of slavery. He had been the great defender of the race, and in the struggle to win from Congress and from the country at large the recognition of the Negro's rights as a man and a citizen he had played an important part. But the long and bitter political struggle in which he had engaged against slavery had not prepared Mr. Douglass to take up the equally difficult task of fitting the Negro for the opportunities and responsibilities of freedom. The same was true to a large extent of other Negro leaders. At the time when I met these men and heard them speak I was invariably impressed, though young and inexperienced, that there was something lacking in their public utterances. I felt that the millions of Negroes needed something more than to be reminded of their sufferings and of their political rights; that they needed to do something more than merely to defend themselves.

Frederick Douglass died in February, 1895. In September of the same year I delivered an address in Atlanta at the Cotton States Exposition.

I spoke in Atlanta to an audience composed of leading Southern white people, Northern white people, and members of my own race. This seemed to me to be the time and the place, without condemning what had been done, to emphasize what ought to be done. I felt that we needed a policy, not of destruction, but of construction; not of defense, but of aggression; a policy, not of hostility or surrender, but of friendship and advance. I stated, as vigorously as I was able, that usefulness in the community where we resided was our surest and most potent protection.

One other point which I made plain in this speech was that, in my opinion, the Negro should seek constantly in every manly, straightforward manner to make friends of the

White man by whose side he lived, rather than to content himself with seeking the good-will of some man a thousand miles away.

While I was fully convinced, in my own mind, that the policy which I had outlined was the correct one, I was not at all prepared for the widespread interest with which my words were received.

I received telegrams and congratulations from all parts of the country and from many persons whose names I did not know or had heard of only indirectly through the newspapers or otherwise. Very soon invitations began to come to me in large numbers to speak before all kinds of bodies and on all kinds of subjects. In many cases I was offered for my addresses what appeared to me almost fabulous sums. Some of the lecture bureaus offered me as high as $300 and $400 a night for as long a period as I would speak for them. Among other things which came to me was an offer from a prominent Western newspaper of $1,000 and all expenses for my services if I would describe for it a famous prize-fight.

I was invited, here and there, to take part in political campaigns, especially in states where the Negro vote was important. Lecture bureaus not only urged upon me the acceptance of their offers through letters, but even sent agents to Tuskegee. Newspapers and magazines made generous offers to me to write special articles for them. I decided, however, to wait until I could get my bearings. Apparently the words which I had spoken at Atlanta, simple and almost commonplace as they were, had touched a deep and responsive chord in the public mind.

One of the most surprising results of my Atlanta speech was the number of letters, telegrams, and newspaper editorials that came pouring in upon me from all parts of the country, demanding that I take the place of "leader of the Negro people," left vacant by Frederick Douglass's death, or assuming that I had already taken this place. Until these suggestions began to pour in upon me, I never had the remotest idea that I should be selected or looked upon, in any such sense as Frederick Douglass had been, as a leader of the Negro people. I was at that time merely a Negro school teacher in a rather obscure industrial school. I had devoted all my time and attention to the work of organizing and bringing into existence the Tuskegee Institute, and I did not know just what the functions and duties of a leader were, or what was expected of him on the part of the colored people or of the rest of the world. It was not long, however, before I began to find out what was expected of me in the new position into which a sudden newspaper notoriety seemed to have thrust me.

I was not a little embarrassed, when I first began to appear in public, to find myself continually referred to as "the successor of Frederick Douglass." Wherever I spoke-whether in the North or in the South, I found, thanks to the advertising I had received, that large audiences turned out to hear me.

It has been interesting, and sometimes amusing, to note the amount and variety of disinterested advice received by a man whose name is to any extent before the public. During the time that my Atlanta address was, so to speak, under discussion, and almost every day since, I have received one or more letters advising me and directing my course in regard to matters of public interest.

One day I receive a letter, or my attention is called to some newspaper editorial, in which I am advised to stick to my work at Tuskegee and put aside every other interest that I may have in the advancement of my race. A day or two later I may receive a letter, or read an editorial in a newspaper, saying that I am making a mistake in confining my attention entirely to Tuskegee, to Negro education, or even to the Negro in the United States. It has been frequently urged upon me, for example, that I ought, in some way or other, to extend the work that we are trying to do at Tuskegee to Africa or to the West Indies, where Negroes are a larger part of the population than in this country.

There has been a small number of white people and an equally small number of colored people who felt, after my Atlanta speech, that I ought to branch out and discuss political questions, putting emphasis upon the importance of political activity and success for the members of my race. Others, who thought it quite natural that, while I was in the South, I should not say anything that would be offensive, expected that I would cut loose in the North and denounce the Southern people in a way to keep alive and intensify the sectional differences which had sprung up as a result of slavery and the Civil War. Still others thought that there was something lacking in my style of defending the Negro. I went too much into the facts and did not say enough about the Rights of Man and the Declaration of Independence.

When these people found that I did not change my policy as a result of my Atlanta speech, but stuck to my old line of argument, urging the importance of education of the hand, the head, and the heart, they were thoroughly disappointed. So far as my addresses made it appear that the race troubles in the South could be solved by education rather than by political measures, they felt that I was putting the emphasis in the wrong place.

I confess that all these criticisms and suggestions were not without effect upon my mind. But, after thinking the matter all over, I decided that, pleasant as it might be to follow the program that was laid out for me, I should be compelled to stick to my original job and work out my salvation along the lines that I had originally laid down for myself.

My determination to stand by the program which I had worked out during the years that I had been at Tuskegee and which I had expressed in my Atlanta speech, soon brought me into conflict with a small group of colored people who sometimes styled themselves "The Intellectuals," at other times "The Talented Tenth." As most of these men were graduates of Northern colleges and made their homes for the most part in the North, it was natural enough, I suppose, that they should feel that leadership in all race matters should remain, as heretofore, in the North. At any rate, they were opposed to any change from the policy of uncompromising and relentless antagonism to the South so long as there seemed to them to be anything in Southern conditions wrong or unjust to the Negro.

My life in the South and years of study and effort in connection with actual and concrete problems of Southern life had given me a different notion, and I believed that I had gained some knowledge and some insight which they were not able to obtain in the same degree at a distance and from the study of books.

The first thing to which they objected was my plan for the industrial education of the Negro. It seemed to them that in teaching colored people to work with the hands I was making too great a concession to public opinion in the South. Some of them thought, probably, that I did not really believe in industrial education myself; but in any case they were opposed to any "concession," no matter whether industrial education was good or bad.

According to their way of looking at the matter, the Southern white man was the natural enemy of the Negro, and any attempt, no matter for what purpose, to gain his sympathy or support must be regarded as a kind of treason to the race.

All these matters furnished fruitful subjects for controversy, in all of which the college graduates that I have referred to were naturally the leaders. The first thing that such a young man was tempted to do after leaving college was, it seems, to start out on a lecturing tour, traveling about from one town to another for the purpose of discussing what are known as "race" subjects.

I remember one young man in particular who graduated from Yale University and afterward took a post graduate course at Harvard, and who began his career by delivering a series of lectures on "The Mistakes of Booker T. Washington." It was not long, however, before he found that he could not live continuously on my mistakes. Then he discovered that in all his long schooling he had not fitted himself to perform any kind of useful and productive labor. After he had failed in several other directions he appealed to me, and I tried to find something for him to do. It is pretty hard, however, to help a young man who has started wrong. Once he gets the idea that because he has crammed his head full with mere book knowledge-the world owes him a living, it is hard for him to change. The last I heard of the young man in question, he was trying to eke out a miserable existence as a book agent while he was looking about for a position somewhere with the Government as a janitor or for some other equally humble occupation.

When I meet cases, as I frequently do, of such unfortunate and misguided young men as I have described, I cannot but feel the most profound sympathy for them, because I know that they are not wholly to blame for their condition. I know that, in nine cases out of ten, they have gained the idea at some point in their career that, because they are Negroes, they are entitled to the special sympathy of the world, and they have thus got into the habit of relying on this sympathy rather than on their own efforts to make their way.

In college they gave little thought or attention to preparing for any definite task in the world, but started out with the idea of preparing themselves to solve the race problem. They learned in college a great deal about the history of New England freedom; their minds were filled with the traditions of the anti-slavery struggle; and they came out of college with the idea that the only thing necessary to solve at once every problem in the South was to apply the principles of the Declaration of Independence and the Bill of Rights. They had learned in their studies little of the actual present-day conditions in the South and had not considered the profound difference between the political problem and the educational problem, between the work of destruction and of construction, as it applies to the task of race building.

Among the most trying class of people with whom I come in contact are the persons who have been educated in books to the extent that they are able, upon every occasion, to quote a phrase or a sentiment from Shakespeare, Milton, Cicero, or some other great writer. Every time any problem arises they are on the spot with a phrase or a quotation. No problem is so difficult that they are not able, with a definition or abstraction of some kind, to solve it. I like phrases, and I frequently find them useful and convenient in conversation, but I have not found in them a solution for many of the actual problems of life.

In college they studied problems and solved them on paper. But these problems had already been solved by some one else, and all that they had to do was to learn the answers. They had never faced any unsolved problems in college, and all that they had learned had not taught them the patience and persistence which alone solve real problems.

I remember hearing this fact illustrated in a very apt way by a colored minister some years ago. After great sacrifice and effort he had constructed in the South a building to be used for the purpose of sheltering orphans and aged colored women. After this minister had succeeded in getting his building constructed and paid for, a young colored man came to inspect it and at once began pointing out the defects in the building. The minister listened patiently for some time and then, turning to the young man, he said: "My friend, you have an advantage over me." Then he paused and looked at the young man, and the young man looked inquiringly at the minister, who continued: "I am not able to find fault with any building which you have constructed."

Perhaps I ought to add, in order that my statements may not be misleading, that I do not mean to say that the type of college man that I have described is confined to the members of my own race. Every kind of life produces its own peculiar kind of failures, and they are not confined to one race. It would be quite as wrong for me to give the impression that the description which I have given applies to all colored graduates of New England or other colleges and to none others. As a matter of fact, almost from the beginning we have had men from these colleges at Tuskegee; I have come into contact with others at work in various institutions of the South; and I have found that some of the sanest and most useful workers were those who had graduated at Harvard and other New England colleges. Those to whom I have referred are the exception rather than the rule.

There is another class of colored people who make a business of keeping the troubles, the wrongs, and the hardships of the Negro race before the public. Having learned that they are able to make a living out of their troubles, they have grown into the settled habit of advertising their wrongs, partly because they want sympathy and partly because it pays. Some of these people do not want the Negro to lose his grievances, because they do not want to lose their jobs.

A story told me by a colored man in South Carolina will illustrate how people sometimes get into situations where they do not like to part with their grievances. In a certain community there was a colored doctor of the old school, who knew little about modern ideas of medicine, but who in some way had gained the confidence of the people and had made considerable money by his own peculiar methods of treatment. In this community there was an old lady who happened to be pretty well provided with this world's goods and who thought that she had a cancer.

For twenty years she had enjoyed the luxury of having this old doctor treat her for that cancer. As the old doctor became thanks to the cancer and to other practice pretty well to do, he decided to send one of his boys to a medical college. After graduating from the medical school, the young man returned home, and his father took a vacation. During this time the old lady who was afflicted with the" cancer" called in the young man, who treated her; within a few weeks the cancer (or what was supposed to be the cancer) disappeared, and the old lady declared herself well.

When the father of the boy returned and found the patient on her feet and perfectly well, he was outraged. He called the young man before him and said: "My son, I find that you have cured that cancer case of mine. Now, son, let me tell you something. I educated you on that cancer. I put you through high school, through college, and finally through the medical school on that cancer. And now you, with your new ideas of practicing medicine, have come here and cured that cancer. Let me tell you, son, you have started all wrong. How do you expect to make a living practicing medicine in that way?"

I am afraid that there is a certain class of race problem solvers who don't want the patient to get well, because as long as the disease holds out they have not only an easy means of making a living, but also an easy medium through which to make themselves prominent before the public.

My experience is that people who call themselves "The Intellectuals" understand theories, but they do not understand things. I have long been convinced that, if these men could have gone into the South and taken up and become interested in some practical work which would have brought them in touch with people and things, the whole world would have looked very different to them. Bad as conditions might have seemed at first, when they saw that actual progress was being made, they would have taken a more hopeful view of the situation.

But the environment in which they were raised had cast them in another world. For them there was nothing to do but insist on the application of the abstract principles of protest. Indignation meetings in Faneuil Hall, Boston, became at one time so frequent as to be a nuisance. It would not have been so bad if the meetings had been confined to the subjects for which they were proposed; but when "The Intellectuals" found that the Southern people rarely, if ever, heard of their protests and, if they did hear of them, paid no attention to them, they began to attack the persons nearer home.

They began to attack the people of Boston because they said that the people of Boston had lost interest in the cause of the Negro. After attacking the friends of the Negro elsewhere, particularly all those who happened to disagree with them as to the exact method of aiding the Negro, they made me a frequent and favorite object of attack not merely for the reasons which I have already stated, but because they felt that if they attacked me in some particularly violent way it would surprise people and attract attention. There is no satisfaction in holding meetings and formulating protests unless you can get them into the newspapers. I do not really believe that these people think as badly of the person whom they have attacked at different times as their words would indicate.

They are merely using them as a sort of sounding board or megaphone to make their own voices carry farther. The persistence and success with which these men sought this kind of advertising has led the general public to believe the number of my opponents among the Negro masses to be much larger than it actually is.

A few years ago when I was in Boston and the subject of those who were opposing me was under discussion, a colored friend of mine, who did not belong to the so called "Talented Tenth," used an illustration which has stuck in my mind. He was originally from the South, although he had lived in Boston for a number of years. He said that he had once lived in Virginia, near a fashionable hotel. One day a bright idea struck him and he went to the proprietor of the hotel and made a bargain to furnish him regularly with a large number of frogs, which were in great demand as a table delicacy. The proprietor asked him how many he could furnish. My friend replied that he felt quite sure that he could furnish him with a cartload, if necessary, once a week. The bargain was concluded. The man was to deliver at the hotel the following day as large a number of frogs as possible.

When he appeared, my friend had just six frogs. The proprietor looked at the frogs, and then at my friend.

"Where are the others?" he said.

"Well, it is this way," my friend replied; "for months I had heard those bull-frogs in a pond near my house, and they made so much noise that I supposed there were at least a million of them there. When I came to investigate, however, I found that there were only six."

Inspired by their ambition to "make themselves heard," and, as they said, compel the public to pay attention to their grievances, this little group kept up their agitation in various forms and at different places, until their plans culminated one night in Boston in 1903. To convince the public how deep and sincere they were in their peculiar views, and how profoundly opposed they were to every one who had a different opinion, they determined to do something desperate. The colored citizens of Boston had asked me to deliver an address before them in one of their largest churches. The meeting was widely advertised, and there was a large audience present.

Unknown to any of my colored friends in Boston, this group, who, as I have stated, were mostly graduates of New England colleges, organized a mob to disturb the meeting and to break it up if possible. The presiding officer at the meeting was the Hon. William H. Lewis, a graduate of Amherst College and of the Harvard Law School. Various members of the group were scattered in different parts of the church. In addition to themselves there were present in the audience and this, better than anything else, shows how far they had been carried in their fanaticism-some of the lowest men and women from vile dens in Boston, whom they had in some way or other induced to come in and help them disturb the meeting.

As soon as I began speaking, the leaders, stationed in various parts of the house, began asking questions. In this and in a number of other ways they tried to make it impossible for me to speak. Naturally the rest of the audience resented this, and eventually it was necessary to call in the police and arrest the disturbers.

Of course, as soon as the disturbance was over, most of those who had participated in it were ashamed of what they had done. Many of those who had classed themselves with "The Intellectuals" before, hastened to disavow any sympathy with the methods of the men who had organized the disturbance. Many who had before been lukewarm in their friendship became my closest friends. Of course the two leaders, who were afterward convicted and compelled to serve a sentence in the Charles Street Jail, remained unrepentant. They tried to convince themselves that they had been made martyrs in a great cause, but they did not get much encouragement in this notion 'from other colored people, because it was not possible for them to make clear just what the cause was for which they had suffered.

The masses of colored people in Boston and in the United States indorsed me by resolution and condemned the disturbers of the meeting. The Negro newspapers as a whole were scathing in their criticism of them. For weeks afterward my mail was filled with letters from colored people, asking me to visit various sections and speak to the people.

I was intensely interested in observing the results of this disturbance. For one thing I wanted to find out whether a principle in human nature that I had frequently observed elsewhere would prove true in this case.

I have found in my dealings with the Negro race-and I believe that the same is true of all races that the only way to hold people together is by means of a constructive, progressive program. It is not argument, nor criticism, nor hatred, but work in constructive effort that gets hold of men and binds them together in a way to make them rally to the support of a common cause.

Before many weeks had passed, these leaders began to disagree among themselves. Then they began to quarrel, and one by one they began to drop away. The result is that, at the present time, the group has been almost completely dispersed and scattered. Many of "The Intellectuals" today do not speak to one another.

The most surprising thing about this disturbance, I confess, is the fact that it was organized by the very people who have been loudest in condemning the Southern white people because they had suppressed the expression of opinion on public questions and denied the Negro the right of free speech.

As a matter of fact, I have talked to audiences in every part of this country; I have talked to colored audiences in the North and to white audiences in the South; I have talked to audiences of both races in all parts of the South; everywhere I have spoken frankly and, I believe, sincerely on everything that I had in my mind and heart to say. When I had something to say about the white people I said it to the white people; when I had something to say about colored people I said it to colored people. In all these years that is the curious thing about it-no effort has been made, so far as I can remember, to interrupt or to break up a meeting at which I was present until it was attempted by "The Intellectuals" of my own race in Boston.

I have gone to some length to describe this incident because it seems to me to show dearly the defects of that type of mind which the so-called "Intellectuals" of the race represent.

I do not wish to give the impression by what I have said that, behind all the intemperance and extravagance of these men, there is not a vein of genuine feeling and even at times of something like real heroism. The trouble is that all this fervor and intensity is wasted on side issues and trivial matters. It does not connect itself with anything that is helpful and constructive. These crusaders, as nearly as I can see, are fighting windmills.

The truth is, I suspect, as I have already suggested, that "The Intellectuals" live too much in the past. They know books but they do not know men. They know a great deal about the slavery controversy, for example, but they know almost nothing about the Negro. Especially are they ignorant in regard to the actual needs of the masses of the colored people in the South today.

There are some things that one individual can do for another, and there are some things that one race can do for another. But, on the whole, every individual and every race must work out its own salvation. Let me add that if one thing more than another has taught me to have confidence in the masses of my own people it has been their willingness (and even eagerness) to learn and their disposition to help themselves and depend upon themselves as soon as they have learned how to do so.

A Commencement Oration on Cabbages

One of the advantages of a new people or a new race, such as, to a very large extent, the American Negroes are, consists in the fact that they are not hampered, as other peoples sometimes are, by tradition. In the matter of education, for example, Negroes in the South are not hampered by tradition, because they have never had any worth speaking of. As a race we are free, if we so choose, to adopt at once the very latest and most approved methods of education, because we are not held back by any worn out tradition; and we have few bad educational habits to be got rid of before we can start in to employ newer and better methods.

I have sometimes regarded it as a fortunate circumstance that I never studied pedagogy. If I had done so, every time I attempted to do anything in a new way I should have felt compelled to reckon with all the past, and in my case that would have taken so much time that I should never have got anywhere. As it was, I was perfectly free to go ahead and do whatever seemed necessary at the time, without reference to whether that same thing had ever been done by anyone else at any previous time or not. As an illustration of the way in which too much learning will hamper a man who finds himself in the presence of a new problem; one not in the books. I recall the fate of the young Harvard graduate who was a teacher at Tuskegee for one or two sessions several years ago. This young man had very little practical experience as a teacher, but he had made a special study of the subject of education while he was in college; largely because of his high scholarship, he was given a position as teacher of education at Tuskegee.

I am afraid that, until he arrived, we knew very little about pedagogy at Tuskegee. He proceeded to enlighten us, however. He lectured and preached to us about Comenius, Rousseau, Pestalozzi, and all the others, and what he said was very interesting. The trouble was that he made a complete failure in his own classes. But that was not all. We were trying to fit our students to go out as teachers in the rural districts. I pointed out to him that if he were going to help them to any great extent it would be necessary for him to study the conditions of the country people and to get acquainted with some of the actual problems of a small, rural Negro community. He did not seem to regard that as important, because, as he said, the principles were the same in every case and all that was necessary was to apply them.

I told him, then, that I thought we had worked out at Tuskegee a number of definite methods of dealing with the problems of these rural communities, and suggested to him that if he wanted to teach the general principles he ought to work out a theory for these methods, so that the teachers and students might understand the principles under which they were actually working. He did not seem to take this suggestion seriously. It seemed absurd to him that anyone should come down to the Black Belt of Alabama to look for anything new in the matter of education. In short, his mind was so burdened with the traditions and knowledge of other systems of education that he could not see anything in any kind of education that seemed to break with these traditions. In fact, he seemed to feel, whenever he did discover anything new or strange about the methods that we employed, that there must be something either wrong or dangerous about them.

My own early experience was, I suppose, like that of most other teachers; I picked up quite naturally those methods of teaching that were in vogue around me or that seemed to be prescribed by the textbooks. My method consisted in asking pupils to learn what was in the book, and then requiring them to recite it.

I shall long remember the time when the folly and uselessness of much of the old time method of teaching first fairly dawned upon me. I was teaching a country school near my old home in West Virginia. This school was located near a piece of land that was wet and marshy, but nevertheless beautiful in appearance. It was June and the day was hot and sultry; when the usual recess or playtime came, I was as anxious as the children were to get outside of the close and stuffy school room into the open air. That day I prolonged the playtime to more than twice the usual period.

The hour previous to recess had been employed by me in trying to get a class of children interested in what proved to be a rather stupid geography lesson. I had been asking my pupils a lot of dull and tiresome questions, getting them to define and name lakes, capes, peninsulas, islands, and so forth. Naturally the answers of the children were quite as dull and stupid as the questions.

As soon as the children were out of doors at playtime, however, they all, as if by common instinct, scampered off into the marshes. In a few seconds they were wading in the cool water, jumping about in the fragrant grass, and enjoying themselves in a way that was in striking contrast to the dull labor of the geography lesson. I soon became infected with the general fever; and in a few minutes I found myself following the children at a rapid rate and entering into the full enjoyment of the contrast between the dull, dead atmosphere of the school room and the vivid tingling sense of the living outdoors.

We had not been out of the school house and away from the old geography lesson long before one of the boys who had been among the dullest in his recitation in the school room became the leader of a sort of exploring party. Under his leadership we began to discover, as we waded along the stream, dozens of islands, capes, and peninsulas, with here and there a little lake or bay, which, as some of the pupils pointed out, would furnish a safe harbor for ships if the stream were only large enough. Soon every one of the children was busy pointing out and naming the natural divisions of land and water. And then, after a few days, we got pieces of wood and bark and let them float down the stream; we imagined them to be great ships carrying their cargoes of merchandise from one part of the world to another. We studied the way the stream wandered about in the level land, and noticed how the little sand bars and the corresponding harbors were formed by the particles of sand and earth which were rolled down by the stream. We located cities on these harbors, and tried to find water power where we might build up manufacturing centers.

Before long I discovered that, quite unconsciously, we had taken up again the lessons in the school room and were studying geography after a new fashion. This time, however, we found a real joy and zest in the work, and I think both teacher and pupils learned more geography in that short period than they ever learned in the same space of time before or since.

For the first time the real difference between studying about things through the medium of books, and studying things themselves without the medium of books, was revealed to me. The children in this recess period had gained more ideas in regard to the natural divisions of the earth than they would have gained in several days by merely studying geography inside the school room. To be sure, they had not learned the names, the locations, nor the definitions of the capes, bays, and islands, but they had learned what was more important to think capes, islands, and peninsulas. From that time on they found no difficulty and were really greatly interested in recognizing the natural divisions of land and water wherever they met them.

The lesson that I learned thus early in my experience as a teacher I have never forgotten. In all my work at Tuskegee Institute I have lost no opportunity to impress upon our teachers the importance of training their students to study, analyze, and compare actual things, and to use what they have learned in the school room and in the textbook, to enable them to observe, think about, and deal with the objects and situations of actual life.

Not long ago I visited the class room of a new teacher at Tuskegee, who was conducting a class in measurements. This teacher had insisted that each member of the class should commit to memory the tables of measurement, and when I came in they were engaged in reciting, singsong, something that sounded like a sort of litany composed of feet, yards, rods, acres, gills, pints, quarts, ounces, pounds, and the rest. I looked on at this proceeding for a few minutes; then a happy thought occurred to me and I asked the teacher to let me take the class in hand. I began by asking if anyone in the class had ever measured the class room 1ll which they were sitting. There was a dumb silence. Then I asked if anyone had ever marked off an acre of actual land, had ever measured a gill of water, or had ever weighed an ounce or a pound of sugar. Not a hand was raised in reply.

Then I told the teacher that I would like to take charge of the class for a few days. Before the week was over I had seen to it that every member of the class had supplied himself with a rule or a measure of some sort. Under my direction the students measured the class room and found what it would cost to paint the walls of the room.

From the class room we went to a part of the farm where the students were engaged in planting sweet potatoes. Soon we had an acre of sweet potatoes measured off. We computed the number of bushels raised on that acre and calculated the cost and profit of raising them.

Before the week was over the whole class had been through the boarding department, where they had an opportunity to weigh actual sugar. From the steward we obtained some interesting figures as to how much sugar was used a day; then we computed how much was used by each student. We went to the farm again and weighed a live pig, and I had the class find out the selling price of pork on that particular day, not in Chicago, but in Alabama. I had them calculate the amount that, not an imaginary pig or a pig in Chicago, the pig that they had weighed would bring that day in the local market. It took some time to go through all these operations, but I think that it paid to do so. Besides, it was fun. It was fun for me, and it was a great deal more fun for the students. Incidentally the teacher got an awakening and learned a lesson that I dare say he has never forgotten.

At the present time all teachers in the academic studies are expected to make a careful study of the work carried on by the students in the industries. Nearly every day, for example, some class in mathematics goes under the charge of a teacher, into the shops or the dairy or out on the farm to get its problems in mathematics at first hand. Students are sent from the English classes to look up the history of some trade, or some single operation performed by students in the shop, and to write out an account of that trade or that operation for the benefit of the other members of the class. In such cases attention is paid not merely to the form in which the report is written, but more especially to the accuracy and clearness of the statement. The student who prepares that kind of paper is writing something in which other students have a practical interest, and if students are not accurate there are always one or more students in the class who know enough about the subject to criticize and correct the statements made. The student in this case finds himself dealing with live matters, and he naturally feels responsibility for the statements that he makes a responsibility that he would not feel if he were merely putting together facts that he had gathered from some encyclopedia or other second hand source of information.

In emphasizing the importance of studying things rather than books, I do not mean to underrate the importance of studying history, general literature, or any of the other so called cultural studies. I do think, however, that it is important that young men and young women should first of all get clear and definite ideas of things right about them, because these are the ideas by which they are going to measure and interpret things farther removed from their practical interests. To young, inexperienced minds there seems to be a kind of fatal charm about the vague, the distant, and the mysterious.

In the early days of freedom, when education was a new thing, the boy who went away to school had a very natural human ambition to be able to come back home in order to delight and astonish the old folks with the new and strange things that he had learned. If he could speak a few words in some strange tongue that his parents had never heard before, or read a few sentences out of a book with strange and mysterious characters, he was able to make them very proud and happy. There was a constant temptation therefore for schools and teachers to keep everything connected with education in a sort of twilight realm of the mysterious and supernatural. Quite unconsciously they created in the minds of their pupils the impression that a boy or a girl who had passed through certain educational forms and ceremonies had been initiated into some sort of secret knowledge that was inaccessible to the rest of the world. Connected with this was the notion that because a man had passed through these educational forms and ceremonies he had somehow become a sort of superior being set apart from the rest of the world; a member of the "Talented Tenth" or some other ill defined and exclusive caste.

Nothing, in my opinion, could be more fatal to the success of a student or to the cause of education than the general acceptance of any such ideas. In the long run it will be found that neither black people nor white people want such an education for their children, and they will not support schools that give it.

My experience has taught me that the surest way to success in education, and in any other line for that matter, is to stick close to the common and familiar things; things that concern the greater part of the people the greater part of the time.

I want to see education as common as grass, and as free for all as sunshine and rain.

The way to open opportunities of education for every one, however, is to teach things that every one needs to know. I venture to say that anything in any school, taught with the object of fitting students to produce and serve food, for example, will win approval and popularity for the school. The reason is simple: every human being is interested, several times a day, in the subject of food; and a large part of the world is interested, either directly or indirectly, in its production and sale.

Not long ago I attended the closing exercises of a high school in a community composed mainly of people in the humble walks of life. The general theme of the graduating addresses was "An Imaginary Trip to Europe." Of course the audience was bored, and I was not surprised that a number of people went to sleep. As a matter of fact, I do not think that the parents of a single student who delivered one of these addresses had ever been to Europe or will have an opportunity to go at any time in the near future. The thing did not touch a common chord. It was too far removed from all the practical, human interests of which they had any experience. The average family in America is not ordinarily engaged in traveling through Europe for any large part of the time. Besides that, none of the members of this graduating class had ever been to Europe; consequently they were not writing about something of which they had any real knowledge.

Some years ago, in an effort to bring our rhetorical and commencement exercises into a little closer touch with real things, we tried the experiment at Tuskegee of having students write papers on some subject of which they had first hand knowledge. As a matter of fact, I believe that Tuskegee was the first institution that attempted to reform its commencement exercises in this particular direction. Ordinarily, at the closing exercises of a high school, graduates are expected to stand up on the platform and, out of all their inexperience, instruct their elders how to succeed in life. We were fortunate at Tuskegee, in the thirty seven industries carried on there and in the thousand acres of land that are cultivated, to be able to give our students, in addition to their general education, a pretty good knowledge of some one of the familiar trades or vocations. They have, therefore, something to talk about in their essays in which all of the audience are interested and with which all are more or less familiar.

Instead of having a boy or girl read a paper on some subject like "Beyond the Alps Lies Italy," we have them explain and demonstrate to the audience how to build a roof, or the proper way to make cheese, or how to hatch chickens with an incubator. Perhaps one of the graduates in the nurses' training school will show how to lend "first aid to the injured." If a girl is taking the course in dairying, she will not only describe what she has learned but will go through, on the platform, the various methods of operating a modern dairy.

Instead of letting a boy tell why one ought to do right, we ask him to tell what he has learned about the feeding of pigs, about their diseases, and the care of them when they are sick. In such a case the student will have the pig on the platform, in order to illustrate the methods of caring for it, and demonstrate to the audience the points that he is trying to make.

One of our students, in his commencement oration last May, gave a description of how he planted and raised an acre of cabbages. Piled high upon the platform by his side were some of the largest and finest cabbages that I have ever seen. He told how and where he had obtained the seed; he described his method of preparing and enriching the soil, of working the land, and harvesting the crop; and he summed up by giving the cost of the whole operation. In the course of his account of this comparatively simple operation, this student had made use of much that he had learned in composition, grammar, mathematics, chemistry, and agriculture. He had not merely woven into his narrative all these various elements that I have referred to, but he had given the audience (which was made up largely of colored farmers from the surrounding country) some useful and practical information in regard to a subject which they understood and were interested in.

I wish that anyone who does not believe it possible to make a subject like cabbages interesting in a commencement oration could have heard the hearty cheers which greeted the speaker when, at the close of his speech, he held up one of the largest cabbages on the platform for the audience to look at and admire. As a matter of fact, there is just as much that is interesting, strange, mysterious, and wonderful; just as much to be learned that is edifying, broadening, and refining in a cabbage as there is in a page of Latin. There is, however, this distinction: it will make very little difference to the world whether one Negro boy, more or less, learns to construe a page of Latin. On the other hand, as soon as one Negro boy has been taught to apply thought and study and ideas to the growing of cabbages, he has started a process which, if it goes on and continues, will eventually transform the whole face of things as they exist in the South today.

I have spoken hitherto about industrial education as a means of connecting education with life. The mere fact that a boy has learned in school to handle a plane or that he has learned something about the chemistry of the soil does not of itself insure that he has gained any new and vital grip upon the life about him. He must at the same time learn to use the knowledge and the training that he has received to change and improve the conditions about him.

In my travels I have come across some very interesting and amusing examples of the failures of teachers to connect their teaching with real things, even when they had a chance right at hand to do so. I recall visiting, not long since, a somewhat noted school which has a department for industrial or hand training, concerning which the officers of the school had talked a great deal. Almost directly in front of the building used for the so called industrial training, I noticed a large brick building in process of erection. In the construction of this building every principle of mechanics taught in the manual training department of this institution was being put into actual use. Notwithstanding this fact, I learned upon inquiry that the teacher had made no attempt to connect what was taught in the manual training department with the work on the brick building across the way. The students had no opportunity to work on this building; they had not visited it with their teacher; they had made no attempt to study the actual problems that had arisen in the course of its construction. As far as they were concerned, there was no relation whatever between the subjects discussed in the class room or the operations carried on in the school shops and the work that was going on outside. All that they were getting in the school was, as far as I was able to learn, just as formal in its character, just as much an educational ceremony, as if they were engaged in diagraming a sentence in English or reciting the parts of a Latin verb.

My experience in the little country school in West Virginia first taught me that it was possible to take teaching outside of the textbook and deal with real things. I have learned from later experience that it is just as important to carry education outside of the school building and take it into the fields, into the homes, and into the daily life of the people surrounding the school.

One of the most important activities of our school at Tuskegee is what we call our Extension Work, in which nearly all the departments of the Institute cooperate. In fact, at the present time more attention, energy, and effort are directed to this work outside the school grounds than to any other branch of work in which the school is engaged.

It would be impossible to describe here all the ramifications or all the various forms which this extension work has taken in recent years. The thing that I wish to emphasize, however, is that we are seeking in this work less to teach (according to the old fashioned notion of teaching) than to improve conditions. We are trying to improve the methods of farming in the country surrounding the school, to change and improve the home life of the farming population, and to establish a model school system not only for Macon but for several other counties in the state.

Perhaps I can best illustrate what I mean when I say that education should connect itself with life, by describing a type of rural school which we have worked out and are seeking to establish in Macon County. There are several schools in our county which might be called, in a certain sense, model country schools. There are nearly fifty communities in which, during the last four or five years, new school buildings have been erected and the school terms lengthened to eight and nine months, largely with funds collected from the Negro farmers under the direction and inspiration of the Tuskegee Institute.

The school that I have in mind is known as the "Rising Star." That is the name that the colored people gave to their church, and that is now the name which has become attached to the little farming community surrounding it. The "Rising Star" community is composed of some score or more of hard working, thrifty, successful Negro farmers; the larger number of whom own their land. There is no wealth in this community; neither is there much, if any, actual want. When I first made the acquaintance of "Rising Star," soon after beginning my work in Alabama, the church which gave the neighborhood its name was an old, dilapidated building, located in a worn out field. It was about the worst looking building that I had ever seen, up to that time, in which to carry on the work of saving men's souls. The condition of the farmhouses, the farms, and the school was in keeping with the condition of the church. This was true also of the minister. He was run down and dilapidated. I used frequently to go Sunday afternoons to hear him preach. His sermons usually held on for about an hour and a half. I remember that I used to study them carefully from week to week in the hope that I might hear him utter, at some time or other, a single sentence that seemed to me to have any practical value to any man, woman, or child in his congregation. I was always disappointed, however. Almost without exception, his sermons related to something that is supposed to have taken place two or three thousand years ago, or else they were made up of a vivid description of the horrors of hell and of the glories of heaven.

Nor far from the church, in another old field, there was a little broken down, unsightly building which had never been touched by paint or whitewash. This was the school. The teacher went with the minister. He had about fifty or sixty children in his school, but the things that he taught them had no more relation to the life of that community than the preacher's sermons had. The weakness and poverty of this little Negro settlement gave me, however, the chance that I wanted. I determined to try there the experiment of building up a model school, one that should actually seek to articulate school life into every day life. I cannot give here a detailed history of this experiment, but I will briefly describe conditions as they exist today.

In place of the old building to which I have referred, there is now a comfortable five room house, resembling in style and general appearance the cottages of the more prosperous farmers of the neighborhood. In this building, surrounded by its garden, with its stable and outbuildings adjoining, the teachers (a man and his wife) live and teach school. All of the rooms, as well as the garden and the stable, are used at different times in the day for teaching pupils the ordinary household duties of a farmer and his wife in that part of the country. Here the children learn to make the beds and to clean, dust, and arrange the sitting room. At noon they go into the kitchen, where they are taught to cook, and into the dining room, where they are taught to lay the table and serve a farmer's meal. The flowers in the front yard are cared for by the children of the school. The vegetables in the garden are those which have been found best adapted to the soil and the needs of the community, and all are planted and cared for by the teachers and students. There is a cow in the barn, and near by are pigs and poultry. The children are taught how to keep the cow house, the pig sty, and the poultry house clean and attractive.

The usual academic studies of a public school are taught in the sitting room. There is, however, this difference: the lessons in arithmetic consist for the most part of problems that have to do with the work that is going on at the time in the house, the garden, or on the farms in the surrounding community. As far as possible, all the English composition work is based on matters connected with the daily life of the community. In addition to the ordinary reading book, pupils in this school spend some time every week reading a little local agricultural newspaper which is published at Tuskegee Institute in the interest of the farmers and schools in the surrounding country.

It is interesting to observe the effect of this teaching on the fathers and mothers of the children who attend this school As soon as fathers discovered that their boys were learning in school to tell how much their pigs, cotton, and corn were worth, the fathers (who had been more or less disappointed with the results of the previous education) felt that the school was really worth something after all. When the girls began to ask their mothers to let them take their dresses to school so that they might learn to patch and mend them, these mothers began to get an entirely new idea of what school meant. Later, when these girls were taught to make simple garments in the school room, their mothers became still more interested. They began to attend the mothers' meetings, and before long there was a genuine enthusiasm in that community; not only for the school and its teachers, but for the household improvement that they taught. The teachers used their influence with the pupils first of all to start a crusade of whitewashing and general cleaning up. Houses that had never known a coat of white wash began to assume a neat and attractive appearance. Better than all else, under the inspiration of this school and of the other schools like it, the whole spirit of this community and the others throughout the county improved.

In a short time a little revolution has taken place in the material, educational, moral, and religious life of "Rising Star." The influence of the school has extended to the minister and to the church. At the present time the sermons that are preached in the church have a vital connection with the moral life of the community. I shall not soon forget one of my recent visits to the church. The minister chose for his text: "The earth is full of Thy riches," and, to illustrate his sermon, he placed on the platform beside the pulpit two bushels of prize corn which he himself had grown on his farm. When he came to expound his text he pointed with pride to his little agricultural exhibit as an indication of the real significance of this sentence from the Bible, which had never before had any definite meaning for him.

Education, such as I have attempted to describe, touches the life of the white man as well as that of the black man. By encouraging Negro farmers to buy land and improve their methods of agriculture, it has multiplied the number of small landowners and increased the tax value of the land. Recent investigations show that the number of Negro landowners in Macon County has grown more in the last five or six years than in the whole previous period since the abolition of slavery. Land that was selling for two and three dollars an acre five years ago is now worth fifteen and twenty dollars an acre. In many parts of the county large plantations have been broken up and sold in small tracts to Negro farmers. At the last annual meeting of the Colored State Teachers' Association, at Birmingham, one teacher from Macon County reported that during the previous year she had organized a club among the farmers through which six hundred acres of land had been purchased in her community.

The struggles of the Negro farmer to lengthen the school term, and the competition among different local communities in the county in the work of building and equipping school buildings, has had the effect of leading the colored people to think about all kinds of matters that concern the welfare of their local communities. For example, Law and Order Leagues have been organized throughout Macon County to assist in enforcing the prohibition law. I do not believe that there is a county in the state where these laws are better enforced than they are in our county at the present time. At the last sitting of the grand jury, only seventeen indictments for all classes of offences were returned. The next session of the criminal court will have, I am told, the smallest docket in its history. I am convinced that there is not a county in that state with so large a Negro population that has so small a number of criminals.

Silently and almost imperceptibly, the work of education has gone on from year to year, slowly changing conditions not only in Macon County, but, to a greater or less extent, in other parts of Alabama and of the South. Education of the kind that I have described has helped to diminish the cost of production on the farm and, at the same time, has steadily increased the wants of the farmers. In other words, it has enabled the Negro farmer to earn more money, and at the same time has given him a reason for doing so.

Farmers have learned to plant gardens, to keep hogs and chickens, and, as far as possible, to raise their own food and fodder. This has led them to increase and sometimes double the annual amount of their labor. Under former conditions, the Negro farmer did not work more than one hundred and fifty days in the year. Merely to plant and harvest the cotton crop, he did not need to do so.

In learning to raise his own provisions, the Negro farmer is no longer dependent to the same extent that he formerly was upon the landlord or the storekeeper. Under the old system the Negro farmer obtained his provisions (or "advances" as they are called) from the storekeeper on credit. In order to carry him through the year until the cotton crop was harvested, the storekeeper borrowed from the local banker. The local banker borrowed, in turn, from the bankers in the city, who, perhaps, obtained a portion of their money from the large money centers of the North. Every time this money passed from one hand to the other, the man who loaned collected toll from the man who borrowed. At the bottom, where the system connected up with the Negro farmer, the planter or storekeeper added something to the costs which had already accumulated-as a sort of insurance, and to pay the expenses of looking after his tenant and seeing that he did his work properly, All this sum, of course, was finally paid by the man on the soil.

The farmer, who has become independent enough to raise his own provisions, or a large portion of them, does not need the supervision of his landlord in his farming operations. At the present time the majority of the Negro farmers in Macon County get their money directly from the bank and pays cash for their provisions. A number have money on deposit in the local banks. The bankers' capital and deposits have increased so that they are not so dependent as they once were upon foreign capital to aid them in carrying on the farming operations in the county.

I do not mean to say that all this has been affected as a direct result of education; I merely wish to point out how intimately the kind of education that we are trying to introduce does, in fact, touch all the fundamental interests of the community.

Naturally the influences that I have referred to do not end with the effects that I have already described. The results obtained have had a reflex influence upon the schools themselves. From the very beginning of my work at Tuskegee I saw that our problem was a double one. We had at first to work out a kind of education which would meet the needs of the masses of the colored people. We had, in the second place, to convince the white people that education could be made of real value to the Negro.

There are many sincere and honest men in the South today who do not believe that education has done or will do the race any good. In my opinion, Negro education will never be an entire success in the South until it gets the sympathy and support of these men. Arguments will not go far toward convincing men like these. It is necessary to show them results.

The people in Macon County are not exceptional in this respect. Until a few years ago I think that I should have described the attitude of a majority of the white people in that county as indifferent. Today I believe that I am safe in saying that nine tenths of the people of Macon County believe in Negro education.

Let me speak of some of the ways in which this attitude of the white people has manifested itself. In the first place, when a school house is to be built or some improvements to be made in the community where the white man lives, he contributes money toward it. One white man in Macon County recently gave $100 toward the erection of such a school. A number of white planters, who a few years ago were indifferent on the subject of Negro education, give annual prizes to the colored people on their plantations. I know one planter who gives an annual prize to the Negro farmer who raises the largest number of bushels of corn on an acre of land. He gives another prize to the colored family which keeps its children in the public school the greatest number of days during the year. He gives another prize to the woman who keeps her front yard in the best condition.

One of the white bankers in Macon County has established an annual prize to be given to the Negro farmer who raises the best oats on a given plot of land. The editor of the county paper gives an annual prize to the school in the county that has the best spelling class, the contest to take place at the annual Macon County Colored Farmers' Fair. At these fairs exhibitions are made of vegetables and grain raised by the children on the school farms. There are also exhibitions of cooking and sewing done by the children in the public schools of the county. Many of the white merchants and white farmers offer prizes for the best exhibition of agricultural products at this fair.

Gradually, as I have said, improved methods of educating the Negro are extending the same influences throughout the state of Alabama and the South. In fact, wherever a school is actually teaching boys and girls to do something that the community wants, it is seldom that that school fails to enlist the interest and cooperation of all the people in that community, whether they be black or white. This is, as definitely as I can express it, my own experience of the way in which educators can and do solve the race problem.

Colonel Roosevelt and What I Have Learned From Him

Some years ago, and not so very many, either I think that I should have been perfectly safe in saying that the highest ambition of the average Negro in America was to hold some sort of office, or to have some sort of job that connected him with the Government. Just to be able to live in the capital city was a sort of distinction, and the man who ran an elevator or merely washed windows in Washington (particularly if the windows or the elevator belonged to the United States Government) felt that he was in some way superior to a man who cleaned windows or ran an elevator in any other part of the country. He felt that he was an office holder!

There has been a great change in this respect in recent years. Many members of my race have learned that, in the long run, they can earn more money and be of more service to the community in almost any other position than that of an employee or office holder under the Government. I know of a number of recent cases in which Negro business men have refused positions of honor and trust in the Government service because they did not care to give up their business interests. Notwithstanding, the city of Washington still has a peculiar attraction and even fascination for the average Negro.

I do not think that I ever shared that feeling of so many others of my race. I never liked the atmosphere of Washington. I early saw that it was impossible to build up a race, of which the leaders were spending most of their time, thought and energy in trying to get into office, or in trying to stay there after they were in. So, for the greater part of my life, I have avoided Washington; and even now I rarely spend a day in that city which I do not look upon as a day practically thrown away.

"I do not like politics...I [seek] no political office of any kind and would accept no position with the Government, unless it were an honorary one."

I do not like politics, and yet, in recent years, I have had some experience in political matters. However, no man who is in the least interested in public questions can escape some sort of connection with politics, I suppose, even if he does not want a political position. As a matter of fact, it was just because it was well known that I sought no political office of any kind and would accept no position with the Government, unless it were an honorary one, that brought my connection with politics about.

One thing that has taught me to dislike politics is the observation that, as soon as any person or thing becomes the subject of political discussion he or it at once assumes in the public mind an importance out of all proportion to his or its real merits. Time and time again I have seen a whole community (sometimes a whole county or state) wrought up to the highest pitch of excitement over the appointment of some person to a political position paying perhaps not more than $25 or $50 a month. At the same time I have seen individuals secure important positions at the head of a manufacturing house or receive an appointment to some important educational position that paid three or four times as much money (or perhaps purchase a farm), where just as much executive ability was required, without arousing public attention or causing comment in the newspapers. I have also seen white men and colored men resign important positions in private life where they were earning much more than they could get under the Government, simply because of the false and mistaken ideas of the importance which they attached to a political position. All this has given me distaste for political life.

In Mississippi, for example, a colored man and his wife had charge, a few years ago, of a post office. In some way or other a great discussion was started in regard to this case, and before long the whole community was in a state of excitement because colored people held that position. A little later the post office was given up and the colored man, Mr. W. W. Cox, started a bank in the same town. At the present time he is the president of the bank and his wife assists him. As bankers they receive three or four times as much pay as they received from the post office. The bank is patronized by both white and colored people and, when last I heard of it, was in a flourishing condition. As president of a Negro bank, Mr. Cox is performing a much greater service to the community than he could possibly render as postmaster. There are, no doubt, a great many people in his town who would be able to fill the position of postmaster, but there are very few who could start and successfully carry on an institution that would so benefit the community as a Negro bank. While he was postmaster, merely because his office was a political one, Mr. Cox occupied for some time the attention of the whole state of Mississippi; in fact, he (or rather his wife) was for a brief space almost a national figure. Now he is occupying a much more remunerative and important position in private life, but I do not think that he has attracted attention to amount to anything outside of the community in which he lives.

The effect of the excitement about this case has been greatly to exaggerate the importance of holding a Government position. The average Negro naturally feels that there must be some special value to him as an individual, as well as to his race, in holding a position which white people don't want him to hold, simply because he is a Negro. It leads him to believe that it is in some way more honorable or respectable to work for the Government as an official than for the community and himself as a private citizen.

Because of these facts, as well as for other reasons, I have never sought nor accepted a political position. During President Roosevelt's administration I was asked to go as a Commissioner of the United Sates to Liberia. In considering whether I should accept this position, it was urged that, because of the work that I had already done in this country for my own people and because my name was already known to some extent to the people of Liberia, I was the person best fitted to undertake the work that the Government wanted done. While I did not like the job and could ill spare the time from the work which I was trying to do for the people of my own race in America, I finally decided to accept the position. I was very happy, however, when President Taft kindly decided to' relieve me from the necessity of making the trip and allowed my secretary, Mr. Emmett J. Scott, to go to Africa in my stead. This was as near as I ever came to holding a Government job. But there are other ways of getting into politics than by holding office.

In the case of the average man, it has seemed to me that as soon as he gets into office he becomes an entirely different man. Some men change for the better under the weight of responsibility; others change for the worse. I never could understand what there is in American politics that so fatally alters the character of a man. I have known men who, in their private life and in their business, were scrupulously careful to keep their word, men who would never, directly or indirectly, deceive anyone with whom they were associated. When they took political office all this changed. I once asked a colored hack driver in Washington how a certain colored man whom I had known in private life (but who was holding a prominent office) was getting on. The old driver had little education but he was a judge of men, and he summed up the case in this way:

"Dere is one thing about Mr. --; you can always depend on him." The old fellow shook his head and laughed. Then he added: "If he tells you he's gwine to do anything, you can always depend upon it that he's not gwine to do it."

This sort of change that comes over people after they get office is not confined, however, to the Negro race. Other races seem to suffer in the same way. I have seen men who, in the ordinary affairs of life, were cool and level headed, grow suspicious and jealous, give up interest in everything, neglect their business, sometimes even neglect their families; in short, lose entirely their mental and moral balance as soon as they started out in quest of an office.

I have watched these men after the political microbe attacked them, and I know all the symptoms of the disease that follows. They usually begin by carefully studying the daily newspapers. They attach great importance to the slightest thing that is said (or not said) by persons who they believe have political influence or authority. These men (the men who dispense the offices) soon come to assume an enormous importance in the minds of office seekers. They watch all the movements of the political leaders with the greatest anxiety, and study every chance word that they let drop, as if it had some dark and awful significance. Then, when they get a little farther along, the office seekers will, perhaps, be found tramping the streets, getting signatures of Tom, Dick, and Harry as a guarantee that they are best qualified to fill some office that they have in view.

I remember the case of a white man who lived in Alabama when President McKinley was first elected. This man gave up his business and went to Washington with a full determination to secure a place in the President's cabinet. He wrote me regularly concerning his prospects. After President McKinley had filled all the places in his cabinet, the same individual applied for a foreign ambassadorship; failing in that, he applied for an auditorship in one of the departments; failing in that, he tried to get a clerkship in Washington; failing in that, he finally wrote to me (and to a number of other acquaintances in Alabama) and asked me to lend him enough money to defray his traveling expenses back to Alabama.

Of course, not all men who go into politics are affected in the way that I have described. Let me add that I have known many public men and have studied them carefully, but the best and highest example of a man that was the same in political office that he was in private life is Col. Theodore Roosevelt. He is not the only example, but he is the most conspicuous one in this respect that I have ever known.

I was thrown, comparatively early in my career, in contact with Colonel Roosevelt. He was just the sort of man to whom anyone who was trying to do work of any kind for the improvement of any race or type of humanity would naturally go to for advice and help. I have seen him and been in close contact with him under many varying circumstances and I confess that I have learned much from studying his career, both while he was in office and since he has been in private life. One thing that impresses me about Mr. Roosevelt is that I have never known him, having given a promise, to overlook or forget it; in fact, he seems to forget nothing, not even the most trivial incidents. I found him the same when he was President that he was as a private citizen, or as Governor of New York, or as Vice-President of the United States. In fact, I have no hesitation in saying that I consider him the highest type of all-round man that I have ever met.

One of the most striking things about Mr. Roosevelt, both in private and public life is his frankness. I have been often amazed at the absolute directness and candor of his speech. He does not seem to know how to hide anything. In fact, he seems to think aloud. Many people have referred to him as being impulsive and as acting without due consideration. From what I have seen of Mr. Roosevelt in this regard, I have reached the conclusion that what people describe as impulsiveness in him is nothing else but quickness of thought. While other people are thinking around a question, he thinks through it. He reaches his conclusions while other people are considering the preliminaries. He cuts across the field, as it were, in his methods of thinking. It is true that in doing so he often takes great chances and risks much. But Colonel Roosevelt is a man who never shrinks from taking chances when it is necessary to take them. I remember that, on one occasion, when it seemed to me that he had risked a great deal in pursuing a certain line of action; I suggested to him that it seemed to me that he had taken a great chance.

"One never wins a battle," he replied, "Unless he takes some risks."

Another characteristic of Colonel Roosevelt, as compared with many other prominent men in public life, is that he rarely forgets or forsakes a friend. If a man once wins his confidence, he stands by that man. One always knows where to find him, and that, in my opinion, accounts to a large degree for his immense popularity. His friend, particularly if he happens to be holding a public position, may become very unpopular with the public, but unless that friend has disgraced himself, Mr. Roosevelt will always stand by him, and is not afraid or ashamed to do so. In the long run the world respects a man who has the courage to stand by his friends, whether in public or private life, and Mr. Roosevelt has frequently gained popularity by doing things that more discreet politicians would have been afraid to do.

I first became acquainted with Mr. Roosevelt through correspondence. Later, in one of my talks with him, and this was at a time when there seemed little chance of his ever becoming President, for it was before he had even been mentioned for that position-he stated to me in the frankest manner that some day he would like to be President of the United States. The average man, under such circumstances, would not have thought aloud. If he believed that there was a remote opportunity of gaining the Presidency, he would have said that he was not seeking the office; that his friends were thrusting it on him; that he did not have the ability to be President, and so forth. Not so with Colonel Roosevelt. He spoke out, as is his custom, that which was in his mind. Even then, many years before he attained his ambition, he began to outline to me how he wanted to help not only the Negro, but the whole South, should he ever become President. I question whether any man ever went into the Presidency with a more sincere desire to be of real service to the South than Mr. Roosevelt did.

That incident will indicate one of the reasons why Mr. Roosevelt succeeds. He not only thinks quickly, but he plans and thinks a long distance ahead. If he had an important state paper to write, or an important magazine article or speech to prepare, I have known him to prepare it six or eight months ahead. The result is that he is at all times master of himself and of his surroundings. He does not let his work push him; he pushes his work.

Practically everything that he tried to do for the South while he was President was outlined in conversations to me many years before it became known to most people that he had the slightest chance of becoming President. What he did was not a matter of impulse but the result of carefully matured plans.

An incident which occurred immediately after he became President will illustrate the way in which Mr. Roosevelt's mind works upon a public problem. After the death of President McKinley I received a letter from him, written in his own hand, on the very day that he took the oath of office at Buffalo as President, or was it the day following, in which he asked me to meet him in Washington. He wanted to talk over with me the plans for helping the South that we had discussed years before. This plan had lain matured in his mind for months and years and, as soon as the opportunity came, he acted upon it.

When I received this letter from Mr. Roosevelt, asking me to meet him in Washington, I confess that it caused me some grave misgivings. I felt that I must consider seriously the question whether I should allow myself to be drawn into a kind of activity that I had definitely determined to keep away from. But here was a letter which, it seemed to me, I could not lightly put aside, no matter what my personal wishes or feelings might be. Shortly after Mr. Roosevelt became established in the White House I went there to see him and we spent the greater part of an evening in talk concerning the South. In this conversation he emphasized two points in particular: First, he said that wherever he appointed a white man to office in the South he wished him to be the very highest type of native Southern white man, one in whom the whole country had faith. He repeated and emphasized his determination to appoint such a type of man regardless of political influences or political consequences.

Then he stated to me, quite frankly, that he did not propose to appoint a large number of colored people, to office in any part of the South, but that he did propose to do two things which had not been done before that time, at least not to the extent and with the definite purpose that he had in mind. Wherever he did appoint a colored man to office in the South, he said that he wanted him to be not only a man of ability, but of character, a man who had the confidence of his white and colored neighbors. He did not propose to appoint a colored man to office simply for the purpose of temporary political expediency. He added that, while he proposed to appoint fewer colored men to office in the South, he proposed to put a certain number of colored men of high character and ability in office in the Northern states. He said that he had never been able to see any good reason why colored men should be put in office in the Southern states and not in the North as well.

As a matter of fact, before Mr. Roosevelt became President, not a single colored man had ever been appointed, so far as I know, to a Federal office in any Northern state. Mr. Roosevelt determined to set the example by placing a colored man in a high office in his own home city, so that the country might see that he did not want other parts of the country to accept that which he himself was not willing to receive. Some months afterward, as a result of this policy, the Hon. Charles W

Anderson was made collector of internal revenues for the second district of New York. This is the district in which Wall Street is located and the district that receives, perhaps, more revenue than any other in the United States. Later on, Mr. Roosevelt appointed other colored men to high office in the North and West, but I think that anyone who examines into the individual qualifications of the colored men appointed to office by Mr. Roosevelt will find, in each case, that they were what he insisted that they should be men of superior ability and of superior character.

President Taft happily has followed the same policy. He has appointed Whitefield McKinlay, of Washington, to the collectorship of the port of Georgetown, a position which has never heretofore been held by a black man. He had designated J. c. Napier, cashier of the One Cent Savings Bank of Nashville, Tenn., to serve as register of the United States treasury; and he has recently announced the appointment of William H. Lewis, assistant United States district attorney, Boston, Mass., to the highest appointive position ever held by a black man under the Federal Government, namely, to a place as assistant attorney general of the United States.

Back of their desire to improve the public service, Mr.

Roosevelt and Mr. Taft have had another purpose in appointing to office the kind of colored people that I have named. They have said that they desire the persons appointed by them to be men of the highest character in order that the younger generation of colored people might see that men of conspicuous ability and conspicuous purity of character are recognized in politics as in other walks of life. They have hoped that such recognition might lead other colored people to strive to attain a high reputation.

Mr. Roosevelt did not apply this rule to the appointments of colored people alone. He believed that he could not only greatly improve the public service, but to some extent could change the tone of politics in the South and improve the relations of the races by the appointment of men who stood high in their professions and who were not only friendly to the colored people but had the confidence of the white people as well. These men, he hoped, would be to the South a sort of model of what the Federal Government desired and expected of its officials in their relations with all parties.

During the first conference with Mr. Roosevelt in the White House, after discussing many matters, he finally agreed to appoint a certain white man, whose name had been discussed, to an important judicial position. Within a few days the appointment was made and accepted. I question whether any appointment made in the South has ever attracted more attention or created more favorable comment from people of all classes than was true of this one.

During the fall of 1901, while I was making a tour of Mississippi, I received word to the effect that the President would like to have a conference with me, as soon as it was convenient, concerning some important matters. With a friend, who was traveling with me, I discussed very seriously the question whether, with the responsibilities I already had, I should take on others. After considering the matter carefully, we decided that the only policy to pursue was to face the new responsibilities as they arose, because new responsibilities bring new opportunities for usefulness of which I ought to take advantage in the interest of my race. I was the more disposed to feel that this was a duty because Mr. Roosevelt was proposing to carry out the very policies which I had advocated ever since I began work in Alabama. Immediately after finishing my work in

Mississippi I went to Washington. I arrived there in the afternoon and went to the house of a friend, Mr. Whitefield McKinlay, with whom I was expected to stop during my stay in Washington.

This trip to Washington brings me to a matter which I have hitherto constantly refused to discuss in print or in public, though I have had a great many requests to do so. At the time, I did not care to add fuel to the controversy which it aroused, and I speak of it now only because it seems to me that an explanation will show the incident in its true light and in its proper proportions.

When I reached Mr. McKinlay's house I found an invitation from President Roosevelt asking me to dine with him at the White House that evening at eight o'clock. At the hour appointed I went to the White House and dined with the President and members of his family and a gentleman from Colorado. After dinner we talked at considerable length concerning plans about the South which the President had in mind. I left the White House almost immediately and took a train the same night for New York. When I reached New York the next morning I noticed that the New York Tribune had about two lines stating that I had dined with the President the previous night. That was the only New York paper, so far as I saw, that mentioned the matter. Within a few hours the whole incident completely passed from my mind. I mentioned the matter casually, during the day, to a friend, Mr. William H. Baldwin, Jr., then president of the Long Island Railroad, but spoke of it to no one else and had no intention of doing so. There was, in fact, no reason why I should discuss it or mention it to anyone.

My surprise can be imagined when, two or three days afterward, the whole press, North and South, was filled with dispatches and editorials relating to my dinner with the President. For days and weeks I was pursued by reporters in quest of interviews. I was deluged with telegrams and letters asking for some expression of opinion or an explanation; but during the whole of this period of agitation and excitement I did not give out a single interview and did not discuss the matter in any way.

Some newspapers attempted to weave into this incident a deliberate and well planned scheme on the part of President Roosevelt to lead the way in bringing about the social intermingling of the two races. I am sure that nothing was farther from the President's mind than this; certainly it was not in my mind. Mr. Roosevelt simply found that he could spare the time best during and after the dinner hour for the discussion of the matters which both of us were interested in.

The public interest aroused by this dinner seemed all the more extraordinary and uncalled for because, on previous occasions, I had taken tea with Queen Victoria at Windsor Castle; I had dined with the governors of nearly every state in the North; I had dined in the same room with President McKinley at Chicago at the Peace jubilee dinner; and I had dined with ex-President Harrison in Paris, and with many other prominent public men.

Some weeks after the incident I was making a trip through Florida. In some way it became pretty generally known along the railroad that I was on the train, and the result was that at nearly every station a group of people would get aboard and shake hands with me. At a little station near Gainesville, Fla., a white man got aboard the train whose dress and manner indicated that he was from the class of small farmers in that part of the country. He shook hands with me very cordially, and said: "I am mighty glad to see you. I have heard about you and I have been wanting to meet you for a long while." I was naturally pleased at this cordial reception, but I was surprised when, after looking me over, he remarked:

"Say, you are a great man. You are the greatest man in this country!" I protested mildly, but he insisted, shaking his head and repeating, "Yes, sir, the greatest man in this country." Finally I asked him what he had against President Roosevelt, telling him at the same time that, in my opinion, the President of the United States was the greatest man in the country.

"Huh! Roosevelt?" he replied with considerable emphasis in his voice. "I used to think that Roosevelt was a great man until he ate dinner with you. That settled him for me."

This remark of a Florida farmer is but one of the many experiences which have taught me something of the curious nature of this thing that we call prejudice-social prejudice, race prejudice, and all the rest. I have come to the conclusion that these prejudices are something that it does not pay to disturb. It is best to "let sleeping dogs lie." All sections of the United States, like all other parts of the world, have their own peculiar customs and prejudices. For that reason it is the part of common sense to respect them. When one goes to European countries or into the Far West, or into India or China, he meets certain customs and certain prejudices which he is bound to respect and, to a certain extent, comply with. The same holds good regarding conditions in the North and in the South. In the South it is not the custom for colored and white people to be entertained at the same hotel; it is not the custom for black and white children to attend the same school. In most parts of the North, a different custom prevails. I have never stopped to question or quarrel with the customs of the people in the part of the country in which I found myself.

Thus, in dining with President Roosevelt, there was no disposition on my part, and I am sure there was no disposition on Mr. Roosevelt's part to attack any custom of the South. There is, therefore, absolutely no ground or excuse for the assertion sometimes made that our dining together was part of a preconcerted and well thought out plan. It was merely an incident that had no thought or motive behind it except the convenience of the President.

I was born in the South and I understand thoroughly the prejudices, the customs, the traditions of the South, and, strange as it may seem to those who do not wholly understand the situation, I love the South. There is no Southern white man who cherishes a deeper interest than I in everything that promotes the progress and the glory of the South. For that reason, if for no other, I will never willingly and knowingly do anything that, in my opinion, will provoke bitterness between the races or misunderstanding between the North and the South.

Now that the excitement in regard to it is all over, it may not be out of place, perhaps, for me to recall the famous order disbanding a certain portion of the Twenty fifth Infantry (a Negro regiment) because of the outbreak at Brownsville, Texas, particularly since this is an illustration of the trait in Mr. Roosevelt to which I have referred. I do not mind stating here that I did not agree with Mr. Roosevelt's method of punishing the Negro soldiers, even supposing that they were guilty. In his usual frank way, he told me several days prior to issuing that order what he was going to do. I urged that he find some other method of punishing the soldiers. While, in some matters, I was perhaps instrumental in getting him to change an opinion that he had formed, in this case he told me that his mind was perfectly clear and that he had reached a definite decision which he would not change, because he was certain that he was right.

At the time this famous order was issued there was no man in the world who was so beloved by the ten millions of Negroes in America as Colonel Roosevelt. His praises were sung by them on every possible occasion. He was their idol. Within a few days, I might almost say hours as a consequence of this order, the songs of praise of ten millions of people were turned into a chorus of criticism and censure.

Mr. Roosevelt was over and over again urged and be sought by many of his best friends, both white and colored, to modify or change this order. Even President Taft, who was at that time Secretary of War, urged him to withdraw the order or modify it. I urged him to do the same thing. He stood his ground and refused. He said that he was convinced that he was right and that events would justify his course.

Notwithstanding the fact that I was deeply concerned in the outcome of this order, I confess that I could not but admire the patience with which Mr. Roosevelt waited for the storm to blow over. I do not think that the criticisms and denunciation which he received had the effect of swerving him in the least from the general course that he had determined to pursue with regard to the colored people of the country. He was just as friendly in his attitude to them after the Brownsville affair as before.

Months have passed since the issuing of the order; the agitation has subsided and the bitterness has disappeared. I think that I am safe in saying that, while the majority of colored people still feel that Colonel Roosevelt made a mistake in issuing the order, there is no individual who is more popular and more loved by the ten millions of Negroes in America than he.

My Educational Campaigns Through the South and What They Taught Me

Several years ago, in company with a few personal friends, most of them Negro business men of Little Rock, Ark., I made a week's journey through Arkansas and Oklahoma, visiting most of the principal cities, speaking, wherever I had time and opportunity along the route, to audiences of both races.

In order to cover as much ground as possible in the eight days we had allotted to the trip, and in order to make the journey as comfortable as possible, we secured a special car in St. Louis and on the night of November 17, 1905, I think it was, we started out on what was one of the most interesting and memorable journeys I have ever made.

For several years my friend, Mr. John E. Bush, receiver of public moneys at Little Rock, and at that time head of the local Negro Business League in that city, had been urging me to come and see for myself the progress which Negroes were making in Little Rock and the neighboring city of Pine Bluff. After I had finally decided to accept his invitation, I made up my mind that I would take advantage of the opportunity to see something, also, of the progress Negroes were making in the neighboring state of Oklahoma and in what was then the Indian Territory.

At that time thousands of Negroes were pouring into this new country from the South. Some of my own students were either in business or teaching school in different parts of the present state of Oklahoma and from them, and from other sources, I had heard much of the progress that colored people were making, particularly at Muskogee and in the booming little Negro town of Boley, where, within a few years, a flourishing little city, controlled entirely by Negroes, and without a single white inhabitant, had sprung into existence.

In the course of my journey I visited not only Little Rock and Pine Bluff, Ark., but Oklahoma City, Guthrie, Muskogee, South McAlester, and several other towns in Oklahoma, and I confess that I was surprised to note the enterprise which these colored immigrants had shown and the progress they were making, particularly in material and business directions. I met successful farmers, who, having sold their farms in Texas or in Kansas at a considerable advance, had come out into this new country to reinvest their money. I made the acquaintance in nearly every part of the state, of successful merchants, bankers, and professional men. At South McAlester I stayed at the home of E. E. McDaniels, a successful railway contractor, the first Negro I ever happened to meet who was engaged in that business. At Oklahoma City I remember meeting Albert Smith, who is known out there as the "Negro cotton king" because he gained the prize at the

Paris Exposition in 1900 for the best bale of cotton. It was a great satisfaction to me to be able to talk with these men, to hear from their own lips the stories of their struggles, of their difficulties, mistakes, and successes. It seemed to me that, after talking with them around the fireside and in the close and intimate way I have suggested, I gained a deeper insight into the forces that were making for the up building of my race than I could have possibly gained in any other way.

One thing that particularly impressed me was the difference between the condition of the colored people who were pouring into this new portion of the Southwest and the condition of those who some thirty years before had poured into Kansas at the time of the famous "exodus." At that time some forty thousand bewildered and helpless colored people, coming for the most part from the plantations of Louisiana, Arkansas, and Mississippi, made their way to Kansas in the hope of finding there greater opportunity and more freedom. It was people from these same regions who, with much the same purpose, were at this time pouring into Oklahoma. The difference was that these later immigrants came with a definite notion of where they were going; they brought a certain amount of capital with them, and had a pretty clear idea of what they would find and what they proposed to do when they reached their destination. The difference in these two movements of the population seemed to me the most striking indication I had seen of the progress which the masses of the Negro people had made in a little more than thirty years.

During the next five years, in company with different parties of Negro business and professional men, I made similar journeys of observation through Mississippi, Tennessee, South Carolina, North Carolina, Delaware, and portions of Virginia and West Virginia. In several instances we made use of special trains to make these trips, and this enabled us to cover longer distances and make the journey practically on our own time. On each of these journeys I took advantage of my opportunities, not only to meet and talk with the people individually, but also to speak to large audiences of white and colored people about many matters which concerned the interests of both races and particularly about the importance to both races, of increasing the efficiency of the Negro schools. In fact, I had not made more than two or three of these trips before they came to be regarded by both white and colored people as the beginning, in each of the states I visited, of a movement or campaign in the interest of Negro education.

Perhaps I can best indicate the character of these campaigns and the sort of information and insight that they gave me in regard to the condition of the colored people in the states I visited by giving a more extended account of my journey in Mississippi in 1908. As an indication of the general interest in the purpose and the success of my visit I ought to say that, while the journey was made under the direction of the Negro Business League of Mississippi, representatives of nearly every important interest among Negroes in the state either accompanied the party for a portion of the journey or assisted in making the meetings successful at the different places at which we stopped. For instance, as I remember, there were not less than eight presidents of Negro banks and many other successful business men in the course of the eight day trip. Among them were Charles Banks, president of the Negro Business League of Mississippi, and one of the most influential colored men of the state. It was he who was more directly responsible than anyone else for organizing and making a success of our journey. Not only the business men, but the representatives of different religious denominations and of the secret organizations, which are particularly strong in Mississippi, united with the members of the business league to make the meetings which we held in the different parts of the state as successful and as influential as it was possible to make them.

It is a matter of no small importance to the success of the people of my race in Mississippi that business men, teachers, and the members of the different religious denominations are uniting disinterestedly in the effort to give the colored children of the state a proper and adequate education, and that they are using their influence to encourage the masses of the people to get property and build homes.

Dr. E. C. Morris, for instance, who was a member of the party, represents the largest Negro organization of any kind in the world-the National Baptist Convention, which has a membership of more than two millions;]. W Straughter, as a member of the finance committee of the Negro Pythians, represented an organization of about seventy thousand persons, owning about three hundred and twenty-two thousand dollars' worth of property. The African Methodist Episcopal Review, of which Dr. H. T. Kealing, now president of the Negro college at Quindaro, Kan., is editor, is probably the best edited and one of the most influential periodicals published by the Negro race. It has been in existence now for more than twenty five years.

I have mentioned the names of these men and have referred to their positions and influence among the Negro people as showing how widespread at the present time is the interest in the moral and material up building of the race.

I had heard a great deal, indirectly, before I reached Mississippi, of the progress that the colored people were making there. I had also heard a great deal through the newspapers of the difficulties under which they were laboring. There are some portions of Mississippi, for instance, where a large part of the colored population has been driven out as a result of white capping organizations. There are other portions of the state where the white people and the colored people seem to be getting along as well as, if not better than, in any other portion of the Union.

After leaving Memphis, the first place at which we stopped was Holly Springs, in Marshall County. Holly Springs has long been an educational center for the colored people of Mississippi. Shortly after the war the Freedman's Aid and Southern Educational Society of the Methodist Church established here Rust University. Until a few years ago the State Normal School for Training Negro Teachers was in existence In Holly Springs, when it was finally abolished by former Governor Vardaman. The loss of this school was a source of great disappointment to the colored people of the state, as they felt that, in vetoing the appropriation, the governor was making an attack upon the Negro education of the state. Under the leadership of Bishop Cottrell, a new industrial school and theological seminary has grown up to take the place of the Normal Training School and do its work. During the previous two years Bishop Cottrell had succeeded in raising more than seventy five thousand dollars, largely from the colored people of Mississippi, in order to erect the two handsome modern buildings which form the nucleus of the new school. In this city there had also been recently established a Baptist Normal School, which is the contribution of the Negro Baptists of the state in response to the abolition of the State Normal School.

The enthusiasm for education that I discovered at Holly Springs is merely an indication of the similar enthusiasm in every other part of the state that I visited. At Utica, Miss., I spoke in the assembly room of the Utica Institute, founded October 27, 1903, by William H. Holtzclaw, a graduate of Tuskegee. After leaving

Tuskegee he determined to go to the part of the country where it seemed to him that the colored people were most in need of a school that could be conducted along the lines of Tuskegee Institute. He settled in Hinds County, where there are forty thousand colored people, thirteen thousand of whom can neither read nor write. In the community in which this school was started the Negroes outnumber the whites seven to one. He began teaching out in the forests. From the very first he succeeded in gaining the sympathy of both races for the work that he was trying to do. In the five years since the school started he has succeeded in purchasing a farm of fifteen hundred acres. He had at that time erected three large and eleven small buildings of various kinds for school rooms, shops, and homes. On the farm there were one large plantation house and about thirty farm houses. He told me that a conservative estimate of the property which the school owned would make the valuation something more than seventy-five thousand dollars. In addition to this, he has already started an endowment fund in order to make the work that he is doing there permanent, and to give aid by means of scholarships to worthy students who are not fully able to pay their own way.

At Jackson, Miss., there are two colleges for Negro students. Campbell College was founded by the African Methodist Episcopal Church; Jackson College, which had just opened a handsome new building for the use of its students, was established and is supported by the Baptist denomination. At Natchez I was invited to take part in the dedication of the beautiful new building erected by the Negro Baptists of Mississippi at a cost of about twenty thousand dollars.

Perhaps I ought to say that, while there has been considerable rivalry among the different Negro churches along theological lines, it seems to me that I can see that, as the leaders of the people begin to realize the seriousness of the educational problem, this rivalry is gradually dying out in a disinterested effort to educate the masses of the Negro children irrespective of denominations. The so called denominational schools are merely a contribution of the members of the different sects to the education of the race.

Nothing indicates the progress which the colored people have made along material lines so well as the number of banks that have been started by colored people in all parts of the South. I have made a special effort recently to learn something of the influence of these institutions upon the mass of the colored people. At the present time there are no less than fifty six Negro banks in the United States.

All but one or two of them are in the Southern States. Of these fifty six banks, eleven are in the state of Mississippi. Not infrequently I have found that Negro banks owe their existence to the secret and fraternal organizations. There are forty two of these organizations, for example, in the state of Mississippi, and they collected $708,670 in 1907, and paid losses to the amount of $522,757. Frequently the banks have been established to serve as depositories for the funds of these institutions. They have then added a savings department, and have done banking business for an increasing number of stores and shops of various kinds that have been established within the last ten years by Negro business men.

A special study of the city of Jackson, Miss., made shortly before I visited the city, showed that there were ninety three businesses conducted by Negroes in that city. Of this number, forty-four concerns did a total annual business of about three hundred and eighty-eight thousand dollars a year. But, of this amount of business, one contractor alone did one hundred thousand dollars' worth. As near as could be estimated, about 73 per cent of the colored people owned or were buying their own homes. It is said that the Negroes, who make up one half of the population, own one third of the area of the city of Jackson. The value of this property, however, is only about one eleventh of the taxable value of the city.

As nearly as could be estimated at that time, Negroes had on deposit in the various banks of the city almost two hundred thousand dollars. Of this amount, more than seventy thousand was in the two Negro banks of the city. I learned that most of these businesses had been started in the previous ten years, but, as a matter of fact, one of the oldest business men in Jackson is a colored man, with whom I stopped during my visit to that city. H. T. Risher is the leading business man in his particular line in Jackson. He has had a bakery and restaurant in that city, as I understand, for more than twenty years. He has one of the handsomest of the many beautiful residences of colored people in Jackson, which I had an opportunity to visit on my journey through the state.

Among the other business enterprises that especially attracted my attention during my journey was the drug store and offices of Dr. A. W Dumas, of Natchez. His store is located in a handsome two story brick block, and although there are a large number of Negro druggists in the United States, I know of no store which is better kept and makes a more handsome appearance.

According to the plan of our journey, I was to spend seven days in Mississippi, starting from Memphis, Tenn., going thence to Holly Springs, Utica, Jackson, Natchez, Vicksburg, Greenville, Mound Bayou, and then, crossing the Mississippi, to spend Sunday in the city of Helena, Ark. As a matter of fact, we did stop at other places and I had an opportunity to speak to audiences of colored people and white people at various places along the railroad, the conductor kindly holding the train for me to do this at several points, so that I think it is safe to say that I spoke to forty or fifty thousand people during the eight days of our journey. Everywhere, I found the greatest interest and enthusiasm among both the white people and colored people for the work that we were attempting to do. In Jackson, which for a number of years had been the center of agitation upon the Negro question, there was some opposition expressed to the white people of the town attending the meeting, but I was told that among the people in the audience were Governor Noel; Lieutenant-Governor Manship; Major R. W Milsaps, who is said to be the wealthiest man in Mississippi; Bishop Charles B. Galloway, of the Methodist Episcopal Church (South), who has since died; United States Marshal Edgar S. Wilson; the postmaster of Jackson, and a number of other prominent persons.

At Natchez, the white people were so interested in the object of the meeting that they expressed a desire to pay for the opera house, in which I spoke, provided that the seating capacity should be equally divided between the two races. At Vicksburg I spoke in a large building that had been used for some time for a roller skating rink. I was informed that hundreds of people who wished to attend the meeting were unable to find places. At Greenville I delivered an address in the courthouse; and there were so many people who were unable to attend the address that, at the suggestion of the sheriff, I delivered a second one from the steps of the courthouse.

The largest and most successful meeting of the trip was held at Mound Bayou, a town founded and controlled entirely by Negroes. This town, also, is the center of a Negro colony of about three thousand people. Negroes own thirty thousand acres of land in direct proximity to the town.

Mound Bayou is in the center of the Delta district, where the colored people outnumber the whites frequently as much as ten to one; and there are a number of Negro settlements besides Mound Bayou in which no white man lives. My audience extended out into the surrounding fields as far as my voice could reach. I was greatly impressed with the achievements and possibilities of this town, where Negroes are giving a striking example of success in self government and in business.

From what I was able to see during my visit to Mississippi, and from what I have been able to learn from other sources, I have come to the conclusion that more has been accomplished by the colored people of that state during the last ten years than was accomplished by them during the whole previous period since the Civil War. To a large extent this has been due to the fact that the colored people have learned that in getting land, in building homes, and in saving their money they can make themselves a force in the communities in which they live. It is generally supposed that the colored man, in his efforts to rise, meets more opposition in Mississippi than anywhere else in the United States, but it is quite as true that there, more than anywhere else, the colored people seem to have discovered that, in gaining habits of thrift and industry, in getting property, and in making themselves useful, there is a door of hope open for them which the South has no disposition to close.

As an illustration of what I mean, I may say that while I was in Holly Springs I learned that, though the whites outnumbered the blacks nearly three to one in Marshall County, there had been but one lynching there since the Civil War. When I inquired of both white people and colored people why it was that the two races were able to live on such friendly terms, both gave almost exactly the same answer. They said that it was due to the fact that in Marshall County so large a number of colored farmers owned their farms. Among other things that have doubtless helped to bring about this result is the fact that the treasurer of the Odd Fellows of Mississippi, who lived in Holly Springs, frequently had as much as two hundred thousand dollars on deposit in the local banks.

My purpose in making the educational campaigns to which I have referred was not merely to see the condition of the masses of my own people, but to ascertain, also, the actual relations existing between the races and to say a word if possible that would bring about more helpful relations between white men and black men in the communities which I visited.

Again and again in the course of these journeys I noticed that, almost invariably, as soon as I began to inquire of some colored school teacher, merchant, banker, physician, how it was he had gotten his start, each one began at once to tell me of some prominent white man in their town who had befriended them. This man had advised them in their business transactions, had, perhaps, loaned them money, or had pointed out to them where they could invest their savings to advantage, and in this way had managed to get ahead. In some cases the very men who had privately befriended these individual colored men were persons who in their public life had the reputation, outside of the community in which they lived, of being the violent opponents and enemies of the Negro race.

These experiences have been repeated so often in my journeys through the South that I have learned that public speeches and newspaper reports are a very poor indication of the actual relations of the races. Somehow when a Southern politician gets upon a platform to make a public speech it comes perfectly natural to him to denounce the Negro. He has been doing it so long that it is second nature.

Now one of the advantages of the educational campaigns I have described is that they have given an opportunity to Southern men to stand up in public and say what was deep down in their hearts with regard to the Negro, to express a feeling toward the Negro that represents another and higher side of Southern character and one which, as a result of sectional feelings and political controversies, has been too long hidden from the world.

After returning from my last educational trip through North Carolina I received letters from prominent people in all parts of the state expressing their approval of what I had said and of the work that my visit was intended to accomplish. These letters came from business men, from men who were or had been in public life, as well as from school superintendents. For example, Charles L. Coon, superintendent of public schools at Wilson, N.C., whose paper before the educational conference in Atlanta, in 1909, was the most convincing plea for the Negro schools I have ever read, wrote as follows:

I write to express my personal appreciation of your visit and its effects here in Wilson. You had a good audience representing all classes of our white and colored population. Numbers of the best white people in town have told me that your address was the very best ever made here. Many of them say you must come back. Some want to get a warehouse so that everybody can hear you.

The Negro school here is stronger in the affections of the colored people, the white people are prouder of it, than before you came. I was delighted that we had a school building in which you could speak. The Negro school will get better each year. It is not doing nearly all it ought to do, but we are moving forward. There will be slight opposition from now on. I am more than ever convinced that white people will believe in and stand for the education of the Negro children, if the matter is put to them in the right shape. Our Negro school has more colored than white opposition. In fact, the last white man in town who counts one was converted by you! I rejoice over this sinner's making his peace with me.

I have quoted Superintendent Coon's letter because it represents the attitude toward Negro education and toward the Negro of an increasing number of thoughtful and earnest men of the younger generation in the South. Perhaps I can give no better idea of how many of the older generation of the Southerners feel toward the Negro than by quoting the words of Judge Bond, of Brownsville, Tenn., in the course of a few remarks he made at the close of my address in his city.

Judge Bond said, according to a short hand report taken at the time and afterward published in the Boston Transcript:

I was born and reared here in the South and have been associated all my life with Negroes. I feel that as a Southern white man I owe a debt to the Negro that I can never pay, that no Southern white man can ever pay. During the war the Southern white man left his home, his wife, and his children to be taken care of by the Negroes, and I have yet to hear of a single instance where that trust was betrayed or where they proved unfaithful; and ever since that time I have sworn by the Most Divine that I shall ever be grateful to the colored people as long as I shall live, and that I shall never be unfair to that race. I have always since thought that a white man is not a man who does not admit that he owes a duty in the sight of God to the colored people of this country; he is not a man if he is not willing at all times and under all circumstances to do all he can to acquit himself of that duty. If there was ever a people in this country who owed a debt to any people, it is the Southern white man to the Southern colored man. The white man who lives on the other side of the Ohio River owes him a debt, too, but, by my honest conviction in the sight of God, his obligation is nothing compared to that of the Southern white man to the colored people, and I have often wondered what will be the judgment on the Southern white man and his children and his grandchildren in failing to discharge his duty toward the old Negro, his children, and his grandchildren for their many years faithful and true service. My mother died at my birth. Now I am growing old. An old black mammy, who, thank God, is living today, took me in her arms and nursed me and cared for me and loved me until I grew strong and to manhood; and there has never been a day since that she has not been willing to do the same for my wife and children, even in spite of her years.

I remember some time ago very well, when I was sitting in a darkened room nursing my youngest child, who was confined with the dreaded disease small pox, my wife in a most distressing manner appeared at the head of the stairs (we had been separated because of our little girl's condition and we were kept from the rest of the family upstairs). My wife called down to me and informed me that she feared another of our children had fallen victim to the small pox. We were in a predicament, you may easily see. It was necessary at once to remove the child from the rest, but there still remained a doubt as to her being a victim, so we could not bring her into the room in which we were and it was also necessary that she be taken out of the room in which she was. She must be kept in a separate room and neither was it safe for her mother or myself to be in the room in which she would be taken. She must remain in this room all night without care or attention from either, but just about that time the old black mammy, this same black mammy who nursed and cared for me, appeared. Black mammy was heard from. "Small pox or no small pox, that child cannot stay in that room by herself to night or no other night, even if I takes the small pox and dies tomorrow"; and she did go into that room and stayed in that room until morning, and was willing to stay there as long as it was necessary. God bless her old soul!

I am glad to see Mr. Washington here and to have him speak to us. He is a credit to his race, and would be a credit to any race. I wish we had many more men like him all over this country.

Mr. Washington, I pray to God that the Spirit may ever guide you in your purpose to lift up your people and that you may inspire all Southern white men as well as Southern colored men to lift up and elevate your race.

These expressions of interest in the welfare of my race and of hearty sympathy with work which others and myself have been trying to do for the up building of the Negro have come to me in recent years from every part of the South. Almost from the beginning of my work in Alabama, however I have had the support and the encouragement, both public and private, not only of my neighbors, but of the best white people everywhere in the South who were acquainted with what I was trying to do. When I have been inclined to be discouraged, the expressions of good will have given me faith. They have taught me that in spite of wrongs and injustices to which members of my race are frequently subjected to, look with confidence to the future and to believe that the Negro has the power within himself to become an indispensable part of the life of the South, not feared and merely tolerated, but trusted and respected by the members of the white rice by whom he is surrounded.

What I Have Learned From Black Men

No single question is more often asked me than this: "Has the pure blooded black man the same ability or the same worth as those of mixed blood?"

It has been my good fortune to have had a wide acquaintance with black as well as brown and even white Negroes. The race to which I belong permits me to meet and know people of all colors and conditions. There is no race or people who have within themselves the choice of so large a variety of colors and conditions as is true of the American Negro. The Japanese, as a rule, can know intimately human nature in only one hue, namely, yellow. The white man, as a rule, does not get intimately acquainted with any other than white men. The Negro, however, has a chance to know them all, because within his own race and among his own acquaintances he has friends, perhaps even relatives, of every color in which mankind has been painted.

Perhaps I can answer the question as to the relative value of the pure Negro and the mixed blood in no better way than by telling what I know concerning, and what I have learned from, some four or five men of the purest blood and the darkest skins of any human beings I happen to know men to whom I am indebted for many things, but most of all for what they have done for me in teaching me to value all men at their real worth regardless of race or color.

Among those black men whom I have known, the one who comes first to my mind is Charles Banks, of Mound Bayou, Miss., banker, cotton broker, planter, real estate dealer, head of a hundred-thousand-dollar corporation which is erecting a cottonseed oil mill, the first ever built and controlled by Negro enterprise and Negro capital, and, finally, leading citizen of the little Negro town of Mound Bayou.

I first met Charles Banks in Boston. As I remember, he came in company with Hon. Isaiah T. Montgomery, the founder of Mound Bayou, to represent, at the first meeting of the National Negro Business League in 1900, the first and at that time the only town in the United States founded, inhabited, and governed exclusively by Negroes. He was then, as he is to-day, a tall, big-bodied man, with a shiny round head, quick, snapping eyes, and a surprisingly swift and quiet way of reaching out and getting anything he happens to want. I never appreciated what a big man Banks was until I began to notice the swift and unerring way in which he reached out his long arm to pick up, perhaps a pin, or to get hold of the buttonhole and of the attention of an acquaintance. He seemed to be able to reach without apparent effort anything he wanted, and I soon found there was a certain fascination in watching him move.

I have been watching Banks reach for things that he wanted, and get them, ever since that time. I have been watching him do things, watching him grow, and as I have studied him more closely my admiration for this big, quiet, graceful giant has steadily increased. One thing that has always impressed itself upon me in regard to Mr. Banks is the fact that he never claims credit for doing anything that he can give credit to other people for doing. He has never made any effort to make himself prominent. He simply prefers to get a job done and, if he can use other people and give them credit for doing the work, he is happy to do so.

At the present time Charles Banks is not, by any means, the wealthiest, but I think I am safe in saying that he is the most influential, Negro business man in the United States. He is the leading Negro banker in Mississippi, where there are eleven Negro banks, and he is secretary and treasurer of the largest benefit association in that state, namely, that attached to the Masonic order, which paid death claims in 1910 to the amount of one hundred and ninety five thousand dollars and had a cash balance of eighty thousand dollars. He organized and has been the moving spirit in the state organization of the Business League in Mississippi and has been for a number of years the vice president of the National Negro Business League.

Charles Banks is, however, more than a successful business man. He is a leader of his race and a broad minded and public spirited citizen. Although he holds no public office, and, so far as I know, has no desire to do so, there are, in my opinion, few men, either white or black, in Mississippi today who are performing, directly or indirectly, a more important service to their state than Charles Banks.

Without referring to the influence that he has been able to exercise in other directions, I want to say a word about the work he is doing at Mound Bayou for the Negro people of the Yazoo Delta, where, in seventeen counties, the blacks represent from seventy-five to ninety-four per cent of the whole population.

As I look at it, Mound Bayou is not merely a town; it is at the same time and in a very real sense of that word, a school. It is not only a place where a Negro may get inspiration, by seeing what other members of his race have accomplished, but a place, also, where he has an opportunity to learn some of the fundamental duties and responsibilities of social and civic life.

Negroes have here, for example, an opportunity, which they do not have to the same degree elsewhere, either in the North or in the South, of entering simply and naturally into all the phases and problems of community life. They are the farmers, the business men, bankers, teachers, preachers. The mayor, the constable, the aldermen, the town marshal, even the station agent, are Negroes.

Black men cleared the land, built the houses, and founded the town. Year by year, as the colony has grown in population; these pioneers have had to face, one after another, all the fundamental problems of civilization. The town is still growing, and as it grows, new and more complicated problems arise. Perhaps the most difficult problem the leaders of the community have to face now is that of founding a school, or a system of schools, in which the younger generation may be able to get some of the kind of knowledge which these pioneers gained in the work of building up and establishing the community.

During the twenty years this town has been in existence it has always had the sympathetic support of people in neighboring white communities. One reason for this is that the men who have been back of it were born and bred in the Delta, and they know both the land and the people.

Charles Banks was born and raised in Clarksdale, a few miles above Mound Bayou, where he and his brother were for several years engaged in business. It was his good fortune, as has been the case with many other successful Negroes, to come under the influence, when he was a child, of one of the best white families in the city in which he was born. I have several times heard Mr. Banks tell of his early life in Clarksdale and of the warm friends he had made among the best white people in that city.

It happened that his mother was cook for a prominent white family in Clarksdale. In this way he became in a sort of a way attached to the family. It was through the influence of this family, if I remember rightly, that he was sent to Rust University, at Holly Springs, to get his education.

In 1900 Mr. Banks, because of his wide knowledge of local conditions in that part of the country, was appointed supervisor of the census for the Third district of Mississippi. In speaking to me of this matter Mr. Banks said that every white man in town endorsed his application for appointment.

Since he has been in Mound Bayou, Mr. Banks has greatly widened his business connections. The Bank of Mound Bayou now counts among its correspondents banks in Vicksburg, Memphis, and Louisville, together with the National Bank of Commerce of St. Louis and the National Reserve Bank of the City of New York. One of the officers of the former institution, Mr. Eugene Snowden, in a recent letter to me, referring to this and another Negro bank, writes:

"It has been my pleasure to lend them $30,000 a year and their business has been handled to my entire satisfaction."

Some years ago, in the course of one of my educational campaigns, I visited Mound Bayou, among other places in Mississippi. Among other persons I met the sheriff of Bolivar County, in which Mound Bayou is situated. Without any suggestion or prompting on my part, he told me that Mound Bayou was one of the most orderly. In fact; I believe he said the most orderly town in the Delta. A few years ago a newspaper man from Memphis visited the town for the purpose of writing an article about it. What he saw there set him to speculating, and among other things he said:

Will the Negro as a race work out his own salvation along Mound Bayou lines? Who knows? These have worked out for themselves a better local government than any superior people has ever done for them in freedom. But it is a generally accepted principle in political economy that any homogeneous people will in time do this. These people have their local government, but it is in consonance with the county, state, and national governments and international conventions, all in the hands of another race. Could they conduct as successfully a county government in addition to their local government and still under the state and national governments of another race? Enough Negroes of the Mound Bayou type, and guided as they were in the beginning, will be able to do so.

The words I have quoted will, perhaps, illustrate the sort of interest and sympathy which the Mound Bayou experiment arouses in the minds of thoughtful Southerners. Now it is characteristic of Charles Banks that, in all his talks with me, he has never once referred to the work he is doing as a solution of the problem of the Negro race. He has often referred to it, however, as one step in the solution of the problem of the Delta. He recognizes that, behind everything else, is the economic problem.

Aside from the personal and business interest which he has in the growth and progress of Mound Bayou, Mr. Banks sees in it a means of teaching better methods of farming, of improving the home life, of getting into the masses of the people greater sense of the value of law and order. I have learned much from studying the success of Charles Banks. Before all else he has taught me the value of common sense in dealing with conditions as they exist in the South. I have learned from him that, in spite of what the Southern white man may say about the Negro in moments of excitement, the sober sentiment of the South is in sympathy with every effort that promises solid and substantial progress to the Negro.

Mal R. R. Moton, of Hampton Institute, is one of the few black men I know who can trace his ancestry in an unbroken line on both sides back to Africa. I have often heard him tell the story, as he had it from his grandmother, of the way in which his great-grandfather, who was a young African chief, had come down to the coast to sell some captives taken in war and how, after the bargain was completed, he was enticed on board the white man's ship and himself carried away and sold, along with these unfortunate captives, into slavery in America. Major Moton is, like Charles Banks, not only a full blooded black man, with a big body and broad Negro features, but he is, in his own way, a remarkably handsome man. I do not think anyone could look in Major Moton's face without liking him. In the first place, he looks straight at you, out of big friendly eyes, and as he speaks to you an expression of alert and intelligent sympathy constantly flashes and plays across his kindly features.

It has been my privilege to come into contact with many different types of people, but I know few men who are so lovable and, at the same time, so sensible in their nature as Major Moton. He is chock full of common sense. Further than that, he is a man who, without obtruding himself and without your understanding how he does it, makes you believe in him from the very first time you see him and from your first contact with him, and, at the same time, makes you love him. He is the kind of man in whose company I always feel like being, never tire of, always want to be around him, or always want to be near him.

One of the continual sources of surprise to people who come for the first time into the Southern States is to hear of the affection with which white men and women speak of the older generation of colored people with whom they grew up, particularly the old colored nurses. The lifelong friendships that exist between these old "aunties" and "uncles" and the white children with whom they were raised is something that is hard for strangers to understand.

It is just these qualities of human sympathy and affection that endeared so many of the older generation of Negroes to their masters and mistresses and which seems to have found expression, in a higher form, in Major Moton. Although he has little schooling outside of what he was able to get at Hampton Institute, Major Moton is one of the best read men and one of the most interesting men to talk with I have ever met. Education has not "spoiled him," as it seems to have done in the case of some other educated Negroes. It has not embittered or narrowed him in his affections. He has not learned to hate or distrust any class of people, and he is just as ready to assist and show a kindness to a white man as to a black man, to a Southerner as to a Northerner.

My acquaintance with Major Moton began, as I remember, after he had graduated at Hampton Institute and while he was employed there as a teacher. He had at that time the position that I once occupied in charge of the Indian students. Later he was given the very responsible position he now occupies, at the head of the institute battalion, as commandant of cadets, in which he has charge of the discipline of all the students. In this position he has an opportunity to exert a very direct and personal influence upon the members of the student body and, what is especially important, to prepare them to meet the peculiar difficulties that await them when they go out in the world to begin life for themselves.

It has always seemed to me very fortunate that Hampton Institute should have had in the position which Major Moton occupies a man of such kindly good humor, thorough self-control, and sympathetic disposition.

Major Moton knows by intuition Northern white people and Southern white people. I have often heard the remark made that the Southern white man knows more about the Negro in the South than anybody else. I will not stop here to debate that question, but I will add that colored men like Major Moton know more about the Southern white man than anybody else on earth.

At the Hampton Institute, for example, they have white teachers and colored teachers; they have Southern white people and Northern white people; besides, they have colored students and Indian students. Major Moton knows how to keep his hands on all of these different elements, to see to it that friction is kept down and that each works in harmony with the other. It is a difficult job, but Major Moton knows how to negotiate it.

This thorough understanding of both races which Major Moton possesses has enabled him to give his students just the sort of practical and helpful advice and counsel that no white man who has not himself faced the peculiar conditions of the Negro could be able to give.

I think it would do anyone good to attend one of Major Moton's Sunday school classes when he is explaining to his students, in the very practical way which he knows how to use, the mistake of students allowing themselves to be embittered by injustice or degraded by calumny and abuse with which every colored man must expect to meet at one time or another. Very likely he will follow up what he has to say on this subject by some very apt illustration from his own experience or from that of some of his acquaintances which will show how much easier and simpler it is to meet prejudice with sympathy and understanding than with hatred; to remember that the man who abuses you because of your race probably hasn't the slightest knowledge of you personally, and, nine times out of ten, if you simply refuse to feel injured by what he says, will feel ashamed about himself later.

I think one of the greatest difficulties which a Negro has to meet is in traveling about the country on the railway trains. For example, it is frequently difficult for a colored man to get anything to eat while he is traveling in the South, because, on the train and at the lunch counters along the route, there is often no provision for colored people. If a colored man goes to the lunch counter where the white people are served he is very likely, no matter who he may be, to find himself roughly ordered to go around to the kitchen, and even there no provision has been made for him.

Time and again I have seen Major Moton meet this situation, and others like it, by going up directly to the man in charge and telling him what he wanted. More than likely the first thing he received was a volley of abuse. That never discouraged Major Moton. He would not allow himself to be disturbed nor dismissed, but simply insisted, politely and good naturedly, that he knew the custom, but that he was hungry and wanted something to eat. Somehow, without any loss of dignity, he not only invariably got what he wanted, but after making the man he was dealing with ashamed of himself, he usually made him his friend and left him with a higher opinion of the Negro race as a whole.

I have seen Major Moton in a good many trying situations in which an ordinary man would have lost his head, but I have never seen him when he seemed to feel the least degraded or humiliated. I have learned from Major Moton that one need not belong to a superior race to be a gentleman.

It has been through contact with men like Major Moton who is a clean, wholesome, high soled gentleman under black skins-that r have received a kind of education no books could impart. Whatever disadvantages one may suffer from being a part 0 what is called an "inferior race," a member of such a race has the advantage of not feeling compelled to go through the world, as some members of other races do, proclaiming their superiority from the house tops. There are some people in this world who would feel lonesome, and they are not all of them white people either, if they did not have some one to whom they could claim

One of the most distinguished black men of my race is George W Clinton, of Charlotte, N. c., bishop of the A. M. E. Zion Church. Bishop Clinton was born a slave fifty years ago in South Carolina. He was one of the few young colored men who, during the Reconstruction days, had an opportunity to attend the University of South Carolina. He prides himself on the fact that he was a member of that famous class of 1874 which furnished one Negro congressman, two United States ministers to Liberia-the most recent of whom is Dr. W D. Crum five doctors, seven preachers, and several business men who have made good in after life. Among others was W McKinlay, the present collector of customs for the port of Georgetown, D. C.

Bishop Clinton has done a great service to the denomination to which he belongs and his years of service have brought him many honors and distinctions. He founded the African Methodist Episcopal Zion Quarterly Review and edited, for a time, another publication of the African Methodist Episcopal Zion denomination. He has represented his church in ecumenical conferences at home and abroad, is a trustee of Livingstone College, chairman of the publishing board, has served as a member of the international convention of arbitration and is vice-president of the international Sunday school union.

Bishop Clinton is a man of a very different type from the other men of pure African blood I have mentioned. Although he says he is fifty years of age, he is in appearance and manner the youngest man in the group. An erect, commanding figure, with a high, broad forehead, rather refined features and fresh, frank, almost boyish manner, he is the kind of man who everywhere wins confidence and respect.

Although Bishop Clinton is by profession a minister, and has been all his life in the service of the Church, he is of all the men I have named the most aggressive in his manner and the most soldierly in his bearing.

Knowing that his profession compelled him to travel about a great deal in all parts of the country, I asked him how a man of his temperament managed to get about without getting into trouble.

"I have had some trouble but not much," he said, "and I have learned that the easiest way to get along everywhere is to be a gentleman. It is simple, convenient, and practicable. "The only time I ever came near having any serious trouble:' continued Bishop Clinton, "was years ago when 1 was in politics." And then he went on to relate the following incident: It seems that at this time the Negroes at the bishop's home in Lancaster, S. c., were still active in politics. There was an attempt at one time to get some of the better class of Negroes to unite with some of the Democrats in order to elect a prohibition ticket. The fusion ticket, with two Negroes and four white men as candidates, was put in the field and elected. It turned out, however, that a good many white people cut the Negroes on the ticket and, at the same time, a good many Negroes cut the whites, so that there was some bad blood on both sides. A man who was the editor of the local paper at that time had accused young Clinton of having advised the Negroes to cut the fusion ticket.

"As 1 knew him well," said the bishop, "I went up to his office to explain. Some rather foolish remark 1 made irritated the editor and he jumped up and came toward me with a knife in his hands."

The bishop added that he didn't think the man really meant anything "because my mother used to cook in his family" and they had known each other since they were boys, so he simply took hold of his wrists and held them. The bishop is a big, stalwart, athletic man with hands that grip like a vise. He talked very quietly and they settled the matter between them.

Bishop Clinton has told me that he has made many life long friends among the white people of South Carolina, but this was the only time that he ever had anything like serious trouble with a white man.

I first made the acquaintance of Bishop Clinton when he came to Tuskegee in 1893 as representative of the African Methodist Episcopal Zion Church, at the dedication of the Phelps Hall Bible training school. The next year he came to Tuskegee as one of the lecturers in that school and he has spent some time at Tuskegee every year since then, assisting in the work of that institution.

Bishop Clinton has been of great assistance to us, not only in our work at Tuskegee, but in the larger work we have been trying to do in arousing interest throughout the country in Negro public schools. He organized and conducted through North Carolina in 1910 what I think was the most successful educational campaign I have yet been able to make in any of the Southern States.

Although he is an aggressive churchman, Bishop Clinton has found time to interest himself in everything that concerns the welfare of the Negro race. He is as interested in the business and economic as he is in the intellectual advancement of the race.

One of the most gifted men of the Negro race whom I ever happened to meet is George W Carver, Professor Carver, as he is called at Tuskegee, where he has for many years been connected with the scientific and experimental work in agriculture carried on in connection with the Tuskegee Institute. I first met Mr. Carver about 1895 or 1896 when he was a student at the State Agricultural College at Ames, Ia. I had heard of him before that time through Hon. James Wilson, now secretary of agriculture, who was for some time one of Mr. Carver's teachers. It was about this time that an attempt was made to put our work in agriculture on a scientific basis, and Mr. Carver was induced to come to Tuskegee to take charge of that work and of the state experiment station that had been established in connection with it. He has been doing valuable work in that department ever since and, as a result of his work in breeding cotton and of the bulletins be has prepared on experiments in building up worn-out soils, he has become widely known to both colored and white farmers throughout the South.

When some years ago the state secretary of agriculture called a meeting at Montgomery of the leading teachers of the state, Professor Carver was the only colored man invited to that meeting. He was at that time invited to deliver an address to the convention and for an hour was questioned on the interesting work he was doing at the experiment station.

Professor Carver, like the other men I have mentioned, is of unmixed African blood, and is one of the most thoroughly scientific men of the Negro race with whom I am acquainted. Whenever anyone who takes a scientific interest in cotton growing, or in the natural history of this part of the world, comes to visit Tuskegee, he invariably seeks out and consults Professor Carver. A few years ago the colonial secretary of the German empire, accompanied by one of the cotton experts of his department, traveling through the South in a private car, paid a visit of several days to Tuskegee largely to study, in connection with the other work of the school, the cotton growing experiments that Professor Carver has been carrying on for some years.

In his book, "The Negro in the New World," Sir Harry Johnston, who has himself been much interested in the study of plant life in different parts of the world, says: "Professor Carver, who teaches scientific agriculture, botany, agricultural chemistry, etc., at Tuskegee, is, as regards complexion and features, an absolute Negro; but in the cut of his clothes, the accent of his speech, the soundness of his science, he might be professor of botany, not at Tuskegee, but at Oxford or Cambridge. Any European botanist of distinction, after ten minutes' conversation with this man, instinctively would treat him as a man on a level with himself." What makes all that Professor Carver has accomplished the more remarkable is the fact that he was born in slavery and has had relatively few opportunities for study, compared with those which a white man who makes himself a scholar in any particular branch of science invariably has.

Professor Carver knows but little of his parentage. He was born on the plantation of a Mr. Carver in Missouri some time during the war.

It was a time when it was becoming very uncomfortable to hold slaves in Missouri, and so he and his mother were sent south into Arkansas. After the war Mr. Carver, the master, sent south to inquire what had become of his former slaves. He learned that they had all disappeared with the exception of a child, two or three years old, by the name of George, who was near dead with the whooping-cough and of so little value that the people in Arkansas said they would be very glad to get rid of him.

George was brought home, but he proved to be such a weak and sickly little creature that no attempt was made to put him to work and he was allowed to grow up among chickens and other animals around the servants' quarters, getting his living as best he could.

The little black boy lived, however, and he used his freedom to wander about in the woods, where he soon got on very good terms with all the insects and animals in the forest and gained an intimate and, I might almost say personal, acquaintance with all the plants and the flowers.

As he grew older he began to show unusual aptitude in two directions: He attracted attention, in the first place, by his peculiar knack and skill in all sorts of household work. He learned to cook, to knit and crochet and he had a peculiar and delicate sense for color. He learned to draw and, at the present time, he devotes a large part of his leisure to making the most beautiful and accurate drawings of different flowers and forms of plant life in which he is interested.

In the second place, he showed a remarkable natural aptitude and intelligence in dealing with plants. He would spend hours, for example, gathering all the most rare and curious flowers that were to be found in the woods and fields. One day some one discovered that he had established out in the brush a little botanical garden, where he had gathered all sorts of curious plants and where he soon became so expert in making all sorts of things grow, and showed such skill in caring for and protecting plants from all sorts of insects and diseases that he got the name of "the plant doctor."

Another direction in which he showed unusual natural talent was in music. While he was still a child he became famous among the colored people as a singer. After he was old enough to take care of himself he spent some years wandering about. When he got the opportunity he worked in greenhouses. At one time he ran a laundry; at another time he worked as a cook in a hotel. His natural taste and talent for music and painting, and, in fact, almost every form of art, finally attracted the attention of friends, through whom he secured a position as church organist.

During all this time young Carver was learning wherever he was able. He learned from books when he could get them; learned from experience always; and made friends wherever he went. At last he found an opportunity to take charge of the greenhouses of the horticultural department of the Iowa Agricultural College at Ames. He remained there until he was graduated, when he was made assistant botanist. He took advantage of his opportunities there to continue his studies and finally took a diploma as a post graduate student, the first diploma of that sort that had been given at Ames.

While he was at the agricultural college in Iowa he took part with the rest of the students in all the activities of college life. He was lieutenant, for example, in the college battalion which escorted Governor Boies to the World's Fair at Chicago. He began to read papers and deliver lectures at the horticultural conventions in all parts of the state. But, in spite of his success in the North, among the people of another race, Mr. Carver was anxious to come south and do something for his own race. So it was that he gladly accepted an invitation to come to Tuskegee and take charge of the scientific and experimental work connected with our department of agriculture.

Although Professor Carver impresses every one who meets him with the extent of his knowledge in the matter of plant life, he is quite the most modest man I have ever met. In fact, he is almost timid. He dresses in the plainest and simplest manner possible; the only thing that he allows in the way of decoration is a flower in his button hole. It is a rare thing to see Professor Carver any time during the year without some sort of flower on the lapel of his coat and he is particularly proud when he has found somewhere in the woods some especially rare specimen of a flower to show to his friends.

I asked Professor Carver at one time how it was, since he was so timid, that he managed to have made the acquaintance of so many of the best white as well as colored people in our part of the country. He said that as soon as people found out that he knew something about plants that was valuable he discovered they were very willing and eager to talk with him.

"But you must have some way of advertising," I said jestingly; "how do all these people find out that you know about plants?"

"Well, it is this way," he said. "Shortly after I came here I was going along the woods one day with my botany can under my arm. I was looking for plant diseases and for insect enemies. A lady saw what she probably thought was a harmless old colored man, with a strange looking box under his arm, and she stopped me and asked if I was a peddler. I told her what I was doing. She seemed delighted and asked me to come and see her roses, which were badly diseased. I showed her just what to do for them in fact, sat down and wrote it out for her.

"In this," he continued, "and several other ways it became noised abroad that there was a man at the school who knew about plants. People began calling upon me for information and advice."

I myself recall that several years ago a dispute arose down town about the name of a plant. No one knew what it was. Finally one gentleman spoke up and said that they had a man out at the normal school by the name of Carver who could name any plant, tree, bird, stone, etc., in the world, and if he did not know there was no use to look farther. A man was put on a horse and the plant brought to Professor Carver at the Institute. He named it and sent him back. Since then Professor Carver's laboratory has never been free from specimens of some kind.

I have always said that the best means which the Negro has for destroying race prejudice is to make himself a useful and, if possible, an indispensable member of the community in which he lives. Every man and every community is bound to respect the man or woman who has some form of superior knowledge or ability, no matter in what direction it is. I do not know of a better, illustration of this than may be found in the case of Professor Carver. Without any disposition to push himself forward into any position in which he is not wanted; he has been able, because of his special knowledge and ability, to make friends with all classes of people, white as well as black, throughout the South. He is constantly receiving inquiries in regard to his work from all parts of the world, and his experiments in breeding new varieties of cotton have aroused the greatest interest among those cotton planters who are interested in the scientific investigation of cotton growing.

There are few colored men in the South today who are better or more widely known than Dr. Charles T. Walker, pastor of the Tabernacle Baptist Church of Augusta, Ga. President William H. Taft, referring to Doctor Walker, said that he was the most eloquent man he had ever listened to. For myself I do not know of any man, white or black, who is a more fascinating speaker either in private conversation or on the public platform.

Doctor Walker's speeches, like his conversation, have the charm of a natural born talker, a man who loves men, and has the art of expressing himself simply, easily, and fluently, in a way to interest and touch them.

On the streets of Augusta, his home, it is no uncommon thing to see Doctor Walker, after the familiar and easy manner of Southern people stand for hours on a street corner or in front of a grocery store, surrounded by a crowd who have gathered for no other purpose than to hear what he will say. It is said that he knows more than half of the fifteen thousand colored people of Augusta by name, and when he meets any of them in the street he is disposed to stop, in his friendly and familiar way, in order to inquire about the other members of the family. He wants to know how each is getting on and what has happened to anyone of them since he saw them last.

If one of these acquaintances succeeds in detaining him, he will, very likely, find himself surrounded by other friends and acquaintances and, when once he is fairly launched on one of the quaintly humorous accounts of his adventures in some of the various parts of the world he has visited, or is discussing, in his vivid and epigrammatic way, some public question, business in that part of the town stops for a time.

Doctor Walker is a great story teller. He has a great fund of anecdotes and a wonderful art in using them to emphasize a point in argument or to enforce a remark. I recall that the last time he was at Tuskegee, attending the Negro conference; he told us what he was trying to do at the school established by the

Walker Baptist Association at Augusta for the farmers in his neighborhood. From that he launched off into some remarks upon the colored farmer, his opportunities, and his progress. He said Senator Tillman had once complained that the colored farmer wasn't as ignorant as he pretended to be, and then he told this story: He said that an old colored farmer in his part of the country had rented some land of a white man on what is popularly known as "fourths." By the term of the contract the white man was to get one fourth of the crop for the use of the land.

When it came time to divide the crop, however, it turned out that there were just three wagon loads of cotton and this the old farmer hauled to his own barn.

Of course the landlord protested. He said: "Look here, Uncle Joe, didn't you promise me a fourth of that cotton for my share?"

"Yes, cap'n," was the reply, "Dat's so. I'se mighty sorry, but dere wasn't no fort'.".

"How is that?" inquired the landlord.

"There wasn't no fort' 'cause dere was just three wagon loads, and dere wasn't no fort' dere."

Doctor Walker is not only a fascinating conversationalist, a warm-hearted friend, but he is, also, a wonderfully successful preacher. During the time when he was in New York, as pastor of the Mount Olivet Baptist Church, his sermons and his wonderful success as an evangelist were frequently reported in the New York papers.

Doctor Walker is not only an extraordinary pulpit orator, but he is a man of remarkably good sense. I recall some instances in particular in which he showed this quality in a very conspicuous way. The first was at a meeting of the National Convention of Negro Baptists at St. Louis in 1886. At this meeting some one delivered an address on the subject, "Southern Ostracism," in which he abused the Southern white Baptists, referring to them as mere figure heads, who believe "there were separate heavens for white and colored people."

Later, in the session Doctor Walker found an opportunity to reply to these remarks, pointing out that a few months before the Southern Baptist Convention had passed a resolution to expend $10,000 in mission work among the colored Baptists of the South. He formulated his protest against the remarks made by the speaker of the previous day in a resolution which was passed by the convention.

His speech and the resolution were published in many of the Southern newspapers and denominational organs and did much to change the currents of popular feeling at that time and bring about a better understanding between the races.

Dr. Charles T. Walker was born at the little town of Hepzibah, Richmond County, Ga., about sixteen miles south of his present home, Augusta. His father, who was his master's coachman, was also deacon in the little church organized by the slaves in 1848, of which his uncle was pastor. Doctor Walker comes of a race of preachers. The Walker Baptist Association is named after one of his uncles, Rev. Joseph T. Walker, whose freedom was purchased by the members of his congregation who were themselves slaves. In 1880, upon a resolution of Doctor Walker, this same Walker Association passed a resolution to establish a normal school for colored children, known as the Walker Baptist Institute. This school has from the first been supported by the constant and unremitting efforts of Doctor Walker.

Meanwhile he has been interested in other good works. He assisted in establishing the Augusta Sentinel, and in 1891, while he was traveling in the

Holy Land, his accounts of his travels did much to brighten its pages and increase its circulation.

In 1893, he was one of a number of other colored people to establish a Negro state fair at Augusta, which has continued successfully ever since. Another of his enterprises started and carried on in connection with his church is the Tabernacle Old Folks' Home. He has taken a prominent part in all the religious and educational work of the state and has even dipped, to some extent, into politics, having been at one time a member of the Republican state executive committee.

Aside from these manifold activities, and beyond all he has done in other directions, Doctor Walker has been a man who has constantly sought to take life as he found it and make the most of the opportunities that he saw about him for himself and his people. He has not been an agitator and has done more than any other man I know to bring about peace and good-will between the two sections of the country and the races. It is largely due to his influence that in Augusta, Ga., the black man and the white man live more happily and comfortably than they do in almost any other city in the United States.

The motto of Doctor Walker's life, I can state in his own words. "I am determined," he has said, "never to be guilty of ingratitude; never to desert a friend; and never to strike back at an enemy."

It is because of such men as Doctor Walker and many others like him that I have learned not only to respect but to take pride in the race to which I belong.

In seeking to answer the question as to the relative value of the man of pure African extraction and the man of mixed blood I have referred to five men who have gained some distinction in very different walks of life. There are hundreds of others I could name, who, though not so conspicuous nor so well known, are performing in their humble way valuable service for their race and country. I might also mention here the fact that at Tuskegee, during an experience of thirty years, we have found that, although perhaps a majority of our students are not of pure black blood, still the highest honors in our graduating class, namely, that of valedictorian, which is given to students who have attained the highest scholarship during the whole course of their studies, has been about equally divided between students of mixed and pure blood.

For my own part, however, it seems to me a rather unprofitable discussion that seeks to determine in advance the possibilities of any individual or any race or class of individuals. In the first place, races, like individuals, have different qualities and different capacities for service and, that being the case; it is the part of wisdom to give every individual the opportunities for growth and development which will fit him for the greatest usefulness.

When any individual and any race is allowed to find that place, freely and without compulsion, they will not only be happy and contented in themselves, but will fall naturally into the happiest possible relations with all other members of the community.

In the second place, it should be remembered that human life and human society are so complicated that no one can determine what latent possibilities any individual or any race may possess. It is only through education, and through struggle and experiment in all the different activities and relations of life, that it is possible for a race or an individual to find the place in the common life in which they can be of the greatest value to themselves and the rest of the world.

To assume anything else is to deny the value of the free institutions under which we live and of all the centuries of struggle and effort it has cost to bring them into existence.

Meeting High and Low in Europe

I have gotten an education by meeting all classes of people in the United States. I have been fortunate in getting much education by coming into contact with different classes of people in Europe.

In the course of my journey across Europe I visited, in the fall of 1910, the ancient city of Cracow, the former capital of Poland. It was evening when we reached our destination, and, as we had been traveling all day without sighting an American or anyone who spoke English, I began to feel more at sea than I had ever felt, before in my life. I was a little surprised, therefore, as I was getting out of the omnibus, to hear some one say in an unmistakable American accent: "Excuse me, but isn't this Booker T. Washington?" I replied that it was, and added that I was very glad to hear that kind of a voice in this remote corner of Europe. In a few minutes I was exchanging notes with a man who once lived, he said, in the same part of the country I came from, in West Virginia. He had come originally from Poland and was, I suspect, a Polish Jew, one of that large number of returned immigrants whom one meets in every part of Eastern and Southern Europe.

The next day I met a very intelligent American lady, though of Polish origin, who turned out to be the wife of the Polish count who was the owner and proprietor of the hotel. It was this lady who advised me to go and visit, while I was in Cracow, the tomb of the Polish patriot, Kosciuszko, whose name I had learned in school as one of those revolutionary heroes who, when there was no longer any hope of liberty for their own people in the old world, had crossed the seas to help establish it in the new:

I knew from my school history what Kosciuszko had done for America in its early struggle for independence. I did not know, however, until my attention was called to it in Cracow, what Kosciuszko had done for the freedom and education of my own people.

After his second visit to this country in 1797 Kosciuszko, I learned, made a will in which he bequeathed part of his property in this country in trust to Thomas Jefferson to be used for the purpose of purchasing the freedom of Negro slaves and giving them instruction in the trades and otherwise.

Seven years after his death a school of Negroes, known as the Kosciuszko school, was established in Newark, N.J. The sum left for the benefit of this school amounted to thirteen thousand dollars.

The Polish patriot is buried in the cathedral at Cracow, which is the Westminster Abbey of Poland, and is filled with memorials of the honored names of that country. Kosciuszko lies in a vault beneath the marble floor of the cathedral. As I looked upon his tomb I thought how small the world is after all and how curiously interwoven are the interests that bind people together. Here I was in this strange land, farther from my home than I had ever expected to be in my life, and yet I was paying my respects to a man to whom the members of my race owed one of the first permanent schools for them in the United States.

When I visited the tomb of Kosciuszko I placed a rose on it in the name of my race. A few days later I took a day's journey by train and wagon into a remote part of the country districts of Poland in order to see something of the more primitive peasant life of that region. Away up in the mountains we stopped at a little group of thatched-roof cottages. As I wanted to see what their homes looked like inside, I knocked at the door of one of them and made some inquiry or other in English, not expecting to get a reply that I could understand. I was surprised to hear a man answer me in fairly good English. He told me that he had lived for a long time in Detroit, Mich. My companion, Dr. Robert E. Park, who had also lived in that city, was soon talking familiarly with him about a famous rebel priest, Kolisinski, who had been a leader of the Polish colony in that city.

A week before that I had visited, in the wildest part of Sicily, the sulphur mines of Campo Franco. In the deepest part of these mines I discovered a man who had been a miner in West Virginia, in the same region in which, years before, I had myself learned to mine coal.

These incidents were characteristic of a kind of experience I had everywhere in Europe. In the most remote parts of the country, where I expected to meet people who had, perhaps, never heard of America, I found people who not only spoke my own language, but welcomed me almost as a fellow countryman. All this led me to realize, as I had not been able to do before, the close and intimate way in which the life, the problems, and the people of Europe were touching and influencing America. But it led me also to notice and study the curious and to me surprising reflex influence of America on Europe.

I have made in all three visits to Europe. On my first visit, a number of years ago, I made the journey with no very definite purpose in mind. I kept in the main line of travel and saw what I may call the polite and official side of life in England and some portions of the continent. In London, for example, I was entertained by the American ambassador, Hon. Joseph H. Choate, had the privilege of attending one of the queen's luncheons at Windsor Castle, and made the acquaintance of Hon. James Bryce, the present ambassador to the United States, besides meeting a number of distinguished men whose names were familiar to me in connection with some important phase of the world's work in which they were engaged.

On my last trip I made up my mind to leave, as far as possible, the main highways of travel and see something of the condition of the poorer people, whose lives are neither polite nor picturesque nor pleasant to look at. My purpose in making this trip was to compare, as far as I was able, the condition of the masses of my own people in this country with the masses of the people in Europe, who are in relatively the same situation in political and economic opportunity. I believed that if the black people in America knew something of the burdens and difficulties under which the masses of the people in Europe live and work, they would see that their own situation was by no means so hopeless as they have been sometimes taught to believe.

I had another reason for desiring to get acquainted with the situation of people at the bottom in Europe. For a number of years I have been convinced that there is a very intimate relation between the work I have been trying to do at Tuskegee Institute for the masses of the Negroes in the South and the work that was being done for the poorer classes of the people in the different parts of Europe. Different as has been the history of the black man in the South and the white man in

Europe, there were, I was convinced, many points in which the life of the one would compare with the life of the other. In the case of the Negro we have a black people struggling up from slavery to freedom: in the other case we have a white man making his way upward through a milder form of subjection and servitude to a position of political and economic independence; and, in each case, the means by which the long journey has been made, in the one instance by a race, in the other by a class, has been, in many respects, the same.

But aside from all that, I was interested in these people for their own sake. An individual or a race that has come up from slavery cannot but feel a peculiar interest and sympathy with any other individual or race that has traveled that same journey or any part of it.

I arrived in London in the late summer. At that time all the polite world, all the distinguished and all the wealthy people, were away in some other part of the world upon their vacations, and the city, as far as these people were concerned, was like a winter residence which had been closed for the summer. But the other six million, whose acquaintance I had determined to make upon this trip, were there.

In one way or another I saw a good deal of the life of the poorer classes, particularly in that vast region inhabited almost wholly by people of the poorer and working classes, which goes under the name of East London. I tramped about at night, visiting the darkest corners of the city I could find. One night I interviewed, on the Thames Embankment, those dreary outcasts of the great city who wander up and down the bank of the river all day and sleep upon the pavement at night. At another time I visited the alehouses and the bar rooms, where men and women of the poorer classes congregate at night to drink and gossip. I went several times to the police courts in some of the poorer parts of the city, where I had a chance to observe the methods by which the police courts of London deal with the failures and unfortunates of the city who in one way or other fall into the hands of the police. It had been my plan to give as large a part of my time as possible to getting acquainted with the working classes in the farming regions of Austria, Italy, and Denmark.

To a certain extent the condition of the urban laborers in London connected itself in my mind with the condition of the rural population in other countries I have mentioned, since London represents the largest city population in the world, and England is the country in which the masses of the people have been most completely detached from the land, while Austria, Italy, and Denmark are distinctly agricultural countries, and leaving out Russia, represent the parts of Europe where the people, to a greater extent than elsewhere, live close to the soil.

It is impossible for me to describe in detail what I learned in regard to the condition of the masses of the people in the different parts of Europe I visited. As a rule I suppose the man on the soil has always represented the most backward and neglected portion of the population. This class has everywhere, until recent years, had fewer opportunities for education than the similar classes in the cities and, where the people who tilled the soil have not succeeded in getting possession of the soil-as is especially true in certain parts of Austria Hungary, and lower Italy. They have remained in a condition of greater or less subjection to the landowning classes. In lower Italy, where the masses of the farming population have neither land nor schools, they have remained in a position not far removed from slavery. In Denmark, on the contrary, where the farming class is, for the most part, made up of independent landowners, not only has agriculture been more thoroughly developed and organized than elsewhere, but farmers are a dominating influence in the political life of the country.

In England, which is the home of political liberty, the working classes have all the political privileges of other Englishmen, although the bulk of the land is in the hands of a comparatively few landowners. On the other hand, the majority of the laborers in the cities have not increased their economic independence. In fact, the English city laborer, from all that I could observe, seemed to be in a position of greater dependence upon his employer and upon the capitalist than is true of any other country I visited.

I recall one incident of my stay in London which emphasized this fact in my mind: I noticed one day a man who was standing, with his hands in his pockets, looking vaguely into the street, one of those types of the casual laborer of whom one meets so many examples in London. I asked if work was plentiful about this time of the year.

"No," he replied. "It is hard to get anything to do; so many people are out of town."

This man looked to me like a dock laborer. I met him somewhere, I think, on or near Mile End Road, in the East End, which is in the center of a district of over a million inhabitants made up entirely of working people. I told him I could not understand how the absence of a few hundred or a few thousand individuals from a great city like London could make much difference to him. "It makes a great difference, sir," he replied. "Everything seems to stop when they go away."

This man was to be sure, a casual laborer, one who had, perhaps, been crowded out by competition from the regular avenues of employment. But there are an enormous number of these casual laborers in England. They seem to be a product of the system.

A week or ten days later I met at Skibo Castle in the Highlands of Scotland, Lord John Morley, at that time secretary of state for India. During the time that I was there the question of the condition of the laboring classes was several times touched upon in conversation and some reference was made to the condition I have referred to. I recall that Lord Morley listened to the discussion for some time without making any comment. Then he said very positively that, in spite of all that had been said, the English laborer was, in his opinion, in a greatly better position today than he had ever been before in his history. I was the more impressed with this statement because it came from a man who has a world wide reputation as a scholar and a writer, and who is at the same time a member of what is the most democratic government that has ever ruled in England, a government, also, that has sought to do more than any other to improve the living conditions of the laboring classes.

The experience I had among the poorer classes in London helped me to realize, as I had not done before, the opportunity that the Negro, in spite of the discriminations and injustices from which he suffers, has in America today, and particularly in the Southern States, where there is still opportunity to get land, to live in God's open country and in contact with simple, natural things, compared with that of the people in the crowded English cities, where hundreds of thousands of them live practically from hand to mouth and where one tenth of the population, according to an investigation some years ago, are living either in poverty or on the edge of destitution.

At the present moment the national government, in conjunction with the city of London, is spending immense sums of money in laying out parks, in building public baths, model tenements and lodging houses in some of the poorer quarters of the city. Better than all else, they are building out in the suburbs, on some of the vacant land outside the city, beautiful garden cities, rows and rows of model houses, each with its little garden in front of it, and each provided with every convenience that modern invention and science can suggest to make it healthful, convenient, and comfortable. As a result of this improvement, thousands of working people are being removed every year from the dark, gloomy, and unhealthy regions of the overcrowded city to these free, open spaces, where they have an opportunity to get in contact with God's free air and sunlight.

I confess that I marveled at the time and interest and money that have been expended not only by the government, but by the philanthropic people of London, in attempting to ameliorate and to raise the level of life among the poorer working classes. I am convinced that if one half or one tenth of the money, interest, and sympathy that have been expended for the education and uplifting of the poorer classes in London were spent upon the Negro in the South, the race problem in our country would be practically solved.

After visiting London, I went, as I have said, to Austria and spent some time in the city of Prague, in Bohemia; in Vienna, Austria, and Budapest, Hungary. While there I had opportunity several times to go out into the country districts and see something of the condition of the farm laborers. From there I went to Sicily. I saw something of the condition of the small farmers in the region of Palermo. I visited the sulphur mines at Campo Franco in the mountainous region of the interior. I passed several days at Catania and saw the grape harvest and the men bare legged treading the wine in the same way I have read in the Bible. From there I returned and passed several days in Austrian Poland and visited the salt mines. I went out into the country districts and saw the condition of the people in the small country towns in the region around Cracow. I crossed the frontier into Russian Poland and visited a Russian village. From, there I went to Copenhagen and gained new acquaintance with the wonderful things that have been accomplished in the way of organizing and developing agricultural life in that little state.

In thinking over all that I saw and learned during my trip abroad, it seemed to me that I could clearly discern, in all those parts of Europe where the people are most backward, the signs of a great, silent revolution. Everywhere, with perhaps the exception of lower Italy and Sicily, I thought I could see that the man at the bottom was making his way upward and, in doing so, was lifting the level of civilization.

Directly and indirectly, this revolution has, to a very considerable extent, been brought about through the influence of the United States. For example, one of the results of the opening up of the great grain fields in the central part of the United States was to break up the whole system of agriculture in every part of Europe where the products of American agriculture come in competition with those of Europe. It was this same competition with American agriculture that provoked the immigration from Austria, Hungary, and southern Italy. I found that wherever the condition of farm labor was particularly bad in Southern Europe the emigration from that part of Europe to America was especially large and increasing. On the other hand, in Denmark, where the agricultural crisis had been overcome by more intensive and intelligent methods of farming, emigration to the United States had almost ceased.

A secondary effect has been to bring about a reorganization of agriculture in such a way as to improve the condition of the farmer. In several countries efforts have been made to break up the large estates and increase the number of small landowners. There has been a very general improvement in the character of the rural schools. The states of Europe, having discovered that their rural population is one of the most important of the natural resources, have begun to take practical measures to educate and improve the neglected masses.

To a large extent, it seemed to me that the older civilization had been built up on the ignorance and the oppression of the masses of the people who were at the bottom. The welfare of the few was obtained at the expense of the many. On the other hand, at the present time, wherever any of these countries are successful and are making progress, they are seeking to do so, not by oppressing and holding down the masses of the people, but by building them up, making them more intelligent, more independent, better able to think and care for themselves.

It was first of all, the competition with America which brought this result about. It was, in the second place, the contact of the masses of the people with life in America which has made the change. I met everywhere in Southern Europe, among the laboring classes of the people, those who had been to America and who had returned. Frequently they had returned with money which they had earned at common labor in America, and had bought and improved property. The number of small landowners has increased greatly in Hungary, Poland, and in southern Italy as the result of the emigration to America. These people came back, sometimes with money, but always with new ideas and new ambitions. They refused to work for the same wages that they had previously worked for. The result was that the price of farm labor has greatly increased, both in Italy and in other parts of Southern Europe.

On the other hand, this compelled the greater use of farm machinery, compelled more intensive and rational methods of agriculture. But nowhere did I find, as some people had expected, that this emigration had had a deterrent effect upon the development of the country. For the laboring masses, particularly in the rural parts of Southern Europe, the journey to America has been a sort of higher education; it has taught them not only to work better and more efficiently, but to have confidence in themselves and to hope and believe in a better future for themselves and their children. In this way the silent revolution to which I refer in Europe has come about.

Now if there is any lesson to be drawn from these facts, it seems to me it is this: that more and more, at the present day, education must take the place of force in the affairs of men. The world is changing. The greatest nation to-day is not the nation with the greatest army, not the nation that can destroy the most, but the nation with the most efficient laborers and the most productive machinery; the nation that can produce the most.

But if labor is to be efficient, it must be trained and it must be free. The school teacher to-day is more important to the state than the soldier, and the aim of the highest statesmanship should be the improvement not so much of the army as of the school.

Although I started out on my last visit to Europe with the determination of getting acquainted with the people at the bottom and made that my main business while I was there, I did, incidentally, have opportunity to see something, also, of the people at the top. In fact, some of the pleasantest and most profitable moments I had during my stay in Europe were those spent in conversation with people who were either interested or actively engaged in some kind of public service which connected itself with the work that I have been trying to do for my own people in America.

For example, I made the acquaintance through my friend, Mr. Jacob Riis, of Mr. V. Cavling, the editor of one of the most important papers in Denmark, the Politiken. It was largely through him that I was able to see and learn as much as I did, during the short time that I was there, of the life of the country people and of the remarkable schools that have been established for their benefit in the country districts. While I was in Copenhagen I was introduced by the American ambassador, Mr. Maurice E Egan, to the king and queen of Denmark. I learned to my surprise that their majesties were perfectly familiar with the work that we are doing at Tuskegee and I found them anxious to talk with me about the possibility of a similar work for the Negroes in the Danish West India Islands, where there are about thirty thousand people of African descent. The queen told me that she had read not only my earlier book "Up From Slavery," but the volume I had just completed, "The Story of the Negro." What surprised me most was to find the king and queen of Denmark so much better informed in regard to the actual condition and progress of the Negro in America than so many Americans I have met.

At another time, I was the guest of Mr. Andrew Carnegie at his summer home in Scotland. Three of the most interesting and restful days I have ever had were spent at Skibo Castle. Although Skibo is situated in the wildest and most Northern part of Scotland, farther removed from the world, it seemed to me, than any other place I had ever visited, I never felt nearer the center of things than I did while I was there. All kinds of people find their way to Skibo Castle, and apparently anyone who has something really valuable to contribute to the world's welfare or progress finds a welcome there.

Naturally, among guests of that sort, conversation and discussion took a wide range. For three days I had an opportunity of hearing great world questions discussed familiarly by men who knew them at first hand. At the time that I met Lord John Morley at Skibo Castle he was still secretary of state for India. I had never been able to get any definite conception, from what I had read in the newspapers, of the actual situation as between the two races in India, the English and the native Indians, and I was very glad to hear Lord Morley comment on that puzzling and perplexing problem. What he said about the matter was the more interesting because he was able to draw parallels between racial conditions in the Eastern and the Western world, between the Indians in India and the Negroes in the United States.

After I returned from the south of Europe I made two addresses in London, one under the auspices of the Anti slavery and Aborigines Protection Society, and the other at the National Liberal Club. At these meetings I had an opportunity to see face to face people who, as missionaries, writers, or government officials, had both in Africa and at home, labored for the welfare and the salvation of the members of my race in parts of the world I had never seen.

For example, at the luncheon given me under the auspices of the Anti slavery and Aborigines Protection Society, Sir T. Folwell Buxton, grandson of the noted abolitionist and statesman who did so much for the abolition of slavery in the British West Indies, was the presiding officer.

It happened that, at this time, the Society of Friends, which has been from the beginning to the present day, both in England and America, the best friend the

Negro has ever had, was holding its annual meeting, and many of the members of this sect were present the day I spoke. Among others I remember, who have distinguished themselves by what they have done for the Negro in Africa were Sir Harry H. Johnston, the noted African explorer; Sir Arthur Conan Doyle, Mr. E. D. Morel, and Rev. J. H. Harris, secretary of the Anti slavery and Aborigines Protection Society, all of whom have had so large a part in the struggle to bring about reform in the Congo Free State.

Among the many pleasant surprises of this luncheon were a large number of letters from distinguished persons who were unable to be present. Among them, I remember, was a very cordial note from the Prime Minister of England, the Rt. Hon. Herbert Henry Asquith, and among others were two from distinguished personal friends which expressed so generous an appreciation of the work I have attempted to do that I am tempted to reproduce them here. These letters were addressed to John H. Harris, secretary of the Anti-Slavery and Aborigines Protection Society, and were as follows:

Skibo Castle, Dornech Sutherland, Sept. 19th, 1910.
Dear Mr. Harris:
I regret exceedingly to miss any opportunity of doing honor to one of the greatest men living, Booker Washington. Taking into account his start in life, born a slave, and now the acknowledged leader of his people, I do not know a parallel to the ascent he has made. He has marched steadily upward to undisputed leadership, carrying with this the confidence and approval of the white race, and winning the warm friendship of its foremost members a double triumph.

Booker Washington is to rank with the few immortals as one who has not only shown his people the promised land, but is teaching them to prove themselves worthy of it-a Joshua and Moses combined.

Very truly yours,
Andrew Carnegie.

The other letter, from the Archbishop of Canterbury, was as follows:

It is a great disappointment to me that paramount engagements far away from London render it impossible for me to be present at the gathering which is to give greeting and Godspeed to Mr. Booker T. Washington's acquaintance, and I share with all those who know the facts, the appreciation of the services he has rendered and is rendering to the solution of one of the gravest and most perplexing problems of our time. He is a man who, in every sense, deserves well of his contemporaries, and I believe that, when hereafter the story is written of Christian people's endeavor in our day to atone for and to amend the racial wrongdoing of the past, Mr. Booker T. Washington's name will stand in the very forefront of those for whom the world will give thanks.

It was a great pleasure and satisfaction to me to meet and speak to these distinguished people and the many others whom I met while I was in London. What impressed me through it all was the wide outlook which they had upon the world and its problems. Questions which we in America are inclined to look upon as local and peculiar to our own country assume in the eyes of Englishmen whose interests are not confined to any single country or continent the character of world problems. I learned in England to see that the race problem in the United States is, as Mr. Herbert Samuels, the English postmaster-general said, "A problem which faces all countries in which races of a widely divergent type are living side by side."

The success of the Negro in America and the progress which has been made here in the solution of the racial problem gained wider and deeper meaning for me as a result of my visit to Europe.

What I Learned About Education in Denmark

On the railway train between Copenhagen, Denmark, and Hamburg, Germany, I fell into conversation with an English traveler who had been in many parts of the world and who, like myself, was returning from a visit of observation and study in Denmark. We exchanged traveler's experiences with each other. I found that he had had opportunity to study conditions in that country a great deal more thoroughly than was true in my case and he gave me much information that I was glad to have about the condition of agriculture and the life of the people.

In return I told him something of the places I had visited before going to Denmark and of the way I had attempted to dig down, here and there in different parts of Europe, beneath the crust and see what was going on in the lower strata of social life. I said to him, finally, that after all I had seen, I had come to the conclusion that the happiest country in Europe, perhaps the happiest country in the world, is Denmark. Then I asked him if he knew any part of the world where the people seemed to come so near to solving all their problems as in Denmark. He seemed a little startled and a little amused at that way of putting the matter, but, after considering the question, he confessed that he had never visited any other part of the world that seemed to be in a more generally healthy and wholesome condition than this same little country which we were just leaving behind us.

Denmark is not rich in the sense that England and the United States are rich. I do not know what the statisticians say about the matter, but I suppose that in Denmark there are few if any such great fortunes as one finds in England, in the United States, and in many parts of Europe. In fact, there is hardly room enough in this little land for a multi millionaire to move about in, as it is less than one third the size of the state of Alabama, although it has one third more population.

Denmark is an agricultural country. About two fifths of the whole population is engaged in some form or other of agriculture. The farms in Denmark have been wonderfully prosperous in recent years. I doubt, however, whether as much money has been made or can be made in Denmark as has been made on the farms in the best agricultural districts in America. The soil is not particularly rich. A large section of the country is, or has been until recent years, made up of barren heath like that in northern Scotland. Within the past few years, as a result of one of the most remarkable pieces of agricultural engineering that has ever been attempted, large tracts of this waste have been made over into fruitful farm land.

In spite of disadvantages, however, the country has greatly prospered for a number of years past. People have been coming from all over the world to study Danish agriculture and they have gone away marveling at the results. I am not going to try to tell in detail what these results were or in what manner they have been obtained. I will merely say that it seems to be generally conceded that, both in the methods of culture and in the marketing of the crops, Denmark has gone farther and made greater progress than any other part of the world. Furthermore, there is no country, I am certain, not even the United States or Canada, where the average farmer stands so high or exercises so large an influence upon political and social life as he does in Denmark at the present time.

"What's back of the Danish farmer?" I said to my English friend. "What is it that has made agriculture in this country?"

"It's the Danish schools," he replied.

I had asked the same question before and received various replies, but they all wound up with a reference to the schools, particularly the country high schools. I had heard much of them in America; I heard of them again in England; for 90 per cent of Denmark's agricultural exports goes to England.

It was not, however, until I reached Denmark, saw the schools themselves, and talked with some of the teachers, not in fact, until after I had left Denmark and had an opportunity to look into and study their history and organization-that I began to comprehend the part that the rural high schools were playing in the life of the masses of the Danish people, and to understand the manner in which they had influenced and helped to build up the agriculture of the country.

There are two things about these rural high schools that were of peculiar interest to me: First, they have had their origin in a movement to help the common people, and to lift the level of the masses, particularly in the rural district; second, they have succeeded. I venture to say that in no part of the world is the general average intelligence of the farming class higher than it is in Denmark. I was impressed in my visits to the homes of some of the small farmers by the number of papers and magazines to be found in their homes.

In recent years there has sprung up in many parts of Europe a movement to improve the condition of the working masses through education. Wherever any effort has been made on a large scale to improve agriculture, it has almost invariably taken the form of a school of some sort or other. For example, in Hungary, the state has organized technical education in agriculture on a grand scale. Nowhere in Europe, I learned, has there been such far reaching effort to improve agriculture through experimental and research stations, agricultural colleges, high schools, and common schools. There is this difference, however: Hungary has tried to improve agriculture by starting at the top, creating a body of teachers and experts who are expected in turn to influence and direct the classes below them. Denmark has begun at the bottom.

One of the principal aims of the Hungarian Government, as appears from a report by the Minister of Agriculture, was "to adapt the education to the needs of the different classes and take care, at the same time, that these different classes did not learn too much, did not learn anything that would unfit them for their station in life."

I notice, for example, that it was necessary to close the agricultural school at Debreczen, which was conducted in connection with an agricultural college at the same place, because, as the report of the Minister of Agriculture states, "the pupils of this school, being in daily contact with the first year pupils of the college, attempted to imitate their ways, wanted more than was necessary for their social position, and at the same time aimed at a position they were unable to maintain."

All this is in striking contrast to the spirit and method of the Danish rural high school, which started among the poorest farming class, and has grown, year by year, until it has drawn within its influence nearly all the classes in the rural community. In this school it happens that the daughters of the peasant and of the nobleman sometimes sit together on the same bench and that the sons of the landlord and of the tenant frequently work and study side by side, sharing the personal friendship of their teacher and not infrequently the hospitality of his home.

The most striking thing about the rural high school in Denmark is that it is neither a technical nor an industrial school and, although it was created primarily for the peasant people, the subject of agriculture is almost never mentioned, at least not with the purpose of giving practical or technical education in that subject.

It may seem strange that, in a school for farmers, nothing should be said about agriculture, and I confess that it took some time for me to see the connection between this sort of school and Denmark's agricultural prosperity. It seemed to me, as I am sure it will seem to most other persons, that the simplest and most direct way to apply education to agriculture was to teach agriculture in the schools.

The real difference between the Hungarian and the Danish methods of dealing with this problem is, however, in the spirit rather than in the form. In Hungary the purpose of the schools seems to be to give each individual such training as it is believed will fit him for the particular occupation which his station in life assigns him, and no more. The government decides. In other words, education is founded on a system of caste. If the man below learns in school to look to the man in station above him, if he begins to dream and hope for something better than the life to which he has been accustomed then, a social and political principle is violated, and, as the Commissioner of Agriculture says, "the government is not deterred from issuing energetic orders."

Of course, the natural result of such measures is to increase the discontent. Just as soon as any class of people feel that privileges granted to others are denied to them, immediately these privileges whether they be the opportunities for education, or anything else assume in the eyes of the people to whom they are denied a new importance and value. The result of this policy is seen in emigration statistics.

I doubt, from what I have been able to learn, whether all the efforts made by the Hungarian Government in the way of agricultural instruction have done very much to allay the discontent among the masses of the farming population. Thousands of these Hungarian peasants every year still prefer to try their fortune in America, and the steady exodus of the farming population continues.

The rural high school in Denmark has pursued just the opposite policy. It has steadily sought to stimulate the ambitions and the intellectual life of the peasant people. Instead, however, of compelling the ambitious farmer's boy, who wants to know something about the world, to go to America, to the ordinary college, or to the city, the schools have brought the learning of the colleges and the advantages of the city to the country.

The most interesting and remarkable thing about these high schools is the success that they have had in presenting every subject that an educated man should know about in such a form as will make it intelligible and interesting to country boys and girls who have only had, perhaps, the rudiments of a common school education.

The teachers in these country high schools are genuine scholars. They have to be, for the reason that the greater part of their teaching is in the form of lectures, without textbooks of any kind, and their success depends upon the skill with which they can present their subjects. In order to awaken interest and enthusiasm, they have to go to the sources for their knowledge.

Most of the teachers whom I met could speak two or three languages. I was surprised at the knowledge which every one I met in Denmark, from the King and Queen to the peasants, displayed in American affairs, and the interest they showed in the progress of the Negro and the work we have been doing at Tuskegee. As an illustration of the wide interests which occupy the teachers in these rural schools, I found one of them engaged in translating Prof. William James's book on "Pragmatism" into the Danish language.

I have heard it said repeatedly since I was in Denmark that the Danish people as a whole were better educated and better informed than any other people in Europe. Statistics seem to bear out this statement; for, according to the immigration figures of 1900, although 24.2 percent of all persons over fourteen years of age coming into the United States as immigrants could neither read, nor write, only .8 percent of the immigrants from Scandinavia were illiterate. Of the Germans, among whom I had always supposed education was more widely diffused than elsewhere in Europe, 5.8 percent. were illiterate.

Before I go farther, perhaps, I ought to give some idea of what these rural high schools look like. One of the most famous of them is situated about an hour's ride from Copenhagen, near the little city of Roskilde. It stands on a piece of rolling ground, overlooking a bay, where the little fisher vessels and small seafaring craft are able to come far inland, almost to the center of the island. All around are wide stretches of rich farm land, dotted here and there with little country villages.

There is, as I remember, one large building with a wing at either end. In one of these wings the head master of the school lives, and in the other is a gymnasium. In between are the school rooms where the lectures are held. Everything about the school is arranged in a neat and orderly manner. They were simple, clean, and sweet-and I was especially impressed by the wholesome, homelike atmosphere of the place. Teachers and pupils eat together at the same table and meet together in a social way in the evening. Teachers and students are thus not merely friends; they are in a certain sense comrades.

In the school at Roskilde there are usually about one hundred and fifty students. During the winter term of five months the young men are in school; in the summer the young women take their turn. Pupils pay for board and lodging twenty crowns, a little more than five dollars a month, and for tuition, twenty crowns the first month, fifteen the second, ten the third, five the fourth, and nothing the fifth. These figures are themselves an indication of the thrift as well as the simplicity with which these schools are conducted.

Twenty years ago, when they were first started, I was told the pupils used to sleep together, in a great sleeping room on straw mattresses, and eat with wooden spoons out of a common dish, just as the peasant people did at that time. This reminds me that just about this same time, at Tuskegee, pupils were having similar hardships. For one thing, I recall that, in those days, the food for the whole school was cooked in one large iron kettle and that sometimes we had to skip a meal because there wasn't anything to put in the kettle. Since that time conditions have changed, not only in the rural high schools of Denmark, but among the country people. At the present day, if not every peasant cottage, at least every cooperative dairy has its shower bath. The small farmer, who, a few years ago, looked upon every innovation with mistrust, is likely now to have his own telephone for Denmark has more telephones to the number of the population than has any other country in Europe, and every country village has its gymnasium and its assembly hall for public lectures.

I have before me, on my desk, a school plan showing the manner in which the day is disposed of. School begins at eight o'clock in the morning and ends at seven o'clock in the evening, with two hours rest at noon. Two thirds of the time of the school is devoted to instruction in the Danish mother tongue, and in history. The rest is given to arithmetic, geography, and the natural sciences.

It is peculiar to these schools that most of the instruction is given in the form of lectures. There are no examinations and few recitations. Not only the natural sciences, but even the higher mathematics, are taught historically, by lectures.

The purpose is not to give the student training in the use of these sciences, but to give him a general insight into the manner in which different problems have arisen and of the way in which the solution of them has widened and increased our knowledge of the world.

In the Danish rural high school, emphasis is put upon the folk songs, upon Danish history and the old Northern mythology. The purpose is to emphasize, in opposition to the Latin and Greek teaching of the colleges, the value of the history and the culture of the Scandinavian people; and, incidentally, to instill into the minds of the pupils the patriotic conviction that they have a place and mission of their own among the people of the world.

There are several striking things about this system of rural high schools, of which there are now 120 in Denmark. The first thing about them that impressed me was the circumstances in which they had their origin. In the beginning, the rural high schools were a private undertaking, as indeed they are still, although they get a certain amount of support from the State. The whole scheme was worked out by a few courageous individuals, who were sometimes opposed, but frequently assisted by the Government. The point which I wish to emphasize is that they did not spring into existence all at once, but that they grew up slowly and are still growing. It took long years of struggles to formulate and popularize the plans and methods which are now in use in these schools. In this work the leading figure was a Lutheran bishop, Nicolai Frederick Severen Grundvig, who is often referred to as the Luther of Denmark. The rural school movement grew out of a non sectarian religious movement and was, in fact, an attempt to revive the spiritual life of the masses of the people.

Rural high schools were established as early as 1844, but it was not until twenty years later, when Denmark, as a result of her disastrous war with Prussia, had lost one third of her richest territory, that the rural high school movement began to gain ground. It was at that time, when affairs were at their lowest ebb in Denmark, that Grundvig began preaching to the Danish people the gospel that what had been lost without, must be regained within; and that what had been lost in battle must be gained in peaceful development of the national resources.

Bishop Grundvig saw that the greatest national resource of Denmark, as it is of any country, was its common people. The schools he started and the methods of education he planned were adapted to the needs of the masses. They were an attempt to popularize learning, put it in simple language, rob it of its mystery and make it the common property of the common people.

Another thing peculiar about these schools is that they were not for children, but for older students. Eighty percent of the students in the rural high schools are from eighteen to twenty five years of age; 12 per cent are more than twenty five years of age and only 8 per cent are under eighteen. These schools are in fact, farmers' colleges. They presuppose the education of the common school. The farmer's son and the farmer's daughter, before they enter the rural high school, have had the training in the public schools and have had practical schooling in the work of the farm and the home. At just about the age when a boy or a girl begins to think about leaving home and of striking out in the world for himself; just at the age when there, comes, if ever, to a youth the desire to know something about the larger world and about all the mysteries and secrets that are buried away in books or handed down as traditions in the schools, just at this time the boys and girls are sent away to spend two seasons or more in a rural high school. As a rule they go, not to the school in their neighborhood but to some other part of the country.

There they make the acquaintance of other young men and women who, like themselves, have come directly from the farms, and this intercourse and acquaintance helps to give them a sense of common interest and to build up what the socialists call a" class consciousness." All of this experience becomes important a little later in the building up of the cooperative societies, cooperative dairies, cooperative slaughter houses, societies for the production and sale of eggs, for cattle raising and for other purposes.

The present organization of agriculture in Denmark is indirectly but still very largely due to the influence of the rural school. The rural high school came into existence, as I have said, as the result of a religious rather than of a merely social or economic movement. Different in methods and in outward form as these high schools are from the industrial schools for the Negro in America, they have this in common, that they are non-sectarian, but in the broadest, deepest sense of that word, religious. They seek not merely to broaden the minds, but to raise and strengthen the moral life of masses of the people. This peculiar character of the Danish rural high school was defined to me in one word by a gentleman I met in Denmark. He called them "inspirational."

It is said of Grundvig that he was one of those who did not look for salvation merely in political freedom. In spite of this fact, the rural high schools have had a large influence upon politics in Denmark. It is due to them, although they have carefully abstained from any kind of political agitation, that Denmark, under the influence of its "Peasant Ministry," has become the most democratic country in Europe. It is certainly a striking illustration of the result of this education that what, a comparatively few years ago, was the lowest and the most oppressed class in Denmark, namely the small farmer, has become the controlling power in the State, as seems to be the case at the present time.

I have gone to some length to describe the plans and general character of the rural high schools because they are the earliest, the most peculiar and unusual feature in Danish rural life and education, and because, although conducted in the same spirit, they are different in form and methods from the industrial schools with which I have been mainly interested during the greater part of my life.

The high schools, however, are only one part of the Danish system of rural schools. In recent years there has grown up side by side with the rural high school another type of school for the technical training in agriculture and in the household arts. For example, not more than half a mile from the rural high school which I visited at Roskilde, there has recently been erected what we in America would call an industrial school, where scientific agriculture, as well as technical training in home keeping are given. In this school, young men and women get much the same practical training that is given our students at Tuskegee, with the exception that this training is confined to agriculture and housekeeping. Besides, there is, in these agricultural schools, no attempt to give students a general education as is the case with the industrial schools in the South. In fact, schools like Hampton and Tuskegee are trying to do for their students at one and the same time, what is done in Denmark through two distinct types of school.

I found this school, like its neighbor the high school, admirably situated, surrounded by beautiful gardens in which the students raised their own vegetables. In the kitchen, the young women learned to prepare the meals and to set the tables. I was interested to see also that, in the whole organization of the school there was an attempt to preserve the simplicity of country life. In the furniture, for example, there was an attempt to preserve the solid simplicity and quaint artistic shapes with which the wealthier peasants of fifty or a hundred years ago furnished their homes. Dr. Robert E. Park, my companion on my trip through Europe, told me when I visited this school that he found one of the professors at work in the garden wearing the wooden shoes that used to be worn everywhere in the country by the peasant people. This man had traveled widely, had studied in Germany, where he had taken a degree in his particular specialty at one of the agricultural colleges.

Perhaps the most interesting and instructive part of my visit was the time that I spent at what is called a husmand's or cotter's school, located at Ringsted and founded by N. J. Nielsen-Klodskov in 1902. At this school I saw such an exhibition of vegetables, grains, and especially of apples, as I think I had never seen before, certainly not at any agricultural school.

I wish I had opportunity to describe in detail all that I saw and learned about education and the possibilities of country life in the course of my visit to this interesting school. What impressed me most with regard to it and to the others that I visited, was the way in which the different types of schools in Denmark have succeeded in working into practical harmony with one another; the way also, in which each in its separate way had united with the other to uplift, vivify, and inspire the life and work of the country people.

For example, the school at Ringsted, in addition to the winter course in farming for men and the summer school in household arts for women, offers, just as we do at Tuskegee, a short course to which the older people are invited. The courses are divided between the men and the women, the men's course coming in the winter and the women's course in the summer. During the period of instruction which lasts eleven days, these older people live in the school, just as the younger students do and gain thus the benefit of an intimate association with each other and with their teachers. To illustrate to what extent this school and the others like it have reached and touched the people, I will quote from a letter written to me by the founder. He says: "The Keorehave Husmandskole (cotter's school) is the first of its kind in Denmark. It is a private undertaking and the buildings erected since 1902 are worth about 400,000 crowns ($100,000). During the seven years in which it has been in operation 631 men and 603 women have had training for six months. In addition 3,205 men and women have attended the eleven day courses."

In addition to the short courses in agriculture and housekeeping, offered by the school at Ringsted, some of the rural high schools hold every fall, great public assembles like our Chautauquas, which last from a few days to a week and are attended by men and women of the rural districts. At these meetings there are public lectures on historical, literary and religious subjects. In the evening there are music, singing, and dancing, and other forms of amusement. These annual assemblies, held under the direction of the rural high schools, have largely taken the place of the former annual harvest home festivals in which there was much eating and drinking, as I understand, but very little that was educational or uplifting. In addition to these yearly meetings, which draw together people from a distance, there are monthly meetings which are held either in the high school buildings, or in the village assembly buildings, or in the halls connected with the village gymnasiums. In the cities these meetings are sometimes held in the "High School Homes" as they are called, which serve the double purpose of places for the meetings of young men's and young women's societies and at the same time as cheap and home like hotels for the traveling country people.

In this way the rural high schools have extended their influence to every part of the country, making the life on the farm attractive, and enabling Denmark to set before the world an example of what a simple, wholesome, and beautiful country life can be.

No doubt there are in the country life of Denmark, as of other countries, some things that cast a shadow here and there on the bright picture I have drawn. New problems always spring up out of the solution of the old ones. No matter how much has been accomplished those who know conditions best will inevitably feel that their work has just been begun. However that may be, I do not believe there will be found anywhere a better illustration of the possibilities of education than in the results achieved by the rural schools of Denmark.

One of the things that one hears a great deal of talk: about in America is the relative value of cultural and vocational education. I do not think that I clearly understood until I went to Denmark what a "cultural" education was. I had gotten the idea, from what I had seen of the so called "cultural" education in America, that culture was always associated with Greek and Latin, and that people who advocated it believed there was some mysterious, almost magical power which was to be gotten from the study of books, or from the study of something ancient and foreign, far from the common and ordinary experiences of men. I found, in Denmark, schools in which almost no text-books are used, which were more exclusively cultural than any I had ever seen or heard of.

I had gotten the impression that what we ordinarily called culture was something for the few people who are able to go to college, and that it was somehow bottled up and sealed in abstract language and in phrases which it took long years of study to master. I found in Denmark real scholars engaged in teaching ordinary country people, making it their peculiar business to strip the learning of the colleges of all that was technical and abstract and giving it, through the medium of the common speech, to the common people.

Cultural education has usually been associated in my mind with the learning of some foreign language, with learning the history and traditions of some other people. I found in Denmark a kind of education which, although as far as it went touched every subject and every land that it was the business of the educated man to know about, sought especially to inspire an interest and enthusiasm in the art, the traditions, the language, and the history of Denmark and in the people by whom the students were surrounded. I saw that a cultural education could be and should be a kind of education that helps to awaken, enlighten, and inspire interest, enthusiasm, and faith in one's self, in one's race and in mankind; that it need not be, as it sometimes has been in Denmark and elsewhere, a kind of education that robs its pupils of their natural independence, makes them feel that something distant, foreign, and mysterious is better and higher than what is familiar and close at hand.

I have never been especially interested in discussing the question of the particular label that should be attached to any form of education; I have never taken much interest, for example, in discussing whether the form of education which we have been giving our students at Tuskegee was cultural, vocational, or both. I have been only interested in seeing that it was the kind that was needed by the masses of the people we were trying to reach, and that the work was done as well as possible under the circumstances. From what I have learned in Denmark, I have discovered that what has been done, for example, by Dr. R. H. Boyd in teaching the Negro people to buy Negro instead of white dolls for their children, "in order," as Dr. Boyd says, "to teach the children to admire and respect their own type"; that what has been done at Fisk University to inspire in the Negro a love of folksongs; that what has been done at Tuskegee in our annual Negro Conferences, and in our National Business League, to awaken an interest and enthusiasm in the masses of the people for the common life and progress of the race has done more good, and, in the true sense of the word, been more cultural than all the Greek and Latin that have ever been studied by all Negroes in all the colleges in the country.

For culture of this kind spreads over more ground; it touches more people and touches them more deeply. My study of the Danish rural schools has not only taught me what may be done to inspire and foster a national and racial spirit, but it has shown how closely interwoven are the moral and material conditions of the people, so that each man responds to and reflects the progress of every other man in a way to bring about a healthful, wholesome condition of national and racial life.

The Mistakes and The Future of Negro Education

During the thirty years I have been engaged in Negro education in the South, my work has brought me into contact with many different kinds of Negro schools. I have visited these schools in every part of the South and have had an opportunity to study their work and learn something of their difficulties as well as of their successes. During the last five years, for example, I have taken time from my other work to make extended trips of observation through eight different states, looking into the condition of the schools and saying a word, wherever I went, in their interest. I have had opportunities, as I went about, to note not merely the progress that has been made inside the school houses, but to observe, also, the effects which the different types of schools have had upon the homes and in the communities by which they are surrounded.

Considering all that I have seen and learned of Negro education in the way I have described, it has occurred to me that I could not do better in the concluding reminiscences of my own larger education than give some sort of summary statement, not only of what has been accomplished, but what seems to be the present needs and prospects of Negro education in general for the Southern States. In view also of the fact that I have gained the larger part of my own larger education in what I have been able to do for this cause, the statement may not seem out of place here. Let me then, first of all, say that never in the history of the world has a people, coming so lately out of slavery, made such efforts to catch up with and attain the highest and best in the civilization about them; never has such a people made the same amount of progress in the same time as is the case of the Negro people of America.

At the same time, I ought to add, also, that never in the history of the world has there been a more generous effort on the part of one race to help civilize and build up another than has been true of the American white man and the Negro. I say this because it should be remembered that, if the white man in America was responsible for bringing the Negro here and holding him in slavery, the white man in America was equally responsible for giving him his freedom and the opportunities by which he has been able to make the tremendous progress of the last forty eight years.

In spite of this fact, in looking over and considering conditions of Negro education in the South today, not so much with reference to the past as to the future, I am impressed with the imperfect, incomplete, and unsatisfactory condition in which that education now is I fear that there is much misconception, both in the North and in the South, in regard to the actual opportunities for education which the Negro has.

In the first place, in spite of all that has been said about it, the mass of the Negro people has never had, either in the common schools or in the Negro colleges in the South, an education in the same sense as the white people in the Northern States have had an education. Without going into details, let me give a few facts in regard to the Negro schools of so-called higher learning in the South. There are twenty five Negro schools which are ordinarily classed as colleges in the South. They have, altogether, property and endowments, according to the report of the United States commissioner of education, of $7,993,028. There are eleven single institutions of higher learning in the Northern States, each of which has property and endowment equal to or greater than all the Negro colleges in the South. There are, for instance, five colleges or universities in the North every one of which has property and endowments amounting to more than $20,000,000; there are three universities which together have property and endowments amounting to nearly $100,000,000.

The combined annual income of twenty-four principal Negro colleges is $1,048,317. There are fifteen white schools that have a yearly income of from one million to five million dollars each. In fact, there is one single institution of learning in the North which, in the year of 1909, had an income, nearly twice as large as the combined income of the one hundred and twenty three Negro colleges, industrial schools, and other private institutions of learning of which the commissioner of education has any report. These facts indicate, I think, that however numerous the Negro institutions of higher learning may be, the ten million Negroes in the United States are not getting from them, either in quality or in quantity, an education such as they ought to have.

Let me speak, however, of conditions as I have found them in some of the more backward Negro communities. In my own state, for example, there are communities in which Negro teachers are now being paid not more than from fifteen dollars to seventeen dollars a month for services covering a period of three or four months in the year. As I stated in a recent open letter to the Montgomery Advertiser, more money is paid for Negro convicts than for Negro teachers. About forty six dollars a month is now being paid for first class, able bodied Negro convicts, thirty six dollars for second-class, and twenty-six dollars for third class, and this is for twelve months in the year. This will, perhaps, at least suggest the conditions that exist in some of the Negro rural schools.

I do not mean to say that conditions are as bad everywhere as these that I refer to. Nevertheless, when one speaks "of the results of Negro education" it should be remembered that, so far as concerns the masses of the Negro people, education has never yet been really tried.

One of the troubles with Negro education at the present time is that there are no definite standards of education among the different Negro schools. It is not possible to tell, for instance, from the name of an institution, whether it is teaching the ordinary common school branches, Greek and Latin, or carpentry, blacksmithing, and sewing. More than that, there is no accepted standard as to the methods or efficiency of the teaching in these schools. A student may be getting a mere smattering, not even learning sufficient reading and writing to be able to read with comfort a book or a newspaper. He may be getting a very good training in one subject and almost nothing in some other. A boy entering such a school does not know what he is going for, and, nine times out of ten, he will come away without knowing what he got. In many cases, the diploma that the student carries home with him at the conclusion of his course is nothing less than a gold brick. It has made him believe that he has gotten an education, when he has actually never had an opportunity to find out what an education is.

I have in mind a young man who came to us from one of those little colleges to which I have referred where he had studied Greek, Latin, German, astronomy, and, among other things, stenography. He found that he could not use his Greek and Latin and that he had not learned enough German to be able to use the language, so he came to us as a stenographer. Unfortunately, he was not much better in stenography and in English than he was in German. After he had failed as a stenographer, he tried several other things, but because he had gone through a college and had a diploma, he could never bring himself to the point of fitting himself to do well any one thing. The consequence was that he went wandering about the country, always dissatisfied and unhappy, never giving satisfaction to himself or to his employers.

Although this young man was not able to write a letter in English without making grammatical errors or errors of some kind or other, the last time I heard of him he was employed as a teacher of business, in fact, he was at the head of the business department in one of the little colleges to which I have referred. He was not able to use his stenography in a well-equipped office, but he was able to teach stenography sufficiently well to meet the demands of the business course as given in the kind of Negro college of which there are, unfortunately, too many in the South.

Now, there was nothing the matter with this young man accepting his education. He was industrious, ambitious, absolutely trustworthy, and, if he had been able to stick at any one position long enough to learn to do the work required of him well, he would have made, in my opinion, a very valuable man. As it was, his higher education spoiled him. In going through college he had been taught that he was getting an education when, as a matter of fact, he really had no education worth the mention.

One of the mistakes that Negro schools have frequently made has been the effort to cover, in some sort of way, the whole school curriculum from the primary, through the college, taking their students, as a friend of mine once said, "From the cradle to the grave." The result is that many of the Negro colleges have so burdened themselves with the work of an elementary grade that they are actually doing no college work at all, although they still keep up the forms and their students still speak of themselves as "college students."

In this way nearly every little school calling itself a college has attempted to set up a complete school system of its own, reaching from the primary grade up through the university. These schools, having set themselves an impossible task, particularly in view of the small means that they have at their command, it is no wonder that their work is often badly done.

I remember visiting one of these institutions in the backwoods district of one of the Southern States. The school was carried on in an old ramshackle building, which had been erected by the students and the teachers, although it was evident that not one of them had more than the most primitive notion of how to handle a saw or a square.

The wind blew through the building from end to end. Heaps of Bibles, which had been presented to the school by some friends, were piled up on the floor in one corner of the building. The dormitory was in the most disorderly condition one could possibly imagine. Half of the building had been burned away and had never been rebuilt. Broken beds and old mattresses were piled helter skelter about in the rooms. What showed as well as anything the total incompetency of everybody connected with the school, were the futile efforts that had been made to obtain a supply of drinking water. The yard around the school, which they called the "campus," was full of deep and dangerous holes, where some one had attempted at different times to dig a well but failed, because, as was evident enough, he had not the slightest idea of how the work should have been done.

At the time I was there the school was supplied with water from an old swamp in the neighborhood, but the president of the college explained to me an elaborate plan which he had evolved for creating an artificial lake and this enterprise, he said, had the added advantage of furnishing work for the students.

When I asked this man in regard to his course of study, he handed me a great sheet of paper, about fifteen inches wide and two feet long, filled with statements that he had copied from the curricula of all sorts of different schools, including theological seminaries, universities, and industrial schools. From this sheet, it appeared that he proposed to teach in his school everything from Hebrew to telegraphy. In fact, it would have taken at least two hundred teachers to do all the work that he had laid out.

When I asked him why it was that he did not confine himself within the limits of what the students needed and of what he would be able to teach, he explained to me that he had found that some people wanted one kind of education and some people wanted another. As far as he was concerned, he took a liberal view and was willing to give anybody anything that was wanted. If his students wanted industrial education, theological education, or college education, he proposed to give it to them.

I suggested to him that the plan was liberal enough, but it would be impossible for him to carry it out. "Yes," he replied, "it may be impossible just now, but I believe in aiming high." The pathetic thing about it all was that this man and the people with whom he had surrounded himself were perfectly sincere in what they were trying to do. They simply did not know what an education was or what it was for.

We have in the South, in general, five types of Negro schools. There are: (1) the common schools, supported in large part by state funds supplemented in many cases by contributions from the colored people; (2) academies and so called colleges, or universities, supported partly by different Negro religious denominations and partly by the contributions of philanthropic persons and organizations; (3) the state normal, mechanical, and agricultural colleges, supported in part by the state and in part by funds provided by the Federal Government; (4) medical schools, which are usually attached to some one or other of the colleges, but really maintain a more or less independent existence; (5) industrial schools, on the model of Hampton and Tuskegee.

Although these schools exist, in many cases, side by side, most of them are attempting to do, more or less, the work of all the others. Because every school is attempting to do the work of every other, the opportunities for cooperation and team work are lost. Instead one finds them frequently quarreling and competing among themselves both for financial support and for students. The colleges and the academies frequently draw students away from the public schools. The state agricultural schools, supported in part by the National Government, are hardly distinguishable from some of the theological seminaries. Instead of working in cooperation with one another and with the public authorities in building up the public schools, thus bringing the various institutions of learning into some sort of working harmony and system, it not infrequently happens that the different schools are spending time and energy in trying to hamper and injure one another.

We have had some experience at Tuskegee of this lack of cooperation among the different types of Negro schools. For some years we have employed as teachers a large number of graduates, not only from some of the better Negro colleges in the South, but from some of the best colleges in the North as well. In spite of the fact that Tuskegee offers a larger market for the services of these college graduates than they are able to find elsewhere, I have yet to find a single graduate who has come to us from any of these colleges in the South who has made any study of the aims or purposes of industrial education. And this is true, although some of the colleges claim that a large part of their work consists in preparing teachers for work in industrial schools.

Not only has it been true that graduates of these colleges have had no knowledge or preparation which fitted them for teaching in an industrial school, but in many cases, they have come to us with the most distorted notions of what these industrial schools were seeking to do.

Perhaps the larger proportion of the college graduates go when they leave college, as teachers into the city or rural schools. Nevertheless, there is the same lack of cooperation between the colleges and the public schools that I have described as existing between the colleges and the industrial schools. It is a rare thing, so far as my experience goes, for students in the Negro colleges to have had an opportunity to make any systematic study of the actual condition and needs of the schools or communities in which they are employed after they graduate. Instead of working out and teaching methods of connecting the school with life, thus making it a center and a source of inspiration that might gradually transform the communities about them, these colleges have too frequently permitted their graduates to go out with the idea that their diploma was a sort of patent of nobility, and that the possessor of it was a superior being who was making a sacrifice in merely bestowing himself or herself as a teacher upon the communities to which he or she was called.

One of the chief hindrances to the progress of Negro education in the public schools in the South is in my opinion due to the fact that the Negro colleges in which so many of the teachers are prepared have not realized the importance of convincing the Southern white people that education makes the same improvement in the Negro that it does in the white man; makes him so much more useful in his labor, so much better a citizen, and so much more dependable in all the relations of life, that it is worth while to spend the money to give him an education. As long as the masses of the Southern white people remain unconvinced by the results of the education which they see about them that education makes the Negro a better man or woman, so long will the masses of the Negro people who are dependent upon the public schools for their instruction remain to a greater or less extent in ignorance.

Some of the schools of the strictly academic type have declared that their purpose in sticking to the old fashioned scholastic studies was to make of their students Christian gentlemen. Of course, every man and every woman should be a Christian and, if possible, a gentleman or a lady; but it is not necessary to study Greek or Latin to be a Christian. More than that, a school that is content with merely turning out ladies and gentlemen who are not at the same time something else; who are not lawyers, doctors, business men, bankers, carpenters, farmers, teachers, not even housewives, but merely ladies and gentlemen. Such a school is bound, in my estimation, to be more or less of a failure. There is no room in this country, and never has been, for the class of people who are merely gentlemen, and, if I may judge from what I have lately seen abroad, the time is coming when there will be no room in any country for the class of people who are merely gentlemen for people, in other words, who are not fitted to perform some definite service for the country or the community in which they live.

In the majority of cases I have found that the smaller Negro colleges have been modeled on the schools started in the South by the anti-slavery people from the North directly after the war. Perhaps there were too many institutions started at that time for teaching Greek and Latin, considering that the foundation had not yet been laid in a good common school system. It should be remembered, however, that the people who started these schools had a somewhat different purpose from that for which schools ordinarily exist today. They believed that it was necessary to complete the emancipation of the Negro by demonstrating to the world that the black man was just as able to learn from books as the white man, a thing that had been frequently denied during the long anti-slavery controversy.

I think it is safe to say that that has now been demonstrated. What remains to be shown is that the Negro can go as far as the white man in using his education, of whatever kind it may be, to make himself a more useful and valuable member of society. Especially is it necessary to convince the Southern white man that education, in the case of the colored man, is a necessary step in the progress and up building, not merely of the Negro, but of the South.

It should be remembered in this connection that there are thousands of white men in the South who are perfectly friendly to the Negro and would like to do something to help him, but who have not yet been convinced that education has actually done the Negro any good. Nothing will change their minds but an opportunity to see results for themselves.

The reason more progress has not been made in this direction is that the schools planted in the South by the Northern white people have remained, not always through their own fault to be sure, in a certain sense, alien institutions. They have not considered, in planning their courses of instruction, the actual needs either of the Negro or of the South. Not infrequently young men and women have gotten so out of touch during the time that they were in these schools with the actual conditions and needs of the Negro and the South that it has taken years before they were able to get back to earth and find places where they would be useful and happy in some form or other of necessary and useful labor.

Sometimes it has happened that Negro college students, as a result of the conditions under which they were taught, have yielded to the temptation to become mere agitators, unwilling and unfit to do any kind of useful or constructive work. Naturally under such conditions as teachers, or in any other capacity, they have not been able to be of much use in winning support in the South for Negro education. Nevertheless it is in the public schools of the South that the masses of the Negro people must get their education, if they are to get any education at all.

I have long been of the opinion that the persons in charge of the Negro colleges do not realize the extent to which it is possible to create in every part of the South a friendly sentiment toward Negro education, provided it can be shown that this education has actually benefitted and helped in some practical way the masses of the Negro people with whom the white man in the South comes most in contact. We should not forget that as a rule in the South it is not the educated Negro, but the masses of the people, the farmers, laborers, and servants, with whom the white people come in daily contact.

If the higher education which is given to the few does not in some way directly or indirectly reach and help the masses, very little will be done toward making Negro education popular in the South, or toward securing from the different states the means to carry it on.

On the other hand, just so soon as the Southern white man can see for himself the effects of Negro education in the better service he receives from the laborer on the farm or in the shop; just so soon as the white merchant finds that education is giving the Negro not only more wants, but more money with which to satisfy these wants, thus making him a better customer; when the white people generally discover that Negro education lessens crime and disease and makes the Negro in every way a better citizen, then the white taxpayer will not look upon the money spent for Negro education as a mere sop to the Negro race, or perhaps as money entirely thrown away.

I said something like this some years ago to the late Mr. H. H. Rogers and together we devised a plan for giving the matter a fair test. He proposed that we take two or three counties for the purpose of the experiment, give them good schools, and see what would be the result.

We agreed that it would be of no use to build these schools and give them outright to the people, but determined rather to use a certain amount of money to stimulate and encourage the colored people in these counties to help themselves. The experiment was started first of all in Macon County, Ala., in the fall of 1905. Before it was completed Mr. Rogers died, but members of his family kindly consented to carry on the work to the end of the term that we had agreed upon-that is to say, to October, 1910.

As a result of this work forty six new school buildings were erected at an average cost of seven hundred dollars each; school terms were lengthened from three and four to eight and nine months, at an average cost to the people themselves of thirty six hundred dollars per year. Altogether about twenty thousand dollars was raised by the people in the course of this five year period. Similar work on a less extensive scale was done in four other counties. As a result we now have in Macon County a model public school system, supported in part by the county board of education, and in part by the contributions of the people themselves.

As soon as we had begun with the help of the colored people in the different country communities to erect these model schools throughout the county, C. J. Calloway, who had charge of the experiment, began advertising in colored papers throughout the South that in Macon County it was possible for a Negro farmer to buy land in small or large tracts near eight-months' schools. Before long the Negro farmers not only from adjoining counties, but from Georgia and the neighboring states, began to make inquiries. A good many farmers who were not able to buy land but wanted to be near a good school began to move into the county in order to go to work on the farms. Others who already had property in other parts of the South, sold out and bought land in Macon County. Mr. Calloway informs me that, during the last five years, he alone has sold land in this county to something like fifty families at a cost of $49,740. He sold during the year 1910 1450 acres at a cost of $21,335.

I do not think that any of us realized the full value of this immigration into Macon County until the census of 1910 revealed the extent to which the dislocation of the farming population has been going on in other parts of the state. The census shows, for example, that a majority of the Black Belt counties in Alabama instead of increasing have lost population during the last ten years. It is in the Black Belt counties which have no large cities that this decrease has taken place. Macon County, although it has no large cities, is an exception, for instead of losing population it shows an increase of more than ten per cent.

I think that there are two reasons for this: In the first place there is very little Negro crime and no mob violence in Macon County. The liquor law is enforced and there are few Negroes in Macon County who do not cooperate with the officers of the law in the effort to get rid of the criminal element.

In the second place, Macon County is provided not only with the schools that I have described, but with teachers who instruct their pupils in regard to things that will help them and their parents to improve their homes, their stock, and their land, and in other ways to earn a better living.

When the facts brought out by the census were published in Alabama they were the subject of considerable discussion among the large planters and in the public press generally. In the course of this discussion I called attention, in a letter to the Montgomery Advertiser, to the facts to which I have referred.

In commenting upon this letter the editor of The Advertiser said:

The State of Alabama makes liberal appropriations for education and it is part of the system for the benefit to reach both white and black children. It must be admitted that there are many difficulties in properly spending the money and properly utilizing it which will take time and the legislature to correct. The matter complained of in the Washington letter could be easily remedied by the various county superintendents and it is their duty to see that the causes for such complaint are speedily removed.

Negro fathers and mothers have shown intense interest in the education of their children and if they cannot secure what they want at present residences they will as soon as possible seek it elsewhere. We commend Booker Washington's letter on this subject to the careful consideration of all the school officials and to all citizens of Alabama.

The value of the experiment made in Macon County is, in my opinion, less in the actual good that has been done to the twenty six thousand people, white and black, who live there, than it is in the showing by actual experiment what a proper system of Negro education can do in a country district toward solving the racial problem.

We have no race problem in Macon County; there is no friction between the races; agriculture is improving; the county is growing in wealth. In talking with the sheriff recently he told me that there is so little crime in this county that he scarcely finds enough to keep him busy. Furthermore, I think I am perfectly safe in saying that the white people in this county are convinced that Negro education pays.

What is true of Macon County may, in my opinion, be true of every other county in the South. Much will be accomplished in bringing this about if those schools which are principally engaged in preparing teachers shall turn about and face in the direction of the South, where their work lies. My own experience convinces me that the easiest way to get money for any good work is to show that you are willing and able to perform the work for which the money is given. The best illustration of this is, perhaps, the success, in spite of difficulties and with almost no outside aid, of the best of the Negro medical colleges. These colleges, although very largely dependent upon the fees of their students for support, have been successful because they have prepared their students for a kind of service for which there was a real need.

What convinces me that the same sort of effort outside of Macon County will meet with the same success is that it has in fact met with the same success in the case of Hampton and some other schools that are doing a somewhat similar work. On "the educational campaigns" which I have made from time to time through the different Southern States I have been continually surprised and impressed at the interest taken by the better class of white people in the work that I was trying to do. Everywhere in the course of these trips I have met with a cordial, even an enthusiastic, reception not only from the colored people but from the white people as well.

For example, during my trip through North Carolina in November of 1910, not only were the suggestions I tried to make for the betterment of the schools and for the improvement of racial relations frequently discussed and favorably commented upon in the daily newspapers, but after my return I received a number of letters and endorsements from distinguished white men in different parts of the state who had heard what I had had to say.

I was asked the other day by a gentleman who has long been interested in the welfare of the colored people what I thought the Negro needed most after nearly fifty years of freedom. I promptly answered him that the Negro needed now what he needed fifty years ago, namely, education. If I had attempted to be more specific I might have added that what Negro education needed most was not so much more schools or different kinds of schools as an educational policy and a school system.

In the last analysis, the work of building up such a school system as I have suggested must fall upon the industrial normal schools and colleges which prepare the teacher, because it is the success or failure of the teacher which determines the success of the school. In order to make a beginning in the direction which I have indicated, the different schools and colleges will have to spend much less time in the future than they have in the past in quarreling over the kind of education the Negro ought to have and devote more time and attention to giving him some kind of education.

In order to accomplish this it will be necessary for these schools to obtain very much larger sums of money for education than they are now getting. I believe, however, if the different schools will put the matter to the people in the North and the people in the South "in the right shape," it will be possible to get much larger sums from every source. I believe the state governments in the South are going to see to it that the Negro public schools get a much fairer share of the money raised for education in the future than they have in the past. At the same time I feel that very few people realize the extent to which the colored people are willing and able to pay, and, in fact, are now paying, for their own education. The higher and normal schools can greatly aid the Negro people in raising among themselves the money necessary to build up the educational system of the South if they will prepare their teachers to give the masses of the people the kind of education which will help them to increase their earnings instead of giving them the kind of education that makes them discontented and unhappy and does not give them the courage or disposition to help themselves.

In spite of all the mistakes and misunderstandings, I believe that the Negro people, in their struggle to get on their feet intellectually and find the kind of education that would fit their needs, have done much to give the world a broader and more generous conception of what education is and should be than it had before.

Education, in order to do for the Negro the thing he most needed, has had to do more and different things than it was considered possible and fitting for a school to undertake before the problem of educating a newly enfranchised people arose. It has done this by bringing education into contact with men and women in their homes and in their daily work.

The importance of the scheme of education which has been worked out, particularly in industrial schools, is not confined to America or to the Negro race. Wherever in Europe, in Africa, in Asia, or elsewhere great masses are coming for the first time in contact with and under the influence of a higher civilization, the methods of industrial education that have been worked out in the South by, with, and through the Negro schools are steadily gaining recognition and importance.

It seems to me that this is a fact that should not only make the Negro proud of his past, brief as it has been, but, at the same time, hopeful of the future.

Character Building

Table of Contents

Two Sides Of Life

There are quite a number of divisions into which life can be divided, but for the purposes of this evening I am going to speak of two; the bright side of life and the dark side.

In thought, in talk, in action, I think you will find that you can separate life into these two divisions—the dark side and the bright side, the discouraging side and the encouraging side. You will find, too, that there are two classes of people, just as there are two divisions of the subject. There is one class that is schooling itself, and constantly training itself, to look upon the dark side of life; and there is another class, made up of people who are, consciously or unconsciously, constantly training themselves to look upon the bright side of life.

Now it is not wise to go too far in either direction. The person who schools himself to see the dark side of life is likely to make a mistake, and the person who schools himself to look only upon the bright side of life, forgetting all else, also is apt to make a mistake.

Notwithstanding. this, I think I am right in saying that persons who accomplish the most in this world, those to whom on account of their helpfulness the world looks most for service those — who are most useful in every way — are those who are constantly seeing and appreciating the bright side as well as the dark side of life.

You will sometimes find two persons who get up in the morning, perhaps a morning that is overcast with shadows—a damp, wet, rainy, uninviting morning—and one of these persons will speak of the morning as being gloomy, will speak of the mud-puddles about the house, of the rain, and of all of the disagreeable features. The second person, the one who has schooled himself to see the brighter side of life, the beautiful things in life, will speak of the beauties that are in the rain drops, and the freshness of the newly bathed flowers, shrubs and trees. Notwithstanding the gloomy and generally disconsolate appearance of things; he will find something attractive in the scene out of doors, and will discover something in the gloomy morning that will cheer him.

Suppose that you see these same two persons eat their breakfast.

Perhaps they will find out that the rolls are bad, but that the coffee is excellent. If the rolls are poor, it is a great deal better in such a case to get into the habit—a habit that you will find pays from every standpoint of being able to forget how unpalatable they are, and to let your thoughts dwell upon the good and satisfactory coffee. Call the attention of your near neighbor at the table to the excellence of the coffee. What is the result of that kind of schooling? You will grow up to be an individual whom people will like to see coming near them—an individual to whom people will go for encouragement when the hours are dark, and when everything seems to be discouraging.

In just the same way, when you go into the class-rooms to recite your lessons, do not dwell upon any mistakes that you may think you see the teacher make, or upon any weakness in the presentation of the lesson. All teachers make mistakes sometimes, and you may depend upon it that it is an excellent teacher and a person of fine character who, when he or she has made a mistake, says frankly and plainly, "I have made a mistake," or "I don't know." It takes a very good and a very bright teacher to say, "I don't know." No teacher knows everything about every subject. A good teacher will say frankly and clearly, "I don't know. I cannot answer that question."

Let me tell you, right here, too, that when you go out from here to become teachers yourselves as a large proportion of you will go—whenever you get to a point where a student asks you a question which you are not able to answer, or asks you something about a subject on which you are not well informed, you will find it better to say frankly and honestly," I am unable to answer your question. "Your students will respect you a great deal more for your frankness and honesty. Education is not what a person is able to hold in his head, so much as it is what a person is able to find. I believe it was Daniel Webster who said that the truly educated man was not the one who had all knowledge in his head, but the one who knew where to look for information upon any subject upon which at any time he might want information. Each individual who wishes to succeed must get that kind of discipline. He must get such training that he will know where to go and get facts, rather than try to train himself to hold all facts in his head.

I want you to go out from this institution so trained and so developed that you will be constantly looking for the bright, encouraging and beautiful things in life.

I want you to go out from this institution so trained and so developed that you will be constantly looking for the bright, encouraging and beautiful things in life. It is the weak individual, as a rule, who is constantly calling attention to the other side—to the dark and discouraging things of life. When you go into your classrooms, I repeat, try to forget and overlook any weak points that you may think you see. Remember, and dwell upon, the consideration that has been given to the lesson, the faithfulness with which it was prepared, and the earnestness with which it is presented. Try to recall and to remember every good thing and every encouraging thing which has come under your observation, whether it has been in the classroom, or in the shop, or in the field. No matter where you are, seize hold on the encouraging things with which you come in contact.

In connection with the personality of their teachers, it is very unfortunate for students to form a habit of continually finding fault, of criticizing, of seeing nothing but what the student may think are weak points. Try to get into a frame of mind where you will be constantly seeing and calling attention to the strong and beautiful things which you observe in the life and work of your teachers. Grow into the habit of talking about the bright side of life. When you meet a fellow student, a teacher, or anybody, or when you write letters home, get into the habit of calling attention to the bright things of life that you have seen; the things that are beautiful, the things that are charming. Just in proportion as you do this, you will find that you will not only influence yourself in the right direction, but that you will also influence others that way. It is a very bad habit to get into, that of being continually moody and discouraged, and of making the atmosphere uncomfortable for everybody who comes within ten feet of you. There are some people who are so constantly looking on the dark side of life that they cannot see anything but that side. Everything that comes from their mouths is unpleasant, about this thing and that thing, and they make the whole atmosphere around them unpleasant for themselves and for everybody with whom they come in contact. Such persons are surely undesirable. Why, I have seen people coming up the road who caused me to feel like wanting to cross over on to the other side of the way so as not to meet them. I didn't want to hear their tales of misery and woe. I had heard those tales so many times that I didn't want to get into the atmosphere of the people who told them.

It is often very easy to influence others in the wrong direction, and to grow into such a moody fault-finding disposition that one not only is miserable and unhappy himself, but makes everyone with whom he comes in contact miserable and unhappy. The persons who live constantly in a fault-finding atmosphere, who see only the dark side of life, become negative characters. They are the people who never go forward. They never suggest a line of activity. They live simply on the negative side of life.

Now, as students, you cannot afford to grow in that way. We want to send each one of you out from here, not as a negative force, but as a strong, positive, helpful force in the world. You will not accomplish the task which we expect of you if you go with a moody, discouraged, faultfinding disposition. To do the most that lies in you, you must go with a heart and head full of hope and faith in the world, believing that there is work for you to do, believing that you are the person to accomplish that work, and the one who is going to accomplish it.

In nine cases out of ten, the person who cultivates the habit of looking on the dark side of life is the little person, the miserable person, the one who is weak in mind, heart and purpose. On the other hand, the person who cultivates the habit of looking on the bright side of life, and who calls attention to the beautiful and encouraging things in life, in nine cases out of ten, is the strong individual, the one to whom the world goes for intelligent advice and support. I am trying to get you to see, as students, the best things in life. Do not be satisfied with second-hand or third-hand things in life. Do not be satisfied until you have put yourselves into that atmosphere where you can seize and hold on to the very highest and most beautiful things that can be got out of life.

Helping Others

There are a few essential things in an institution of this kind that I think it is well for you to keep ever before you.

This institution does not exist for your education alone; it does not exist for your comfort and happiness altogether, although those things are important, and we keep them in mind; it exists that we may give you intelligence, skill of hand, and strength of mind and heart; and we help you in these ways that you, in turn, may help others. We help you that you may help somebody else, and if you do not do this, when you go out from here, then our work here has been in vain.

You would be surprised to know how small a part of your own expenses you pay here. You pay but little; and—by reason of that fact it follows that as trustees of the funds which are given to this institution, we have no right to keep an individual here who we do not think is going to be able to go out and help somebody else. We have no right to keep a student here who we do not think is strong enough to go out and be of assistance to somebody else. We are here for the purpose of educating you, that you may become strong, intelligent and helpful.

If you were paying the cost of your board here, and for your tuition, and fuel and lights, then we should have a different problem. But so long as it is true that you pay so small a proportion of your expenses as you do, we must keep in view the fact that we have no right to keep a student here, no matter how much we may sympathize with him or her, unless that student is going to be able to do somebody else some good. Every young man and every young woman should feel that he or she is here on trust, that every day here is a sacred day; that it is a day that belongs to the race. Our graduates, and the majority of the students that have gone out from here, have ever had an unselfish spirit, and have been willing to go out and work at first for small salaries, and in uncomfortable places, where in a large degree conditions have been discouraging

and desolate. We believe that kind of spirit will continue to exist in this institution, and that we shall continue to have students who will go out from here to make other persons strong and useful.

Now no individual can help another individual unless he himself is strong. You notice that the curriculum here goes along in three directions along the line of labor, of academic training, and of moral and religious training. We expect those who are here to keep strong, and to make themselves efficient in these three directions, in each of which you are to learn to be leaders.

Some people are able to do a thing when they are directed to do it, but people of that kind are not worth very much. There are people in the world who never think, who never map out anything for themselves, who have to wait to be told what to do. People of that kind are not worth anything. They really ought to pay rent for the air they breathe, for they only vitiate it. Now we do not want such people as those here. We want people who are going to think, people who are going to prepare themselves. I noticed an incident this morning. Did you ever hear that side door creak on its hinges before this morning? The janitor ought to have noticed that creaking and put some oil on the hinges without waiting to be told to do it. Then, again, this morning I noticed that after it had been raining hard for twenty-four hours, when it was wet and muddy, no provision had been made to protect the hogs at the sty, and they were completely covered with mud. Now the person who had charge of the sty should not have waited for some one to tell him to go down there and put some straw in for bedding and put boards over the sty to keep the animals dry. No one in charge of the hogs ought to have waited to be told to do a thing like that. The kind of persons we want here are those who are not going to wait for you to tell them to do such things, but who will think of them for themselves and do them. If we cannot turn out a man here who is capable of taking care of a pig sty, how can we expect him to take care of affairs of State?

Then, again, some of you are expected to take care of the roads. I should have liked to have seen boys this morning so much interested in working on the roads that they would have put sawdust from this building to the gate. I should have liked to see them put down some boards, and arrange for the water to drain off. We want such fellows as those here. The ones we want are the ones who are going to think of such things as these without being told. That is the only kind of people worth having.

Those who have to wait to have somebody else put ideas into their minds are not worth much of anything. And, to be plain with you, we cannot have such people here. We want you to be thinkers, to be leaders.

Yesterday, and the night before, I traveled on the Mobile and Ohio railroad from St. Louis to Montgomery, and there was a young man on the same train who was not more than twenty years old, I believe, who recently had been appointed a special freight agent of the road. All his conversation was about freight. He talked freight to me and to everybody else. He would ask this man and that man if they had any freight, and if so he would tell them that they must have it shipped over the Mobile and Ohio railroad. Now that man will be general freight agent of that road some day: he may be president of the road. But suppose he had sat down and gone to sleep, and had waited for some one to come to him to inquire the best way to ship freight. Do you suppose he would ever have secured any freight to ship?

Begin to think. If you cannot learn to think, why, you will be of no use to yourself or anybody else. Every once in a while; about every three months, we have to go through the process of "weeding out" among the students. We are going to make that "weeding out" process stricter this year than ever before. We are compelled to get rid of every student here who is weak in mind, weak in morals, or weak in industry. We cannot keep a student here unless he counts for one. You must count one yourself. You eat for one, you drink for one, and you sleep for one; and so you will have to count for one if you are going to stay here.

I want you to go out into the world, not to have an easy time, but to make sacrifices, and to help somebody else. There are those who need your help and your sacrifice. You may be called upon to sacrifice a great deal; you may have to work for small salaries; you may have to teach school in uncomfortable buildings; you may have to work in desolate places, and the surroundings may be in every way discouraging. And when I speak of your going out into life, I do not confine you to the schoolroom. I believe that those who go out and become farmers, and leaders in other directions, as well as teachers, are to succeed.

The most interesting thing connected with this institution is the magnificent record that our graduates are making. As the institution grows larger, we do not want to lose the spirit of self-sacrifice, the spirit of usefulness which the graduates and the students who have gone out from here have shown. We want you to help somebody else. We want you not to think of yourselves alone. The more you do to make somebody else happy, the more happiness will you will receive in turn. If you want to be happy, if you want to live a contented life, if you want to live a life of genuine pleasure, do something for somebody else. When you feel unhappy, disagreeable and miserable, to some one else who is miserable and to that person an act of kindness, you will find that you will be made happy. The miserable persons in this world are the ones whose hearts are narrow and hard; the happy ones are those who have great big hearts. Such persons are always happy.

Some Rocks Ahead

I feel sure that I can be of some degree of service to you tonight, in helping you to anticipate some of the troubles that you are going to meet during the coming year. "Do not look for trouble" is a safe maxim to follow, but it is equally safe to prepare for trouble.

All of you realize, of course, that where we have so large a machine as we happen to have here— when I speak of machine in this way you will understand that I refer to the school — it takes some time to get it into perfect order, or anything bordering upon perfect running order. Now, I repeat, it is the wise individual who prepares him-self beforehand for the day of difficulties, for the day of discouragements, for the rainy day. It is the wise individual, who makes up his mind that life is not going to be all sunshine, that all is not going to be perpetual pleasure. What is true of everyday life is true of school life; there are a number of difficulties which it is probable you are going to meet or which are going to meet you.

During the coming school year, and which, if possible, I want you to prepare yourselves against as wisely as you can.

In the first place, a great many of you are going to be disappointed — if this has not already been the case — in the classes to which you will be assigned. The average individual thinks he knows a great deal more than he does know. The individual who really knows more than he thinks he knows is very rare indeed. When a student gets to the point where he knows more than he knows a great deal more thank he does know. The individual who really knows more thank he thinks he knows is very rare indeed. When a student gets to the point where he knows more than he thinks he knows, that student is about ready to leave school. I wish a very large number of you had reached that point. I repeat, 'numbers of you are going to be disappointed during the year as to the classes to which you are going to be assigned.'

Now, I want to give you this advice, before you go to an institution. Examine the catalogue of that school. The catalogue will give you all the information about the school. Then make up your mind whether or not you have faith in that institution. Find out if it is the school you wish to attend, and then decide if you have faith enough in it to become its pupil. Then if you have once done this, make up your mind that those who are placed over you as your teachers have had more experience than you can have had, and that they are therefore able to advise you as to your classes. Make up your mind that if you are asked to go into a lower class than you think your ability entitles you to go into, you are going to follow the advice and instruction of the people who are older thank you and who have more education than you have.

Another way in which you are going to be disappointed, and be made homesick, perhaps, if you have not already so, is in the rooms to which you are going to be assigned. You are going to get rooms that you do not like. They will not be, perhaps, as attractive as you desire, or they will be too crowded. You are going to be given persons for room mates with whom you think it is going to be impossible to get along pleasantly, people who are not congenial to you. During the hot months your rooms are going to be too hot, and during the cold months they are going to be too cold. You are going to meet with all these difficulties in your rooms. Make up your mind that you are going to conquer them. I have often said that the students who in the early years of this school had such hard times with their rooms have succeeded grandly. Many of you now live in palaces, compared to the rooms which those students had. I am sure that the students who attend this school find that the institution is better fitted every year to take care of them than it was the year previous. From year to year there has been a steady growth in the accommodations, and that is all that we can wish or expect. From year to year we do not forget that it is our duty to make students more comfortable than in previous years, and we are steadily growing in that direction. But notwithstanding all this we cannot do all that we want to do.

Make up your minds, then, that you are going to find difficulties in your room, in reference to your room mates, the heat, the cold, and any number of things that concern your stay in the buildings. But in all these matters keep in mind the high purpose for which you came here—to get an education. Get that thought into your heart and body, and it will enable you to be the master of all these little things, all these minor and temporary obstacles.

Many of you are going to be disappointed in regard to your food. Notwithstanding all the care we may try to take, and want to take, many of you are going to be disappointed in this respect. But how little is the meaning of one meal, how little a thing is being inconvenienced by one meal, as compared with something that is going to be a part of you all the remainder of your lives. It is not for the food, the room, or the minor things that you have come here; it is to get something into your minds and hearts that will make you better, that will stand by you and hold you up, and make you useful all through life.

Some of you are going to find it difficult to obey orders. Sometimes orders will be given you which you think are wrong and unjust. Perhaps orders will be given you sometimes that really are unjust. In that respect no institution is perfect. But I want to learn this lesson in respect to orders — that it is always best to learn to obey orders and respect authority — that it is better ten time over for you to obey an order that you know is wrong, and which perhaps was given you in a wrong spirit or with a mistaken motive. It is better for you to obey even such an order as that, thank it is for any individual to get into the habit of disobeying and not respecting those in authority.'

Make up your mind that if you want to add to your happiness and strength of character, you are, before all things else, going to learn to obey. If it should happen that for a minute, or five minutes, one of your fellow students is placed in authority over you, that student's commands should be sacred. You should obey his commands just as quickly as you would obey those of the highest officer in this institution. Learn that it is no disgrace to obey those in authority. One of the highest and surest signs of civilization is that a people have learned to obey the commands of those who are placed over them. I want to add here that it is to the credit of this institution that, with very few exceptions, the students have always been ready and willing to respect authority.

I want you to see, as I think you will see, that having a hard time, running up against difficulties here and there, helps to make an individual strong, and also helps to make him powerful. This is the point I want to make with you; that .one of the reasons you are here is that you may learn to overcome difficulties. I have named some that you may expect to meet, but I have not named them all. They will keep springing up all the time. Just in proportion as you learn to rise above them and trample them under your feet, just in that proportion—will you accomplish the high purpose for which you came here, and help to accomplish the purpose for which this institution exists.

On Influencing By Example

A few evenings ago, while in Cincinnati, I was very pleasantly surprised after speaking at, a large meeting to be invited by a company of young colored men to attend for a few minutes a reception at their club room. I expected, when I went to the place designated, to find a number of young men who, perhaps, had hired a room and fitted it up for the purpose of gratifying their own selfish pleasures. I found that this was not the case. Instead, I found fifteen young men whose ages ranged from eighteen to twenty years, who had banded themselves together in a club known as the "Winona Club," for the purpose of improving themselves, and further, for the purpose, so far as possible, of getting hold of other young colored men in the city who were inclined in the wrong direction. I found a room beautifully fitted up, with a carpet on the floor, with beautiful pictures 'upon the walls, with books and pictures in their little library, and with fifteen of the brightest, most honest, and cleanest looking young men that it has been my pleasure to meet for a long time.

It was a very pleasant surprise to find these young men, especially in the midst of the temptations of a Northern city, in the midst of evil surroundings, banded together for influencing others in the right direction.

These young men came together, and at their first meeting said that they were going to band themselves together for the purpose of improving themselves and helping others. They said that the first article in their constitution should be to the effect that there should be no gambling in that club; that there must be no strong drink allowed in that club, and that there should be nothing there that was not in keeping with the life of a true and high-minded gentleman.

I repeat that it was very pleasant and encouraging for me to find such work as this going on in Cincinnati. What was equally gratifying, and surprising, was that at the close of the reception they presented me with a neat sum of money which they had collected, and asked that this money be used to defray the expenses of some student at the school here.

Now the point I especially want to make tonight is this: all of you must bear in mind the fact that you are not only to keep yourselves clean, and pure, and sober, and true, in every respect, but you owe a constant responsibility to yourself to see that you exert a helpful influence on others also.

A large proportion of you are to go from here into great cities. Some of you will go into such cities as Montgomery, and some, perhaps, will go into the cities of the North—although I hope that the most of you will see your way clear to remain in the South. I believe that you will do better to remain in the country districts than to go into the cities. I believe that you will find it to your advantage in every way to try to live in a small town, or in a country district, rather than in a city. I believe that we are at our best in country life—in agricultural life—and too often at our worst in city life. Now when you go out into the world for yourselves, you must remember in the first place that you cannot hold yourselves up unless you keep engaged and out of idleness. No idle person is ever safe, whether he be rich or poor. Make up your minds, whether you are to live in the city, or in the country that you are going to be constantly employed.

In a rich and prosperous country like America there is absolutely no excuse for persons living in idleness. I have little patience with persons who go around whining that they cannot find anything to do. Especially is this true in the South. Where the soil is cheap there is little or no excuse for any man or woman going about complaining that he or she cannot find work. You cannot set proper examples unless you, yourself, are constantly employed. See to it, then, whether you live in a city, a town, or in a country district, that you are constantly employed when you are not engaged in the proper kind of recreation, or in rest. Unless you do this you will find that you will go down as thousands of our young men have gone down—as thousands of our young men are constantly going down who yield to the temptations which beset them.

Refrain from staking your earnings upon games of chance. See to it that you pass by those things which tend to your degradation. Teach this to others. Teach those with whom you come in contact that they cannot lead strong, moral lives unless they keep away from the gambling table. See to it that you regulate your life properly; that you regulate your hours of sleep.

Have the proper kinds of recreation. Quite a number of our young men in the cities stay up until twelve, one and two o'clock each night. Sometimes they are at a dance, and sometimes at the gambling table, or in some brothel, or drinking in some saloon. As a result they go late to their work, and in a short time you hear them complaining about having lost their positions. They will tell you that they have last their jobs on account of race prejudice, or because their former employers are not going to hire colored help any longer. But you will find, if you learn the real circumstances, that it is much more likely they have lost their jobs because they were not punctual, or on account of carelessness.

Then, too, you will find that you will go down if you yield to the temptation of indulging in strong drink. That is a thing that is carrying a great many of our young men down. I do not say that all of our men are of this class or that all of them yield to temptations, because I can go into many of the large cities and find just such men as those in Cincinnati to whom I have referred. You cannot hope to succeed if you keep bad company. As far as possible, try to form the habit of spending your nights at home. There is nothing worse for a young man or young woman than to get into the habit of thinking that he or she must spend every night on the street or in some public place.

I want you, as you go out from this institution, whether you are graduates or not, whether you have been here one year or four years—to go out with the idea that you must set a high example for everyone in your community. You must remember that the people are watching you every day. If you yield to the temptation of strong drink, of going into bad company, others will do the same thing. They will shape their lives after yours. You must so shape your lives that the hundreds and thousands of those who are looking to you for guidance may profit by your example.

The Virtue Of Simplicity

I hope that you all paid strict attention to what Mr. William H. Baldwin, Jr., who recently spoke to you, had to say. In the few words that he spoke, I think he told you the platform upon which this institution has been built. You will remember that he laid a great deal of stress upon the importance of the institution remaining simple, of keeping that degree of simplicity and thoroughness that it has always possessed.

It is true that in the last few months the institution has come into a great deal of prominence, and is meeting with what the world calls" success." But we must remember that very often it is with institutions as it is with individuals—success may injure them more than poverty. Now, this institution will continue to succeed, will continue to have the good will and confidence, the co-operation of the best and wisest and most generous people in the country, just so long as its faculty, its students, and all connected with it, remain simple, earnest and thorough. Just as soon as in any department there are indications that we are beginning to become what the world calls "stuck up," just so soon will the people lose confidence in us, and will fail to support us, and just so soon will the institution begin to decay. We will grow in buildings, in industries, in apparatus, in the number of teachers and of students, and in the confidence of the people, just in proportion as we do what the institution has set out to do; that is, teach young men and women how to live simple, plain and honorable lives by learning how to do something uncommonly well.

When I speak of humbleness and simplicity, I do not mean that it is necessary for us to lose sight of what the world calls manhood and womanhood; that it is necessary to be cringing and unmanly; but you will find, in the long run, that the people who have the greatest influence in the world are the humble and simple ones.

Now, we must not only remain humble, but we must be very sure that whatever is done in every department of the school is thoroughly done. Any institution runs a great risk when it begins to grow—to grow larger in numbers or larger in any respect. It can succeed then only in proportion as those who have responsibilities are conscientious in the highest degree. We can succeed in putting up good buildings only in proportion as everyone performs well his part in the erection of each building. We can succeed only in proportion as the student who makes the mortar, who lays the bricks, puts his whole conscience into that work, and does it just as thoroughly as it is possible; for him to do it. If he is mixing mortar, he must do it just as well as he can, and then, tomorrow, must do it still better than he did it to-day, and the next week better than he did it this week. The student who lays the bricks must learn to lay each brick as well as it is possible for him to lay it, and then do still better work on the morrow.

We must remember, too, that we have a certain amount of responsibility to care for our buildings, and that a great deal of interest should be taken not only in putting up all our buildings thoroughly, but in looking out for their preservation as well. We must see to it that the buildings which the students have worked so hard to erect, and which generous friends have so kindly enabled us to secure, are not marred in any way. You must make new students know that this property is yours, and that every building here is yours. No student has any right to mar in any way what you have worked so hard to erect, and your friends have been generous enough to provide If you find a student drawing a lead pencil across a piece of plastering which you have put on, you must let that student know that he is destroying what you have worked hard to create, and that when he destroys that building he is destroying something which students yet to come should have the opportunity of enjoying.

We want to be sure that in every industry, in every department of the institution, there is simplicity, humbleness, and thoroughness. Whatever is entrusted to you to do in the industrial departments, in the class rooms, be sure that you put your whole heart into that thing.

We do not expect to have fine, costly buildings, nor do we want to have them. But we do expect to have well-constructed buildings, and attractive buildings; and, if we can go on in this simple, humble way, the time will come when we shall have all the buildings we need. Just in proportion as our friends see that we are worthy of these good things, they will come to us.

We want to be sure; also, that in no department is there any wastefulness. We must try to make every dollar go as far as possible. "We must stretch a dollar," as I have heard Mr. Baldwin say, "Until it can be stretched no further." Now, there will be waste unless we put' our conscience into everything that we do. There will be: waste in the boarding department, in the academic department, in the industrial department, in the religious department, in all the departments about us, unless we put our conscience into everything that we do. Let us be sure that not a single dollar that is given to us is wasted, because the same people who give to us are called upon almost every day in the week, each year, to give for hundreds of purposes, and they have to choose which they will support. They must decide whether they want to give to this cause, or to that cause, and they will give to us if we make them feel that we are more worthy than other similar institutions.

We want, also, to be sure that we remain simple in our dress and in all our outward appearance. I do not. like to see a young man who is poor, and whose tuition is being paid by some one, and who has no books, sometimes has no socks, sometimes has no decent shoes, wearing a white, stiff, shining collar which he has sent away to be laundered. I do not like to ask people to give money for such a young man as that. It is much better for a young man to learn to launder his collars himself, than to pretend to the world that he is what he is not. When you send a collar to the city laundry, it indicates that you have a bank account; it indicates that you have money ahead, and can afford that luxury. Now I do not believe that you can afford it; and that kind of pretense and that kind of acting do not pay.

Get right down to business, and, as I have said, if we cannot do up your collars well enough here to suit you, why, get some soap and water, and starch, and an iron, and learn to launder your own collars, and keep on laundering them until you can do them better than anybody else.

I am not trying to discourage you about wearing nice collars. I like to see every collar shine. I like to see every collar as bright as possible. I like to see you wear good, attractive collars. I do not, however, want you to get the idea that collars make the man. You quite often see fine cuffs and collars, when there is no real man there. You want to be sure to get the man first. Be sure that the man is there, and if he is, the collars and the cuffs will come in due time. If there is no man there, we may put on all the collars and cuffs we can get, and we shall find that they will not make the man.

When you have finished school, after you have gone out and established yourselves in some kind of business, after you have learned to save money, and have got a good bank account ahead, if you are where the laundering is not sufficiently well done to suit you, why perhaps you can afford to send your collars forty or fifty miles away. But as I see you young men, I do not believe you can afford it. And if you can afford it, why, I should like to have you pay that money for a part of your tuition, which we now have to get some one else to pay for you.

You want to be very sure, too, that as you go out into the world, you go out not ashamed to work; not ashamed to put in practice what you have learned here. As I come in contact with our graduates, I am very glad to be able to say that in almost no instance have I found a student who has been at Tuskegee long enough to learn the ways of the institution, or a graduate who has been ashamed to use his hands. Now that reputation we want to keep up. We want to be sure that such a reputation as this follows every student who goes out.

And then be very sure that you are simple in your words and your language. Write your letters in the simplest and plainest manner possible. Who of you did not understand what was said by Mr. John D. Rockefeller, Jr., when he spoke from this platform a few evenings ago? Was there a single word, or a single reference, or figure of speech that he used that you did not understand the full force of, or did not appreciate? Here is a man whose father is perhaps the richest man in the world, and yet there was no "tomfoolery" about his speech. Every word was simple and plain, and everybody could understand everything that he said. He used no Latin or Greek quotations.

Some people get the idea that if they can get a little education, and a little money ahead, and can talk so that no one can understand them, they are educated. That is a great mistake, because nobody understands them, and they do not understand themselves. Now, the world has no sympathy with that kind of thing. If you have anything to write, write it in the plainest manner possible. Use just as few words as possible, and as simple words as possible. If you can get a word with one syllable that will express your meaning, use it in preference to one of two syllables. If you can not get a suitable word of one syllable, try to get one of two syllables instead of three or four. At any rate make your words just as short as possible, and your sentences as short and simple as you can make them. There is great power in simplicity, simplicity of speech, simplicity of life in every form. The world has no patience with people who are superficial, who are trying to show off, who are trying to be what the world knows they are not.

You know you sometimes get frightened and discouraged about the laws that some of the States are inclined to pass, and that some of them are passing, but there is no State, there is no municipality, there is no power on earth that can neutralize the influence of a high, pure, simple and useful life. Every individual who learns to live such a life will find an opportunity to make his influence felt.

No one can in any way permanently hold back a race of people who are getting those elements of strength which the world recognizes, which the world has always recognized, and which it always will recognize, as indicating the highest type of manhood and womanhood. There is nothing, then, to be discouraged about. We are going forward, and we shall keep going forward if we do not let these difficulties which sometimes occur discourage us. You will find that every man and every woman who is worthy to be respected and praised and recognized will be respected and praised and recognized.

Have You Done Your Best?

[This talk was given at the middle of the school year.]

If you have not already done so—and I hope you have— I think that you will find this a convenient season for each one of you to stop and to consider your school-year very carefully; to consider your life in school from every point of view; to place yourselves, as it were, in the presence of your parents, or your friends at home; to place yourselves in the presence of those who stand by and support this institution; to place yourselves in the presence of your teachers and of all who are in any way interested in you.

Now, suppose you were to-night sitting down by your parents' side, by their fireside, looking them in the face, or by the side of your nearest and dearest friends, those who have done the most for you, those who have stood by you most closely. Suppose you were in that position. I want to ask you to answer this question, In considering your school life in your studies, for example—during the year, thus far, have you done your best?

Have you been really honest with your parents, who have struggled, who have sacrificed, who have toiled for years, in ways you do not know of, in order that you might come here, and in order that you might remain here? Have you really been interested in them? Have you really been honest with your teachers? Have you been honest with those who support this institution? Have you really, in a word, in the preparation and recitation of your lessons, done your level best? Right out from your hearts, have you done your best? I fear that a great many of you, when you look your conscience squarely in the face, when you get right down to your real selves, at the bottom of your lives, must answer that you have not done your best. There have been precious minutes, there have been precious hours, that you have completely thrown away, hours for which you cannot show a single return.

Now, if you have not done your level best, right out straight from your heart, in the preparation and recitation of your lessons, and in all your work, it is not too late for you to make amends. I should be very sorry if I waited until the end of the term to remind you of this, because it would then be too late. There would be many of you with long faces, who would say, if you were reminded then, that you could have done so much better, would have been so much more honest with your parents and friends, if you had only been reminded earlier; and that in every way you would have made your lives so different from what they had been. Now, it isn't too late.

Grant, as I know that numbers of you will grant, that you have thrown away precious time, that you have been indifferent to the advice of your teachers, that you really haven't been honest with yourselves in the preparation of your lessons, that you have been careless in your recitations. I want you to be really honest with yourselves and say, from tonight on, "I am going to take charge of myself. I am not going to drift in this respect. I am going to row up the stream; and my life, as a schoolboy or a schoolgirl, is going to be different from what it has been."

Now place yourselves again in the presence of your parents, of those who are dearest to you, and answer this question, in your work, in your industrial work here, have you done your real best? In the field and in the shop, with the plough, the trowel, the hammer, the saw, have you done your level best? Have you done your best in the sewing room and in the cooking classes? Have you justified your parents in the sacrifice of time and money which they have made in order to allow you to come here? If you haven't done your best in these respects—and many of you haven't there is still time for you to become a different man or woman. It isn't too late. You can turn yourselves completely around. Those of you who have been indifferent and slow, those of you who have been thoughtless and slovenly, those of you who have tried to find out how little effort of body or mind you could put into your industrial work here,—it isn't too late for you to turn yourselves completely around in that respect, and to say that from to-night you are going to be a different man or woman.

Have you done your level best in making your surroundings what the school requires, what your school life should be, in learning how to take care of your bodies, in learning how to keep your bodies clean and pure, in the conscientious, systematic use of the tooth brush? Have you done your best? Have you been downright honest in that respect, alone? Have you used the tooth brush just because you felt it was a requirement of the school, or because you felt that you could not be clean or honest with your room-mates, that you could not be yourself in the sight of God, unless you used the tooth brush? Have you used it in the dark, as well as in the light? Have you learned that, even if your room was not going to be inspected on a certain day, it was just as important that you learn the lesson of being conscientious about keeping it in order as if you knew it was going to be inspected? Have you been careful in this respect? Have you shifted this duty, or neglected that duty? Have you thrown some task off on to your room-mates? Have you tried to "slide out" of it, or, as it were, "to get by," as the slang phrase goes, without doing really honest, straightforward work, as regards the cleanliness of your room, the improvement of it, the making of it more attractive?

Have you been really honest with yourselves and your parents, and with those who spend so much money for the support of this institution? Above all, have you been really true to your parents and to your best selves in growing in strength of character, in strength of purpose, in being downright honest? Those of you who came here, for instance, with the habit of telling falsehoods, of deceiving in one way or another; those of you who came here with the temptation, perhaps, in too many cases, overshadowing you and overpowering you, to take property which does not belong to you; have you been really honest in overcoming habits of this kind? Are you building character? Are you less willing to yield to temptation? Are you more able to overcome temptation now than you were? If you are not more able, you have not grown in this respect.

But it is not too late. If there are some of you who have been unfortunate enough to allow little mean habits, mean dispositions, mean acts, mean thoughts, mean words, to get the uppermost of you—in a word, if your life thus far has been a little, dried-up, narrow life, get rid of that life. Throw open your heart. Say now, "I am not going to be conquered by little, mean thoughts, words and acts any longer. Hereafter all my thoughts, all my words, all my acts, shall be large, generous, high, pure."

In a word, I want you to get hold of this idea, that you can make the future of your lives just what you want to make it. You can make it bright, happy, useful, if you learn this fundamental lesson, and stick to it while in school, or after you go away from here, that it doesn't pay any individual to do any less than his very best. It doesn't pay to be anything else but downright honest in heart. Any person who is not honest, who is not trying to do his very best in the classroom or in the shop, no matter where he may be, will find out that it does not pay in the long run. You may think it best for a little while, but permanently it does not pay any man or woman to be anything but really, downright honest, and to do his or her level best.

Now I want you to think about these things, not only here in the chapel to-night, but to-morrow in your class-rooms, and with reference to everything you touch. I want to, see you let it shine out, even at the very ends of your fingers, that you are doing your best in everything. Do this, and you will find at the end of the year that you are growing stronger, purer, and brighter, that you are making your parents and those interested in you happier, and that you are preparing yourselves to do what this institution and the country expect you to do.

Don't Be Discouraged

Last Sunday evening I spoke to you for a few minutes regarding the importance of determining to do the right thing in every phase of your school life. There are a few things that enter into student life which, in a very large degree, cause the untrue to fall by the wayside, and which prevent students from doing their very best. Among these things is the disposition to grow discouraged. Very many people, very many students, who otherwise would succeed, who would go through school creditably, graduating with honors, have failed to succeed because they became discouraged.

Now there are a number of things in school life that cause a student to become discouraged, and I am going to try to enumerate a few of them, although I do not know that I shall mention nearly all of them.

Students frequently become discouraged on account of their industrial work. It is not of the character that they want it to be, or they do not get assigned to the trade they want to work at. Still others become discouraged because of their classroom studies. They find that their studies are difficult; that their lessons are too long and their memories too short. They find that they cannot understand the teacher, or they think they find that the teacher does not understand them. Some become discouraged because they think that they are entirely misunderstood, are misunderstood by their classmates and by their teachers. They think that their efforts in the classroom and in the shop are not properly appreciated.

Others become discouraged because they feel that they are without friends. It seems to them that other students have friends on every hand who are encouraging them, who send them money, who supply them with clothing, and that they themselves have no such friends.

You become discouraged for such reasons as these. You feel that your highest and best efforts are not appreciated. This tends to discourage you. There are not a few of you who get discouraged because you feel that you belong to a despised race; that for a long time you have been trampled upon because of your color, and because of certain peculiar characteristics; that you have been neglected or oppressed, and that there is no reason why you should make an effort to go forward; that you belong to a race that is doomed to disappointment, to stay under, and to not succeed.

Some of you become discouraged and despondent because of poverty. Perhaps here I strike the basis of the reason for most of the discouragement. You come here, and your parents disappoint you. They do not supply you with money. You become discouraged because they do not supply you with proper clothing, or with what you think you ought to have, and, very often, with such as you really ought to have, and that disheartens you. You find that other students have money, and you have none. They have money not only for the necessities of school life, but for some of the luxuries, while you have not enough for even the bare necessities.

Other students are more than supplied with clothing, while you are very scantily supplied. You shiver, in many cases, by reason of the cold, while others are comfortable and nicely dressed. Sometimes you are even ashamed to show yourself in public, because of the appearance of the old coat, or trousers, or shoes that you have to wear.

Some of you become discouraged because you find yourselves without the proper books. Some of you cannot get the, money needed to purchase books, a tooth brush, and other necessary things. You find yourselves cramped and hampered on every hand. You are discouraged at this point and at that point, and you feel that nobody's lot is as hard as your own. You become discouraged, you become dissatisfied, and you feel like giving up.

Now I want to suggest to you tonight that this very thing of discouragement, as an element in life, is for a purpose. I do not believe that anything, any element of your lives, is put into them without a purpose. I believe that every effort that we are obliged to make to overcome obstacles will give us strength, and will also give us a confidence in ourselves, that nothing else can give us. I would ten times rather see you having a hard struggle to elevate yourselves, having a hard time either at work on the farm, or on the buildings, or in the shops, without money and without clothes, than to see you here having too much money, and having everything that you want come to you without any effort on your part. You are blessed, as compared with some people. The man or woman who has money, without having had to work for it, who has all the comforts of life, without effort, and who saves his own soul and perhaps the soul of somebody else, such an individual is rare, very rare indeed.

Now it is not a curse to be situated as some of you are, and if you will make up your minds that you are going to overcome the obstacles and the difficulties by which you are surrounded, you will find that in every effort you make to overcome these difficulties you are growing in strength and confidence. Make up your minds that you are not going to allow anything to discourage you. Make up your minds that poor lessons, scoldings on the part of your teachers, want of money, and want of books; that none of these shall discourage you. Make up your mind that in spite of race and color, in spite of the obstacles that surround you, in spite of everything, you are going to succeed in your school life, and are going to prepare yourself for usefulness hereafter.

Every person who has grown to any degree of usefulness, every person who has grown to distinction, almost without exception has been a person who has risen by overcoming obstacles, by removing difficulties, by resolving that when he met discouragements he would not give up. Make up your minds that you are going to overcome every discouragement, and that you are not going to let any discouragement overcome you. Those of you who have been inclined to be moody and morose, or have been inclined to feel that the whole world is against you, that there is no use for you to try to elevate yourselves, make up your minds that your future is just as bright as that of anybody else Do this, and you will find that you have it in your own power to make your future bright or gloomy, just as you desire.

On Getting A Home

Every colored man owes it to himself and to his children as well, to secure a home just as soon as possible. No matter how small the plot of ground may be, or how humble the dwelling placed on it, something that can be called a home should be secured without delay.

A home can be secured much easier than many imagine. A small amount of money saved from week to week, or from month to month, and carefully invested in a piece of land, will soon secure a site upon which to build a comfortable house. No individual should feel satisfied until he has a comfortable home. More and more the Southern States are making one of the conditions for voting, the ownership of at least $300 worth of property, so that persons who own homes will not only reap the benefits that come from owning a home, in other directions, but will also find themselves entitled to cast their ballot.

Care should be taken as to the location of the land. It is of little advantage to secure a lot in some crowded, filthy alley. One should try to secure a lot on a good street, a street that is carefully and well worked, so that the surroundings of the home will be enjoyable. Even if one has to go a good ways into the country to secure such a lot, it is much better than to buy a building spot on an unsightly, undesirable alley.

I believe that our people do best, as a rule, to buy land in the country instead of in the city; but in either-case we should not rest until we have secured a home in one place or the other. No man has a right to marry and run the risk of leaving his wife at his death without a home.

I notice with regret that there are many of our people who have already bought homes, who, after they have secured the land, paid for it and built a cabin containing two or three rooms, do not seek to go any further in the improvement of the property. In the first place, in too many cases, the house and yard, especially the yard, are not kept clean. The fences are not kept in repair. Whitewash and paint are not used as they should be. No matter if the house is paid for, the greatest care should be exercised to see that it is kept in first -class repair; that the walls of the house and the fences are kept neatly painted or whitewashed; that no palings are allowed to fall off the fence, or if they do falloff, to remain off. If there is a barn or a henhouse, these should be kept in repair, and should, like the house, be made to look neat and attractive by paint and whitewash.

Paint and whitewash add a great deal to the value of a house. If persons would learn to use even a part of the time they spend in idle gossip or in standing about on the streets, in whitewashing or painting their houses, it would make a great difference in the appearance of the buildings, as well as add to their value.

Only a short time ago, near a certain town, I visited the house— I could not call it a home — of a presiding elder, a man who had received considerable education, and who spent his time in going about over his district preaching to hundreds and thousands of colored people; and yet the home of this man was almost a disgrace to him and to his race. The house was not painted or whitewashed; the fence was in the same condition; the yard was full of weeds; there were no walks laid out in the yard; there were no flowers in it. — In fact everything on the outside of the house and in the yard presented a most dismal and discouraging appearance. So far as I could see there was not a single vegetable around this house, nor did I see any chickens or fowls of any kind.

This is not the way to live, and especially is it not the way for a minister or a teacher to live, for they are men who are supposed to lead their people not only by word but by example. Every minister and every teacher should make his home, his yard, and his garden, models for the people whom he attempts to teach and lead. I confess that I have no confidence in the preaching of a minister whose home is in the condition of the one I have described. There is no need why, as a race, we should get into the miserable and unfortunate habit of living in houses that are out of repair, that are not whitewashed or painted, that are not comfortable, and above all else, in houses that we do not own. There is no reason why we should not make our homes not only comfortable, but attractive, so that no one can tell from the outside appearance, at least, whether the house is occupied by a white family or a black family.

After a house has been paid for, it not only should be improved from year to year and kept in good repair, but, as the family grows, new rooms should be added. The house should not only be made comfortable, but should be made convenient. fu soon as possible there should be a sitting room, where books and papers can be found, a room in which the whole family may read and study during the winter nights. I do not believe that any house is complete without a bathroom. As soon as possible every one of our houses should be provided with a bathroom, so that the body of every member of the family can be baptized every morning in clean, invigorating, fresh water. Such a bath puts one in proper condition for the work of the day, and not only keeps one well physically, but strong morally and religiously.

Another important part of the home is the dining-room. The dining room should be the most attractive and most comfortable room in the house. It should be large and airy, a room into which plenty of sunlight can come, and a room that can be kept comfortable both in the summer and in the winter.

These suggestions are made to you with the hope that you will put them into practice, and also that you will influence others to do the same.

They are all suggestions that we, as a race, notwithstanding our poverty, in most cases can find a way to put into practice. Every one of them should be taken up by our teachers, our ministers and by our educated young people. They should be taught and urged in school, in church, in farmers' meetings, in women's meetings, and, in fact, wherever the people of the race come together.

Calling Things By Their Right Name

A few evenings ago I talked with you about the importance of learning to be simple, humble and child-like before going out into the world. You should remain in school until you get to the point where you feel that you do not know anything, where you feel that you are willing to learn from anyone who can teach you.

Unfortunately there are many things here in the South which tends to lead away from this simplicity to which I have referred. There is a great inclination to make things appear what they are not. For example: take the schools. There is a great tendency to call schools by names which do not belong to them, and which do not correctly represent that which in reality exists. You will find the habit growing more prevalent every year, I fear, of calling a school a university, or a college, or an academy, or a high-school. In fact we seldom hear of a plain, common, public or graded school.

We do ourselves no good when we yield to that temptation. If a school is a public school, call it one; but do not think that we gain anything by calling a little country school, with two or three rooms and one or two teachers, where some of the students are studying the alphabet, a university. And still this is too often done throughout the South, as you know. No respect or confidence is gained by the practice, but, on the contrary, sensible people get disgusted with such false pretenses. When you go out into the world and meet with such cases as this, try to make the people see that it is a great deal better to call their small public school by a name which truly represents it, than to call it a high-school or an academy. I do not by any means intend to say that schools do not have the right to aspire to become high-schools and colleges. What I mean to say is that it is hurtful to the race to get into the habit of calling every little institution of learning that is opened, a college or a university. It weakens us and prevents us from getting a solid, sure foundation.

Again, we make the same mistake when we call every preacher or person who stands in a pulpit to read from it, "Doctor," whether or not that degree has been conferred upon him. Sensible people get tired of that kind of thing. The degree of Doctor of Divinity was once held in the highest esteem, and was conferred only upon those ministers who had really become entitled to it because of some original research or other work of high scholarship. Among highly educated people this rule holds still. But to-day, especially in the South, many a little institution that opens its doors and calls itself a college or a university, is beginning to confer degrees, and make doctors of divinity of persons who are unworthy of degrees. And sometimes, should these persons fail to get an institution to confer a degree on them, they confer it on themselves! The habit is getting to be so common that in little towns the ministers are calling themselves Doctors. One pastor will meet another and say, "Good morning, Doctor," and the other, wishing to be as polite as his friend, will say, "How are you, Doctor?" and so it goes on, until both begin to believe they really are Doctors. Now this practice is not only ridiculous, but it is very hurtful to us as a race, and it should be discouraged.

Much the same criticism may be made of many of those who teach. A person who teaches a little country school, perhaps in a brush arbor, is called "Professor." Every person who leads a string band is called "Professor." I was in a small town not long ago, and I heard the people speaking of some one as "the professor." I was anxious to know who the professor was. So I waited a few minutes, and finally the professor came up, and I recognized him as a member of one of our preparatory classes. Now, don't suffer the world to put you in this silly, ridiculous position. If people attempt to call you "Professor," or by any other title that is not yours, tell them that you are not a professor, that you are a simple mister. That is a good enough title for anyone. We have the same right to become professors as any other people, when we occupy positions which entitle us to that name, but we drag that title, which ought to be a badge of scholarship, down into the mud and mire when we allow it to be misapplied.

We carry a similar kind of deception into our school work when, in the essays which we read and the orations which we deliver, we simply rehearse matter a great deal of which has been copied from some one else. Go into almost any church where there is one of the doctors of divinity to whom I have referred, and you will hear sermons copied out of books and pamphlets. The essays, the orations, the sermons that are not the productions of the people who pretend to write them, all come from this false foundation.

Then there is another error to which I wish to call your attention. In many parts of the South, especially in the cities and towns, there are excellent public schools, well equipped in every way with apparatus and material, and provided with good, competent teachers, but in some cases these schools are crippled by reason of the fact that there are little denominational schools which deprive the public schools of their rightful attendance. If the school can't be in the church of some particular denomination, it must be near it. In the average town there may be the denominational school of the United Methodist Episcopal church, of the Zion church, of the Baptist church, of the Wesleyan Methodist church, and so on, all in different parts of the town. Instead of supporting one public school, provided at the expense of the town or city, there exists this little, narrow denominational spirit, which is robbing these innocent children of their education. We want to say to such people as these, people who are content so to deprive their children, and have them taught by some second-rate teacher, that they are wrong. We want you to let the people know that the great public-school system of America is the nation's greatest glory, and that we do not help matters when we attempt to tear down the public school. Of course it is the right and the duty of every denomination to erect its own theological seminaries and its colleges, where the special tenets of that denomination are taught to those who are preparing for its pulpit; but no one has a right to let this denominational spirit defeat the work of a public school to which all should be free to go.

I have in mind a place where the colored people have an excellent school, equal to that of the whites. I went through the building and found it supplied with unproved apparatus and capable teachers, and saw that first-class work was done there. Later, I was taken about a mile outside the city, where there was a school with all incapable teachers, and some sixty or seventy pupils being poorly taught.

Here was a third-rate teacher in a third-rate building, poor work, and the children suffering for lack of proper instruction. Why? This was simply because the people wanted a school of their own denomination in that part of the city.

Now you want to cultivate courage, and see to it that you are brave enough to condemn these wrongs and to show the people the mistakes which they make in these matters.

I mention all these things because they hinder us from getting a solid foundation. They hinder us, further, in that in many cases they prevent us from getting the right power of leadership in teaching, in the work of the ministry, and in many other respects. Wherever you go, then, make up your minds that you are going to make your influence felt in favor of better prepared teachers and preachers-in better preparation of all those who stand for leaders of the people. Just in proportion as you set your lives right in this matter, will the masses of the race be inclined to follow you.

European Impressions

Some people here in America think that some of us make too much ado over the matter of industrial training for the Negro. I wish some of the skeptics might go to Europe and see what races that are years ahead of us are doing there in that respect. I shall not take the time here to outline what is being done for men in the direction of industrial training in Europe, but I shall give some account of what I saw being done for women in England.

Mrs. Washington and I visited the Agricultural College for women, at Swanley, England, where we found forty intelligent, cultivated women, who were most of them graduates from high schools and colleges, engaged in studying practical agriculture, horticulture, dairying and poultry raising. We found the women in the laboratory and classrooms, studying agricultural chemistry, botany, zoology, and applied mathematics, and we also saw these same women in the garden, planting vegetables, trimming rose bushes, scattering manure, growing grapes and raising fruit in the hot-houses and in the field.

As another suggestion for our people, I might mention that while I was in England I knew of one of the leading members of Parliament leaving his duties in that body for three days to preside at a meeting of the National Association of Poultry Raisers, which was largely attended by people from all parts of the United Kingdom.

In the trip which Mrs. Washington and I made through Holland, we saw much which may be of interest to you. It has been said that, God made the world, but the Dutch made Holland. For one to fully realize the force of this one must see Holland for himself. One of the best ways to see the interior of Holland, and the peasant life, is to take a trip, as we did, on one of the canal boats plying between Antwerp, in Belgium, and Rotterdam, in Holland.

It was especially interesting for me to compare the rural life in Holland with the life of the country colored people in the South. Holland has been made what it is very largely, by the unique system of dykes or levees which have been built there to keep out the water of the ocean, and thus enable the people to use to advantage all the land there is in that small country.

The great lesson which our colored farmers can learn from the Dutch, is how to make a living from a small plot of ground well cultivated, instead of from forty or fifty acres poorly tilled. I have seen a whole family making a comfortable living by cultivating two acres of land there, while our Southern farmers, in too many cases, try to till fifty or a hundred acres, and find themselves in debt at the end of the year. In all Holland, I do not think one can find a hundred acres of waste land; every foot of land is covered with grass, vegetables, and grain or fruit trees. Another advantage which our Southern farmers might have in trying to pattern after the farmers of Holland, would be that they would not be obliged to go to so much additional expense for horse or mule power. Most of the cultivating of the soil there is done with a hoe and spade.

I saw the people of Holland on Sunday and on week days, but I did not see a single Dutch man, woman or child in rags. There were practically no beggars and no very poor people. They owe their prosperity, too, very largely to their thorough and intelligent cultivation of the soil.

Next to the thorough tilling of the soil, the thing of most interest there, from which the colored people in America may learn a lesson, is the fine dairying which has made Holland famous throughout the world. Even the poorest family has its herd of Holstein cattle, and they are the finest specimens of cattle that it has ever been my pleasure to see. To watch thousands of these cattle grazing on the fields is worth a trip to Holland. As the result of the attention which they have given to breeding Holstein cattle, Dutch butter and cheese are in demand all through Europe. The most ordinary farmer there has a cash income as the result of the sale of his butter and milk.

Many of these people make more out of the wind that blows over the fields than our poor Southern people make out of the soil. The old-fashioned windmill is to be seen on every farm. This mill not only pumps the water for the live stock, but, in many cases, is made to operate the dairy, to saw the wood, to grind the grain, and to run the heavy machinery. These people are, however, not unlike our Southern people in one respect, and that is in having their women and children work in the fields. This, I think, is done in a larger measure even than in the South among the colored people.

An element of strength in the farming and dairying interests of these people is to be found in the fact that many of the farmers have received a college or university training. After this they take a special course in agriculture and dairying. This is as it should be. Our people in the South will prosper in proportion as a larger number of university men take up agriculture and kindred callings after they have finished their academic education.

In the matter of physical appearance, including grace, beauty, and carriage of the body, I think our own people are far ahead of the Dutch. But the Dutch are a hardy, rugged, industrious race of people. In our trip in the canal boat we saw the men at the landings in large numbers, in their wooden shoes, and the women and children in their beautiful, old-fashioned head-dresses, each community having its own style of head-dress, which has been handed down from one generation to another.

We were in Rotterdam over Sunday. The free and rather boisterous commingling of the sexes on the street was noteworthy. In this, also, our people in the United States could set an example to the Dutch.

The foundation of the civilization of these people is in their regard for and respect for the law, and their observance of it. This is the great lesson which the entire South must learn before it can hope to receive the respect and confidence of the world. Europeans do not understand how the South can disregard its own laws as it so often does. If you ask any man on that side of the Atlantic why he does not emigrate to the Southern part of the United States, he shrugs his shoulders and says, "No law; they kill." I pray God that no part of our country may much longer have such a reputation as that in any part of the world.

From Holland we went to Paris. On a beautiful, sunny day, if you could combine the whirl of fashion and gaiety of New York City, Boston and Chicago on a prominent avenue, you would have some idea of what is to be seen in Paris upon one of her popular boulevards. Fashion seemed to sway everything in that great city; for example, when I went into a shoe store to purchase a pair of shoes, I could not find a pair large enough to be comfortable. I was gently told that it was not the fashion to wear large shoes there.

One of the things I had in mind when I went to France was to visit the tomb of Toussaint L'Ouverture, but I learned from some Haitian gentlemen residing in Paris that the grave of that general was in the northern part of France, and these same gentlemen informed me that his burial place is still without a monument of any kind. It seems that it has been in the minds of the Haitians for some time to remove his body to Haiti, but thus far it has been neglected. The Haitian Government and people owe it to themselves; it appears to me, to see to it that the resting place of this great hero is given a proper memorial, either in France or on the island of Haiti.

Speaking of the Haitians, there are a good many well educated and cultivated men and women of that nationality in Paris. Numbers of them are sent there each year for education, and they take high rank in scholarship. It is greatly to be regretted, however, that some of these do not take advantage of the excellent training which is given there in the colleges of physical science, agriculture, mechanics and domestic science. They would then be in a position to return home and assist in developing the agricultural and mineral resources of their native land. Haiti will never be what it should be until a large number of the natives receive an education which will enable them to develop agriculture, build roads, start manufactories, build railroads and bridges, and thus keep on the island the large amount of money which is now being sent outside for productions which these people themselves could supply.

In all the European cities which we visited, we compared the conduct of the rank and file of the people on the streets and in other places with that of our own people in the United States, and we have no hesitation in saying that, in all that marks a lady or gentleman, our people in the South do not suffer at all by the comparison. Even at the camp-meetings and other holiday gatherings in the South, the deportment of the masses of the colored people is quite up to the standard of that of the average European in the larger cities which we saw.

I should strongly advise our people against going to Europe, and especially to Paris, with, the hope of securing employment, unless fortified by strong friends and a good supply of money. In one week, in Paris, three men of my race called to see me, and in each case I found the man to be practically in a starving condition. They were well-meaning, industrous men, who had gone there with the idea that life was easy and work sure; but notwithstanding the fact that they walked the streets for days, they could get no work. The fact that they did not speak the language, nor understand the customs of the people, made their life just so much the harder. With the assistance of other Americans, I secured passage for one of these men to America. His parting word to me was, "The United States is good enough for me in the future."

The Value Of System In Home Life

Most of you are going out from Tuskegee sooner or later to exert your influence in the home life of our people. You are going to have influence in homes of your own; you are going to have influence in the homes of your mothers and fathers, or in the homes of your relatives. You are going to exert an influence for good or for evil in the homes wherever you may go. Now the question how to bring about the greatest amount of happiness in these homes is one that should concern every student here. I say this because I want you to realize that each one of you is to go out from here to exert an influence. You are to exercise this influence in the communities where you go; and if you fail to exercise it for the good of other individuals, you have failed to accomplish the purpose for which this institution exists.

In the first place you want to exert your influence in those directions that will bring about the best results; among these, it is important that the people have presented to them the highest forms of home life.

Very often I find it true—and especially the more I travel about among our people—that many persons have the idea that they cannot have comfortable homes unless they have a great amount of money. Now some of the happiest and most comfortable homes I have ever been in have been homes where the people have but little money; in fact, they might well be called poor people. But in these homes there was a certain degree of order and convenience which made you feel as comfortable as if you were in the homes of people of great wealth.

I want to speak plainly. In the first place there must be promptness in connection with everything in the life of the home. Take the matter of the meals, for instance. It is impossible for a home to be properly conducted unless there is a certain time for each meal, and promptness must be insisted on. In some homes the breakfast may be eaten at six o'clock one morning, at eight o'clock the next morning, and, perhaps, at nine o'clock the morning after that. Dinner may be served at twelve, one, or two o'clock, and supper may be eaten at five, six or seven; and even then one-half the members of the family are absent when the meal is served. There is useless waste of time and energy in this, and an unnecessary amount of worry. It saves time, and it saves a great amount of worry, to have it understood that there is to be a certain time for each meal, and that all the members of the family are to be present at that time. In this way the family will get rid of a great deal of annoyance, and precious time will be saved to be used in reading or in some other useful occupation.

Then as to the matter of system, no matter how cheap your homes are, no matter how poverty-stricken you may be in regard to money, it is possible for each home to have its affairs properly systematized. I wonder how many housekeepers can go into their homes on the darkest night there is, and put their hands on the box of matches without difficulty. That is one way to test a good housekeeper. If she cannot do this, then there is a waste of time. It saves time and it saves worry, too, if you have a certain place in which the matches are to be kept, and if you teach all the members of the family that the matches are always to be kept in that place. Oftentimes you find the match box on the table, or on a shelf in the corner of the room, or perhaps on the floor; sometimes here, sometimes there.

In many homes five or ten minutes are wasted every day just on account of the negligence of the housekeeper or the wife in this little matter.

Then as to the matter of the dish cloth, you should have a place for your dish cloth, and put it there every day. The persons who do not have a place for an article are the persons who are found looking in-doors and out-of-doors for it, from five to ten minutes every time that article is needed. They will be saying, "Johnnie," or "Jennie, where is it? Where did you put it the last time you had it?" and all that kind of thing.

The same thing is true of the broom. In the first place, in the home where there is system, you do not find the broom left standing on the wrong end. I hope all of you know which the right end of the broom is in this respect. You do not find the broom on the wrong end, and you always find that there is a certain place for it, and that it is kept there. When things are out of place and you have to hunt for them, you are spending not only time, but you are spending strength that should be used in some more profitable way. There should be a place for the coat and the cloak, for the hat, and, in fact, a place for everything in the house.

The people who have a place for everything are the people who will find time to read, and who will have time for recreation. You wonder sometimes how the people in New England can afford to have so much time for reading books and newspapers, and still have sufficient money to send as much as they do here to this institute to be used in our education. These people find time to keep themselves thus intelligent, and to keep themselves in touch with all that takes place in the world, because everything is so well systematized about their homes that they save the time which you and I spend in worrying about something which we should know all about.

I have very rarely gone into a boarding house kept by our people and found the lamp in its proper place. When you go into such a house it is too apt to be the case that the people there will have to look for the lamp; then, when they have found it, it is not filled; somebody forgot to put the oil in it in the morning; then they have to go and hunt up a wick, and then they must get a chimney. Then, when they get all these things, they must hunt for the matches to light the lamp. I wonder how many girls there are here now who can go into a room and arrange it properly for an individual to sleep in—that is, provide the proper number of towels, the soap and matches, and have everything that should be provided for the comfort of the person who is to use the room, put in the room and put in its proper place. I should be afraid to test some of you. You mush learn to be able to do such things before you leave here, in order that you may be of some use to yourself and to others. If you are not able to do this, you will be a disappointment to us.

What Will Pay

I wish to talk with you for a few minutes upon a subject that is much discussed, especially by young people—What things pay in life? There is no question, perhaps, which is asked oftener by a person entering upon a career than this—What will pay? Will this course of action, or that business? What will pay?

Let us see if we can answer that question, a question which every student in this school should ask himself or herself. What will profit me most? What will make my life most useful? What will bring about the greatest degree of happiness? What will pay best?

Not long ago a certain minister secured the testimony of forty men, who had been successful in business, persons who beyond question had been pronounced to be business men of authority. The question which this minister put to these business men was, whether under any circumstances it paid to be dishonest in business; whether they had found, in all their business career, that under any circumstances it paid to cheat, swindle or take advantage of their fellow-men, or in any way to deceive those with whoa} they came in contact. Every one of the forty answered, without hesitation that nothing short of downright honesty and fair dealing ever paid in any business. They said that no one could succeed permanently in business that was not honest in dealing with his fellowmen, to say nothing of the future life or of doing right for right's sake.

It does not pay an individual to do anything except what his conscience will approve of every day, and every hour and minute in the day.

I want you to put that question to yourselves to-night: ask yourselves what course of action will pay.

You may be tempted to go astray in the matter of money. Think when you are tempted to do that: "Will it pay?" Persons, who are likely to go astray in the matter of money, furthermore are likely to do so in the matter of dress, tampering with each other's property; and the matter of acting dishonestly with each other's books. Such persons will be dishonest in the matter of labor, too.

It pays an individual to be honest with another person's money. It never pays to be dishonest in taking another person's clothes or books. None of these things ever pays, and when you have occasion to yield or not to yield to such a temptation, you should ask yourself the question: "Will it pay me to do this?" Put that question constantly to yourself.

Whenever you promise, moreover, to do a piece of work for a man, there is a contract binding you to do an honest day's labor-and the man to pay you for an honest day's labor. If you fail to give such service, if you break that contract, you will find that such a course of action never pays. It will never pay you to deal dishonestly with an individual, or to permit dishonest dealing. If you fail to give a full honest day's work, if you know that you have done only three-quarters of a day's work, or four fifths, it may seem to you at the time that it has paid, but in the long run you lose by it.

I regret to say that we sometimes have occasion to meet students here who are inclined to be dishonest. Such students come to Mr. Palmer or to me, and say they wish to go home. When they are asked why they wish to go home, some of them say they wish to go because they are sick. Then, when they have been talked with a few minutes, they may say that they do not like the food here, or perhaps that some disappointment has befallen their parents. In some cases I have had students give me half a dozen excuses in little more than the same number of minutes.

The proper thing for students to do, when they wish to go home, is to state the exact reason, and then stick to it. The student who does that is the kind that will succeed in the world. The students, who are downright dishonest in what they say, will find out that they are not strong in anything, that they are not what they ought to be. The time will come when that sort of thing will carry them down instead of up.

In a certain year— I think it was 1857— there was a great financial panic in the United States, especially in the city of New York. A great many of the principal banks in the country failed, and others were in daily danger of failure. I remember a story that was told of one of the bank presidents of that time, William Taylor, I believe. All the bank presidents in the city of New York were having meetings every night to find out how well they were succeeding in keeping their institutions solvent. At one of these meetings, after a critical day in the most trying period of the panic, when some men reported that they had lost money during that day, and others that so much money had been withdrawn from their banks during the day that if there were another like it they did not see how they could stand the strain, William Taylor reported that money had been added to the deposits of his bank that day instead of being withdrawn.

What was behind all this? William Taylor had learned in early life that it did not pay to be dishonest, but that it paid to be honest with all his depositors and with all persons who did business with his bank. When other people were failing in all parts of the country, the evidence of this man's character, his regard for truth and honest dealing, caused money to come into his bank when it was being withdrawn from others.

Character is a power. If you want to be powerful in, the world, if you want to be strong, influential and useful, you can be so, in no better way than by having strong character; but you cannot have a strong character if you yield to the temptations about which I have been speaking.

Some one asked some time ago, what it was that gave such a power to the sermons of the late Dr. John Hall. In the usual sense he was not a powerful speaker; but everything he said carried conviction with it. The explanation was that the character of the man was behind the sermon. You may go out and make great speeches, you may write books or addresses which are great literature, but unless you have character behind what you say and write, it will amount to nothing; it will all go to the winds.

I leave this question with you, then. When you are tempted to do what your conscience tells you is not right, ask yourself: "Will it pay me to do this thing which I know is not right?" Go to the penitentiary. Ask the people there who have failed, who have made mistakes, why they are there, and in every case they will tell you that they are there because they yielded to temptation, because they did not ask themselves the question "Will it pay?"

Go ask those people who have no care for life, who have thrown away their virtue, as it were, ask them why they are without character, and the answer will be, in so many words, that they sought but temporary success. In order to find some short road to success, in order to have momentary happiness, they yielded to temptation. We want to feel that in every student who goes out from here there is a character which can be depended upon in the night as well as in the day. That is the kind of young men and young women we wish to send out from here. Whenever you are tempted to yield a hair's breadth in the direction which I have indicated, ask yourself the question over and over again: "Will it pay me in this world? Will it pay me in the world to come?"

Education That Educates

This talk was given soon after the visit of President McKinley to Tuskegee Institute in the fall of 1898.

Perhaps I am safe in saying that during the last ten days you have not given much systematic effort to book study in the usual sense. When interruptions come such as we have just had, taking you away from your regular routine work and study, and the preparation of routine lessons is interrupted, the first thought to some may be that this time is lost, in so far as it relates to education in the ordinary sense; that it is so," much time taken away from that part of one's life that should be devoted to acquiring education. I suppose that during the last few days the questions have come to many of you: "What are we gaining? What are we getting from the irregularity that has characterized the school grounds within the last week that will in any degree compensate for the amount of book study that we have lost?"

To my mind I do not believe that you have lost anything by the interruption. On the other hand, I am convinced that you have got the best kind of education. I do not mean to say that we can depend upon it for all time to come for systematic training of the mind, but so far as real education, so far as development of the mind and heart and body are concerned, I do not believe that a single student has lost anything by the irregularity of the last week or more.

You have gained in this respect: in preparing for the reception and entertainment of the President of the United States and his Cabinet, and the distinguished persons who accompanied the party you have had to do an amount of original thinking which you, perhaps, have never had to do before in your lives. You have been compelled to think; you have been compelled to put more than your bodily strength into what you have been doing.

You could not have made the magnificent exhibition of our work which you have made if you had not been compelled to do original thinking and execution. Most of you never saw such an exhibition before; I never did. Those of you who had to construct floats that would illustrate our agricultural work and our mechanical and academic work, had to put a certain amount of original thought into the planning of these floats, in order to make them show the work to the best advantage; and two-thirds of you—yes, practically all of you—had never seen anything of the kind before. For this reason it was a matter that had to be thought out by you and planned out by you, and then put into visible shape.

Now compare that kind of education with the mere committing to memory of certain rules, or something which some one else thought out and executed a thousand years ago perhaps—and that is what a large part of our education really is... Education in the usual sense of the word is the mere committing to memory of something which has been known before us. Now during the last ten days we have had to solve problems of our own, not problems and puzzles that some one else originated for us. I do not believe that there is a person connected with the institution who is not stronger in mind, who is not more self-confident and self-reliant, so far as the qualities relate to what he is able to do with his mind or his hands, than he was ten or twelve days ago. There is the benefit that came to all of us. It put us to thinking and planning; it brought us in to contact with things that are out of the ordinary; and there is no education that surpasses this. Those people who came here to visit us knew perfectly well that we could commit to memory certain lines of poetry, they knew we were able to solve certain problems in algebra and geometry, they understood that we could learn certain rules in chemistry and agriculture; but what interested them most was to see us put into visible form the results of our education. Just in proportion as an individual is able to do that, he is of value to the world. That is the object of the work which we are trying to do here. We are trying to turn out men and women who are able to do something that the world wants done, that the world needs to have done. Just in proportion as you can comply with that demand you will find that there is a place for you there is going to be standing room. By the training we are giving you here we are preparing you for a place in the world. We are going to train you so that when you get to that place, if you fail in it, the failure will not be our fault.

It is a great satisfaction to have connected with a race men and women who are able to do something, not merely to talk about doing it, not to the study of men and of things, rather than to the study of mere books. You will find more and more as the years go by, that people will gradually lay aside books, and study the nature of man in a way they have never done as yet. I tell you, then, that in this interruption of the regular school work you have not lost anything you have gained; you have had your minds awakened, your faculties strengthened, and your hands guided.

I do not wish to speak of this matter egotistically, but it is true that I have heard a great many persons from elsewhere mention the pleasure which they have received in meeting Tuskegee students, because when they come in contact with a student who has been here, they are impressed with the fact that he or she does not seem to be dead or sleepy. They say that when they meet a Tuskegee boy or girl they find a person who has had contact with real life. The education that you have been getting during the last few days, you will find, as the years go by, has been of a kind that will serve you in good stead all through your lives.

Just in proportion as we learn to execute something, to put our education into tangible form—as we have been doing during the last few days—in just the same proportion will we find ourselves of value as individuals and as a race. Those people who came here to visit us knew perfectly well that we could commit to memory certain lines of poetry, they knew we were able to solve certain problems in algebra and geometry, they understood that we could learn certain rules in chemistry and agriculture; but what interested them most was to see us put into visible form the results of our education. Just in proportion as an individual is able to do that, he is of value to the world. That is the object of the work which we are trying to do here. We are trying to turn out men and women who are able to do something that the world wants done, that the world needs to have done. Just in proportion as you can comply with that demand you will find that there is a place for you there is going to be standing room. By the, training we are giving you here we are preparing you for a place in the world. We are going to train you so that when you get to that place, if you fail in it, the failure will not be our fault.

It is a great satisfaction to have connected with a race of men and women who are able to do something, not merely to talk about doing it, not merely to theorize about doing it, but actually to do something that makes the world better to live in, something that enhances the comforts and conveniences of life. I had a good example of this last week. I wanted something done in my office which required a practical knowledge of electricity. It was a great satisfaction when I called upon one of the teachers, to have him do the work in a careful, praiseworthy manner. It is very well to talk or lecture about electricity, but it is better to be able to do something of value with one's knowledge of electricity.

And so, as you go on, increasing your ability to do things of value, you will find that the problem which often now-a-days looks more and more difficult of solution will gradually become easier. One of the Cabinet members who were here a few days ago said, after witnessing the exhibition which you made here, that the islands which this country had taken into its possession during the recent war are soon going to require the service of every man and woman we can turn out from this institution. You will find it true, not only in this country but in other countries, that the demand will be more and more for people who can do something. Just in proportion as we can, as a race, get the reputation which I spoke to you about a few days ago, you will find there will be places for us. Regardless of color or condition, the world is going to give the places of trust and remuneration to the men and women who can do a certain thing as well as anybody else or better. This is the whole problem. Shall we prepare ourselves to do something as well as anybody else or better? Just in proportion as we do this, you will find that nothing under the sun will keep us back.

The Importance of Being Reliable

I am going to call your attention this evening to a tendency of the people of our race which I had occasion to notice in the course of a visit recently made to certain portions of North Carolina and South Carolina.

I find that with persons who are the employers or who might be the employers of numbers of our people, there is a very general impression that as a race we lack steadiness—that we lack steadiness as laborers. Now you may say that this is not true, and you may cite any number of instances to show that we are not unreliable in that respect; whether it is true or not, the results are the same; —it works against us in the matter of securing paying employment.

Almost without exception, in talking with persons who are in a position to employ us, or who have been employing us, or who are thinking of employing us, I have found that this objection has been very largely in their minds, that we cannot be depended upon, that we are unsteady and unreliable in matters of labor. I am speaking, of course, of that class of people of our race who depend mainly upon a day's work — working by the day, as we call it — for their living. These men with whom I talked gave several illustrations of this tendency. In the first place, I think they mentioned, without exception, this fact—that if the colored people are employed in a factory, they work well and steadily for a few days, say until Saturday night comes, and they are paid their week's wages. Then they cannot be depended upon to put in an appearance the following Monday morning.

That special criticism was made without exception. The colored people, these men said, would work earnestly, and give good satisfaction until they got a little money ahead, and got food enough assured to last them two or three weeks; then they would give up the job, or simply remain away from the factory until others had been put in their places. That was one of the statements that was made to me over and over again.

People also mentioned to me as an unfavorable tendency the inclination which the people of our race have to go on excursions. They said that if an excursion were going to Wilmington or Greensboro, or Charleston, and the colored people had a little money on hand, you could not depend on their going to work instead of going on the excursion; that people would say that they must go on this or that excursion, and that nothing should stop them. A great many people lose employment and money because of this tendency to go on excursions.

Another thing that was mentioned to me was the Sunday dinners. Our people are too likely to starve all through the week, and then on Sunday invite all the neighbors to come in and eat up what they have made through the week. People say that we take our week's earnings on Saturday night, and go to the market and spend it all, and then invite all of our kindred and neighbors to come in on Sunday to have a great party. Then by Monday morning we have made ourselves so ill by over-eating that we are unfit for work. This was given as one of the reasons which cause people to complain of our race for unsteadiness.

Then there was complaint of a general lack of perseverance, of an unwillingness to be steady, to put money into the bank, to begin at the bottom and gradually work toward the top. You can easily see some of the results of such a reputation as this. I have noticed some of the results in many of the places where our people have been securing paying employment. One result is a general distrust of the entire race in matters pertaining to industry. Another is that people are not going to employ persons on whom they cannot depend, to fill responsible positions. Employers are not likely to employ for responsible positions persons who are likely to go away unexpectedly on excursions.

Another result is loss of money. You will find many of our people in poverty simply because, in so large a measure, we have got this reputation of being unsteady and unreliable. Wherever our people are not getting regular, paying employment, it is largely on account of these things of which I have been speaking; and gradually the opportunities for employment are slipping into the hands of the people of other races. You can easily understand that where people are not getting steady employment — but a job this week and a job next week — and perhaps nothing the week after — it is impossible for them to put money in the bank, impossible to acquire homes and property, and to settle down as reliable, prosperous citizens.

Now, how are we going to change all these things? I do not see any hope unless we can depend upon you to change them, you young men and young women who are being educated in institutions of learning. It rests largely with you to change public sentiment among our people in all these directions, to a point where we shall feel that we must be as reliable and as responsible as it is possible for the people of any other race to be. But in order to do this it is necessary for you to learn how to control yourselves in these respects.

Young men come here and want to work at this industry or that, for a while, and then get tired and want to change to something else. Some come with a strong determination to work, and stay until something happens that is not quite pleasant, and then they want to leave and go to some other school or go back home. Now we cannot make the leaders and the examples of our people that we should make, if we are going to be guilty of these same weaknesses in these institutions. Let each of you take control of himself or herself, and determine that whatever you plan to be you are going to be; you are going to keep driving away, pegging away, moving on and on each hour, each day, until you have accomplished the purpose for which you came here.

Such are the persons, the men and women, that the world is looking for. These are the men and women we want to send to North Carolina and South Carolina, to Georgia, to Mississippi, and about in our own State of Alabama, to reach hundreds and thousands of our people, and to bring about such a sentiment that these people can control themselves in the directions I have mentioned and become steady and reliable along all the avenues of industry.

I have spoken very plainly about these things, because I believe that they are matters to which as a race we ought to give more attention. No race can thrive and prosper and grow strong if it is living on the outer edges of the industrial world, is jumping here and there after a job that somebody else has given up. At the risk of repeating myself, I say that we must give attention to this matter, we must be more trustworthy and more reliable in matters of labor. As you go home, and go into your churches, your schools and your families, preach, teach and talk from day to day the doctrine that our people must become steady and I reliable, must become worthy of confidence in all their occupations.

I am sorry to say that it is too often true of young people that they overlook these matters in their conversation. We are always ready to talk about Mars and Jupiter, about the sun and moon, and about things under the earth and over the earth—in fact about everything except these little matters that have so much to do with our real living. Now if we cannot put a spirit of determination into you to go out and change public sentiment, then the future for us as a race is not very bright.

But I have faith in you to believe that you are going to set a high standard for yourselves in all these matters, and that if you can stay here two, four, five years, some of you will control yourselves, in all those respects, and will bring yourselves to be examples of what we hope and expect the people whom you are going to teach are to become. If you will do this you will find that in a few years there will be a decided change for the better in the things of which I have spoken, a change in regard to these matters that will make us as a race firmer and stronger in these important directions.

The Highest Education

It may seem to some of you that I am continually talking to you about education—the right kind of education, how to get an education, and such kindred subjects—but surely no subject could be more pertinent, since the object for which you all are here is to get an education; and if you are to do this, you wish to get the best kind possible.

You will understand, then, I am sure, if I speak often about this, or refer to the subject frequently, that it is because I am very anxious that all of you go out from here with a definite and correct idea of what is meant by education, of what an education is meant to accomplish, what it may be expected to do for one.

We are very apt to get the idea that education means the memorizing of a number of dates, of being able to state when a certain battle took place, of being able to recall with accuracy this event or that event. We are likely to get the impression that education consists in being able to commit to memory a certain number of rules in grammar, a certain number of rules in arithmetic, and in being able to locate correctly on the earth's surface this mountain or that river, and to name this lake and that gulf.

Now I do not mean to disparage the value of this kind of training, because among the things that education should do for us is to give us strong, orderly and well developed minds. I do not wish to have you get the idea that I undervalue or overlook the strengthening of the mind. If there is one person more than another who is to be pitied, it is the individual who is all heart and no head. You will see numbers of persons going through the world whose hearts are full of good things—running over with the wish to do something to make somebody better, or the desire to make somebody happier—but they have made the sad mistake of being absolutely without development of mind to go with this willingness of heart. We want development of mind and we want strengthening of the mind.

I have often said to you that one of the best things that education can do for an individual is to teach that individual to get hold of what he wants, rather than to teach him how to commit to memory a number of facts in history or a number of names in geography. I wish you to feel that we can give you here orderliness of mind—I mean a trained mind—that will enable you to find dates in history or to put your finger on names in geography when you want them. I wish to give you an education that will enable you to construct rules in grammar and arithmetic for yourselves. That is the highest kind of training.

But, after all, this kind of thing is not the end of education. What, then, do we mean by education? I would say that education is meant to give us an idea of truth. Whatever we get out of text books, whatever we get out of industry, whatever we get here and there from any sources, if we do not get the idea of truth at the end, we do not get education. I do not care how much you get out of history, or geography, or algebra, or literature, I do not care how much you have got out of all your text books:—unless you have got truth, you have failed in your purpose to be educated. Unless you get the idea of truth so pure that you cannot be false in anything, your education is .a failure.

Then education is meant to make us just in our dealings with our fellow men. The man or woman who has learned to be absolutely just, so far as he can interpret, has, in that degree, an education, is to that degree an educated man or woman. Education is meant to make us change for the better, to make us more thoughtful, to make us so broad that we will not seek to help one man because he belongs to this race or that race of people, and seek to hinder another man because he does not belong to this race or that race of people.

Education in the broadest and truest sense will make an individual seek to help all people, regardless of race, regardless of color, regardless of condition. And you will find that the person who is most truly educated is the one who is going to be kindest, and is going to act in the gentlest manner toward persons who are unfortunate, toward the race or the individual that is most despised. The highly educated person is the one who is the most considerate of those individuals who are less fortunate. I hope that when you go out from here, and meet persons who are afflicted by poverty, whether of mind or body, or persons who are unfortunate in any way, that you will show your education by being just as kind and just as considerate toward those persons as it is possible for you to be. That is the way to test a person with education. You may see ignorant persons, who, perhaps, think themselves educated, going about the street, who, when they meet an individual who is unfortunate—lame, or with a defect of body, mind or speech—are inclined to laugh at and make sport of that individual. But the highly educated person, the one who is really cultivated, is gentle and sympathetic to everyone.

Education is meant to make us absolutely honest in dealing with our fellows. I don't care how much arithmetic we have, or how many cities we can locate—it all is useless unless we have an education that makes us absolutely honest.

Education is meant to make us give satisfaction, and to get satisfaction out of giving it. It is meant to make us get happiness out of service for our fellows. And until we get to the point where we can get happiness and supreme satisfaction out, of helping our fellows, we are not truly educated. Education is meant to make us generous. In this connection let me say that I very much hope that when you go out from here you will show that you have learned this lesson of being generous in all charitable objects, in the support of your churches, your Sunday schools, your hospitals, and in being generous in giving help to the poor.

I hope, for instance, that a large proportion of you—in fact all of you—will make it a practice to give something yearly to this institution. If you cannot give but twenty-five cents, fifty cents, or a dollar a year, I hope you will put it down as a thing that you will not forget, to give something to this institution every year. We want to show to our friends who have done so much for us, who have supported this school so generously, how much interest we take in the institution that has given us so nearly all that we possess. I hope that every senior, in particular, will keep this in mind. I am glad to say that we have many graduates who send us such sums, even if small; and one graduate who for the last eight or ten years has sent us ten dollars annually. I hope a number of you in the senior class that I see before me will do the same thing.

Education is meant to make us appreciate the things that are beautiful in nature. A person is never educated until he is able to go into the swamps and woods and see something that is beautiful in the trees and shrubs there, is able to see something beautiful in the grass and flowers that surround him, is, in short, able to see something beautiful, elevating and inspiring in everything that God has created. Not only should education enable us to see the beauty in these objects which God has put about us, but it is meant to influence us to bring beautiful objects about us. I hope that each one of you, after you graduate, will surround himself at home with what is beautiful, inspiring and elevating. I do not believe that any person is educated so long as he lives in a dirty, miserable shanty. I do not believe that any person is educated until he has learned to want to live in a clean room made attractive with pictures and books, and with such surroundings as are elevating.

In a word, I wish to say again, that education is meant to give us that culture, that refinement, that taste which will make us deal truthfully with our fellow men, and will make us see what is beautiful, elevating and inspiring in what God has created. I want you to bear in mind that your text books, with all their contents, are not an end, but a means to an end, a means to help us get the highest, the best, the purest and the most beautiful things out of life.

Unimproved Opportunities

Several of the things which I shall say to you to-night may not sound very agreeable or encouraging to many of you, yet I think you will agree with me that they are facts that cannot be denied.

We must recognize the fact, in the first place, that our condition as a race is, in a large measure, different from the condition of the white race by which we are surrounded; that our capacity is very largely different from that of the people of the white race. I know we like to say the opposite. It sounds well in compositions, does well in rhetoric, and makes a splendid essay, for us to make the opposite assertion. It does very well in a newspaper article, but when we come down to hard facts we must acknowledge that our condition and capacity are not equal to those of the majority of the white people with whom we come in daily contact.

Of course that does not sound very well; but to say that we are equal to the whites is to say that slavery was no disadvantage to us. That is the logic of it. To illustrate, suppose a person has been confined in a sick room, deprived of the use of his faculties, the use of his body and senses, and that he comes out and is placed by the side of a man who has been healthy in body and mind. Are these two persons in the same condition? Are they equal in capacity? Is the young animal of a week old, although he has all the characteristics that his mother has, as strong as she? With proper development he will be, in time, as strong as she, but it is unreasonable to say that he is as strong at present. And so, I think, this is all that we can say of ourselves—with proper development our condition and capacity will be the same as those of the people of any other race.

Now, the fact that our capacity as a people is different, and that the conditions which we must meet are different, makes it reasonable for us to believe that, when the question of education is considered, we shall find that different educational methods are desirable for us from those which would be appropriate to the needs of a people whose capacity and conditions are different from ours. What we most need, in my opinion, for the next few generations, is such an education as will help us most effectually to conquer the forces of nature;—I mean in the general sense of supplying food, clothing, homes, and a substantial provision for the future.

Do not think that I mean by this that I do not believe in every individual getting all the education he or she can get,—for I do. But since for some years to come, at least, it must of necessity be impossible for all of our young people to get all the education possible, or even all they may want to get, I believe they should apply their energies to getting such a training as will be best fitted to supply their immediate needs.

In Scotland, for instance, where higher education has been within reach of the people for many years, and where the people have reached a high degree of civilization, it is not out of place for the young people to give their time and attention to the study of metaphysics and of law and the other professions. Of course I do not mean to say that we shall not have lawyers and metaphysicians and other professional men after a while, but I do mean to say that I think the efforts of a large majority of us should be devoted to securing the material necessities of life.

When you speak to the average person about labor—industrial work, especially—he seems to get the idea at once that you are opposed to his head being educated—that you simply wish to put him to work. Anybody that knows anything about industrial education knows that it teaches a person just the opposite—how not to work. It teaches him to make water work for him, air, steam, and all the forces of nature. That is what is meant by industrial education.

Let us make an illustration. Yesterday I was over in the creamery and became greatly interested in the process of separating the cream. The only energy spent was that required to turn a crank. The apparatus had been so constructed as to utilize natural forces. Now compare the old process of butter-making with the new. Before, you had to go through a long process of drudgery before the cream could be separated from the milk, and then another long process before the cream could be turned into butter, and then, even after churning three or four hours at a time, you got only a small portion of butter. Now what we mean by giving you an industrial education is to teach you so to put brains into your work that if your work is butter-making, you can make butter simply by standing at a machine and turning a crank.

If you are studying chemistry, be sure you get all you can out of the course here, and then go to a higher school somewhere else. Become as proficient in the science as you can. When you have done this, do not sit down and wait for the world to honor you because you know a great deal about chemistry—you will be disappointed if you doubt if you wish to make the best use of your knowledge of chemistry, come back here to the South and use it in making this poor soil rich, and in making good butter where the farmers have made poor butter before. Used in this way you will find that your knowledge of chemistry will cause others to honor you.

During the last thirty years we, as a race, have let some golden opportunities slip from us, and partly, I fear, because we have not had enough plain talk in the direction I am following with you tonight. If you ever have an opportunity to go into any of the large cities of the North you will be able to see for yourselves what I mean. I remember that the first time I went north —and it was not so very many years ago—it was not an uncommon thing to see the barber shops in the .hands of colored men. I know colored men who in that way could have become comfortably rich. You cannot find to-day in the city of New York or Boston a first-class barber shop in the hands of colored men. That opportunity is gone, and something is wrong that it is so. Coming nearer home; go to Montgomery, Memphis, New Orleans, and you will find that the barber shops are gradually slipping away from the hands of the colored men, and they are going back into dark streets and, opening little holes. These opportunities have slipped from us largely because we have not learned to dignify labor. The colored man puts a dirty little chair and a pair of razors into a dirtier looking hole, while the white man opens his shop on one of the principal streets, or in connection with some fashionable hotel, fits it up luxuriously with carpets, handsome mirrors and other attractive furniture, and calls the place a "tonsorial parlor." The proprietor sits at his desk and takes the cash. He has transformed what we call drudgery into a paying business.

Still another instance, you can remember that only a few years ago one of the best paying positions that a large number of colored men filled was that of doing whitewashing. A few years ago it would not have been hard to see colored men in Boston, Philadelphia or Washington carrying a whitewash tub and a long pole into somebody's house to do a job of whitewashing. You go into the North to-day, and you will find very few colored men at that work. White men learned that they could dignify that branch of labor, and they began to study it in schools. They gained knowledge of chemistry which would enable them to understand the mixing of the necessary ingredients; they learned decorating and frescoing; and now they call themselves "house decorators." Now that job is gone, perhaps to come no more; for now that these men have elevated this work, and introduced more intelligent skill into it, do you suppose anyone is going to allow some old man with a pole and a bucket to come into the house?

Then there is the field occupied by the cooks. You know that all over the South we have held and still hold to a large extent—the matter of cooking in our hands. Wherever there was any cooking to be done, a colored man or a colored woman did it. But while we still have something of a monopoly of this work, it is a fact that even this is slipping away from us. People do not wish always to eat fried meat, and bread that is made almost wholly of water and salt. They get tired of such food, and they desire a person to cook for them who will put brains into the work. To meet this demand white people have transformed what was once the menial occupation of cooking into a profession; they have gone to school and studied how to elevate this work, and if we can judge by the almost total absence of colored cooks in the North, we are led to believe that they have learned how. Even here in the South colored cooks are gradually disappearing, and unless they exert themselves they will go entirely. They have disappeared in the North because they have not kept pace with the demand for the most improved methods of cooking, and because they have not realized that the world is moving forward rapidly in the march of civilization. A few days ago, when in Chicago, I noticed in one of the fashionable restaurants a fine-looking man, well dressed, who seemed to be the proprietor. I asked who he was, and was told that he was the "chef," as he is called—the head cook. Of course I was surprised to see a man dressed so stylishly and presenting such an air of culture, filling the place of chief cook in a restaurant, but I remembered then, more forcibly than ever, that cooking had been transformed into a profession into dignified labor.

Still another opportunity is going, and we laugh when we mention it, although it is really no laughing matter. When we think of what we might have done to elevate it in the same way that white persons have elevated it, we realize that it was an opportunity after all. I refer to the opportunity which was in boot-blacking. Of course, here in the South, we have that yet, to a large extent, because the competition here is not quite so sharp as in the North. In too many Southern towns and cities, if you wish your shoes blacked, you wait until you meet a boy with a box slung over his shoulder. When he begins to polish your shoes you will very likely see that he uses a much-worn shoe brush, or, worse still, a scrubbing brush, and unless you watch him closely there is a chance that he will polish your shoes with stove polish. But if you go into a Northern city you will find that such a boy as this does not stand a chance of making a living. White boys and even men have opened shops which they have fitted up with carpets, pictures, mirrors, and comfortable chairs, and sometimes their brushes are even run by electricity. They have the latest newspapers always within reach for their patrons to read while their work is being done, and they grow rich. The man who owns and runs such a place as that is not called a "bootblack"; he is called the proprietor of such and such a "Shoe-blacking Emporium." And that chance is gone to come no more. Now there are many colored men who understand about electricity, but where is the colored man who would apply his knowledge of that science to running brushes in a boot-black stand?

In the South it was a common thing when anybody was taken ill to notify the old mammy nurse. We had a monopoly of the nursing business for many years, and up to a short time ago it was the common opinion that nobody could nurse but one of those old black mammies. But this idea is being dissipated. In the North, when a person gets ill, he does not think of sending for anyone but a professional nurse, one who has received a diploma from some nurse-training school, or a certificate of proficiency from some reputable institution.

I hope you have understood me in what I have been trying to say of these little things. They all tend to show that if we are to keep pace with the progress of civilization, we must pay attention to the small things as well as the larger and more important things in life. They go to prove that we must put brains into what we do. If education means anything at all, it means putting brains into the common affairs of life and making something of them. That is just what we are seeking to tell to the world through the work of this institution.

There are many opportunities all about us where we can use our education. You very rarely see a man idle who knows all about house building, who' knows how to draw plans, to test the strength of materials that enter into the making of a first class house. Did you ever see such a man out of a job? Did you ever see such a man as that writing letters to this place and that place applying for work? People are wanted allover the world who can do work well, Men and women are wanted who understand the preparation and supplying of food—I don't mean in the small menial sense—but people who know all about it. Even in this there is a great opportunity. A few days ago I met a woman who had spent years in this country and in Europe studying the subject of food economics in all its details. I learn that this person is in constant demand by institutions of learning and other establishments where the preparation and the serving of food are important features. She spends a few months at each institution. She is wanted everywhere, because she has applied her education to one of the most important necessities of life.

And so you will find it all through life—those persons who are going to be constantly sought after, constantly in demand, are those who make the best use of their opportunities, who work unceasingly to become proficient in whatever they attempt to do. Always be sure that you have something out of which you can make a living, and then you will not only be independent, but you will be in a much better position to help your fellow-men.

I have spoken about these matters at this length because I believe them to be the foundation of our future success. We often hear a man spoken of as having moral character. A man cannot have moral character unless he has something to wear, and something to eat three hundred and sixty-five days in a year... he cannot have any religion either. You will find at the bottom of much crime the fact that the criminals have not had the common necessities of life supplied them. Men must have some of the comforts and conveniences—certainly the necessities of life—supplied them before they can be morally or religiously what they ought to be.

Keeping Your Word

I do not want to speak to you continually upon subjects that tend to show up the weaker traits of character which our race has, but there are some characteristic points in our life so important that it seems to me well that we emphasize those which are especially weak just now.

A few weeks ago I mentioned two or three examples which had come under my own personal observation, of the unreliability of the race, and to those I now add one or two more.

On three distinct occasions, while traveling, I have found it necessary to make engagements with hack men to call at a certain hour in the morning to take me to an early train, and on no one of these occasions has the hack man kept his word. In the first case the man disappointed me entirely, so that I had to walk to the station, a distance of a mile or more. In the second instance the hack man was to come at six o'clock, and did not come until half-past six. By that time I had started to walk, and had gone two or three squares, meeting him on the way to the place where I had stopped. In the third case the man was at least an hour late when we met him, after we had walked over half the distance to the station.

I have spoken at another time of the fact that men who employ colored workmen have complained to me that after these men had drawn a week's pay, they could not be depended upon to return to work the next Monday morning. In the city of Savannah, Georgia, there are a great many colored men employed as stevedores men who load and unload ships. If you have read the newspapers carefully you will have noticed that recently the persons who employ these men have made a new rule, by which they refuse to pay the stevedores all of their wages at the end of the week, but retain two days' payout of each week, from every individual who works for them, to be paid to them at the end of the next week. Of course the men do not lose anything in the end by this method; it simply means that so long as they work for one employer there are at least two days' pay due them. Of course the laborers whose wages were thus kept back have made a great noise about it, but when their employers were asked for an explanation, they said: "We find by experience that if we pay you all that we owe you on Saturday night, we cannot depend upon your returning on Monday morning to continue your work. You are apt to get drunk, or to debauch yourselves on Sunday so that you are unfitted for your work the next day." This is the decision these men have arrived at after having employed these men for a number of years.

Now think of the things I have spoken to you about. You may say with regard to the last, that to a great extent this action on the part of the Savannah employers was due to prejudice, to a desire to use the . money withheld for their own selfish purposes, and because they had the power to do so, but you can very easily understand that if a person goes on being disappointed month after month in his business, he will soon conclude that it is best for him to try a hack man of some other color and disposition, and that if these Savannah employers find year after year that they cannot depend on colored men to give them thorough, regular, systematic labor, they are going to look out for persons of another race who will do their work properly.

It is not necessary for me to continue in this strain, and to call attention to other incidents of this kind, to show, as I have told you before, that one of the weak points which we as a race must fight against, is that of not being reliable. Of course I understand that it is not always possible for a person to keep an engagement, but if he cannot, it is very rarely the case that he cannot send word to the person with whom he has made the engagement of his inability to keep his part of it. In the case of the hack men who disappointed me, if they had sent word two or three hours ahead of the time, that they could not come, or if they had sent another hack man to fill the engagement for them, I should have thought nothing about it. In the case of those Savannah laborers, when they found they could not go back to their work promptly, if they had sent word to that effect, their absence, perhaps, could have been excused. But it is this habit of disappointing people in business matters without apparent care or concern that has given the race the damaging reputation which it has for unreliability.

I speak of these things repeatedly and so plainly because I am constantly meeting persons who are employers or who would be employers of our people, and they tell me every time when I speak to them about work, that their only objection to employing colored labor is this very matter I have been speaking of, its unreliability. Many of them say that they want to employ colored people, would be glad to give them places of responsibility, but that they cannot find men who will stick to their work.

You may say that it is impossible for us to grow and develop, to get positions of trust and responsibility that will pay good wages, simply because we are colored. I will give you an example on this very point. A few days ago I was in New Orleans, visiting a large sugar refinery. The firm which operates this refinery employs from two hundred to three hundred men. I found the young man who has charge of all the bookkeeping of the firm, through whose hands all the business and cash of the firm pass—I found this man to be colored, and that all the other persons filling responsible positions under him were white.

I remember some two or three years ago having met one of the partners of this firm in the White Mountains, and he told me at that time of this young man. He told me that a great many persons came to him and said: "You ought not to have this colored man filling this position when there are so many white persons who want the place."He told me that he said to these persons" This young man does my work better than anyone else I have yet found, and so long as he does this, so long shall I employ him." This gentleman has since died, but the business is in the hands of his widow, who has so much confidence in the ability of this young colored man to manage the affairs of a great business— Mr. Lewis is his name ; perhaps some of you know him that he is retained, practically at the head of this great establishment. This single instance shows that notwithstanding his color a man can rise for what is in him; that he can advance when he shows that he can be depended upon.

Remember that whether you are hack men, or business men, it pays whenever you cannot fill an engagement to explain beforehand why you cannot, and that unless you make a practice of doing this, it will be impossible for you to get ahead or to attain to places of trust and responsibility, no matter how much education you may have.

As I have so often said before, if we cannot send out from Tuskegee and similar schools young men and women who can be depended upon, our reputation as a race, for the years that are to come, is not going to be very bright. On the other hand, if we can succeed in sending out young men and women with a high sense of responsibility, who can at all times be relied upon to be prompt in business matters, we shall have gone a long way in redeeming the character of the race and in lifting it up. In this important matter all of you can help. Do not wait until you go out from Tuskegee, but begin to-morrow morning, every boy and girl, to be reliable and to keep at it until reliability becomes a part of you.

Some Lessons Of The Hour

This evening I am going to remind you of a few things which you should get out of the school year, but it will be of very little use for me to do this unless you make up your minds to do two things.

In the first place you must resolve that you are going to remember the things I am going to say, and in the second place you must put my suggestions into practice. If you will make up your minds, then, that you are going to hold on to these suggestions, so far as your memory is concerned, and then so far as possible put them into practice, we shall be able to discuss something that will be of profit to you during the year.

I want you to get it firmly fixed in your minds that books, industries, or tools of any character, no matter how thoroughly you master them, do not within themselves constitute education. Committing to memory pages of written matter, or becoming deft in the handling of tools, is not the supreme thing at which education aims. Books, tools, and industries are but the means to fit you for something that is higher and better. All these are not ends within themselves; they are simply means. The end of all education, whether of head or hand or heart, is to make an individual good, to make him useful, to make him powerful; is to give him goodness, usefulness and power in order that he may exert a helpful influence upon his fellows.

One of the things I want you to get out of this year is the ability to put a proper value upon time. If there is any one lesson that we all of us need to have impressed upon us more thoroughly and more constantly than any other, it is that each minute of our "lives is of supreme value, and that we are committing a sin when we allow a single minute to go to waste. Remember that every five minutes of time you are spending at this institution is worth so much money to you. How many people there are who, after they have arrived at the ages of sixty, seventy, or eighty years, look back with regret and say, "I wish I could live the years over again." But they cannot. All they can do is to regret that they have wasted precious minutes, precious hours.

Now your lives are yet before you, not, as in the case of these people, behind you. Your lives are yet to be lived, and they will be made successful lives just in proportion as you learn to place a value upon the minutes. Spend every minute here in hard, earnest study, or in helpful recreation. Be sure that none of your time is thrown away.

Among other things, you should get out of the year the habit of reading. Any individual who has learned to love good books, to love the best newspapers, the best magazines, and has learned to spend some portion of the day in communication with them, is a happy individual. You should get yourselves to the point where you will not be happy unless you do spend a part of each day in this way.

You should get out of the year the habit of being kind and polite to every individual. As a general thing it is not difficult for a person to be polite in words and courteous in actions to individuals who are classed in the same social scale, or who, perhaps, are above him in wealth and influence. The test of a true lady or gentleman comes when that individual is brought in contact with some one who is considered beneath her or him, some one who is ignorant or poor. Show me a man who is himself wealthy, and who is gentle and polite to the ignorant about him, and to the poor people about him, and I will show you every time a true gentleman. When Prince Henry of Prussia was in this country, I remember reading this description of one of the prominent public men who received him: "He is such a true gentleman that he can meet a prince without himself being embarrassed, and can meet a poor man without embarrassing the poor man."

Learn to speak kindly to every individual, white or black. No man loses anything by being gentlemanly, by learning to be polite, by treating the most unfortunate individual with the highest deference.

We want you to learn to control your temper. Some one has said that the difference between an animal and a man is that the beast has no method of learning to control his temper. With the individual, the human being, there is education and training. He learns to master himself, to have an even temper; learns to master his temper completely. Now if any of you have a temper that often gets to be your master, make up your mind that it is a part of your duty here to learn to control it. Step upon it, as it were, and say: "I will be master of my temper, instead of letting it be my master."

You want to have that kind of courage that is going to make you able to speak .the truth at all times, no matter what it may seem to cost you. This may, for the time being, seem to make you unpopular; it may inconvenience you, it may deprive you of something that you count dear; but the individual who cultivates that kind of courage, who, at the cost of everything, always speaks the truth, is the individual who in the end will be successful, is the one who in the end will come out the conqueror. You cannot afford to learn to speak anything but the absolute truth. One of the most beautiful things that I have seen printed about President Roosevelt was where someone wrote of him that one of the President's greatest faults was that he did not know when to lie when to deceive people—but that he always spoke the absolute, frank truth. As a result of his honesty, his truth speaking, he is at the head of the nation.

We also want you to learn to be absolutely honest in all your dealings with other people's property. We may just as well speak plainly and emphatically. One of our worst sins, one of our weaknesses, is that of not being able to handle other people's property and be honest with it.

You should learn to be absolutely honest with the property of your room-mates, school-mates and teachers. Make up your minds that nothing is going to tempt you from the path of absolute honesty. There is no man or woman who begins with meddling with other people's property and affairs, who begins to learn to take that which does not belong to him or her, who is not beginning in a downward path ending in misery, sorrow and disappointment. Make up your minds that you are going to be absolutely honest and truthful in all cases. There is no way to get happiness out of life, there is no way to get satisfaction out of your school career, except by following the lessons that I have here tried to emphasize.

When we speak of honesty, the first thought may be that the word applies only to the taking of property that does not belong to us, but this is not so. It is possible for a person to be dishonest by taking time or energy that belongs to someone else, just as much as tangible property. In going into a class-room, office, store or shop, one man may ask himself the question:" How little can I do to-day and still get through the day?" Another man will have constantly before him the question: "How much can I put into this hour or this day?" Now we expect every student who goes out from Tuskegee to be, not the man who tries to see how little he can do, or the average man who proposes to do merely his duty, but the man above the average, who will do more than his duty. And you will disappoint us unless you are above the average man, unless you go out from here with the determination that you are going to perform more than your duty.

I like to see young men or young women who, if employed in any capacity, no matter how small or unimportant that capacity may be, if the hour is eight o'clock at which they must come to work, I like to see them at work ten or fifteen minutes before that hour. I like to see a man or woman who, if the closing hour is five o'clock or six o'clock, goes to the person in charge and says "Shall I not stay longer? Is there not something else I ought to do before I go?" Put your whole souls into whatever you attempt to do. That is honesty.

Another thing you should learn this year is to get into touch with the best people there are in the world. You should learn to associate with the best students in the institution. Take them as models, and say that you are going to improve from month to month, and from year to year, until you are as good as they are, or better. You cannot reach these things all at once, but I hope that each one of you will make up his mind or her mind that from to-night, throughout the year and throughout life, there is going to be a hard striving on your part toward reaching the best results. If you do this, when you get ready to leave this institution, you will find that it has been worth your while to have spent your time here.

The Gospel Of Service

The subject on which I am going to speak to you for a few minutes to-night, "The Gospel of Service," may not, when you first hear it, strike a very responsive chord in your hearts and minds, but I assure you I have nothing but the very highest and best interest of the race at heart when I select this subject to talk about..

The word "service" has too often been misunderstood, and on this account it has in too many cases carried with it a meaning which indicates degradation. Every individual serves another in some capacity, or should do so. Christ said that he who would become the greatest of all must become the servant of all; that is, He meant that in proportion as one renders service he becomes great. The President of the United States is a servant of the people, because he serves them; the Governor of Alabama is a servant, because he renders service to the people of the State ; the greatest merchant in Montgomery is a servant, because he renders service to his customers; the school teacher is a servant, because it is his duty to serve the best interests of his pupils; the cook is a servant, because it is her duty to serve those for whom she works; the housemaid is a servant, because it is her duty to care for the property entrusted to her in the best manner in which she is able.

In one way or another, every individual who amounts to anything is a servant. The man or the woman who is not a servant is one who accomplishes nothing. It is very often true that a race, like an individual, does not appreciate the opportunities that are spread out before it until those opportunities have disappeared. Before us, as a race in the South to-day, there is a vast field for service and usefulness which is still in our hands, but which I fear will not be ours to the same extent very much longer unless we change our ideas of service, and put new life, put new dignity and intelligence into it.

Perhaps I am right in thinking that in no department of life has there been such great progress and such changes for the better during the last ten years as in the department of domestic service, or housekeeping. The cook who does not make herself intelligent, who does not learn to do things in the latest, and in the neatest and cleanest manner, will soon find herself without employment, or will at least find herself a "drug on the market," instead of being sought after and paid higher wages. The woman who does not keep up with all the latest methods of decorating and setting her table, and of putting the food on it properly, will find her occupation gone within a few years. The same is true of general housekeeping, of laundering and of nursing.

All the occupations of which I have been talking are at present in our hands in the South; but I repeat that very great progress is being made in all of them in every part of the world, and we shall find that we shall lose them unless our women go forward and get rid of the old idea that such occupations are fit only for ignorant people to follow. At the present time scores of books and magazines are appearing bearing upon every branch of domestic service. People are learning to do things in an intelligent and scientific manner. Not long ago I sat for an hour and listened to a lecture delivered upon the subject of dusting, and it was one of the most valuable hours I ever spent. The person who gave this lecture upon dusting was a highly educated and a cultivated woman, and her audience was composed of wealthy and cultivated people. We must bring ourselves to the point where we can feel that one who cooks, and does it well, should be just as much honored as the person who teaches school.

What I have said in regard to the employments of our women is equally true of the occupations followed by our men. It is true that at the present we are largely cultivating the soil of the South, but if other people learn to do this work more intelligently, learn more about laborsaving machinery, and become more conscientious about their work than we, we shall find our occupation departing. It used to be the case in many parts of the North that the Negro was the coachman; but in a very large degree, in cities like New York and Philadelphia, the Negro has lost this occupation, and lost it, in my opinion, not because he was a Negro, but because in many cases he did not see that the occupation of coachman was constantly being improved. It has been improved and lifted up until now it has almost become a profession. The Negro who expects to remain a coachman should learn the proper dress for a coachman, and learn how to care for horses and vehicles in the most approved.

What is true of the coachman is true of the Butler. In too many cases, I fear, we use these occupations merely as stepping stones, holding on to them until we can find something else to do, in a careless and ship shod manner. We want to change all this, and put our whole souls into these occupations, and in a large degree make them our life-work. In proportion as we do this, we shall lay a foundation upon which our children and grandchildren are to rise to higher things. The foundation of every race must be laid in the common every-day occupations that are right about our doors. It should not be our thought to see how little we can put into our work, but how much; not how quickly we can get rid of our tasks, but how well we can do them. I often wish that I had the means to put into every city a large training-school for giving instruction in all lines of domestic service. Few things would add more to the fundamental usefulness of the race than such a school. Perhaps it may be suggested that my argument has reference only to our serving while people. It has reference to doing whatever we do in the best manner, no matter whom we serve. The individual who serves a black man poorly will serve a white man poorly. Let me illustrate what I mean. In a Southern city, a few days ago, I found a large hotel conducted by colored people. It is one of the very cleanest and best and most attractive hotels for colored people that I have found in any part of the country. In talking with the proprietors I asked them what was the greatest obstacle they had had to overcome, and they told me it was in finding colored women to work in the house who would do their work systematically and well, women who would, in a word, keep the rooms in every part of the hotel thoroughly swept and cleaned. This hotel had been opened three months, and I found that during that time the proprietors had employed fifteen different chambermaids, and they had got rid of a large proportion of these simply because they were determined not to have people in their employment who did not do their work well.

One weakness pertaining to the whole matter of domestic employment in the South, at present, is this: it is too easy for our people to find work. If there was a rule followed in every family that employs persons, that no man or woman should be hired unless he or she brought a letter of recommendation from the last employer, we should find that the whole matter of domestic service would be lifted up a hundred per cent. So long as an individual can do poor work for one family, and perhaps be dishonest at the same time, and be sure that he or she will be employed by some other family, without regard to the kind of service rendered the last employer, so long will domestic service be poor and unsatisfactory.

Many white, people seldom come in contact with the Negro in any other capacity than that of domestic service. If they get a poor idea of our character and service in that respect, they will infer that the entire life of the Negro is unsatisfactory from every point of view. We want to be sure that wherever our life touches that of the white man, we conduct ourselves so that he will get the best impression possible of us.

In spite of all the fault I have found, I would say this before I stop. I recognize that the people of no race, under similar circumstances, have made greater progress in thirty-five years than is true of the people of the Negro race. If I have spoken to you thus plainly and frankly, it is that our progress in the future may be still greater than it has been in the past.

Your Part In The Negro Conference

For eight or nine years, now, it has been our custom to hold here what is known as the Tuskegee Negro Conference. A number of years ago it occurred to some of us that instead of confining the work of this institution to the immediate body of students gathered within its walls, we perhaps could extend and broaden its scope so as to reach out to, and try to help, the parents of the students and the older people in the country districts, and, to some extent, if possible, in the cities also.

With this end in view, we, some years ago, invited a number of men and women to come and spend the day with us, and, while here, to tell us in a very plain and straightforward manner something about their material, moral and religious condition. Then the afternoon of that same day was spent in hearing from these same~ men and women suggestions as to how they thought this institution and other institutions might help them, and also how they thought they might help themselves.

Out of these simple and small meetings has grown what we now call "The Tuskegee Negro Conference," which, in the last few years, has grown until it numbers from nine hundred to twelve hundred persons. We not only have that large number of persons, most of whom come from farms and are engaged in farm work, but we now also have "The Workers' Conference," which meets on the day following the Negro Conference. This Workers Conference brings together representatives from all the larger institutions for the education of the Negro in the South.

Now these meetings for this year begin next Wednesday morning, and the practical question that I wish to discuss with you to-night is what can we do to make that Conference a success? What can you do for the Conference, and what can the Conference do for you?

I wish you to grasp the idea that is growing through the country— that very few institutions now confine themselves and their work to mere teaching in the class-room, in the old-fashioned manner. Very few now confine themselves and their work to the comparatively small number of students that they can reach in that way, as they did a few years ago. In many cases they have their college extension work. In one way or another they are reaching out and getting hold of the young people—and getting a hold on the older people as well. And just so, to a very large degree, through this Conference, Tuskegee is doing something of the same kind of thing.

During these few days we shall have hundreds of the farmers, with their wives and daughters, gathered here. We want each and every one of you here in the institution to make up your mind that you can do something to help these people. We want each one of you here to-night to feel that he or she has a special responsibility during the time these' people are gathered together at Tuskegee. We sometimes speak of it as their one day of schooling in the whole year,—that is, the one day out of the whole three hundred and sixty-five days in the year when, perhaps, they will give the greatest amount of attention to matters pertaining to themselves. In inviting them here, not only the teachers and officers of this institution have a responsibility, but each and every student here also has a responsibility. I want you to feel that, and see to what extent you can take hold of these people while they are here, to inspire and encourage them, so as to have them go away from here feeling that it is worth their while to come to the Institute for this meeting, even if as is true of some of them—they have come a long distance.

Some of these people who will come here are ignorant, so far as books are concerned, but I want you to know that not every person who cannot read and write is ignorant. Some of the persons, whom I have met and from whom I have learned much, are persons who cannot write a word. Very many of the people who will come here may not be able to read or write, but we can learn something from them notwithstanding, while they are here, and they can learn something from us.

I want you to take delight in getting hold of these people and taking them through our shops, guiding them through our various agricultural and mechanical departments. Be sure that you exert every effort possible to make them comfortable and happy while they are here. Heretofore the students have been so generous, at the time of this meeting, that many of them, if necessary, have given up their rooms that these people might have a comfortable night's rest. I do not know where you have slept, but I do not think that in the history of the school a student was ever asked to give up his room to any of these people that he did not gladly and freely do so. I believe that you are going to do the same thing this year.

I want you, also, to remember that you not only can help the Conference to he a success by being polite and kindly to the farmers who come from this and other Southern States, but also by being polite and attentive to the representatives from the large institutions that will be here. We will have present representatives from every large institution engaged in the education of our people. It means much for the principals and instructors in these large colleges and industrial schools to leave their work and come as far as many of them do, to spend these days here. We have a responsibility on their account; we desire them to feel that it has been worth their while to leave their work and spend their time and money to come here for these meetings. We wish them to get something out of our industries here; we wish them to get something out of the training here, in every department, something which they can take back to their own institution to make their work there stronger and better.

Now as to yourselves, you can get something out of this Conference for yourselves, by getting hold of everything possible, so that when you go out from Tuskegee you will have just that much more helpful information to put into practice. I want to see you go out through the South and establish local conferences. Call them together, and teach the same kind of lessons that we teach at these gatherings at Tuskegee. You can get the most out of this Conference by putting into practice this effort to make other people happy. To get the greatest happiness out of life is to make somebody else happy. To get the greatest good out of life is to do something for somebody else. I want you to find the persons who are most ignorant and most poverty stricken; I want you to find the persons who are most forlorn and most discouraged, and do something for them to make their hours happy. In doing that, you will do the most for yourselves.

I want each boy and each girl who belongs to this institution to be deep down in his or her heart a gentleman or a lady. A gentleman means simply this: a generous person; one who has learned to be kind; one who has learned to think not of himself first, but of the happiness and welfare of others. Let us put this spirit into our Conference day the coming week, and the day and week will be the greatest and most successful and we have ever had. Let our resolution be that the persons who come here, whether they represent a university, a college, an industrial school, a farm, or a shop—let our resolve be that when these people leave here they shall take away with them from Tuskegee something that will make their lives happier, brighter, stronger and more useful.

What Is To Be Our Future?

Last Thursday afternoon I received a telegram from a gentleman stopping for a time in a city in Georgia, asking me to come there at once on important business; and being rather curious to know what he wanted of me, I went. I found that this man was in the act of making his will, and that he had in mind the putting aside of a considerable sum in his will—some $20,000, in fact—for this institution.

The special point upon which this gentleman wished to consult me was the future of the Institution. He said that he had worked very hard for his money, that it had come as a result of much sacrifice and hard effort, and that there were friends of his who were beseeching him to use his money in other directions, because they thought it would be more likely to do permanent good elsewhere. And so he wished to know what the future of this Institution is likely to be, because he did not care to risk his money upon an uncertain venture, one that was likely to prosper for a few years, and then fail. He said that he would not like to give his money to an institution where it would not go on through the years, accomplishing a certain amount of good. Accordingly the question he repeated to me over and over again was: "What is to be the future of Tuskegee?" He wished to know whether, if we were given the money, it would go on from year to year, blessing one generation after another.

My point in speaking to you to-night is to emphasize what I think our good friend Professor Brown has already brought to our attention in one or two of his talks to us this week, the importance of making this institution what it ought to be, what its reputation gives it, and what its name implies.

More and more I realize—and I remember that the gentleman of whom I have spoken repeated this to me with great emphasis—that so far as the outside world is concerned, Tuskegee is sure; you need not have the least doubt that the institution will be supported. If we keep things right at the institution, if it is worthy of support, the moneyed people of the country will support it and stand by it. More and more each year this impression grows upon me, and more and more each year there are convincing evidences of the fact that the permanence and growth of this institution do not rest upon whether the people of the South or the people of the North are going to support it with their means. I have the most implicit confidence that the institution is going to be supported. But the question that comes to us with the greatest force is: "Are we going to be worthy of that support? Shall we be worthy of the confidence of the public?" That is the question that is most serious; that is the question that presses most heavily upon my heart, and upon the hearts of the other teachers here.

Now these questions can be answered satisfactorily only by evidence that each student, each individual connected with the school in any way, no matter in how low or high a capacity, is putting his or her whole conscience into the work here. When I say work, I mean study of books, work of the hand, effort of the body, willingness of the heart. No matter what the thing is, put your conscience into it; do your best. Let it be possible for you to say: "I have put my whole soul into my study, into my work, into whatever I have attempted. Whatever I have done I have honestly endeavored to do to the best of my ability. "

The questions which this gentleman asked me, and similar kinds of questions, are being asked over and over again by people all over the country. The question can be answered only by our putting our consciences into our work, and by our being entirely unselfish in it. Let every person get into the habit of planning every day for the comfort and welfare of others, let each one try to live as unselfishly as possible, remembering that the Bible says: "He that would save his life, must lose it." And you never saw a person save his life in this higher sense, in the Christ—like sense, unless that person was willing, day by day, to lose himself in the interest of his fellow-men. Such persons save their own lives, and in saving them save thousands of other lives.

Such questions as these can be satisfactorily answered not merely by our putting our consciences into every effort, no matter what the effort may be, but by improving, day by day, upon what has been done the day before. In large institutions and establishments it is comparatively easy to find persons who will sweep a room day by day, or plough a field during certain seasons of the year, and do other work at certain other seasons of the year, but the difficulty comes in finding persons who make improvements in the manner of sweeping rooms, of plowing fields and planting corn. The question for us is: "Are we going to put so many brains into our efforts every year that we are going to go on steadily and constantly improving from year to year?" Are you going to get into the habit of so thinking about your work here that the habit will become, as it were, a part of yourself, so that when you go out into the world you will not be satisfied to take a position and go on in the same humdrum manner, but will not be satisfied until your work has been improved in every possible detail, and made easier, more systematic, and more convenient?

We must put brains into our work. There must be improvement in every department of this institution every year. It is absolutely impossible for an institution to stand still; it must go forward or backward, grow better or worse each year. An institution grows stronger and more useful each year, or weaker and less useful.

This institution can grow only by each person putting his thought into his work, by planning how he can improve the work of his particular department, by constantly striving to make his work more useful to the institution, by keeping the place where he works cleaner, and making his work more business—like and more systematic. That is the only way in which the questions which people all over the country are asking about this institution can be satisfactorily answered.

You will find that people will look to us more and more for tangible results. Not only here, but all over the country, our race is going to be called on to answer the question: "What can the race really accomplish?" It is perfectly well understood by our friends as well as by our enemies that we can write good newspaper articles and make good addresses, that we can sing well and talk well, and all that kind of thing is perfectly well understood and conceded. But the question that will be more and more forced upon us for an answer is: "Can we work out our thoughts; can we put them into tangible shape, so that the world may see from day to — day actual evidences of our intellectuality?"

Last winter I was in the town of Clinton, Iowa. I think I had never heard of the place before, and when I got there I was surprised to find it a place of more than 16,000 inhabitants. The gentleman who was to entertain me wanted to take me to a colored restaurant. I expected to go into a restaurant of the kind operated by our people generally, and I was very much surprised when he took me into a large, two-story building. I found the floors carpeted, and everything about the place as pleasant and attractive as it was possible to make it. In fact the restaurant compared very favorably with many in the largest cities in the country. I found the waiters clean, the service good, and everything conducted in the most systematic manner. And there was not the least thing, except the color of the proprietor's skin, to show that the place was operated by colored people.

Afterward my friend took me into another establishment of the same size, operated in the same creditable manner by another colored man. In both I found that these gentlemen not only carried on a regular restaurant business, but manufactured their own candies and ice cream, and did a sort of wholesale catering business. I asked the white people there what they thought of the colored people, and I did not find a single white person who did not have the most implicit confidence in the colored people. The trouble was that there were not many colored people there. That accounts possibly for the good opinion which the white people have of them. But you see what just two black men can do. These people had never seen many black people, but fortunately for us they had with them two of the best specimens of our race that I have ever seen anywhere in this country. As a result you do not find anyone cursing the black man in that town. Everybody had the utmost confidence in black people, and respected them.

Just in proportion as we can establish object lessons of this kind all over the country, you will find that the problem that now is so perplexing will disappear. Until we do this, we shall not be able to talk away, or to argue away, this prejudice. We cannot talk our way into our rights; we must work our way, think our way, into them. And you will find that just in proportion as we do this, we are going to get all we deserve.

Some Great Little Things

I am going to speak to you for a few minutes tonight upon what I shall term "Some Great Little Things." I speak of them as great, because of their supreme importance, and I speak of them as little, because they come in a class of things which are usually looked upon by many people as small and unimportant. But in an institution like this I think they often hold first place — certainly they come under the head of important things that we can learn.

You will remember that in the sermon the Chaplain preached this morning, he mentioned the three-fold division of our nature; the physical part, the mental part, and the spiritual part. What I shall refer to to-night has largely to do with the material, the physical part of our natures. There are certain little things that each one of you can learn now, in connection with the care of your bodies, which, if left unlearned now, will perhaps go without being learned all your lives. You are now, as it were, at the parting of the ways—you are going to make these habits a part of yourselves, or you are going to let them escape you forever, and be weak in a measure all your lives for not having made them a part of yourselves.

I am going to speak very plainly, because I feel that such talk means nothing unless it is in language which everyone can appreciate and understand. Now, among the first things that a person going to a, boarding school should learn, if he has not already learned it at home—and I am constantly being surprised at the number who seem to have thus left it unlearned—is the habit of regular and systematic bathing. No person who has left this habit unlearned can reach the highest success in life. I mean by that, that a person who does not get into the habit of keeping the body clean, cannot do the highest work and the greatest amount of work in the world. When it comes to competing with persons who have learned the habit of keeping the body in good condition, you will find that the first named persons usually win in the race of life. I think many of you have already learned from your physiologies that when it comes to the combating of disease, where two persons are on a sick-bed with the same disease, the one who is habitually clean in his personal habits Thus a far greater chance for recovery than the one who has not learned the habit of cleanliness. You will also find that the person who is in the habit of caring for his body is in a better condition for study; he is in a condition to bear prolonged and severe exertion, while the person whose body is unclean is in a weak condition.

Take the matter of the teeth. Persons cannot call themselves educated and refined who do not make the matter of the cleanliness and proper care of their teeth an important part of themselves. When I speak of making such a thing a part of yourselves, I mean that you should make it such a strong habit that to leave it undone would seem unnatural. Some person has defined man as a bundle of habits. There are many habits that I wish you to make a part of yourselves, by practicing so constantly that they may really be said to have become that.

There is the matter of the care of the hair, which everyone should make a part of himself. There is also the proper care of the fingernails.

Now all of these are common things, but they are great things. I should not recommend very highly a young man or young woman who went out from this institution as a graduate, and had not learned the habit of caring for the teeth, hair and nails systematically. Are you making these lessons a part of yourself?

Take the young men and young women who have been here two or three years. Have you grown to the point where you are dissatisfied and all out of sorts when your hair is not combed, your finger nails dirty, and your body not in the condition it should be in? If you have not reached that point, when you come to graduate, then there will be something wrong with your education, and you are not ready to go out from this institution, whether you are in the senior class or in the preparatory class.

Another thing; I confess that I cannot have the highest kind of respect for the person who is in the habit of going day after day with buttons off his clothes. There is no excuse for it, when buttons are so cheap. I wonder how many of you could stand, if I were now to ask all to stand who have every button in its place. I cannot have the best opinion of a girl who will let a hole remain in her apron day after day. Nor can I think well of a man who does not remove a grease spot from his coat as soon as he discovers it.

You have more respect for yourselves, and other people have more respect for you, when you get into the habit of polishing your shoes, no matter where you are, but especially when you are at school. Every man should get into the habit of polishing his shoes. See to it that they are in proper condition at all times.

I need not repeat here, after what I have said that it is of the utmost importance that every person wears the cleanest of linen. If I speak to you so plainly, it is because I want you to make these matters a part of yourselves to such an extent that they will be essential to your happiness and success. I want every girl who goes away from here to be so nearly perfect in her dress that she cannot be happy if there is any detail unattended to; and I want the same thing to be true of the young men. Let these things have an important bearing on your education here, and on your life hereafter.

And then, above all things, although on account of the number of students here you are very much crowded in your rooms and will have to make all the harder effort on that account, get into the habit of being orderly and neat. School your room-mates to the point where they will have a place for everything. Always know where to put your hands on anything you may want in your room, whether in the light or in the dark.

Then there are one or two other little things. You should have quiet in your rooms, at your work or in your talk with your fellow students. Do your work quietly. Get into the habit of closing doors quietly. You cannot realize how much all these little things add to your happiness and to the manhood and womanhood which you are going to build up as the years go on.

And then, in conclusion, so order your lives that you can form the habit of reading. Set aside a certain amount of time each day, even if it be not more than four or five minutes, for reading and studying aside from your lessons. Read books of travel, history and biography. I want you to patronize the library this year as never before. In it are great numbers of books by authors of the highest rank.

Be regular in all your habits. Have a regular time for studying, for recreation, and for sleeping.

And last, but far from least, set aside a regular time for thinking, for meditating with yourself. Take yourself up, pick yourself to pieces, see wherein you are weak and need strengthening. Analyze yourself. Get rid, as it were, of all the weights that have been holding you back, and resolve at the end of each week that you will walk upon your dead selves of the week before. If you will go on, making that kind of progress, you will find at the end of the nine school months that you are stronger in everything essential to good manhood and good womanhood.

To Would-Be Teachers

Since very many of you whom I see before me to-night will spend some part of your lives after you leave here as teachers, even if you do not make teaching your life work, I am going to talk over with you again a subject on which I have spoken elsewhere—How to build up a good school in the South.

The colored schools of the South, especially in the country districts and smaller towns, are not kept open by the State fund, as a rule, longer than three or four months in the year. One of the great questions, then, willing teachers and parents, is how to extend the school term to seven or eight months, so that the school shall really do some good.

I want to give a few plain suggestions, which will, I think, if carefully followed, result in placing a good school in almost every community. In this I am not speculating, because more than one Tuskegee graduate has built up a good school on the plan I outline.

In the first place the teacher must be willing to settle down in the community, and feel that that is to be his home, and teaching there his chief object in life while he is there. Not only must he not feel that he can move about from place to place every three months, but he must feel that he is not working for his salary alone. He must be willing to sacrifice for the good of the community.

The next thing is to get a convenient schoolhouse. Usually, in the far South, the State has not been able to build a school-house. How is it to be secured? A good school-house should be carefully planned. Then the teacher or some one else should go among the people in the community, colored and white, and get each individual to give something, no matter how small an amount if in money, or, if not in money, how little in value, for purchasing lumber. When we were getting started here at Tuskegee one old colored woman brought me six eggs as her contribution to our work.

If enough money cannot be secured by subscription and collection to pay for the lumber, a supper, a festival, entertainment or church collection will help out. After the lumber is secured, the parents should be asked to "club in" with their wagons and haul it free. Then at least one good carpenter should be secured to take the lead in building. Each member of the community should agree to give a certain number of days' work in helping to put up the structure. In this work of building, the larger pupils can help a good deal, and they will have all the more interest in the school-house because they have had a hand in its erection. In these ways, by patient effort, a good frame school-house can be secured in almost any community.

Where it is possible, take a three or four months' public school as a starting point, and work in cooperation with the school officers, but do not let the school close at the end of these three or four months, because if that is done it will amount to almost nothing.

As soon as the teacher goes into a community, he should organize the people into an educational society or club, and there should be regular meetings once a week, or once in two weeks, at which plans for the improvement of the school should be discussed.

There are a number of ways for extending the school term. One is for each parent to pay ten, fifteen, twenty-five or fifty cents each month during the whole time the school is in session. Frequently parents who cannot pay in cash can let the teacher have eggs, chickens, butter, sweet potatoes, corn or some other kind of produce which will help to supply the teacher with food. Another plan is for each farmer to set aside a portion of land and give all that is raised upon it to the school. Still another plane and one that is being successfully carried out in at least one place; and one that I think much of, is for the teacher to secure, either by renting or purchase, a small tract of land say from two to five acres—and let the children cultivate this land while they are attending school. If, in this way, three bales of cotton can be raised, and a variety of vegetables and grain also; the produce can be sold and the school term extended from three months to six or seven months.

Some parents may object to this at first, but they will soon see that it is better to let the school close at one o'clock or two o'clock in the afternoon, so that the children may work on the school land for an hour or two, and in this way keep the school open six or seven months, than to let it close entirely at the end of three months. There is another advantage in this latter plan. The teacher can in this way teach the students, in a practical way, better methods of farming. Short talks on the principles of agriculture are worth much more to them than time spent in committing to memory the names of mountain peaks in Central Africa. Very often there is enough land right around the schoolhouse for the pupils to cultivate.

In every case where it is possible, the teacher should buy a home in the community, and make his home in every way a model for those of the people who live around him. The teacher should cultivate a farm, or follow some trade while not teaching. This not only helps him, but sets a good example for the people in the community. If the teacher be a woman, there are few communities where she cannot add much to her income by sewing, dressmaking or poultry-raising.

The Cultivation Of Stable Habits

I am going to speak with you a few minutes this evening upon the matter of stability. I want you to understand when you start out in school, that no individual can accomplish anything unless he means to stick to what he undertakes. No matter how many possessions he may have, no matter how much he may have in this or that direction, no matter how much learning or skill of hand he may possess, an individual cannot succeed unless, at the same time, he possesses that quality which will enable him to stick to what he undertakes. In a word he is not to be jumping from this thing to that thing.

That is the reason why so many ministers fail. They preach awhile, and then jump to something else. They do not stick to one thing. It is the same with many lawyers and doctors. They do not stick to what they undertake. Many business men fail for the same reason. When an individual gets a reputation—no matter what he has undertaken—of not having the quality of sticking to a thing until he succeeds in reaching the end, that reputation nullifies the influence for good of the better traits of his character in every direction. It is said of him that he is unstable.

I want you to begin your school life with the idea that you are going to stick to whatever you undertake until you have completed it. I take it for granted that all of you have come here with that idea in mind; that before you came here you sat down and talked the matter over with your father and mother, read over the circulars giving information about the school, and then deliberately decided that this institution was the one whose course of study you wished to complete. I take it for granted that you have come here with that end in view, and I want to say to you now, that you will injure yourselves, your parents, and the institution—and you will hurt your own reputation—unless, after having come here with the determination to succeed, you remain here for that purpose, and remain for the full time, until you receive your diploma. I hope every individual here, every young man and woman at the school, is here with the determination that he or she will not give up the struggle until the object aimed at has been attained.

You are at a stage now, when, if you begin jumping about here and there, if you begin in this course of study and then go to that course of study, you will very likely be jumping about from one thing to another all your life. You must make up your minds, after coming here, to do well whatever you undertake. This is a good rule not only to begin your school life with, but also to begin your later life with.

Perhaps I was never more interested than I was last evening in Montgomery, while standing on one of the streets there for an hour. I seldom stand on any street for an hour, but last night I did stand on that street for an hour, in front of a large, beautiful store that is owned by Mr. J. W. Adams, and watched the notice taken of the display of millinery made in his store windows by two girls that finished their academic and industrial courses at this school—Miss Jemmie Pierce and Miss Lydia Robinson. The first Monday in October is always the day in

Montgomery for what they call the millinery openings; on that day the stores which handle such goods all make a great display of ladies' hats and bonnets. It was surprising and interesting to note how these two girls had entered a great city like Montgomery and had taken entire charge of the millinery department in a large store. Hundreds of people stopped to comment favorably upon the taste that was displayed in the decoration of those windows.

Now, all this work was done by two Tuskegee graduates. And the complimentary remarks that were made came not only from colored people but from white people as well. No one could tell from the windows of that store whether it was a colored or a white establishment. Many of the white ladies who were standing there did not know that they were standing in front of a store that was owned by a black man. It had none of the usual earmarks about it. Usually when you go into colored establishments you see grease on the doors or on the counters; or you see this sign or that sign that this is a colored man's establishment. Those of you here who are going to go into business after you leave school do not want to have any such earmarks about your establishments. Such a store as that of Mr. Adams is the kind of a store to have.

Now, these two young women have made a reputation for themselves. They went into the millinery division while they were here, and they remained until they graduated. One of them, I believe had not finished in the millinery department when she received her academic diploma, and so she came back last year and took a postgraduate course in millinery. It is interesting and encouraging to see these two young women succeeding in their work, and it all comes from their determination to succeed, and because they had sense enough to finish what they had undertaken.

That is the lesson that you all want to learn. If you do not learn it now, in a large degree you will be failures in life. You want to be like these young women. You want to fight it out. Now if you mean to get your diploma, you are going to have a hard time. Some of you are going to be without shoes, without a hat, without proper clothing of any kind. You will get discouraged because you have not as nice a dress or as nice a hat as this person or that person. I would not give a snap of my finger for a person who would give up for that. The thing for you to do is to fight it out. Get something in your head, and don't worry about what you can get to put on it. The clothes will come afterward.

You are going to be greatly discouraged sometimes, but if you will heed the lesson of fighting out what you have undertaken, that same disposition will follow you all through life, and you will get a reputation, because people will say of you that there is a person who sticks to whatever he or she undertakes. One of the saddest things in life is to see an individual who has grown to old age, with no profession, with no calling whatever from which he is sure of getting an independent living. It is sad to see such individuals without money, without homes, in their old age, simply because they did not learn the lesson of saving money and getting for themselves a beautiful home when they ought to have done this. And so, all through life~ we can point to many people who have not learned this lesson that for whatever they undertake they must pay the price which the world asks of them if they would succeed. If we are going to succeed we trust pay the price for what we get; and he who accomplishes the most, accomplishes it in an humble and straightforward way, by sticking to what he has, undertaken. He who does this finds in the end that he has achieved a tremendous success.

What You Ought To Do

It is comparatively easy to perform almost any kind of work, but the value of any work is in having it performed so that the desired results may be most speedily reached and in having the means with which the worker labors arranged so as to meet certain ends. It is the constant problems of those organs which have charge of the well being of the body, to cause digestion to take place, so that what is nourishing in tie food may reach every part of the body; not only the portions near the organs in which digestion takes place, but also the most extreme parts of the different members.

Just so it is the aim of all persons who are accustomed to making public addresses to try to make those who are far away from them hear them as well as those who sit near. In this same way, it seems to me more and more every year, it is going to be the main object of all our schools in the South to make their influence felt most forcibly among those who are remote from them.

How can we reach the masses who are remote— I mean remote from educational advantages and from opportunities for encouragement and enlightenment? The problem in the rural districts is difficult because of the vastness of the number to be reached, and of the frequent difficulty of reaching them. We must keep this fact before us, then; that institutions of this kind are of little value unless they can pave the way to make the results of their work felt among the masses of the people who are especially remote from these institutions.

It is a fact, as most of you know, that we very seldom meet with a thoroughly well-educated teacher in the rural districts, in spite of the passing of over thirty years since we became men and women. You know, too, that the same thing is, in too large a measure, true of the ministry. The responsibility for reaching these people, for, affecting them for good, rests upon the young men and young women who are being educated in these Southern institutions today.

What are you going to do as your part towards reaching these people, towards carrying to them the light which they need so much and so earnestly long for? Difficult as this problem is, it is not a discouraging one, because these people are ready to follow the light as soon as they are sure that the right kind of light is set up before them. You very seldom meet with a colored man who is not conscious of his ignorance, and who is not anxious to get up as soon as he finds himself down. In this respect the problem is encouraging.

One of the ways in which the problem is serious is with respect to labor. In almost every city and town in the South a large proportion of the colored people are shiftless so far as manual labor is concerned, although I think there is already improvement. The masses of our people are given to thrift and industry, and to unremitting toil, in their way. The hard thing about it, the discouraging thing, is that they do not know how to realize on the results of their toil; because they have no education and little idea of industrial development, they do not know how to make their work tell for what it ought to. As a general thing the people—those in the country especially —do not ask anybody to come and give them food, clothing and houses; all they ask is for some person, some honest, upright man or woman who is interested in their welfare, to come among them and show them how to direct their efforts and their energy, show them how best to realize an .the results of their work, so that they can supply their own moral, religious and material needs and educate their children.

And you will find that wherever this institution, Hampton, Talladega, Fisk, Atlanta or any other, can put in the midst of the people young men and young women who will settle down among them and make their lives object lessons for the people —plant a good school and convince the people that the teacher has settled down there to stay through encouraging or discouraging circumstances—you will find that such a teacher will not only be encouraged, but will be supported materially. In every way there will be an opportunity for that person to revolutionize the community. That opportunity is open to you. It is an opportunity which is being opened to no other set of young men and young women who are being educated anywhere else in the world. Are you going to appreciate the beauty and grandeur of this opportunity?

I was talking with a gentleman last night who has recently spent some time in one of the Southern states, and he told me that in hardly any country district in that state was there a public school which is kept open longer than four months. He tells me that the average salary in some of those districts is little more than fifteen dollars a month. In another state the condition of the people is about the same. In our own state perhaps the conditions are worse even than in the states referred to. In some counties in Alabama, the people are this year receiving no money to run their schools more than three and a half months in the year; except, of course, in the cities and towns. In some counties the teachers are being paid only twelve to twenty dollars, and there are possibly some where the teachers get not more than ten dollars from the state fund.

I was talking with a gentleman from another state not long ago about the material condition of the people in that state, and he told me that so far as their industrial life is concerned, the masses are in a very bad condition this year; that they are too often at the mercy of the landowners— I refer to the persons who run the large plantations and that the same thing is largely true of all of the cotton-raising states. I need not go on to describe to you the moral results that must inevitably follow such a condition of things. I need not take your time to tell you that there can be little morality or religion among people who are so ignorant as these people, and who do not know where they are going to get anything to eat. It is needless to describe the train of moral evils that must follow such conditions as these.

What I have attempted to describe to you as existing to-day in these country districts may not be very encouraging, but it seems to me that every young man and young woman who has enjoyed the privileges afforded by this and by other institutions in the South— I speak especially now to the members of the next graduating class should feel that such conditions as these present one of the most inviting fields possible for labor. Every young man and woman here is being educated by money that is given by others. None of you are paying for the education you are receiving. You might pay for your board, but you would have to do that elsewhere. Everyone must pay for his or her own clothing, but the cost of buildings, rent, tuition, expenses and other matters pertaining to the institution you do not pay. Your education, in a large measure, is a gift from the public, and it seems to me that one of the first things you should do is to repay, to as large an extent as is possible with your services, what has been spent in giving you so large a part of your education.

This is a debt that you owe not only to yourselves, but to our race and our country. It is a religious debt as well, that you be willing to go out into these country districts and suffer, as it were, for a few years, until you can get a foothold, so that you can plant yourselves in one of these dark communities. I feel sure that you would not have to suffer very long. I believe that the hardest part of the struggle would come during the first two or three years. When you can convince the people that you are in earnest, the battle is won. When you can convince them that it is cheaper to keep an educated teacher than to keep one who is ignorant, and when you can once demonstrate your value to them not only in an educational respect but industrially and morally, the battle is won, and these people will stand by you and support you. In many cases, it is my belief that you will eventually find yourselves better supported financially than you would if you had gone to work in cities and large towns. No matter from which side you look at this problem, good is bound to come from it.

And while we ate talking about the reward that will come as a result of your services, let me tell you that no greater satisfaction can come to anyone than that which you will get from the worship and praise which will come to you from these old mothers and fathers who will be benefitted by your services. I know of instances where teachers have gone and planted themselves in these country districts who, even if they do not make such a very great success financially, receive the love and most sincere worship from year to year, because of the feeling of gratitude which the people among whom they have settled have for them on account of their having helped them in so many ways.

This same kind of pioneer work had to be done all over the world before the right kind of civilization was planted. It was such work as this that the people did who settled the great West, where they were deprived of the comforts of life. The people who planted Oberlin College lit what was then a wilderness had to suffer many such hardships. The men who went to Washington, Oregon, and California and established what now large Cities there are, had to suffer many such hardships; they had to suffer just what you must and should suffer. Are you going to suffer for your own people until they can receive the light which they so much need? If the young men and women before me have the right kind of stuff in them they will do this. Most certainly do I hope that you are going to carry out into these dark communities the light which you receive here from day to day. I hope you will fill these districts with men and women of education. When you go out from here with your diploma, whether it be next Mayor at some other time, resolve to plant yourself in one community and stay there. No matter what your work is, you cannot accomplish much if you become the wandering Jew. Find the community where you think you can use your life to the best advantage, and then stay there.

In the time that has elapsed since this talk was given, I think there has been improvement in many of the country schools in the South, and in the general condition of the people as described to me then—B. T. W.

Individual Responsibility

I have referred in a general way, before this, when I have been speaking to you, to the fact that each one of you ought to feel an interest in whatever task is set you to do here over and above the mere bearing which that task has on your own life. I wish to speak more specifically to-night on this subject—on what I may term the importance of your feeling a sense of personal responsibility not only for the successful performance of every task set you, but for the successful outcome of every worthy undertaking with which you come in contact.

You ought to realize that your actions will not affect yourselves alone. In this age it is almost impossible for a man to live for himself alone. On every side our lives touch those of others; their lives touch ours. Even if it were possible to live otherwise, few would wish to. A narrow life, a selfish life, is almost sure to be not only unprofitable but unhappy. The happy people and the successful people are those who go out of their way to reach and influence for good as many persons as they can. In order to do this, though, in order best to fit one's self to live this kind of life, it is important that certain habits be acquired; and an essential one of these is the habit of realizing one's responsibility to others.

Your actions will affect other people in one way or another, and you will be responsible for the result. You ought always to remember this, and govern yourselves accordingly. Suppose it is the matter of the recitation of a lesson, for instance. Some one may say: "It is nobody's business but my own if I fail in a recitation. Nobody will suffer but me." This is not so. Indirectly you injure your teacher also, for while a conscientious, hard-working teacher ought not to be blamed for the failures of pupils who do not learn simply because they do not want to, or are too lazy to try, it is generally the case that a teacher's reputation gains or loses as his or her class averages high or low. And each failure in recitation, for whatever cause, brings down the average. Then, too, you are having an influence upon your classmates, even if it be unconscious. There is hardly ever a student who is not observed by some one at some time as an example. "There is such a boy," some other student says to himself. "He has failed in class ever so many times, and still he gets along. It can't make much difference it I fail once." And as a result he neglects his duty, and does fail.

The same thing is true of work in the industrial departments. Too many students try to see how easily they can get through the day, or the work period, and yet not get into trouble. Or even if they take more interest than this, they care for their work only for the sake of what they can get out of it for themselves, either as pay, or as instruction which will enable them to work for pay at some later time. Now there ought to be a higher impulse behind your efforts than that. Each student ought to feel that he or she has a personal responsibility to do each task in the very best manner possible. You owe this not only to your fellow students, your teachers, the school, and the people who support the institution, but you owe it even more to yourselves. You owe it to yourselves because it is right and honest, because nothing less than this is right and honest, and because you never can be really successful and really happy until you do study and work and live in this way.

I have been led to speak specifically on this subject to-night on account of two occurrences here which have come to my notice. One of these illustrates the failure on the part of students to feel this sense of responsibility to which I have referred. The other affords an illustration of the possession by a student of a feeling of personal interest and personal responsibility which has been very gratifying and encouraging. The first incident, I may say, occurred some months ago. It is possible that the students who were concerned in it may not be here now or, if they are, that it would not happen again. I certainly hope not.

A gentleman who had been visiting here was to go away. He left word at the office of his wish, saying that he planned to leave town on the five o'clock train in the afternoon. A boy was sent from the office early in the afternoon with a note to the barn ordering a carriage to take this gentleman and his luggage to the station. Half-past four came, and the man had his luggage brought down to the door of the building in which he had been staying, so as to be ready when the team came. But no team came. The visitor finally became so anxious that he walked over to the barn himself. Just as he reached the barn he met the man who was in charge there, with the note in his hand. The note had only just that moment reached this man, and of course no carriage had been sent because the first person who felt that he had any responsibility in the matter had only just learned that a carriage was wanted. The boy who had brought the note had given it to another boy, and he to someone else, and he, perhaps, to someone else. At any rate it had been delayed because no one had taken enough interest in the errand to see that whatever business the note referred to received proper attention. This occurred, as I have said, several months ago, before the local train here went over to Chehaw to meet all of the trains. It happened that this particular passenger was going north, and it was possible by driving to Chehaw for him to get there in time to take the northbound train. 1fhe had been going the other way, though, towards Montgomery, he would have lost the train entirely, and, as chanced to be the case, would have been unable to keep a very important engagement. As it was, he was obliged to ride to Chehaw in a carriage, and the time of a man and team, which otherwise would have been saved, was required to take him there.

Now when such a thing as this happens, no amount of saying, "I am sorry," by the person or persons to blame, will help the matter any. It is too late to help it then. The thing to do is to feel some responsibility in seeing that things are done right yourself. Take enough interest in whatever you are engaged in to see that it is going to come out in the end just as nearly right, just as nearly perfect, as anything you can do will go towards making it right or perfect. And if the task or errand passes out of your hands before it is completed, do not feel that your responsibility in the matter ends until you have impressed it upon the minds and heart of the person to whom you turn over the further performance of the duty.

The world is looking for men and women who can tell one why they can do this thing or that thing, how a certain difficulty was surmounted or a certain obstacle removed. But the world has little patience with the man or woman who takes no real interest in the performance of a duty, or who runs against a snag and gets discouraged, and then simply tells why he did not do a, thing, and gives excuses instead of results. Opportunities never come a second time, nor do they wait for our leisure. The years come to us but once, and they come then only to pass swiftly on, bearing the ineffaceable record we have put upon them. If we wish to make them beautiful years or profitable years, we must do it moment by moment as they glide before us.

The other case to which I have referred is pleasanter to speak about. One day this spring, after it had got late enough in the season so that it was not as a general thing necessary to have fires to heat our buildings, a student passing Phelps Hall noticed that there was a volume of black smoke pouring out of one of the chimneys there. Some boys might not have noticed the smoke at all; others would have said that it came from the chimney; still others would have said that it was none of their business anyway, and would have gone along. This boy was different. He noticed the smoke, and although he saw, or thought he saw that it came from the chimney, and if so was probably no sign of harm, he felt that any smoke at all there at that time was such an unusual thing that it ought to be investigated for fear it might mean danger to the building. He was not satisfied until he had gone into the building and had inspected every floor clear up to the attic, to see that the chimney and the building were not in danger. As it happened, the janitor had built a fire in the furnace in the basement for some reason, so that the young man's anxiety fortunately was unfounded, but I am heartily glad he had such an anxiety, and that he could not rest until he found out whether there was any foundation for it or not. I shall feel that all of our buildings are safer for his being here, and when he graduates and goes away I hope he will leave many others here who will have the same sense of personal responsibility which he had. Let me tell you, here and now, that unless you young men and young women come to have this characteristic, your lives are going to fall far short of the best and noblest achievement possible.

We frequently hear the word "lucky" used with reference to a man's life. Two boys start out in the world at the same time, having the same amount of education. When twenty years have passed, we find one of them wealthy and independent; we find him a successful professional man with an assured reputation, or perhaps at the head of a large commercial establishment employing many men, or perhaps a farmer owning and cultivating hundreds of acres of land. We find the second boy, grown now to be a man, working for perhaps a dollar or a dollar and a half a day, and living from hand to mouth in a rented house. When we remember that the boys started out in life equal handed, we may be tempted to remark that the first boy has been fortunate, that fortune has smiled on him; and that the second has been unfortunate. There is no such nonsense as that. When the first boy saw a thing that he knew he ought to do, he did it; and he kept rising from one position to another until he became independent. The second boy was an eye-servant who was afraid that he would do more than he was paid to do—he was afraid that he would give fifty cents' worth of labor for twenty-five cents. He watched the clock, for fear that he would work one minute past twelve o'clock at noon and past six o'clock at night. He did not feel that he had any responsibility to look out for his employer's interests. The first boy did a dollar's worth of work for fifty cents. He was always ready to be at the store before time; and then, when the bell rang to stop work, he would go to his employer and ask him if there was not something more that ought to be done that night before he went home.

It was this quality in the first boy that made him valuable and caused him to rise. Why should we call him "fortunate" or "lucky?" I think it would be much more suitable to say of him "He is responsible."

Getting On In The World

It is natural and praiseworthy for a person to be looking for a higher and better position than the one he occupies. So long as a man does his whole duty in what he is engaged in, he is not to be condemned for looking for something better to do. Now the question arises:—How are you going to put yourself in a condition to be in demand for these higher and more important positions?

In the first place you should be continually on the lookout for opportunities to improve yourselves in your present work. You should be constantly on the lookout for chances to make yourselves more valuable to your present employer, and more efficient in your work for him. Suppose you are engaged in the work of milking cows —I think it better to talk of practical things with which you all are acquainted, although I know that many of you boys had rather I would tell you how to go to Congress than how to become successful milkers. Inasmuch, though, as I suspect a good many more of us will have to milk cows than can go to Congress, I think it will not hurt us to talk about milking. If the boy who milks cows now does that thoroughly, by doing it he may lay the foundation to go to Congress later. The point is that we want to be constantly on the lookout for ways of improving whatever work we are engaged in, whether that work be milking cows or doing something else.

In whatever you are doing, there are a great many improvements which you want to become acquainted with. If your work is dairying, read the dairy journals. Get hold of every book or paper that you can which has anything to do with your line of work. Be sure that you know all or as nearly as possible all—there is to be known about milking cows. And then don't be content with what you get out of books and newspapers, for that information is only the result of some other person's experience. By conversing with intelligent and experienced persons, and by your own experiments, you can get much valuable information about your work. Never get to the point where you are ashamed to ask somebody else for information. The ignorant: man will always be ignorant, if he fears that by asking for information he will betray his lack of knowledge.

Know all there is to be known about the position you occupy, but ever feel that there is more for you to learn. There is no person who makes himself of so little use in the world as the one who feels that he knows all there is to be known about his work. If you are milking cows, and feel that you know all there is to be known about that subject, you have simply reached a point where you are practically useless and unfitted for the work. Feel that you can always learn something from somebody else. It is a mark of intelligence to learn, even from the humblest person. I do not mean for you always to put into practice every suggestion that is made to you, or to agree with every statement made to you; but listen to what people say, weigh their plans alongside of your own, and then profit by the one which you are convinced is the best. Persevere in such conversation, and in reading. You will constantly be surprised to find how little you really know about your work, and how much more somebody else knows about it than you do.

You want to get to the point where you can anticipate the wants of your employer. In this way you will make yourself of great service to him. You do not know how vexing and discouraging it is to a man to be compelled to say every morning to those in his employ: "Do this at nine o'clock, and that at twelve o'clock, and the other at five;" or how pleasant it is to have a person with whom you come in contact anticipate the needs of the man who employs him.

Then you can make yourself valuable and in demand just in proportion as you consider that the work you are performing is your own. Do not consider that it is being performed for a certain man or a particular organization. Make haste and get to the point where you can feel that everything connected with the shop in which you work, or in the office, or in the stable, is under your care, and that you alone are responsible for it. If you are at the head of a stable or barn, plan day by day how you can best provide for the well-being of your cows and horses. When you make yourself master of these humble positions, you will find that the calls to higher places will come to you. The men you see spending most of their times looking for higher and more lucrative positions are, nine times out of ten, men who have made worthless failures in other places.

Each One His Part

I desire to call your attention for a few minutes to-night to the fact that one thing is dependent for success upon another; one individual is dependent for success upon another, one family in a community upon other families for their mutual prosperity, one part of a State upon the other parts for the successful government of the State. The same thing is true in nature. One thing cannot exist unless another exists; cannot succeed without the success of something else. The very forces of nature are dependent upon other forces for their existence. Without vegetable life we could not have animal life; without mineral life we could not have vegetable life. So, throughout all kinds of life, as throughout the life of nature, everything is dependent upon something else for its success.

The same thing is true of this institution and of every institution. The success of the whole depends upon having every person connected with the institution do his or her whole duty.

We are very apt to get the idea that there are high positions and that there are low positions, that there is important service and unimportant service; but I believe that God expects the same amount of conscientious work from a person in a low position as from one in a high position, that He expects the same conscientious service whether the work be a big task or a little one. We are dependent as an institution—every institution is dependent—for success, upon the individual consciences of those connected with it as teachers and students; and there is nothing that gives me more satisfaction and pleasure, and more faith in the future of the school, than to see examples of conscientious work here.

I remember a special instance of this kind that occurred at one of our Commencements. I believe that Commencement, more than any other time in the school year, is an occasion when there is excitement and a desire to witness the exercises. After the exercises of that year were over, I had occasion to go to the dining room, and I found there one of the teachers who from her appearance I thought had not attended the exercises. When I asked her about this, she said: "No. I intended to go, but at the last minute I saw that there were some dishes here that needed to be washed, and I stayed here to see that they were washed."

Now that was one of the finest exhibitions of conscientious regard for duty that I ever saw, and there are very few persons who would have done a thing like that. That we have teachers here whose hearts are so much in their work that they are willing to do such things as this gives me great faith in the future of this school as the years go on.

It takes a person with a conscience, when there are public men of note here, a great many strangers and many things to attract attention, to be so mindful of her duty that she will stay behind and wash dishes when everyone else is in attendance upon the exercises and seeking enjoyment. When the people connected with this institution can bring themselves up to that point, I have no fear for the success of the institution; and it can succeed only as they do bring their consciences up to that point.

If I were to ask you individually as students to deliver an address upon this platform, or to read an essay, I should not be at all afraid that you would fail. I believe that you would carefully prepare that address or essay. You would look up all the references necessary in order to give you what information you needed, and then you would get up here and speak or read successfully. I feel sure that I would hear something that I should not be ashamed of. The average man and woman do succeed when before the public. But where I fear for your success is when you come to the performance of the small duties—the duties which you think no one else will know about, the things which no one will see you do. It is when you think that no one is going to see you washing dishes, or getting dirt out of crevices, that I am afraid you are going to fail.

I remember that some time ago when I was traveling in a buggy from one New England village to another, after we had gone some miles on our way, the young man who was driving me stopped the horse and got out. I asked him what was the matter, and he said that something was the matter with the harness. I looked with all the eyes I had, and yet I could see nothing at fault. Still the man mended a piece of harness that he said was not as it should be. It had not seemed to me that this fault in the harness had been irritating the horse or hindering him from going so fast as he ought, but after it had been repaired I could see a difference for the better. That, to my mind, was a great lesson. It taught me how the people of New England have educated their consciences so that they cannot allow themselves to let even the smallest thing go undone or be improperly done. It is this trait in the New England character that has come to make the very name itself of that part of the country a synonym for success. Don't we wish that we had a hundred such men as that driver here 1 If I could put my hand on a thousand such persons as that, we could find employment for all of them as soon as they got their diplomas.

One learns to judge persons by their character in this respect. Not long ago I had an opportunity to go through the jail of this county. As the sheriff showed me through the building I was impressed to see how clean everything was, and I noticed that the man who seemed to be the janitor of the jail, although he too was a prisoner, seemed to take a great deal of pride in showing me the cleanness of the corners and the general good appearance of the place. He seemed to put his whole heart into the keeping of that jail clean.

"Who is that man?" I asked the sheriff, after we had got out of the janitor's hearing.

"He is a prisoner," the sheriff replied, "but I believe he is innocent. I do not believe that a man can be so honest and faithful about his work and be guilty of a crime. When I see how well he does his work here, notwithstanding the fact that he is shut up here in prison, I believe that he is an honest man and deserves his freedom."

In plain words, then, the problem we must work out here is not: Can you master algebra, or literature? We know you can do that. We know you can master the sciences. The general problem we have to work out here, and work it out with fear and trembling, is: —Can we educate the individual conscience? Can we so educate a group of students that there will be in every one of them a conscience on which we can depend. Can we educate a class of girls here who will not be satisfied when sweeping their rooms to make the middle of the rooms look clean, but leave a trail of dirt in the corners and under the furniture? Will they see to it that everything is properly cleaned and put in its appropriate place? Can we educate a class of young men who will do their duty on the farm as they would do it on this platform? Can we educate your consciences so that you will do certain things, not because it is the rule that they should be done, but because they should be done? These are the problems we must work out here.

What Would Father And Mother Say?

I think there is no more important or more critical time in a person's life than when he or she leaves home for the first time, to enter school, or to go to work, or to go into business. I think that as a general thing you can judge pretty accurately what a person is going to amount to in life by the way he or she acts during the first year or two after leaving home.

You will find, usually, that if a young man is able during this time to stand up against temptation, is able to practice the lessons that his father and mother have taught him, and instead of falling by the wayside gains help and inspiration as he goes along from these lessons, he is almost sure to prove himself a valuable citizen, one who not only will be a help to his parents in their old age, but a help to the community in which he lives.

There is no better way to test an act than to ask yourself the question: "What would my father or my mother think of this? Would they approve, or should I be ashamed to let them know that I have done this thing?" If you will ask yourselves these questions day by day, I think you will find that you will get a great deal of assistance from them in the shaping of your lives while you are here at school.

I want you to put that question to yourselves with regard to deportment, because that is a thing on which we must lay emphasis. We can fill your heads with knowledge, and we can train your hands, to work with skill, but unless all this training of head and hand is based upon high, upright character, upon a true heart, it will amount to nothing. You will be no better off than the most ignorant.

Now, one of the ways in which young people are likely to go astray, especially when they first go away from home to school, is in yielding to a temptation to spend their time with persons who have mean and low dispositions; persons whom you would be ashamed to have your parents know that you kept company with. Avoid that. Be sure that the young men and women with whom you associate are persons who are able to raise you up, persons who will help to make you stronger in every way.

I do not need to tell you, I am sure, of the consequences of association with persons who will have a bad influence upon you, or the results of a disregard of admonitions for good. A student who persistently keeps bad company, who breaks rules, who is constantly disobedient, who is repeatedly behind at roll call, who time after time has to be called up by the officer of the day, or watched in the dining room or on the parade ground, is the student who in a few years is going to bring sorrow to the hearts of his parents. There is no getting away from that.

Only today the mother of one of the students came here with a message from another mother whose son had been sent here. She told me how this anxious mother had told her to impress upon her son the necessity of obeying every rule here and how she wanted him to put in every moment in hard study and honest work. She wanted this woman to impress upon the boy how hard his mother was struggling every day so that she could keep him here, and at the same time provide for the younger children of the family at home. Now, when this message was delivered, where was that boy? Was he doing as his mother was so earnestly praying him to do? No. He had already disgraced himself, and had been sent away from the institution. How much sorrow will he bring to his poor mother's heart when she knows! No wonder he was trying to conceal his misconduct and disgrace from her.

Let me entreat you, then, if you are inclined to fritter away the best hours of your lives, think how the news of your misconduct will act upon the hearts of your parents, those fathers and mothers whose every thought is of you.

I have spoken of these as some of the things that we do not want to have you do at school. What are some of the things that we do want you to learn to do? We want to have you learn to see and appreciate the practical value of the religion of Christ. We hope to help you to see that religion, that Christianity, is not something that is far off, something in the air, that it is not something to be enjoyed only after the breath has left the body. We want to have you see that the religion of Christ is a real and helpful thing; that it is something which you can take with you into your class-rooms, into your shops, on to the farm, into your very sleeping rooms, and that you do not have to wait until to-morrow before you can find out about the power and helpfulness of Christ's religion.

We want to have you feel that this religion is a part of your lives, and that it is meant to be a. help to you from day to day. We hope to have you feel that the religious services that we have you attend here are not burdens, but that it is a privilege, greatly to be desired, to come to these, meetings, and into the prayer meetings of the various societies on the grounds, and there commune, not in a far-off, imaginary way, but in an humble but intimate way, with the spirit of Jesus. We want you to feel that religion is something to make you happier, brighter and more hopeful, not something to make you go about with long, solemn faces. We want you to learn, if you do not already know, that in order to be Christ like one does not have to be unnatural.

Then we want to have you to learn to govern your actions, not alone for the sake of the result which they will have upon yourself and those who are near and dear to you, but for the sake of your influence upon all with whom you will come in contact. Your life here will be largely wasted. I am tempted to say wholly wasted—if you fail to learn that higher, broader, and far more important lesson of your relations to your fellow—students and to all the persons by whom you are going to be daily surrounded. Your life will be wasted if you go away from here and have not learned that the greatest lesson of all is the lesson of brotherly love, of usefulness and of charity. I want to see young men who are here realizing this spirit to such an extent that they will rise in chapel and give their seats to students who are strangers at the school. I want to have you get to the point where you will go to the matron in the dining room and ask her permission to have some new student who has not had a chance to get acquainted take his meals at a seat beside you.

Of the many noble traits exhibited by the late General Armstrong, none made a deeper impression upon me than his supreme unselfishness. I do not believe that I ever saw in all my association with General Armstrong anything in his life or actions which indicated in the slightest degree that he was selfish. He was interested not only in the black South, but in the white South, not only in his own school, but in all schools. Anything which he could do or say to benefit another institution seemed to give him as much pleasure as if he were speaking or acting directly for the benefit of Hampton Institute.

I had a pleasant experience of this spirit of a desire to be helpful to others a little while ago, when I was visiting a certain theological seminary in Pennsylvania. I think I was never in such an atmosphere as during the two days I spent in that institution. I was surrounded by a crowd of young men whose sole object seemed to be to make me comfortable and happy. Most of these young men were far advanced in the study of theology and the sciences, and yet they were not above serving me, even to the extent of offering to black my boots. When I came' away several wished to carry my luggage to the station. This is the kind of thoughtfulness we want to have in every corner of this institution. Get hold of the spirit of wanting to help somebody else. Seek every opportunity possible to make somebody happy and comfortable. Do all this, and you will find that the years will not be many before we will have one of the best institutions on the face of the globe, and that you, in helping to make it such, have been doing things that, when you ask yourselves: "What would father and mother say about my doing this?" will enable you to answer the question with pride and satisfaction.

Object Lessons

Not long ago an old colored man living in this State said to me: "I's done quit libin' in de ashes. I's got my second freedom."

That remark meant, in this case, that that old man by economy, hard work and proper guidance, after twenty years of struggle, had freed himself from debt, had paid for fifty acres of land, had built a comfortable house, and was a tax-payer. It meant that his two sons had been educated in academic and agricultural branches, that his daughter had received mental training in connection with lessons in sewing and cooking. Within certain limitations here was a Christian, American home, the result of industrial effort and philanthropy. This Negro had been given a chance to get upon his feet. That is all that any Negro in America asks. That is all that you in this school ask.

What position in State, in letters, or in commerce and in business the offspring of that man is to occupy must be left to the future and the capacity of the race. What position you are to occupy must be left to your future and to your capacity. During the days of slavery we were shielded from competition. To-day, unless we prepare ourselves to compete with the world, we must go to the wall as a race.

If I were to go into certain communities in the United States and say that the German is ignorant, I should be pointed to the best paying truck-farm in that neighborhood, owned and operated by a German. If I said that the German is without skill, I should be shown the largest machine-shop in the city, owned and operated by a German. If I said the German is lazy, I should be shown the largest and finest residence on the most fashionable avenue, built from the savings of a German who began life in poverty. If I said that the German could not be trusted, I should be introduced to a man of that race who is the president of the largest bank in the city. If I said that the German is not fitted for citizenship, I should be shown a German who is a respected and influential member of the city government.

Now, when your critics say that the Negro is lazy, I want you to be able to show them the finest farm in the community owned and operated by a Negro. When they ask if the Negro is honest, I want you to show them a Negro whose note is acceptable at the bank for $5,000. When they say that the Negro is not economical, I want you to show them a Negro with $50,000 in the bank. When they say that the Negro is not fit for citizenship, I want you to show them a man of our race paying taxes on a cotton factory. I want you to be able to show them Negroes who stand in the front in the affairs of State, of religion, of education, of mechanics, of commerce and of household economy. You remember the old admonition: "By this sign we shall conquer." Let it be our motto.

There are people in the North who have been aiding in the matter of Negro education in the South during the last ten, twenty, or even thirty years. It is in part the money of those people that has made this institution possible. Those people have a right, as a plain matter of business, to ask," what are the results," of this aid they have been giving. What evidences can we present to prove to them that their investments in this direction have been paying ones? It is, in no small measure, the duty of you, as students of Tuskegee Institute, to answer, and to answer satisfactorily, such a question as that.

We have reached a point, largely through the aid which the North has given to the South during the last thirty years, where there is little opposition in the South to the people of the Negro race receiving any form of education. You can go out from here and plant a school in. any county in the South, which will not meet with opposition from the white residents of the community. What is more, in many cases it will receive encouragement, and in some a hearty sympathy and support. Not long ago I received fifty dollars from a white man in Mississippi to pay for the education of a black boy. This man was formerly a slave-holder, and at first he was not inclined to encourage the education of the Negro, but he stated to me frankly, in his letter, that he now believes that Tuskegee and similar institutions are doing the work that the Negro most needs to have done. He wanted to show the people of the North, he said, that Southern white men are as deeply interested in the development of the Negro as they are. I have in mind another case, of a Southern white man in Alabama who during the last year contributed out of his own pocket nearly $2,000 for the building and maintenance of a Negro school in his county. Still another Southern white man, Mr. Belton Gilreath, of Birmingham, Alabama, recently sent, the Institute his check for $500—up to that time the largest sum which the school had received from a Southern man—with this letter:

"As a Southern man and the son of one of the largest slave owners of the South, I am anxious for our people to do all that can reasonably be expected of them for the education of the Negroes, thereby making them more content and useful citizens and friends.

"Furthermore, I think the time has come in the South for all our people to consider more fully than they have ever done before the question of the education of all of our population; and, wherever practicable, to give attention in our schools to teaching the art of saving also."

More recently still, Mr. H. M. Atkinson, of Atlanta, one of the most successful business men in the entire South, came to Tuskegee Institute and made a thorough inspection of our work. After he returned to Atlanta I received a letter from him from which I quote one paragraph: "I enclose my check for $ion, for the benefit of your school, to be used as your judgment dictates. I was very much impressed by what I saw. I will not forget it."

These white people are beginning to see the difference between the value of an educated Negro and one who is not educated. It is for you to demonstrate to them this value more and more clearly every year.

Substance VS. Shadow

You are here for the purpose of getting an education. Now, one of the results of an education is to increase a person's wants. You take the ordinary person who lives on a plantation, and so long as that person is ignorant, he is content to live in a cabin with one room, in which he has a skillet, a bedstead —or an apology for one—a table, and a few chairs or stools. He is content if he has fat meat, corn bread and peas on the table to eat, and for clothing he is satisfied to wear jeans and osnaburg himself, and to have his wife wear a calico dress and a twenty-five cent hat.

But, as soon as that man becomes educated, he feels that he must have a house with at least two or three rooms in it, furnished with neat and substantial furniture. Instead of jeans and osnaburg for clothes, he wants decent woolen cloth, neat fitting shoes, and a white collar and a necktie, things which he never thought of wearing before he became educated. Sometimes he even thinks that he must have jewelry.

So you see the result of education is to increase a person's wants. Now, the crisis in that person's affairs comes when the question arises whether his education has increased his ability to supply his wants. Such ability, I claim, is one of the results of industrial education. By such an education as that, while we are getting culture along all the lines that in any degree tend to increase the wants of a, person, we are, in the meantime, getting skill to increase our ability to supply these wants. And, unless we have this ability, we will find, sooner or later, that instead of going forward we are going backward.

I think that the temptation for us, especially for those who are only half educated, is to try to get hold of a certain kind of shallow culture, instead of getting the substantial—instead of getting hold of real education, of property and material prosperity.

You who study history know how the Pilgrim Fathers, who landed at Plymouth Rock in the bleak winter of 1620, were willing to wear homespun clothes, and to be married in them, if necessary, and to have a wedding that in all would not cost more than four dollars, I suppose. On the other hand, when one of our boys wants to get married now, he must have a wedding that costs not less than one hundred and fifty dollars. His wife must have a dress with a long train, and he must have a Prince Albert, broadcloth coat that he either rents, or buys on the installment plan. They think that they must have a bevy of waiting bridesmaids, and there must be a line of hacks standing on the outside of the church door that will cost him not less than twenty-five dollars. Then, after the ceremony, where do these people go to live? The chances are the young man who has been to all this expense for the sake of the show of it, takes his bride to live in a small cabin with only two rooms—sometimes only one room rented at that.

This is what I mean by getting the superficial culture before the dollars are made; grasping at the shadow instead of the substance. Now what we want to do here is to send out a set of young men and young women who will go into the communities where such mistakes as these are made, and show the people by example and by work how much better it is to get married for four dollars, and to pay as you go, than to get married for a hundred and fifty dollars, and then pay four dollars a month to live in a rented cabin. When I go to New York, or to any large city, there is nothing more discouraging than to see people of this very class I am speaking of, people who seek the superficial culture, the shadow, rather than the substantial dollars and education. If you stand for a few minutes on any of the fashionable streets in the Northern cities, you will see these elaborately dressed men, wearing five dollar hats on heads that at most are not worth more than fifty cents. This is the class of people who have got just enough education to make them want everything they see, but who have not got enough to make them able to get what they want unless they go beyond their means to do so.

A superficial education, too, makes us inclined to seek show in other things besides dress. We are inclined, for one thing, to seek to show off in the use of titles. I remember that once I was introduced to a company of about sixty men, and out of the whole number there were only six who were not doctors, professors, or colonels, or who did not have some title. I must say I thought more of the six who were just plain misters than I did of all the rest, for among the others there were some very hard-looking doctors and professors. An over desire for these things' shows a shallowness in us which makes us ridiculous. We want to stop making that kind of mistake. If you are a mister, encourage the people to call you by that title. If you are a minister and preach interesting and instructive sermons, people are going to be impressed by what you say and not by the title you bear. The title is the shadow; what you say is the substance.

When a person is simple, he is on the strong side. People not only have more respect for him, but he accomplishes more. I was once at a memorial meeting held in honor of a man who had done a great and useful work, not only for the race but for the school with which he had been connected. After about two hours of speech making, somebody took the platform and said that a collection ought to be taken up for the benefit of the school which this man had worked so hard for, to show the appreciation which those present felt for this man's services. After a good deal of talk, $6.65 was collected. Then the question was raised again as to what was going to be done with this money—just how it was to be donated to the school.

The meeting had passed a set of resolutions testifying to the high character of the man and the worth of his work. Somebody suggested that— these resolutions be engrossed and sent to the school. This was a big word, and the people liked the sound of it. Upon inquiry it was found that it would cost $6.00 to have the resolutions engrossed. It was voted to have this done, and it was done; when the resolutions would have done just as much good typewritten, at a cost of twenty-five cents. But the meeting paid out the $6.00, and sent the engrossed copy of the resolutions down to the school, along with the sixty-five cents left to be expended for the help of the school. That, it seemed to me, was another case of grasping the shadow instead of the substance. The engrossed resolutions were the shadow; the sixty-five cents were all that was left of the substance.

In all these matters we need speedy and effective reforms. We want you to go out into the world and use your influence toward securing these reforms. There are too many people in the world who give their whole lives to grasping at the shadow instead of the substance—grasping at a sham instead of real worth. We want you to teach by word and action simple, right and honest living.

Character As Shown In Dress

It is surprising how much we can tell about a person's character by his dress. I think it is very seldom that we cannot tell whether a person is ignorant or educated, simply by his dress; and there are some few, plain facts about dress that I am going to mention to you tonight. While it is hard to lay down any rules as to how we must dress, I think there are some well-defined principles of dress to which all well-educated persons will conform.

I think we will all agree that our dress should be clean. There is little excuse for persons wearing filthy clothes— I think we all will agree as to that. It is disgraceful for a man to go about with ragged clothes or with clothes fastened together with pins where buttons ought to be. It is disgraceful for a girl to go about with a soiled apron, or with her clothes pinned together. Our clothes should be kept clean and in good repair. Thus far, I think, we shall have no disagreement.

But there are some people who make the mistake of giving their whole mind to the subject of dress. From the very beginning of the week you will find that a great part of their thought and attention is given to planning what they are going to wear the next Sunday. Some people will go in rags all through the week, in order to have something showy to wear on Sunday. I think we should respect Sunday by putting on something different from what we wear during the week if we can—although of course these things are largely governed by our station in life—but even then it certainly is inappropriate to wear our most showy clothes on that day.

Dress in the way that your pocket will allow. There are some persons who not only employ all their thoughts in considering what they shall wear, but also spend all their money on their clothes.

There are some persons who live for the sake of dress. These persons are usually denominated "fops." I think the people in the Northern cities are the worst in this respect. If you go through Sixth Avenue, in New York, or Cambridge Street, in Boston, you will see many of these fops, who perhaps earn about twenty dollars a month, standing on the street corners with kid gloves on, cigars between their lips, and high hats. Now that kind of a person is a foolish fop, and one whom we do not care to have in this institution. There is no more foolish person than the one who spends all he makes, and sometimes more, on dress.

Then, too, I think there are persons who make mistakes in the matter of ornaments—what we call jewelry. You will find many a man whose, income is not twenty dollars a month wearing a great brass watch chain with so much brass in it that you can almost smell it. You will see men and women with three or four brass finger rings, or women with brass ear-rings. Do you know that one of the most common mistakes among the masses of our people in, the country is throwing away their money on cheap jewelry? Do, you know that they will come in to town to the stores, and spend their money on jewelry worth about ten cents apiece, jewelry that you actually can get for six dollars and a bushel seven dollars at wholesale? Our people spend thousands of dollars every year for this cheap jewelry. If there is a young man or a young woman here who likes jewelry, and is going to indulge in it, be sure to get that which is modest.

Another mistake that some of our people make is in wearing flashy or loud dressy clothing. Dress in which bright colors and red ribbons predominate, our dress should be modest; with few colors.

We often make a mistake in getting shoes about two sizes too small. I saw a girl this morning in perfect misery, simply because she had bought, and was trying to wear, a pair of shoes about two sizes too small. Such people simply punish their feet to make people think they have small feet, though it is just as honorable to have a large foot as a small one; there is no difference. Then we make another mistake in buying cheap, showy shoes simply because they have a gloss on them. Such shoes are made to attract attention, and not for comfort or durability. When you are spending your money for shoes, be sure that you get something good, something that will last you. Do not buy those worthless things, which, when they come in contact with water, will shrivel up because they are made of cheap material. A man cannot respect a girl who punishes her feet in-order to make them look small.

Then, another thing some of us think we can improve our color. Some get flour, and others get other kinds of mixtures which are called face powders. There is no use for this. Any man will lose respect for a girl who abuses herself in this way. Only get something into your head, and then you will find that these matters of dress will adjust themselves. While some of you do not dress so well as you might, yet, if you will give the contents of your heads the proper attention, you will find that the matter of dress will not trouble you. You can get dresses and clothes after you have secured your education, but now is the only time that you have in which to secure the education.

Sing The Old Songs

There is no part of our chapel exercises that gives me more pleasure than the beautiful Negro melodies which you sing. I believe there is no part of the service more truly spiritual, more elevating. Wherever you go, after you leave this school, I hope that you will never give up the singing of these songs. If you go out to have schools of your own, have your pupils sing them as you have sung them here, and teach them to see the beauty which dwells in these songs. When in New York, not long ago, I had the pleasure of conversing with Prince Henry of Prussia; he spoke particularly of the beauty of these songs, and said that in his own home, in Germany, he and his family often sing them. He asked if there was any printed collection of these songs, that a copy might be sent him, and I have since then forwarded to him a copy of the book of plantation melodies collected and published under the auspices of Hampton Institute.

When Christ was upon this earth He said: "A little child shall lead them." Whence comes this supreme power of leadership? In this age, when we hear so much said about leaders of men, about successful leadership, we do well to stop to consider this admonition of the Savior. Some are said to lead in business, others in education, others in politics, or in religion. What is the explanation of "A little child shall lead them?" Simply this, a little child, under all circumstances, is its simple, pure, sweet self; never appearing big when it is little; never appearing learned when it is ignorant; never appearing wealthy when it is in poverty; never appearing important when it is unimportant. In a word, the life of the child is founded upon the great and immutable, and yet simple, tender and delicate laws of nature. There is no pretense. There is no mockery.

There is an unconscious, beautiful, strong clinging to truth; and it is this divine quality in child or in man, in Jew or Gentile, in Christian or Mohammedan, in the ancient world or in the modern world, in a black man or in a white man, that always has led men and molded their activity. The men who have been brave enough, wise enough, simple enough, self-denying enough to plant themselves upon this rock of truth and there stand, have, in the end, drawn the world unto them, even as Christ said: "I will draw all men unto me." Such a man was Luther, such a man was Wesley, such a man was Carlyle, such a man was Cromwell, such were Garrison and Phillips, such was Abraham Lincoln, and such was our own great Frederick Douglass.

The thing aimed at by all great souls has been to bring men and races back to the simplicity and purity of childhood—back to reality.

What is the most original product with which the Negro race stands accredited? Yes, I am almost ready to add, with which America stands accredited? Without hesitation I answer — Those beautiful, weird, quaint, sweet melodies which were the simple, child-like expression of the anguish, the joy, the hopes, the burdens, the faith, the trials of our forefathers who wore the yoke of slavery.

Why are they the admiration of the world? Why does every attempt at improvement spoil them? Why do they never fail to touch the tenderest chord—to bring tears from the eyes 'of rich and poor—from king and humblest toiler alike?

Listen how in this beautiful song the soul in trouble is told not to go to houses and temples made by man, but to get close to Nature

If yer want to see Jesus Go in de wilderness, Go in de wilderness, Go in de wilderness, Go in de wilderness. 1f yer want to see Jesus, Go in de wilderness Leanin' on de Lord.

Oh brudder, how d'ye feel, when ye come out de wilderness, Come out de wilderness, Come out de wilderness,

Oh, brudder, how d'ye feel, when ye come out de wilderness, Leanin' on de Lord?

Then, in another, hear how our fore parents broke through all the deceptions and allurements of false wealth, and in their long days of weariness expressed their faith in a place where every day would be one of rest.

Oh, religion is a fortune,
I raly do believe.
Oh, religion is a fortune,
I r'a'ly do believe.
Oh, religion is a fortune,
I r'a'ly do believe,
Whar Sabbaths hab no end.
Whar yo' been, poor mourner, whar yo' been so long?
" Been down in de valley, for to pray; An' I ain't done prayin' yet."

Then, how, when oppressed by years of servitude to which others thought there would be no end, we hear them break out into quaint and wild bursts of appeal to fact?

My Lord delibered Daniel, My Lord delibered Daniel, My
Lord delibered Daniel;
Why can't He deliber me?
I met pilgrim on de way, an' I ask him where he's gwine.
'I'm bound for Canaan's happy lan',
An' dis is de shoutin' band.
Go on."
He delibered Daniel from de lion's den,
Jonah from de belly ob de whale,
An' de Hebrew children from de fiery furnace.
Den why not ebery man?"
Or when the burden seemed almost too great for human body to endure, there carne this simple, child-like prayer
O Lord, 0, my Lord, 0, my good Lord, Keep me from sinkin' down.
O Lord, 0 my Lord, 0 my good Lord, Keep me from sinkin' down.
I tell yo' what I mean to do. Keep me from sinkin' down.
I mean to go to hebben, too. Keep me from sinkin' down.

Or what could go more directly to Nature's heart than the pathetic yet hopeful, trustful outburst of the little slave boy who was to be taken from his mother to be sold into the far South, when it seemed to him that all earthly happiness was forever blighted. Hear him:

I'm gwine to jine de great 'sociation, I'm gwine to jine de great 'sociation, I'm gwine to jine de great 'sociation.
Den my little soul's gwine to shine, shine;
Den my little soul's gwine to shine along. Oh I
I'm gwine to climb up Jacob's ladder.
Den my little soul's gwine to shine, shine.
Den my little soul's gwine to shine along. Oh I
I'm gwine to climb up higher an' higher. Den my little soul's gwine , etc
I'm gwine to sit at de welcome table I'm gwine to feast off milk an' honey.
I'm gwine to tell God how—a' you sarved me. Den my little
soul's gwine to shine, shine. Den my little soul's gwine to shine along. Oh!

And so it has ever been, so it is, and ever will be. The world, regardless of race, or color, or condition, admires and approves a real thing. But sham, buffoonery, mere imitation, mere superficiality, never has brought success and never will bring it.

An individual or a race that is strong enough, is wise enough, to disregard makeshifts, customs, prejudices, alluring temptations, deceptions, imitations—to throw off the mask of unreality and plant itself deep down in the clay, or on the solid granite of nature, is the individual or the race that will crawl up, struggle up, yes, even burst up; and in the effort of doing so will gain a strength that will command for it respect and recognition. Before an individual or a race thus equipped, race prejudice, senseless customs, oppressions, will hide their faces forever in blushing shame.

Getting Down To Mother Earth

One of the highest ambitions of every man leaving Tuskegee Institute should be to help the people of his race find bottom—find bed-rock and then help them to stand upon that foundation. If we who are interested in the school can help you to do this, we shall count ourselves satisfied. And until the bed-rock of our life is found, and until we are planted thereon, all else is but plaster, but make-believe, but the paper on the walls of a house without framework.

That is one of the stepping stones with which nature has provided us. Here the path is plain, if we have the courage to follow it. Eighty-five per cent of the people of the Negro race live —or attempt to live by some form of agriculture. If we would save the race, and lift it up, here is the great opportunity around which, in a large measure, individual, organized, religious and secular effort should center for the next fifty years.

But to do this we must take advantage of the forces at hand. We must stand upon our own feet, and not upon a foundation supplied by another. We must begin our growth where our civilization finds us, and not try to begin on some other civilization.

To illustrate what I mean, we need not go to another race, nor very far from home. In a little town in Alabama there was a sturdy, industrious black man who for nearly twenty years had lived upon rented land, had hired mules and horses to work that land, and had mortgaged his crops to secure food and clothes. He had driven to church on Sunday in a buggy that was not his, and he wore good-looking clothes that were not paid for. In outward appearance he seemed to prosper. He seemed to be what the white men about him were.

But this black man knew that he was trying—to stand upon an imperfect basis. And so, one day about a dozen years ago, he made up his mind that henceforth he would be himself— that he would stand upon his own foundation. He told the white man to take back his mules, to take back his wagon and buggy; and he gave up the rented land. He had resolved to be a man.) A few acres of land were secured. He made his bed in the cotton seed at night. He hired a boy to come to his place at night, and by moonlight he pulled a plough which the boy guided. In this way a cotton crop was made free from debt. With the small surplus which he got from this he bought an ox, and with this beast made a second crop free from debt. A mule was bought, and then another. To-day this man is the owner of a comfortable home, is a stockholder in one of the banks of his county, and his note or check will be honored by any business house there. While others were talking, or debating over second-hand doctrines learned by rote, this strong son of nature had found himself and solved his own problem.

I might tell you the story of another man of our race who began his successful business life in the hollow of a tree for his home; without furniture or bed-clothing. But that tree, and the land on which it stood, were his own. You had better begin life in a hollow tree and be a man, than begin it in a rented house and be a mere tool, the imitation of a man. If you were to go into the Western part of this country you would find it filled with men of the highest culture, profound scholarship, and enduring wealth, whose ancestors a few generations ago began life in a dug-out, in a hay loft, or in a hole in the side of a mountain. Young men and young women, there is no escape. If I we would be great, and good, and useful; we must pay the price. And remember that when we get down to the fundamental principles of truth, nature draws no color line.

I do not want to startle you when I say it, but I should like to see during the next fifty years every colored minister and teacher, whose work lies outside the large cities, armed with a thorough knowledge of theoretical and practical agriculture, in connection with his theological and academic training. This, I believe, should be so because the race is an agricultural one, and because my hope is that it will remain such. Upon this foundation almost every race in history has got its start. With cheap lands, a beautiful climate and a rich soil, we can lay the foundation of a great and powerful race. The question that confronts us is whether we will take advantage of this opportunity?

In a recent number of the New York Independent, Rev. Russell H. Conwell, the pastor of the great Temple Baptist Church, in Philadelphia, a church that has a membership of three thousand persons, tells of the pastor of a small country church in Massachusetts who, in perplexity at the eternally recurring question of how to make his church pay its expenses, asked Mr. Conwell's advice. "I advised him," Mr. Conwell says, "to study agricultural chemistry, dairy farming and household economy. I meant the advice seriously, and he took it seriously. He made his studies, and he made them thoroughly. On the Sunday when he preached his first practical sermon which was the outgrowth of his helpful learning, its topic was scientific manures, with appropriate scriptural allusions. He had just seventeen listeners. These seventeen, however, were greatly interested. Later on, they discussed the remarkable departure with their friends who had not attended the service. The result was that within five Sundays the church was packed with worshipers, who had discovered that heaven is not such a long distance from earth after all."

In the present condition of our race, what an immense gain it would be if from every church in the vast agricultural region of the South there could be preached every Sunday two sermons on religion, and a lesson or lecture given on the principles of intelligent agriculture, on the importance of the ownership of land, and on the importance of building comfortable homes. I believe that if this policy could be pursued, instead of the now too often poorly clothed, poorly fed, and poorly housed ministers, with salaries ranging from one hundred to three hundred dollars a year, we should soon have communities and churches on their feet, to such are extent that hundreds of ministers who now live at a dying rate would be supported in a manner commensurate with the dignity of the profession. Not, only this, but such a policy would result in giving the ministry such an ideal of the dignity of labor and such a love for it, that the minister's own home and garden and farm would be constant object lessons for his followers, and at the .same time sources from which he could draw a support which would make him in a large measure independent.

One of the most successful and most honored ministers I know is a man who owns and cultivates fifty acres of land. This land yields him an income sufficient to live on each year. This man's note or check is gladly honored at the bank

Because of his independence he leads his people instead of having to cater to their whims. It may be suggested that what I plead for has not been done by others, after this fashion. It was done in the early years of the settlement of New England, and persevered in by the ministers there until the people of the country had become sufficiently prosperous to support their ministers suitably. Besides, if one race of people, or one individual, is simply to follow in the steps of another, no progress would ever be possible in the world. Let us remember that no other race of people ever had just such a problem to work out as we have.

What I have tried to say to you to-night about agricultural life may be said with equal emphasis about city occupations. Show, me the race that leads in work in wood and in metal, in the building of houses and factories, and in the constructing and operating of machinery, and I will show you the race that in the long run molds public thought, that; controls government, that leads in commerce, in the sciences, in the arts and in the professions.

What we should do in all our schools is to turn out fewer jobseekers and more job-makers. Anyone can seek a job, but it requires a person of rare ability to create a job.

If it may seem to some of you that what I have been saying overlooks the development of the race in morals, ethics, religion and statesmanship, my answer would be this. You might as well argue that because a tree is planted deep down in Mother Earth, because it comes in contact with clay, and rocks, and sand, and water that through its graceful branches, its beautiful leaves and its fragrant blossoms it teaches no lesson of truth, beauty and divinity. You cannot plant a tree in air, and have it live. Try it. No matter how much we may praise its proportions and enjoy its beauty, it dies unless its roots and fibers touch and have their foundation in Mother Earth. What is true of the tree is true of a race.

A Penny Saved

A large proportion of you, for one reason or another, will not be able to return to this institution after the close of the present year. On that account there are some central thoughts which I should like to impress upon your minds this evening, and which I wish you to take with you into the world, whether you go out from the school as graduates or whether you go as undergraduates.

I have often spoken to you about the matter of learning to economize your time, to save your time, the matter of trying to make the most of every minute and hour of your existence. I have often spoken to you about the hurtful reputation which a large proportion of the people of our race get in one way or another because of this seeming inability to put a proper value upon time, or a proper value upon the importance of keeping one's word in connection with obligations.

You know to what a large extent the feeling prevails—whether justly or unjustly—that as a people we cannot be depended upon to keep our word; that if we are hired to work in a mill or a factory, we work until we have got three dollars or four dollars in wages ahead, and then go on an excursion, or go to town, and do not return to work until what we have earned has been consumed.

And so, in one way or another, a large proportion of us get the reputation that we cannot be depended upon for faithful, regular, efficient service; and that hurts the race. Wherever you go, we wish you by your own actions, by your advice, by your influence, to try and disprove and counteract that hurtful reputation. You can do this in the most efficient manner by yourselves being the highest possible example.

The people who succeed are, very largely, those who learn to economize time, in the ways I have referred to, and those who also have learned to save, not only time, but money.

Now this may seem to you a very materialistic thought for me to emphasize this evening—the saving of money—but to us, as a race, it is of vital importance. I have heard it expressed recently on several occasions that the Negro was becoming too much materialized, too much industrialized. Too much attention, it has been said, is given to the material side of life. Now it seems to me that I have as yet seen very little that need arouse our fears in that direction. I am not able to understand how a race that does not own a single steam railroad, that does not own a single street-car line, that owns hardly a bank:, that does not own a single block of houses in a large city— I am not able to understand how such a race as that is in danger of becoming materialized. When you get millions of dollars in banks, when you get millions of dollars invested in railroad stocks, when you get other millions invested in street-car lines, or in the control of large factories, great plantations, or in other great industrial enterprises in the South, then I shall say that there are signs of your becoming too materialistic, of your getting to be too rich; but I do not see any such signs yet. And until we do see such signs, we can rest ourselves in peace, I think, so far as that danger is concerned.

But there is a certain influence of money that I do not think we emphasize enough. In the first place the getting hold of money, the getting hold of a competency, insures us the possession of certain influences that we can get in no other way. In order to get hold of the spiritually best and highest things in life there are certain material things that we are compelled to have first. In the first place the getting hold of money and the saving of this money will assure the possession of decent comfortable houses to live in. No person can do his best work, or can be of the greatest service to himself and to his fellow beings, until he is able to live in a decent, comfortable house. You will not be ready for life until you own such a house, whether you live in it or not. Even if you own such a house and rent it out, you are that much more of a man. I often hear people say that they do not own a house, or property, because they do not expect to live long in this place or that place. I have known such people to move six times in six years. They never will own a house, simply because they have got into the habit of giving excuses, instead of trying to get to own a home.

The possession of a decent house insures us a certain amount of proper comfort. No person can do the best work, can think well, can get along well, unless he has a certain amount of comfort, and, I may add, a certain amount of good, nourishing food, well cooked. The person who is not sure where he is going to get his breakfast, or the one who is not sure where he is going to get the money to pay his next week's board, is the individual who cannot do the best work, whether the work be physical, mental or spiritual. The possession of money enables us to be sure that we are going to have comfortable clothing, clothing enough to keep the body warm and vigorous, and in good, healthy condition.

The possession of money enables us to get to the point where we can do our part in the building of school-houses, churches, hospitals; it enables us to do our part in all these directions. Money not only enables us to get upon our feet in these material directions, but it has another value. The getting of it develops foresight on our part. People cannot get money, without learning to exercise forethought, without planning to-day for to-morrow, this week for the next week, and this year for next year. People cannot get hold of money—or at least cannot keep hold of it—who have not learned to exercise self-control. They must be able to say "No." I want you students, when you go out from here, to be able to say "No." I want you to be able to go by a store and, as you notice the things in that store—whether candy or spring hats, or whatever it is that attracts you—to be able, notwithstanding the fact that you have the money in your pockets to buy, to exercise a self-control that will enable you to pass these things by and save your money to invest it in a home. Persons cannot get hold of money without learning to exercise economy, without learning to make everything go just as far as it is possible to make it go.

Then, again, the getting money enables a person to become a good, steady, safe citizen. The people who kill and are killed, nine times out of ten, whether they are black or white, are people who do not own a home, who do not have money in the bank. They are people who live in their gripsacks. They are gripsack leaders. If their gripsacks are in Montgomery to-night, there is their home. If they are in Opelika the next night, there is their home that night. There are numbers of these people who have no home except their gripsacks. Now I don't want you to go out from here to be that kind of men and women. I want to see you own land. I want to see you own a decent home. And let me say right here that your home is not decent or complete unless it contains a good, comfortable bath-tub. Of the two, I believe I would rather see you own a bathtub without a house, than a house without a bathtub. If you get the tub you are sure to get the house later. So when you go out from here, buy a bathtub, even if you cannot afford to buy anything else.

The possession of money, the having of a bank account, even if small, gives us a certain amount of self-respect. An individual who has a bank account walks through a street so much more erect; he looks people in the face. The people in the community in which he lives have a confidence in him and a respect for him which they would not have if he did not possess the bank account.

Now one great mistake that we make in striving to reach these things is that we keep putting off beginning. The young man says that he will begin when he gets married. The young woman says that she will begin when she gets dressed well enough, or gets a little further on in life. Yielding to this temptation or to that, they keep putting off beginning to save. It makes one sick at heart, as he goes into the cities, to see young men on Sunday afternoons paying two or three dollars for a hack or carriage to take young women out to drive, when in too many cases the men do not earn a salary of more than four dollars a week. Young women, don't go driving with such men. A man who goes driving on a salary of four dollars a week cannot own a home or possess a bank account. When you are asked to go to drive by such a man as that, tell him you would rather he would put his money in the bank, because you know he is not able to afford to spend it in that way.

I like to see people comfortably and neatly dressed; but there is no sadder sight than to see young men and women yielding to the temptation to spend all they earn upon clothes. Then when they die in many, many cases—somebody has to pass around a hat to take up a collection in order that they may be decently put away. Do not make that mistake. Resolve that no matter how little you may earn, you will put a part of the money in the bank. If you earn five dollars a week, put two dollars in the bank. If you earn ten dollars, save four of them. Put the money in the bank. Let it stay there. When it begins to draw interest you will find that you will appreciate the value of money.

A little while ago I was in the city of New Bedford, ford, the city which was formerly the home of Mrs. Hetty Green, who is said to be the richest woman in the world. I want to tell you a story about her that was told me by a gentleman who lived in New Bedford, and who knew Mrs. Green when she lived there. For many years they had in New Bedford no savings bank that would take a very small deposit. Finally a five-cent savings bank was opened there. Just after this had been done, Mrs. Green told this gentleman that she was glad they had opened a five-cent bank, so that now she would be able to put that amount in and have it draw interest. You who are here do not think about five cents as a sum to be saved. You think of it only as money to buy peanuts and candy, or cheap ribbons, or cheap jewelry.

On last Sunday evening I was in the home of a gentleman in New York who has in his family a girl who is now only eighteen years old, and who, when she came to this country a few years ago and went to work in this family as a maid, could not speak a word of English. This girl now has fifteen hundred dollars in the bank. Think of it! A young woman coming to this country poor, and unable to speak a word of English, has saved in a short time fifteen hundred dollars! I wonder how many of you, five years from now, will have fifteen hundred dollars in the bank or in some other safe kind of property.

The civilization of New England and of other such prosperous regions rests more, perhaps, upon the savings banks of the country than upon any other one thing. You ask where the wealth of New England is. It is not in the hands of millionaires. It is in the hands of individuals, who have a few hundreds or a few thousands of dollars put safely away in some bank or banks. You will find that the savings banks of New England, and of all countries that are prosperous, are filled with the dollars of poor people, dollars aggregating millions in all.

We cannot get upon our feet, as a people, until we learn the saving habit; until we learn to save every nickel, every dime and every dollar that we can spare.

Growth

I want to impress upon you this evening the importance of continued growth. I very much, wish that each one of you might imagine, this evening, your father and your mother to be looking at you and examining into every act of your life while here, I wish that you might feel, as it were, their very heart throbs. I wish that you might realize, perhaps as you have never realized before, how anxious they are that you should succeed here. I wish that you could know how many prayers they send up, day after day, that your school life may be more and more successful as one day succeeds another, that you may grow to be successful, studious, strong men and women, who will reflect credit upon yourselves and honor upon your families.

Each one of you must have had some thoughts about those who are anxious about you; some thought for those persons whose hearts are very often bowed down in anxiety because they fear your school life here will not be successful. Not only for your own sake, but for the sake of those who are near and dear to you, those who have done more for you than anybody else, I want you to make up your minds that this year is going to be the best one of your liven.

I want you to resolve that you are going to put into this year the hardest and the most earnest work that you have ever done in your life, to resolve that this is going to be the greatest, the most courageous and the most sinless year of life that you have ever lived; I want you to make up your minds to do this; to decide that you are going to continually grow-and grow more tomorrow than to-day. There are but two directions in this life in which you can grow; backward or forward. You can grow stronger, or you can grow weaker; you can grow greater, or smaller; but it will be impossible for you to stand still.

Now in regard to your studies— your lessons, I want you to make up your minds that you are going to be more and more thorough in your lessons each day you remain here; that you are going to so discipline yourselves that each morning will find you in the recitation rooms with your lessons more thoroughly and more conscientiously prepared for the day's work than they were for the work of the day before. I want you to make up your minds that you are going to be more nearly perfect, are going to put more manly and womanly strength into the preparation of your lessons each day, that you may be more useful. Then you will find yourselves wanting to grow, I hope; will find yourselves learning the dignity of labor, and that no class of people can get up and stay up, can be strong and useful and respected, until they learn that there is no disgrace in any form of labor.

I hope you are learning that labor with the hand, in any form whatever, is not disgraceful. I hope that you are learning, day by day, that all kinds of labor—whether with the mind or with the hand—are honorable, and that people only disgrace themselves by being and keeping in idleness.

I want you to go forward by thoroughness in your work; by being more conscientious in your work; by loving your work more to-day than you did yesterday. If you are not growing in these respects—that is, if you are not going forward—you are going backward, and are not answering the purpose for which this institution was established, are not answering the purpose for which your parents sent you here.

I want to emphasize the fact that we want you to grow in the direction of character—to grow stronger each day in the matter of character. When I say character, here, I mean to use the word in its broadest sense. The institution wants to find you growing more polite to your fellows every day, as you come in contact with them, whether it be in the class-room, in the shop, in the field, in the dining-room, or in your bedroom. No matter where you are, I want you to find yourselves growing more polite and gentlemanly. Notice I do not say merely that I want your teachers—those who are over you—to find you growing more polite; I want you to find yourselves so. If you are not doing this, you are going backward; you are going in the wrong direction.

I want to find you each day more thoughtful of others, and less selfish. I want you to be more conscientious in your thoughts and in your work, and with regard to' your duty toward others. This is growing in the right direction; not doing this is growing in the wrong direction. Nor do I want you to feel that you are to strive for this spirit of growth for this one year alone, or for the time that you are here. I hope that you will continue to grow in the forward direction.

Then, and this is more important still, we want you to take this habit of growth—this disposition to grow in the right direction—out with you from the school, and scatter it as an influence for good wherever you go. We want you to take it into your schools; for many of you are going to become teachers. We want you not only to begin it when you begin teaching in a humble way, but we want to see you grow and improve in it every year. We want to see you make your schoolhouses more attractive; to see you make everything in connection with your schools and your teaching better and stronger; to see you make a school more useful every year that you remain as its teacher.

Then, too, when you go out and get employment—no matter of what kind it may be—we want to see you grow better in that employment; we want to see you advance in ability, commanding always a larger salary, advancing in value to those who employ you. We want to see you grow in reputation for being honest, conscientious, intelligent, hard-working; no matter in what capacity you are employed.

Some of you are going out to establish homes and settle down in home life. We want to see you grow in that direction. Nothing is so disheartening—there is nothing so discouraging as to see a man or woman settle down in a home, and then not to see that home grow more beautiful, inside and outside;—to see it, instead of this, each year grow dingy and dirty, because it each year receives less and less attention.

We want Tuskegee students to go out from here and establish homes that will be models in every respect for those about them homes that will show that the lives of the persons who have established them are models for the lives of those who live about them. If you do this, your lives are going —to be a constant going forward for, I repeat, your lives are going to be one thing or the other, continually going backward or continually going forward.

Last Words

We have come to the close of another school year. Some of you will go out from among us now, not to return. Others will go home for the summer vacation and return at the end of that for the next school year.

As you go out, there is one thing that I want to especially caution you about. Don't go home and feel that you are better than the rest of the folks in your neighborhood because you have been away at school. Don't go home and feel ashamed of your parents because you think they don't know as much as you think you know. Don't think that you are too good to help them. It would be better for you not to have any education, than for you to go home and feel ashamed of your parents, or not want to help them.

Let me tell you of one of the most encouraging and most helpful things that I have known of in connection with the life of our students after they leave this institution. I was in a Southern city and going about among the homes of the people of our race. Among these homes I noticed one which was so neat looking that it was conspicuous. I asked the person who was with me, "How is it that this house is in such good condition, looks so much better than some of the others in the neighborhood?" "It is like this," said the man who was accompanying me. "The people who live there have a son whom they sent to your school, at considerable self denial to themselves. This young man came home from school a few weeks ago. For some time after he came back he did not have work to keep him busy, and so he employed his spare time in fixing up his parents' home. He fixed the roof and chimney, put new palings in the fence where they were needed and did such things as that. Then he got a stock of paint and painted the house thoroughly, two coats, outside and in. That is why the place looks so neat."

Such testimony as that is very helpful. It shows that the students carry out from here the spirit which we try to inculcate.

Another thing, go home and lead a simple life. Don't give the impression that you think education means superficiality and dress.

Be polite; to white and colored people, both.

It is possible for you, by paying heed to this, to do a great deal toward securing and preserving pleasant relations between the people of both races in the South. Try to have your manners in this respect so good that people will notice them and ask where you have been, at what school you learned to be so polite. You will find that politeness counts for a great deal, not only in helping you to get work, but in helping you to keep it.

Don't be ashamed to go to church and Sunday school, to the Young Men's Christian Association and the Christian Endeavor Society. Show that education has only deepened your interest in such things. Have no going backward. Be clean, in your person, your language and in your thoughts.

It seems appropriate during these closing days of the school year to re-emphasize, if possible, that for which the institution stands. We want to have every student get what we have—in our egotism, perhaps called the "Tuskegee spirit"; that is, to get hold of the spirit of the institution, get hold of that for which it stands; and then spread that spirit just as widely as possible, and plant it just as deeply as it is possible to plant it.

In addition to the members of our graduating class, we have each year a large number of students who go out to spend their vacations. Some of these will return at the close of vacation, but some, for various reasons, will not return. Whether you go out as graduates, whether you go out to return or not to return, it is important that all of you get hold of the "Tuskegee spirit"; the spirit of giving yourselves, in order that you may help lift up others. In no matter how small a degree it may be, see that you are assisting someone else.

Now, after a number of years' experience, the institution feels that it has reached a point where it can, with some degree of authority, give advice as to the best way in which you can spend your life.

In the first place, as to your location-the place where you shall work, I very much hope that the larger part of the students who go out from Tuskegee will choose the country districts for their place of work; rather than the large cities. For one thing, you will find that the larger places are much better supplied with workers and helpers than is true of the towns, and especially of the country districts. The cities are better supplied with churches and schools, with everything that tends to uplift people; and they are at the same time much more prolific of those agencies which tend to pull people down. Notwithstanding this latter fact, the greater portion, by far, of those who need help live in the country districts. I think a census report will show that eighty per cent of our people are to be found in the country and small towns. I advise you, then, to go into the country and the towns, rather than into the cities.

Then, as to the manner of work, you must make up your minds in the first place, as I have said before, that you are going to make some sacrifice that you are going to live your lives in an unselfish way, in order that you may help some one. Go out with a spirit that will not allow you to become discouraged when you have opposition, when you meet with obstacles to be overcome. You must go with a determination that you are going to succeed in whatever undertaking you have entered upon.

I do not attempt to give you specific advice as to the kind of work you shall do, but I should say that in a general way I believe that you can accomplish more good—and perhaps this will hold good for the next fifty years here in the South—by taking a country school for your nucleus. Take three months school, and gradually impress upon the people of the community the need of having a longer school. Get them to add one month to three months, and then another month, until they get to the point where they will have six, seven or eight months of school in a year. Then get them to where they will see the importance of building a decent school-house—getting out of the one room log cabin school-house—and of having suitable apparatus for instruction.

There are two things you must fix your mind on — the building of a suitable school-house and the arousing in the people, at the same time, a spirit that will make them support your efforts: In order to do this you must go into the country with the idea of staying there for some time at least. Plant yourself in the community, and by economical living, year by year; manage to buy land for yourself, on which to build a nice and comfortable home. You will find that the longer you stay there the more the people will give you their confidence, and the more they will respect and love you.

I find that many of our graduates have done excellent work by having a farm in connection with their schools. This is true, also, of many who did not remain here to graduate. I have in mind such a man. He has been teaching school in one of the counties of this State for seven or eight years. He has lengthened the school year to eight months. He has a nice cottage with four rooms in it, and a beautiful farm of forty acres. This man is carrying out the "Tuskegee idea."

There will be some of you who can spend your life to better advantage by devoting it to farming than to any other industry. I speak of farming particularly, because I believe that to be the great foundation upon which we must build for the future. I believe that we are coming to the point where we are going to be recognized for our worth in the proportion that we secure an agricultural foundation. Throughout the South we can give ourselves in a free, open way to getting hold of property and building homes, in a way that we cannot do in any other industry. In farming, as in teaching, no matter where you go, remember to go with the "Tuskegee spirit."

I want the boys to go out and do as Mr. N. E. Henry is doing; I want the girls to go out and do as Miss Anna Davis and Miss Lizzie Wright are doing. I want you to go out into the country districts and build up schools. I would not advise you to be too ambitious at first. Be willing to begin with a small salary and work your way up gradually. I have in mind one young man who began teaching school for five dollars a month; another who began teaching in the open air under a tree.

Then, too, I want you to go out in a spirit of liberality toward the white people with whom you come in contact. That is an important matter. When I say this I do not mean that you shall go lowering your manhood or your dignity. Go in a manly way, in a straightforward and honorable way, and then you will show the white people that you are not of a belittling race that the prejudice which so many people possess cannot come among you and those with whom you work. If you can extend a helping hand to a white person, feel just as happy in doing so as in helping a black person.

In, the sight of God there is no color line, and we want to cultivate a spirit that will make us forget that there is such a line anywhere. We want to be larger and broader than the people who would oppress us on account of our color.

No one ever loses anything by being a gentleman or a lady. No person ever lost anything by being broad. Remember that if we are kind and useful, if we are moral, if we go out and practice these traits, no matter what people say about us, they cannot pull us down. But, on the other hand, if we are without the spirit of usefulness, if we are without morality, without liberality, without economy and property, without all those qualities which go to make a people and a nation great and strong, no matter what we may say about ourselves and what other people may say about us, we are losing ground. Nobody can give us those qualities merely by praising us and talking well about us; and when we possess them, nobody can take them from us by speaking ill of us.

The Negro Problem

Table of Contents

Industrial Education for the Negro

By Booker T. Washington

The necessity for the race's learning the difference between being worked and working. He would not confine the Negro to industrial life, but believes that the very best service which any one can render to what is called the "higher education" is to teach the present generation to work and save. This will create the wealth from which alone can come leisure and the opportunity for higher education.

One of the most fundamental and far-reaching deeds that has been accomplished during the last quarter of a century has been that by which the Negro has been helped to find himself and to learn the secrets of civilization—to learn that there are a few simple, cardinal principles upon which a race must start its upward course, unless it would fail, and its last estate be worse than its first.

It has been necessary for the Negro to learn the difference between being worked and working—to learn that being worked meant degradation, while working means civilization; that all forms of labor are honorable, and all forms of idleness disgraceful. It has been necessary for him to learn that all races that have got upon their feet have done so largely by laying an economic foundation, and, in general, by beginning in a proper cultivation and ownership of the soil.

Forty years ago my race emerged from slavery into freedom. If, in too many cases, the Negro race began development at the wrong end, it was largely because neither white nor black properly understood the case. Nor is it any wonder that this was so, for never before in the history of the world had just such a problem been presented as that of the two races at the coming of freedom in this country.

For two hundred and fifty years, I believe the way for the redemption of the Negro was being prepared through industrial development. Through all those years the Southern white man did business with the Negro in a way that no one else has done business with him. In most cases if a Southern white man wanted a house built he consulted a Negro mechanic about the plan and about the actual building of the structure. If he wanted a suit of clothes made he went to a Negro tailor, and for shoes he went to a shoemaker of the same race. In a certain way every slave plantation in the South was an industrial school. On these plantations young colored men and women were constantly being trained not only as farmers but as carpenters, blacksmiths, wheelwrights, brick masons, engineers, cooks, laundresses, sewing women and housekeepers.

I do not mean in any way to apologize for the curse of slavery, which was a curse to both races, but in what I say about industrial training in slavery I am simply stating facts. This training was crude, and was given for selfish purposes.

It did not answer the highest ends, because there was an absence of mental training in connection with the training of the hand. To a large degree, though, this business contact with the Southern white man, and the industrial training on the plantations, left the Negro at the close of the war in possession of nearly all the common and skilled labor in the South. The industries that gave the South its power, prominence and wealth prior to the Civil War were mainly the raising of cotton, sugar cane, rice and tobacco. Before the way could be prepared for the proper growing and marketing of these crops forests had to be cleared, houses to be built, public roads and railroads constructed. In all these works the Negro did most of the heavy work. In the planting, cultivating and marketing of the crops not only was the Negro the chief dependence, but in the manufacture of tobacco he became a skilled and proficient workman, and in this, up to the present time, in the South, holds the lead in the large tobacco manufactories.

In most of the industries, though, what happened? For nearly twenty years after the war, except in a few instances, the value of the industrial training given by the plantations was overlooked. Negro men and women were educated in literature, in mathematics and in the sciences, with little thought of what had been taking place during the preceding two hundred and fifty years, except, perhaps, as something to be escaped, to be got as far away from as possible. As a generation began to pass, those who had been trained as mechanics in slavery began to disappear by death, and gradually it began to be realized that there were few to take their places. There were young men educated in foreign tongues, but few in carpentry or in mechanical or architectural drawing. Many were trained in Latin, but few as engineers and blacksmiths. Too many were taken from the farm and educated, but educated in everything but farming. For this reason they had no interest in farming and did not return to it. And yet eighty-five per cent. of the Negro population of the Southern states lives and for a considerable time will continue to live in the country districts. The charge is often brought against the members of my race—and too often justly, I confess—that they are found leaving the country districts and flocking into the great cities where temptations are more frequent and harder to resist, and where the Negro people too often become demoralized. Think, though, how frequently it is the case that from the first day that a pupil begins to go to school his books teach him much about the cities of the world and city life, and almost nothing about the country. How natural it is, then, that when he has the ordering of his life he wants to live it in the city.

Only a short time before his death the late Mr. C.P. Huntington, to whose memory a magnificent library has just been given by his widow to the Hampton Institute for Negroes, in Virginia, said in a public address some words which seem to me so wise that I want to quote them here:

"Our schools teach everybody a little of almost everything, but, in my opinion, they teach very few children just what they ought to know in order to make their way successfully in life. They do not put into their hands the tools they are best fitted to use, and hence so many failures. Many a mother and sister have worked and slaved, living upon scanty food, in order to give a son and brother a "liberal education," and in doing this have built up a barrier between the boy and the work he was fitted to do. Let me say to you that all honest work is honorable work. If the labor is manual, and seems common, you will have all the more chance to be thinking of other things, or of work that is higher and brings better pay, and to work out in your minds better and higher duties and responsibilities for yourselves, and for thinking of ways by which you can help others as well as yourselves, and bring them up to your own higher level."

Some years ago, when we decided to make tailoring a part of our training at the Tuskegee Institute, I was amazed to find that it was almost impossible to find in the whole country an educated colored man who could teach the making of clothing. We could find numbers of them who could teach astronomy, theology, Latin or grammar, but almost none who could instruct in the making of clothing, something that has to be used by every one of us every day in the year. How often have I been discouraged as I have gone through the South, and into the homes of the people of my race, and have found women who could converse intelligently upon abstruse subjects, and yet could not tell how to improve the condition of the poorly cooked and still more poorly served bread and meat which they and their families were eating three times a day. It is discouraging to find a girl who can tell you the geographical location of any country on the globe and who does not know where to place the dishes upon a common dinner table. It is discouraging to find a woman who knows much about theoretical chemistry, and who cannot properly wash and iron a shirt.

In what I say here I would not by any means have it understood that I would limit or circumscribe the mental development of the Negro-student. No race can be lifted until its mind is awakened and strengthened. By the side of industrial training should always go mental and moral training, but the pushing of mere abstract knowledge into the head means little. We want more than the mere performance of mental gymnastics. Our knowledge must be harnessed to the things of real life. I would encourage the Negro to secure all the mental strength, all the mental culture—whether gleaned from science, mathematics, history, language or literature that his circumstances will allow, but I believe most earnestly that for years to come the education of the people of my race should be so directed that the greatest proportion of the mental strength of the masses will be brought to bear upon the every-day practical things of life, upon something that is needed to be done, and something which they will be permitted to do in the community in which they reside. And just the same with the professional class which the race needs and must have, I would say give the men and women of that class, too, the training which will best fit them to perform in the most successful manner the service which the race demands.

I would not confine the race to industrial life, not even to agriculture, for example, although I believe that by far the greater part of the Negro race is best off in the country districts and must and should continue to live there, but I would teach the race that in industry the foundation must be laid—that the very best service which any one can render to what is called the higher education is to teach the present generation to provide a material or industrial foundation. On such a foundation as this will grow habits of thrift, a love of work, economy, ownership of property, bank accounts. Out of it in the future will grow practical education, professional education, positions of public responsibility. Out of it will grow moral and religious strength. Out of it will grow wealth from which alone can come leisure and the opportunity for the enjoyment of literature and the fine arts.

In the words of the late beloved Frederick Douglass: "Every blow of the sledge hammer wielded by a sable arm is a powerful blow in support of our cause. Every colored mechanic is by virtue of circumstances an elevator of his race. Every house built by a black man is a strong tower against the allied hosts of prejudice. It is impossible for us to attach too much importance to this aspect of the subject.

Without industrial development there can be no wealth; without wealth there can be no leisure; without leisure no opportunity for thoughtful reflection and the cultivation of the higher arts."

I would set no limits to the attainments of the Negro in arts, in letters or statesmanship, but I believe the surest way to reach those ends is by laying the foundation in the little things of life that lie immediately about one's door. I plead for industrial education and development for the Negro not because I want to cramp him, but because I want to free him. I want to see him enter the all-powerful business and commercial world.

It was such combined mental, moral and industrial education which the late General Armstrong set out to give at the Hampton Institute when he established that school thirty years ago. The Hampton Institute has continued along the lines laid down by its great founder, and now each year an increasing number of similar schools are being established in the South, for the people of both races.

Early in the history of the Tuskegee Institute we began to combine industrial training with mental and moral culture. Our first efforts were in the direction of agriculture, and we began teaching this with no appliances except one hoe and a blind mule. From this small beginning we have grown until now the Institute owns two thousand acres of land, eight hundred of which are cultivated each year by the young men of the school. We began teaching wheelwrighting and blacksmithing in a small way to the men, and laundry work, cooking and sewing and housekeeping to the young women. The fourteen hundred and over young men and women who attended the school during the last school year received instruction—in addition to academic and religious training—in thirty-three trades and industries, including carpentry, blacksmithing, printing, wheelwrighting harnessmaking, painting, machinery, founding, shoemaking, brickmasonry and brick making, plastering, sawmilling, tinsmithing, tailoring, mechanical and architectural drawing, electrical and steam engineering, canning, sewing, dressmaking, millinery, cooking, laundering, housekeeping, mattress making, basketry, nursing, agriculture, dairying and stock raising, horticulture.

Not only do the students receive instruction in these trades, but they do actual work, by means of which more than half of them pay some part or all of their expenses while remaining at the school. Of the sixty buildings belonging to the school all but four were almost wholly erected by the students as a part of their industrial education. Even the bricks which go into the walls are made by students in the school's brick yard, in which, last year, they manufactured two million bricks.

When we first began this work at Tuskegee, and the idea got spread among the people of my race that the students who came to the Tuskegee school were to be taught industries in connection with their academic studies, were, in other words, to be taught to work, I received a great many verbal messages and letters from parents informing me that they wanted their children taught books, but not how to work. This protest went on for three or four years, but I am glad to be able to say now that our people have very generally been educated to a point where they see their own needs and conditions so clearly that it has been several years since we have had a single protest from parents against the teaching of industries, and there is now a positive enthusiasm for it. In fact, public sentiment among the students at Tuskegee is now so strong for industrial training that it would hardly permit a student to remain on the grounds who was unwilling to labor.

It seems to me that too often mere book education leaves the Negro young man or woman in a weak position. For example, I have seen a Negro girl taught by her mother to help her in doing laundry work at home. Later, when this same girl was graduated from the public schools or a high school and returned home she finds herself educated out of sympathy with laundry work, and yet not able to find anything to do which seems in keeping with the cost and character of her education. Under these circumstances we cannot be surprised if she does not fulfill the expectations made for her. What should have been done for her, it seems to me, was to give her along with her academic education thorough training in the latest and best methods of laundry work, so that she could have put so much skill and intelligence into it that the work would have been lifted out from the plane of drudgery. The home which she would then have been able to found by the results of her work would have enabled her to help her children to take a still more responsible position in life.

Almost from the first Tuskegee has kept in mind—and this I think should be the policy of all industrial schools—fitting students for occupations which would be open to them in their home communities. Some years ago we noted the fact that there was beginning to be a demand in the South for men to operate dairies in a skillful, modern manner. We opened a dairy department in connection with the school, where a number of young men could have instruction in the latest and most scientific methods of dairy work. At present we have calls—mainly from Southern white men—for twice as many dairymen as we are able to supply. What is equally satisfactory, the reports which come to us indicate that our young men are giving the highest satisfaction and are fast changing and improving the dairy product in the communities into which they go. I use the dairy here as an example. What I have said of this is equally true of many of the other industries which we teach. Aside from the economic value of this work I cannot but believe, and my observation confirms me in my belief, that as we continue to place Negro men and women of intelligence, religion, modesty, conscience and skill in every community in the South, who will prove by actual results their value to the community, I cannot but believe, I say, that this will constitute a solution to many of the present political and social difficulties.

Many seem to think that industrial education is meant to make the Negro work as he worked in the days of slavery. This is far from my conception of industrial education. If this training is worth anything to the Negro, it consists in teaching him how not to work, but how to make the forces of nature—air, steam, water, horse-power and electricity—work for him. If it has any value it is in lifting labor up out of toil and drudgery into the plane of the dignified and the beautiful. The Negro in the South works and works hard; but too often his ignorance and lack of skill causes him to do his work in the most costly and shiftless manner, and this keeps him near the bottom of the ladder in the economic world.

I have not emphasized particularly in these pages the great need of training the Negro in agriculture, but I believe that this branch of industrial education does need very great emphasis. In this connection I want to quote some words which Mr. Edgar Gardner Murphy, of Montgomery, Alabama, has recently written upon this subject:

"We must incorporate into our public school system a larger recognition of the practical and industrial elements in educational training. Ours is an agricultural population. The school must be brought more closely to the soil. The teaching of history, for example, is all very well, but nobody can really know anything of history unless he has been taught to see things grow—has so seen things not only with the outward eye, but with the eyes of his intelligence and conscience. The actual things of the present are more important, however, than the institutions of the past. Even to young children can be shown the simpler conditions and processes of growth—how corn is put into the ground—how cotton and potatoes should be planted—how to choose the soil best adapted to a particular plant, how to improve that soil, how to care for the plant while it grows, how to get the most value out of it, how to use the elements of waste for the fertilization of other crops; how, through the alternation of crops, the land may be made to increase the annual value of its products—these things, upon their elementary side are absolutely vital to the worth and success of hundreds of thousands of these people of the Negro race, and yet our whole educational system has practically ignored them.

"Such work will mean not only an education in agriculture, but an education through agriculture and education, through natural symbols and practical forms, which will educate as deeply, as broadly and as truly as any other system which the world has known. Such changes will bring far larger results than the mere improvement of our Negroes. They will give us an agricultural class, a class of tenants or small land owners, trained not away from the soil, but in relation to the soil and in intelligent dependence upon its resources."

I close, then, as I began, by saying that as a slave the Negro was worked, and that as a freeman he must learn to work. There is still doubt in many quarters as to the ability of the Negro unguided, unsupported, to hew his own path and put into visible, tangible, indisputable form, products and signs of civilization. This doubt cannot be much affected by abstract arguments, no matter how delicately and convincingly woven together. Patiently, quietly, doggedly, persistently, through summer and winter, sunshine and shadow, by self-sacrifice, by foresight, by honesty and industry, we must re-enforce argument with results. One farm bought, one house built, one home sweetly and intelligently kept, one man who is the largest tax payer or has the largest bank account, one school or church maintained, one factory running successfully, one truck garden profitably cultivated, one patient cured by a Negro doctor, one sermon well preached, one office well filled, one life cleanly lived—these will tell more in our favor than all the abstract eloquence that can be summoned to plead our cause. Our pathway must be up through the soil, up through swamps, up through forests, up through the streams, the rocks, up through commerce, education and religion!

The Talented Tenth
By Prof. W.E. Burghardt Dubois

A strong plea for the higher education of the Negro, which those who are interested in the future of the freedmen cannot afford to ignore. Prof.
DuBois produces ample evidence to prove conclusively the truth of his statement that "to attempt to establish any sort of a system of common and industrial school training, without *first* providing for the higher training of the very best teachers, is simply throwing your money to the winds."

The Negro race, like all races, is going to be saved by its exceptional men. The problem of education, then, among Negroes must first of all deal with the Talented Tenth; it is the problem of developing the Best of this race that they may guide the Mass away from the contamination and death of the Worst, in their own and other races. Now the training of men is a difficult and intricate task. Its technique is a matter for educational experts, but its object is for the vision of seers. If we make money the object of man-training, we shall develop money-makers but not necessarily men; if we make technical skill the object of education, we may possess artisans but not, in nature, men. Men we shall have only as we make manhood the object of the work of the schools—intelligence, broad sympathy, knowledge of the world that was and is, and of the relation of men to it—this is the curriculum of that Higher Education which must underlie true life. On this foundation we may build bread winning, skill of hand and quickness of brain, with never a fear lest the child and man mistake the means of living for the object of life.

If this be true—and who can deny it—three tasks lay before me; first to show from the past that the Talented Tenth as they have risen among American Negroes have been worthy of leadership; secondly, to show how these men may be educated and developed; and thirdly, to show their relation to the Negro problem.

You misjudge us because you do not know us. From the very first it has been the educated and intelligent of the Negro people that have led and elevated the mass, and the sole obstacles that nullified and retarded their efforts were slavery and race prejudice; for what is slavery but the legalized survival of the unfit and the nullification of the work of natural internal leadership? Negro leadership, therefore, sought from the first to rid the race of this awful incubus that it might make way for natural selection and the survival of the fittest. In colonial days came Phillis Wheatley and Paul Cuffe striving against the bars of prejudice; and Benjamin Banneker, the almanac maker, voiced their longings when he said to Thomas Jefferson, "I freely and cheerfully acknowledge that I am of the African race, and in color which is natural to them, of the deepest dye; and it is under a sense of the most profound gratitude to the Supreme Ruler of the Universe, that I now confess to you that I am not under that state of tyrannical thraldom and inhuman captivity to which too many of my brethren are doomed, but that I have abundantly tasted of the fruition of those blessings which proceed from that free and unequaled liberty with which you are favored, and which I hope you will willingly allow, you have mercifully received from the immediate hand of that Being from whom proceedeth every good and perfect gift.

"Suffer me to recall to your mind that time, in which the arms of the British crown were exerted with every powerful effort, in order to reduce you to a state of servitude; look back, I entreat you, on the variety of dangers to which you were exposed; reflect on that period in which every human aid appeared unavailable, and in which even hope and fortitude wore the aspect of inability to the conflict, and you cannot but be led to a serious and grateful sense of your miraculous and providential preservation, you cannot but acknowledge, that the present freedom and tranquility which you enjoy, you have mercifully received, and that a peculiar blessing of heaven.

"This, sir, was a time when you clearly saw into the injustice of a state of Slavery, and in which you had just apprehensions of the horrors of its condition. It was then that your abhorrence thereof was so excited, that you publicly held forth this true and invaluable doctrine, which is worthy to be recorded and remembered in all succeeding ages: 'We hold these truths to be self evident, that all men are created equal; that they are endowed with certain inalienable rights, and that among these are life, liberty and the pursuit of happiness.'"

Then came Dr. James Derham, who could tell even the learned Dr. Rush something of medicine, and Lemuel Haynes, to whom Middlebury College gave an honorary A.M. in 1804. These and others we may call the Revolutionary group of distinguished Negroes—they were persons of marked ability, leaders of a Talented Tenth, standing conspicuously among the best of their time. They strove by word and deed to save the color line from becoming the line between the bond and free, but all they could do was nullified by Eli Whitney and the Curse of Gold. So they passed into forgetfulness.

But their spirit did not wholly die; here and there in the early part of the century came other exceptional men. Some were natural sons of unnatural fathers and were given often a liberal training and thus a race of educated mulattoes sprang up to plead for black men's rights. There was Ira Aldridge, whom all Europe loved to honor; there was that Voice crying in the Wilderness, David Walker, and saying:

"I declare it does appear to me as though some nations think God is asleep, or that he made the Africans for nothing else but to dig their mines and work their farms, or they cannot believe history, sacred or profane. I ask every man who has a heart, and is blessed with the privilege of believing—Is not God a God of justice to all his creatures? Do you say he is? Then if he gives peace and tranquility to tyrants and permits them to keep our fathers, our mothers, ourselves and our children in eternal ignorance and wretchedness to support them and their families, would he be to us a God of Justice? I ask, O, ye Christians, who hold us and our children in the most abject ignorance and degradation that ever a people were afflicted with since the world began—I say if God gives you peace and tranquility, and suffers you thus to go on afflicting us, and our children, who have never given you the least provocation—would He be to us a God of Justice? If you will allow that we are men, who feel for each other, does not the blood of our fathers and of us, their children, cry aloud to the Lord of Sabaoth against you for the cruelties and murders with which you have and do continue to afflict us?"

This was the wild voice that first aroused Southern legislators in 1829 to the terrors of abolitionism.

In 1831 there met that first Negro convention in Philadelphia, at which the world gaped curiously but which bravely attacked the problems of race and slavery, crying out against persecution and declaring that "Laws as cruel in themselves as they were unconstitutional and unjust, have in many places been enacted against our poor, unfriended and unoffending brethren (without a shadow of provocation on our part), at whose bare recital the very savage draws himself up for fear of contagion—looks noble and prides himself because he bears not the name of Christian." Side by side this free Negro movement, and the movement for abolition, strove until they merged into one strong stream. Too little notice has been taken of the work which the Talented Tenth among Negroes took in the great abolition crusade. From the very day that a Philadelphia colored man became the first subscriber to Garrison's "Liberator," to the day when Negro soldiers made the Emancipation Proclamation possible, black leaders worked shoulder to shoulder with white men in a movement, the success of which would have been impossible without them. There was Purvis and Remond, Pennington and Highland Garnett, Sojourner Truth and Alexander Crummel, and above all, Frederick Douglass—what would the abolition movement have been without them? They stood as living examples of the possibilities of the Negro race, their own hard experiences and well wrought culture said silently more than all the drawn periods of orators—they were the men who made American slavery impossible. As Maria Weston Chapman once said, from the school of anti-slavery agitation "a throng of authors, editors, lawyers, orators and accomplished gentlemen of color have taken their degree! It has equally implanted hopes and aspirations, noble thoughts, and sublime purposes, in the hearts of both races. It has prepared the white man for the freedom of the black man, and it has made the black man scorn the thought of enslavement, as does a white man, as far as its influence has extended. Strengthen that noble influence! Before its organization, the country only saw here and there in slavery some faithful Cudjoe or Dinah, whose strong natures blossomed even in bondage, like a fine plant beneath a heavy stone. Now, under the elevating and cherishing influence of the American Anti-slavery Society, the colored race, like the white, furnishes Corinthian capitals for the noblest temples."

Where were these black abolitionists trained? Some, like Frederick Douglass, were self-trained, but yet trained liberally; others, like Alexander Crummell and McCune Smith, graduated from famous foreign universities. Most of them rose up through the colored schools of New York and Philadelphia and Boston, taught by college-bred men like Russworm, of Dartmouth, and college-bred white men like Neau and Benezet.

After emancipation came a new group of educated and gifted leaders: Langston, Bruce and Elliot, Greener, Williams and Payne. Through political organization, historical and polemic writing and moral regeneration, these men strove to uplift their people. It is the fashion of to-day to sneer at them and to say that with freedom Negro leadership should have begun at the plow and not in the Senate—a foolish and mischievous lie; two hundred and fifty years that black serf toiled at the plow and yet that toiling was in vain till the Senate passed the war amendments; and two hundred and fifty years more the half-free serf of to-day may toil at his plow, but unless he have political rights and righteously guarded civic status, he will still remain the poverty-stricken and ignorant plaything of rascals, that he now is. This all sane men know even if they dare not say it.

And so we come to the present—a day of cowardice and vacillation, of strident wide-voiced wrong and faint hearted compromise; of double-faced dallying with Truth and Right. Who are to-day guiding the work of the Negro people? The "exceptions" of course. And yet so sure as this Talented Tenth is pointed out, the blind worshipers of the Average cry out in alarm: "These are exceptions, look here at death, disease and crime—these are the happy rule." Of course they are the rule, because a silly nation made them the rule: Because for three long centuries this people lynched Negroes who dared to be brave, raped black women who dared to be virtuous, crushed dark-hued youth who dared to be ambitious, and encouraged and made to flourish servility and lewdness and apathy. But not even this was able to crush all manhood and chastity and aspiration from black folk. A saving remnant continually survives and persists, continually aspires, continually shows itself in thrift and ability and character. Exceptional it is to be sure, but this is its chiefest promise; it shows the capability of Negro blood, the promise of black men. Do Americans ever stop to reflect that there are in this land a million men of Negro blood, well-educated, owners of homes, against the honor of whose womanhood no breath was ever raised, whose men occupy positions of trust and usefulness, and who, judged by any standard, have reached the full measure of the best type of modern European culture? Is it fair, is it decent, is it Christian to ignore these facts of the Negro problem, to belittle such aspiration, to nullify such leadership and seek to crush these people back into the mass out of which by toil and travail, they and their fathers have raised themselves?

Can the masses of the Negro people be in any possible way more quickly raised than by the effort and example of this aristocracy of talent and character? Was there ever a nation on God's fair earth civilized from the bottom upward? Never; it is, ever was and ever will be from the top downward that culture filters. The Talented Tenth rises and pulls all that are worth the saving up to their vantage ground. This is the history of human progress; and the two historic mistakes which have hindered that progress were the thinking first that no more could ever rise save the few already risen; or second, that it would better the unrisen to pull the risen down.

How then shall the leaders of a struggling people be trained and the hands of the risen few strengthened? There can be but one answer: The best and most capable of their youth must be schooled in the colleges and universities of the land. We will not quarrel as to just what the university of the Negro should teach or how it should teach it—I willingly admit that each soul and each race-soul needs its own peculiar curriculum. But this is true: A university is a human invention for the transmission of knowledge and culture from generation to generation, through the training of quick minds and pure hearts, and for this work no other human invention will suffice, not even trade and industrial schools.

All men cannot go to college but some men must; every isolated group or nation must have its yeast, must have for the talented few centers of training where men are not so mystified and befuddled by the hard and necessary toil of earning a living, as to have no aims higher than their bellies, and no God greater than Gold. This is true training, and thus in the beginning were the favored sons of the freedmen trained. Out of the colleges of the North came, after the blood of war, Ware, Cravath, Chase, Andrews, Bumstead and Spence to build the foundations of knowledge and civilization in the black South. Where ought they to have begun to build? At the bottom, of course, quibbles the mole with his eyes in the earth. Aye! truly at the bottom, at the very bottom; at the bottom of knowledge, down in the very depths of knowledge there where the roots of justice strike into the lowest soil of Truth. And so they did begin; they founded colleges, and up from the colleges shot normal schools, and out from the normal schools went teachers, and around the normal teachers clustered other teachers to teach the public schools; the college trained in Greek and Latin and mathematics, 2,000 men; and these men trained full 50,000 others in morals and manners, and they in turn taught thrift and the alphabet to nine millions of men, who to-day hold $300,000,000 of property. It was a miracle—the most wonderful peace-battle of the 19th century, and yet to-day men smile at it, and in fine superiority tell us that it was all a strange mistake; that a proper way to found a system of education is first to gather the children and buy them spelling books and hoes; afterward men may look about for teachers, if haply they may find them; or again they would teach men Work, but as for Life—why, what has Work to do with Life, they ask vacantly.

Was the work of these college founders successful; did it stand the test of time? Did the college graduates, with all their fine theories of life, really live? Are they useful men helping to civilize and elevate their less fortunate fellows? Let us see. Omitting all institutions which have not actually graduated students from a college course, there are to-day in the United States thirty-four institutions giving something above high school training to Negroes and designed especially for this race.

Three of these were established in border States before the War; thirteen were planted by the Freedmen's Bureau in the years 1864-1869; nine were established between 1870 and 1880 by various church bodies; five were established after 1881 by Negro churches, and four are state institutions supported by United States' agricultural funds. In most cases the college departments are small adjuncts to high and common school work. As a matter of fact six institutions—Atlanta, Fisk, Howard, Shaw, Wilberforce and Leland, are the important Negro colleges so far as actual work and number of students are concerned. In all these institutions, seven hundred and fifty Negro college students are enrolled. In grade the best of these colleges are about a year behind the smaller New England colleges and atypical curriculum is that of Atlanta University. Here students from the grammar grades, after a three years' high school course, take a college course of 136 weeks. One-fourth of this time is given to Latin and Greek; one-fifth, to English and modern languages; one-sixth, to history and social science; one-seventh, to natural science; one-eighth to mathematics, and one-eighth to philosophy and pedagogy.

In addition to these students in the South, Negroes have attended Northern colleges for many years. As early as 1826 one was graduated from Bowdoin College, and from that time till to-day nearly every year has seen elsewhere, other such graduates. They have, of course, met much color prejudice. Fifty years ago very few colleges would admit them at all. Even to-day no Negro has ever been admitted to Princeton, and at some other leading institutions they are rather endured than encouraged. Oberlin was the great pioneer in the work of blotting out the color line in colleges, and has more Negro graduates by far than any other Northern college.

The total number of Negro college graduates up to 1899, (several of the graduates of that year not being reported), was as follows:

Negro Colleges.			White Colleges.
Before '76		137	75
'75-80		143	22
'80-85		250	31
'85-90		413	43
'90-95		465	66
'96-99		475	88
Class Unknown		57	64
Total		1,914	390

Of these graduates 2,079 were men and 252 were women; 50 per cent. of Northern-born college men come South to work among the masses of their people, at a sacrifice which few people realize; nearly 90 per cent. of the Southern-born graduates instead of seeking that personal freedom and broader intellectual atmosphere which their training has led them, in some degree, to conceive, stay and labor and wait in the midst of their black neighbors and relatives.

The most interesting question, and in many respects the crucial question, to be asked concerning college-bred Negroes, is: Do they earn a living? It has been intimated more than once that the higher training of Negroes has resulted in sending into the world of work, men who could find nothing to do suitable to their talents. Now and then there comes a rumor of a colored college man working at menial service, etc. Fortunately, returns as to occupations of college-bred Negroes, gathered by the Atlanta conference, are quite full—nearly sixty per cent. of the total number of graduates.

This enables us to reach fairly certain conclusions as to the occupations of all college-bred Negroes. Of 1,312 persons reported, there were:

	Per Cent.
Teachers	53.4
Clergymen	16.8
Physicians, etc.	6.3
Students	5.6
Lawyers	4.7
In Govt. Service	4.0
In Business	3.6
Farmers and Artisans	2.7
Editors, Secretaries and Clerks	2.4
Miscellaneous	.5

Over half are teachers, a sixth are preachers, another sixth are students and professional men; over 6 per cent. are farmers, artisans and merchants, and 4 per cent. are in government service. In detail the occupations are as follows:

Occupations of College-Bred Men.

Teachers:

Presidents and Deans		19
Teacher of Music		7
Professors, Principals and Teachers,		675
	Total	701

Clergymen:

Bishop		1
Chaplains U.S. Army		2
Missionaries		9
Presiding Elders		12
Preachers		197
	Total	221

Physicians,

Doctors of Medicine		76
Druggists		4
Dentists		3
	Total	83

Students	74
Lawyers	62

Civil Service:

U.S. Minister Plenipotentiary		1
U.S. Consul		1
U.S. Deputy Collector		1
U.S. Gauger		1
U.S. Postmasters		2
U.S. Clerks		44
State Civil Service		2
City Civil Service		1
	Total	53

Business Men:

Merchants, etc.		30
Managers		13
Real Estate Dealers		4
	Total	47

Farmers	26

Clerks and Secretaries:

Secretary of National Societies		7
Clerks, etc.		15
	Total	22

Artisans	9

These figures illustrate vividly the function of the college-bred Negro. He is, as he ought to be, the group leader, the man who sets the ideals of the community where he lives, directs its thoughts and heads its social movements. It need hardly be argued that the Negro people need social leadership more than most groups; that they have no traditions to fall back upon, no long established customs, no strong family ties, no well defined social classes. All these things must be slowly and painfully evolved. The preacher was, even before the war, the group leader of the Negroes, and the church their greatest social institution. Naturally this preacher was ignorant and often immoral, and the problem of replacing the older type by better educated men has been a difficult one. Both by direct work and by direct influence on other preachers, and on congregations, the college-bred preacher has an opportunity for reformatory work and moral inspiration, the value of which cannot be overestimated.

It has, however, been in the furnishing of teachers that the Negro college has found its peculiar function. Few persons realize how vast a work, how mighty a revolution has been thus accomplished. To furnish five millions and more of ignorant people with teachers of their own race and blood, in one generation, was not only a very difficult undertaking, but a very important one, in that, it placed before the eyes of almost every Negro child an attainable ideal. It brought the masses of the blacks in contact with modern civilization, made black men the leaders of their communities and trainers of the new generation. In this work college-bred Negroes were first teachers, and then teachers of teachers. And here it is that the broad culture of college work has been of peculiar value. Knowledge of life and its wider meaning, has been the point of the Negro's deepest ignorance, and the sending out of teachers whose training has not been simply for bread winning, but also for human culture, has been of inestimable value in the training of these men.

In earlier years the two occupations of preacher and teacher were practically the only ones open to the black college graduate. Of later years a larger diversity of life among his people, has opened new avenues of employment. Nor have these college men been paupers and spendthrifts; 557 college-bred Negroes owned in 1899, $1,342,862.50 worth of real estate, (assessed value) or $2,411 per family. The real value of the total accumulations of the whole group is perhaps about $10,000,000, or $5,000 a piece. Pitiful, is it not, beside the fortunes of oil kings and steel trusts, but after all is the fortune of the millionaire the only stamp of true and successful living? Alas! it is, with many, and there's the rub.

The problem of training the Negro is to-day immensely complicated by the fact that the whole question of the efficiency and appropriateness of our present systems of education, for any kind of child, is a matter of active debate, in which final settlement seems still afar off. Consequently it often happens that persons arguing for or against certain systems of education for Negroes, have these controversies in mind and miss the real question at issue. The main question, so far as the Southern Negro is concerned, is: What under the present circumstance, must a system of education do in order to raise the Negro as quickly as possible in the scale of civilization? The answer to this question seems to me clear: It must strengthen the Negro's character, increase his knowledge and teach him to earn a living. Now it goes without saying, that it is hard to do all these things simultaneously or suddenly, and that at the same time it will not do to give all the attention to one and neglect the others; we could give black boys trades, but that alone will not civilize a race of ex-slaves; we might simply increase their knowledge of the world, but this would not necessarily make them wish to use this knowledge honestly; we might seek to strengthen character and purpose, but to what end if this people have nothing to eat or to wear? A system of education is not one thing, nor does it have a single definite object, nor is it a mere matter of schools. Education is that whole system of human training within and without the school house walls, which molds and develops men. If then we start out to train an ignorant and unskilled people with a heritage of bad habits, our system of training must set before itself two great aims—the one dealing with knowledge and character, the other part seeking to give the child the technical knowledge necessary for him to earn a living under the present circumstances. These objects are accomplished in part by the opening of the common schools on the one, and of the industrial schools on the other. But only in part, for there must also be trained those who are to teach these schools—men and women of knowledge and culture and technical skill who understand modern civilization, and have the training and aptitude to impart it to the children under them. There must be teachers, and teachers of teachers, and to attempt to establish any sort of a system of common and industrial school training, without *first* (and I say *first* advisedly) without *first* providing for the higher training of the very best teachers, is simply throwing your money to the winds. School houses do not teach themselves—piles of brick and mortar and machinery do not send out *men*. It is the trained, living human soul, cultivated and strengthened by long study and thought, that breathes the real breath of life into boys and girls and makes them human, whether they be black or white, Greek, Russian or American. Nothing, in these latter days, has so dampened the faith of thinking Negroes in recent educational movements, as the fact that such movements have been accompanied by ridicule and denouncement and decrying of those very institutions of higher training which made the Negro public school possible, and make Negro industrial schools thinkable. It was Fisk, Atlanta, Howard and Straight, those colleges born of the faith and sacrifice of the abolitionists, that placed in the black schools of the South the 30,000 teachers and more, which some, who depreciate the work of these higher schools, are using to teach their own new experiments. If Hampton, Tuskegee and the hundred other industrial schools prove in the future to be as successful as they deserve to be, then their success in training black artisans for the South, will be due primarily to the white colleges of the North and the black colleges of the South, which trained the teachers who to-day conduct these institutions. There was a time when the American people believed pretty devoutly that a log of wood with a boy at one end and Mark Hopkins at the other, represented the highest ideal of human training. But in these eager days it would seem that we have changed all that and think it necessary to add a couple of saw-mills and a hammer to this outfit, and, at a pinch, to dispense with the services of Mark Hopkins.

I would not deny, or for a moment seem to deny, the paramount necessity of teaching the Negro to work, and to work steadily and skillfully; or seem to depreciate in the slightest degree the important part industrial schools must play in the accomplishment of these ends, but I *do* say, and insist upon it, that it is industrialism drunk with its vision of success, to imagine that its own work can be accomplished without providing for the training of broadly cultured men and women to teach its own teachers, and to teach the teachers of the public schools.

But I have already said that human education is not simply a matter of schools; it is much more a matter of family and group life—the training of one's home, of one's daily companions, of one's social class. Now the black boy of the South moves in a black world—a world with its own leaders, its own thoughts, its own ideals. In this world he gets by far the larger part of his life training, and through the eyes of this dark world he peers into the veiled world beyond. Who guides and determines the education which he receives in his world? His teachers here are the group-leaders of the Negro people—the physicians and clergymen, the trained fathers and mothers, the influential and forceful men about him of all kinds; here it is, if at all, that the culture of the surrounding world trickles through and is handed on by the graduates of the higher schools. Can such culture training of group leaders be neglected? Can we afford to ignore it? Do you think that if the leaders of thought among Negroes are not trained and educated thinkers, that they will have no leaders? On the contrary a hundred half-trained demagogues will still hold the places they so largely occupy now, and hundreds of vociferous busy-bodies will multiply. You have no choice; either you must help furnish this race from within its own ranks with thoughtful men of trained leadership, or you must suffer the evil consequences of a headless misguided rabble.

I am an earnest advocate of manual training and trade teaching for black boys, and for white boys, too. I believe that next to the founding of Negro colleges the most valuable addition to Negro education since the war, has been industrial training for black boys. Nevertheless, I insist that the object of all true education is not to make men carpenters, it is to make carpenters men; there are two means of making the carpenter a man, each equally important: the first is to give the group and community in which he works, liberally trained teachers and leaders to teach him and his family what life means; the second is to give him sufficient intelligence and technical skill to make him an efficient workman; the first object demands the Negro college and college-bred men—not a quantity of such colleges, but a few of excellent quality; not too many college-bred men, but enough to leaven the lump, to inspire the masses, to raise the Talented Tenth to leadership; the second object demands a good system of common schools, well-taught, conveniently located and properly equipped.

The Sixth Atlanta Conference truly said in 1901:

"We call the attention of the Nation to the fact that less than one million of the three million Negro children of school age, are at present regularly attending school, and these attend a session which lasts only a few months.

"We are to-day deliberately rearing millions of our citizens in ignorance, and at the same time limiting the rights of citizenship by educational qualifications. This is unjust. Half the black youth of the land have no opportunities open to them for learning to read, write and cipher. In the discussion as to the proper training of Negro children after they leave the public schools, we have forgotten that they are not yet decently provided with public schools.

"Propositions are beginning to be made in the South to reduce the already meager school facilities of Negroes. We congratulate the South on resisting, as much as it has, this pressure, and on the many millions it has spent on Negro education. But it is only fair to point out that Negro taxes and the Negroes' share of the income from indirect taxes and endowments have fully repaid this expenditure, so that the Negro public school system has not in all probability cost the white taxpayers a single cent since the war.

"This is not fair. Negro schools should be a public burden, since they are a public benefit. The Negro has a right to demand good common school training at the hands of the States and the Nation since by their fault he is not in position to pay for this himself."

What is the chief need for the building up of the Negro public school in the South? The Negro race in the South needs teachers to-day above all else. This is the concurrent testimony of all who know the situation. For the supply of this great demand two things are needed—institutions of higher education and money for school houses and salaries. It is usually assumed that a hundred or more institutions for Negro training are to-day turning out so many teachers and college-bred men that the race is threatened with an over-supply. This is sheer nonsense. There are to-day less than 3,000 living Negro college graduates in the United States, and less than 1,000 Negroes in college. Moreover, in the 164 schools for Negroes, 95 per cent. of their students are doing elementary and secondary work, work which should be done in the public schools. Over half the remaining 2,157 students are taking high school studies. The mass of so-called "normal" schools for the Negro, are simply doing elementary common school work, or, at most, high school work, with a little instruction in methods. The Negro colleges and the post-graduate courses at other institutions are the only agencies for the broader and more careful training of teachers. The work of these institutions is hampered for lack of funds. It is getting increasingly difficult to get funds for training teachers in the best modern methods, and yet all over the South, from State Superintendents, county officials, city boards and school principals comes the wail, "We need *Teachers!*" and teachers must be trained. As the fairest minded of all white Southerners, Atticus G. Haygood, once said: "The defects of colored teachers are so great as to create an urgent necessity for training better ones. Their excellencies and their successes are sufficient to justify the best hopes of success in the effort, and to vindicate the judgment of those who make large investments of money and service, to give to colored students opportunity for thoroughly preparing themselves for the work of teaching children of their people."

The truth of this has been strikingly shown in the marked improvement of white teachers in the South. Twenty years ago the rank and file of white public school teachers were not as good as the Negro teachers. But they, by scholarships and good salaries, have been encouraged to thorough normal and collegiate preparation, while the Negro teachers have been discouraged by starvation wages and the idea that any training will do for a black teacher. If carpenters are needed it is well and good to train men as carpenters. But to train men as carpenters, and then set them to teaching is wasteful and criminal; and to train men as teachers and then refuse them living wages, unless they become carpenters, is rank nonsense.

The United States Commissioner of Education says in his report for 1900: "For comparison between the white and colored enrollment in secondary and higher education, I have added together the enrollment in high schools and secondary schools, with the attendance on colleges and universities, not being sure of the actual grade of work done in the colleges and universities. The work done in the secondary schools is reported in such detail in this office, that there can be no doubt of its grade."

He then makes the following comparisons of persons in every million enrolled in secondary and higher education:

Whole Country. Negroes.

1880	4,362	1,289
1900	10,743	2,061

And he concludes: "While the number in colored high schools and colleges had increased somewhat faster than the population, it had not kept pace with the average of the whole country, for it had fallen from 30 per cent. to 24 per cent. of the average quota. Of all colored pupils, one (1) in one hundred was engaged in secondary and higher work, and that ratio has continued substantially for the past twenty years. If the ratio of colored population in secondary and higher education is to be equal to the average for the whole country, it must be increased to five times its present average." And if this be true of the secondary and higher education, it is safe to say that the Negro has not one-tenth his quota in college studies. How baseless, therefore, is the charge of too much training! We need Negro teachers for the Negro common schools, and we need first-class normal schools and colleges to train them. This is the work of higher Negro education and it must be done.

Further than this, after being provided with group leaders of civilization, and a foundation of intelligence in the public schools, the carpenter, in order to be a man, needs technical skill. This calls for trade schools. Now trade schools are not nearly such simple things as people once thought. The original idea was that the "Industrial" school was to furnish education, practically free, to those willing to work for it; it was to "do" things—i.e.: become a center of productive industry, it was to be partially, if not wholly, self-supporting, and it was to teach trades. Admirable as were some of the ideas underlying this scheme, the whole thing simply would not work in practice; it was found that if you were to use time and material to teach trades thoroughly, you could not at the same time keep the industries on a commercial basis and make them pay. Many schools started out to do this on a large scale and went into virtual bankruptcy. Moreover, it was found also that it was possible to teach a boy a trade mechanically, without giving him the full educative benefit of the process, and, vice versa, that there was a distinctive educative value in teaching a boy to use his hands and eyes in carrying out certain physical processes, even though he did not actually learn a trade. It has happened, therefore, in the last decade, that a noticeable change has come over the industrial schools. In the first place the idea of commercially remunerative industry in a school is being pushed rapidly to the back-ground. There are still schools with shops and farms that bring an income, and schools that use student labor partially for the erection of their buildings and the furnishing of equipment. It is coming to be seen, however, in the education of the Negro, as clearly as it has been seen in the education of the youths the world over, that it is the *boy* and not the material product, that is the true object of education. Consequently the object of the industrial school came to be the thorough training of boys regardless of the cost of the training, so long as it was thoroughly well done.

Even at this point, however, the difficulties were not surmounted. In the first place modern industry has taken great strides since the war, and the teaching of trades is no longer a simple matter. Machinery and long processes of work have greatly changed the work of the carpenter, the ironworker and the shoemaker. A really efficient workman must be to-day an intelligent man who has had good technical training in addition to thorough common school, and perhaps even higher training. To meet this situation the industrial schools began a further development; they established distinct Trade Schools for the thorough training of better class artisans, and at the same time they sought to preserve for the purposes of general education, such of the simpler processes of elementary trade learning as were best suited therefor. In this differentiation of the Trade School and manual training, the best of the industrial schools simply followed the plain trend of the present educational epoch. A prominent educator tells us that, in Sweden, "In the beginning the economic conception was generally adopted, and everywhere manual training was looked upon as a means of preparing the children of the common people to earn their living. But gradually it came to be recognized that manual training has a more elevated purpose, and one, indeed, more useful in the deeper meaning of the term. It came to be considered as an educative process for the complete moral, physical and intellectual development of the child."

Thus, again, in the manning of trade schools and manual training schools we are thrown back upon the higher training as its source and chief support. There was a time when any aged and worn-out carpenter could teach in a trade school. But not so to-day. Indeed the demand for college-bred men by a school like Tuskegee, ought to make Mr. Booker T. Washington the firmest friend of higher training. Here he has as helpers the son of a Negro senator, trained in Greek and the humanities, and graduated at Harvard; the son of a Negro congressman and lawyer, trained in Latin and mathematics, and graduated at Oberlin; he has as his wife, a woman who read Virgil and Homer in the same class room with me; he has as college chaplain, a classical graduate of Atlanta University; as teacher of science, a graduate of Fisk; as teacher of history, a graduate of Smith,—indeed some thirty of his chief teachers are college graduates, and instead of studying French grammars in the midst of weeds, or buying pianos for dirty cabins, they are at Mr. Washington's right hand helping him in a noble work. And yet one of the effects of Mr. Washington's propaganda has been to throw doubt upon the expediency of such training for Negroes, as these persons have had.

Men of America, the problem is plain before you. Here is a race transplanted through the criminal foolishness of your fathers. Whether you like it or not the millions are here, and here they will remain. If you do not lift them up, they will pull you down. Education and work are the levers to uplift a people. Work alone will not do it unless inspired by the right ideals and guided by intelligence. Education must not simply teach work—it must teach Life. The Talented Tenth of the Negro race must be made leaders of thought and missionaries of culture among their people. No others can do this work and Negro colleges must train men for it. The Negro race, like all other races, is going to be saved by its exceptional men.

The Disfranchisement
of the Negro
By Charles W. Chesnutt

In this paper the author presents a straightforward statement of facts
concerning the disfranchisement of the Negro in the Southern States. Mr.
Chesnutt, who is too well known as a writer to need any introduction to an
American audience, puts the case for the Negro to the American people very
plainly, and spares neither the North nor the South.

The right of American citizens of African descent, commonly called Negroes, to
vote upon the same terms as other citizens of the United States, is plainly declared
and firmly fixed by the Constitution. No such person is called upon to present
reasons why he should possess this right: that question is foreclosed by the
Constitution. The object of the elective franchise is to give representation. So long
as the Constitution retains its present form, any State Constitution, or statute,
which seeks, by juggling the ballot, to deny the colored race fair representation, is
a clear violation of the fundamental law of the land, and a corresponding injustice
to those thus deprived of this right.

For thirty-five years this has been the law. As long as it was measurably
respected, the colored people made rapid strides in education, wealth, character
and self-respect. This the census proves, all statements to the contrary
notwithstanding. A generation has grown to manhood and womanhood under the
great, inspiring freedom conferred by the Constitution and protected by the right
of suffrage—protected in large degree by the mere naked right, even when its
exercise was hindered or denied by unlawful means. They have developed, in
every Southern community, good citizens, who, if sustained and encouraged by
just laws and liberal institutions, would greatly augment their number with the
passing years, and soon wipe out the reproach of ignorance, unthrift, low morals
and social inefficiency, thrown at them indiscriminately and therefore unjustly,
and made the excuse for the equally undiscriminating contempt of their persons
and their rights. They have reduced their illiteracy nearly 50 per cent. Excluded
from the institutions of higher learning in their own States, their young men hold
their own, and occasionally carry away honors, in the universities of the North.
They have accumulated three hundred million dollars worth of real and personal
property. Individuals among them have acquired substantial wealth, and several
have attained to something like national distinction in art, letters and educational
leadership. They are numerously represented in the learned professions. Heavily
handicapped, they have made such rapid progress that the suspicion is justified
that their advancement, rather than any stagnation or retrogression, is the true
secret of the virulent Southern hostility to their rights, which has so influenced

Northern opinion that it stands mute, and leaves the colored people, upon whom the North conferred liberty, to the tender mercies of those who have always denied their fitness for it.

It may be said, in passing, that the word "Negro," where used in this paper, is used solely for convenience. By the census of 1890 there were 1,000,000 colored people in the country who were half, or more than half, white, and logically there must be, as in fact there are, so many who share the white blood in some degree, as to justify the assertion that the race problem in the United States concerns the welfare and the status of a mixed race. Their rights are not one whit the more sacred because of this fact; but in an argument where injustice is sought to be excused because of fundamental differences of race, it is well enough to bear in mind that the race whose rights and liberties are endangered all over this country by disfranchisement at the South, are the colored people who live in the United States to-day, and not the low-browed, man-eating savage whom the Southern white likes to set upon a block and contrast with Shakespeare and Newton and Washington and Lincoln.

Despite and in defiance of the Federal Constitution, to-day in the six Southern States of Mississippi, Louisiana, Alabama, North Carolina, South Carolina and Virginia, containing an aggregate colored population of about 6,000,000, these have been, to all intents and purposes, denied, so far as the States can effect it, the right to vote. This disfranchisement is accomplished by various methods, devised with much transparent ingenuity, the effort being in each instance to violate the spirit of the Federal Constitution by disfranchising the Negro, while seeming to respect its letter by avoiding the mention of race or color.

These restrictions fall into three groups. The first comprises a property qualification—the ownership of $300 worth or more of real or personal property (Alabama, Louisiana, Virginia and South Carolina); the payment of a poll tax (Mississippi, North Carolina, Virginia); an educational qualification—the ability to read and write (Alabama, Louisiana, North Carolina). Thus far, those who believe in a restricted suffrage everywhere, could perhaps find no reasonable fault with any one of these qualifications, applied either separately or together.

But the Negro has made such progress that these restrictions alone would perhaps not deprive him of effective representation. Hence the second group. This comprises an "understanding" clause—the applicant must be able "to read, or understand when read to him, any clause in the Constitution" (Mississippi), or to read and explain, or to understand and explain when read to him, any section of the Constitution (Virginia); an employment qualification—the voter must be regularly employed in some lawful occupation (Alabama); a character qualification—the voter must be a person of good character and who "understands the duties and obligations of citizens under a republican (!) form of government" (Alabama).

The qualifications under the first group it will be seen, are capable of exact demonstration; those under the second group are left to the discretion and judgment of the registering officer—for in most instances these are all requirements for registration, which must precede voting.

But the first group, by its own force, and the second group, under imaginable conditions, might exclude not only the Negro vote, but a large part of the white vote. Hence, the third group, which comprises: a military service qualification—any man who went to war, willingly or unwillingly, in a good cause or a bad, is entitled to register (Ala., Va.); a prescriptive qualification, under which are included all male persons who were entitled to vote on January 1, 1867, at which date the Negro had not yet been given the right to vote; a hereditary qualification, (the so-called "grandfather" clause), whereby any son (Va.), or descendant (Ala.), of a soldier, and (N.C.) the descendant of any person who had the right to vote on January 1, 1867, inherits that right. If the voter wish to take advantage of these last provisions, which are in the nature of exceptions to a general rule, he must register within a stated time, whereupon he becomes a member of a privileged class of permanently enrolled voters not subject to any of the other restrictions.

It will be seen that these restrictions are variously combined in the different States, and it is apparent that if combined to their declared end, practically every Negro may, under color of law, be denied the right to vote, and practically every white man accorded that right. The effectiveness of these provisions to exclude the Negro vote is proved by the Alabama registration under the new State Constitution. Out of a total, by the census of 1900, of 181,471 Negro "males of voting age," less than 3,000 are registered; in Montgomery county alone, the seat of the State capital, where there are 7,000 Negro males of voting age, only 47 have been allowed to register, while in several counties not one single Negro is permitted to exercise the franchise.

These methods of disfranchisement have stood such tests as the United States Courts, including the Supreme Court, have thus far seen fit to apply, in such cases as have been before them for adjudication. These include a case based upon the "understanding" clause of the Mississippi Constitution, in which the Supreme Court held, in effect, that since there was no ambiguity in the language employed and the Negro was not directly named, the Court would not go behind the wording of the Constitution to find a meaning which discriminated against the colored voter; and the recent case of Jackson vs. Giles, brought by a colored citizen of Montgomery, Alabama, in which the Supreme Court confesses itself impotent to provide a remedy for what, by inference, it acknowledges *may* be a "great political wrong," carefully avoiding, however, to state that it is a wrong, although the vital prayer of the petition was for a decision upon this very point.

Now, what is the effect of this wholesale disfranchisement of colored men, upon their citizenship. The value of food to the human organism is not measured by the pains of an occasional surfeit, but by the effect of its entire deprivation. Whether a class of citizens should vote, even if not always wisely—what class does?—may best be determined by considering their condition when they are without the right to vote.

The colored people are left, in the States where they have been disfranchised, absolutely without representation, direct or indirect, in any law-making body, in any court of justice, in any branch of government—for the feeble remnant of voters left by law is so inconsiderable as to be without a shadow of power. Constituting one-eighth of the population of the whole country, two-fifths of the whole Southern people, and a majority in several States, they are not able, because disfranchised where most numerous, to send one representative to the Congress, which, by the decision in the Alabama case, is held by the Supreme Court to be the only body, outside of the State itself, competent to give relief from a great political wrong. By former decisions of the same tribunal, even Congress is impotent to protect their civil rights, the Fourteenth Amendment having long since, by the consent of the same Court, been in many respects as completely nullified as the Fifteenth Amendment is now sought to be. They have no direct representation in any Southern legislature, and no voice in determining the choice of white men who might be friendly to their rights. Nor are they able to influence the election of judges or other public officials, to whom are entrusted the protection of their lives, their liberties and their property. No judge is rendered careful, no sheriff diligent, for fear that he may offend a black constituency; the contrary is most lamentably true; day after day the catalogue of lynchings and anti-Negro riots upon every imaginable pretext, grows longer and more appalling. The country stands face to face with the revival of slavery; at the moment of this writing a federal grand jury in Alabama is uncovering a system of peonage established under cover of law.

Under the Southern program it is sought to exclude colored men from every grade of the public service; not only from the higher administrative functions, to which few of them would in any event, for a long time aspire, but from the lowest as well. A Negro may not be a constable or a policeman. He is subjected by law to many degrading discriminations. He is required to be separated from white people on railroads and street cars, and, by custom, debarred from inns and places of public entertainment. His equal right to a free public education is constantly threatened and is nowhere equitably recognized. In Georgia, as has been shown by Dr. DuBois, where the law provides for a pro rata distribution of the public school fund between the races, and where the colored school population is 48 per cent. of the total, the amount of the fund devoted to their schools is only 20 per cent. In New Orleans, with an immense colored population, many of whom are persons of means and culture, all colored public schools above the fifth grade have been abolished.

The Negro is subjected to taxation without representation, which the forefathers of this Republic made the basis of a bloody revolution.

Flushed with their local success, and encouraged by the timidity of the Courts and the indifference of public opinion, the Southern whites have carried their campaign into the national government, with an ominous degree of success. If they shall have their way, no Negro can fill any federal office, or occupy, in the public service, any position that is not menial. This is not an inference, but the openly, passionately avowed sentiment of the white South. The right to employment in the public service is an exceedingly valuable one, for which white men have struggled and fought. A vast army of men are employed in the administration of public affairs. Many avenues of employment are closed to colored men by popular prejudice. If their right to public employment is recognized, and the way to it open through the civil service, or the appointing power, or the suffrages of the people, it will prove, as it has already, a strong incentive to effort and a powerful lever for advancement. Its value to the Negro, like that of the right to vote, may be judged by the eagerness of the whites to deprive him of it.

Not only is the Negro taxed without representation in the States referred to, but he pays, through the tariff and internal revenue, a tax to a National government whose supreme judicial tribunal declares that it cannot, through the executive arm, enforce its own decrees, and, therefore, refuses to pass upon a question, squarely before it, involving a basic right of citizenship. For the decision of the Supreme Court in the Giles case, if it foreshadows the attitude which the Court will take upon other cases to the same general end which will soon come before it, is scarcely less than a reaffirmation of the Dred Scott decision; it certainly amounts to this—that in spite of the Fifteenth Amendment, colored men in the United States have no political rights which the States are bound to respect. To say this much is to say that all the privileges and immunities which Negroes henceforth enjoy, must be by favor of the whites; they are not *rights*. The whites have so declared; they proclaim that the country is theirs, that the Negro should be thankful that he has so much, when so much more might be withheld from him. He stands upon a lower footing than any alien; he has no government to which he may look for protection.

Moreover, the white South sends to Congress, on a basis including the Negro population, a delegation nearly twice as large as it is justly entitled to, and one which may always safely be relied upon to oppose in Congress every measure which seeks to protect the equality, or to enlarge the rights of colored citizens. The grossness of this injustice is all the more apparent since the Supreme Court, in the Alabama case referred to, has declared the legislative and political department of the government to be the only power which can right a political wrong. Under this decision still further attacks upon the liberties of the citizen may be confidently expected. Armed with the Negro's sole weapon of defense, the white South stands ready to smite down his rights. The ballot was first given to the Negro to defend him against this very thing. He needs it now far more than then, and for even stronger reasons. The 9,000,000 free colored people of to-day have vastly more to defend than the 3,000,000 hapless blacks who had just emerged from slavery. If there be those who maintain that it was a mistake to give the Negro the ballot at the time and in the manner in which it was given, let them take to heart this reflection: that to deprive him of it to-day, or to so restrict it as to leave him utterly defenseless against the present relentless attitude of the South toward his rights, will prove to be a mistake so much greater than the first, as to be no less than a crime, from which not alone the Southern Negro must suffer, but for which the nation will as surely pay the penalty as it paid for the crime of slavery. Contempt for law is death to a republic, and this one has developed alarming symptoms of the disease.

And now, having thus robbed the Negro of every political and civil *right*, the white South, in palliation of its course, makes a great show of magnanimity in leaving him, as the sole remnant of what he acquired through the Civil War, a very inadequate public school education, which, by the present program, is to be directed mainly towards making him a better agricultural laborer. Even this is put forward as a favor, although the Negro's property is taxed to pay for it, and his labor as well. For it is a well settled principle of political economy, that land and machinery of themselves produce nothing, and that labor indirectly pays its fair proportion of the tax upon the public's wealth. The white South seems to stand to the Negro at present as one, who, having been reluctantly compelled to release another from bondage, sees him stumbling forward and upward, neglected by his friends and scarcely yet conscious of his own strength; seizes him, binds him, and having bereft him of speech, of sight and of manhood, "yokes him with the mule" and exclaims, with a show of virtue which ought to deceive no one: "Behold how good a friend I am of yours! Have I not left you a stomach and a pair of arms, and will I not generously permit you to work for me with the one, that you may thereby gain enough to fill the other? A brain you do not need. We will relieve you of any responsibility that might seem to demand such an organ."

The argument of peace-loving Northern white men and Negro opportunists that the political power of the Negro having long ago been suppressed by unlawful means, his right to vote is a mere paper right, of no real value, and therefore to be lightly yielded for the sake of a hypothetical harmony, is fatally short-sighted. It is precisely the attitude and essentially the argument which would have surrendered to the South in the sixties, and would have left this country to rot in slavery for another generation. White men do not thus argue concerning their own rights. They know too well the value of ideals. Southern white men see too clearly the latent power of these unexercised rights. If the political power of the Negro was a nullity because of his ignorance and lack of leadership, why were they not content to leave it so, with the pleasing assurance that if it ever became effective, it would be because the Negroes had grown fit for its exercise? On the contrary, they have not rested until the possibility of its revival was apparently headed off by new State Constitutions. Nor are they satisfied with this. There is no doubt that an effort will be made to secure the repeal of the Fifteenth Amendment, and thus forestall the development of the wealthy and educated Negro, whom the South seems to anticipate as a greater menace than the ignorant ex-slave. However improbable this repeal may seem, it is not a subject to be lightly dismissed; for it is within the power of the white people of the nation to do whatever they wish in the premises—they did it once; they can do it again. The Negro and his friends should see to it that the white majority shall never wish to do anything to his hurt. There still stands, before the Negro-hating whites of the South, the specter of a Supreme Court which will interpret the Constitution to mean what it says, and what those who enacted it meant, and what the nation, which ratified it, understood, and which will find power, in a nation which goes beyond seas to administer the affairs of distant peoples, to enforce its own fundamental laws; the specter, too, of an aroused public opinion which will compel Congress and the Courts to preserve the liberties of the Republic, which are the liberties of the people. To wilfully neglect the suffrage, to hold it lightly, is to tamper with a sacred right; to yield it for anything else whatever is simply suicidal. Dropping the element of race, disfranchisement is no more than to say to the poor and poorly taught, that they must relinquish the right to defend themselves against oppression until they shall have become rich and learned, in competition with those already thus favored and possessing the ballot in addition. This is not the philosophy of history. The growth of liberty has been the constant struggle of the poor against the privileged classes; and the goal of that struggle has ever been the equality of all men before the law. The Negro who would yield this right, deserves to be a slave; he has the servile spirit. The rich and the educated can, by virtue of their influence, command many votes; can find other means of protection; the poor man has but one, he should guard it as a sacred treasure. Long ago, by fair treatment, the white leaders of the South might have bound the Negro to themselves with hoops of steel. They have not chosen to take this course, but by assuming from the beginning an attitude hostile to his rights, have never gained his confidence, and now seek by foul means to destroy where they have never sought by fair means to control.

I have spoken of the effect of disfranchisement upon the colored race; it is to the race as a whole, that the argument of the problem is generally directed. But the unit of society in a republic is the individual, and not the race, the failure to recognize this fact being the fundamental error which has beclouded the whole discussion. The effect of disfranchisement upon the individual is scarcely less disastrous. I do not speak of the moral effect of injustice upon those who suffer from it; I refer rather to the practical consequences which may be appreciated by any mind. No country is free in which the way upward is not open for every man to try, and for every properly qualified man to attain whatever of good the community life may offer. Such a condition does not exist, at the South, even in theory, for any man of color. In no career can such a man compete with white men upon equal terms. He must not only meet the prejudice of the individual, not only the united prejudice of the white community; but lest some one should wish to treat him fairly, he is met at every turn with some legal prohibition which says, "Thou shalt not," or "Thus far shalt thou go and no farther." But the Negro race is viable; it adapts itself readily to circumstances; and being thus adaptable, there is always the temptation to

"Crook the pregnant hinges of the knee,
Where thrift may follow fawning."

He who can most skillfully balance himself upon the advancing or receding wave of white opinion concerning his race, is surest of such measure of prosperity as is permitted to men of dark skins. There are Negro teachers in the South—the privilege of teaching in their own schools is the one respectable branch of the public service still left open to them—who, for a grudging appropriation from a Southern legislature, will decry their own race, approve their own degradation, and laud their oppressors. Deprived of the right to vote, and, therefore, of any power to demand what is their due, they feel impelled to buy the tolerance of the whites at any sacrifice. If to live is the first duty of man, as perhaps it is the first instinct, then those who thus stoop to conquer may be right. But is it needful to stoop so low, and if so, where lies the ultimate responsibility for this abasement?

I shall say nothing about the moral effect of disfranchisement upon the white people, or upon the State itself. What slavery made of the Southern whites is a matter of history. The abolition of slavery gave the South an opportunity to emerge from barbarism. Present conditions indicate that the spirit which dominated slavery still curses the fair section over which that institution spread its blight.

And now, is the situation remediless? If not so, where lies the remedy? First let us take up those remedies suggested by the men who approve of disfranchisement, though they may sometimes deplore the method, or regret the necessity.

Time, we are told, heals all diseases, rights all wrongs, and is the only cure for this one. It is a cowardly argument. These people are entitled to their rights to-day, while they are yet alive to enjoy them; and it is poor statesmanship and worse morals to nurse a present evil and thrust it forward upon a future generation for correction. The nation can no more honestly do this than it could thrust back upon a past generation the responsibility for slavery. It had to meet that responsibility; it ought to meet this one.

Education has been put forward as the great corrective—preferably industrial education. The intellect of the whites is to be educated to the point where they will so appreciate the blessings of liberty and equality, as of their own motion to enlarge and defend the Negro's rights. The Negroes, on the other hand, are to be so trained as to make them, not equal with the whites in any way—God save the mark! this would be unthinkable!—but so useful to the community that the whites will protect them rather than to lose their valuable services. Some few enthusiasts go so far as to maintain that by virtue of education the Negro will, in time, become strong enough to protect himself against any aggression of the whites; this, it may be said, is a strictly Northern view.

It is not quite clearly apparent how education alone, in the ordinary meaning of the word, is to solve, in any appreciable time, the problem of the relations of Southern white and black people. The need of education of all kinds for both races is woefully apparent. But men and nations have been free without being learned, and there have been educated slaves. Liberty has been known to languish where culture had reached a very high development. Nations do not first become rich and learned and then free, but the lesson of history has been that they first become free and then rich and learned, and oftentimes fall back into slavery again because of too great wealth, and the resulting luxury and carelessness of civic virtues. The process of education has been going on rapidly in the Southern States since the Civil War, and yet, if we take superficial indications, the rights of the Negroes are at a lower ebb than at any time during the thirty-five years of their freedom, and the race prejudice more intense and uncompromising. It is not apparent that educated Southerners are less rancorous than others in their speech concerning the Negro, or less hostile in their attitude toward his rights. It is their voice alone that we have heard in this discussion; and if, as they state, they are liberal in their views as compared with the more ignorant whites, then God save the Negro!

I was told, in so many words, two years ago, by the Superintendent of Public Schools of a Southern city that "there was no place in the modern world for the Negro, except under the ground." If gentlemen holding such opinions are to instruct the white youth of the South, would it be at all surprising if these, later on, should devote a portion of their leisure to the improvement of civilization by putting under the ground as many of this superfluous race as possible?

The sole excuse made in the South for the prevalent injustice to the Negro is the difference in race, and the inequalities and antipathies resulting therefrom. It has nowhere been declared as a part of the Southern program that the Negro, when educated, is to be given a fair representation in government or an equal opportunity in life; the contrary has been strenuously asserted; education can never make of him anything but a Negro, and, therefore, essentially inferior, and not to be safely trusted with any degree of power. A system of education which would tend to soften the asperities and lessen the inequalities between the races would be of inestimable value. An education which by a rigid separation of the races from the kindergarten to the university, fosters this racial antipathy, and is directed toward emphasizing the superiority of one class and the inferiority of another, might easily have disastrous, rather than beneficial results. It would render the oppressing class more powerful to injure, the oppressed quicker to perceive and keener to resent the injury, without proportionate power of defense. The same assimilative education which is given at the North to all children alike, whereby native and foreign, black and white, are taught side by side in every grade of instruction, and are compelled by the exigencies of discipline to keep their prejudices in abeyance, and are given the opportunity to learn and appreciate one another's good qualities, and to establish friendly relations which may exist throughout life, is absent from the Southern system of education, both of the past and as proposed for the future. Education is in a broad sense a remedy for all social ills; but the disease we have to deal with now is not only constitutional but acute. A wise physician does not simply give a tonic for a diseased limb, or a high fever; the patient might be dead before the constitutional remedy could become effective. The evils of slavery, its injury to whites and blacks, and to the body politic, was clearly perceived and acknowledged by the educated leaders of the

South as far back as the Revolutionary War and the Constitutional Convention, and yet they made no effort to abolish it. Their remedy was the same—time, education, social and economic development;—and yet a bloody war was necessary to destroy slavery and put its spirit temporarily to sleep. When the South and its friends are ready to propose a system of education which will recognize and teach the equality of all men before the law, the potency of education alone to settle the race problem will be more clearly apparent.

At present even good Northern men, who wish to educate the Negroes, feel impelled to buy this privilege from the none too eager white South, by conceding away the civil and political rights of those whom they would benefit. They have, indeed, gone farther than the Southerners themselves in approving the disfranchisement of the colored race. Most Southern men, now that they have carried their point and disfranchised the Negro, are willing to admit, in the language of a recent number of the *Charleston Evening Post*, that "the attitude of the Southern white man toward the Negro is incompatible with the fundamental ideas of the republic." It remained for our Clevelands and Abbotts and Parkhursts to assure them that their unlawful course was right and justifiable, and for the most distinguished Negro leader to declare that "every revised Constitution throughout the Southern States has put a premium upon intelligence, ownership of property, thrift and character." So does every penitentiary sentence put a premium upon good conduct; but it is poor consolation to the one unjustly condemned, to be told that he may shorten his sentence somewhat by good behavior. Dr. Booker T. Washington, whose language is quoted above, has, by his eminent services in the cause of education, won deserved renown. If he has seemed, at times, to those jealous of the best things for their race, to decry the higher education, it can easily be borne in mind that his career is bound up in the success of an industrial school; hence any undue stress which he may put upon that branch of education may safely be ascribed to the natural zeal of the promoter, without detracting in any degree from the essential value of his teachings in favor of manual training, thrift and character-building. But Mr. Washington's prominence as an educational leader, among a race whose prominent leaders are so few, has at times forced him, perhaps reluctantly, to express himself in regard to the political condition of his people, and here his utterances have not always been so wise nor so happy. He has declared himself in favor of a restricted suffrage, which at present means, for his own people, nothing less than complete loss of representation—indeed it is only in that connection that the question has been seriously mooted; and he has advised them to go slow in seeking to enforce their civil and political rights, which, in effect, means silent submission to injustice. Southern white men may applaud this advice as wise, because it fits in with their purposes; but Senator McEnery of Louisiana, in a recent article in the *Independent*, voices the Southern white opinion of such acquiescence when he says: "What other race would have submitted so many years to slavery without complaint? *What other race would have submitted so quietly to disfranchisement?* These facts stamp his (the Negro's) inferiority to the white race." The time to philosophize about the good there is in evil, is not while its correction is still possible, but, if at all, after all hope of correction is past. Until then it calls for nothing but rigorous condemnation. To try to read any good thing into these fraudulent Southern constitutions, or to accept them as an accomplished fact, is to condone a crime against one's race. Those who commit crime should bear the odium. It is not a pleasing spectacle to see the robbed applaud the robber. Silence were better.

It has become fashionable to question the wisdom of the Fifteenth Amendment. I believe it to have been an act of the highest statesmanship, based upon the fundamental idea of this Republic, entirely justified by conditions; experimental in its nature, perhaps, as every new thing must be, but just in principle; a choice between methods, of which it seemed to the great statesmen of that epoch the wisest and the best, and essentially the most just, bearing in mind the interests of the freedmen and the Nation, as well as the feelings of the Southern whites; never fairly tried, and therefore, not yet to be justly condemned. Not one of those who condemn it, has been able, even in the light of subsequent events, to suggest a better method by which the liberty and civil rights of the freedmen and their descendants could have been protected. Its abandonment, as I have shown, leaves this liberty and these rights frankly without any guaranteed protection. All the education which philanthropy or the State could offer as a *substitute* for equality of rights, would be a poor exchange; there is no defensible reason why they should not go hand in hand, each encouraging and strengthening the other. The education which one can demand as a right is likely to do more good than the education for which one must sue as a favor.

The chief argument against Negro suffrage, the insistently proclaimed argument, worn threadbare in Congress, on the platform, in the pulpit, in the press, in poetry, in fiction, in impassioned rhetoric, is the reconstruction period. And yet the evils of that period were due far more to the venality and indifference of white men than to the incapacity of black voters. The revised Southern Constitutions adopted under reconstruction reveal a higher statesmanship than any which preceded or have followed them, and prove that the freed voters could as easily have been led into the paths of civic righteousness as into those of misgovernment. Certain it is that under reconstruction the civil and political rights of all men were more secure in those States than they have ever been since. We will hear less of the evils of reconstruction, now that the bugaboo has served its purpose by disfranchising the Negro, it will be laid aside for a time while the nation discusses the political corruption of great cities; the scandalous conditions in Rhode Island; the evils attending reconstruction in the Philippines, and the scandals in the postoffice department—for none of which, by the way, is the Negro charged with any responsibility, and for none of which is the restriction of the suffrage a remedy seriously proposed. Rhode Island is indeed the only Northern State which has a property qualification for the franchise!

There are three tribunals to which the colored people may justly appeal for the protection of their rights: the United States Courts, Congress and public opinion. At present all three seem mainly indifferent to any question of human rights under the Constitution. Indeed, Congress and the Courts merely follow public opinion, seldom lead it. Congress never enacts a measure which is believed to oppose public opinion;—your Congressman keeps his ear to the ground. The high, serene atmosphere of the Courts is not impervious to its voice; they rarely enforce a law contrary to public opinion, even the Supreme Court being able, as Charles Sumner once put it, to find a reason for every decision it may wish to render; or, as experience has shown, a method to evade any question which it cannot decently decide in accordance with public opinion. The art of straddling is not confined to the political arena. The Southern situation has been well described by a colored editor in Richmond: "When we seek relief at the hands of Congress, we are informed that our plea involves a legal question, and we are referred to the Courts. When we appeal to the Courts, we are gravely told that the question is a political one, and that we must go to Congress. When Congress enacts remedial legislation, our enemies take it to the Supreme Court, which promptly declares it unconstitutional." The Negro might chase his rights round and round this circle until the end of time, without finding any relief.

Yet the Constitution is clear and unequivocal in its terms, and no Supreme Court can indefinitely continue to construe it as meaning anything but what it says. This Court should be bombarded with suits until it makes some definite pronouncement, one way or the other, on the broad question of the constitutionality of the disfranchising Constitutions of the Southern States. The Negro and his friends will then have a clean-cut issue to take to the forum of public opinion, and a distinct ground upon which to demand legislation for the enforcement of the Federal Constitution. The case from Alabama was carried to the Supreme Court expressly to determine the constitutionality of the Alabama Constitution. The Court declared itself without jurisdiction, and in the same breath went into the merits of the case far enough to deny relief, without passing upon the real issue. Had it said, as it might with absolute justice and perfect propriety, that the Alabama Constitution is a bold and impudent violation of the Fifteenth Amendment, the purpose of the lawsuit would have been accomplished and a righteous cause vastly strengthened.

But public opinion cannot remain permanently indifferent to so vital a question. The agitation is already on. It is at present largely academic, but is slowly and resistlessly, forcing itself into politics, which is the medium through which republics settle such questions. It cannot much longer be contemptuously or indifferently elbowed aside. The South itself seems bent upon forcing the question to an issue, as, by its arrogant assumptions, it brought on the Civil War. From that section, too, there come now and then, side by side with tales of Southern outrage, excusing voices, which at the same time are accusing voices; which admit that the white South is dealing with the Negro unjustly and unwisely; that the Golden Rule has been forgotten; that the interests of white men alone have been taken into account, and that their true interests as well are being sacrificed. There is a silent white South, uneasy in conscience, darkened in counsel, groping for the light, and willing to do the right. They are as yet a feeble folk, their voices scarcely audible above the clamor of the mob. May their convictions ripen into wisdom, and may their numbers and their courage increase! If the class of Southern white men of whom Judge Jones of Alabama, is so noble a representative, are supported and encouraged by a righteous public opinion at the North, they may, in time, become the dominant white South, and we may then look for wisdom and justice in the place where, so far as the Negro is concerned, they now seem well-nigh strangers. But even these gentlemen will do well to bear in mind that so long as they discriminate in any way against the Negro's equality of right, so long do they set class against class and open the door to every sort of discrimination. There can be no middle ground between justice and injustice, between the citizen and the serf.

It is not likely that the North, upon the sober second thought, will permit the dearly-bought results of the Civil War to be nullified by any change in the Constitution. As long as the Fifteenth Amendment stands, the *rights* of colored citizens are ultimately secure. There were would-be despots in England after the granting of Magna Charta; but it outlived them all, and the liberties of the English people are secure. There was slavery in this land after the Declaration of Independence, yet the faces of those who love liberty have ever turned to that immortal document. So will the Constitution and its principles outlive the prejudices which would seek to overthrow it.

What colored men of the South can do to secure their citizenship to-day, or in the immediate future, is not very clear. Their utterances on political questions, unless they be to concede away the political rights of their race, or to soothe the consciences of white men by suggesting that the problem is insoluble except by some slow remedial process which will become effectual only in the distant future, are received with scant respect—could scarcely, indeed, be otherwise received, without a voting constituency to back them up,—and must be cautiously made, lest they meet an actively hostile reception. But there are many colored men at the North, where their civil and political rights in the main are respected. There every honest man has a vote, which he may freely cast, and which is reasonably sure to be fairly counted. When this race develops a sufficient power of combination, under adequate leadership,—and there are signs already that this time is near at hand,—the Northern vote can be wielded irresistibly for the defense of the rights of their Southern brethren.

In the meantime the Northern colored men have the right of free speech, and they should never cease to demand their rights, to clamor for them, to guard them jealously, and insistently to invoke law and public sentiment to maintain them. He who would be free must learn to protect his freedom. Eternal vigilance is the price of liberty. He who would be respected must respect himself. The best friend of the Negro is he who would rather see, within the borders of this republic one million free citizens of that race, equal before the law, than ten million cringing serfs existing by a contemptuous sufferance. A race that is willing to survive upon any other terms is scarcely worthy of consideration.

The direct remedy for the disfranchisement of the Negro lies through political action. One scarcely sees the philosophy of distinguishing between a civil and a political right. But the Supreme Court has recognized this distinction and has designated Congress as the power to right a political wrong. The Fifteenth Amendment gives Congress power to enforce its provisions. The power would seem to be inherent in government itself; but anticipating that the enforcement of the Amendment might involve difficulty, they made the supererogatory declaration. Moreover, they went further, and passed laws by which they provided for such enforcement. These the Supreme Court has so far declared insufficient. It is for Congress to make more laws. It is for colored men and for white men who are not content to see the blood-bought results of the Civil War nullified, to urge and direct public opinion to the point where it will demand stringent legislation to enforce the Fourteenth and Fifteenth Amendments. This demand will rest in law, in morals and in true statesmanship; no difficulties attending it could be worse than the present ignoble attitude of the Nation toward its own laws and its own ideals—without courage to enforce them, without conscience to change them, the United States presents the spectacle of a Nation drifting aimlessly, so far as this vital, National problem is concerned, upon the sea of irresolution, toward the maelstrom of anarchy.

The right of Congress, under the Fourteenth Amendment, to reduce Southern representation can hardly be disputed. But Congress has a simpler and more direct method to accomplish the same end. It is the sole judge of the qualifications of its own members, and the sole judge of whether any member presenting his credentials has met those qualifications. It can refuse to seat any member who comes from a district where voters have been disfranchised: it can judge for itself whether this has been done, and there is no appeal from its decision.

If, when it has passed a law, any Court shall refuse to obey its behests, it can impeach the judges. If any president refuse to lend the executive arm of the government to the enforcement of the law, it can impeach the president. No such extreme measures are likely to be necessary for the enforcement of the Fourteenth and Fifteenth Amendments—and the Thirteenth, which is also threatened—but they are mentioned as showing that Congress is supreme; and Congress proceeds, the House directly, the Senate indirectly, from the people and is governed by public opinion. If the reduction of Southern representation were to be regarded in the light of a bargain by which the Fifteenth Amendment was surrendered, then it might prove fatal to liberty. If it be inflicted as a punishment and a warning, to be followed by more drastic measures if not sufficient, it would serve a useful purpose. The Fifteenth Amendment declares that the right to vote *shall not* be denied or abridged on account of color; and any measure adopted by Congress should look to that end. Only as the power to injure the Negro in Congress is reduced thereby, would a reduction of representation protect the Negro; without other measures it would still leave him in the hands of the Southern whites, who could safely be trusted to make him pay for their humiliation.

Finally, there is, somewhere in the Universe a "Power that works for righteousness," and that leads men to do justice to one another. To this power, working upon the hearts and consciences of men, the Negro can always appeal. He has the right upon his side, and in the end the right will prevail. The Negro will, in time, attain to full manhood and citizenship throughout the United States. No better guaranty of this is needed than a comparison of his present with his past. Toward this he must do his part, as lies within his power and his opportunity. But it will be, after all, largely a white man's conflict, fought out in the forum of the public conscience. The Negro, though eager enough when opportunity offered, had comparatively little to do with the abolition of slavery, which was a vastly more formidable task than will be the enforcement of the Fifteenth Amendment.

The Negro and the Law
By Wilford H. Smith

The law and how it is dodged by enactments infringing upon the rights guaranteed to the freedmen by constitutional amendment. A powerful plea for justice for the Negro.

The colored people in the United States are indebted to the beneficent provisions of the 13th, 14th and 15th amendments to the Constitution of the United States, for the establishment of their freedom and citizenship, and it is to these mainly they must look for the maintenance of their liberty and the protection of their civil rights. These amendments followed close upon the Emancipation Proclamation issued January 1st, 1863, by President Lincoln, and his call for volunteers, which was answered by more than three hundred thousand negro soldiers, who, during three years of military service, helped the Union arms to victory at Appomattox. Standing in the shadow of the awful calamity and deep distress of the civil war, and grateful to God for peace and victory over the rebellion, the American people, who upheld the Union, rose to the sublime heights of doing justice to the former slaves, who had grown and multiplied with the country from the early settlement at Jamestown. It looked like an effort to pay them back for their years of faithfulness and unrequited toil, by not only making them free but placing them on equal footing with themselves in the fundamental law. Certainly, they intended at least, that they should have as many rights under the Constitution as are given to white naturalized citizens who come to this country from all the nations of Europe.

The 13th amendment provides that neither slavery nor involuntary servitude, except as a punishment for crime, whereof the party shall have been duly convicted, shall exist in the United States or any place subject to their jurisdiction.

The 14th amendment provides in section one, that all persons born or naturalized in the United States and subject to the jurisdiction thereof, are citizens of the United States, and of the State wherein they reside. No State shall make or enforce any law which shall abridge the privileges or immunities of citizens of the United States, nor shall any State deprive any person of life, liberty or property without due process of law, nor deny to any person within its jurisdiction the equal protection of the law.

The 15th amendment provides that the right of citizens of the United States to vote shall not be denied or abridged by the United States, or by any State on account of race, color, or previous condition of servitude.

Chief Justice Waite, in the case of the United States vs. Cruikshank, 92nd U.S. 542, said:—

"The 14th amendment prohibits a State from denying to any person within its jurisdiction the equal protection of the law. The equality of the rights of citizens is a principle of republicanism. Every Republican government is in duty bound to protect all its citizens in the enjoyment of this principle if within its power."

The same Chief Justice, in the case of the United States vs. Reese, 92nd U.S. 214, said:

"The 15th amendment does not confer the right of suffrage upon anyone. It prevents the States or the United States from giving preference in this particular to one citizen of the United States over another, on account of race, color or previous condition of servitude. Before its adoption this could be done. It was as much within the power of a State to exclude citizens of the United States from voting on account of race and color, as it was on account of age, property or education. Now it is not."

Notwithstanding the manifest meaning of equality of citizenship contained in the constitutional amendments, it was found necessary to reinforce them by a civil rights law, enacted by the Congress of the United States, March 1st, 1875, entitled, "An Act To Protect All Citizens In Their Civil and Legal Rights." Its preamble and first section are as follows:—Preamble: "Whereas, it is essential to just government we recognize the equality of all men before the law, and hold that it is the duty of government in its dealings with the people to mete out equal and exact justice to all, of whatever nativity, race, color or persuasion, religious or political, and it being the appropriate object of legislation to enact great fundamental principles into law, therefore,

"Be it enacted that all persons within the jurisdiction of the United States shall be entitled to the full and equal enjoyment of the accommodations, advantages, facilities and privileges of inns, public conveyances on land or water, theaters and other places of public amusement, subject only to the conditions and limitations established by law, and applicable alike to citizens of every race and color, regardless to any previous condition of servitude."

The Supreme Court of the United States has held this salutary law unconstitutional and void as applied to the States, but binding in the District of Columbia, and the Territories over which the government of the United States has control.—Civil Rights cases 109 U.S. 63. Since the Supreme Court's ruling, many Northern and Western States have enacted similar civil rights laws. Equality of citizenship in the United States suffered a severe blow when the civil rights bill was struck down by the Supreme Court. The colored people looked upon the decision as unsound, and prompted by race prejudice. It was clear that the amendments to the Constitution were adopted to secure not only their freedom, but their equal civil rights, and by ratifying the amendments the several States conceded to the Federal government the power and authority of maintaining not alone their freedom, but their equal civil rights in the United States as well.

The Federal Supreme Court put a narrow interpretation on the Constitution, rather than a liberal one in favor of equal rights; in marked contrast to a recent decision of the Appellate Division of the Supreme Court of New York in a civil rights case arising under the statute of New York, Burks vs. Bosso, 81 N.Y. Supp, 384. The New York Supreme Court held this language: "The liberation of the slaves, and the suppression of the rebellion, was supplemented by the amendments to the national Constitution according to the colored people their civil rights and investing them with citizenship. The amendments indicated a clear purpose to secure equal rights to the black people with the white race. The legislative intent must control, and that may be gathered from circumstances inducing the act. Where that intent has been unvaryingly manifested in one direction, and that in the prohibition of any discrimination against a large class of citizens, the courts should not hesitate to keep apace with legislative purpose. We must remember that the slightest trace of African blood places a man under the ban of belonging to that race. However respectable and whatever he may be, he is ostracized socially, and when the policy of the law is against extending the prohibition of his civil rights, a liberal, rather than a narrow interpretation should be given to enactments evidencing the intent to eliminate race discrimination, as far as that can be accomplished by legislative intervention."

The statutory enactments and recent Constitutions of most of the former slave-holding States, show that they have never looked with favor upon the amendments to the national Constitution. They rather regard them as war measures designed by the North to humiliate and punish the people of those States lately in rebellion. While in the main they accept the 13th amendment and concede that the negro should have personal freedom, they have never been altogether in harmony with the spirit and purposes of the 14th and 15th amendments. There seems to be a distinct and positive fear on the part of the South that if the negro is given a man's chance, and is accorded equal civil rights with white men on the juries, on common carriers, and in public places, that it will in some way lead to his social equality. This fallacious argument is persisted in, notwithstanding the well-known fact, that although the Jews are the leaders in the wealth and commerce of the South, their civil equality has never, except in rare instances, led to any social intermingling with the Southern whites.

Holding these views the Southern people in 1875, found means to overcome the Republican majorities in all the re-constructed States, and practically drove the negroes out of the law-making bodies of all those States. So that, now in all the Southern States, so far as can be ascertained, there is not one negro sitting as a representative in any of the law-making bodies. The next step was to deny them representation on the grand and petit juries in the State courts, through Jury Commissioners, who excluded them from the panels.

To be taxed without representation is a serious injustice in a republic whose foundations are laid upon the principle of "no taxation without representation." But serious as this phase of the case must appear, infinitely more serious is the case when we consider the fact that they are likewise excluded from the grand and petit juries in all the State courts, with the fewest and rarest exceptions. The courts sit in judgment upon their lives and liberties, and dispose of their dearest earthly possessions. They are not entitled to life, liberty or property if the courts should decide they are not, and yet in this all-important tribunal they are denied all voice, except as parties and witnesses, and here and there a negro lawyer is permitted to appear. One vote on the grand jury might prevent an indictment, and save disgrace and the risk of public trial; while one vote on the petit jury might save a life or a term of imprisonment, for an innocent person pursued and persecuted by powerful enemies.

With no voice in the making of the laws, which they are bound to obey, nor in their administration by the courts, thus tied and helpless, the negroes were proscribed by a system of legal enactments intended to wholly nullify the letter and spirit of the war amendments to the national organic law. This crusade was begun by enacting a system of Jim-Crow car laws in all the Southern States, so that now the Jim-Crow cars run from the Gulf of Mexico into the national capital. They are called, "Separate Car Laws," providing for separate but equal accommodations for whites and negroes. Though fair on their face, they are everywhere known to discriminate against the colored people in their administration, and were intended to humiliate and degrade them.

Setting apart separate places for negroes on public carriers, is just as repugnant to the spirit and intent of the national Constitution, as would be a law compelling all Jews or all Roman Catholics to occupy compartments specially set apart for them on account of their religion. If these statutes were not especially aimed at the negro, an arrangement of different fares, such as first, second and third classes, would have been far more just and preferable, and would have enabled the refined and exclusive of both races to avoid the presence of the coarse and vicious, by selecting the more expensive fare. Still these laws have been upheld by the Federal Supreme Court, and pronounced not in conflict with the amendments to the Constitution of the United States.

City ordinances providing for separate street cars for white and colored passengers, are in force in Atlanta, New Orleans, and in nearly all the cities of the South. In all the principal cities of Alabama, a certain portion of the street cars is set apart and marked for negroes. The conductors are clothed with the authority of determining to what race the passenger belongs, and may arrest persons refusing to obey his orders. It is often a very difficult task to determine to what race some passengers belong, there being so many dark-white persons that might be mistaken for negroes, and persons known as negroes who are as fair as any white person.

In the State of Georgia, a negro cannot purchase a berth in a sleeping car, under any circumstances, no matter where his destination, owing to the following statute enacted December 20th, 1899: "Sleeping car companies, and all railroads operating sleeping cars in this State, shall separate the white and colored races, and shall not permit them to occupy the same compartment; provided, that nothing in this act shall be construed to compel sleeping car companies or railroads operating sleeping cars, to carry persons of color in sleeping or parlor cars; provided also, that this act shall not apply to colored nurses or servants traveling with their employers." The violation of this statute is a misdemeanor.

Article 45, section 639 of the statutes of Georgia, 1895, makes it a misdemeanor to keep or confine white and colored convicts together, or to chain them together going to and from work. There is also a statute in Georgia requiring that a separate tax list be kept in every county, of the property of white and colored persons. Both races generally approve the laws prohibiting inter-marriages between white and colored persons, which seem to be uniform throughout the Southern States.

Florida seems to have gone a step further than the rest, and by sections 2612 and 2613, Revised Statutes, 1892, it is made a misdemeanor for a white man and a colored woman, and vice versa, to sleep under the same roof at night, occupying the same room. Florida is entitled to credit, however, for a statute making marriages between white and colored persons prior to 1866, where they continue to live together, valid and binding to all intents and purposes.

In addition to this forced separation of the races by law, "from the cradle to the grave," there is yet a sadder and more deplorable separation, in the almost universal disposition to leave the negroes wholly and severely to themselves in their home life and religious life, by the white Christian people of the South, distinctly manifesting no concern in their moral and religious development.

In Georgia and the Carolinas, and all the Gulf States (except Texas, where the farm labor is mostly white) the negroes on the farms are held by a system of laws which prevents them from leaving the plantations, and enables the landlord to punish them by fine and imprisonment for any alleged breach of contract. In the administration of these laws they are virtually made slaves to the landlord, as long as they are in debt, and it is wholly in the power of the landlord to forever keep them in debt.

By section 355, of the Criminal Code of South Carolina, 1902, it is made a misdemeanor to violate a contract to work and labor on a farm, subject to a fine of not less than five dollars, and more than one hundred dollars, or imprisonment for not less than ten days, or more than thirty. It is also made a misdemeanor to employ any farm laborer while under contract with another, or to persuade or entice a farm laborer to leave his employer.

The Georgia laws are a little stronger in this respect than the laws of the other States. By section 121, of the Code of Georgia, 1895, it is provided, "that if any person shall, by offering higher wages, or in any other way entice, persuade or decoy, or attempt to entice, persuade or decoy any farm laborer from his employer, he shall be guilty of a misdemeanor." Again, by act of December 17th, 1901, the Georgia Legislature passed a law making it an offense to rent land, or furnish land to a farm laborer, after he has contracted with another landlord, without first obtaining the consent of the first landlord.

The presence of large numbers of negroes in the towns and cities of the South and North can be accounted for by such laws as the above, administered by ignorant country magistrates, in nearly all cases the pliant tools of the landlords.

The boldest and most open violation of the negro's rights under the Federal Constitution, was the enactment of the grand-father clauses, and understanding clauses in the new Constitutions of Louisiana, Alabama, the Carolinas, and Virginia, which have had the effect to deprive the great body of them of the right to vote in those States, for no other reason than their race and color. Although thus depriving him of his vote, and all voice in the State governments at the South, in all of them his property is taxed to pay pensions to Confederate soldiers, who fought to continue him in slavery. The fact is, the franchise had been practically taken from the negroes in the South since 1876, by admitted fraudulent methods and intimidation in elections, but it was not until late years that this nullification of the amendments was enacted into State Constitutions.

This brings me to the proposition that it is mainly in the enforcement, or the administration of the laws, however fair and equal they may appear on their face, that the constitutional rights of negroes to equal protection and treatment are denied, not only in the South but in many Northern States. There are noble exceptions, however, of high-toned honorable gentlemen on the bench as trial judges, and Supreme Court justices, in the South, who without regard to consequences have stood for fairness and justice to the negro in their courts.

With the population of the South distinctly divided into two classes, not the rich and poor, not the educated and ignorant, not the moral and immoral, but simply whites and blacks, all negroes being generally regarded as inferior and not entitled to the same rights as any white person, it is bound to be a difficult matter to obtain fair and just results, when there is any sort of conflict between the races. The negro realizes this, and knows that he is at an immense disadvantage when he is forced to litigate with a white man in civil matters, and much more so when he is charged with a crime by a white person.

The juries in the South almost always reject the testimony of any number of negroes if given in opposition to that of a white witness, and this is true in many instances, no matter how unreasonable or inconsistent the testimony of the white witness may be. Jurors in the South have been heard to admit that they would be socially ostracized if they brought in a verdict upon colored testimony alone, in opposition to white testimony.

Perhaps it can be best explained how the negro fares in the courts of the South by giving a few cases showing how justice is administered to him:

A negro boy was brought to the bar for trial before a police magistrate, in a Southern capital city, charged with assault and battery on a white boy about the same age, but a little larger. The testimony showed that the white boy had beat the negro on several previous occasions as he passed on his way to school, and each time the negro showed no disposition to fight. On the morning of the charge he attacked the negro and attempted to cut him with a knife, because the negro's mother had reported to the white boy's mother the previous assaults, and asked her to chastise him. The colored boy in trying to keep from being cut was compelled to fight, and got the advantage and threw the white boy down and blacked his eyes. The magistrate on this evidence fined the negro twenty-five dollars. The mother of the negro having once been a servant for the magistrate, found courage to rise, and said: "Jedge, yo Honer, can I speak?" The magistrate replied, "Yes, go on." She said, "Well, Jedge, my boy is ben tellin' me about dis white boy meddlin' him on his way to school, but I would not let my boy fight, 'cause I 'tole him he couldn't git no jestice in law. But he had no other way to go to school 'ceptin' gwine dat way; and den jedge, dis white chile is bigger an my chile and jumped on him fust with a knife for nothin', befo' my boy tetched him. Jedge I am a po' woman, and washes fur a livin', and ain't got nobody to help me, and can't raise all dat money. I think dat white boy's mammy ought to pay half of dis fine." By this time her voice had become stifled by her tears. The judge turned to the mother of the white boy and said, "Madam, are you willing to pay half of this fine?" She answered, "Yes, Your Honor." And the judge changed the order to a fine of $12.50 each, against both boys.

A celebrated case in point reported in the books is, George Maury vs. The State of Miss., 68 Miss. 605. I reproduce the court's statement of the case:—"This is an appeal from the Circuit Court of Kemper County. Appellant was convicted of murder and sentenced to imprisonment for life. He appears in this court without counsel. The facts are briefly these: One, Nicholson, a white man, accompanied by his little son seven years old, was driving an ox team along a public road; he had occasion to stop and the oxen were driven by his son; defendant, a negro, also in an ox wagon, was going along the road in an opposite direction, and met Nicholson's wagon in charge of the little boy. It was after dark, and when the wagons met, according to the testimony of Nicholson, the defendant insultingly demanded of the boy to give the way, and cursed and abused him. Nicholson, hearing the colloquy, hurried to the scene and a fight ensued between him and Maury, in which the latter got the advantage, inflicting severe blows upon Nicholson. This occurred on Thursday, and on the following Sunday night, Nicholson, in company with eleven or twelve of his friends, rode to the farm of Maury, and after sending several of their number to ascertain if he was at home, rode rapidly into his yard and called for him. Not finding him, they proceeded to search the premises, and found several colored men shut up in the smoke house, the door of which some of the searching party had broken open. Maury, the accused, was not found there, and about that time some one called out, "Here is George." Some of the party then started in the direction of the cotton house from which the voice proceeded, when a volley was fired from it, and two of the searching party were killed, one of whom was the son of the former owner of the defendant, and the other a brother-in-law of Nicholson. The members of the raiding party testified that their purpose in going to the home of the defendant was merely to arrest him. It was, however, shown that Nicholson, immediately after the fight on Thursday, informed Cobb, and Cobb between Thursday and Sunday night collected the men who joined in the raid. No affidavit for the arrest of Maury had been made, and none of the party had any warrant, or made any announcement to the defendant or his family, of the object of their visit. The accused who testified in his own behalf, denied that he was at home at the time of the shooting, and says he fled before the raiding party arrived. He also contradicted Nicholson in his account of the difficulty with him, and denies that he spoke harshly to the child." Chief Justice Campbell, in delivering the opinion of the court said, "It is inconceivable that the crime of murder is predicable of the facts disclosed by the evidence in this case. The time and place and circumstances of the killing forbid any such conclusion as a verdict of guilty of murder." The judgment of the trial court was reversed.

This same Chief Justice, in the case of Monroe vs. Mississippi, 71 Miss. 201, where a negro was convicted of rape, makes use of the following brave and noble language, reversing the case on the ground of the insufficiency of the evidence: "We might greatly lighten our labors by deferring in all cases to the verdict approved by the presiding judge as to the facts, but our duty is to administer justice without respect of persons, and do equal right to the poor and the rich. Hence the disposition, which we are not ashamed to confess we have, to guard jealously the rights of the poor and friendless and despised, and to be astute as far as we properly may, against injustice, whether proceeding from wilfulness or indifference."

The country has produced no abler jurist, nor the South no greater man than Ex-Chief Justice Campbell of Mississippi. If the counsel of such men as he and Chief Justice Garret of the Court of Civil Appeals of Texas, could obtain in the South, there would be no problem between the races. All would be contented because justice would be administered to the whites and blacks alike.

In the administration of the suffrage sections under the new Constitutions of the South by the partisan boards of registrars, the same discrimination against negroes was practiced. Their methods are of more or less interest. The plan was to exclude all negroes from the electorate without excluding a single white man. Under the Alabama Constitution, a soldier in the Civil War, either on the Federal or Confederate side, is entitled to qualification. When a negro goes up to register as a soldier he is asked for his discharge. When he presents it he is asked, "How do we know that you are the man whose name is written in this discharge? Bring us two white men whom we know and who will swear that you have not found this paper, and that they know that you were a soldier in the company and regiment in which you claim to have been." This, of course, could not be done, and the ex-soldier who risked his life for the Union is denied the right to vote.

The same Constitution provides that if not a soldier or the legal descendant of one, an elector must be of good character and understand the duties and obligations of citizenship under a Republican form of government. When a negro claims qualifications under the good character and understanding clauses he is put through an examination similar to the following:

"What is a republican form of government?

"What is a limited monarchy?

"What islands did the United States come into possession of by the Spanish-American War?

"What is the difference between Jeffersonian Democracy and Calhoun principles, as compared to the Monroe Doctrine?

"If the Nicaragua Canal is cut, what will be the effect if the Pacific Ocean is two feet higher than the Atlantic?" Should these questions be answered satisfactorily, the negro must still produce two white men known to the registrars to testify to his good character. A remarkable exception in the treatment of negroes by the registrars of Dallas county, Alabama, is shown in the following account taken from the Montgomery Advertizer:—

"An old negro barber by the name of Edward E. Harris, stepped in before the registrars, hat in hand, humble and polite, with a kindly smile on his face. He respectfully asked to be registered. He signed the application and waited a few minutes until the registrars had disposed of some other matters, and being impressed with his respectful bearing, some member of the board commenced to ask a few questions. The old man told his story in a straight forward manner. He said: "Gentlemen, I am getting to be a pretty old man. I was born here in the South, and I followed my young master through all of the campaigns in Virginia, when Mas' Bob Lee made it so warm for the Yankees. But our luck left us at Gettysburg. The Yankees got around in our rear there, and I got a bullet in the back of my head, and one in my leg before I got out of that scrape. But I was not hurt much, and my greatest anxiety was about my young master, Mr. John Holly, who was a member of the Bur Rifles, 18th Mississippi. He was a private and enlisted at Jackson, Miss.

"He could not be found the first day; I looked all among the dead on the battle field for him and he was not there. Next day I got a permit to go through the hospitals, and I looked into the face of every soldier closely, in the hope of finding my young master. After many hours of searching I found him, but he was dangerously wounded. I stayed by his side, wounded as I was, for three long weeks, but he gradually grew worse and then he died. I went out with the body and saw it buried as decently as I could, and then I went back to Jackson and told the young mistress how brave he was in battle, how good he was to me, and told her all the words he had sent her, as he lay there on that rude cot in the hospital. That is my record as a Confederate soldier, and if you gentlemen care to give me a certificate of registration, I would be much obliged to you." It is needless to say that old Ed. Harris got his certificate.

It is insisted upon by the leaders of public opinion at the South, that negroes should not be given equal political and civil rights with white men, defined by law and enforceable by the courts; but that they should be content to strive to deserve the good wishes and friendly feeling of the whites, and if the South is let alone, they will see to it that negroes get becoming treatment.

While there is a large number of the high-toned, chivalrous element of the old master class yet living, who would stand by the negro and not permit him to be wronged if they could prevent it, yet they are powerless to control the great mass of the poor whites who are most bitter in their prejudices against the negro. They should also bear in mind that the old master class is rapidly passing way, and that there is constantly an influx of foreigners to the South, and in less than fifty years the Italians, or some other foreign nationality, may be the ruling class in all the Southern States; and the negro, deprived of all political and civil rights by the

Constitution and laws, would be wholly at the mercy of a people without sympathy for him.

In order to show the fallacy and the wrong and injustice of this doctrine, and how helplessly exposed it leaves the negro to the prejudices of the poor whites, I relate a tragedy in the life of a friend of mine, who was well known and respected in the town of Rayville, Louisiana.

Sewall Smith, for many years ran the leading barber shop for whites in the town of Rayville, and was well-liked and respected by the leading white men of the entire parish. At the suggestion of his customers he bought Louisiana state lands while they were cheap, before the railroad was put through between Vicksburg and Shreveport; and as the road passed near his lands he was thereby made a rich man, as wealth goes in those parts. His good fortune, however, did not swell his head and he remained the same to his friends. He became so useful in his parish that there was never a public gathering of the leading white business men that he was not invited to it, and he was always on the delegations to all the levee or river conventions sent from his parish. He was chosen to such places by white men exclusively; and in his own town he was as safe from wrong or injury, on account of his race or color, as any white man.

After the trains began to run through Rayville, on the Shreveport road, he had occasion to visit the town of Ruston, in another parish some miles in the interior, and as he got off at the depot, a barefoot, poor white boy asked to carry his satchel. Smith was a fine looking mulatto, dressed well, and could have easily been taken for a white man, and the boy might not have known at the time he was a negro. When he arrived at his stopping place he gave the boy such a large coin that he asked permission to take his satchel back to the train on the following day when he was to return. The next day the boy came for the satchel, and they had nearly reached the depot about train time, when they passed a saloon where a crowd of poor whites sat on boxes whittling sticks. The sight of a negro having a white boy carrying his satchel quite enraged them, and after cursing and abusing Smith and the boy, they undertook to kick and assault Smith. Smith defended himself. The result was a shooting affair, in which Smith shot two or three of them and was himself shot. The train rolled up while the fight was in progress, and without inquiring the cause or asking any questions whatever, fully a hundred white men jumped off the train and riddled Smith with bullets. That was the end of it. Nobody was indicted or even arrested for killing an insolent "nigger" that did not keep his place. That is the way the affair was regarded in Ruston. Of course, the people of Rayville very much regretted it, but they could not do anything, and could not afford to defend the rights of a negro against white men under such circumstances, and the matter dropped.

I have preferred not to mention the numerous ways and many instances in which the rights of negroes are denied in public places, and on the common carriers in the South, under circumstances very humiliating and degrading. Nor have I cared to refer to the barbarous and inhuman prison systems of the South, that are worse than anything the imagination can conceive in a civilized and Christian land, as shown by reports of legislative committees.

If the negro can secure a fair and impartial trial in the courts, and can be secure in his life and liberty and property, so as not to be deprived of them except by due process of law, and can have a voice in the making and administration of the laws, he shall have gone a great way in the South. It is to be hoped that public opinion can be awakened to this extent, and that it may assist him to attain that end.

The Characteristics of the Negro People

By H.T. Kealing

A frank statement of the virtues and failings of the race, indicating
very clearly the evils which must be overcome, and the good which must
be developed, if success is really to attend the effort to uplift them.

The characteristics of the Negro are of two kinds—the inborn and the inbred.
As they reveal themselves to us, this distinction may not be seen, but it exists.
Inborn qualities are ineradicable; they belong to the blood; they constitute
individuality; they are independent, or nearly so, of time and habitat. Inbred
qualities are acquired, and are the result of experience. They may be overcome by
a reversal of the process which created them. The fundamental, or inborn,
characteristics of the Negro may be found in the African, as well as the American,
Negro; but the inbred characteristics of the latter belong to the American life
alone.

There is but one human nature, made up of constituent elements the same in
all men, and racial or national differences arise from the predominance of one or
another element in this or that race. It is a question of proportion. The Negro is
not a Caucasian, not a Chinese, not an Indian; though no psychological quality in
the one is absent from the other. The same moral sense, called conscience; the
same love of harmony in color or in sound; the same pleasure in acquiring
knowledge; the same love of truth in word, or of fitness in relation; the same love
of respect and approbation; the same vengeful or benevolent feelings; the same
appetites, belong to all, but in varying proportions. They form the indicia to a
people's mission, and are our best guides to God's purpose in creating us. They
constitute the material to be worked on in educating a race, and suggest in every
case where the stress of civilization or education should be applied in order to
follow the lines of least resistance.

But there are also certain manifestations, the result of training or neglect,
which are not inborn. As they are inculcable, so they are eradicable; and it is only
by a loose terminology that we apply the term characteristics to them without
distinction between them and the inherent traits. In considering the
characteristics of the Negro people, therefore, we must not confuse the
constitutional with the removable. Studied with sympathy and at first hand, the
black man of America will be seen to possess certain predominant idiosyncrasies
of which the following form a fair catalogue:

He is intensely religious. True religion is based upon a belief in the
supernatural, upon faith and feeling. A people deeply superstitious are apt to be
deeply religious, for both rest upon a belief in a spiritual world. Superstition differs

from religion in being the untrained and unenlightened gropings of the human soul after the mysteries of the higher life; while the latter, more or less enlightened, "feels after God, if haply," it may find Him. The Negro gives abundant evidence of both phases. The absolute inability of the master, in the days of slavery, while successfully vetoing all other kinds of convocation, to stop the Negro's church meetings, as well as the almost phenomenal influence and growth of his churches since; and his constant referring of every event, adverse or favorable, to the personal ministrations of the Creator, are things unique and persistent. And the master class reposed more faith in their slaves' religion ofttimes than they did in their own. Doubtless much of the reverential feeling that pervades the American home to-day, above that of all other nations, is the result of the Negro mammy's devotion and loyalty to God.

He is imaginative. This is not evinced so much in creative directions as in poetical, musical, combinatory, inventional and what, if coupled with learning, we call literary imagination. Negro eloquence is proverbial. The crudest sermon of the most unlettered slave abounded in tropes and glowing tongue pictures of apocalyptic visions all his own; and, indeed, the poetic quality of his mind is seen in all his natural efforts when the self-consciousness of education does not stand guard. The staid religious muse of Phillis Wheatley and the rollicking, somewhat jibing, verse of Dunbar show it equally, unpremeditated and spontaneous.

I have heard by the hour some ordinary old uneducated Negro tell those inimitable animal stories, brought to literary existence in "Uncle Remus," with such quaint humor, delicious conceit and masterly delineation of plot, character and incident that nothing but the conventional rating of Aesop's Fables could put them in the same class. Then, there are more Negro inventors than the world supposes. This faculty is impossible without a well-ordered imagination held in leash by a good memory and large perception.

He is affectionate and without vindictiveness. He does not nurse even great wrongs. Mercurial as he is, often furiously angry and frequently in murderous mood, he comes nearer not letting the sun go down upon his anger than any other man I know. Like Brutus, he may be compared to the flint which,

"Much enforced, shows a hasty spark,
And straight is cold again."

His affection is not less towards the Caucasian than to his own race. It is not saying too much to remark that the soul of the Negro yearns for the white man's good will and respect; and the old ties of love that subsisted in so many instances in the days of slavery still survive where the ex-slave still lives. The touching case of a Negro Bishop who returned to the State in which he had been a slave, and rode twenty miles to see and alleviate the financial distress of his former master is an exception to numerous other similar cases only in the prominence of the Negro concerned. I know of another case of a man whose tongue seems dipped in hyssop when he begins to tell of the wrongs of his race, and who will not allow anyone to say in his presence that any good came out of slavery, even incidentally; yet he supports the widowed and aged wife of his former master. And, surely, if these two instances are not sufficient to establish the general proposition, none will gainsay the patience, vigilance, loyalty and helpfulness of the Negro slave during the Civil War, and of his good old wife who nursed white children at her breast at a time when all ties save those of affection were ruptured, and when no protection but devoted hearts watched over the "great house," whose head and master was at the front, fighting to perpetuate slavery. Was it stupidity on the Negro's part? Not at all. He was well informed as to the occurrences of the times. A freemasonry kept him posted as well as the whites were themselves on the course of the war and the issue of each battle. Was it fear that kept him at the old home? Not that, either. Many thousands *did* cross the line to freedom; many other thousands (200,000) fought in the ranks for freedom, but none of them—those who went and those who stayed—those who fought and those who worked,—betrayed a trust, outraged a female, or rebelled against a duty. It was love, the natural wellings of affectionate natures.

He has great endurance, both dispositional and physical. So true is the first that his patience has been the marvel of the world; and, indeed, many, regarding this trait manifested in such an unusual degree, doubted the Negro's courage, till the splendid record of the '60's and the equal, but more recent, record of the '90's, wrote forbearance as the real explanation of an endurance seemingly so at variance with manly spirit.

Of his physical powers, his whole record as a laborer at killing tasks in the most trying climate in America speaks so eloquently that nothing but the statistics of cotton, corn, rice, sugar, railroad ties and felled forests can add to the praise of this burden-bearer of the nation. The census tables here are more romantic and thrilling than figures of rhetoric.

He is courageous. His page in the war record of this country is without blot or blemish. His commanders unite in pronouncing him admirable for courage in the field, commendable for obedience in camp. That he should exhibit such excellent fighting qualities as a soldier, and yet exercise the forbearance that characterizes him as a citizen, is remarkable.

He is cheerful. His ivories are as famous as his songs. That the South is "sunny" is largely due to the brightness his rollicking laugh and unfailing good nature bring to it. Though the mudsill of the labor world, he whistles as he hoes, and no dark broodings or whispered conspirings mar the cheerful acceptance of the load he bears. Against the rubber bumper of his good cheer things that have crushed and maddened others rebound without damage. When one hears the quaint jubilee songs, set to minor cadence, he might suppose them the expressions of a melancholy people. They are not to be so interpreted. Rather are they the expression of an experience, not a nature. Like the subdued voice of a caged bird, these songs are the coinage of an occasion, and not the free note of nature. The slave sang of griefs he was not allowed to discuss, hence his songs. This cheerfulness has enabled the Negro to live and increase under circumstances which, in all other instances, have decimated, if not exterminated, inferior peoples. His plasticity to mauling forces and his resiliency against crushing ones come from a Thalian philosophy, unconscious and unstudied, that extracts Epicurean delights from funeral meats.

The above traits are inborn and fundamental, belonging to the race everywhere, in Africa as well as America. Strict correctness requires, however, that attention be called to the fact that there are tribal differences among African Negroes that amount almost to the national variations of Europe; and these are reflected in American Negroes, who are the descendants of these different tribes. There is as much difference between the Mandingo and the Hottentot, both black, as between the Italian and the German, both white; or between the Bushman and the Zulu, both black, as between the Russian and the Englishman, both white.

Scientific exactness, therefore, would require a closer analysis of racial characteristics than an article of this length could give; but, speaking in a large way, it may be said that in whatever outward conformity may come to the race in America by reason of training or contact, these traits will lie at the base, the very warp and woof of his soul texture.

If, now, we turn to consider his inbred traits, those the result of experience, conditions and environments, we find that they exist mainly as deficiencies and deformities. These have been superimposed upon the native soul endowment. Slavery has been called the Negro's great schoolmaster, because it took him a savage and released him civilized; took him a heathen and released him a Christian; took him an idler and released him a laborer. Undoubtedly it did these things superficially, but one great defect is to be charged against this school—it did not teach him the meaning of home, purity and providence. To do this is the burden of freedom.

The emancipated Negro struggles up to-day against many obstacles, the entailment of a brutal slavery. Leaving out of consideration the many who have already emerged, let us apply our thoughts to the great body of submerged people in the congested districts of city and country who present a real problem, and who must be helped to higher things. We note some of the heritages under which they stagger up into full development:

Shiftlessness. He had no need to devise and plan in bondage. There was no need for an enterprising spirit; consequently, he is lacking in leadership and self-reliance. He is inclined to stay in ruts, and applies himself listlessly to a task, feeling that the directive agency should come from without.

Incontinence. It is not to the point to say that others are, too. Undoubtedly, example has as much to do with this laxity as neglect. We simply record the fact. A slave's value was increased by his prolificacy. Begetting children for the auction block could hardly sanctify family ties. It was not nearly so necessary for a slave to know his father as his owner. Added to the promiscuity encouraged and often forced among this class, was the dreadful license which cast lustful Caucasian eyes upon "likely" Negro women.

Indolence. Most men are, especially in a warm climate: but the Negro acquired more than the natural share, because to him as a bondman laziness was great gain, for he had no pecuniary interest in his own labor. Hence, holidays were more to be desired than whole labor days, and he learned to do as little as he might, be excused as often as he could, and hail Saturday as the oasis in a desert week. He hails it yet. The labor efficiency of the Negro has greatly increased since the emancipation, for self-interest is a factor now. In 1865, each Negro produced two-thirds of a bale of cotton; now he produces an average of one whole bale to the man. But there is still woeful waste of productive energy. A calculation showing the comparative productive capacity, man for man, between the Northern and Southern laborer would be very interesting.

Improvidence and Extravagance. He will drop the most important job to go on an excursion or parade with his lodge. He spends large sums on expensive clothing and luxuries, while going without things necessary to a real home. He will cheerfully eat fat bacon and "pone" corn-bread all the week in order to indulge in unlimited soda-water, melon and fish at the end. In the cities he is oftener seen dealing with the pawn-broker than the banker. His house, when furnished at all, is better furnished that that of a white man of equal earning power, but it is on the installment plan. He is loath to buy a house, because he has no taste for responsibility nor faith in himself to manage large concerns; but organs, pianos, clocks, sewing-machines and parlor suits, on time, have no terrors for him. This is because he has been accustomed to think in small numbers. He does not regard the Scotchman's "mickle," because he does not stop to consider that the end is a "muckle." He has amassed, at full valuation, nearly a billion dollars' worth of property, despite this, but this is about one-half of what proper providence would have shown.

Untidiness. Travel through the South and you will be struck with the general misfit and dilapidated appearance of things. Palings are missing from the fences, gates sag on single hinges, houses are unpainted, window panes are broken, yards unkempt and the appearance of a squalor greater than the real is seen on every side. The inside of the house meets the suggestions of the outside. This is a projection of the slave's "quarters" into freedom. The cabin of the slave was, at best, a place to eat and sleep in; there was no thought of the esthetic in such places. A quilt on a plank was a luxury to the tired farm-hand, and paint was nothing to the poor, sun-scorched fellow who sought the house for shade rather than beauty. Habits of personal cleanliness were not inculcated, and even now it is the exception to find a modern bath-room in a Southern home.

Dishonesty. This is the logic, if not the training, of slavery. It is easy for the unrequited toiler in another's field to justify reprisal; hence there arose among the Negroes an amended Commandment which added to "Thou shalt not steal" the clause, "except thou be stolen from." It was no great fault, then, according to this code, to purloin a pig, a sheep, a chicken, or a few potatoes from a master who took all from the slave.

Untruthfulness. This is seen more in innocent and childish exaggeration than in vicious distortion. It is the vice of untutored minds to run to gossip and make miracles of the matter-of-fact. The Negro also tells falsehoods from excess of good nature. He promises to do a piece of work on a certain day, because it is so much easier and pleasanter to say Yes, and stay away, than it is to say No.

Business Unreliability. He does not meet a promise in the way and at the time promised. Not being accustomed to business, he has small conception of the place the promise has in the business world. It is only recently he has begun to deal with banks. He, who has no credit, sees no loss of it in a protested note, especially if he intends to pay it some time. That chain which links one man's obligation to another man's solvency he has not considered. He is really as good and safe a debt-payer when he owes a white man as the latter can have, but the methods of the modern bank, placing a time limit on debts, is his detestation. He much prefers the *laissez-faire* of the Southern plantation store.

Lack of Initiative. It was the policy of slavery to crush out the combining instinct, and it was well done; for, outside of churches and secret societies, the Negro has done little to increase the social efficiency which can combine many men into an organic whole, subject to the corporate will and direction. He has, however, made some hopeful beginnings.

Suspicion of his own race. He was taught to watch other Negroes and tell all that they did. This was slavery's native detective force to discover incipient insurrection. Each slave learned to distrust his fellow. And added to this is the knowledge one Negro has that no other has had half sufficient experience in business to be a wise counselor, or a safe steward of another man's funds. Almost all Negroes who have acquired wealth have entrusted its management to white men.

Ignorance. The causes of his ignorance all know. That he has thrown off one-half of it in forty years is a wonderful showing; but a great incubus remains in the other half, and it demands the nation's attention. What the census calls literacy is often very shallow. The cause of this shallowness lies, in part, in the poor character and short duration of Southern schools; in the poverty that snatches the child from school prematurely to work for bread; in the multitude of mushroom colleges and get-smart-quick universities scattered over the South, and in the glamour of a professional education that entices poorly prepared students into special work.

Add to this, too, the commercialism of the age which regards each day in school as a day out of the market. Boys and girls by scores learn the mechanical parts of type-writing and stenography without the basal culture which gives these callings their greatest efficiency. They copy a manuscript, Chinese-like, mistakes and all; they take you phonetically in sense as well as sound, having no reserve to draw upon to interpret a learned allusion or unusual phrase. Thus while prejudice makes it hard to secure a place, auto-deficiency loses many a one that is secured.

We have discussed the leading characteristics of the Negro, his inborn excellencies and inbred defects, candidly and as they are to be seen in the great mass whose place determines the status of the race as a whole. It would, however, be to small purpose if we did not ask what can be done to develop the innate good and correct the bad in a race so puissant and numerous? This mass is not inert; it has great reactionary force, modifying and influencing all about it. The Negro's excellences have entered into American character and life already; so have his weaknesses. He has brought cheer, love, emotion and religion in saving measure to the land. He has given it wealth by his brawn and liberty by his blood. His self-respect, even in abasement, has kept him struggling upward; his confidence in his own future has infected his friends and kept him from nursing despondency or planning anarchy. But he has laid, and does lay, burdens upon the land, too: his ignorance, his low average of morality, his low standards of home, his lack of enterprise, his lack of self-reliance—these must be cured.

Evidently, he is to be "solved" by educational processes. Everyone of his inborn traits must be respected and developed to proper proportion. Excesses and excrescences must not be carelessly dealt with, for they mark the fertility of a soil that raises rank weeds because no gardener has tilled it. His religion must become "ethics touched with feeling"—not a paroxysm, but a principle. His imagination must be given a rudder to guide its sails; and the first fruits of its proper exercise, as seen in a Dunbar, a Chesnutt, a Coleridge-Taylor and a Tanner, must be pedestaled along the Appian Way over which others are to march. His affection must be met with larger love; his patience rewarded with privilege; his courage called to defend the rights of others rather than redress his own wrongs. Thus shall he supplement from within the best efforts of good men without.

To cure the evils entailed upon him by an unhappy past, he must be educated to work with skill, with self-direction, in combination and unremittingly. Industrial education with constant application, is the slogan of his rise from racial pauperism to productive manliness. Not that exceptional minds should not have exceptional opportunities (and they already exist); but that the great majority of awkward and unskilled ones, who must work somehow, somewhere, all the time, shall have their opportunities for training in industrial schools near them and with courses consonant with the lives they are to lead. Let the ninety and nine who must work, either with trained or fumbling hands, have a chance. Train the

Negro to accept and carry responsibility by putting it upon him. Train him, more than any schools are now doing, in morals—to speak the truth, to keep a promise, to touch only his own property, to trust the trustworthy among his own race, to risk something in business, to strike out in new lines of endeavor, to buy houses and make homes, to regard beauty as well as utility, to save rather than display. In short, let us subordinate mere knowledge to the work of invigorating the will, energizing productive effort and clarifying moral vision. Let us make safe men rather than vociferous mountebanks; let us put deftness in daily labor above sleight-of-hand tricks, and common sense, well trained, above classical smatterings, which awe the multitude but butter no parsnips.

If we do this, America will have enriched her blood, ennobled her record and shown the world how to deal with its Dark Races without reproach.

Representative American Negroes

By Paul Laurence Dunbar

An enumeration of some of the noteworthy American Negroes of to-day and yesterday, with some account of their lives and their work. In this paper Mr. Dunbar has turned out his largest and most successful picture of the colored people. It is a noble canvas crowded with heroic figures.

In considering who and what are representative Negroes there are circumstances which compel one to question what is a representative man of the colored race. Some men are born great, some achieve greatness and others lived during the reconstruction period. To have achieved something for the betterment of his race rather than for the aggrandizement of himself, seems to be a man's best title to be called representative. The street corner politician, who through questionable methods or even through skillful manipulation, succeeds in securing the janitorship of the Court House, may be written up in the local papers as "representative," but is he?

I have in mind a young man in Baltimore, Bernard Taylor by name, who to me is more truly representative of the race than half of the "Judges," "Colonels," "Doctors" and "Honorables" whose stock cuts burden the pages of our negro journals week after week. I have said that he is young. Beyond that he is quiet and unobtrusive; but quiet as he is, the worth of his work can be somewhat estimated when it is known that he has set the standard for young men in a city that has the largest colored population in the world.

It is not that as an individual he has ridden to success one enterprise after another. It is not that he has shown capabilities far beyond his years, nor yet that his personal energy will not let him stop at one triumph. The importance of him lies in the fact that his influence upon his fellows is all for good, and in a large community of young Negroes the worth of this cannot be over-estimated. He has taught them that striving is worth while, and by the very force of his example of industry and perseverance, he stands out from the mass. He does not tell how to do things, he does them. Nothing has contributed more to his success than his alertness, and nothing has been more closely followed by his observers, and yet I sometimes wonder when looking at him, how old he must be, how world weary, before the race turns from its worship of the political janitor and says of him, "this is one of our representative men."

This, however, is a matter of values and neither the negro himself, his friends, his enemies, his lauders, nor his critics has grown quite certain in appraising these. The rabid agitator who goes about the land preaching the independence and glory of his race, and by his very mouthings retarding both, the saintly missionary, whose only mission is like that of "Pooh Bah," to be insulted; the man of the cloth who thunders against the sins of the world and from whom honest women draw away their skirts, the man who talks temperance and tipples high-balls—these are not representative, and whatever their station in life, they should be rated at their proper value, for there is a difference between attainment and achievement.

Under the pure light of reason, the ignorant carpet bagger judge is a person and not a personality. The illiterate and inefficient black man, whom circumstance put into Congress, was "a representative" but was not representative. So the peculiar conditions of the days immediately after the war have made it necessary to draw fine distinctions.

When Robert Smalls, a slave, piloted the Confederate ship Planter out of Charleston Harbor under the very guns of the men who were employing him, who owned him, his body, his soul, and the husk of his allegiance, and brought it over to the Union, it is a question which forty years has not settled as to whether he was a hero or a felon, a patriot or a traitor. So much has been said of the old Negro's fidelity to his masters that something different might have been expected of him. But take the singular conditions: the first faint streaks of a long delayed dawn had just begun to illumine the sky and this black pilot with his face turned toward the East had no eye for the darkness behind him. He had no time to analyze his position, the right or wrong of it. He had no opportunity to question whether it was loyalty to a union in which he aspired to citizenship, or disloyalty to his masters of the despised confederacy. It was not a time to argue, it was a time to do; and with rare power of decision, skill of action and with indomitable courage, he steered the good ship Planter past Fort Johnson, past Fort Sumter, past Morris Island, out where the flag, the flag of his hopes and fears floated over the federal fleet. And Robert Smalls had done something, something that made him loved and hated, praised and maligned, revered and despised, but something that made him representative of the best that there is in sturdy Negro manhood.

It may seem a far cry from Robert Smalls, the pilot of the Planter, to Booker T. Washington, Principal of the Institute at Tuskegee, Alabama. But much the same traits of character have made the success of the two men; the knowledge of what to do, the courage to do it, and the following out of a single purpose. They are both pilots, and the waters through which their helms have swung have been equally stormy. The methods of both have been questioned; but singularly neither one has stopped to question himself, but has gone straight on to his goal over the barriers of criticism, malice and distrust. The secret of Mr. Washington's power is organization, and organization after all is only a concentration of force. This concentration only expresses his own personality, in which every trait and quality tend toward one definite end. They say of this man that he is a man of one idea, but that one is a great one and he has merely concentrated all his powers upon it; in other words he has organized himself and gone forth to gather in whatever about him was essential.

Pilot he is, steadfast and unafraid, strong in his own belief,—yes strong enough to make others believe in him. Without doubt or skepticism, himself he has confounded the skeptics.

Less statesmanlike than Douglass, less scholarly than DuBois, less eloquent than the late J.C. Price, he is yet the foremost figure in Negro national life. He is a great educator and a great man, and though one may not always agree with him, one must always respect him. The race has produced no more adroit diplomatist than he. The statement is broad but there is no better proof of it than the fact that while he is our most astute politician, he has succeeded in convincing both himself and the country that he is not in politics. He has none of the qualities of the curb-stone politician. He is bigger, broader, better, and the highest compliment that could be paid him is that through all his ups and downs, with all he has seen of humanity, he has kept his faith and his ideals. While Mr. Washington stands pre-eminent in his race there are other names that must be mentioned with him as co-workers in the education of the world, names that for lack of time can be only mentioned and passed.

W.H. Council, of Normal, Alabama, has been doing at his school a good and great work along the same lines as Tuskegee. R.R. Wright, of the State College of Georgia, "We'se a-risin' Wright," he is called, and by his own life and work for his people he has made true the boyish prophecy which in the old days inspired Whittier's poem. Three decades ago this was his message from the lowly South, "Tell 'em we'se a-risin'," and by thought, by word, by deed, he has been "Tellin' em so" ever since. The old Southern school has melted into the misty shades of an unregretted past. A new generation, new issues, new conditions, have replaced the old, but the boy who sent that message from the heart of the Southland to the North's heart of hearts has risen, and a martyred President did not blush to call him friend.

So much of the Negro's time has been given to the making of teachers that it is difficult to stop when one has begun enumerating some of those who have stood out more than usually forceful. For my part, there are two more whom I cannot pass over. Kelly Miller, of Howard University, Washington, D.C., is another instructor far above the average. He is a mathematician and a thinker. The world has long been convinced of what the colored man could do in music and in oratory, but it has always been skeptical, when he is to be considered as a student of any exact science. Miller, in his own person, has settled all that. He finished at Johns Hopkins where they will remember him. He is not only a teacher but an author who writes with authority upon his chosen themes, whether he is always known as a Negro writer or not. He is endowed with an accurate, analytical mind, and the most engaging blackness, for which some of us thank God, because there can be no argument as to the source of his mental powers.

Now of the other, William E.B. DuBois, what shall be said? Educator and author, political economist and poet, an Eastern man against a Southern back-ground, he looms up strong, vivid and in bold relief. I say looms advisedly, because, intellectually, there is something so distinctively big about the man. Since the death of the aged Dr. Crummell, we have had no such ripe and finished scholar. Dr. DuBois, Harvard gave him to us, and there he received his Ph.D., impresses one as having reduced all life and all literature to a perfect system. There is about him a fascinating calm of certain power, whether as a searcher after economic facts, under the wing of the University of Pennsylvania, or defying the "powers that be" in a Negro college or leading his pupils along the way of light, one always feels in him this same sense of conscious, restrained, but assured force.

Some years ago in the course of his researches, he took occasion to tell his own people some plain hard truths, and oh, what a howl of protest and denunciation went up from their assembled throats, but it never once disturbed his magnificent calm. He believed what he had said, and not for a single moment did he think of abandoning his position.

He goes at truth as a hard-riding old English squire would take a difficult fence. Let the ditch be beyond if it will.

Dr. DuBois would be the first to disclaim the name of poet but everything outside of his statistical work convicts him. The rhythm of his style, his fancy, his imagery, all bid him bide with those whose souls go singing by a golden way. He has written a number of notable pamphlets and books, the latest of which is "The Soul of the Black Folk," an invaluable contribution to the discussion of the race problem by a man who knows whereof he speaks.

Dr. DuBois is at Atlanta University and has had every opportunity to observe all the phases of America's great question, and I wish I might write at length of his books.

It may be urged that too much time has already been taken up with the educational side of the Negro, but the reasonableness of this must become apparent when one remembers that for the last forty years the most helpful men of the race have come from the ranks of its teachers, and few of those who have finally done any big thing, but have at some time or other held the scepter of authority in a school. They may have changed later and grown, indeed they must have done so, but the fact remains that their poise, their discipline, the impulse for their growth came largely from their work in the school room.

There is perhaps no more notable example of this phase of Negro life than the Hon. Richard Theodore Greener, our present Consul at Vladivostok. He was, I believe, the first of our race to graduate from Harvard and he has always been regarded as one of the most scholarly men who, through the touch of Negro blood, belongs to us. He has been historian, journalist and lecturer, but back of all this he was a teacher; and for years after his graduation he was a distinguished professor at the most famous of all the old Negro colleges. This institution is now a thing of the past, but the men who knew it in its palmy days speak of it still with longing and regret. It is claimed, and from the names and qualities of the men, not without justice, that no school for the higher education of the black man has furnished a finer curriculum or possessed a better equipped or more efficient faculty. Among these, Richard T. Greener was a bright, particular star.

After the passing of the school, Mr. Greener turned to other activities. His highest characteristics were a fearless patience and a hope that buoyed him up through days of doubt and disappointment. Author and editor he was, but he was not satisfied with these. Beyond their scope were higher things that beckoned him. Politics, or perhaps better, political science, allured him, and he applied himself to a course that brought him into intimate contact with the leaders of his country, white and black. A man of wide information, great knowledge and close grasp of events he made himself invaluable to his party and then with his usual patience awaited his reward.

The story of how he came to his own cannot be told without just a shade of bitterness darkening the smile that one must give to it all. The cause for which he had worked triumphed. The men for whom he had striven gained their goal and now, Greener must be recognized, but—

Vladivostok, your dictionary will tell you, is a sea-port in the maritime Province of Siberia, situated on the Golden Horn of Peter the Great. It will tell you also that it is the chief Russian naval station on the Pacific. It is an out of the way place and one who has not the world-circling desire would rather hesitate before setting out thither. It was to this post that Mr. Greener was appointed.

"Exile," his friends did not hesitate to say. "Why didn't the Government make it a sentence instead of veiling it in the guise of an appointment?" asked others sarcastically.

"Will he go?" That was the general question that rose and fell, whispered and thundered about the new appointee, and in the midst of it all, silent and dignified, he kept his council. The next thing Washington knew he was gone. There was a gasp of astonishment and then things settled back into their former state of monotony and Greener was forgotten.

But in the eastern sky, darkness began to arise, the warning flash of danger swept across the heavens, the thunder drum of war began to roll. For a moment the world listened in breathless suspense, the suspense of horror. Louder and louder rose the thunder peal until it drowned every other sound in the ears of the nation, every other sound save the cries and wails of dying women and the shrieks of tortured children. Then France, England, Germany, Japan and America marshaled their forces and swept eastward to save and to avenge. The story of the Boxer uprising has been told, but little has been said of how Vladivostok, "A sea-port in the maritime Province of Siberia," became one of the most important points of communication with the outside world, and its Consul came frequently to be heard from by the State Department. And so Greener after years of patience and toil had come to his own. If the government had wished to get him out of the way, it had reckoned without China.

A new order of things has come into Negro-American politics and this man has become a part of it. It matters not that he began his work under the old regime. So did Judge Gibbs, a man eighty years of age, but he, too, has kept abreast of the times, and although the reminiscences in his delightful autobiography take one back to the hazy days when the land was young and politics a more strenuous thing than it is even now, when there was anarchy in Louisiana and civil war in Arkansas, when one shot first and questioned afterward; yet because his mind is still active, because he has changed his methods with the changing time, because his influence over young men is greatly potent still; he is, in the race, perhaps, the best representative of what the old has brought to the new.

Beside him strong, forceful, commanding, stands the figure of George H. White, whose farewell speech before the Fifty-sixth Congress, when through the disfranchisement of Negroes he was defeated for re-election, stirred the country and fired the hearts of his brothers. He has won his place through honesty, bravery and aggressiveness. He has given something to the nation that the nation needed, and with such men as Pinchback, Lynch, Terrell and others of like ilk, acting in concert, it is but a matter of time when his worth shall induce a repentant people, with a justice built upon the foundation of its old prejudice, to ask the Negro back to take a hand in the affairs of state.

Add to all this the facts that the Negro has his representatives in the commercial world: McCoy and Granville T. Woods, inventors; in the agricultural world with J.H. Groves, the potato king of Kansas, who last year shipped from his own railway siding seventy-two thousand five hundred bushels of potatoes alone; in the military, with Capt. Charles A. Young, a West Pointer, now stationed at the Presidio; that in medicine, he possesses in Daniel H. Williams, of Chicago, one of the really great surgeons of the country; that Edward H. Morris, a black man, is one of the most brilliant lawyers at the brilliant Cook County bar; that in every walk of life he has men and women who stand for something definite and concrete, and it seems to me that there can be little doubt that the race problem will gradually solve itself.

I have spoken of "men and women," and indeed the women must not be forgotten, for to them the men look for much of the inspiration and impulse that drives them forward to success. Mrs. Mary Church Terrell upon the platform speaking for Negro womanhood and Miss Sarah Brown, her direct opposite, a little woman sitting up in her aerie above a noisy New York street, stand for the very best that there is in our mothers, wives and sisters. The one fully in the public eye, with learning and eloquence, telling the hopes and fears of her kind; the other in suffering and retirement, with her knowledge of the human heart and her gentleness inspiring all who meet her to better and nobler lives. They are both doing their work bravely and grandly. But when the initiate ask who is "la Petite Reine," we think of the quiet little woman in a New York fifth floor back and are silent.

She is a patron of all our literature and art and we have both. Whether it is a new song by Will Marion Cook or a new book by DuBois or Chestnut, than whom no one has ever told the life of the Negro more accurately and convincingly, she knows it and has a kindly word of praise or encouragement.

In looking over the field for such an article as this, one just begins to realize how many Negroes are representative of something, and now it seems that in closing no better names could be chosen than those of the two Tanners.

From time immemorial, Religion and Art have gone together, but it remained for us to place them in the persons of these two men, in the relation of father and son. Bishop Benj. Tucker Tanner, of the A.M.E. Church, is not only a theologian and a priest, he is a dignified, polished man of the higher world and a poet. He has succeeded because he was prepared for success. As to his writings, he will, perhaps, think most highly of "His Apology For African Methodism;" but some of us, while respecting this, will turn from it to the poems and hymns that have sung themselves out of his gentle heart.

Is it any wonder that his son, Henry O. Tanner, is a poet with the brush or that the French Government has found it out? From the father must have come the man's artistic impulse, and he carried it on and on to a golden fruition. In the Luxembourg gallery hangs his picture, "The Raising of Lazarus." At the Academy of Fine Arts, Philadelphia, I saw his "Annunciation," both a long way from his "Banjo Lesson," and thinking of him I began to wonder whether, in spite of all the industrial tumult, it were not in the field of art, music and literature that the Negro was to make his highest contribution to American civilization. But this is merely a question which time will answer.

All these of whom I have spoken are men who have striven and achieved and the reasons underlying their success are the same that account for the advancement of men of any other race: preparation, perseverance, bravery, patience, honesty and the power to seize the opportunity.

It is a little dark still, but there are warnings of the day and somewhere out of the darkness a bird is singing to the Dawn.

The Negro's Place in American Life at the Present Day

By T. Thomas Fortune

Considering the two hundred and forty-five years of his slavery and the comparatively short time he has enjoyed the opportunities of freedom, his place in American life at the present day is creditable to him and promising for the future.

There can be no healthy growth in the life of a race or a nation without a self-reliant spirit animating the whole body; if it amounts to optimism, devoid of egotism and vanity, so much the better. This spirit necessarily carries with it intense pride of race, or of nation, as the case may be, and ramifies the whole mass, inspiring and shaping its thought and effort, however humble or exalted these may be,—as it takes "all sorts and conditions of men" to make up a social order, instinct with the ambition and the activity which work for "high thinking and right living," of which modern evolution in all directions is the most powerful illustration in history. If pride of ancestry can, happily, be added to pride of race and nation, and these are re-enforced by self-reliance, courage and correct moral living, the possible success of such people may be accepted, without equivocation, as a foregone conclusion. I have found all of these requirements so finely blended in the life and character of no people as that of the Japanese, who are just now emerging from "the double night of ages" into the vivifying sunlight of modern progress.

What is the Negro's place in American life at the present day?

The answer depends entirely upon the point of view. Unfortunately for the Afro-American people, they have no pride of ancestry; in the main, few of them can trace their parentage back four generations; and the "daughter of an hundred earls" of whom there are probably many, is unconscious of her descent, and would profit nothing by it if this were not true. The blood of all the ethnic types that go to make up American citizenship flows in the veins of the Afro-American people, so that of the ten million of them in this country, accounted for by the Federal census, not more than four million are of pure negroid descent, while some four million of them, not accounted for by the Federal census, have escaped into the ranks of the white race, and are re-enforced very largely by such escapements every year. The vitiation of blood has operated irresistibly to weaken that pride of ancestry, which is the foundation-stone of pride of race; so that the Afro-American people have been held together rather by the segregation decreed by law and public opinion than by ties of consanguinity since their manumission and enfranchisement. It is not because they are poor and ignorant and oppressed, as a mass, that there is no such sympathy of thought and unity of effort among them as among Irishmen and Jews the world over, but because the vitiation of blood, beyond the honorable restrictions of law, has destroyed, in large measure, that pride of ancestry upon which pride of race must be built. In no other logical way can we account for the failure of the Afro-American people to stand together, as other oppressed races do, and have done, for the righting of wrongs against them authorized by the laws of the several states, if not by the Federal Constitution, and sanctioned or tolerated by public opinion. In nothing has this radical defect been more noticeable since the War of the Rebellion than in the uniform failure of the people to sustain such civic organizations as exist and have existed, to test in the courts of law and in the forum of public opinion the validity of organic laws of States intended to deprive them of the civil and political rights guaranteed to them by the Federal Constitution. The two such organizations of this character which have appealed to them are the National Afro-American League, organized in Chicago, in 1890, and the National Afro-American Council, organized in Rochester, New York, out of the League, in 1898. The latter organization still exists, the strongest of its kind, but it has never commanded the sympathy and support of the masses of the people, nor is there, or has there been, substantial agreement and concert of effort among the thoughtful men of the race along these lines. They have been restrained by selfish, personal and petty motives, while the constitutional rights which vitalize their citizenship have been "denied or abridged" by legislation of certain of the States and by public opinion, even as Nero fiddled while Rome burned. If they had been actuated by a strong pride of ancestry and of race, if they had felt that injury to one was injury to all, if they had hung together instead of hanging separately, their place in the civil and political life of the Republic to-day would not be that, largely, of pariahs, with none so poor as to do them honor, but that of equality of right under the law enjoyed by all other alien ethnic forces in our citizenship. They who will not help themselves are usually not helped by others. They who make a loud noise and courageously contend for what is theirs, usually enjoy the respect and confidence of their fellows and get, in the end, what belongs to them, or a reasonable modification of it.

As a consequence of inability to unite in thought and effort for the conservation of their civil and political rights, the Afro-American Negroes and colored people have lost, by fundamental enactments of the old slave-holding States, all of the civil and political rights guaranteed them by the Federal Constitution, in the full enjoyment of which they were from the adoption of the War Amendments up to 1876-7, when they were sacrificed by their Republican allies of the North and West, in the alienation of their State governments, in order to save the Presidency to Mr. Rutherford B. Hayes of Ohio. Their reverses in this matter in the old slave-holding States, coupled with a vast mass of class legislation, modeled on the slave code, have affected the Afro-American people in their civil and political rights in all of the States of the Republic, especially as far as public opinion is concerned. This was inevitable, and follows in every instance in history where a race element of the citizenship is set aside by law or public opinion as separate and distinct from its fellows, with a fixed status or caste.

It will take the Afro-American people fully a century to recover what they lost of civil and political equality under the law in the Southern States, as a result of the reactionary and bloody movement begun in the Reconstruction period by the Southern whites, and culminating in 1877,—the excesses of the Reconstruction governments, about which so much is said to the discredit of the Negro, being chargeable to the weakness and corruption of Northern carpet-baggers, who were the master and responsible spirits of the time and the situation, rather than to the weakness, the ignorance and venality of their Negro dupes, who, very naturally, followed where they led, as any other grateful people would have done. For, were not these same Northern carpet-baggers the direct representatives of the Government and the Army which crushed the slave power and broke the shackles of the slave? Even so. The Northern carpet-baggers planned and got the plunder, and have it; the Negro got the credit and the odium, and have them yet. It often happens that way in history, that the innocent dupes are made to suffer for the misdeeds and crimes of the guilty.

The recovery of civil and political rights under the Constitution, as "denied or abridged" by the constitutions of the States, more especially those of the old slave holding ones, will be a slow and tedious process, and will come to the individual rather than to the race, as the reward of character and thrift; because, for reasons already stated, it will hardly be possible in the future, as it has not been in the past, to unify the mass of the Afro-American people, in thought and conduct, for a proper contention in the courts and at the ballot-box and in the education of public opinion, to accomplish this purpose. Perhaps there is no other instance in history where everything depended so largely upon the individual, and so little upon the mass of his race, for that development in the religious and civic virtues which makes more surely for an honorable status in any citizenship than constitutions or legislative enactments built upon them.

But even from this point of view, I am disposed to believe that the Negro's civil and political rights are more firmly fixed in law and public opinion than was true at the close of the Reconstruction period, when everything relating to him was unsettled and confused, based in legislative guarantees, subject to approval or disapproval of the dominant public opinion of the several States, and that he will gradually work out his own salvation under the Constitution,—such as Charles Sumner, Thaddeus Stevens, Benjamin F. Butler, Frederick Douglass, and their co-workers, hoped and labored that he might enjoy. He has lost nothing under the fundamental law; such of these restrictions, as apply to him by the law of certain of the States, necessarily apply to white men in like circumstances of ignorance and poverty, and can be overcome, in time, by assiduous courtship of the schoolmaster and the bank cashier. The extent to which the individual members of the race are overcoming the restrictions made a bar to their enjoyment of civil and political rights under the Constitution is gratifying to those who wish the race well and who look beyond the present into the future: while it is disturbing the dreams of those who spend most of their time and thought in abortive efforts to "keep the 'nigger' in his place"—as if any man or race could have a place in the world's thought and effort which he did not make for himself! In our grand Republic, at least, it has been so often demonstrated as to become proverbial, that the door of opportunity shall be closed to no man, and that he shall be allowed to have that place in our national life which he makes for himself. So it is with the Negro now, as an individual. Will it be so with him in the future as a race? To answer that we shall first have to determine that he has a race.

However he may be lacking in pride of ancestry and race, no one can accuse the Negro of lack of pride of Nation and State, and even of county. Indeed, his pride in the Republic and his devotion to it are among the most pathetic phases of his pathetic history, from Jamestown, in 1620, to San Juan Hill, in 1898. He has given everything to the Republic,—his labor and blood and prayers. What has the Republic given him, but blows and rebuffs and criminal ingratitude! And he stands now, ready and eager, to give the Republic all that he has. What does the Republic stand ready and eager to give him? Let the answer come out of the mouth of the future.

It is a fair conclusion that the Negro has a firmer and more assured civil and political status in American life to-day than at the close of the Reconstruction period, paradoxical as this may appear to many, despite the adverse legislation of the old slave-holding States, and the tolerant favor shown such legislation by the Federal Supreme Court, in such opinions as it has delivered, from time to time, upon the subject, since the adoption of the War amendments to the Federal Constitution. Technically, the Negro stands upon equality with all other citizens under this large body of special and class legislation; but, as a matter of fact, it is so framed that the greatest inequality prevails, and was intended to prevail, in the administration of it by the several States chiefly concerned. As long as such legislation by the States specifies, on the face of it, that it shall operate upon all citizens equally, however unequally and unjustly the legislation may be interpreted and administered by the local courts, the Federal Supreme Court has held, time and again, that no hardship was worked, and, if so, that the aggrieved had his recourse in appeal to the higher courts of the State of which he is a citizen,—a recourse at this time precisely like that of carrying coal to New Castle.

Under the circumstances, there is no alternative for the Negro citizen but to work out his salvation under the Constitution, as other citizens have done and are doing. It will be a long and tedious process before the equitable adjustment has been attained, but that does not much matter, as full and fair enjoyment of civil and political rights requires much time and patience and hard labor in any given situation, where two races come together in the same governmental environment; such as is the case of the Negro in America, the Irishman in Ireland, and the Jew everywhere in Europe. It is just as well, perhaps, that the Negro will have to work out his salvation under the Constitution as an individual rather than as a race, as the Jew has done it in Great Britain and as the Irishman will have to do it under the same Empire, as it is and has been the tendency of our law and precedent to subordinate race elements and to exalt the individual citizens as indivisible "parts of one stupendous whole." When this has been accomplished by the law in the case of the Negro, as in the case of other alien ethnic elements of the citizenship, it will be more gradually, but assuredly, accomplished by society at large, the indestructible foundation of which was laid by the reckless and brutal prostitution of black women by white men in the days of slavery, from which a vast army of mulattoes were produced, who have been and are, gradually, by honorable marriage among themselves, changing the alleged "race characteristics and tendencies" of the Negro people. A race element, it is safe and fair to conclude, incapable, like that of the North American Indian, of such a process of elimination and assimilation, will always be a thorn in the flesh of the Republic, in which there is, admittedly, no place for the integrality and growth of a distinct race type. The Afro-American people, for reasons that I have stated, are even now very far from being such a distinct race type, and without further admixture of white and black blood, will continue to be less so to the end of the chapter. It seems to me that this view of the matter has not received the consideration that it deserves at the hands of those who set themselves up as past grand masters in the business of "solving the race problem," and in accurately defining "The Negro's Place in American Life at the Present Day." The negroid type and the Afro-American type are two very distinct types, and the sociologist who confounds them, as is very generally done, is bound to confuse his subject and his audience.

It is a debatable question as to whether the Negro's present industrial position is better or worse than it was, say, at the close of the Reconstruction period. As a mass, I am inclined to the opinion that it is worse, as the laws of the States where he is congregated most numerously are so framed as to favor the employer in every instance, and he does not scruple to get all out of the industrial slave that he can; which is, in the main, vastly more than the slave master got, as the latter was at the expense of housing, feeding, clothing and providing medical service for his chattel, while the former is relieved of this expense and trouble. Prof. W .E.B. DuBois, of Atlanta University, who has made a critical study of the rural Negro of the Southern States, sums up the industrial phase of the matter in the following ("The Souls of Black Folk," pp. 39-40):

"For this much all men know: Despite compromise, war and struggle, the Negro is not free. In the backwoods of the Gulf States, for miles and miles, he may not leave the plantation of his birth; in well-nigh the whole rural South the black farmers are peons, bound by law and custom to an economic slavery, from which the only escape is death or the penitentiary. In the most cultured sections and cities of the South the Negroes are a segregated servile caste, with restricted rights and privileges. Before the courts, both in law and custom, they stand on a different and peculiar basis. Taxation without representation is the rule of their political life. And the result of all this is, and in nature must have been, lawlessness and crime."

It is a dark and gloomy picture, the substitution of industrial for chattel slavery, with none of the legal and selfish restraints upon the employer which surrounded and actuated the master. And this is true of the entire mass of the Afro-American laborers of the Southern States. Out of the mass have arisen a large number of individuals who own and till their own lands. This element is very largely recruited every year, and to this source must we look for the gradual undermining of the industrial slavery of the mass of the people. Here, too, we have a long and tedious process of evolution, but it is nothing new in the history of races circumstanced as the Afro-American people are. That the Negro is destined, however, to be the landlord and master agriculturist of the Southern States is a probability sustained by all the facts in the situation; not the least of which being the tendency of the poor white class and small farmers to abandon agricultural pursuits for those of the factory and the mine, from which the Negro laborer is excluded, partially in the mine and wholly in the factory. The development of mine and factory industries in the Southern States in the past two decades has been one of the most remarkable in industrial history.

In the skilled trades, at the close of the War of the Rebellion, most of the work was done by Negroes educated as artisans in the hard school of slavery, but there has been a steady decline in the number of such laborers, not because of lack of skill, but because trade unionism has gradually taken possession of such employments in the South, and will not allow the Negro to work alongside of the white man. And this is the rule of the trade unions in all parts of the country. It is to be hoped that there may be a gradual broadening of the views of white laborers in this vital matter and a change of attitude by the trade unions that they dominate. Can we reasonably expect this? As matters now stand, it is the individual Negro artisan, often a master contractor, who can work at his trade and give employment to his fellows. Fortunately, there are a great many of these in all parts of the Southern States, and their number is increasing every year, as the result of the rapid growth and high favor of industrial schools, where the trades are taught. A very great deal should be expected from this source, as a Negro contractor stands very nearly on as good footing as a white one in the bidding, when he has established a reputation for reliability. The facts obtained in every Southern city bear out this view of the matter. The individual black man has a fighting chance for success in the skilled trades; and, as he succeeds, will draw the skilled mass after him. The proper solution of the skilled labor problem is strictly within the power of the individual Negro. I believe that he is solving it, and that he will ultimately solve it.

It is, however, in the marvelous building up of a legal, comfortable and happy home life, where none whatever existed at the close of the War of the Rebellion; in the no less stupendous development of the church life, with large and puissant organizations that command the respect and admiration of mankind, and owning splendid church property valued at millions of dollars; in the quenchless thirst of the mass of the people for useful knowledge, displayed at the close of the War of the Rebellion, and abating nothing of its intense keenness since, with the remarkable reduction in the illiteracy of the mass of the people, as is eloquently disclosed by the census reports—it is in these results that no cause for complaint or discouragement can be found. The whole race here stands on improved ground over that it occupied at the close of the War of the Rebellion; albeit, even here, the individual has outstripped the mass of the race, as it was but natural that he should and always will. But, while this is true and gratifying to all those that hope the Afro-American people well, it is also true, and equally gratifying that, as far as the mass is concerned, the home life, the church and the school house have come into the life of the people, in some sort, everywhere, giving the whole race a character and a standing in the estimation of mankind which it did not have at the close of the war, and presaging, logically, unless all signs fail, a development along high and honorable lines in the future; the results from which, I predict, at the end of the ensuing half century, built upon the foundation already laid, being such as to confound the prophets of evil, who never cease to doubt and shake their heads, asking: "Can any good thing come out of Nazareth?" We have the answer already in the social and home life of the people, which is so vast an improvement over the conditions and the heritage of slavery as to stagger the understanding of those who are informed on the subject, or will take the trouble to inform themselves.

If we have much loose moral living, it is not sanctioned by the mass, wedlock being the rule, and not the exception; if we have a vast volume of illiteracy, we have reduced it by forty per cent. since the war, and the school houses are all full of children eager to learn, and the schools of higher and industrial training cannot accommodate all those who knock at their doors for admission; if we have more than our share of criminality, we have also churches in every hamlet and city, to which a vast majority of the people belong, and which are insistently pointing "the way, the light and the truth" to higher and nobler living.

Mindful, therefore, of the Negro's two hundred and forty-five years of slave education and unrequited toil, and of his thirty years of partial freedom and less than partial opportunity, who shall say that his place in American life at the present day is not all that should be reasonably expected of him, that it is not creditable to him, and that it is not a sufficient augury for better and nobler and higher thinking, striving and building in the future? Social growth is the slowest of all growth. If there be signs of growth, then, there is reasonable hope for a healthy maturity. There are plenty of such signs, and he who runs may read them, if he will.

A Helping Hand

A sure way for one to lift himself
up is by lifting up someone else.

The harder the work required on account of the depth or unpopularity
of the individual to be helped, the greater will be the strength and
happiness gained.

Daily Resolves

To keep in mind that no one ever makes a sacrifice
who does every day
the simple, plain duty of lifting up the unfortunate.

To do a common thing in an uncommon way.

To do our work so well that it will be a difficult task
for anyone to improve upon what we have done.

To live up to the high-water mark of daily duty.

Whoever does this will meet with constant unexpected happiness and
encouragement.

To keep in mind that service to our fellows
will always be Our greatest protection,
and will bring our greatest happiness.

Remember that the only way
to show ourselves superior to others
Is to excel them in kindlier impulses
and more generous deeds.

To realize that the surest way to lift up ourselves, is to lift up someone
else.

CPSIA information can be obtained
at www.ICGtesting.com
Printed in the USA
LVOW01s1626030816

498915LV00018B/912/P